PENSION SCHEMES AND PENSION FUNDS
IN THE UNITED KINGDOM

PENSION SCHEMES AND PENSION FUNDS IN THE UNITED KINGDOM

David Blake

Barclays Bank Reader in Financial Economics

Birkbeck College

University of London

CLARENDON PRESS · OXFORD

OXFORD

UNIVERSITY PRESS

Great Clarendon Street, Oxford OX2 6DP

Oxford University Press is a department of the University of Oxford
It furthers the University's objective of excellence in research, scholarship,
and education by publishing worldwide in

Oxford New York

Athens Auckland Bangkok Bogotá Buenos Aires Calcutta
Cape Town Chennai Dar es Salaam Delhi Florence Hong Kong Istanbul
Karachi Kuala Lumpur Madrid Melbourne Mexico City Mumbai
Nairobi Paris São Paulo Singapore Taipei Tokyo Toronto Warsaw

and associated companies in Berlin Ibadan

Oxford is a registered trade mark of Oxford University Press
in the UK and in certain other countries

Published in the United States
by Oxford University Press Inc., New York

ISBN 0-19-828623-6

Printed in Great Britain
on acid-free paper by
Biddles Short Run Books
King's Lynn

In memory of my beloved father,
Peter Blake,
1920–1994.

PREFACE

This book has had a long gestation period. Its origins go back to 1978 when I began a Ph.D at the London School of Economics on modelling pension-fund investment behaviour. At that time the market value of UK pension funds stood at £34bn., but there was very little publicly available information about them. Similarly, while there was a good deal of information about UK pension schemes, very little of this information was either easily accessible or presented in a convenient form.

In undertaking research for my thesis, I was constantly coming across bits and pieces of information from diverse sources. What soon became evident was that the pensions industry was a vast, rapidly changing leviathan. While there were experts on parts of the beast, few people really understood the entire animal: an animal that embraces actuarial science, law, economics, industrial relations, accounting and auditing, taxation, marketing, finance, investment, insurance, demographic science, politics, and social policy (both domestic and European). The speed with which the pensions industry changes from one year to the next is also quite astonishing. Almost every year there is a new Social Security Act or a new Finance Act that affects pension schemes or pension funds. Roughly once a decade pensions policy is radically changed as a result of a change in the political party running the government. Similarly, with increasing frequency, the European Commission or the European Court of Justice does something that has consequences for the UK pensions industry.

What I have attempted to do in this book is bring together a mass of information and organize it in a coherent manner. The subject-matter is arranged in four sections: the history of pensions and pension schemes; the types of pensions and pension schemes; the structure, management, and performance of pension funds; and future developments. Having done that, I conduct a thorough analysis of the information. For example, I analyse the role of the state in the development of pensions and pension schemes, I discuss the pension choices and retirement decisions that individuals are now able to make, I examine the public-policy issues surrounding pensions and pension schemes, and I investigate the consequences of pension funds for capital markets. Finally, in the light of the weaknesses revealed by the above analysis, I propose a reform of the pensions system in the UK.

In the UK today, the total working population (including the self-employed) is 24 million. Of these, 6.75 million employees work for companies which do not offer pension schemes at all and therefore have to rely on the state pension scheme. There are 1.5 million employees in occupational pension schemes that are contracted into the State Earnings-Related Pension Scheme (or SERPS) and 9.5 million employees in occupational pension schemes that are contracted out of SERPS. There are 3.75 million employed people with personal pension schemes. There are also 1.25 million self-employed people with personal pension schemes, and another 1.25 million self-employed people without a personal pension other than the basic state pension. In addition, about 10 million people are currently receiving a basic state pension and, of these, about 3 million are also receiving a SERPS pension and about 6 million are also receiving an occupational pension. By the time that I had finished this book the value of UK pension funds had increased to £400bn., about two-thirds of the value of UK gross domestic product.

Despite this large number of people with a huge vested interest in UK pensions and pension schemes, and despite the huge sum of money invested on their behalf, the UK pensions industry is surprisingly secretive. For example, I was unable to get hold of a copy of the current actuarial valuation report of the pension fund of a major UK bank (that had recently been a building society), even though I was a shareholder in the bank, on the grounds that the trustees 'are unwilling to disclose such information to persons to whom they do not have a statutory duty'. Even with my own pension scheme, the Universities Superannuation Scheme, I had to give a detailed explanation of why I wanted to see the latest actuarial valuation report before it would give me a copy.

Pension funds have an enormous influence on our lives, even though most of us do not realize it. I hope that this secrecy will soon end. In the light of the Maxwell scandal, I believe it will have to.

CONTENTS

LIST OF ABBREVIATIONS

ABI	Association of British Insurers
AGE	Americans for Generational Equity
ARP	accrued-rights premium
ASB	Accounting Standards Board
AVC	additional voluntary contribution
BCIAPS	British Clothing Industry Association's Pension Scheme
BIM	Bishopsgate Investment Management
bn.	billion
BR	British Rail
C.	Command paper
CAPM	capital-asset pricing model
CAPS	Combined Actuarial Performance Services
CBOE	Chicago Board Options Exchange
Cd.	Command paper
CD	certificate of deposit
CIMPS	contracted-in money-purchase scheme
CINVEN	CIN Venture Managers
Cmd.	Command paper
CME	Chicago Mercantile Exchange
Cmnd.	Command paper
CMO	collateralized mortgage obligation
c/o	care of
COEG	Contracted Out Employment Group
COFSS	contracted-out final-salary scheme
COMPS	contracted-out money-purchase scheme
Corp.	Corporation
CP	commercial paper
CPS	Centre for Policy Studies
CTD	cheapest-to-deliver
DHSS	Department of Health and Social Security
DSS	Department of Social Security
ECU	European Currency Unit
EIPS	Engineering Industry Pension Scheme
EIRIS	Ethical Investment Research and Information Service
ERISA	Employee Retirement Income Security Act
EU	European Union
FASB87	Financial Accounting Standards Board's Statement of Financial Accounting Standards No. 87

FIMBRA	Financial Intermediaries, Managers and Brokers Regulatory Association
FRA	forward-rate agreement
FRN	floating-rate note
FSA	Financial Services Act
FSAVC	free-standing additional voluntary contribution
FT	Financial Times
FT-A	FT-Actuaries
FTSE100	Financial Times Stock Exchange 100 Index
FURBS	funded unapproved retirement benefit scheme
GASOPS	government actuary's survey of occupational pension schemes for 1987
Geo.	George
GIC	guaranteed income contract
GMC	guaranteed minimum contribution
GMP	guaranteed minimum pension
GPPS	group personal pension scheme
HC	House of Commons paper
HMSO	Her Majesty's Stationery Office
IDS	Income Data Services
IDS188	Income Data Services Study 188
IMM	International Monetary Market
IMRO	Investment Managers Regulatory Organization
LAPR	life-assurance premium relief
LAUTRO	Life Assurance and Unit Trust Regulatory Organization
LBO	leveraged buy-out
LEL	lower earnings limit
LIBID	London Inter-Bank Bid Rate
LIBOR	London Inter-Bank Offered Rate
LIFFE	London International Financial Futures and Options Exchange
LT	London Transport
m.	million
MBO	management buy-out
MCC	Maxwell Communication Corporation
MGN	Mirror Group Newspapers
MLI	market-level indicator
MP	Member of Parliament
MPT	modern portfolio theory
NAO	National Audit Office
NAPF	National Association of Pension Funds
NCB	National Coal Board
NHS	National Health Service

NIC	national-insurance contribution
NUM	National Union of Mineworkers
OPAS	Occupational Pensions Advisory Service
OPB	Occupational Pensions Board
OTC	over-the-counter
p.a.	per annum
PAYE	pay-as-you-earn
PAYG	pay-as-you-go
PBGC	Pension Benefit Guaranty Corporation
PLC	Public Limited Company
PPM	Personal Pension Management
PRP	pensioner's-rights premium
PSO	Pension Schemes Office
QC	Queen's Counsel
RPI	retail price index
SEAQ	Stock Exchange Automated Quotations System
SEPC	self-employed premium certificate
SERPS	state earnings-related pension scheme
SGRPS	state graduated retirement pension scheme
SIB	Securities and Investments Board
SIPPS	self-invested personal pension scheme
SML	security-market line
SRI	socially responsible investment
SRO	self-regulatory organization
SSAP24	Statement of Standard Accounting Practice 24
SSAPS	small self-administered pension scheme
TB	Treasury bill
UEL	upper earnings limit
UKAEA	UK Atomic Energy Authority
USM	unlisted securities market
VAT	value added tax
WM	World Markets

PART I

THE HISTORICAL DEVELOPMENT OF PENSIONS AND PENSION SCHEMES IN THE UNITED KINGDOM

In Part I we examine the historical development of pensions and pension schemes in the UK. Chapter 1 looks at the development of state pensions for public servants and for members of the public. In Chapter 2 we review the development of occupational pension schemes by the state, both for public servants and for members of the public, and also by the private sector for its own employees. We also consider the recent development of personal pension schemes. Chapter 3 examines the close historical connection between the development of state pensions and pension schemes and those in the private sector, and the ways in which the state, through competition, co-operation, legislation, and taxation, has influenced private-sector schemes.

1

The Development of State Pensions

The earliest attempts by the state to guarantee a minimum standard of living at the subsistence level were the Poor Laws of 1597 and 1601 under the reign of Elizabeth I, which resulted from the threat to law and order caused by roaming bands of poor, starving people. Each local authority became responsible for collecting funds through a poor rate and for allocating poor-law relief to deserving individuals. Parts of the Poor Laws were still in operation until the National Assistance Act came into force in 1948.

1.1. State Pensions for Public Servants

The first direct concern by the state for the explicit provision of pensions was with its own employees, that is, civil and other public servants. This was in an act of parliament in 1810 (50 Geo. III, c. 117),[1] and the first act to establish non-contributory pensions for all civil servants was the Superannuation Act of 1834. This was the first time in Britain that a comprehensive scheme had been established for any group of former employees.

This initial development was not an altruistic act by the state but resulted from an attempt to improve the civil service in several ways. First, there was a need to retire, without hardship, civil servants who were no longer able to perform their duties efficiently. Secondly, the payment of civil servants at this time was a very confused and haphazard affair, and needed to be reorganized. Some civil servants were paid fees, not salaries; others held sinecures with an income but no duties; others had life offices but paid an assistant to do their work. So there was no clear division between work and retirement, between salary and pension. The first recorded state pensioner was a Martin Horsham, a civil servant who retired on 10 March 1684 with a pension of £40 per year. This was half his final salary, even though he had been a civil servant for less than two years. His successor was a Mr G. Scope, and Mr Horsham's pension was paid out of Mr Scope's £80 per year salary.

[1] An Act to direct that Accounts of Increase and Diminution of Public Salaries, Pensions and Allowances shall be annually laid before Parliament and to regulate and control the granting and paying of such Salaries, Pensions and Allowances.

In 1785 a committee was appointed to inquire into the 'fees, gratuities, perquisites and emoluments' of civil servants and to make recommendations to improve the 'managing of the business transacted in the said offices'. The committee was therefore concerned with pension provision only to the extent that the existing system gave rise to inefficiency or corruption, and its recommendation was to improve the arrangements for both salary and superannuation. This resulted in a Treasury minute, dated 1803, which established a scale of allowances for those officers of the customs who had served 'with diligence and fidelity' and were 'absolutely incapable', from infirmity of mind or body, to perform their duties. The acts of 1810 and 1834 followed later.

There was much discussion during the remainder of the nineteenth century on the effects and implications of providing pensions for public servants. An important consideration was that of cost. The Select Committee on the Public Income and Expenditure of the United Kingdom, 1808, which was established to make recommendations about reductions in public expenditure, approved the pensions arrangements established by the Treasury minute of 1803 'as uniting a due consideration towards long and meritorious service, with a just attention to economy' (*Report*, Parliamentary Paper 331, 1808). By 1822 a contributory system for paying for pensions had been introduced. Nevertheless, expenditure on superannuation continued to rise, and this led the Select Committee on the Public Income and Expenditure of the United Kingdom to attribute this rise to the propensity of heads of departments to use the provisions relating to infirmity 'to hasten the removal of the less useful of their clerks', and it had also found cases where 'persons superannuated as unfit for public service had enjoyed health and strength long afterwards, and have discharged active duties in other public offices or in private business' (*Report*, Parliamentary Paper 480, 1828).

Apart from concern with cost, consideration was also given to the effect of pensions in improving efficiency. For instance, in 1857 the Royal Commission to Inquire into the Operation of the Superannuation Act of 1834 decided that the public interest at large was served by public servants being retired with pensions before they had 'become incompetent to perform their duties', since 'the evil consequences of retaining a single civil servant in an important post for which he had become incompetent, cannot be estimated in money and may be much more than an equivalent for the expense of the superannuation of a whole department' (*Report of the Commissioners*, 1857).

It was also being recognized that pensions were becoming an important part of the conditions of service of employees. In 1888 the Royal Commission to Inquire into Civil Establishments (Ridley) recognized that civil-service pensions 'help to retain in the service men who might otherwise be tempted elsewhere' (*Report of the Commissioners*, C. 5545, 1888). Further, the Royal Commission on Superannuation in the Civil Service (Courtney) in 1903 argued: 'It is advantageous to the state . . . as there is thus secured an inducement to maintain continuous service on the part of the servant and a facility on the part of the state to dispense with further services if age or infirmity renders them less efficient' (*Report of the Commissioners*, Cd. 1744, 1903).

Despite the acknowledged advantages to the state of having a superannuation scheme for its own civil servants, it proved quite difficult for other public servants to gain a pensions entitlement and, for many years after the achievements of civil servants, they were dependent on the goodwill of their employers for a pension. The main reason for this seems to have been the desire to hold down costs and also to encourage self-help, one of the great principles of the Victorian era. It was felt that providence and thrift would not be adequately rewarded if pensions were provided on a general and universal basis. This view is summarized by Sir Edward Brabrook, chief registrar of friendly societies, who, in the minority report of the Courtney Commission in 1903, argued that to provide against death by life insurance required 'but a little self-denial in the early years of life', whereas a general pension scheme 'seems to offer a premium on improvidence'.

More than thirty years after civil servants had achieved a universal pension scheme, teachers, for example, were told that: 'It has never been proposed that the government should make a general offer of pensions. In one form or another, it has always been assumed that the teachers were to make provision for themselves' (circular letter to HM Inspectors of Education, 12 June 1857). However, after various parliamentary select committees in which witnesses argued that pension provision would 'attract a better class of teachers, and keep them longer', or would enable the government to 'escape from the embarrassment consequent on the absence of any provision for the old age of 30,000 teachers', the House of Commons appointed the Select Committee on the Elementary Education (Teachers' Superannuation) in 1892 to find 'the best system of providing for the superannuation of public elementary teachers'. It recommended that the Education Department should set up a fund financed by contributions from both teachers and the Exchequer (*Report of the Select Committee*, HC 231, 1892). But it was not until 1898 that an act was passed setting up a universal, compulsory scheme for elementary schoolteachers. This was nearly eighty years after the original civil servants scheme, and other schoolteachers had to wait even longer.

There was a similarly uneven and piecemeal development of the provision of pensions for other public servants. For example, in 1829 in the metropolis, and by the County Police Act of 1839 for the rest of the country, pensions could be provided to policemen who were 'worn out by length of service'. But it was not until 1890 that a universal police pension scheme was established.

Since the turn of the twentieth century there has been a series of measures dealing with public-sector pensions. These have been embodied in various Superannuation Acts. The most recent is the Superannuation Act of 1972. This was designed to enable the minister for the civil service in future to prescribe pension schemes for the civil service via non-statutory instruments and not by acts of parliament. Secondly, the act created a single consistent pattern of control in relation to the pension schemes of other public servants (local government, health- and fire-service employees, teachers, and the police). Finally, the act completed the process of removing from ministerial control the terms and conditions of the pension funds of employees of the nationalized industries and public corporations.

1.2. State Pensions for Members of the Public

Despite the existence and continuation of poor-law relief, it was believed in the Victorian age that poverty was largely due to idleness. Poverty was not a condition to be pitied and relieved, but a moral failing to be despised and condemned. These attitudes, together with the wish to keep the cost of poor-law relief under control, influenced government policy for most of the nineteenth century. For example, the Poor Law Reforms of 1834 were designed to relieve temporary distress but not to end poverty, and the conditions in workhouses were to be made even harsher in order to discourage the idle. When in work, it was believed that a man should exercise thrift in order to avoid the workhouse in his old age. Even the Church shared this view. The Revd T. R. Malthus, for example, argued that 'the quantity of provisions consumed in the workhouse, upon a part of society that cannot in general be considered as the most valuable part, diminishes the share that would otherwise belong to the more industrious and worthy members'.

Opponents of this manifestation of the Protestant ethic were led to argue that in many cases the extent of poverty was so great that the poor were simply not able to provide for their old age, and that therefore their arrival at the workhouse was not necessarily a consequence of their lack of foresight. Indeed, it was even possible to demonstrate that some people had attempted to save for their old age but had been thwarted in their efforts through no fault of their own. A specific example of this was saving with friendly societies, through which individuals saved regular amounts to provide for future sickness, old age, and funeral costs. But because of mismanagement or fraud many of these societies failed, and the savings of the poor were lost completely. Eventually it was recognized that such failures discouraged thrift, and this was officially confirmed by the Royal Commission on Friendly Societies in 1874.

Furthermore, surveys were made which suggested that old age itself was one of the primary causes of poverty. The principal architect of this approach was the Liverpool shipowner Charles Booth, who published his results in *The Aged Poor* (1894) and *Life and Labour of the People in London* (1903). They indicated that as many as one-third of the population of London were living below the poverty line, and that old age was undoubtedly the chief cause of this poverty; in Stepney, for instance, Booth found that one-third of those who were poor were so merely because they were old. As a solution to this problem, Booth suggested that the state should grant pensions of 5*s*. per week to all over 65 years at an estimated cost to the Exchequer of £17m. per year.

At the same time, the government became more interested in the plight of the aged poor. In 1885 the government appointed a select committee to suggest 'the best system of national provident insurance against pauperism'. In 1893 the Royal Commission on Poor Law Relief and People Destitute from Old Age was appointed under the chairmanship of Lord Aberdare, whose terms of reference were 'to consider whether any alterations in the system of poor-law relief are desirable in the case of persons whose destitution is occasioned by incapacity for work resulting from old age or whether assistance could otherwise be afforded in those cases'. Charles Booth was a member, as was Joseph Chamberlain. Chamberlain's evidence included the observation that, although poverty was only 8 per cent among those under 65, it was 25 per cent among those older than 65. He also showed how difficult it was for working men to save, however thrifty they might be (*Report of the Commissioners*, C. 7684, 1895). Finally, in 1899 a select committee, under the chairmanship of Lord Rothschild, was appointed to find 'the best means of improving the conditions of the aged deserving poor'. It was estimated that there were 2 million people older than 65 years, and that two-thirds required aid, with about one-third receiving poor-law relief of around 2*s*. 6*d*. per week, and it recommended that a non-contributory system of old-age pensions should be established.

There were other pressures besides those of royal commissions and select committees. Some of these were domestic, such as those resulting from the extension of the electoral franchise in 1867 and 1885 and the growth of the trade-union movement, all of which led to demands for some positive measures of social assistance. Other pressures were external, the most important being the introduction of social-insurance provision, including pensions, in Germany in the 1880s under Bismarck.

Introducing his Workman's Compensation Bill in 1881, Bismarck reasoned that 'anyone with the prospect of a pension in old age or infirmity is happier, more content with his lot and more tractable . . . the chief cause of anxiety among artisans is uncertainty as to their future. Remove that and we shall remove their hatreds, and avert more serious troubles'.

The introduction of state pensions eventually came when the Old Age Pensions Act was passed in 1908, under the auspices of Lloyd George as Liberal chancellor of the exchequer. Its objective was as follows: 'every person in whose case the conditions laid down by this act for the receipt of an old age pension are fulfilled shall be entitled to receive such a pension under this act so long as those conditions continue to be fulfilled.' The conditions were that the person must be more than 70 years old with an income of less than 12*s*. per week. The pension was to be 5*s*. per week if other income was less than 8*s*. per week, falling to 1*s*. per week if other income was between 11*s* and 12*s*. per week. The average weekly wage at that time was about 30*s*. per week. However, the pension was not available to people who had repeatedly refused to work when given the chance, and was only granted following a means test of applicants. The pensions were non-contributory and were financed from general taxation. The estimated annual cost to the Exchequer was £6m., sufficient to finance half-a-million pensioners. But such was the extent of the poverty amongst the aged that by 1911 there were 900,000 pensioners, costing nearly £12m. per year.

The 1908 Old Age Pensions Act provided financial aid to those who were already old and unable to keep themselves. The natural concomitant to this was to remove the problem of the aged poor in the future by making adequate provision for those who were still in work in anticipation of their old age. The system adopted was known as *national insurance*, and was a form of compulsory saving. This idea was first embodied in the National Insurance Act of 1911, again under the instigation of Lloyd George. While this act did not deal explicitly with pensions, it did deal with sickness and unemployment benefit. In particular, it granted 10*s*. a week sickness benefit for male employees (7*s*. 6*d*. for female employees), provided they earned less than £160 per year. By 1914 13.5 million people were covered under this part of the act. The act also granted 7*s*. per week unemployment benefit for both men and women. By 1914 2.5 million people, mostly skilled workers, were covered under this part of the act. As far as contributions were concerned, these were made up as follows: the employee paid 4*d*. per week for *national-health insurance* and $2\frac{1}{2}d$. per week for *unemployment insurance*; the employer paid respectively 3*d*. and $2\frac{1}{2}d$.; while the Exchequer paid 2*d*. and $1\frac{2}{3}d$. The total contributions paid into the two national funds providing the benefits were respectively 9*d*. and $6\frac{2}{3}d$., the former amount giving rise to the Liberal Party slogan 'nine pence for four pence'. The joint contributions by employee and employer to the National Health Fund was calculated to be the actuarial contribution necessary for a male starting work at 16 and paying into the fund for the remainder of his working life. However, because the scheme was to be open to people of all ages, who were to pay the same contribution regardless of age, the funds would be in deficit from the start, and so an Exchequer supplement was necessary to keep the funds solvent.

The 1919 Departmental Committee on Old Age Pensions, chaired by Ryland Adkins (*Report*, Cmd. 410, 1919), was much impressed by the examples of national-health and unemployment insurance, and recommended that a similar insurance scheme should be established for pensioners. This would have the desirable effects of making people save (if compulsorily rather than voluntarily) for their old age, guaranteeing them some certain income when they did retire, and permitting the abolition of the means test, since access to a pension would now be a right that has been paid for and not a privilege.

The government was also under pressure for a different reason to reassess the existing means of providing pensions. The reason was the rapidly increasing costs. Pensions were costing the Exchequer £18m. in 1919 and £27m. in 1927, and costs were expected to continue to rise because the number of old people in the population was increasing and also their life expectancy was rising. It was estimated that costs would be doubled if the means test was abolished and pensions were paid to everyone over 70.

The Conservative government, under Baldwin, was no longer prepared to finance a non-contributory pension scheme, and in 1925 Neville Chamberlain, as minister of health, passed the Widows', Orphans' and Old Age Contributory Pensions Act. The purpose of the act was to provide a pension of 10s. per week to all people who were already insured under the national-health scheme. Since this was a right, the means test was no longer necessary. The act was to apply to all people over the age of 65 years, constituting a reduction in the pensionable age of five years. It also gave a pension of 10s. per week to the employee's wife when she reached 65 years. There was also a child allowance for children under 14, providing 5s. for the first and 3s. for each subsequent child. In addition, there was a widow's pension of 10s. and an orphan's pension of 7s. 6d. per week. Nevertheless, despite the large increase in numbers entitled to receive a pension, the pension was not intended to be adequate to live on by itself. The huge inflation produced as a result of the Great War had seen to that. Chamberlain stressed that the government's intention was to provide only a basic pension which was to be supplemented by other means, especially additional pensions provided by employers. The contributions were 9*d*. per week for men, with the employee and employer each paying 4½*d*., and 4½*d*. per week for women, made up of 2*d*. from the employee and 2½*d*. from the employer. Again, these contributions were calculated actuarially as the amounts required from the age of 16 to pay the given pension from the age of 65. By 1926 17 million people were contributing to the pension scheme. But people were also entitled to a pension from 1926, and since they had not made the necessary contributions, the Old Age Pensions Fund was immediately in deficit. The government realized this and made provisions for this deficit to be covered by an Exchequer supplement of £4m. per year for ten years. The contributions were to be raised three times every ten years, so that by 1956 the fund would be self-supporting. However, by 1938 the annual Exchequer supplement was greater than the combined contributions of both employees and employers. By 1938 there were still 600,000 pensioners who were receiving non-contributory pensions under the old 1908 scheme and, in addition, there were 2 million contributory pensioners, more than half of whom were over 70.

In 1937 the Widows', Orphans' and Old Age Contributory Pensions (Voluntary Contributors) Act widened the scope of the 1925 Act to include workers who were not insured under the national-health scheme, mainly self-employed men and women earning respectively less than £400 and £250 per year. This was on a voluntary basis, with such workers paying higher contributions: 1*s*. 3*d*. for men and 6*d*. for women. With these additional contributors, the total number eligible for state pensions rose to 21 million in 1938.

In 1940 the Old Age and Widows' Pensions Act reduced the pensionable age for women to 60 years on the grounds that, because married women were, on average, four years younger than their husbands, they would be able to draw pensions at about the same time as their husbands retired at 65 years. The act also provided pensions for single women and widows over 60 years. So, since 1940 the *state-pension age* has been 65 for men and 60 for women.

As a result of injuries caused during the Second World War, the Pension Appeals Tribunals Act of 1943 provided for appeals to be brought by members of the armed services against the rejection by the minister of pensions of certain claims for war pensions in respect of incapacity for work, disablement, or death arising out of the war. The grounds for rejection by the minister, against which appeals could be lodged under the act, arose in those cases where the award was withheld or reduced on grounds of serious negligence or misconduct, or where there was dissatisfaction with the assessment of the extent of disablement. This act was extended by the Pension Appeals Tribunals Act of 1949 to include claims arising other than out of war service.

In 1942 the Beveridge Report, *Social Insurance and Allied Services* (Cmd. 6404, 1942), was published. It had two main recommendations. The first was administrative, with the report calling for all the separate branches of national insurance to be consolidated in a single unified system, 'so that existing social services . . . [may] be made at once more beneficial and intelligible to those whom they serve and more economical in their administration'. The second recommendation signalled an important change of principle in the provision of social benefits. Social benefits should not only be provided universally, they should also be 'sufficient without further resources to provide the minimum income needed for subsistence in all normal cases'. This meant that pensions had to be increased to ensure that this condition was achieved. Beveridge recommended pensions of 24*s.* per week for a single man and £2 per week for a married couple. These amounts were based on the evaluation of minimum subsistence levels made from social surveys carried out in the 1930s, with 25 per cent added on for wartime inflation.

Beveridge recognized that there were two further problems which would have to be faced. One was that the assessment of minimum subsistence levels was very difficult because of the large differences in rents which people paid. The other was the effect of continuing inflation in reducing the real value of pensions over time. However, it must be remembered that Beveridge recommended that pensions be provided at the subsistence level only, and that individuals who wished to enjoy their retirement at a higher living standard should make adequate provision. In the words of the report:

social insurance and national assistance organised by the state are designed to guarantee, on condition of service, a basic income for subsistence. The actual incomes and, by consequence, the normal standards of expenditure of different sections of the population differ greatly. Making provision for these higher standards is primarily the function of the individual, that is to say, it is a matter for free choice and voluntary insurance.

The main recommendations of the Beveridge Report were contained in the National Insurance Act of 1946, passed by the post-war Labour government. It also established a retirement pension of £1. 6*s.* per week for a single man and £2. 2*s.* per week for a married couple. The act came into operation in July 1948 and made national insurance compulsory for everyone who, regardless of earnings or nature of employment, was below state-pension age at that date. It gave the new level of pension to existing national-insurance pensioners immediately and to the rest after a ten-year period of qualifying contributions. The contributions were again calculated actuarially, and the Exchequer supplement was fixed at one-sixth of the contributions. The government actuary predicted that the

Exchequer's share of the cost of national-insurance benefits would rise from 26 per cent in 1948 to 56 per cent in 1978.

In 1948 the National Assistance Act finally consolidated the pensions provision for the aged. Until the passing of the 1946 National Insurance Act, the old-age pension was not designed to provide even a minimum standard of living. If the pensioner had no other means to support himself, he could apply for poor-law relief to supplement his state pension. In 1900, before state pensions had been introduced, poor-law relief amounted to £3m.; by 1940 the amount was £25m. as a result of the easier qualifications for relief. So until 1948 there were two systems for helping the aged—state pensions and poor-law relief. The National Assistance Act ended this bipartite system and set up a National Assistance Board to take complete responsibility for paying pensions, both contributory and non-contributory.

By the beginning of the 1950s Britain had a unified and co-ordinated system for providing state pensions at the subsistence level along the lines of the Beveridge Report. They were flat-rate pensions paid for by flat-rate contributions and related to what the state considered to be a person's very basic needs, not to the earnings he received when he was working. Beveridge had argued that if individuals wanted to enjoy a living standard higher than the subsistence level, then they must provide it for themselves. Higher-paid employees were beginning to do this via *occupational pension schemes*, but it was argued that lower-paid employees would not be able to afford the contributions to both occupational and national-insurance pension schemes. However, in 1954 the Committee to Review the Economic and Financial Problem of the Provision for the Old Age, chaired by Sir Thomas Phillips, felt that adequate provision for the aged could only be met by extending occupational pension schemes to all employees, and discussed ways of integrating occupational pension schemes with state-pension policy.

The principle of flat-rate pensions from flat-rate contributions was first questioned by Brian Abel-Smith and Peter Townsend in *New Pensions for Old* (Fabian Tract, No. 171) in 1955. Instead, they recommended the introduction of earnings-related or graduated pensions. The Labour Party accepted the idea of graduated pensions in its policy document *National Superannuation: Labour Policy for Security in Old Age* in 1957. This suggested that the existing national-insurance pension should become the foundation for a larger earnings-related pension, with the two components providing a pension equal to half the earnings of the average earner, more than half for the lower paid and less than half for the higher paid. These would be financed from earnings-related contributions, and those covered by adequate private occupational schemes could contract out of the state scheme.

In 1958 the Conservative government also produced proposals for a graduated pension scheme, together with plans for reconstituting the financial basis of the existing national-insurance schemes. These were contained in the white paper *Provision for Old Age* (Cmnd. 538, 1958). The government's three objectives were: (i) to place the national-insurance scheme on a sound financial basis; (ii) to make provision for employed persons who cannot be covered by an appropriate occupational scheme to obtain some pension benefits related to their earnings; (iii) to preserve and encourage the best development of occupational pension schemes.

It had been clear for several years that the financial structure of the national-insurance scheme was unsound. The growth of pensions in line with living standards, the increase in numbers of eligible pensioners, and the way in which pensions had been granted to people with incomplete contributions had all combined to produce large deficits in the National Insurance Fund. The capital fund required to generate interest from its investments in government stock sufficient to pay for the pensions was £8.5bn. in 1948, and rose to £15bn. in 1957. But the actual fund available to finance these pensions was only about one-tenth of this sum, despite the annual Exchequer supplement. The fund was no longer growing as a result of expenditure on pensions exceeding the income from contributions. On existing trends, the fund would vanish altogether by 1970. Even in 1946 the government, on predictions by the government actuary, realized that its share of the cost of national insurance would continue to increase. So over the years the method of financing national-insurance benefits had changed, almost by default, from one of *funding* to one of *pay-as-you-go*.

The government's first objective, therefore, was to design a graduated scheme that would both clear the existing deficit and also keep itself in balance in the future and so avoid the permanent increase in the deficit that would otherwise have arisen. Pay-as-you-go was, therefore, for the first time officially sanctioned as the method by which pensions would be financed in the future. The growing income from the graduated contributions was to be used to reduce the proportion of costs borne by the Exchequer: the government actuary predicted that the proportion would be under 15 per cent by 1981. The second objective of the white paper was to provide graduated state pensions for people who could not be covered by private occupational schemes. The Labour opposition scheme had been designed to prevent a 'catastrophic fall in living standards' on retirement, and to allow pensions to grow in line with average earnings and thereby be automatically related to rising living standards. This scheme, therefore, regarded state pensions as an alternative to private occupational pensions. The Conservative government's plan for national superannuation, on the other hand, was to provide less-generous benefits, on the grounds that

it would not be right to force everyone to contribute more through a state scheme than would be needed for a reasonable provision for old age. For the state to go further would be to arrogate to itself the individual's right to dispose of his income in what he thinks the right way, and would seriously undermine the individual's sense of responsibility for his own affairs.

The government favoured less-generous state benefits for another reason: it did not wish, in any way, to discourage private pension schemes, and this was the third objective of the white paper. Up till then national insurance had been universal and compulsory, but the government recommended that national superannuation should be selective, applying only to those who were not members of an equivalent private occupational scheme. The government therefore gave the option of *contracting out* of the state scheme to members of private schemes providing benefits as good as those of the state scheme: 'no employee who was a member of a contracted-out scheme could be in a less favourable pension position than if he had been in the state scheme at the maximum rate.' The choice was to be made by the individual worker, conditional on the employer's willingness and ability to continue operating his scheme. It was estimated that 2.5 million workers would contract out.

The government's proposals were implemented in the National Insurance Act 1959. There was to be a graduated or earnings-related addition to the state flat-rate pension. The scheme was of the average-salary type, that is, the pension was related to the average salary over the career of the individual. But the contribution rate, and therefore the earnings-related pension, were low. The contributions were as follows: the first £9 per week of earnings attracted the flat-rate contribution; between £9 and £15 per week there was a proportional or graduated contribution of 8.5 per cent divided evenly between employee and employer; and the contribution with more than £15 per week was also a flat rate. The pension ranged from £2. 10s. per week for the flat-rate part of the scheme, up to £6 per week for people earning more than £15 per week. The Exchequer supplement was limited to £170m. per year, and to ensure that this was held it was planned that contributions would grow at four intervals of five years to raise the contribution from 8.5 per cent to 9.5 per cent. Private-sector employers were permitted to contract out of the graduated part of the state scheme so long as their pension arrangements guaranteed sufficient benefits (called *equivalent pension benefits*), were financially sound, and ensured the continuity of rights for persons changing their employment. In return, both employees and employers paid lower national-insurance contributions.

The 1959 act was amended by the National Insurance Act 1960 which raised flat-rate contributions and benefits. The *State Graduated Retirement Pension Scheme* (SGRPS) (also known as the Boyd Carpenter scheme after the minister who introduced it) eventually came into operation in April 1961. About 4.5 million employees had been contracted out. These, nearly twice the number expected, included most public-service and nationalized-industry workers, and about a quarter of the employees who were members of private occupational schemes.

The first act to increase contributions and benefits after the introduction of the SGRPS was the National Insurance Act of 1963. Both flat-rate and graduated contributions were increased, and the upper limit for the latter was raised from £15 to £18 per week. The basic benefits were raised from £2. 17s. 6d. to £3. 7s. 6d. for a single person, and from £4. 12s. 6d. to £5. 9s. for a married couple, at an additional cost of £200m. The National Insurance Act of 1966 introduced earnings-related unemployment, sickness, and widows' benefits, which have, in turn, affected the amount of graduated pension that individuals can earn.

The Ministry of Social Security Act of 1966 transferred the functions of the Ministry of National Insurance and of the National Assistance Board to a new Ministry of Social Security. At the same time, the Supplementary Benefits Commission was set up to pay a new kind of non-contributory pension and other benefits. The old type of non-contributory pension embodied in the various National Insurance Acts ceased, and 63,000 pensioners had their pensions transferred to the Supplementary Benefits Commission from the National Assistance Board.

In 1970 the National Insurance (Old Persons' and Widows' Pension and Attendance Allowance) Act provided for the payment of pensions and widows' benefits under the National Insurance Act 1965 to people over pensionable age in July 1948, and reduced from 50 to 40 years the qualifying age for widows' pensions under section 28 of that act. The National Insurance Act of 1971 again raised benefits and contributions to compensate for increases in the cost of living.

The 1973 Social Security Act established statutory annual reviews of the contributions and benefits of the state pension scheme. Before this, reviews had taken place on an irregular basis. But so endemic was inflation that, from 1973, contributions and benefits were to be uprated in line with the increase in the general level of prices. More significantly, the act also intended to replace most of the existing SGRPS. There was to be a new *Social Security Pensions Scheme*, in which a system of wholly earnings-related contributions for employees would replace the existing combination of flat-rate and graduated contributions, with further contributions to the SGRPS ceasing in April 1975. The act was designed to come into force in April 1975, but by this time the Conservative government which introduced the act had been replaced by a Labour government which intended to introduce a more generous scheme.

The Labour government's first measure in respect of pensions was the 1974 National Insurance Act. This established a relaxation of the *earnings rule*[2] for pensioners to take account of inflation. The act also amended the Social Security Act of 1973 so that the annual review of long-term benefits would be related to the general level of earnings rather than prices, unless this would be disadvantageous to recipients. National-insurance contributions and benefits were increased on these new terms. Since wages increase by more than prices on average, tying pensions to wages allowed pensioners to share in the rising living standards of the economy.

The Social Security Pensions Act 1975 introduced SERPS—the *State Earnings-Related Pension Scheme* that still operates in the UK. It followed from the 1974 white paper *Better Pensions* (Cmnd. 5713). Most of the provisions of the act came into force in April 1978. The objective was to improve the benefits provided by the social-security pension scheme established by the 1973 Social Security Act. In particular, a general pension (known as a category A pension) was established consisting of two elements, a *basic pension*, and an *additional pension* which was related to a person's earnings factors over his working life. The *earnings factors* were equal to *band earnings*, that is, annual earnings between a *lower* and *upper earnings limit*. The band earnings are revalued by the increase in national average earnings up to the state-pension age. The additional pension was equal to 1.25 per cent of the average of the best twenty years' earnings factors for each year of membership of SERPS up to a maximum of twenty years. The maximum additional pension was therefore 25 per cent of earnings. This pension was exempted from the earnings rule. The act again determined that the basic pension would be uprated in line with the general level of earnings or prices, whichever was greater, while the revaluation of the additional pension would be in line with prices only. National-insurance contributions towards SERPS were also changed by the act, which specified guidelines for changing lower and upper earnings limits for each tax year. It also exempted employed earners from paying contributions after they had reached pensionable age, and increased the deferred pensions that such people would receive when they retired. It was possible for occupational pension schemes to *contract out* of SERPS, as long as they provided a *guaranteed minimum pension* which was equivalent to the additional pension under

---

[2] The earnings rule was the rule that reduced the pensions of retired workers by £1 for every £1 of earned income above an earnings limit. The earnings rule was abolished in October 1989.

SERPS; in return, both employees and employers paid lower national-insurance contributions. To contract out of SERPS, an occupational pension scheme had to apply for a *contracting-out certificate* from the Occupational Pensions Board which was set up by the 1973 Social Security Act.

The act also introduced major changes in the treatment of women. It abolished the reduced rates of national-insurance contributions for married women and widows. Women who married or began working after April 1977 had to contribute in full to the social-security scheme, and in return acquired entitlements to full benefits in their own right. From April 1978 women, regardless of marital status, received the same sickness and unemployment benefits as men, so long as the contribution conditions were satisfied. From April 1979 a rule (known as the *half-test rule*), requiring married women to work for half the number of years between their marriage and 60 years in order to qualify for a pension, was abolished. Instead, women required the same earnings record as men in order to receive the same additional pension. Women who interrupted their employment to start families were credited with up to twenty years' contributions to the basic flat-rate pension. Therefore they had to work for only twenty years before retirement in order to acquire the right to an earnings-related pension. A married woman who had paid insufficient contributions for a full, basic category A pension in her own right could make up the deficiency by drawing on her husband's contributions and instead receive a category B pension. From April 1978 women were given the right to join occupational pension schemes on an equal basis with men. This was formulated in the Occupational Pension Schemes (Equal Access to Membership) Regulations of 1976. Further, once they were members of the scheme, women could not be discriminated against on the grounds of sex, although discrimination was possible due to the 'nature of employment'; for example, the scheme could exclude part-time employees, of whom women form the majority. Where a woman was widowed after reaching pensionable age, she would receive a *widow's pension* (category B pension) based on her late husband's entitlements. A widow over age 50 years would receive 100 per cent of her late husband's earnings-related pension. A widow who was ill when widowed would be eligible for an invalidity pension based on her spouse's earnings record, if this was better than her own.

The Supplementary Benefits Act of 1976 gave to every person over the age of 16 years whose resources were insufficient to meet his or her basic needs the right to claim a *supplementary pension* if he or she had reached state-pension age, and a supplementary allowance if he or she was less than this age.

The Social Security Act of 1979 made amendments to certain sections of the Social Security Pensions Act of 1975. One amendment enabled previous years' earnings factors to be increased by a consolidated percentage which took account of the fall in their value since the last review. The act also amended the Supplementary Benefits Act of 1976 by providing for appeals to be made from supplementary-benefits appeals tribunals to a national-insurance commissioner, for a new schedule dealing with the constitution and proceedings of supplementary-benefits appeals tribunals, for the suspension of the payment of benefits during an investigation, for the repayment of overpaid benefit to be made by a decision of the adjudicating authority other than a review or appeal, and for solicitors of more than ten years' standing to be eligible for appointment as national-insurance commissioners.

The Conservative government's Social Security Act of 1980 made further miscellaneous amendments to the existing law on social security. The act provided that in future the increase in social-security benefits necessary to restore their real value would be related to the general level of prices only, rather than as before, to prices or wages, whichever was more advantageous to the pensioner. This meant that pensions would be constant in real terms and would no longer grow in line with the increases in real earnings. In addition, the act amended the Supplementary Benefits Act of 1976 by abolishing the Supplementary Benefits Commission and replacing it with a system of supplementary-benefit officers as the initial determining authority of claims for benefit. The act set up a new advisory body, the Social Security Advisory Committee, to advise the secretary of state for social services on all matters of social security (including supplementary benefits, child benefit, and family income supplement). At the same time, the National Insurance Advisory Committee was abolished. The act changed the title of national-insurance commissioners to social-security commissioners, and required that the maximum age for retirement of a commissioner should be 72 years. Finally, the act amended the Pension Appeals Tribunals Acts of 1943 and 1949 to enable an appeal to be brought or continued after the death of a claimant for pensions or to enable an appeal for disablement or death due to service in the armed forces. These changes followed from the 1979 white paper *The Reform of the Supplementary Benefits Scheme* (Cmnd. 7773).

There was another act in 1980 dealing with social security and designated the Social Security (No. 2) Act. The preamble stated that this was 'an act to amend the law relating to social security for the purpose of reducing or abolishing certain benefits and of relaxing or abolishing certain duties to increase sums'. In other words, this act permitted the government not to fully compensate social-security claimants for the loss in the real value of their benefits caused by inflation, an obligation which the government had fully accepted since the Social Security Act of 1973, although it had repeatedly changed the index (either of prices and/or of wages) against which to compare the real value of benefits. In particular, the act made the following changes. It permitted the secretary of state for social services to reduce, by up to 5 per cent in each of the tax years 1979–80, 1980–1, 1981–2, the amount of compulsory up-rating of benefits. It provided for the abolition of the compulsory up-rating of the earnings limit. The act changed the definition of the period of interruption to employment, whether through unemployment or incapacity, for the purpose of calculating entitlement to benefit. It provided for the reduction of, and then the abolition of, the earnings-related supplement to unemployment benefit, sickness benefit, maternity allowance, and to the addition of the widow's allowance.

The Social Security (Contributions) Acts of 1981 and 1982 raised the lower and upper earnings limits for contributions and reduced the Exchequer supplement to national-insurance contributions from 18 per cent to 14.5 per cent (in 1981) and to 13 per cent (in 1982). The Social Security Act of 1981 enabled the secretary of state to alter the increase in social-security benefits and guaranteed minimum pensions in 1981 so as to take account of the fact that they had been uprated in 1980 by 1 per cent more than would have been the case if the estimate of the increase in the general level of prices had been more accurate.

So from the very start of SERPS, governments began tinkering around with it. This initially included the Conservative government under Mrs Margaret Thatcher that came into power in 1979. But in its second term the Thatcher government undertook a review of the entire social-security system. The results were published in 1985 by the Department of Health and Social Security (DHSS) in a green paper called *Reform of Social Security—Programme for Change* (Cmnd. 9517–19). The green paper's main recommendation was the total abolition of SERPS. The most important reason for this was doubts (also raised from sources such as the Institute for Fiscal Studies) concerning the long-term financial viability of SERPS. In 1985 there were 2.3 workers to finance each pension. By 2035 it was estimated that there would only be 1.7 workers for each pension, as a result of the increased longevity of retired workers. This was felt to be an insufficient ratio to finance the existing scheme on a pay-as-you-go basis.

However, there was widespread criticism of the green paper, and the subsequent white paper *Reform of Social Security—Programme for Action* (Cmnd. 9691, 1985) proposed that SERPS should only be modified rather than abolished. The 1986 Social Security Act introduced these modifications by preserving the pay-as-you-go status of SERPS but reducing the benefits. It bases the earnings-related pension on *career revalued band earnings*, that is, lifetime average band earnings (revalued by the annual increase in national average earnings), rather than on the best twenty years' earnings. The pension will equal 1 per cent of average revalued earnings for each year of membership of SERPS up to a maximum of twenty years. The maximum SERPS pension will therefore be only 20 per cent of earnings, instead of 25 per cent as before. These changes are planned to come into effect over a ten-year period, beginning on 6 April 1999. The current and modified SERPS schemes are analysed in considerable detail in Chapter 5. In the next chapter we discuss the historical development of both occupational and personal pension schemes.

2

The Development of Occupational Pension Schemes and Personal Pension Schemes

Occupational pension schemes are pension schemes that are related to a particular occupation or contract of employment. When an individual leaves that occupation, he will generally leave the pension scheme and have his accumulated pension rights transferred to the scheme of his new employer. *Personal pension schemes*, on the other hand, are not tied to a specific contract of employment. Rather, personal pensions are particular to the individual and the individual can keep his own personal pension scheme operating however many times he changes jobs. In addition, occupational pension schemes generally offer pensions that are related to the salary that was earned at or near retirement, and are therefore known as *final-salary* or *defined-benefit* schemes. In contrast, personal pension schemes generally offer pensions that depend on the contributions that are paid into them and are therefore known as *money-purchase* or *defined-contribution* schemes.

2.1. The Development of State Occupational Pension Schemes

2.1.1. OCCUPATIONAL PENSION SCHEMES FOR CIVIL SERVANTS

The first attempt by the state to establish an occupational pension scheme was in 1712, when a superannuation fund was set up by Treasury warrant so that HM Customs and Excise officers in London could contribute sixpence in the pound from their salaries. In return, when they retired, they received a pension from the fund rather than, as before, having to rely on their immediate successors to pay directly over to them half their salaries. The scheme was a pay-as-you-go (PAYG) scheme, since the contribution-rate was fixed and did not depend on the numbers receiving pensions. By 1725 the fund was in deficit and began receiving subsidies from the receiver-general of customs. The fund was eventually put on a sounder financial basis and extended to include other civil servants across the country. By 1765 the fund was again in surplus, and this was being used to purchase 3 per cent government stock.

The first general comprehensive pension scheme for civil servants came in an Act of 1810 (50 Geo. III, c. 117). The scheme was made non-contributory, being financed from public funds. It had three main characteristics: (i) pensions were paid only to those who were older than a minimum retirement age or were physically incapable of work; (ii) there was a minimum qualifying period of ten years' service; and (iii) the pension increased with years of service but never exceeded the salary of the recipient. A man with forty years' service received a pension equal to three-quarters of his final salary, while in the rare case of a man with fifty years' service, he received his whole final salary as pension.

The government soon became concerned with the escalating cost of this non-contributory pension scheme. In August 1821 a Treasury minute, in looking at ways of 'limiting this branch of the public expenditure in future', recommended that 'the individuals who may hereafter enjoy the benefit of superannuation allowances, should be called upon to contribute to a superannuation fund'. Contributions were introduced in an act of 1822 (3 Geo. IV, c. 113). They were at the rate of 2.5 per cent for salaries between £100 and £200 per year, and 5 per cent for salaries higher than £200. These contributions were not designed to finance the entire cost of pensions, only about half the cost.

Even so, there was much opposition to the payment of contributions since this was considered to be a violation of the original terms of employment of civil servants, and in 1824 the system of contributions was abolished and existing contributions were repaid. The problem of cost did not disappear, however, and in 1828 the Select Committee on the Public Income and Expenditure of the United Kingdom recommended the reintroduction of contributions sufficient to finance the entire cost of pensions, which were now recommended not to exceed two-thirds of final salary, and, in order to overcome the earlier opposition, the committee suggested that contributions should only be paid by newly appointed civil servants. Some of the committee's recommendations were implemented in a Treasury minute of August 1829. The rate of contributions was higher than before, 2.5 per cent of salaries up to £100 and 5 per cent above £100. But no fund was established and so the contributions were used to finance current pension-holders and not to provide for future pensions. These contributions applied only to new appointments made after August 1829. The remaining recommendations were contained in the Superannuation Act of 1834, which also granted less-generous pensions for new entrants, with rates rising to a maximum of two-thirds of final salary on completion of forty-five or more years' service. The raising of the contribution and the reduction of the pension benefit were clear attempts to save costs.

So the overall effect of these arrangements was to establish a set of principles which came to be embodied in many future (especially public-sector) schemes, particularly final-salary schemes: a minimum retirement age (which later became 60 for civil servants), a minimum qualifying period, a pension that was calculated as some proportion of the final salary for each year worked, a pension never exceeding the final salary 'because it is expedient to establish a marked distinction between the official duties and the non-performance of them from whatever cause the cessation may arise' (*Report of the Select Committee*, Parliamentary Paper 480, 1828), and the principle of 'no detriment', that is, no existing member of a pension scheme would be made worse off by the introduction of changes to the scheme.

In 1857, by a private member's act, the civil servants' contribution was finally abolished and the civil-service scheme remained non-contributory until 1972, and was the only major public-sector scheme to do so. The Royal Commission to Inquire into the Operation of the Superannuation Act of 1834, which reported in 1857, criticized the existing system of financing pensions since no separate fund was established and allowed to grow to provide the revenues for future pensions. As a result, the commission felt that salaries were lower than they otherwise could have been. The Superannuation Act of 1859 completed the framework of the modern civil-service pension scheme. It established a pension-rate in sixtieths of final salary for each year worked, and a minimum retirement age of 60.

The next major change did not take place until the Superannuation Act of 1909, which introduced death benefit equal to one year's salary and allowed for part of the pension to be commuted in order to provide a tax-free lump sum of money on retirement. If this option was chosen, the pension scale was reduced from one-sixtieth to one-eightieth for each year of service, thereby providing after forty years of service a pension equal to half of final salary together with the lump sum. Another change took place in 1949 when pensions were introduced for widows and other dependants, but civil servants had to pay half the cost of this improvement either through a special contribution or through a reduction in the lump sum on retirement.

The inflation-proofing of civil-service pensions began with the Superannuation Act of 1972.

2.1.2. OCCUPATIONAL PENSION SCHEMES FOR LOCAL-GOVERNMENT OFFICERS

The development of occupational pension schemes for local-government officers took place much later than for central-government civil servants, principally because the organization of local-government activities into a modern system began only with the Local Government Acts of 1888 and 1894, when the separate municipal corporations were replaced by a unified system of counties, county boroughs, and county districts.

Before this, the functions of local administration were carried out by a diverse group of institutions, one of the most important of which was the Board of Guardians of the Poor Law which employed the poor-law officers. In 1864 the Poor Law Officers' Superannuation Act was passed, granting pensions on a discretionary basis to officers who had completed twenty years' service. There was no specified scale of pensions, but the maximum was, as with the civil servants' scheme, two-thirds of final pay, and the minimum age for retirement was again 60 years. Further, the pension was non-contributory, being paid from the same fund as salaries. In 1880 the rate for poor-law officers' pensions was determined by the sixtieths scale, the same as that for civil servants, but the granting of the pension nevertheless remained discretionary in an effort to save on costs. In 1896, by a private member's act, poor-law officers gained the right to have pensions based on the sixtieths scale but, unlike the civil servants, had to pay contributions towards them. Also, unlike the civil servants, the normal age for retirement was set at 65 years rather than 60 years, again to reduce the cost of pension provision. The scale of contributions was set at 2.5 per cent of salaries and this, it was hoped, would be sufficient to pay the complete cost of pensions. But by 1913 these pensions were costing £220,000, while the contributions were raising only £63,000, and the difference was being financed directly from local rates.

The remainder of local-government employees received their pensions in a somewhat piecemeal fashion, with different municipal corporations sponsoring private acts of parliament for the purpose of establishing superannuation funds. These funds were financed by contributions for employees and employers (between 2 per cent and 4 per cent of salary each), offered guaranteed pensions based on the sixtieths scale, and provided deficits to be paid out of the rates. Such acts were passed for Liverpool in 1882, Southport in 1900, and Newcastle upon Tyne in 1904.

In 1922 the Local Government and Other Officers' Superannuation Act was passed. This was another private member's act, the sponsor being Sir Herbert Nield. It established a uniform system of separate local-authority schemes on a voluntary basis. The schemes were of the final-salary type, based on a scale of sixtieths, with a compulsory retirement age of 65. The contributions were equal to 5 per cent of salaries for both employees and employers, but the important point was that, for the first time, the contributions were to be accumulated in funds, the investment of which would generate interest income to contribute towards the provision of pensions. This was the first example in the state sector of an explicitly funded pension scheme. Nield proposed that the scheme should be non-compulsory, which was against the recommendations of the earlier Norman

Committee which had found chaos in the existing pension arrangements for local-government officers: they were 'incomplete, overlapping and conflicting' (*Report*, Cmd. 329, 1919). The voluntary nature of the proposals was advocated on the grounds of cost. A universal compulsory scheme would have to involve all local-government employees, including the more numerous 'servants' (manual workers) as well as 'officers' (salaried staff), and this would inevitably raise the cost of provision. The act permitted each local authority to set up its own scheme along the lines of the above recommendations, without having to introduce a private act of parliament. It also allowed employees to transfer their pension rights with them when they moved between local authorities.

Local-authority pensions were finally made compulsory by an act of 1937, as well as having contributions increased to 6 per cent. In 1953 another act gave final shape to the local-authority scheme, by establishing a widow's pension for a deceased member's wife.

2.1.3. OCCUPATIONAL PENSION SCHEMES FOR OTHER PUBLIC-SECTOR EMPLOYEES

Pension schemes for the police were arranged at the same time as regular police forces were established by acts of parliament: the Metropolitan Police Act 1829 and the County Police Act of 1839. But the schemes were not made obligatory until 1856 for the county police and 1859 for the city police. At first the pensions were discretionary, depending on the watch committees for city police and on justices of the peace for county police. When pensions were granted they were limited to two-thirds of salary, and no police officer was eligible before he reached 60 years unless he was in poor health. The more dangerous conditions of service for police officers meant that the maximum pension could be earned after only twenty years' service, compared with forty-five years for the civil servants. Also, if an officer had to retire through injury he might be given a pension equal to his entire pay.

Police pensions were financed by contributions of up to 2.5 per cent of wages (despite the fact that pensions were discretionary) and also certain court fines, which together were accumulated in funds for investment, the return on which would help pay for pensions, with the deficit being subsidized from the police rate. The police pension scheme was therefore one of the earliest funded schemes in which an explicit fund was established to generate capital and income for the purpose of providing future pensions.

However, the rate of contribution was so small that the funds were soon in deficit. In 1890, for example, the home secretary estimated that the contributions by the metropolitan police, 'if capitalised and invested, would not pay one-tenth part of the proposed pension'. But there was no attempt to increase the rate of contribution. Instead, the government passed the Police Pensions Act of 1890 (covering both England and Wales, and Scotland) which sought to reduce the burden on rates by transferring to the police superannuation funds £300,000 per annum from the collection of certain customs-and-excise duties. The act also gave policemen the right to receive pensions, but the amount of the pension was, within the limits, discretionary; for example, the minimum pension attainable after twenty-five years, varied between 25/50ths and 31/50ths of final salary.

The deficits persisted and in 1921, following the Desborough Committee on Police Affairs, another Police Pensions Act was passed which abolished the separate police superannuation funds in favour of a uniform police pension scheme for the whole of Britain, with pensions again being provided exclusively from contributions and the police rate. The pensions were based on the sixtieths rate, giving a pension equal to half pay after twenty-five years and equal to two-thirds pay after thirty years. Also the police became the first public service to have widows' pensions. All subsequent legislation dealing with police pensions has been based on this 1921 Act. The most important change has been periodic increases in the rate of contribution.

The Elementary School Teachers (Superannuation) Act of 1898 followed from the introduction of compulsory education and the development of state schools. The teachers' scheme under this act, which was different from all other state schemes, was a *money-purchase* scheme, since the pension depended on the number of years that contributions were paid (at the fixed amount of £3 per year for men and £2 a year for women), together with the interest earned on those contributions, and not on the final salary earned. This scheme survived only until 1918, when it was superseded by the Teachers (Superannuation) Act which established a non-contributory, unfunded scheme based on that of the civil service. The teachers' pension scheme soon became contributory but has otherwise remained close to that of the civil service.

A unified scheme for the fire service was introduced by the Fire Brigade Pensions Act 1925. Superannuation funds were established and were financed by both employee and employer contributions, but were later abolished on the same grounds as the police funds.

The establishment of the *national health service* (NHS) by the National Health Service Act 1946 led to pension arrangements being formulated in the NHS (Superannuation) Regulations of 1947–8 for doctors, dentists, nurses, and other NHS employees. These schemes, which were contributory and unfunded, were closely related to existing public-service schemes, especially those of local-government officers, because most NHS employees had previously belonged to such schemes.

The pension schemes that were established for employees of the nationalized industries such as coal, gas, electricity, rail, and air had no previous connections with existing public-sector schemes, and so could more easily develop their own characteristics. However, most schemes provided final-salary pensions based on the scale of sixtieths (or eightieths plus a lump sum). The main difference concerned the method of financing which, for nationalized industries and public corporations, was mainly contributory and funded.

2.2. The Development of Private Occupational Pension Schemes

The earliest recorded private occupational pension schemes were organized by the medieval guilds of artisans in order to provide for the old age of members whose incomes ceased when they retired. This was long before state pension schemes were established. The first recorded occupational pension scheme was that of the Guild of St James at Garlekhithe of London in 1375. However, the artisans' pensions were organized by the artisans themselves. The more usual case was for employers to provide pensions for their employees. To begin with this was done on a discretionary, charitable basis. Only later did a pension become an acknowledgement of previous service (and indeed an inducement to provide loyal service), and even later still did a pension come to be considered a deferred remuneration for which the worker was willing to save.

The next development in the private sector came with the growth of life-assurance companies in the eighteenth century, especially the Equitable Life Assurance Society in 1762 which established *premium tables* based on actuarial calculations. This, in turn, permitted the development of *endowment-assurance pension schemes*, so that individuals were able to save for their old age and at the same time provide security for their families.

The earliest private-sector schemes to be based on life-assurance principles were those of the East India Company and the Bank of England. The Gas, Light and Coke Company introduced a contributory scheme for salaried staff in 1842 and for manual workers in 1870. Prudential Assurance introduced a widows' scheme in 1866 and a retirement-pension scheme in 1872. Siemens Brothers of Woolwich introduced a pension scheme in 1872. Lever Brothers introduced injury, illness, and retirement benefits in 1904, and in 1906 a retirement scheme was established by Rowntrees of York. In 1854 the London and North Western Railway Company established a contributory scheme, and by 1908 about thirty pension schemes covering 90,000 salaried staff had been established by independent railway companies on the argument, according to A. Kaye Butterworth, general manager of the North Eastern Railway Company, that 'the pension . . . is an act of business common sense . . . not philanthropy . . . Unless you have something like an efficient pension fund, the directors would be under a constant compulsion to keep on the men' (evidence to the Departmental Committee on Railway Superannuation Funds, Cd. 5484, 1911). The earliest pension schemes were therefore associated with the largest employers in the nineteenth century: railways, gas companies, banking, insurance, and manufacturing.

The gradual recognition by both employees and employers that pensions were equivalent to deferred salary payments led to the introduction of formal pension schemes with investment funds based on workers' and employers' contributions as a safeguard for those contributions. The system of funded pension schemes began to grow slowly after the First World War. Most occupational pension schemes in the UK have been set up as *pension trust funds* under the Superannuation and Other Trust Funds (Validation) Act of 1927. A pension scheme is established under *irrevocable trust* using a *trust deed* and run by *trustees*, with the employee being a beneficiary under the trust.

The decentralized and piecemeal growth of private-sector pension schemes, even when compared with those in the public sector, resulted in a much greater variety of schemes in the former than in the latter in the early years. For example, one particular feature of the early private-sector schemes was the different types of scheme for salaried staff and wage-earning manual employees. In general, salaried staff made contributions that were a fixed percentage of their salaries and received pensions based on the average salaries earned during their working lives and on the number of years of service. Manual employees, on the other hand, paid a fixed amount in contributions and, in turn, received a flat-rate pension. They also, generally, received their pensions at a later age than salaried staff. However, average-salary schemes were likely to result in a lower average pension than the final-salary schemes enjoyed by most public-sector workers. Another type of scheme found in the private sector was the money-purchase scheme. Money-purchase pensions tended to be lower even than average-salary pensions. Eventually, final-salary pensions came to be preferred to both average-salary and money-purchase pensions. Clearly employees were going to favour final-salary schemes, but many employers favoured them as well: they made it much easier to implement mandatory retirement policies than either average-salary or money-purchase schemes.

Other aspects of private-sector occupational pension schemes began to converge as well, usually on the model provided by public-sector occupational schemes. For example, contributions were set at a fixed proportion of income, pension accruals were proportional to the number of years' service (up to a maximum of forty years), and the normal age of retirement was usually 65 for men and 60 for women.

However, virtually all of the pension schemes that developed in the private sector were funded schemes, usually with contributions from both employees and employers. This compares with the quite wide variety of means of financing pensions in the public sector, resulting from the public sector's unlimited ability to finance its expenditure, derived from its powers of taxation.

Further, most of the funded schemes were assured with life companies; the rest were self-administered and, as a consequence, self-assured. The first company to assure pension funds in Britain was the Metropolitan Life Insurance Company of New York, which in the 1920s began to organize the funds of British subsidiaries of American companies (such as Woolworth and General Motors) which had similar schemes for their employees in the USA. Early in the 1930s Metropolitan Life stopped transacting business in Britain and transferred its existing pension schemes to the Legal and General Assurance Society, which was one of the earliest British insurance companies to offer pension-fund assurance. The first large British pension fund to be assured with an insurance company was that of the Gramophone Company (later renamed Electrical and Musical Industries); this was in 1930 and the insurance company concerned was Legal and General.

The early pension schemes, administered by insurance companies, were based on insurance policies taken out for each employee separately. Such policies could provide pensions from the purchase of deferred annuities or could provide against the risk of death with endowment assurance. However, individual policies proved to be a costly means of giving pensions, because of the problems of staff turnover. They also restricted pensions to those of the money-purchase type. These problems were largely overcome and the administration of pension schemes greatly improved by the introduction from the USA of the *group life pension scheme* in the 1920s. The insurance company agreed to underwrite a single policy covering all the employees in a company, and also took away the burden of administration of the scheme from the company.

Funded pension schemes (as with occupational pension schemes in general) began among the larger companies, and these have tended to run their own schemes. Smaller companies, on the other hand, which were clearly always in the majority, have tended to use the specialist investment services provided by life companies, stockbrokers, or pension consultants; this is because their funds were too small to provide a sufficient degree of risk diversification. The leading life companies involved in providing group pension schemes to smaller companies were the Prudential, Legal and General, Eagle Star, Friends' Provident, and Standard Life. By 1934 these five companies had sold group life pension schemes covering 120,000 workers. In 1958 the government actuary estimated that 76 per cent of large schemes (with more than 500 members) were self-administered, while 24 per cent were assured with life companies. For smaller schemes, only 34 per cent were self-administered. By 1975 the government actuary's survey indicated that virtually all small schemes were assured with life companies, and that about half of the large schemes were too.

The first survey of occupational pension schemes was made by the Ministry of Labour in 1936, and the results were published in 1938 ('Schemes Providing Pensions for Employees on Retirement from Work', *Ministry of Labour Gazette*, May 1938). It showed that 1.6 million employees in the private sector were members of occupational schemes, with about 90,000 people already receiving pensions, half of these being manual workers. There was a large increase in the number of pension schemes after the Second World War as a result of the high taxation of profits and the tax concessions on contributions to pension schemes. By 1956 when the government actuary undertook his first survey of occupational pension schemes (*Occupational Pension Schemes*, Government Actuary's Department, 1958) there were 4.3 million members in the private sector and 300,000 pensioners, again only half of whom were wage-earners, despite the fact that two-thirds of all employees were wage-earners. There were also 2.3 million members in the public services (including the armed services) and 1.4 million in the nationalized industries. The government actuary's third survey, carried out in 1967 (*Occupational Pension Schemes 1967*, Government Actuary's Department, 1968) indicated that the total membership of occupational pension schemes had grown to an historical high of 12.2 million (9.9 million men and 2.3 million women). The public sector provided about 4 million members, and the membership of the private sector, at about 8 million, had doubled between 1956 and 1967. The latest survey from the Government Actuary's Department, carried out in 1987 (*Occupational Pension Schemes 1987*, Government Actuary's Department, 1991) revealed that total membership of occupational pension schemes had fallen somewhat to 10.6 million (7.2 million men and 3.4 million women), with 4.8 million in the public sector and 5.8 million in the private sector, reflecting the decline in the total employed population, especially in the private sector, following the 1980–1 recession. The membership of public-sector schemes, while higher than in 1967, had fallen from the 1979 historical high of 5.5 million, reflecting the Thatcher government's privatization policy.

2.3. The Development of Personal Pension Schemes

Money-purchase pensions have had a long history in the UK. Indeed, some of the earliest funded pensions were not related to salary at all, but were of the money-purchase variety. However, the persistence of inflation and the attraction of a pension related to earnings near retirement led to the virtual demise of money-purchase schemes in the twentieth century. But in recent years money-purchase pensions have made a dramatic comeback and with a new name—*personal pensions*.

Personal pension schemes are pension schemes that are organized for individuals or groups of individuals by financial institutions (such as insurance companies and banks) rather than by the companies for which these individuals work. Personal pensions are designed to be portable, that is, not related to the place of employment. They are now the only type of pension available for the *self-employed*.

The Conservative government that came to power in 1979 had the aim of reducing public expenditure and promoting individual choice. In 1984 the Department of Health and Social Security published *Personal Pensions—A Consultative Document*. It was proposed that personal pensions should be available to all employees if they wanted them. The personal pensions would be of the money-purchase type. This was in contrast with the earnings-related or defined-benefit pensions of SERPS. The consultative document also proposed that the personal pensions should be eligible for contracting out of SERPS, with the qualifying test based on the level of contributions necessary to deliver an adequate level of pension. Given that the pension would be based on the invested contributions, the employee would have to bear the risk that the resulting pension might be smaller than that available from his employer's earnings-related scheme or from SERPS. The right to take out a defined-contribution pension was enshrined in the 1986 Social Security Act. Personal pension schemes first became available on 1 July 1988.

With a personal pension scheme, the pension relates to the size of the fund accumulated; so there is no limit to the size of the pension that can be received. The pension can normally start between the ages of 50 and 75, and must be inflation-proofed up to a maximum of 3 per cent per annum. Up to 25 per cent of the value of the fund accumulated by the time of retirement can be taken as a tax-free lump sum. The 1987 Finance (No. 2) Act placed an upper limit on the size of the lump sum at £150,000, although this upper limit was subsequently removed by the 1989 Finance Act. The 1987 act also allowed money-purchase schemes to be contracted out of SERPS as long as they provided a *protected rights pension* which is equivalent to the SERPS pension given up. In addition, the act allowed employers to establish *contracted-out money-purchase schemes* (COMPSs). Most personal pension schemes have been set up using the Inland Revenue's *model rules*, since any scheme adopting the model rules is automatically granted contracting-out approval from SERPS. Under the model rules, the pension scheme can either be put *in trust* or formed using a *deed poll*.

The 1986 Social Security Act allowed all members of occupational pension schemes to make *additional voluntary contributions* (or AVCs) to their existing schemes in order to enhance their pension benefits. In addition, following the 1987 Finance (No. 2) Act, it has been possible to make *free-standing additional voluntary contributions* (FSAVCs) outside the employer's scheme. The FSAVCs are fully portable when an individual changes occupational schemes.

By 1993 5 million people were contributing towards a personal pension scheme and making annual contributions of £6.4 billion. It is quite clear that the state has played a significant role in the development of both occupational and personal pension schemes. This role is discussed in some detail in the next chapter.

3

The Role of the State in the Development of Pensions and Pension Schemes

The development of UK pensions and pension schemes has been very much a British affair. With some exceptions, there have been no significant outside influences on that development. The exceptions have been few and far between, for example, the introduction of group life pension schemes from the USA in the 1920s and the European Community's (and since 1 November 1993 the European Union's) various rulings on the equal treatment of men and women from the 1970s. The single most important influence on the development of UK pensions and pension schemes has been the state itself. In this chapter we analyse in more detail the role of the state in this respect.

3.1. The Purposes behind the State's Provision of Pensions

The state has been providing some form of retirement assistance since the end of the sixteenth century. However, the first organized provision of pensions was that for public servants in 1810. Members of the public, on the other hand, had to wait another century to receive old-age pensions from the state.

From the beginning, *economy* and *efficiency* were the constant themes underlying the state provision of pensions, both for public servants and for members of the public. For example, a pension came to be regarded both as an important condition of service for, and as a guarantee of loyal service by, public servants. In the beginning, the state's provision of pensions to members of the public was based on a mixture of concern about the plight of the aged poor, belief in the virtue of thrift, and a contempt for idleness. Such considerations of efficiency led to pensions being provided initially only in extreme cases, and then only at a sub-sistence level. As late as the 1940s, Beveridge was able to argue that provision above the subsistence level was a matter for free choice and voluntary insurance. Even more concern was placed on the cost of state-pension provision. To begin with, pensions were non-contributory, but continually rising costs led to the introduction of contributions paid through national insurance. The original aim of the national-insurance scheme was complete funding (as with all insurance schemes), apart from an Exchequer supplement to cover the deficit during the start-up phase. However, the deficit continued to build up to such an extent that, eventually, pay-as-you-go contributions were introduced and all pretence at funding ceased. At the same time, there were pressures both to in-crease choice in pension provision and to link pensions more closely to the changes in the fortunes of the economy as a whole. There was also a change in attitudes towards pensions: from viewing pensions as a relief from poverty to viewing them as a form of income replacement. As a result we have moved from a universal compulsory scheme with flat-rate contributions and benefits to a mixed flat-rate and graduated or earnings-related scheme (with the possibility of contracting out of the earnings-related component), and with benefits linked fully or partially to wages or prices depending on which government was in power. In addition, the demands for increased choice and flexibility led to the introduction of personal pension schemes in 1988.

The importance of the state pension scheme has been to provide a series of bench-marks of minimal standards of living in retirement against which the provision of both occupational pensions and personal pensions could be compared. Viewed as a whole, the history of state-pension provision reflects: (i) the development of society's awareness and concern (especially by the political leaders of society) about the conditions of the aged and, particularly, the aged poor; (ii) the maintenance through the twentieth century of the nineteenth-century Protestant ethic of self-help, together with a concern for economy and efficiency, with the resulting implications for minimal pension provision; and (iii) the changing econ-omic fortunes of the country and how these are shared by pensioners (and other social-security beneficiaries), who constitute a large but also a broadly weak section of society, both economically and politically. Thus, for example, we have witnessed the establishment and then the gradual erosion of the real value of certain social-security benefits. (However, in the future the relative power of the pensioner population is likely to increase as a result of demographic and other factors; the consequences of this are discussed in Chapter 10.)

3.2. The State's Influence on the Development of Occupational Pension Schemes and Personal Pension Schemes

3.2.1. INDIRECT INFLUENCES

Formal occupational pension schemes were first established in 1712 in the public sector and in 1762 in the private sector, although some provision for old age can be traced back to the guilds of artisans in the Middle

Ages. Initially, the development of occupational pension schemes took place in a piecemeal fashion, but eventually the most important aspects of the occupational pension schemes developed by the state for its own employees became incorporated into private-sector schemes.

Occupational pension schemes for public servants took on many different forms during their long historical development. However, they eventually converged into a few distinct types, the differences depending mainly on the nature of the financing of the schemes rather than on the benefits provided, with a principal consideration being that of the cost of the scheme. The typical final form of the pension was a mandatory (that is, non-discretionary) benefit, depending both on the final salary and on the number of years' service, providing an annuity until the death of the pensioner (or commutation of part of that annuity to a lump sum at the beginning of retirement), together with a widow's and later a widower's benefit for the surviving spouse. There was also an invalidity pension in the case of forced early retirement through injury.

The means of financing the schemes differed for different sections of the public service. Civil servants, for example, paid no contributions until their pensions were index-linked in 1972; their scheme was unfunded, the pensions being paid directly by the Exchequer. The pension schemes as finally developed for the police, firemen, teachers, health-service workers, and others were contributory but unfunded, the contributions of current employees being sufficient to provide pay-as-you-go pensions for retired workers. Finally, the pension schemes of both local-authority officers and the employees of nationalized industries and public corporations were both contributory and funded, with the income from the fund contributing to the cost of pensions. The principal importance of public-sector occupational schemes and their different ways of providing and financing pension benefits has been, like state pensions themselves, to provide a comparison with the costs and benefits of private-sector occupational schemes.

Private-sector occupational pension schemes have an even more disorganized history than public-sector ones. There was initially a much larger range of schemes, with different schemes for salaried staff as against manual employees, and with many different ways of calculating benefits, such as flat-rate, average-salary, final-salary, and money-purchase. Eventually, private-sector pension schemes began to converge on a single format, namely, a final-salary structure, with a constant proportion of final salary (typically one-sixtieth) for each year of service, up to a maximum of two-thirds of final salary for forty years' service, but with the possibility of taking a lump sum equal to one-and-a-half times final salary and a lower annual pension based on the eightieths scale. However, there was one thing which virtually all private-sector schemes had in common in contrast with public-sector schemes: they were nearly all funded, usually with contributions from both employers and employees. Also, most large private-sector schemes were self-administered (that is, self-assured), while almost all small schemes were assured with insurance companies on a group life basis.

So by taking the best features of the occupational schemes developed by the state, private occupational pension schemes converged on a single type. The most pervasive influences of the state, then, have been the indirect ones, namely those arising from the powerful forces of *competition* and *comparability*.

3.2.2. DIRECT INFLUENCES

There have been three main direct influences of the state on the development of private pension schemes, both occupational and personal: (i) the tax concessions available to private-sector schemes; (ii) the co-operation between the state and private-sector schemes; and (iii) the legislative controls on private-sector schemes.

3.2.2.1. *Tax Concessions*

The state has done much to influence directly the development of private-sector pension schemes, because tax concessions have only been available on schemes approved by the Inland Revenue. With the high level of progressive taxation experienced in Britain for much of the twentieth century, the tax concessions have made approved pension schemes a more efficient way of remunerating workers than paying them higher salaries and allowing them to save for their own retirements out of these. Indeed, pension schemes are an extremely tax-efficient savings vehicle. However, the state has also been concerned to prevent pension schemes being used as vehicles for tax avoidance.

Tax relief on life-assurance premiums had been available ever since the introduction of income tax itself in the Income Tax Act of 1799. Income tax was abolished after the Napoleonic Wars but reintroduced by Gladstone in his 1853 Budget, when he established the principle of full tax relief on both life assurance and deferred annuities. In 1916 the tax concession was reduced from full relief to a lower rate, called the *life-assurance relief rate*. This concession was consolidated in the Income Tax Act of 1918, and subsequently pension schemes based on deferred annuities, where contributions received relief at the life-assurance relief rate, became known as *1918 act schemes*.[1] *Income-tax allowances* were introduced in 1920.

---

[1] Income-tax relief on life-assurance premiums was eventually abolished in the 1984 Finance Act.

The Finance Act of 1921 introduced tax relief on employees' contributions to pension trust funds approved by the Inland Revenue under the terms of the act, and such funds became known as *1921 act schemes*. In addition, investment income on the funds was free of tax, and income tax was payable on pensions only when they were paid. The pressure for this relief came from the Conference of Superannuation Funds, which was formed in 1917 to lobby for changes in the tax treatment of pension funds.[2]

The Finance Act of 1947 changed the tax treatment of employers' contributions to pension schemes which were not approved under the 1921 Finance Act. Under the 1947 act, any contribution made by an employer to a pension scheme for the benefit of an employee was taxed as if it were the income of that employee. Further, if an employer agreed to provide a pension to an employee but the agreement was not explicitly funded through the purchase of an endowment-assurance policy, then the employee would be taxed on the notional amount that the employer would have paid had the agreement been funded. The act put an end to the growth of the so-called *top-hat schemes*, whereby senior executives were paid relatively low salaries, but had large endowment-assurance policies with premiums paid by employers, and received lump sums entirely free of tax when the policies matured.

The Income Tax Act of 1952 consolidated all previous income-tax legislation, including that dealing with pension schemes. The 1921 act schemes were re-approved, under section 379 of the 1952 act, and became known as *section 379 schemes*. Similarly the 1918 act schemes were re-approved under section 388 of the 1952 act and became known as *section 388 schemes*, with tax relief available on two-fifths of the amount of contribution paid.

In 1954 the Millard Tucker Committee, set up in 1950 to investigate the different tax treatments of the provision of pensions especially for the self-employed and others with no pension scheme, presented its report. Some of the committee's recommendations appeared in the 1956 Finance Act. For example, the act helped the self-employed by re-establishing both full tax relief on contributions and tax-exempt investment income for approved deferred-annuity contracts (these concessions had been available on pension trust funds since 1921). It also removed the tax liability on the interest earned by insurance companies from section 379 funds, thereby raising the effective yield of the funds' investments. This made section 379 schemes, which now enjoyed both complete tax relief on contributions and no tax liability on interest earned, considerably more

---

[2] The Conference changed its name to the Association of Superannuation and Pension Funds in 1923, and in 1962 to the National Association of Pension Funds.

attractive than section 388 schemes, and led to a wholesale conversion of the latter into the former. Despite the administrative burden of this change-over, many pensioners began to receive increased benefits. Section 388 schemes still survived however. They were used by firms with less than ten eligible employees, since insurance companies would not operate section 379 schemes with fewer than this number of members. Also, section 388 schemes could provide commutable pensions whereas section 379 schemes could not.

The Finance Act of 1965 introduced the taxation of capital gains in section 20. But under section 36 most superannuation funds were exempted from the payment of this tax, and such funds were designated *gross funds*. However, to warrant the tax exemptions under section 36, the funds had to engage in investment and not trading or property development.

The Income and Corporation Taxes Act of 1970 (known as the Taxes Act 1970) consolidated all previous income-tax legislation, including that dealing with pension schemes. Pension schemes were granted *exempt approved* status under sections 208 and 209. Under section 208 the schemes enjoyed tax relief on contributions by employers against corporation tax, and by employees against income tax. Under section 209 funds were also exempted from the payment of both income and capital-gains tax. Under section 220 the directors and employees of certain schemes were liable to have their retirement benefits under those schemes treated as income and hence assessable for income tax under Schedule E (that is, pay-as-you-earn), as detailed in sections 181 and 204. However, under section 221 the benefits accruing from approved section 208 schemes were exempted from this liability. Under section 226 certain types of *retirement annuity contracts* were approved for the self-employed, and the premiums paid on these contracts, known as *qualifying premiums*, were eligible for income-tax relief in amounts specified in section 227.[3] The main restrictions were that the benefit did not commence before the individual had reached the age of 60, and that the benefit was by way of an annuity exclusively to that particular individual or his widow, and not by any other means, such as by commutation of the whole or part of the annuity to a third party. However, the Inland Revenue could, if it thought proper, approve annuity contracts which did not satisfy these restrictions. Retirement-trust schemes were also approved under this section, with the income from investments and the capital gains derived from the disposal of investments under these schemes exempted from taxation. Under section 314 the pension business of life companies was exempted from corporation tax

---

[3] *Section 226 schemes* for the self-employed were replaced by personal pension schemes on 1 July 1988.

in respect of income from, and chargeable gains on, investments and deposits exclusively for the purpose of pensions business.

In the Finance Act 1970, section 19 was designed to supersede section 208 of the Taxes Act 1970, in changing the conditions for approval of superannuation schemes by the Inland Revenue. The 'prescribed conditions' were that the scheme was established for the sole purpose of providing retirement benefits for an employee and his dependants; that the scheme was recognized by both employers and employees, and that every employee who was a member of the scheme had been given written particulars of all essential features of the scheme; that the administration of the scheme would be undertaken by residents of the UK; that the employer was a contributor to the scheme; that the scheme was established in connection with some trade or undertaking carried out in the UK by a resident of the UK; and that, under no circumstances or at any time, could the employees' contributions be repaid. Violation of any of these conditions could lead to the Inland Revenue withdrawing approval. Exempt approved status was granted under section 21. Under section 21 certain approved schemes were exempted from income tax in respect of income derived from investments or deposits and from capital-gains tax on the disposal of investments held for the purposes of the scheme. The contributions by employers (up to specified limits) were allowed to be deducted as an expense of management for the purposes of evaluating Schedule D liability under the Taxes Act, and the contributions of employees (up to specified limits) were allowed to be deducted as an expense for the purposes of assessing Schedule E liability. Sections 23 and 24 were designed to supersede sections 220 and 221 of the Taxes Act, the former in assessing the retirement benefits of certain schemes as income and therefore liable to taxation under Schedule E, and the latter in exempting the benefits of approved schemes from this liability.

The Finance Act 1971 amended the conditions of approval of occupational pension schemes made under section 19 of the Finance Act 1970. In particular, the following additional conditions for an approved scheme to satisfy were made: that the benefit was considered to be a retirement pension only if it commenced not earlier than 60 years for a man (55 years for a woman) nor later than 70 years, and did not exceed one-sixtieth of the employee's final remuneration for each year of service up to a maximum of forty years; that the benefit payable to a widow of an employee on his death did not exceed two-thirds of the benefit payable to the employee; and that commutation of part of the pension was permitted only if the lump sum resulting did not exceed three-eightieths of the employee's final remuneration for each year of service up to a maximum of forty years (giving a maximum lump sum of one-and-a-half times final salary).

The 1988 Income and Corporation Taxes Act (known as the Taxes Act 1988) consolidated all previous income-tax legislation, including granting exempt approved status to occupational pension schemes under section 592. The 1989 Finance Act introduced new limits on both earnings and contributions that qualify for tax relief in occupational pension schemes. The earnings limit on which a final-salary pension can be based was set at £60,000 (in 1989 prices), implying a maximum pension, at two-thirds of final salary, of £40,000 (in 1989 prices). The maximum lump sum that could be commuted at retirement was £90,000 (in 1989 prices). The maximum contribution rate into an occupational scheme is 15 per cent of earnings, while the maximum combined employee and employer contribution rate is 17.5 per cent of earnings. Higher combined limits apply to employees over 50, ranging from 20 per cent for a 51-year-old to 27.5 per cent for a 74-year-old.

Since August 1989 occupational schemes have been able to provide *top-up schemes* on top of their main schemes. The top-up schemes can provide additional pension benefits above the tax-approved limits, but do not enjoy any tax advantages on contributions or investment income above the tax-approved limits.

One interesting tax anomaly which has remained purely for historical reasons is the tax-free lump sum that is available on retirement. Civil servants were granted a lump sum on retirement in return for a lower pension thereafter as a result of the Superannuation Act of 1909. The Inland Revenue (whose civil servants could also have the lump sum) was asked whether the lump sum would be taxable, and it said that it would not be. It gave no reason for this decision, although presumably the reason was that the lump sum was a capital payment, not income, and hence not taxable (in 1909).

While there is no real logic to this argument, the lump sum (where a lump sum has been permitted) has remained free of tax ever since, although there have been legislative measures to deal with the permissible size of the lump sum. The 1921 Finance Act established tax-exempted pension trust funds which were exempted from tax on both contributions and investment income; but pensions were fully taxable as income and lump sums were not permitted. However, lump sums were payable on the endowment-assurance schemes of life companies known as top-hat schemes, and these lump sums were entirely free of tax, whatever their size. The tax-avoidance abuses under these schemes were partially rectified by the 1947 Finance Act, which limited the tax-free lump sum to 25 per cent of the value of the fund. The 1970 Finance Act permitted tax-free lump sums with a maximum equal to one-and-a-half times final salary (approximately equal to the 1947 limit of 25 per cent of the fund value) after twenty years' service to all tax-exempt schemes. The act applied to all new schemes from 1973 and to all existing schemes from 1980. So, rather than withdraw the lump-sum privileges of civil servants, those privileges have applied to everyone else since 1980.

The tax treatment of personal pension schemes is governed by the 1987 (No. 2) and 1989 Finance Acts. The 1987 act allows full tax relief on contributions up to 17.5 per cent of salary as the maximum combined employer and employee contributions. The Inland Revenue also allows unused tax relief on employees' contributions to be carried forward for up to six years. The investment income and realized capital gains from the fund are exempt from income and capital-gains taxes. The lump sum payable on retirement is tax-free up to a limit of £150,000, while the annuity pension is taxed as earned income. The 1989 act introduced new limits on contributions that qualify for tax relief in personal pension schemes, but also removed the £150,000 limit on the lump sum. The act introduced new contribution limits for those aged 36 and over, ranging from 20 per cent of earnings for a 36-year-old to 35 per cent for someone above 56 years. The earnings limit on which contributions qualify for tax relief was set at £60,000 (in 1989 prices).

So the state has done much to provide concessions in the form of tax relief on contributions by both employers and employees, not treating employers' contributions as the income of employees and hence subject to income tax, and tax relief on dividends and capital gains for exempt approved schemes. There is also the possibility of a tax-free lump sum at retirement. Only the pension annuity itself is subject to income tax.

3.2.2.2. *Co-operation between the State and Private Schemes*

The state has also done much to influence the development of private-sector occupational pension schemes by establishing greater co-operation between these and the state social-security pension scheme. This was first done in the National Insurance Act of 1959, which permitted private employers to contract out of the graduated part of the state scheme so long as their pension schemes were recognized as being equivalent alternatives to the state scheme, as being financially sound, and as providing a sufficient guarantee of the occupational pension rights of people changing employment.

The partnership between the state and private schemes was further reinforced by the Social Security Pensions Act of 1975, which established SERPS (the state earnings-related pension scheme). It was possible to contract out of SERPS (by applying for a contracting-out certificate from the Occupational Pensions Board) so long as the contracted-out occupational pension scheme provided equivalent benefits expressed in terms of a guaranteed minimum pension. The act reduced the contributions to and the benefits under the state scheme for employees of contracted-out occupational pension schemes. Schemes which ceased to be contracted-out remained supervised by the Occupational Pensions Board until the guaranteed minimum pension rights of their members had been secured and the payments of contributions to the state scheme had begun. The act also guaranteed that if a company went into liquidation, the contributions to its occupational pension scheme would be given priority over other creditors.

The Social Security Act of 1980 made some minor amendments to the Social Security Pensions Act 1975. For example, the Occupational Pensions Board was given the right to withdraw its approval of occupational pension scheme arrangements and could refuse or cancel a contracting-out certificate if the rules of a scheme excluded employees over certain ages. Also, transfers of accrued rights between schemes were permissible only where the employee was in contracted-out employment in the receiving scheme.

The partnership between the state and personal pension schemes was established in the 1986 Social Security Act. This act, for example, allowed members of contracted-out personal pension schemes to re-contract into the state scheme.

3.2.2.3. *Legislative Controls*

The state has also sought to control the activities of pension schemes and to improve the rights of scheme members through a set of legislative measures. These measures have covered such areas as the rights of early leavers, the disclosure of information, the equal treatment of men and women, pension-fund surpluses, and investor protection.

Until fairly recently, pension schemes faced very few direct controls on their activities. They had to comply with the requirements of the 1927 Superannuation and Other Trust Funds (Validation) Act if they wished to be validated as a pension trust fund, and they had to achieve exempt approved status from the Inland Revenue in order to qualify for tax relief.

3.2.2.3.1. *The Rights of Early Leavers* However, in recent years pension schemes have been faced with a wider range of controls. The first set of measures dealt with the *rights of early leavers*. These were first established in the National Insurance Act 1959 and subsequently reinforced in the Social Security Acts of 1973, 1985, 1986, and 1990, and the Health and Social Security Act of 1984.

The 1973 Social Security Act, for example, required that pension schemes provide *deferred pensions* to those early leavers who were at least 26 years of age and who had accumulated at least five years' service; those with less than five years' scheme membership could have a refund of contributions. However, the deferred pension was not indexed for inflation between the date of leaving and the date of retirement. The huge inflation of the 1970s showed the inadequacy of the 1973 act. The position was improved first by the 1985 act and subsequently by the 1986 and 1990 acts. These acts required the deferred pensions of early leavers with at least two years' scheme membership to be uprated each year by the annual rate of inflation up to a maximum of 5 per cent per annum compound from April 1978 for those leaving occupational schemes after January 1991. And as an alternative to a deferred pension, the 1985 act allowed early leavers to take their pension entitlement with them. This is achieved through a *transfer value* calculated as the cash equivalent of the accrued rights under the scheme. The transfer value is paid to another scheme (either occupational or personal) or into an insurance policy known as a *section 32 buy-out policy* after section 32 of the 1981 Finance Act which first permitted buy-outs.

The 1984 Health and Social Security Act amended the Social Security Pensions Act of 1975 in order to protect the accrued rights to the requisite benefits under a contracted-out pension scheme or transfer to another contracted-out scheme, whether or not the member was in current employment.

In recent years the inequitable treatment of early leavers has been widely recognized, and the government's aim has been to correct this inequity as well as to promote and encourage job mobility, especially through the development of personal pensions. But this is very much a new view. A much earlier view of pensions (and one that was prevalent as late as the 1950s) saw them as inducements to remain loyal to the same employer; there was even talk of the economic benefits of reducing labour turnover. This, in turn, required early leavers to be badly penalized in terms of their future pensions from their former employers.

3.2.2.3.2. *The Disclosure of Information*   The government was also concerned that there was widespread ignorance amongst members about their pension schemes. The government therefore decided that members had to be provided with much more information about their schemes. This was achieved in the 1978 Employment Protection Act, the 1985 and 1990 Social Security Acts, the 1986 Occupational Pension Schemes (Disclosure of Information) Regulations, and the 1992 Occupational and Personal Pension Schemes (Miscellaneous Amendments) Regulations. These acts and regulations require that new entrants to a scheme be provided with basic information about their scheme (for example, concerning benefits while they are members and benefits if they subsequently leave) within thirteen weeks of joining. Existing members are entitled to this information on request. An annual trustees' report which includes details of the audited accounts must also be prepared. This must also be made available to scheme members on request. The 1990 Social Security Act introduced a *pensions ombudsman* and a *tracing service* to help early leavers establish their pension rights in former pension schemes.

3.2.2.3.3. *The Equal Treatment of Men and Women*   Another aspect of government intervention in the running of pension schemes concerned the *equal treatment of men and women*. The 1980 Social Security Act amended the 1975 Social Security Act to take account of the Council of the European Communities' directive on the *Equal Treatment for Men and Women in Social Security* (Dir. 79/7/EEC). Under the 1986 Sex Discrimination Act, it became illegal from November 1987 to discriminate between men and women in respect of the age of retirement. The act therefore required pension schemes (although the state scheme is exempted from this act's provisions) to have the same date of normal retirement for both men and women. In addition, the Council of the European Communities issued a directive in July 1986 on the *Implementation of the Principle of the Equal Treatment for Men and Women in Occupational Social Security Schemes* (Dir. 86/378/EEC). The directive required occupational pension schemes to provide equal benefits for men and women after July 1989. Mandatory widowers' pensions were not introduced until April 1989, for example. It also required equal contributions from male and female employees to defined-contribution (that is, money-purchase) schemes from 1999. However, the directive allowed for the possibility of employer contributions to defined-contribution schemes to differ between male and female employees. The directive's aim was still to provide equal benefits, but because women live longer than men on average, the actuarial cost of providing equal benefits is higher for women's schemes than for men's. While employees were not permitted to make different contributions, it remained possible for employers to make different contributions in order that all employees end up with equal benefits. The directive was implemented by the 1989 Social Security Act.

3.2.2.3.4. *Pension-Fund Surpluses*   The 1986 Finance Act introduced criteria for measuring and dealing with the actuarial *surpluses* in defined-benefit occupational pension funds. An actuarial surplus arises whenever the current value of the investments in a fund exceeds the current value of the future pension liabilities. During the 1980s actuarial surpluses had built up in a large number of pension schemes. This was for two reasons. First, the stock-market boom between 1974 and 1987 had led to huge increases in asset values. Secondly, the 1980–1 recession had caused substantial redundancies, especially in manufacturing. These redundancies led to corresponding departures from pension schemes, with the result that the actuarial liabilities of those schemes were substantially reduced. The presence of the surpluses was causing the Inland Revenue some concern. Contributions into the schemes were attracting tax relief, the returns on the invested contributions were free of tax, and now surpluses were accruing to the schemes which were not taxed either. Pension funds were turning into vehicles for tax avoidance. The 1986 Finance Act required that the surpluses had to be reduced to no more than a 5 per cent excess over liabilities within five years. Four methods of doing this were permitted: (i) a reduction or suspension of contributions from the employer; (ii) a reduction or suspension of contributions from employees; (iii) an increase in benefits to existing pensioners up to the limits approved by the Inland Revenue; or (iv) a repatriation of the surplus to the parent company. In the latter case, the repatriated funds would be taxed at a special rate of 40 per cent.

3.2.2.3.5. *Investor Protection*   Finally, the government was concerned with *investor protection*. Trustees had a fiduciary duty under the 1925 Trustee Act to preserve the trust capital and to apply the capital and its income according to the trust deed. Without specific provision in the trust deeds, the 1925 act limited the *authorized investments* of the pension fund to British government or government-guaranteed securities and to the stocks of local authorities and certain railways and utilities. The 1925 act was replaced by the 1961 Trustee Investments Act, which considerably widened the scope of authorized investments to include company securities and unit trusts. Trustees are required to *invest* in assets for the long-term benefits of their pensioners, and not to *trade* in assets for short-term speculative gains. However, the 1990 Finance Act exempts from tax pension funds' trading income from futures and options contracts. This allows pension funds to use futures and options contracts for risk-management purposes without fear of a tax charge.

Despite their wide investment powers, trustees do face a number of restrictions on their investments. For example, the 1990 Social Security Act placed limits on the amount of self-investment by pension funds in parent companies to 5 per-cent of fund assets. The 5 per-cent ceiling covers shares, loans, property, and also money owed by the company to the scheme. The ceiling is designed to protect pension schemes from the failure of the parent company and also from hostile take-overs.

When personal pension schemes first started, the categories of eligible securities that could be invested in were quite restrictive, mainly quoted UK shares and investment trusts. This was changed by the 1989 Finance Act. It became possible to invest in overseas shares, unquoted UK shares, unit trusts, gilts, and commercial property.

A new regulatory framework (involving the setting-up of the Securities and Investments Board along similar lines to the Securities and Exchange Commission in the USA) was established by the 1986 Financial Services

Act, as part of the wider changes in the City of London known as the *Big Bang*. The act requires the authorization of everyone carrying on investment business or giving investment advice. The way in which the act affects pension schemes was contained in a guidance note entitled *Pensions Advice and Management Authorisation under the Financial Services Act*, issued by the Securities and Investments Board in February 1987.

Pension-scheme trustees and employers can advise employees on the merits of joining a scheme without being authorized. They can also compare the advantages and disadvantages of scheme membership versus other forms of pension provision, such as personal pensions, without being authorized. This is because discussing a class of investment (and personal pensions are regarded as a class of investment) is not regarded under the act as giving investment advice. However, trustees and employers could not advise on or recommend specific pension plans without being authorized, as this does constitute investment advice under the act.

As far as managing the investments of the fund is concerned, trustees will not have to be authorized if all the day-to-day investment-management decisions are taken on behalf of the trustees by an authorized person. If this is not the case, then the trustees themselves will have to be authorized.

These legislative measures have been designed either to improve the position of scheme members *vis-à-vis* the employers and trustees or to correct taxation abuses that have occurred. The measures have been introduced largely on an *ad hoc* basis, and it is not clear whether members know or even care much more about their schemes.

3.3. Conclusion

The state has exerted a substantial influence both directly and indirectly on the development of private-sector occupational pension schemes. The main indirect influences derived from competition and comparability with its own schemes, whilst the main direct influences were those dealing with: (i) the tax concessions available on pension-scheme contributions and investment income, which have done so much to encourage pension savings, although not at the expense of pension schemes being used for tax avoidance; (ii) the co-operation between the private-sector and the state schemes in terms of transferability between the schemes, and guaranteeing the minimum level of benefits of members of contracted-out occupational and personal pension schemes; and (iii) legislative measures that have improved the rights of scheme members.

Selected References for Part I

BENJAMIN, B., HABERMAN, S., HELOWICZ, G., KAYE, G., and WILKIE D. (1987), *Pensions: The Problems of Today and Tomorrow* (Allen and Unwin, London).

GILBERT, B. E. (1965), 'The Decay of Nineteenth Century Provident Institutions and the Coming of Old Age Pension Institutions in Great Britain', *Economic History Review* 17, 551–8.

—— (1966), *The Evolution of National Insurance in Great Britain* (Michael Joseph, London).

GILLING-SMITH, D. (1967), *The Complete Guide to Pensions and Superannuation* (Penguin, Harmondsworth).

Halsbury's Statutes of England (1970), 3rd edn. plus current statutes service (Butterworths, London).

HANNAH, L. (1986), *Inventing Retirement: The Development of Occupational Pension Schemes in Britain* (Cambridge University Press, Cambridge).

RHODES, G. (1965), *Public Sector Pensions* (Allen and Unwin, London).

RICHARDSON, J. H. (1960), *Economic and Financial Aspects of Social Security* (Allen and Unwin, London).

SELDON, A. (1960), *Pensions for Prosperity* (Institute of Economic Affairs, London).

STEAD, F. H. (1909), *How Old Age Pensions Began to Be* (Methuen, London).

PART II

PENSIONS AND PENSION SCHEMES IN THE UNITED KINGDOM

In this part of the book we discuss the system of pension schemes operating in the UK. Beginning with the basic state pension scheme (Chapter 4) and the state earnings-related pension scheme (Chapter 5), we move on to examine occupational pension schemes in Chapter 6 and personal pension schemes in Chapter 7. In Chapter 8 we consider the different pension schemes available for the self-employed and partners, and for the directors and senior executives of companies. In Chapter 9 we discuss the now quite numerous choices that individuals can exercise in respect of their pensions and their retirement. Finally, in Chapter 10 we examine some of the most important public-policy issues surrounding pensions and pension schemes in the UK today.

Pension payments are now very substantial in the UK. For example, in 1991–2, state expenditure on pensions amounted to £26bn., while pension payments from occupational schemes amounted to £15bn. The following table gives the capitalized value of state and occupational pensions in relation to total personal wealth for each year between 1976 and 1989.

Capitalized value of state and occupational pensions in relation to total personal wealth 1976–89

Year	Wealth and pensions (£bn.)					%age of personal wealth attributable to:		
	Personal wealth*	Basic pension	SERPS	Total state pensions	Occupational pensions	Marketable wealth	State pensions	Occupational pensions
1976	472	138.1	—	138.1	50	59	30	11
1977	544	145.6	—	145.6	65	61	27	12
1978	637	164.5	—	164.5	90	59	27	14
1979	756	189.1	5.6	194.7	120	58	26	16
1980	919	228.2	12.3	240.5	150	57	27	16
1981	1,036	263.9	19.5	283.4	180	55	28	17
1982	1,156	288.0	26.8	314.8	215	53	28	19
1983	1,328	320.0	35.0	355.0	255	53	27	19
1984	1,470	346.8	43.8	390.6	295	53	27	20
1985	1,628	365.2	53.5	418.7	330	53	26	20
1986	1,784	391.1	65.7	456.8	360	54	26	20
1987	2,080	421.8	78.8	500.6	400	56	25	19
1988	2,331	440.9	91.7	532.6	440	58	23	19
1989	2,648	468.9	104.3	573.2	477	60	22	18

Note: * Personal wealth is defined to be marketable wealth plus occupational pension rights plus state pension rights.

Source: Economic Trends, Nov. 1991.

4

The Basic State Pension Scheme

The *basic state pension* (also known as the *social-security retirement pension*) is based on the state pension scheme that was introduced by the 1975 Social Security Act and came into effect on 6 April 1978. Legislation concerning the state pension scheme has been consolidated in the Social Security Contributions and Benefits Act 1992 and the Social Security Administration Act 1992. These acts established the Benefits Agency and the Contributions Agency as autonomous executive agencies of the Department of Social Security.

4.1. Entitlement to the Basic State Pension

The basic state pension is a *flat-rate* pension that can be received by eligible people when they reach *state-pension age* (65 for men and 60 for women). The pension is paid by the Benefits Agency of the Department of Social Security (DSS). It is payable for the life of the claimant and is liable for income tax. To receive the pension, claim form BR1 must be signed. About 10 million people receive the basic pension in Britain. Since October 1989 people do not have to be retired from regular employment in order to receive the pension. Nor are people obliged to accept the pension at state-pension age: they are entitled to defer the receipt of their pension for up to five years.

As a result of rulings by the European Court of Justice, men have been given the right to retire at the same age as women without diminishing their pension rights, and women have been given the right to retire at the same age as men. These rulings follow from the 1976 European Commission directive on the equal treatment of men and women at work. The UK government intends to introduce a common state-pension age of 65 for men and women between 2010 and 2020.

Entitlement to the basic pension is based on the payment of *national-insurance contributions* (NICs) to the Contributions Agency of the DSS (which also administers DSS rebates). Certain conditions in respect of these contributions have to be satisfied in order to qualify for the basic pension. But anyone paying these contributions, including the self-employed, is entitled to the basic pension.

A person's contribution record must show a minimum number of *qualifying years* in a *working life*. A *qualifying year* is a tax year in which the person has paid or been credited with Class 1, Class 2, or Class 3 NICs on earnings of at least fifty-two times the weekly *lower earnings limit* (for making NICs) for that tax year. Between 6 April 1975 and 5 April 1978 the required figure was fifty times the weekly lower earnings limit. Before 5 April 1975 the total number of qualifying years was found by dividing the total number of *flat-rate contributions* paid by or credited to the person by fifty. In addition, in at least one of those qualifying years all the contributions must have been actually paid and not just credited.

A *working life* begins with the tax year in which the person turns 16 and comprises every tax year until the person dies or reaches pension age, but excludes the tax year in which the person dies or retires. No further NICs are necessary once a person has reached pension age. The required number of qualifying years is related to the length of the working life as follows:

Length of working life in years:	Required number of qualifying years = length of working life *less*:
0–10	1 year
11–20	2 years
21–30	3 years
31–40	4 years
41+	5 years

A person is eligible for the full rate of basic pension only if the contribution record has the required number of qualifying years. A reduced-rate pension is payable if the contribution record has less than the required number of qualifying years but more than one-quarter of the required number of qualifying years. The maximum working life for a man would normally be forty-nine years, while that for a woman would be forty-four years. Therefore the maximum required number of qualifying years is normally forty-four for a man and thirty-nine for a woman. For every additional year not worked, the pension is reduced on a pro-rata basis. So if a man worked for forty-three years and a woman worked for thirty-eight years, they would get pensions based on the fractions 43/44ths and 38/39ths respectively. Because these fractions are rounded up, they would each get pensions equal to 98 per cent of the full pension. Each additional year not worked leads to a further reduction in the pension of 2 per cent or 3 per cent. No pension is paid if the percentage falls below 24 per cent. If a person has paid insufficient contributions, then he or she has to rely on *income support* and possibly *housing benefit*. Alternatively, he/she can increase his/her pension entitlement by making additional NICs.

Someone wanting to calculate his or her pension entitlement can get a *pension forecast* from the DSS. The forecast is given in percentage terms and anyone with a full record of NICs will get a pension forecast of 100 per cent. Anyone with a forecast of less than 100 per cent can ask how many additional qualifying years and what additional contributions are needed to make up 100 per cent.

Missing contributions can be paid up to six years late. So, for example, missing contributions for 1989–90 could be paid as late as 5 April 1996. However, if the missing contributions are paid more than two years late, they must be paid at the rate ruling at the time that they are paid, rather than at the original rate. For example, voluntary contributions for 1989–90 would have cost £4.15 for each missing week if they were paid before 6 April 1992, but would have cost £5.25 for each missing week if they were paid in the 1992–3 tax year.

The required number of qualifying years will be reduced if there'are *years of home responsibility*. A year of home responsibility is defined as a full tax year in which a person was

- receiving *child benefit* for a child under 16;
- engaged for at least thirty-five hours per week in caring for a person who was receiving *attendance allowance*;
- receiving income support without being required to be *available for work* because he or she was caring for an elderly, sick, or disabled person.

Each year of home responsibility is subtracted from the required number of qualifying years, although the required number of years for a full-rate pension cannot be less than half the number that would be required otherwise. This means that a married woman bringing up a family need only work for half her working life to be eligible for a full-rate pension. Credits are also given to people aged 16 and 17 and to those who are claiming unemployment benefit and are available for work.

4.2. Types of Basic State Pension

4.2.1. THE CATEGORY A PENSION

The pension that a person receives on the basis of his/her own contributions is called a *category A pension*. The full category A pension in 1990–1 was £46.90 per week. The lower earnings limit is always equal to the integer part of the full pension (that is, £46 in 1990–1).

The pension is fully linked to the *retail price index* (or RPI) and so is fixed in real terms for the life of the claimant. State pensions are increased in April each year, that is, at the start of the tax year. The announcement of the increase is made the previous October, and is based on the increase in retail prices over the twelve months to the previous September. Before 1987 the increase took place in November every year, but this had the administrative inconvenience of requiring an adjustment to the pensioner's notice of tax coding twice a year.

Where a reduced-rate pension is payable, this is calculated as a proportion of the full-rate pension equal to the ratio of the actual number of qualifying years to the required number of qualifying years. No pension is payable at all if less than one-quarter of the required number of qualifying years have been worked. Individuals reaching pension age have the right to defer taking their state pension for a period up to five years. By doing this their state pension will be enhanced by 1 per cent for every seven weeks deferred or by approximately 7.5 per cent per year. If they defer for the full five years, their state pension will be enhanced by 38.3 per cent.

4.2.2. THE CATEGORY B PENSION

A *category B pension* is a pension that is awarded on the basis of the NICs of a spouse, a former spouse, or a deceased spouse. This is the pension typically claimed by a married woman who has insufficient contributions to claim an adequate category A pension on her own contributions. She can, therefore, claim a pension based on her husband's contributions. The husband must be over 65 and claiming his pension and the wife must be over 60. The pension is paid at the *married woman's rate*, which is 60 per cent of the full rate. In 1990–1 the married woman's pension was £28.20. This meant that the total pension available to a married couple was £75.10 in 1990–1.

The category B pension is payable to a married woman who has never worked and consequently made no NICs. It is also payable to a married woman who did work between 1948 and 1977 but who elected to pay *reduced-rate NICs* (also known as the *small stamp*) rather than the full rate.

A category B pension may also be payable in the event of divorce. A divorced woman may be entitled to a retirement pension at age 60 using not only her own NICs, but also those of her ex-husband up to the time of the divorce. If she subsequently remarries after 60 she is entitled to keep all of this pension, although she will lose it if she remarries before 60.

A category B pension may also be payable in the case where the spouse dies. The position is different for widows and widowers. In the case of a widow, she will receive *widow's benefit* if her husband died before she reached 40. If her husband died after she reached 40, she may be entitled to a category B *widow's pension* based on her late husband's contribution record. She will lose the pension if she remarries before 60. In the case of a widower, a category B *widower's pension* may be payable on the basis of his late wife's contributions, if both he and his late wife had reached pension age before her death. The widower's pension has only been available since April 1979.

It is possible to combine both category A and category B pensions, so long as the combined pension does not exceed the full-rate basic pension or, in the case of a married woman, the married woman's rate. This means, for example, that a woman might receive a full pension as a result of:

- the woman's own NICs;
- the husband's contributions plus the woman's contributions before her marriage and/or after her marriage has ended, either through divorce or the husband's death;
- the woman's own contributions being sufficient to give only a small pension, but when combined with a widow's pension, becoming sufficient to give a full pension; or
- converting the widow's pension into a retirement pension at the same rate if she had been widowed after she had turned 55.

4.2.3. THE CATEGORY C AND D PENSIONS AND THE AGE ADDITION

The basic state pension scheme also has two non-contributory pensions, known as category C and category D pensions.

The *category C* pension was introduced in 1970 for people who were already of pension age in July 1948, when the integrated social-security system came into effect. Very few people now receive this pension and it will end when all current claimants die. In 1990–1 the pension was £28.20 per week.

The *category D* pension (also known as the *old person's pension*) was introduced in 1971 for a person aged 80 or over who before this age was receiving either no basic pension or a very low basic pension as a result of a poor record of contributions. In 1990–1 the pension was £28.20 per week. If, before reaching 80, the person was receiving income support, the pension merely replaces the income support and the person is no better off. However, the person will be better off if he or she is receiving other forms of income (including other types of pension), because the pension is not means-tested and so can be received in addition to these other forms of income.

The *age addition* was a flat-rate benefit of 25p per week in 1990–1 paid to people who have reached the age of 80 and who are receiving the basic pension or income support.

4.3. Invalidity Benefit

People receiving *invalidity benefit* when they reach normal retirement age can choose to continue receiving invalidity benefit or to replace this with a retirement pension.

Invalidity benefit is paid to men below 65 and women below 60 who are incapacitated for work through illness and have received *statutory sickness benefit* for twenty-eight weeks. Invalidity benefit which is tax-free has three components:

* *invalidity pension*: which is worth the same as retirement pension: £46.90 per week in 1990–1 for the claimant and £28.20 for the spouse (if the spouse earned less than £37.35), and £9.65 for each dependent child;
* *invalidity allowance*: which depends on the age of the individual at the time of incapacity for work: for example, £10.00 per week in 1990–1 for people under 40, and £6.20 per week for people between 40 and 50;
* *additional pension*: which is related to earnings after 6 April 1978. It is only paid to those who first claimed invalidity benefit after 5 April 1979 and belong to either SERPS or an occupational pension scheme (see Chapters 5 and 6).

For people first claiming after 16 September 1985, only the higher of the invalidity allowance and the additional pension is paid. At normal retirement age, the DSS offers the choice of a switch to normal retirement pension. However, invalidity benefit has three advantages over the retirement pension:

* invalidity benefit is tax-free, while retirement pension is taxable;
* people on invalidity benefit are eligible for higher levels of housing benefit and income support;
* people retaining invalidity benefit are immune from previous benefit cuts, such as those that occurred in September 1985.

Even if people do not switch from invalidity benefit to retirement pension at normal retirement age, their total benefit can fall. This is because the additional pension can be withdrawn, although in some cases it is replaced by the (possibly lower) invalidity allowance.

Whatever choice was made between invalidity benefit and retirement pension at normal retirement age, everyone has to switch to the taxable retirement pension after five years: that is, at 65 for women and 70 for men. However, the entitlement to the higher level of housing benefit and income support remains, as does any invalidity allowance or additional pension that is received, although they become taxable also. Between the ages of 60 and 65 for women and 65 and 70 for men it is possible to switch back from retirement pension to invalidity pension, but this can only be done once.

From April 1995 invalidity benefit (and sickness benefit) will be replaced with an *incapacity benefit*. Incapacity benefit will be taxable and more tightly controlled than invalidity benefit. Entitlement to the benefit will be determined by the Benefits Agency Medical Service and will be restricted to those genuinely incapable of work.

4.4. Duty of Care in Providing Information to Potential Pensions Claimants and the DSS Compensation Scheme

In February 1988 the DSS accepted for the first time that it had a duty of care to potential claimants and that its failure previously to volunteer certain information to potential claimants had been a breach of this duty.

The particular case that led to the change in policy concerned advice given to many women when they reached 60. The women had asked the DSS whether they were entitled to a pension. They were told that they were not entitled to a pension because they had paid insufficient NICs during their working lives (say, because they had left jobs to have a family). They were not told, however, that if they now paid the missing NICs they could indeed receive a pension. In some cases, for a payment of as little as £200 in NICs, a woman could receive a pension of £10 per week until her husband retired aged 65. While the DSS had correctly answered the questions asked, it was the failure to volunteer this additional information that was accepted as a breach of the duty of care.

The DSS also operates a compensation scheme for people whose pensions or other social-security benefits have been paid late. The scheme was introduced in 1977 following a recommendation by the House of Commons Select Committee on the Ombudsman. It provides compensation only in limited circumstances:

- the delay in payment must have been for more than a year;
- the payment must be for more than £50;
- the delay must be the result of 'a clear and unambiguous error by the Department'.

The amount of compensation is calculated as follows:

- the arrears due in each tax year are determined and interest is calculated from the beginning of the following tax year until the date of payment using the following interest rates (in percentages):

prior to 6/4/66	3.00
6/4/66–5/4/74	6.00
6/4/74–5/1/80	9.00
6/1/80–5/12/82	12.00
6/12/82–5/5/85	8.00
6/5/85–5/9/87	11.00
6/9/87–6/7/89	9.00
7/7/89–5/11/89	12.25
6/11/89–5/11/90	13.00
6/11/90 to 5/12/92	12.25
6/12/92 to date	7.00

- no compensation is paid on the arrears in the tax year that payment is made;
- if the delay is for more than ten years, compound interest is paid.

The compensation scheme is non-statutory, operates in secret, and has no right of appeal. It was relaunched as part of the Citizen's Charter in February 1992. The Benefits Agency Charter sets out national standards for the time it takes to deal with a benefit claim, ranging from four days for an income support claim to nine months for war pensions. It also gives a commitment to provide a service that is courteous, fair, prompt, and accurate. Complaints can be made to a customer-services manager who must reply to them within seven days.

4.5. Pension Rights in Hospital or on Holidays Abroad

If a pensioner has to go into hospital for free in-patient treatment, his or her pension will be reduced if his or her stay in hospital lasts for more than six weeks.

Extended holidays abroad can affect a pensioner's state-pension rights, especially if the DSS is not informed. The general rule is that a pensioner can go abroad for up to three months without this affecting his or her entitlement. However, if a pensioner goes abroad for more than three months without informing the local DSS office, he or she will lose all his or her entitlement after the three-month limit. On the other hand, if he or she does inform the DSS before going abroad, the local office can arrange for the pension to be deposited with a bank or building society, or even transferred to the pensioner's address abroad. Pensioners intending to go abroad for up to two years can leave their pensions to accumulate in the UK and be paid in a lump sum when they return.

People claiming invalidity pensions face even more restrictions. This is because, in order to be eligible for the pension, a person must have been continuously incapable of work for a period of at least six months.

However, if a person leaves the country for medical treatment he or she can continue to receive his or her pension. People who leave the country for more than two years are deemed to have emigrated and different rules apply (see Section 4.6). However, if they still keep a home in the UK and persuade the DSS that they intend to return, it is still possible to receive the state pension.

4.6. Pension Rights of British Pensioners Resident Overseas

Many British pensioners reside and receive their UK pensions outside Britain. They live in at least 169 of the world's 200 countries. Britain has full social-security agreements with about thirty countries (see Table 4.1). If a British pensioner resides in any one of those countries (and about

TABLE 4.1. *Countries with which the UK has full social-security agreements*

European Union member states	*Other countries*
Belgium	Austria
Denmark	Finland
France	Iceland
Germany	Israel
Greece	Norway
Holland	Philippines
Ireland	Sweden
Italy	Switzerland
Luxembourg	Turkey
Portugal	USA
Spain	Yugoslavia (former states of)
Commonwealth countries	
Alderney	
Barbados	
Bermuda	
Cyprus	
Gibraltar	
Guernsey	
Isle of Man	
Jamaica	
Jersey	
Malta	
Mauritius	
Sark	

Source: Overseas Branch of the Department of Social Security, Newcastle upon Tyne, NE99 1YX.

260,000 did in 1992), any state pension that he or she receives from the UK will be uprated in line with UK inflation. However, if he or she lives anywhere else, his or her pension will be frozen, even if it is a Commonwealth country or overseas dependency. In 1992 there were about 350,000 British pensioners resident overseas receiving foreign pensions, that is, about 60 per cent of the total: 144,000 in Australia, 108,000 in Canada, 32,000 in South Africa, and 31,000 in New Zealand. For example, a pensioner who moved to Australia in 1962 was still getting the same pension of £2.88 per week in 1992, when the comparable pension in the UK was £54.15.

If a person has been resident in Australia for less than ten years, his or her UK pension is topped up by the Australian government to the level of the equivalent Australian pension: £63 per week for single pensioners and £105 for married pensioners in 1989. The equivalent UK pensions were £43.60 and £69.80. If the pensioner has been resident in Australia for more than ten years, he or she gets the full Australian state pension in addition to his or her UK pension so long as his or her total income is below a certain threshold; the pension is reduced by 50 cents for every dollar that the income exceeds the threshold. The total cost to the Australian government of uprating the British pensioners living in Australia is £107m. per year in 1989 prices. The British government has consistently refused to make any contribution to this uprating. If the British government index-linked pensions of all the British pensioners resident overseas, it would cost £275m. per annum (in 1992 prices).

4.7. Pension Rights Earned Overseas

British people who temporarily work abroad will often earn pension rights in these countries. The pensions can be claimed after they retire in Britain.

For example, people working in any European Union country or in Gibraltar can contribute to a state pension scheme and subsequently draw a pension (or pensions if they worked in more than one country) anywhere in the EU. A pension can be claimed from every country worked in, even if the country was not then a member of the EU, although the period of work must be after the member state began its own pension scheme.

The person claiming a pension has to satisfy the conditions ruling in the country concerned. For instance, retirement ages range from 60 for men and 55 for women in Italy to 67 for both men and women in Denmark. Also, the minimum period of work to qualify for a full pension varies from five to fifteen years. Nevertheless, it is possible to combine contributions from all countries worked in to qualify for a pro-rata pension from each country if less than the minimum period has been worked.

The UK has similar agreements with a number of other countries; these are listed in Table 4.1. Again, it is possible to combine contributions that have been paid in each country worked in and receive a pro-rata pension from each country. The agreement with the USA, for example, only became fully operational in January 1988. It permits contributions that have been paid in both the UK and USA to count towards the calculation of a US pension. Anyone who has worked at least eighteen months in the USA since 1937 can, therefore, apply for a US pension from the age of 62. The pension is not subject to US tax, but 90 per cent of it counts as taxable income in the UK in the year after it is received. The pension is increased every January in line with increases in the consumer price index. There is also a spouse's pension equal to half the main pension. In 1991 more than 15,000 people in the UK were claiming US pensions worth more than £40m. per year.

The UK has partial agreements with Australia, Canada, New Zealand, and Norway. In the case of Australia and New Zealand, the agreements permit anyone who has been resident in either country to count this time towards qualifying for a UK pension. In the case of Canada, anyone who has worked there since 1966 can claim a Canadian pension in the UK. With the other countries of the world the UK has no specific agreements, and practices differ. Some countries pay pensions to non-nationals whether or not they live in the country. Others only pay pensions to residents. Yet others will pay pensions to qualifying people who were living in the country at the time of retirement, and will continue to pay their pensions if they subsequently leave the country.

4.8. The Taxation of Pensions

All state pensions are taxable generally as *Schedule E* income at the highest marginal rate of tax applicable to the individual after taking into account *income-tax allowances*. The *lower rate* of tax is 20 per cent, the *basic rate* of tax is 25 per cent, while the *higher rate* of tax is 40 per cent. In this section we examine how the tax system in Britain affects pensions that are received in Britain.

4.8.1. INDEPENDENT TAXATION AND PENSIONS

A new system of *independent taxation* of husbands and wifes was introduced in April 1990. It could lead to substantial benefits for pensioners. The system gives married women independence and privacy in their tax affairs. In addition, husband's and wife's incomes and capital gains are taxed separately.

If a man or his wife is aged over 65, the man receives a higher income-tax allowance, known as the *married couple's age allowance* (formerly known as the *married man's age allowance*). In 1990–1, the first tax year of independent taxation, the allowance was £5,815. If the man or wife is more than 75 there is an even higher tax allowance, which was £6,005 in 1990–1. These compare with the standard married couple's allowance in 1990–1 of £4,725.

However, there is an *income limit* for the age allowance, which in 1990–1 was £12,300. If the individual's income is above this limit, the age allowance is reduced by £1 for every £2 that the individual's income is above the limit, until it reaches the standard married couple's allowance. This occurred at an income level of £14,480 for a married man aged 65–74 and at an income level of £14,860 for a married man aged 75 or over.

The income that is used to determine the entitlement to age allowance is referred to as *total income* by the Inland Revenue: it is defined as total taxable income before tax reliefs are deducted. Before independent taxation, a married man's total income included not only his own earned income or pension, but also his wife's earned income or pension. It also included any interest income from the savings of both partners. Since interest from a bank or building society is received net of basic-rate tax, it has to be grossed up before including in total income. With a basic rate of tax of 25 per cent, the grossed-up interest is calculated by dividing net interest by 0.75 (that is, 1 − 0.25).

Before independent taxation, married men could cease to be eligible for age allowance at fairly low levels of total income. For example, assuming the 1990–1 allowances, a 70-year-old married man with a 66-year-old wife would cease to be eligible for age allowance if his total income comprised:

Husband's pension		£9,000
Wife's pension		£3,500
Net building society interest	£1,487	
Gross building society interest (= Net interest/0.75)		£1,982
Total income		£14,482

With the introduction of independent taxation, however, the following benefits operate:

- each partner receives an income limit for age allowance;
- the wife's income is no longer included as part of the husband's total income when the entitlement to age allowance is determined;
- interest from a joint account at a bank or a building society is divided equally between the partners;

- there is still a married couple's allowance which will go to the husband, but if he has insufficient income to use it in full, any surplus can be transferred to the wife;
- the wife receives in her own right a personal allowance (this replaces the *wife's earned income allowance*) that is age-related: in 1990–1 the personal allowance was £3,005 if she was below 65, £3,670 if she was between 65 and 74, and £3,820 if she was 75 or over.

The resulting changes mean that, in the above example, the husband's total income is £9,991 (that is, £9,000 + £1,982/2), and the wife's total income is £4,491 (that is, £3,500 + £1,982/2). Both partners receive the full age allowance, since each partner's total income was below the £12,300 limit for 1990–1. The husband, therefore, had a married age allowance before taxation of £5,815, while the wife had a personal age allowance before taxation of £3,670. The husband's tax bill was:

$$(£9,991 - £5,815) \times 0.25 = £1,044.00$$

while the wife's tax bill was:

$$(£4,491 - £3,670) \times 0.25 = £205.25,$$

a total tax bill of £1,249.25. The comparable tax bill before independent taxation would have been:

$$(£14,482 - £4,725) \times 0.25 = £2,439.25.$$

So independent taxation has led to a reduction in taxation of £1,190 in this example.

Tax relief on the married couple's age allowance was restricted to 20 per cent from April 1994 and to 15 per cent from April 1995.

4.8.2. PENSIONS RECEIVED FROM OVERSEAS

A British resident who receives a pension from abroad has to pay UK income tax on it. Where *double taxation agreements* exist between the UK and the overseas country in which the pension originated, the pension will not also be taxed in the overseas country. There is a liability to UK taxation, even if the pension is not repatriated. However, some overseas pensions are liable to UK taxation under Schedule E, while others are liable under Schedule D. Schedule E is the schedule to the 1970 Income and Corporation Taxes Act that deals with earned income, while Schedule D is the schedule dealing with investment income.

Pensions paid by private companies and state pensions paid to people as citizens rather than as ex-employees of the state are always taxed under Schedule D. The pension is assessed for taxation when it arises in the overseas country and not when it is repatriated to the UK. The pension is converted by the Inland Revenue into a sterling equivalent at the rate of exchange ruling on the date the pension arises, although taxpayers can ask for the pension to be converted at the average exchange rate for the year. Before the tax is deducted the pensions are subject to a special deduction of 10 per cent under section 2 of the 1988 Income and Corporation Taxes Act, so that only 90 per cent of it is liable for taxation.

Most overseas pensions are taxed under Schedule D. However, pensions paid to former public servants in about fifty current or former UK

TABLE 4.2. *Countries where Schedule E operates in respect of pensions received*

Aden	Mauritius
Antigua	Monserrat
Bahamas	New Hebrides
Barbados	Nigeria
Belize	Pakistan
Bermuda	Palestine
Botswana	St Helena
British Virgin Islands	St Kitts
Burma	St Lucia
Cayman Island	St Vincent
Cyprus	Sabah
Dominica	Sarawak
East Africa	Seychelles
Falklands	Sierra Leone
Fiji	Singapore
Gambia	Solomons
Ghana	Somalia
Gibraltar	South Georgia
Grenada	South Yemen
Guyana	Sri Lanka
Hong Kong	Sudan
India	Swaziland
Jamaica	Tanzania
Kenya	Trinidad and Tobago
Kiribati	Turks and Caicos
Lesotho	Uganda
Malawi	Zambia
Malaysia	

Note: Some countries appear under both their old and their new names.

Source: Inland Revenue.

colonies are taxed under Schedule E (see Table 4.2). Where the pensions are still paid by the overseas government, a 10 per-cent special deduction is made under section 196 of the 1988 Income and Corporation Taxes Act before the pension is taxed. However, in 1973 the UK government took over the responsibility for paying some of these pensions. These pensions are paid directly by the UK government in sterling and, unless the pension was already being paid in 1973, the 10 per-cent special deduction is not made before the pension is taxed under Schedule E.

The two tax schedules D and E operate as follows in respect of pensions. With Schedule E, the liability is assessed in the year that the pension is received. The tax is due in four quarterly instalments beginning thirty days after the assessment is made. With Schedule D, the liability does not arise until the following tax year, when the tax is payable in two equal instalments in July and January. However, for the first two years of a Schedule D liability the pension is taxed in the year in which it arises instead of a year in arrears. Thereafter, the tax is levied on the previous year's pension. This means that the second year's pension is taxed twice. This practice follows from a convention which states that tax is not levied after a source of income has ceased. This means that the final year's income under a Schedule D liability is never taxed. To counterbalance this, the Inland Revenue taxes the second year's income twice.

4.9. The Earnings Rule

On 1 October 1989 the *earnings rule* was abolished; the announcement of the abolition was made in the 1989 Budget and put into effect by the 1989 Social Security Act. Under the earnings rule, anyone who continued working up to five years after state-pension age (that is, between 65 and 70 for men and between 60 and 65 for women) began losing state pension at the rate of nearly £1 for £1 if they earned more than £75 per week and lost it completely if they earned more than £120.60 per week. (The exact rule was: for every 10p earned between £75 and £79 per week, 5p was deducted from the state pension; for every 10p earned above £79 per week, the pension was reduced by 10p.)

At the time of the abolition, the social security secretary, Tony Newton, argued that people of pension age wanted the freedom to choose how much they earned, how many hours they worked, and when they retired from full-time employment. It was to everyone's advantage that pensioners were encouraged to remain active participants in society. People who wanted to go on working after retirement age would no longer be penalized by having their state pension reduced if their earnings exceeded £75 per week.

TABLE 4.3. *Penalties for pensioners who work after retirement* (£ per week)

Allowance	Amount in 1990–1	Allowance lost if income exceeds
Age allowance with wife under 60	28.20	37.35 (wife's income)
Severe disablement allowance	28.20	37.35 (dependant's income)
Invalid care allowance	28.20	20

It was estimated that up to 400,000 people above pension age would benefit from the abolition of the earnings rule, at a cost to the Exchequer of £375m. per year. Of this group, about 200,000 had delayed claiming their state pension for up to the maximum allowable period of five years (although the pension was increased at the rate of 7.5 per cent per annum until they claimed it). This group could now draw their full state pension in addition to their salary (although the option to delay receipt of the pension for up to five years remains). Another 200,000 people earned less than £75 per week but were expected to increase their earnings following the abolition of the earnings rule.

The earnings rule that was abolished in October 1989 was the main earnings rule, but there are seventeen other earnings rules that remain. They all involve penalties or lost allowances for pensioners who work after retirement. Table 4.3 shows a few examples.

4.10. The Effect of Pensions on Unemployment Benefit

If a person is receiving a pension, this can affect his or her entitlement to certain state benefits, especially unemployment benefit. Before 1981 the entitlement to unemployment benefit was not affected by the receipt of an occupational pension. However, from 6 April 1981 a new Department of Social Security rule stipulated that any person aged 60 or over in receipt of an occupational pension of more than £35 per week had his or her unemployment benefit reduced at the rate of £1 for each £1 that the pension exceeded £35. At this time the unemployment benefit was £20.65, and this was lost completely if the pension exceeded £55.65.

From 1 January 1989 the rule was extended to cover everyone over 55. As a consequence, 34,000 people lost their unemployment benefit either in whole or in part. On 9 October 1989 the rule was further extended to include personal pensions in addition to occupational pensions. While unemployment benefit has increased over the years, the £35 threshold has remained constant.

4.11. Comparison with the European Union

Britain's state pension compares very unfavourably with those in other European Union member states, according to a number of different measures.

Britain increases its pensions annually, but most other countries increase their pensions more frequently (Table 4.4). Greece and Italy raise them three times per year, while Luxembourg increases them whenever the cost of living rises by 2.5 per cent, and Belgium increases them each month if inflation is more than 2 per cent a month. Britain links its pension increases to prices, as is the case in most other EU countries, but in Germany, Italy, and the Netherlands pensions are linked to increases in wages, which are generally larger than increases in prices.

Not only are Britain's state pensions uprated on a less favourable basis than those of other EU countries, they are also amongst the lowest, both in absolute terms and relative to average wages. This is shown in Table 4.5. Column 1 shows the single-person pension received in different EU

TABLE 4.4. *European Union increases in state pensions*

Country	Frequency	Date(s)	Special conditions	Basis
Belgium	annually	1 Jan.	monthly if inflation more than 2% a month	prices
Denmark	biannually	1 Apr.; 1 Oct.		prices
France	biannually	1 Jan.; 1 July		prices
Germany	annually	1 July		wages
Greece	triannually	1 Jan.; 1 May; 1 Sept.		prices
Ireland	annually	end of July		prices
Italy	triannually	1 Jan.; 1 May; 1 Nov.		prices or wages
Luxembourg	irregular	variable	when cost of living rises by 2.5%	prices
Netherlands	biannually	1 Jan.; 1 July		wages
Spain	annually	1 Jan.		prices
Portugal	annually	1 Jan.		prices
UK	annually	first Monday in tax year		prices

Sources: Tables of Social Security Benefits in the European Communities, Jan. 1988 (Department of Social Security); Portuguese Embassy; Irish Department of Social Welfare.

TABLE 4.5. *Comparing pensions across Europe*

	Single pension (£ per week, 1985 prices)*	Single pension as proportion of average wages (%, 1985)†
Luxembourg	104	84
Netherlands	101	93
Germany	86	82
Italy	85	81
France	73	79
Denmark	66	61
Belgium	63	69
UK	53	46
Ireland	43	49
Portugal	NA	88
Greece	NA	78
Spain	NA	NA

Notes: * The figures are for the gross pension plus other transfers and less taxes paid to someone on average manufacturing wages retiring in January 1985. Figures have been converted to weekly amounts in £ sterling taking account of the purchasing power of each currency in its own country at January 1985 (purchasing-power standard). No figures are available for Spain, Greece, or Portugal.

† The figures are the ratio of net pension to previous earnings for a person on average manufacturing wages retiring in January 1985. Figures for Greece and Portugal are estimates. The estimate for Spain of 188% was omitted as unreliable.

Source: European Parliament, Written Answer 2620/88, 26 May 1989.

countries by a new pensioner who had received the average wage in manufacturing industry in 1985. The pensions are deflated by a purchasing-power standard (to reflect the cost of living in each country) and converted into sterling. The British pension was £53 per week, higher only than that of Ireland at £43. The pension in Luxembourg was the highest at £104, nearly double the UK pension in real terms. The average pension was £75.

Column 2 shows the pensions given in column 1 as a proportion of average wages in the respective countries (after taking into account income tax). The figures represent the *net replacement ratio*, with a value of 100 per cent implying that pensioners receive a pension equal to their wages. Britain comes out bottom of the league, with a state pension only equal to 46 per cent. The best pensions are from the Netherlands, where a typical pensioner receives a pension only 7 per cent less than his wage. The average net replacement ratio is 74 per cent.

Some EU countries pay an annual bonus to pensioners. Again, the

TABLE 4.6. *European state-pension ages*

	Men	Women
Belgium	65	60
Denmark	67	67
France	60	60
Germany	65	65
Greece	65	60
Ireland	65	65
Italy	60	55
Luxembourg	65	65
Netherlands	65	65
Portugal	65	62
Spain	65	65
UK	65	60

Source: *Daily Telegraph*, 29 June 1991.

UK is the least generous. It pays a £10 bonus at Christmas, but Portugal pays an extra month's pension at Christmas. In Belgium and Denmark pensioners receive a summer-holiday bonus equal to a month's pension.

The main reason for the low pensions in the UK, both absolutely and relatively, is that most British pensioners receive most of their state pension in the form of a flat-rate pension that is independent of previous earnings. In 1994 7 million out of 10 million pensioners did not receive an earnings-related supplement. In all other EU states, apart from Ireland and Denmark, pensions are exclusively earnings-related.

Although British pensions are amongst the lowest in Europe, the contributions paid towards them are amongst the highest. In Denmark the contribution-rate is 3.5 per cent of earnings; in Ireland it is 5.5 per cent; in Portugal, 11 per cent; in Germany, 11.5 per cent; and in Belgium and the Netherlands it is 12 per cent. In Britain, NICs vary between 5 per cent and 9 per cent of earnings between the lower and upper earnings limits of £46 and £350 per week (1990–1 limits), although these contributions entitle contributors to all state benefits and not just state pensions.

Finally, we note that the UK is in a minority in the EU in having different state-pension ages for men and women, as Table 4.6 shows. However, a common state-pension age of 65 is being introduced in the UK between 2010 and 2020, as the following table shows:

The Basic State Pension Scheme

Date of birth	Pension age	Pension year
Apr 1950	60yr 1m	2010
Oct 1950	60yr 7m	2011
Apr 1951	61yr 1m	2012
Oct 1951	61yr 7m	2013
Apr 1952	62yr 1m	2014
Oct 1952	62yr 7m	2015
Apr 1953	63yr 1m	2016
Oct 1953	63yr 7m	2017
Apr 1954	64yr 1m	2018
Oct 1954	64yr 7m	2019
Apr 1955	65yr	2020

5

The State Earnings-Related Pension Scheme

The *State Earnings-Related Pension Scheme* (SERPS) was established by the secretary of state for social services (Barbara Castle) in the Social Security Pensions Act 1975 (following the 1974 white paper *Better Pensions*), and came into operation on 6 April 1978. Legislation concerning the state pension scheme has been consolidated in the Social Security Contributions and Benefits Act 1992 and the Social Security Administration Act 1992.

All employed workers are entitled to receive the basic state pension for which they make national-insurance contributions (NICs) (see Chapter 4). In addition, all employed workers whose earnings are above the lower earnings limit for the payment of NICs will automatically be members of SERPS unless they or their employers have specifically *contracted out* of SERPS.[1] Individuals who are not contracted out of SERPS are entitled to receive a state pension that is related to earnings, known as the *additional pension*. About 2.5 million people in the UK are in receipt of a SERPS pension.

It is planned that SERPS will remain in its present form until 1999, from which time it will be modified with its benefits reduced. In this chapter we will discuss both the current SERPS and the modified SERPS. We will also discuss the immediate earnings-related predecessor to SERPS, the *State Graduated Retirement Pension Scheme* (SGRPS), since some people still receive a pension from this scheme.

5.1. The State Earnings-Related Pension Scheme 1978–1999

The current SERPS began on 6 April 1978 and is due to continue in its present form until 6 April 1999.

5.1.1. THE ENTITLEMENT TO A SERPS PENSION

The SERPS pension is payable to employees in contracted-in employment who, together with their employers, have paid Class 1 NICs on

---

[1] Occasionally we hear people saying that they are in *contracted-in* pension schemes (indeed, we frequently use the term below and in subsequent chapters). But strictly speaking, we should say that they are in *non-contracted-out* schemes.

earnings between the *lower* and *upper earnings limits* in one or more tax years since 6 April 1978, and who have reached state-pension age on or after 6 April 1979. The SERPS pension is paid in addition to the basic state pension. As with the basic pension, the SERPS pension is uprated annually in line with increases in the *retail price index*. Widows and widowers are entitled to receive the full SERPS pension earned by their spouse. The SERPS pension is not payable in respect of tax years in which the employee was in a contracted-out occupational scheme or an appropriate personal pension scheme (see Chapters 6 and 7).

The NIC rates for contracted-in and for contracted-out employment for both employees and employers are given in Table 5.1 for 1990–1. From the table, we can see that the cost of SERPS is 2 per cent of employee earnings between the earnings limits (sometimes stated as 2 per cent of *band earnings*) for employees and 3.8 per cent of employee earnings for employers, a total of 5.8 per cent. These figures are known as the *contracted-out rebates*. From April 1993 the contracted-out rebate was reduced to 4.8 per cent (1.8 per cent for employees and 3 per cent for employers).

NICs by both employers and employees applied only up to the upper earnings limits operating between 1978 and 1985. From October 1985 the employer has had to pay contributions at the full rate on all the earnings of the employee, regardless of whether the scheme is contracted in or contracted out of SERPS. In addition, the employer has to pay contributions for all employees, regardless of age, whereas the employee ceases paying contributions on reaching normal pension age.

TABLE 5.1. *National-insurance contribution-rates, 1990–1 (%)*

Weekly gross earnings level	Contracted-in		Contracted-out	
	up to £46*	above £46[†]	up to £46*	above £46[†]
Employees				
£46.00–£350.00	2	9	2	7
Employers				
£46.00–£79.99	5	5	5	1.2
£80.00–£124.99	7	7	7	3.2
£125.00–£174.99	9	9	9	5.2
£175.00–£350.00	10.45	10.45	10.45	6.65
Above £350.00	10.45	10.45	10.45	10.45

Notes: * Percentage of £46 (lower earnings limit); e.g. 2% of £46 is £0.92.
   [†] Percentage of balance in excess of £46: up to £350 (upper earnings limit) for employees, with no upper limit for employers.

5.1.2. CALCULATING THE SERPS PENSION

The amount of the SERPS pension is calculated as follows: the pension is equal to 1.25 per cent (that is, 1/80th) of *total revalued earnings* within the earnings band between the lower and upper earnings limits during the period of membership of SERPS (beginning in 1978) up to a maximum of twenty years. This is equivalent to 1.25 per cent of average revalued earnings within the earnings band for each year of membership of SERPS up to a maximum of twenty years. Each year's earnings are revalued (or indexed) in line with increases in *national average earnings* up to, but not including, the year of retirement, as specified in section 148 of the Social Security Administration Act 1992. If an employee had been a member of SERPS for more than twenty years, then the pension would have been based on the best twenty years. The maximum SERPS pension for someone retiring after 6 April 1999 is, therefore, 25 per cent of revalued earnings within the earnings band. In addition, a widow or widower can receive the whole of the spouse's SERPS pension so long as this together with any SERPS pension he or she is entitled to on the basis of his or her own contributions does not exceed the maximum SERPS pension based on the upper earnings limit.

Table 5.2 provides an example of how the SERPS pension is calculated. The illustration is for a man who retired aged 65 in October 1989. We will assume that throughout his working life the man's income was between

TABLE 5.2. *Calculating the SERPS pension of a man aged 65 in October 1989*

Year	Earnings (£)	Earnings revalued by wage inflation (%)	Revalued earnings (£)	Basic pension (£)	Surplus (£)
1978–9	3,300	195.9	9,765	2,236	7,529
1979–80	3,700	156.3	9,483	2,236	7,247
1980–1	4,500	112.2	9,549	2,236	7,313
1981–2	5,400	88.1	10,157	2,236	7,921
1982–3	6,100	71.9	10,486	2,236	8,250
1983–4	6,900	58.5	10,937	2,236	8,701
1984–5	7,400	49.6	11,070	2,236	8,834
1985–6	7,900	37.9	10,894	2,236	8,658
1986–7	8,500	27.8	10,863	2,236	8,627
1987–8	9,300	18.6	11,030	2,236	8,794
1988–9	10,000	9.1	10,910	2,236	8,674
1989–90	10,900	—	10,900	2,236	8,664
TOTAL					99,212

the lower and upper earnings limits for NICs. In 1989–90 the lower earnings limit was £43 per week or £2,236 per year, while the upper earnings limit was £325 per week or £16,900 per year. Had his earnings been below the lower earnings limit, he would not have been eligible for a SERPS pension, only the flat-rate basic pension. Had his earnings been above the upper earnings limit, only earnings up to the upper earnings limit in any year are included in the calculation of SERPS. Similarly, contributions towards the SERPS pension are payable only on earnings between the lower and upper earnings limits.

The SERPS pension is based on the employee's best twenty years' earnings beginning with the tax year 1978–9. The earnings in each year are revalued by the increase in national average earnings between that year and the year of retirement. So, for example, the earnings of £3,300 in 1978–9 are increased by 195.9 per cent to give real or *revalued earnings* of £9,765. From each year's revalued earnings, the basic pension for 1989–90 of £2,236 (equal to the lower earnings limit) is deducted, to give a figure known as the *surplus*. The surplus was equal to £7,529 in 1978–9 and £8,664 in 1989–90. The surplus for each year is added together to give £99,212. The annual SERPS pension is equal to 1.25 per cent of this sum, that is, £1,240.15, implying a weekly SERPS pension of £23.85. The basic pension was £43 per week, so the total pension for this individual was £66.85 in 1989–90.

The maximum SERPS pension in 1990–1 was £52.23 per week. This was the pension paid to someone who had been a member of SERPS from the start and whose earnings were equal to or exceeded the upper earnings limit for every year of SERPS membership.

5.1.3. THE SERPS PENSION IN THE CASE OF CERTAIN MARRIED WORKING WOMEN

Before April 1977 all married working women were able to pay a reduced rate of NICs, but in exchange lost their entitlement to a state pension at the age of 60 (and also to unemployment benefit or invalidity benefit). Since April 1977 all women have had to pay full contributions (known as Full Class 1 contributions), except those married women who had been paying the reduced rate of contributions and have been in continuous employment since 1977. In 1990 there were more than a million such women in Britain. By paying the full rate of contributions, women in jobs that are contracted into SERPS can receive an earnings-related and index-linked pension from the age of 60. This is in addition to any entitlement to a basic state pension based on their own or their husband's contributions.

In October 1989 full-rate contributions were reduced, while the married woman's rate remained the same. For low-paid women it actually became cheaper to pay the full rate, while for most higher-paid women the benefits of paying the full contracted-in rate exceeded the cost. Therefore the majority of married women not in a contracted-out occupational scheme gain by paying full contributions as Table 5.3 indicates.

In the tax year beginning in April 1990 the full contracted-in rate of NICs was £0.92 per week (that is, 2 per cent of the lower earnings limit of £46), plus 9 per cent of earnings between the lower and upper earnings limits of £46 and £350 per week. This compared with the married woman's rate of 3.85 per cent of all earnings up to £350 per week. Columns 2 and 3 of Table 5.3 show respectively the married woman's reduced rate and the full contracted-in rate of NICs. Column 4 shows the net cost of switching to the full rate. Women earning less than £62 per week were actually better off by switching to full-rate contributions. A woman earning £100 per week had to pay an extra £1.93 per week in contributions, but in return could expect a pension of £5.40 per week when she retired if she was aged 51 in 1990, a pension of £6.62 per week if she was aged 40 in

TABLE 5.3. *Married women's pensions options from 1990 (£)*

Earnings per week	Married woman's NICs	Full Class 1 contracted-in NICs	Net cost	SERPS earned by contributing from April 1990 until pension age, by woman aged		
				51	40	30
46	1.77	0.92	−0.85	0.00	0.00	0.00
50	1.93	1.28	−0.65	0.40	0.49	0.57
60	2.31	2.18	−0.13	1.40	1.72	2.00
62	2.41	2.41	0.00	1.66	2.03	2.37
70	2.69	3.08	0.39	2.40	2.94	3.43
85	3.27	4.43	1.16	3.90	4.78	5.57
100	3.85	5.78	1.93	5.40	6.62	7.71
125	4.81	8.03	3.22	7.90	9.68	11.29
150	5.78	10.28	4.50	10.40	12.75	14.86
175	6.74	12.53	5.79	12.90	15.81	18.43
200	7.70	14.78	7.08	15.40	18.88	22.00
250	9.62	19.28	9.66	20.40	25.01	29.14
300	11.55	23.78	12.23	25.40	31.14	36.29
350	13.47	28.28	14.81	30.40	37.26	43.43

Note: All figures represent weekly rates for female employees.

Source: *Daily Telegraph*, 28 Apr. 1990.

1990, and a pension of £7.71 per week if she was aged 30 in 1990. These pensions are fully indexed against wage inflation until the retirement date, and against price inflation thereafter. A woman who reaches the age of 60 can expect to live until she is 82. Women aged 51 in 1990 will be the last group of women to receive a full SERPS pension before the SERPS system changes on 6 April 1999 (see Section 5.2.2). Thereafter less-favourable pensions are given. Nevertheless, the pension remains generous compared with the contribution level.

5.2. The State Earnings-Related Pension Scheme after 1999

5.2.1. THE PROPOSED CHANGES TO SERPS

In June 1985 the secretary of state for health and social security (Norman Fowler), in his green paper on the *Reform of Social Security—Programme for Change* (Cmnd. 9517–19), announced his intention to abolish SERPS and replace it with compulsory private-insurance schemes. His reason for doing this was the mounting burden placed on the working population by the projected growth in the number of pensioners, especially in the next century. In 1985 there were 9.3 million pensioners and 21.8 million workers, so that there were 2.3 workers to finance each pension. By 2035 the government actuary estimated that there would be 13.2 million pensioners and still only 21.8 million workers, so there will be only 1.7 workers for each pensioner. The situation becomes even worse if the rate of unemployment increases, and more individuals cease to be net contributors to the National Insurance Fund and instead become net beneficiaries. The reason for the increased number of pensioners is both increased longevity, which has resulted from improved diet and health care (such as reduced smoking), and earlier retirement. Apart from the increased number of pensioners, there is also the increased cost which results from the indexation of the state scheme. With full indexation based on prices, it was estimated that the cost of the basic state pension will rise from £15.3bn. in 1985 to between £45bn. and £67bn. in 2035 (in 1985 prices). SERPS adds a further £23bn. to these costs. If the indexation was based on earnings rather than prices, then the cost of state pensions rises four times during the period. Between 1951 and 1985 the basic pension increased from 30 per cent to more than 50 per cent of the post-tax earnings of the average male manual worker. But the real problem, according to the secretary of state, was not that pensions are relatively high or low, but that they are not being funded adequately under the present system. The existing system of financing was not strictly based on the National Insurance Fund as envisaged by Beveridge in 1942, but rather is based on pay-as-you-go, so that each generation pays for the pensions of the previous generation and relies on the next generation to pay for its pensions. If every generation awards itself more and more generous pensions, the whole system tends to become more unmanageable over time.

Under the secretary of state's proposals, the basic flat-rate pension would remain intact, but the earnings-related component would be phased out from April 1987. It would be replaced by a compulsory additional pension arranged through an occupational pension scheme or a personal pension scheme (with the individual having the right to opt out of his employer's scheme), into either of which both employees and employers would be obliged to contribute, with a minimum level of contribution of 2 per cent of salary from each employee and employer. The aim was to encourage private-sector pensions as well as to make them more portable. In addition, by concentrating on the basic pension alone, the government would be able to raise the living standards of all pensioners when the nation's wealth increased, and not just the living standards of those who had recently retired.

There was to be a twenty-year transition period before the new scheme came into full effect. The change-over would begin in April 1987. Men over 50 and women over 45 would remain with SERPS, whether or not they were contracted into the existing state scheme. With younger age-groups SERPS would be phased out over a three-year period, during which rights would continue to be earned at a reduced rate of accrual. Existing SERPS rights would be enhanced for men aged 40 to 49 and women aged 35 to 44. For example, men aged 40 (women aged 35) would receive a 10 per-cent bonus benefit in terms of extra years of SERPS rights, while men aged 49 (women aged 44) would receive a 75 per-cent bonus benefit. In short, all existing pension entitlements earned under the state scheme would be honoured.

The new scheme would operate on a defined-contribution basis, so that contributions paid are invested and the accumulated sum at retirement used to buy an annuity (in other words, the pension would be a money-purchase type). For the employer, this would involve a fixed level of financial liability, without the open-ended commitment to an unknown level of pension benefits. For the employee, there would be a known sum of pension savings which belonged exclusively to him. The existing tax-relief arrangements for contributions would remain. With the ending of SERPS, the differential rate of NICs between contracted-in and contracted-out employees would also end. The green paper proposed a single common rate of contributions of 16.5 per cent of salary for the employer and employee combined, compared with the existing 19.45 per-cent combined contracted-in rate and 13.2 per-cent combined contracted-out rate. The move to this common rate would take place over the three-year phasing-in period, during which time the minimum combined contribution requirements for the occupational scheme or the personal pension would be 2 per cent in the first year, 3 per cent in the second year, and 4 per cent in the third and subsequent years.

The green paper envisaged that existing occupational pension schemes might change in the light of the proposals contained in it. Existing defined-benefit schemes (based, for example, on final salary) would still be able to conform with the new scheme so long as they complied with the new contributions tests. All employees in defined-benefit occupational schemes would be given the right to boost their pensions through additional contributions. Under existing arrangements, these additional voluntary contributions could be made only at the discretion of the trustees of the schemes. It was expected that many employees and employers would opt for the personal pension contract, so there will be more 'limited-liability' money-purchase type schemes and fewer 'open-ended' final-salary type schemes after the abolition of SERPS.

The green paper came under considerable criticism. It was argued that it exaggerated the worsening ratio of contributors to pensioners. In the 1982 quinquennial review of the National Insurance Fund by the government actuary, it had been predicted that the ratio of contributors to pensioners would be 2.1 in 2025, but the green paper predicted that it would be only 1.7. Similarly, the increase in national-insurance costs between 1985 and 2025 was estimated to be 7.4 percentage points in the green paper, but between 5 and 6.5 percentage points in the 1982 review. 'It is difficult not to believe that the [green paper] projections were deliberately made to look as gloomy as possible, in order to provide spurious justification for these unnecessary cuts', claimed John Cullen, pensions officer of the General, Municipal and Boilermakers and Allied Trades Union (letter to the *Financial Times*, 26 February 1985). The green paper was also criticized for failing to offer any estimates of the expected public-expenditure savings, since it was the necessity of making such savings that had been at the heart of the review in the first place. It has been claimed that this is because the government was afraid to identify winners and losers from the changes. On the other side of the fence, the green paper was criticized for not being sufficiently radical. The radical left (for example, the Labour Party) wanted a system of universal benefits regardless of circumstances, while on the radical right, some (for example, the Institute for Fiscal Studies) wanted a wholly means-tested social-security system to encourage self-help, while others (for example, the Adam Smith Institute) wanted the abolition of state pensions and benefits, and their replacement with competing bank and insurance schemes, at an estimated saving to the Exchequer of £12bn. per year at current prices.

By December 1985 the criticism of the plans for social-security reform was felt to be so overwhelming that the secretary of state was forced to withdraw and revise his complete set of proposals. He had received over 7,000 submissions on the green paper, which dealt with the full range of proposed reforms, such as a discretionary (or means-tested) social fund for the poor, a new family credit benefit to replace family income supplement, income support to replace supplementary benefit, and housing-benefit cuts, in addition to the abolition of SERPS. As many as 98 per cent of the submissions were opposed to some of the proposals, while the best-supported proposals had only 10 per-cent support overall. Nevertheless, the radical right accused the government of losing its nerve. Sir John Hoskyns, director-general of the Institute of Directors, argued that the failure to abolish SERPS was a 'major admission of defeat'. On the left, the Labour Party argued that whatever modifications were made, the effect would be that people would be paying the same NICs but getting smaller benefits in return. The centre parties (the Liberal and Social Democrats) argued that SERPS should be modified to do more for the low-paid, or alternatively that SERPS should indeed be abolished and that instead there should be a 25 per-cent increase in the basic state pension.

5.2.2. THE ACTUAL CHANGES TO SERPS

The Social Security Act of 1986 led to SERPS being modified to reduce its costs rather than abolished outright. The act also provided incentives for the creation of personal pensions (see Chapter 7).

The main modifications to SERPS are as follows. The earnings-related pension will be based on *career-revalued earnings* (that is, lifetime average earnings revalued in line with increases in national average earnings), rather than on the best twenty years' earnings. However, married women, single parents, and disabled people would only have to work for twenty years to be eligible for the maximum SERPS pension. The pension will equal 1 per cent (that is, 1/100th) of average career-revalued earnings in the earnings band between the lower and upper earnings limits for each year of membership of SERPS up to a maximum of twenty years. The maximum SERPS pension will therefore be 20 per cent of band earnings, compared with 25 per cent currently. In addition, the widow or widower's pension will be one-half of the deceased spouse's pension. This compares with a full widow/er's pension currently.

The SERPS pension as calculated above is (with appropriate modifications) the pension that is operative when the changes have been fully implemented. This will be for a person who joins SERPS after 6 April 2009. Anyone who is a member of SERPS before that date will be subject to transitional arrangements. The modifications to SERPS will be phased in over a ten-year period, beginning on 6 April 1999. The change to the widow/er's pension, however, occurs abruptly on 6 April 2000.

The SERPS pension during the transitional period is calculated as follows: the pension will equal the sum of two components divided by the number of years between 1978 and the year before the one in which the person reaches state-pension age. The first component is equal to 25 per cent of total revalued earnings in the earnings band between 1978–9 and 1987–8 (revalued to the date of retirement). The second component is equal to a given percentage of total revalued earnings in the earnings band between 1988–9 and the year before the one in which the person reaches state-pension age, where the given percentage depends on the financial year in which the individual reaches state-pension age as follows:

	(%)
1999–2000	25
2000–1	24.5
2001–2	24
2002–3	23.5
2003–4	23
2004–5	22.5
2005–6	22
2006–7	21.5
2007–8	21
2008–9	20.5
2009–10 or later	20

5.2.3. THE EFFECTS OF THE CHANGES TO SERPS

The changes to SERPS are expected to lead to substantial reductions in the cost of state-pension provision by the time they are fully implemented well into the next century. Table 5.4 shows the estimated cost of the original and modified schemes in the financial year 2033–4 in £bn. at 1985 prices.

While there is no change to the cost of basic pensions, the cost of providing earnings-related pensions is reduced by almost half, from £25.5bn. to £13.2bn., and the overall cost of pension provision is reduced by a quarter, from £55.5bn. to £42bn.

The following examples show how substantial the reductions in pensions will be after the changes in SERPS are fully implemented:

● *Male aged 65 with forty years' service, career-revalued earnings of £8,000 p.a., and twenty best years of £12,000 p.a.*:
Before the change: £3,000 p.a. SERPS pension;
After the change: £1,600 p.a. SERPS pension;
Reduction: 47 per cent.

TABLE 5.4. *The cost of SERPS before and after the change* (£bn., 1985 prices)

	Original scheme	Modified scheme
Retirement pensions		
Basic pensions	23.4	23.4
Earnings-related pensions	25.5	13.2
Widows' pensions	1.3	0.8
Invalidity pensions	3.5	3.0
Other pensions	1.8	1.6
TOTAL	55.5	42.0

- *Female aged 60 with thirty years' service, career-revalued earnings of £5,000 p.a., and twenty best years of £14,000 p.a.*:
  Before the change: £3,500 p.a. SERPS pension;
  After the change: £1,000 p.a. SERPS pension;
  Reduction: 71 per cent.
- *Widow of male in first example*:
  Before the change: £3,000 p.a. SERPS pension;
  After the change: £800 p.a. SERPS pension;
  Reduction: 73 per cent.

5.3. The State Graduated Retirement Pension Scheme

SERPS is not the first earnings-related pension scheme operated by the state. It has a predecessor. This was the *state graduated retirement pension scheme* (SGRPS), which operated from April 1961 to April 1975. People paying into SGRPS still receive a pension based on it when they retire. It was also possible to contract out of SGRPS.

Members of SGRPS paid both a weekly *flat-rate* national-insurance contribution and a *graduated* (that is, earnings-related) contribution. The contributions were used to buy *units* of the graduated pension. The amount of pension received depends on the number of units purchased. The cost of units differed for men and women. Men received one unit for each £7.50 of contributions, while women received one unit for each £9 of contributions. Women were deliberately penalized by SGRPS by having their graduated pension entitlement accrue at a lower rate than men. This was because women took their pension from the age of 60 and also lived longer than men, and so in the long run received a larger overall pension than men.

The total number of units purchased is found by taking the total value

TABLE 5.5. *Units purchased and resultant pensions in SGRPS*

	Number of units		Pension (£ per week, 1990–1)	
	Minimum	Maximum	Minimum	Maximum
Contracted-in				
Men	1	86	0.06	5.28
Women	1	72	0.06	4.42
Contracted-out				
Men	1	48	0.06	2.95
Women	1	40	0.06	2.46

of graduated contributions (in pounds) and dividing this number by 7.5 in the case of a man and 9 in the case of a woman. The value of a unit is up-rated annually on the same basis as other state pension benefits. In 1990–1, the value of a unit was £0.0614 per week. The minimum and maximum number of units that could have been purchased during the life of SGRPS and also the minimum and maximum pensions are as shown in Table 5.5.

The pension is very small, at best only about £5 per week, at worst only 6p per week. The graduated pension is payable from state-pension age for the remaining life of the claimant. The pension is not affected by any other earnings received after retirement, but is taxable.

There is a widow's pension equal to half the deceased husband's pension, payable to the widow from age 60. There has also been, since April 1979, a widower's pension, also 50 per cent of the deceased wife's pension but payable only if both the husband and wife had reached pension age before the wife died.

6

Occupational Pension Schemes

Occupational pension schemes are pension schemes that are organized or sponsored by the companies or organizations for which people work. The pensions offered by such schemes are generally related to employees' earnings or salaries at or near retirement; such pensions are known as *defined-benefit* or *final-salary* pensions. As we saw in Chapter 5, the state also operates a pension scheme in which the pensions are related to earnings, that is, the State Earnings-Related Pension Scheme or SERPS.

More than half of all pensioners and about 80 per cent of newly retired pensioners have an occupational pension in addition to the basic pension. These proportions may actually fall if the success of *personal pensions* (see Chapter 7) continues at the present rate. In this chapter we provide a detailed examination of the occupational pension schemes that operate in the UK. In 1992 there were about 120,000 of them, of which only 20,000 are of any size, the rest having only a few members each. About 6 million people draw occupational pensions.

6.1. The Legal Structure of Occupational Pension Schemes

6.1.1. THE TRUST FUND

Most occupational pension schemes in the UK have been set up as *pension trust funds*. A *trust* is a legal relationship between individuals and assets, by which assets provided by one individual (the *settlor*) are held by another group of individuals (*trustees*) for the benefit of a third group of individuals (the *beneficiaries*). The interests of the beneficiaries are set out in the trust deed. If the trust is a *discretionary trust*, the trustees have the freedom of action to dispose the income and capital of the trust as they see fit. The trust serves three functions: it is the primary source of payment of pension entitlements; it is a security for payment; and it is a vehicle for the collective protection and enforcement of the rights of individual scheme members. The first scheme to adopt this legal vehicle was that of Colmans, the mustard manufacturer, in 1900.

There are several reasons why a *trust fund* came to be preferred to a *statutory fund*, its main alternative. A trust fund was much cheaper to set up than a statutory fund. It was also much more flexible: the trust deed could be drawn up in virtually any way that suited the employer, and the employer could ensure effective control of the fund through his appointment of the trustees. Nevertheless, a trust is also a useful vehicle for protecting pension benefits. This is because a trust is a means of attaching to assets the interests of a wide class of beneficiaries, including those not yet born. The presence of a trust also separates the assets of the trust from those of the employer, a valuable feature in the case of default. Further, trustees operate under strict obligations so that their actions can be scrutinized in court. (The implications of the Maxwell Pension Fund Affair are discussed in Chapter 10!)

Since trust law had not originally been established to validate pension schemes, it soon became necessary to put the arrangements on a formal basis. This was done in the Superannuation and Other Trust Funds (Validation) Act of 1927, which permitted the formal validation of trust funds.

In order to receive *exempt approved* status (see Section 6.2.1) from the Inland Revenue, a pension scheme must be established under *irrevocable trust*, with the employee being a beneficiary under the trust, and the employer being a contributor. However, the word 'irrevocable' is not crucial, since the trust deed can provide for the alteration and winding-up of the scheme. But the sole purpose of the scheme must be to provide 'relevant benefits' in respect of service as an employee, where benefits are defined as pensions and lump sums payable on or in anticipation of retirement or on death. The benefits must be made available to the member or widow/er, children, or dependants.

The pension scheme must also appoint an *administrator* to manage the scheme. Under the 1970 Finance Act, the administrator must be a resident of the United Kingdom. Typically the trustees, so long as they are resident in the UK, are appointed as administrator to the scheme.

6.1.2. TRUSTEES

The role of the trustees is to operate the pension scheme in the best interests of its beneficiaries and to act impartially between the interests of different classes of beneficiaries. They have to act in accordance with the trust deed and rules of the scheme, within the framework of the law. They also have to act prudently, conscientiously, honestly, and with the utmost good faith. But there is no requirement for there to be a minimum number of trustees or for the scheme to have an independent trustee. There is also no requirement for a trustee to have any special training or to meet any professional standard. Individuals with criminal records are not barred from being trustees. However, a trustee who has been declared bankrupt or who has been convicted of dishonesty can be removed by court order. It is possible for the trustee to be a limited company: indeed more than half of existing pension schemes have corporate trustees (although most of these are not independent of the employer).

Trustees have a fiduciary duty under the 1961 Trustee Investments Act to preserve the trust capital and to apply the capital and its income according to the trust deed. Trustees generally have wide investment powers, including powers to borrow. Indeed, the failure to invest, or at least place funds on deposit, might make trustees liable to make up the lost income. Scheme members can sue for compensation if they suffer loss as a result of negligence by trustees under the 1925 Trustee Act.

Trustees (and their investment advisers) also have to abide by the Financial Services Act 1986. It is a criminal offence to carry on investment business in the UK unless either *authorized* to do so or *exempted* from the provisions of the act. Pension-fund managers are regulated by IMRO (the Investment Managers Regulatory Organization). Under section 19 of the act, trustees who are not involved in daily investment decision-taking for their schemes do not have to be regulated under the act. Instead they are subject to chapter 11 of the rule-book of IMRO. IMRO makes regular inspection visits to occupational pension schemes. In general, it finds that most schemes are well-run, although some schemes have been criticized for inadequate record-keeping and failing to ensure that administrative staff are properly trained. (However, see Section 10.2.3.7 for an account of IMRO's role in the Maxwell Affair.)

Trustees have substantial discretion over who benefits in the event of a member dying, especially if the member was unmarried or had no one who was financially dependent on him or her. If, for example, a man was married (even if the wife was financially independent) or had parents, or children up to the age of 18, who were financially dependent on him, the case would be clear-cut: they would receive a widow's or dependant's pension. If the man had a financially independent common-law wife, the case is also clear-cut: the common-law wife would not receive a widow's pension. If, however, the common-law wife was financially dependent, she might receive a pension at the trustees' discretion.

There is no restriction on who receives the tax-free lump sum in the event of death in service. It can go to whoever is nominated by the member. If no one is nominated and there are no dependent relatives, it will go into the member's estate and be taxed.

Since trustees can find themselves liable to being sued, they tend to take out *liability insurance* to indemnify them against this possibility. For example, when section 32 buy-out policies first became available in 1986 for those changing jobs (see Section 6.4.2.5 below), many trustees refused to grant transfer values to the job-changers. This was because the trustees found it difficult to determine whether the buy-out policies 'corresponded' with Inland Revenue requirements. Many insurance companies offering buy-out policies were forced to indemnify trustees before they would release an ex-employee's transfer value. Alternatively, trustees obliged the employee and his or her spouse to sign a disclaimer.

6.1.3. WINDING UP A PENSION SCHEME

In the event of the sponsoring company becoming insolvent under the 1986 Insolvency Act, it is likely that the pension scheme will be wound up. The liabilities of the scheme will have to be either bought back from insurance companies or transferred to another approved scheme, except for the *guaranteed minimum pension* (GMP) which can be bought back from the state by payment of *accrued-rights premiums* and *pensioners'-rights premiums*. Pension-scheme members rank as unsecured creditors and so rank behind the Inland Revenue, HM Customs and Excise, secured lenders, and debenture holders. In the event that there are insufficient funds to pay everyone in full, the priority of claims of scheme members is as follows: first existing pensioners, followed by early leavers with deferred benefits, and finally current employees.

The administrator appointed under the Insolvency Act will attempt to recover any arrears of contributions, both employee and employer. Any arrears become preferred claims on the assets of the employer, under the terms of the Companies Act 1985. Alternatively, it is possible to establish a claim on the Redundancy Fund (which is financed from national-insurance contributions) under the terms of the Employment Protection Act 1978. A *group deferred annuity scheme* may be established for current employees with whatever resources remain.

From the beginning of 1991 an independent trustee has to be appointed to schemes where the company is in liquidation. But the only requirement of a contracted-out scheme is to provide a guaranteed minimum pension equivalent to the SERPS benefits forgone, so any new company taking over the insolvent company would be liable only for this commitment and not for the full extent of the shortfall in pension-fund assets. However, the 1990 Social Security Act included provisions to create a debt on the employer when schemes are wound up; but these provisions have not yet come into force.

6.2. Inland Revenue Approval

6.2.1. EXEMPT APPROVED SCHEMES

Only *exempt approved* occupational pension schemes (as defined in sections 590–612 of the 1988 Income and Corporation Taxes Act) are eligible for tax relief. An exempt approved scheme is one that has been established under *irrevocable trust* and has been approved by the *Pension Schemes Office* (PSO) of the Inland Revenue. The tax position of occupational schemes is governed by the 1988 Income and Corporation Taxes Act and the 1989 Finance Act, and is discussed in Section 6.2.4 below.

The main requirements for a scheme to be granted exempt approved status are:

- the scheme is established for the sole purpose of providing *relevant benefits* in respect of service as an employee, where relevant benefits cover any financial benefit offered in respect of the termination of an employee's service;
- the scheme is established in connection with a business carried out in the UK by a person resident in the UK;
- the employer is a contributor to the scheme, making contributions of at least 10 per cent of total contributions;
- there can be no refund of employee contributions;
- there are limits on pension benefits as specified in Section 6.2.3 below.

A scheme that was only *approved* by the PSO rather than *exempt approved* would only be eligible for tax relief on employees' contributions and not for any of the other reliefs.

6.2.2. LIMITS ON CONTRIBUTIONS

There are Inland Revenue limits on the level of contributions that can be made to an occupational pension scheme for the purpose of attracting tax relief. For an employee below the age of 50, the maximum employee's contribution is 15 per cent of the employee's *net relevant earnings* or *pensionable earnings* (broadly, taxable earnings, but it may exclude overtime and bonuses). In addition, for an employee below the age of 50 the maximum combined employee and employer contribution is 17.5 per cent of the employee's pensionable earnings. Included in this limit, members can pay up to 5 per cent of earnings towards death-in-service benefits. These benefits are provided through a term insurance policy and the contributions attract tax relief (one of the few cases remaining of life-assurance premiums attracting tax relief; life-assurance premium relief was abolished in 1984).

There are higher contribution limits for older employees (when they first join the scheme):

Age range	Contribution limits (% of earnings)
50 or less	17.5

51–55	20.0
56–60	22.5
61–74	27.5

The maximum age for making contributions is 74. This is because the payment of a pension annuity cannot be delayed beyond the seventy-fifth birthday.

The scheme will appoint actuaries to determine what contribution level is necessary to keep the scheme solvent. The PSO permits the following assumptions to be used for this purpose: prices increase at 7 per cent p.a. compound; earnings increase at 8.5 per cent p.a. compound; and investment returns are 9 per cent p.a. compound (that is, 0.5 per cent in excess of earnings growth rates).

Nevertheless, defined-benefit schemes operate on a *balance of cost* basis, so that the employer will pay whatever sum in excess of employee contributions the scheme actuary considers necessary to ensure that the scheme has adequate assets to meet its liabilities.

6.2.3. LIMITS ON PENSIONS

It is generally not possible to take a pension before the age of 50 (45 for women), nor to delay taking a pension beyond the age of 75 (70 for women). In terms of the pension at retirement, this is based on the *final salary* or the *average salary*. The Inland Revenue permits two principal definitions of final salary:

- basic salary for any one of the five years preceding the normal retirement date plus an average over three or more years of any bonuses or commissions received. The chosen salary can be uprated by the increase in national average earnings to the date of retirement;
- the average of total salary over three or more consecutive years out of the ten years preceding normal retirement. Again, the chosen salary can be indexed to the date of retirement.

The average salary is defined as total pensionable earnings divided by the number of years of service in the scheme, with the earnings in each year uprated by the increase in national average earnings.

If no lump sum is taken, the typical pension will be based on the *sixtieths scale*, that is, 1/60th (1.67 per cent) of final salary for each year of service, up to a maximum of forty years' service. This gives a maximum pension of two-thirds (that is, 40/60ths) of final salary. Alternatively, a tax-free lump sum can be taken by commuting part of the pension. In this case the pension is calculated on the *eightieths scale*, that is, 1/80th (1.25 per cent) of final salary for each year of service up to a maximum of forty years' service, together with a lump sum of 3/80ths (3.75 per cent) of final salary for each year of service. This gives a maximum pension of half (that is, 40/80ths) of final salary, and a maximum lump sum of 1.5 (that is, 120/80ths) times final salary. The 1992 National Association of Pension Funds survey found that 70 per cent of schemes paid benefits on the sixtieths scale, while 20 per cent of schemes were more generous than this and 10 per cent were less generous.

Occupational pension schemes also provide for widow/ers' or dependants' pensions; widowers' pensions have been mandatory since April 1989. The maximum widow/er's pension is two-thirds of the member's pension. The maximum possible widow/er's pension is therefore 4/9ths (that is, 2/3rds of 2/3rds) of the member's salary at retirement. The widow/er's pension can start from the date of the member's death, and can continue for life, or cease or reduce on remarriage. Any pension paid to a dependent child must cease when the child reaches the age of 18 or finishes full-time education. In the case of death in service, a maximum lump sum can be provided equal to four times the earnings of the member at the time of death, together with a refund of employee contributions, with or without interest. The maximum widow/er's pension is 4/9ths of the member's salary at time of death.

The Inland Revenue also permits the pension to be calculated on a scale higher than the sixtieths scale for those with sufficiently long, but less than full, pensionable service. For employees who were members of schemes before 17 March 1987., this scale is known as the *uplifted sixtieths* scale and is as follows:

Years of pensionable service	Fraction of final salary (for each year of service)
1–5	1/60
6	8/60
7	16/60
8	24/60
9	32/60
10 or more	40/60

This meant, for example, that an employee with only ten years' pensionable service could nevertheless be awarded the maximum possible pension of two-thirds of final salary so long as he had no benefits from a pension scheme from an earlier period of employment; if he had such benefits, these would have to be deducted from the pension.

The 1987 Finance Act replaced the uplifted sixtieths scale with a new *accelerated scale* for employees joining schemes after 17 March 1987. The accelerated scale is simply 1/30th of final salary for each year of service. This has had the effect of improving benefits for employees with less than six years' service, but reducing them for employees with longer service as Table 6.1 shows. Since 17 March 1987 the maximum two-thirds pension

TABLE 6.1. *Comparison between the uplifted sixtieths and accelerated scales*

Years of service	Uplifted sixtieths scale		Accelerated scale	
	Fraction of final salary	%age of final salary	Fraction of final salary	%age of final salary
1	1/60	1.66	2/60	3.33
2	2/60	3.33	4/60	6.66
3	3/60	5.00	6/60	10.00
4	4/60	6.66	8/60	13.33
5	5/60	8.33	10/60	16.66
6	8/60	13.33	12/60	20.00
7	16/60	26.66	14/60	23.33
8	24/60	40.00	16/60	26.66
9	32/60	53.33	18/60	30.00
10	40/60	66.66	20/60	33.33
11	40/60	66.66	22/60	36.66
12	40/60	66.66	24/60	40.00
13	40/60	66.66	26/60	43.33
14	40/60	66.66	28/60	46.66
15	40/60	66.66	30/60	50.00
16	40/60	66.66	32/60	53.33
17	40/60	66.66	34/60	56.66
18	40/60	66.66	36/60	60.00
19	40/60	66.66	38/60	63.33
20	40/60	66.66	40/60	66.66

takes a minimum of twenty years' service to achieve. Individuals such as sportsmen who have short working lives have special rules which enable them to build up full pension benefits during their short careers.

The Inland Revenue allows a similar uplifting of the scale for commutation of the pension. The *uplifted eightieths* scale is as follows:

Years of pensionable service	Fraction of final salary (for each year of service)
1–8	3/80
9	30/80
10	36/80
11	42/80
12	48/80
13	54/80
14	63/80
15	72/80
16	81/80

17	90/80
18	99/80
19	108/80
20 or more	120/80

So, for example, an employee with only twenty years' service could achieve the maximum lump-sum payment of 1.5 times final salary in return for accepting a pension reduced from the sixtieths to the eightieths scale. The 1987 Finance Act replaced the uplifted eightieths scale with a new accelerated scale for employees joining schemes after 17 March 1987. But so long as the accelerated scale of 1/30th was used to calculate the pension, the lump sum could still be calculated using the uplifted eightieths scale. If, however, the pension fraction was between 1/60th and 1/30th, the new accelerated scale provided a lower lump sum than before.

It is possible for members of occupational pension schemes to work beyond normal retirement age and to have their pensions enhanced as a result. The maximum pension accrual rate permitted by the Inland Revenue is 40/60ths of final salary at the normal retirement age, with an additional 1/60th for each year of service beyond this up to a maximum of 45/60ths of final salary. When a lump sum is given, the maximum permissible pension is 45/80ths with a maximum lump sum of 135/80ths of final salary.

The 1989 Finance Act introduced new limits on earnings and contributions that qualify for tax relief in occupational pension schemes. The earnings limit (or *earnings cap*) on which a final-salary pension can be based was set at £60,000 (in 1989 prices). However, this limit could be doubled if the individual had two jobs with unconnected employers. (The Inland Revenue estimated that only 50,000 people earned more than £60,000 in Britain in 1989.) The maximum pension at two-thirds of final salary was therefore £40,000 (in 1989 prices). In addition, if the pension is based on anything other than the sixtieths or eightieths scale, a *retained-benefits rule* comes into operation; this requires pension entitlements from previous employments to be taken into account, so that the two-thirds limit (with a maximum of £40,000 in 1989 prices) is not breached. The lump sum is calculated as the larger of 3/80ths of final salary for each year of service and 2.25 times the pension (before commutation). The maximum lump sum that can be commuted at retirement was £90,000 (in 1989 prices). The maximum contribution-rate is 15 per cent of pensionable earnings. Given that there is also an earnings limit of £60,000, this implies that the maximum level of contributions into a scheme was set by the act at £9,000 (all in 1989 prices). All these limits are indexed in line with prices, rather than earnings. Since earnings-growth on average exceeds price inflation by about 2 per cent, this means that in thirty years' time the £60,000 ceiling will be equivalent to a salary limit of £30,000 in

1989 prices. The new limits apply to members of pension schemes set up after 14 March 1989 and to those joining existing schemes after 1 June 1989.

If an employer makes contributions to a scheme, he receives tax relief on those contributions as a result of the 1970 Finance Act. The employer's contribution is not treated as a benefit by the Inland Revenue, so is not taxable, even though the employer can offset it against corporation tax. However, if the employer withdraws money from the scheme, he is taxed at the rate of 40 per cent as a result of the Finance Act 1986. In addition, this tax liability cannot be offset against any trading losses that the employer is making.

The tax position established by the 1986 Finance Act had initially been designed to deal with the pension-fund surpluses that had arisen during the early 1980s as a result of the combined effects of redundancies during the 1980–1 slump and the global stock-market boom (for more details, see Chapter 11). In 1986 the government decided that the pension-fund surpluses (in excess of 5 per cent of the value of the liabilities) should be eliminated by any of the following methods:

- payment to the employer;
- reduction or suspension for up to five years of the employer's contribution;
- reduction or suspension for up to five years of employees' contributions;
- improvement of benefits; or
- provision of new benefits.

6.2.4. TAXATION ISSUES

6.2.4.1. *Income and Capital-Gains Taxes*

With exempt approved occupational pension schemes, the position with respect to income taxes and capital-gains taxes is clear and simple.

An exempt approved scheme has the following set of tax reliefs. Both the employee's and the employer's contributions attract tax relief at the highest marginal tax rate respectively of the employee and employer so long as the contribution of the employee does not exceed 15 per cent of the employee's salary and so long as the combined contributions of employee and employer do not exceed 17.5 per cent of the employee's salary for an employee aged 50 or less (under the Income and Corporation Taxes Act 1988). In addition, the employer's contribution is not treated for tax purposes as the employee's income (on the grounds that the pension is treated for tax purposes as deferred income). Further, the investment income and realized capital gains from the fund are exempt from income and capital-gains taxes (so long as the fund does not engage in trading or property development). Finally, any lump sum payable on retirement is also tax-free and any lump sum paid to a beneficiary on the death of the employee is free of inheritance tax. Only the final pension itself is taxable as earned income.

6.2.4.2. *Inheritance Tax*

When an individual dies, any pension benefits that he or she may have built up (such as death benefits) will become part of his or her estate, unless prior arrangements have been made to put the pension into a trust and the beneficiaries nominated. The difference can have a substantial effect on both the level of inheritance tax that might be paid and the speed with which payments to beneficiaries are made. This is true for both occupational pension schemes and personal pensions.

Most occupational pensions are payable through discretionary trusts. This means that the benefits will not form part of the pension-holder's estate and will not therefore attract inheritance tax. Although this is not directly useful in the case where the beneficiary is the pension-holder's spouse (since transfers between husbands and wives do not attract inheritance tax), it could be important when the beneficiary is someone else, such as the pension-holder's children. Another important advantage of payment through a trust is that it avoids the delays in the deceased person's estate being granted probate.

It is important that all parts of the pension package should be put in trust. For example, the death benefits might be payable through a life-assurance policy that is separate from the main pension scheme. These benefits should also be placed in a trust and the beneficiaries nominated.

It is also important that the pension-holder's nominated beneficiaries are updated as circumstances change. For example, a single man joining a pension scheme for the first time might name his parents as beneficiaries. Later, when he marries, he might want to make his wife a beneficiary. Unless he does this the trustees will have to exercise discretion in deciding whether the parents or the widow is more deserving of the benefits, in the event that the pension-holder dies.

Even where a beneficiary has been nominated in a pension scheme that has been placed in trust, it is up to the trustees to decide who actually receives the benefits. This is the nature of a discretionary trust. The benefits cannot be assigned. This means, for example, that any life cover that is linked to a pension plan cannot be used in conjunction with a mortgage. However, if a pension in trust does not have a nominated beneficiary, it will be included in the person's estate for inheritance-tax purposes.

The self-employed with their own pension schemes can also avoid inheritance tax and ensure a rapid pay-out by placing their death benefits in trust.

6.2.5. UNAPPROVED SCHEMES

Since August 1989, as a result of the 1989 Finance Act, occupational schemes have been able to establish *unapproved* pension schemes on top of their main schemes. These schemes can provide additional pension benefits above the tax-approved limits but do not enjoy any tax advantages on contributions or investment income above these limits (these schemes are known as *top-up schemes* or *funded unapproved retirement benefit schemes* (or FURBSs)). Unapproved schemes can also be used to provide more flexible compensation packages for high earners who would otherwise be restricted by the earnings cap imposed by the 1989 Finance Act and for employees with less than twenty years' service to retirement who would not be able to achieve the maximum permitted pension.

Contributions by an employer into an unapproved scheme do not qualify for tax relief automatically, as they do for exempt approved schemes, but they might be relievable under the standard rules for corporation tax. For an expense to be tax-deductible, it has to be incurred wholly and exclusively for the purposes of the business, and be an income item and not a capital item. For the Inland Revenue to allow employer contributions into an unapproved scheme to be relieved, it is necessary that: the assets of the scheme be put outside the control of the employer (for example, in a trust for the benefit of employees); the level of benefits is not 'unreasonable', since this could not be justified as being wholly and exclusively for the purposes of the business; and the company does not set up a book reserve to pay for the pension, as this would not be accepted as expenditure.

Contributions by the employer into an unapproved scheme are treated as benefits in kind to the employee and hence taxable in the hands of the employee if the employee has an 'absolute right' to the benefits from the fund. Contributions by the employee do not attract tax relief.

In the case of unapproved schemes that build up funds of investment assets, tax will be payable on investment income and chargeable capital gains. However, the lump-sum benefits payable with unapproved schemes are tax-free, since they involve the receipt of money to which the employee is absolutely entitled and on which tax has already been paid. Any pension from the scheme would be taxed as Schedule E income. It would, therefore, be more tax-efficient for the employee to take the entire pension benefits as a lump sum and buy a purchased life annuity (see

Section 9.2.2). It is also possible that there is a liability to inheritance tax, although this liability may be avoided if death benefits are discretionary and not payable only to the deceased's estate.

6.3. Types of Schemes and Eligibility for Membership

Occupational pension schemes can be classified in a number of ways. The two main classifications are between schemes that are contracted out of and those that are not contracted out of SERPS, the State Earnings-Related Pension Scheme; and between schemes in the private sector and those in the public sector. In this section we analyse schemes according to these classifications. We also consider the different types of eligibility requirements for membership of occupational schemes.

6.3.1. CONTRACTED-OUT AND NON-CONTRACTED-OUT SCHEMES

6.3.1.1. *What is Contracting Out?*

One of the most important distinctions between occupational pension schemes is whether or not they are *contracted out* of the *State Earnings-Related Pension Scheme* (SERPS) which came into operation on 6 April 1978 and is paid for through *national-insurance contributions* (NICs). In *non-contracted-out* occupational pension schemes (more commonly known as *contracted-in* schemes), both employees and employers pay the full rate of NICs. Employees will automatically be contracted into SERPS, unless their pension scheme has been specifically contracted out. Contracted-in schemes can provide just the SERPS pension or, for additional contributions, they can provide a pension in addition to the SERPS pension. In this case, the individual would end up getting three pensions: the basic state pension, a SERPS pension, and an occupational pension. The 1988 Finance Act introduced the *contracted-in money purchase scheme* (CIMPS), which allows employees to belong to a contracted-in occupational pension scheme but also to take out a minimum contribution (that is, rebate-only) personal pension for the purpose of contracting out of SERPS (see Section 7.4.2). In contracted-out schemes, on the other hand, members forfeit their right to receive the SERPS pension and in return both they and their employers pay reduced NICs. The reduction in contributions is known as the *contracted-out rebate*. The current contracted-out rebate is 1.8 per cent of earnings for employees and 3 per cent of earnings for employers, a combined rebate of 4.8 per cent. The contracted-out rebate has been reduced over the years. When

SERPS first started the rebate was 2.5 per cent for employees and 4.5 per cent for employers, a total rebate of 7 per cent; in 1982 the rebate was reduced to 2.15 per cent for employees and 4.1 per cent for employers, giving a total rebate of 6.25 per cent; in 1988 the rebate was reduced to 2 per cent for employees and 3.8 per cent for employers, giving a total rebate of 5.8 per cent. The current rebates have been in effect since 6 April 1993.

The *Occupational Pensions Board* (OPB) has to ensure that a scheme satisfies certain minimum conditions concerning benefits and the preservation of those benefits before it can grant a *contracting-out certificate* for the scheme. In particular, the scheme must provide benefits that are at least equivalent to those provided by the SERPS pension, and this is known as the *guaranteed minimum pension* (GMP). The GMP element of the occupational pension is offset from any SERPS entitlement. On the other hand, the PSO has to ensure that the scheme's benefits do not exceed certain limits that it lays down. This is to prevent schemes circumventing the Inland Revenue's regulations on tax avoidance and to prevent schemes breaking an incomes policy when one is in operation.

6.3.1.2. *The Procedure and Requirements for Contracting Out*

The procedure for contracting out of SERPS is as follows. Once the company has announced its intention to contract out of SERPS, there has to be a three-month consultation period with employees. Following this, the employer applies to the OPB for a contracting-out certificate and submits a copy of the announcement to employees, a *solvency certificate* from an actuary with the recommended funding rate, and an *interim trust deed*. At a later stage the *definitive trust deed* and the scheme's *rules* are lodged with the OPB. The final task of the OPB is to confirm that the GMP is being provided.

The minimum requirements necessary to satisfy the OPB are the following. The pension must be based on the eightieths scale, that is, 1/80th (1.25 per cent) of *pensionable earnings* for each year of service. Pensionable earnings must be based on the *final salary* or the *average salary* as defined in Section 6.2.3 above.

The GMP is the pension calculated on the basis of the same *earnings band* used to calculate the earnings-related component of the state pension (namely, that between the *lower* and *upper earnings limits*) and must not be less than the state pension. The scheme must provide a widow/er's pension that is related to the amount of the GMP of the spouse at the time of his or her death. Widow/ers with children or who are older than 45 years at the time their spouse dies will be awarded a pension equal to the full amount of the GMP; from 6 April 2000 this will be reduced to half the GMP. The OPB must ensure that the resources of the scheme are sufficient to meet both the GMP and the widow/er's pension. Every employee with more than two years' pensionable service has the right to have his or her pension benefit preserved if he or she changes jobs or is made redundant (this is known as the *preserved pension*). The pension must be preserved in such a way that it is not less than the GMP for the same period of service.

The GMP is calculated as follows. For men above 50 and women above 45 on 6 April 1988, the GMP is 1.25 per cent of total *revalued earnings* (between the lower and upper earnings limits, with revaluation based on increases in national average earnings) between 6 April 1978 and 5 April 1988, *plus* 1 per cent of total revalued earnings between 6 April 1988 and state-pension age. For younger men and women the GMP is 25 per cent of total revalued earnings between 6 April 1978 and 5 April 1988, *plus* 20 per cent of total revalued earnings between 6 April 1988 and state-pension age, all *divided by* the number of years between 1978–9 and state-pension age.

When an individual leaves a scheme his or her GMP must be preserved in the scheme from the date of leaving to the date of retirement using one of the procedures listed in Section 6.4.2.2 below. As an alternative to having the benefit preserved if an employee changes jobs and joins another scheme, his or her benefit could be transferred to the new scheme in return for a *transfer payment* from the old scheme (see Sections 6.4.2.3 and 6.4.2.4).

The OPB allows an employer to contract out a particular group of employees on the basis of the *nature of employment*, for example, full-time employees only, or even on the basis of age, such as employees with less than five years to retirement, but not on the grounds of sex.

6.3.1.3. *Re-Contracting Into the State Scheme*

It is possible for contracted-out schemes to re-contract into the state scheme through the payment of premiums to the state which enable the scheme to buy back its members' rights. These payments are known as *accrued-rights premiums* (ARPs) for members below retirement age and *pensioners'-rights premiums* (PRPs) for currently retired members. They are based on some measure of the cost that the state itself will have to pay in order to provide the subsequent earnings-related pensions. First the long-run normal actuarial costs are calculated on the basis that nominal yields on long-term gilts and equities are 9 per cent and 4 per cent respectively. These are then rescaled by a *market-level indicator* (MLI) to give the actual premiums payable in a way which gives some protection against short-term market-value fluctuations. The MLI for ARPs is calculated as the weighted sum of two components: an equity component (with a weight of 0.65) taken as the ratio of 4 per cent to the gross dividend yield on the FT-Actuaries All Share Index, and a fixed-interest component (with a weight of 0.35) taken as the ratio of 9 per cent to the FT-Actuaries gross redemption yield on a 13 per-cent-coupon twenty-five-year gilt. The MLI for PRPs depends only on the yield on gilts and not equities, and is calculated as above, but uses the gross redemption yield for fifteen-year gilts rather than twenty-five-year ones.

6.3.1.4. *Simplified Contracted-Out Occupational Pension Schemes*

The 1986 Social Security Act introduced two new types of contracted-out occupational pension schemes. The scheme arrangements were subsequently amended by the Finance Act 1987. The two new schemes are:

- a simplified defined-benefit scheme, known as a *contracted-out final-salary scheme* (COFSS);
- a simplified defined-contribution scheme known as a *contracted-out money-purchase scheme* (COMPS).

Each scheme is designed to offer 'no frills' pensions and to obtain Inland Revenue tax-relief approval on the basis of a simplified set of rules. Standardized documentation is provided by the Inland Revenue. If these documents are used, tax-relief approval is granted automatically. This contrasts with the complex set of rules that are required for tailor-made occupational pension schemes. The simplified schemes are designed principally for small employers.

There are certain conditions that have to be met in order for the schemes to be approved. The principal ones are as follows. Scheme members cannot belong to any other occupational scheme. Controlling directors (that is, those holding more than 20 per cent of the equity in a firm) cannot be members of these schemes. The schemes cannot be self-administered, that is, they can only invest with approved insurance companies, banks, building societies, or unit trusts.

The COFSS offers pensions based on the final salary at retirement, with the maximum accrual rate being 1/60th of final salary for each year of service. However, it is possible for a COFSS to be established in such a way that individual members are given notional money-purchase accounts, so that each member would get the larger of the pension based on final salary and the pension based on the value of the assets in the money-purchase account. The COMPS is a money-purchase occupational scheme with an overall limit on contributions of 17.5 per cent of salary. As with all money-purchase schemes, there is no limit on total pension benefits. Commutation rights and death benefits will be the same as for personal pensions (see Chapter 7).

With a COMPS, the employee and the employer will pay the contracted-out rate of national-insurance contributions, as in the case of contracted-out final-salary schemes. The employer will make *guaranteed minimum contributions* (GMCs) to the COMPS equal to the contracted-out rebate on NICs; he will be able to recoup the employee's share of this from the employee's salary. It is also possible to set up a COMPS providing a *guaranteed minimum pension* (GMP). With a GMC-COMPS contributions have to be invested monthly. With a GMP-COMPS, it is not necessary to ensure that contributions are invested monthly, since what is guaranteed is that the pension at retirement is no lower than under SERPS. However, a GMP-COMPS can be more expensive to operate because of this guarantee, especially if the scheme's members are old. It has been estimated that the additional cost can be as much as 2–3 per cent of payroll.

In addition, there has been a government incentive to start a COMPS in the form of an extra 2 per-cent national-insurance rebate for the five financial years 1988–9 to 1992–3, reducing to a 1 per-cent rebate between 1993–4 and 1995–6. This additional rebate is available only if the category of employment to which an individual belongs has not been included in the employer's contracted-out occupational scheme for a continuous period of two years or more ending in April 1988. So although an individual might have joined his firm's scheme less than two years before April 1988, if the position had been previously held by someone who was in a contracted-out scheme, then there was no additional rebate into a COMPS.

6.3.2. PRIVATE-SECTOR AND PUBLIC-SECTOR SCHEMES

Another important distinction is between occupational pension schemes in the private sector and those in the public sector. The private sector comprises the personal and company sectors and includes companies, unincorporated businesses, and non-profit-making bodies outside government control, such as universities. The public sector consists of central government, local government, and public corporations.

Most contracted-out private-sector schemes provide pensions based on the sixtieths scale rather than the minimum scale of eightieths; there is also provision for part of the benefit to be commuted as a lump sum on retirement. Most public-sector schemes, on the other hand, use the eightieths scale, but, with an additional lump sum on retirement, this makes the benefit equivalent to one based on the sixtieths scale. Most schemes in both the private and public sectors provide a widow/er's pension of one-third or half of the member's pension, together with a lump sum on death in service of one to two years' salary.

The *Government Actuary's Survey of Occupational Pension Schemes* for 1987 (Government Actuary's Department, 1991; hereafter referred to as GASOPS) estimated (see Table 6.2) that in 1987 10.6 million employees were members of occupational pension schemes, about half the total in employment (GASOPS does not cover the self-employed). There were 7.2 million male and 3.4 million female members. The table also shows that there were 5.8 million members of private-sector schemes from total private-sector employment of 15.2 million, giving a rate of coverage of 38 per cent (49 per cent for men and 22 per cent for women). In the public sector there were 4.5 million members out of a total of 6.1 million employees, giving a much higher rate of coverage of nearly 74 per cent (89 per cent for men and 61 per cent for women). The rates of coverage for the components of the public sector were respectively 90 per cent for public corporations, 85 per cent for central government, and 61 per cent for local authorities.

Table 6.3 shows the growth of pension-scheme membership since estimates were first made for 1936 (see *Ministry of Labour Gazette*, May 1938). Starting with 2.6 million members in 1936, there was rapid growth during the post-war period, reaching 8 million in 1956, stabilizing at between 11 million and 12 million members during the 1960s and 1970s, but falling slightly during the 1980s. Up till 1979 there was a reduction in the relative proportion of private-sector membership, which reached a maximum of 8.1 million in 1967. The relative size of public-sector membership increased as more manual workers were transferred from the private to the public sector as a result of nationalization; the last being the 150,000 workers in the shipbuilding and aerospace industries transferred in 1977. Since 1979 (a year which saw public-sector membership at its maximum of 5.5 million), the privatization policies of the Thatcher and Major governments have led to a relative contraction of public-sector membership, as companies such as British Aerospace, British Telecom, British Airways, British Gas, National Power, and PowerGen have been transferred to the private sector.

Since the passing of the Social Security Pensions Act of 1975 which gave women equal access to occupational pension schemes from April 1978, there has been an increase in the coverage of women employees, from 2.8 million in 1975 to 3.4 million in 1987 (which is over half the number of women in full-time employment). Table 6.4 gives the number of private-sector employees with a pension scheme in 1987 according to size of company. It shows that only about a quarter of employees in small firms were members of schemes, whereas over 80 per cent of employees in large firms were members.

In the public sector there were about 1 million employees in public corporations, 2 million in central government, and 3 million in local government, a total of 6 million employees or just under 30 per cent

TABLE 6.2. *Pension-scheme coverage, 1987, United Kingdom* (millions)

Sector	Men		Women		Total	
	Employees	Members	Employees	Members	Employees	Members
Civil employment:						
Private sector	8.9	4.4	6.3	1.4	15.2	5.8
Public sector:						
Public corporations	0.8	0.8	0.2	0.1	1.0	0.9
Central government	0.6	0.6	1.4	1.1	2.0	1.7
Local authorities	1.4	1.1	1.7	0.8	3.1	1.9
Total public sector	2.8	2.5	3.3	2.0	6.1	4.5
Total civilians	11.7	6.9	9.6	3.4	21.3	10.3
HM Forces:	0.3	0.3	—	—	0.3	0.3
TOTALS	12.0	7.2	9.6	3.4	21.6	10.6

Source: GASOPS, Table 2.2.

TABLE 6.3. *Employees in pension schemes, 1936–1987 (millions)*

Year	Private sector		Public sector		Total members	Total employed	%age employed who are members		
	Men	Women	Men	Women			Men	Women	Total
1936	1.3	0.3	0.8	0.2	2.6	NA	NA	NA	NA
1953	2.5	0.6	2.4	0.7	6.2	21.9	34	18	28
1956	3.5	0.8	2.9	0.8	8.0	22.7	43	21	35
1963	6.4	0.8	3.0	0.9	11.1	22.9	63	21	48
1967	6.8	1.3	3.1	1.0	12.2	23.2	66	28	53
1971	5.5	1.3	3.2	1.1	11.1	22.5	62	28	49
1975	4.9	1.1	3.7	1.7	11.4	23.1	63	30	49
1979	4.6	1.5	3.7	1.8	11.6	23.4	62	35	50
1983	4.4	1.4	3.4	1.9	11.1	21.1	64	37	52
1987	4.4	1.4	2.8	2.0	10.6	21.6	60	35	49

Source: Ministry of Labour Gazette, May 1938, and GASOPS, Table 2.1.

TABLE 6.4. *Private-sector pension-scheme coverage, 1987* (thousands)

Size of establishment	Employees	Members	Non-members	%age of members
Number of employees				
1–2	390	80	310	21
3–24	3,590	890	2,700	25
25–99	2,990	1,270	1,720	42
100–999	3,680	2,290	1,390	62
1,000 and over	1,250	1,040	210	83
TOTALS	11,900	5,570	6,330	47

Source: GASOPS, Table 2.5.

TABLE 6.5. *Public-corporation pension-scheme coverage, 1987*

Employer	Number of schemes	Number of employees (thousands)	Number of members (thousands)	%age coverage
Nationalized industries	20	870	815	94
Other public corporations	20	125	110	88
TOTALS	40	995	925	93

Source: GASOPS, Table 2.6.

of total employment in Britain at 21 million. The public corporations included (in 1987) the nationalized industries such as post, coal, rail, steel, shipbuilding, electricity, waterways, and airports, and other public corporations such as the regional water authorities, the broadcasting authorities, and the Bank of England. Their pension coverage, which is very high, is given in Table 6.5. The rest of the public sector comprises central government ('all bodies for whose activities a minister of the crown is accountable to parliament'), local authorities ('the elected councils for defined areas of the UK'), and Her Majesty's Armed Forces. The pension-scheme coverage of employees in these subsectors is given in Table 6.6. The range of coverage is from 53 per cent for the Local Government Superannuation Scheme (due to the large number of part-time employees who were not members of the scheme) to 100 per cent for regular firemen. The rate of coverage for general government (that is, central and local government combined) is 73 per cent.

Occupational Pension Schemes

TABLE 6.6. *Central- and local-government pension-scheme coverage, 1987*

Employer	Number of different arrangements	Number of employees (thousands)	Number of members (thousands)	Coverage (%)
Central government:				
HM Forces	1	320	320	100
Civil service and other central-government bodies	15	775	730	94
Health authorities	1	1,210	925	76
Local authorities:				
Lecturers and teachers	1	735	600	82
Police officers (regular)	1	135	135	100
Firemen (regular)	1	40	40	100
Other employees of local authorities	2	2,145	1,140	53
TOTALS	22	5,360	3,890	73

Source: GASOPS, Table 2.4.

Table 6.7 gives membership details for contracted-out and non-contracted-out schemes in the private and public sectors in 1987. There were 4.5 million employees in contracted-out schemes in the private sector; these were concentrated mostly in the larger-sized schemes of over 1,000 members. There were 4.8 million employees in 180 public-sector schemes. There were 1.3 million employees, mostly in the smaller schemes of the private sector (that is, with less than 1,000 members), who were not contracted out of the state scheme, and none in the public sector. (Under the Social Security Pensions Act 1975 the government decided not to make public-sector schemes part of the state scheme and instead decided to allow them to contract out.) The contracted-in employees receive the complete benefits of the state scheme (that is, both flat-rate and earnings-related components), together with any additional benefit derived from their own schemes.

Tables 6.8 and 6.9 show occupational-pension-scheme coverage by occupation, for men and women. The figures are derived from the 1985 *General Household Survey*. We see that for the same occupation type, pension-scheme coverage is always higher in the public sector compared with the private sector. We also see that scheme coverage is generally higher amongst management grades compared with skilled manual grades, which in turn are higher than semi-skilled or unskilled manual grades. Coverage is highest of all amongst professional grades, and lowest of all for part-time manual-grade women.

TABLE 6.7. *Numbers of schemes and of members by sector and size of membership and whether contracted-out, 1987*

Sector	Contracted-out		Not contracted-out		Total	
	Schemes	Members (thousands)	Schemes	Members (thousands)	Schemes	Members (thousands)
Private sector, by number of members in scheme:						
1–12	*	50	*	230	*	280
13–99	10,400	390	8,500	280	18,900	670
100–999	2,900	780	900	230	3,800	1,010
1,000–4,999	520	1,040	110	210	630	1,250
5,000–9,999	70	490	10	80	80	570
10,000 and over	70	1,750	10	270	80	2,020
TOTALS		4,500		1,300		5,800
Public sector	180	4,800	—	—	180	4,800
Total members		9,300		1,300		10,600

Note: * The small number of schemes with twelve or fewer members yielded by the sampling method and the relatively low response rate to the questionnaires sent to such schemes do not allow an accurate estimate of their number, but it appears likely that in total there are between 50,000 and 100,000 of them.

Source: GASOPS, Table 5.1.

TABLE 6.8. *Occupational pension-scheme coverage: men, 1985 (%)*

Occupation type	Private sector	Public sector
Engineering, management	81	89
Engineering, skilled manual	51	82
Engineering, semi- and unskilled manual	46	75
Construction, skilled manual	25	83
Energy, skilled manual	61	94
Energy/construction, semi- and unskilled manual	45	82
Distribution, management	52	
Distribution, manual/clerical/shop assistants	32	
Financial services, telecommunications etc., professional, technical, and management	77	
Services, manual	48	
Transport, professional and skilled manual	60	
Food/drink, manual	46	
Teacher		97
Other, education		94
Public sector, professional		97
Public sector, administration		96
Other, management	79	
Other, clerical	64	
Other, manual	49	57

Source: *General Household Survey*, 1985.

TABLE 6.9. *Occupational pension-scheme coverage: women, 1985 (%)*

Occupation type	Private sector		Public sector	
	Full-time	Part-time	Full-time	Part-time
Distribution, management	60	15		
Shop assistants	7	1		
Food/drink, manual	31	6		
Hotel and catering, manual	35	6		
Services, clerical	37	8		
Other clerical, private sector	37	8		
Teacher			97	14
Other, education			94	13
Other, clerical, public sector			86	9
Health, professional			100	60
Health, manual			72	11
Other, management			41	10
Other, manual			21	4

Source: *General Household Survey*, 1985.

TABLE 6.10. *Numbers of pensions in payment, 1936–1987* (millions)

Year	Private sector		Public sector		Total	Pensioners as %age of members
	Former employees	Widows and other dependants	Former employees	Widows and other dependants		
1936	0.1	—	0.1	—	0.2	8
1953	0.2	—	0.6	0.1	0.9	15
1956	0.3	—	0.7	0.1	1.1	14
1963	0.6	0.1	0.9	0.2	1.8	16
1967	0.8	0.2	1.1	0.2	2.3	19
1971	1.1	0.2	1.3	0.3	2.9	26
1975	1.1	0.2	1.7	0.4	3.4	30
1979	1.2	0.2	1.8	0.5	3.7	32
1983	1.8	0.3	2.2	0.7	5.0	45
1987	2.3	0.6	2.4	0.7	6.0	57

Source: Ministry of Labour Gazette, May 1938, and GASOPS, Table 3.1.

Table 6.10 shows that there were 6 million occupational-scheme pensioners in 1987, half from the private sector and half from the public sector. Beginning with only 200,000 pensioners in 1936, there has been rapid growth since then, with the number of pensioners doubling between 1971 and 1987. Pensions for widows and dependants did not become a significant feature until about 1953 in the public sector and about 1963 in the private sector. The table also shows the rapid growth in the *dependency ratio* (the ratio of pensioners to active members). Beginning at 8 per cent in 1936, the dependency ratio rose to 57 per cent in 1987, demonstrating the increasing maturity of UK pension funds. Table 6.11 shows a more detailed breakdown of the number of occupational pensions in payment in 1987.

6.3.3. THE ELIGIBILITY FOR MEMBERSHIP OF OCCUPATIONAL PENSION SCHEMES

There are several reasons why employers might exclude some of their employees from particular or even all the pension schemes that they operate. It has also been possible since August 1988 for employees to choose to exclude themselves from their employer's pension scheme, because membership of the employer's scheme has been voluntary since that date.

Table 6.12 shows that about half the work-force (11 million people out

TABLE 6.11. *Numbers of pensions in payment, 1987* (millions)

	Former employees		Widows and other dependants	Total
	Men	Women		
Private sector	1.6	0.7	0.6	2.9
Public sector:				
Public corporations	0.6	0.05	0.25	0.9
Central government	0.6	0.35	0.3	1.25
Local authorities	0.5	0.3	0.15	0.95
Total public sector	1.7	0.7	0.7	3.1
TOTAL	3.3	1.4	1.3	6.0

Source: GASOPS, Table 3.2.

TABLE 6.12. *Numbers of employees not in pension schemes by cause of exclusion and according to whether in full-time or part-time employment, 1987* (millions)

Reason for exclusion	Full-time		Part-time		Total
	Men	Women	Men	Women	
Employer has no scheme	2.9	1.5	0.3	2.2	6.9
Employer has a scheme, but the employee:					
is too young or has service too short	0.6	0.3	—	—	0.9
has opted not to join, or is ineligible because part-time or for other reasons	0.9	0.5	0.1	1.7	3.2
Total numbers not in pension schemes	4.4	2.3	0.4	3.9	11.0
Total numbers who are in schemes	7.1	3.0	0.1	0.4	10.6
Total numbers of employees	11.5	5.3	0.5	4.3	21.6
Percentage in schemes	62	57	20	9	49
Percentage not in schemes	38	43	80	91	51

Source: GASOPS, Table 5.4.

of 21.6 million workers) were not members of occupational schemes. This breaks down into the following categories: 38 per cent and 43 per cent respectively of full-time men and women and 80 per cent and 91 per cent of part-time men and women were not members of occupational schemes. Nearly 7 million people were not members of an occupational scheme because their employer had no scheme.

The most frequently occurring reason for employees being excluded altogether from their employer's pension scheme is related to the nature of their employment. This covers temporary and part-time workers in particular, and about 3.2 million such workers were excluded for this reason. *Income Data Services Study 188* (hereafter referred to as IDS188) found that the schemes of the BBC, coal (staff), electricity (staff), gas (staff), rail, and London Transport (staff and manual) were open only to full-time employees. The local-government and water-workers' schemes required an employee to work for at least thirty hours per week before being eligible, steel (staff and manual) required at least twenty-one hours, the civil service at least eighteen hours, and the post office required a minimum of sixteen hours per week.

Another reason is that employees have to satisfy a minimum period of service and/or a minimum age before becoming eligible. During this waiting period the employee neither pays contributions nor accrues any pension rights. Having been admitted to the pension scheme, employees may have to complete an additional minimum period of service before qualifying for a normal retirement pension, although they may be entitled to death-in-service benefits from the time they join the scheme. In small companies with less than 100 workers, about 40 per cent of the employees joined their pension scheme at the same time as taking up employment, while in large companies with over 10,000 employees the figure was 80 per cent. Overall, 73 per cent of scheme members have no waiting period, 15 per cent have a waiting period of less than one year, and 12 per cent have more than one year to wait. The public sector has a generally shorter waiting period than the private sector. Similarly, the public sector has a generally lower minimum entry age into schemes than the private sector. Nearly 90 per cent of those in the public sector become eligible by the age of 18, while nearly 50 per cent in the private sector have to wait until they have reached the age of 21 years. IDS188 found the following minimum age requirements in selected schemes:

- *No minimum age*: civil service, coal (mineworkers), rail;
- *Minimum age 16*: steel (staff and manual);
- *Minimum age 18*: local government, teachers, National Health Service (NHS), airways, BBC (optional), Post Office, London Transport (staff), water;
- *Minimum age 20*: coal (staff), electricity (staff), gas (staff and manual);
- *Minimum age 21*: BBC (compulsory);
- *Minimum age 25*: London Transport (wages grades).

At the other end of the age range, there is a further reason for employees being excluded from their company's pension scheme. This is the requirement that a minimum period of service must be completed before a normal retirement pension is granted, and this is generally ensured by having a maximum entry age into the pension scheme. For more than 60 per cent of occupational-pension-scheme members, there is no minimum-service requirement, but for the remaining 40 per cent of members, the most frequent minimum requirement covering 30 per cent of members is five years' service, implying a maximum entry age of 55 years for women and 60 for men.

Many employers operate different schemes for different categories of staff, and this provides another reason for some employees being excluded from certain schemes. The three main categories of scheme are senior-management schemes, staff schemes, and works schemes. In 1987 in the private sector, there were 120,000 members in senior-management schemes, 1.17 million members in staff schemes, 0.51 million in works schemes, and 3.68 million in combined schemes. In the public sector there were no schemes exclusively for senior management, but there were 700,000 members in staff schemes, 200,000 in works schemes, and 3.70 million in combined schemes. In general, the senior-management schemes provided more generous benefits than the other schemes. For example, in the private sector, 75 per cent of the members of senior-management schemes enjoyed a pensions fraction of 1/60th or better, compared with 60 per cent in staff schemes and 55 per cent in works schemes; and 20 per cent of members of senior-management schemes made no contributions, compared with 10 per cent in staff and 15 per cent in works schemes.

Finally, there are the different eligibility requirements for employed and self-employed workers. Most employed workers are members of occupational schemes that are either contracted into or contracted out of SERPS. Self-employed workers, on the other hand, are not only not entitled to receive the state pension, they are by definition ineligible to join an employer's pension scheme. Instead, they have to make their own personal pension arrangements. According to *Inland Revenue Statistics*, about 1.3 million people were contributing to personal pension schemes in 1987.

6.4. The Rights of Pension-Scheme Members

In this section we examine the rights that members or potential members have in respect of their pension schemes in addition to the right to receive a pension (which is considered in Section 6.6 below). These rights can be divided into four categories: (i) the rights of existing members; (ii) the rights of members who leave schemes when changing employment; (iii) the rights of members who leave schemes involuntarily; and (iv) statutory rights established by act of parliament.

6.4.1. THE RIGHTS OF EXISTING MEMBERS

6.4.1.1. *The Participation Rights of Members*

The contracting-out procedure requires employers to undertake consultations with their employees and to publish their scheme's rules. But in 1987 only 30 per cent of members in the private sector (only 3 per cent in the public sector) were able to elect directly a member to the board of trustees or the management committee of their pension scheme. Another 33 per cent and 12 per cent respectively of members were in schemes in which a member was nominated to the board or committee by the employer or a trade union as a representative of the employees. The remaining members were in schemes with either no representative or no specific board of trustees or management committee apart from the employer acting as trustee himself or a corporate trustee, such as an insurance company, acting for a number of schemes.

6.4.1.2. *The Right to Consultation and to Receive Information*

The 1975 Social Security Pensions Act required that employers consult with recognized trade unions about whether or not to contract out of SERPS. There was no duty to consult non-unionized members, although there was a requirement to inform them of any intention to contract out.

The 1986 Occupational Pension Schemes (Disclosure of Information) Regulations as amended by the 1992 Occupational and Personal Pension Schemes (Miscellaneous Amendments) Regulations impose certain obligations on scheme trustees (rather than employers). For example, there is an obligation on trustees to disclose trust deeds and rules on request to members, prospective members, their spouses, dependants receiving pensions, and recognized trade unions. New members must be given basic information about the scheme within thirteen weeks of joining. Retiring members and early leavers must be given information about the options available to them.

Annual reports must be made available to each scheme member free of charge. The reports must contain information about the trustees, the actuaries, the fund managers, the number of beneficiaries, the contributions paid into the scheme, the rate of increase in (but not the level of) benefits provided to existing beneficiaries, and the distribution of assets across thirteen different sectors, such as UK shares, overseas shares, gilts, and property. The report must also contain an *actuarial certificate* from the scheme's actuaries. The certificate states to what degree the scheme is financially viable in the sense of being able to pay the promised future benefits. For example, the certificate might say that the benefits are funded '90 per cent', '100 per cent', or 'more than 100 per cent'. In the first case the scheme has an actuarial deficit that needs to be funded by the employer. In the third case the fund has an actuarial surplus. The annual report also has to present the results from any performance-measurement service that the scheme subscribes to. In addition, the way in which the fund managers and others are remunerated (for example, by flat fee or by commission) has to be reported, although the actual value of the remuneration does not have to be revealed. Every three years or so the actuaries must publish a *valuation report*. This is the scheme's long-term budget forecast, and indicates how viable the pension scheme is on a long-term basis. Members must also receive an annual statement of the value of their pension savings in occupational schemes.

Consulting actuaries William Mercer Fraser suggest that scheme members should ask the following types of questions about their pension schemes:

If I stay until my pension age:
What will my pension be if my salary stays the same?
What will my pension be if my salary grows by 5pc a year?
What will my pension be if my salary grows by 10pc a year?
Does the pension scheme guarantee my pension will be increased for inflation? By how much?
What track record has the pension scheme for discretionary (one-off) increases for inflation? What is it likely to be in the future?
What is the maximum lump sum I can take and how will it affect my pension?
What would my widow/er's pension be if I died after retirement?
Can a pension be paid to other dependants, e.g. children?
How do pensions for widow/er's or dependants increase?

If I die within the next year:
What would my widow/er's pension be?
Can the pension be paid to anyone other than my widow/er?
Does the pension scheme guarantee the pension will be increased for inflation? By how much?
What track record has the pension scheme for discretionary increases for inflation?
What lump sum is payable?
To whom is the lump sum payable? Can I nominate someone e.g. common law wife or children for inheritance tax planning purposes?

If I leave the company within the year:
Can my contributions be refunded?
What is my deferred pension?
What lump sum is available at retirement age?
Does the deferred pension get any increases?
What happens if I die before retirement age?
What happens if I die after retirement age?
What happens if I die early through ill health? Can I take a deferred pension early if I am in good health?[1]

---

[1] William Mercer Fraser, *Daily Telegraph*, 27 Sept. 1986.

Despite all this information, there remains widespread ignorance about pensions. A typical survey of 1,000 employees in twenty-seven major companies by actuaries Towers, Perrin, Forster and Crosby in 1987 found that 80 per cent of members had never read their pension booklet, 30 per cent did not know what their retirement benefit would be, and 20 per cent did not know how much they paid in contributions.

6.4.2. THE RIGHTS OF MEMBERS WHO LEAVE SCHEMES WHEN CHANGING EMPLOYMENT

Most people change jobs at least once during their careers, and a typical person will change jobs four times. In respect of their pension schemes, job-changers are known as *early leavers*.

The rights of members leaving occupational pension schemes are determined by the 1973, 1985, 1986, and 1990 Social Security Acts and the Health and Social Security Act of 1984. The most important in this respect is the 1985 act which came into effect on 1 January 1986 and has become known as the 'early leavers' act'. These acts give early leavers the right to a *transfer value* which represents the *cash equivalent* of the accrued pension rights in the scheme they are leaving. However, the transfer value generally excludes the value of discretionary benefits. Trustees have to provide a statement of the transfer value within six months of a request for one, otherwise a 'penal rate of interest' will be imposed on them. The transfer value is determined at the date the transfer occurs and not the date that the employee leaves the scheme.

Depending on their circumstances, early leavers can have the transfer value returned to them in cash, preserved in the scheme that they are leaving, transferred to a new contracted-in occupational scheme, transferred to a new contracted-out occupational scheme, invested in a section 32 buy-out policy, or invested in a personal pension. We will consider these possibilities in turn.

6.4.2.1. *Return of Contributions*

If an employee leaves a scheme before completing two years of qualifying service, he is entitled to a lump-sum cash payment equal to the contributions that he has paid into the scheme. But he is not entitled to any interest on the contributions. Also he is not entitled to the contributions that have been made on his behalf by his employer. In addition, the lump sum is taxed at 20 per cent. Since the original contribution was relieved at 25 per cent for a basic-rate payer, this means that every £100 of contributions cost £75 and returns £80 if this right is exercised.

This right has been available in this form since April 1988. Before April 1988 the qualifying period was five years rather than two, and the rate of tax was 10 per cent rather than 20 per cent. Before January 1986 this option could only be exercised if the member was below 26 years of age.

6.4.2.2. *Preserved Pension*

If a member leaves a scheme after 1 January 1991 he is entitled to a preserved (or frozen or deferred) pension known as a *protected rights pension* in the scheme that he is leaving. This is calculated using the same accrual rate as for those who remain but is based on earnings at the date of leaving. The protected rights pension is subject to *limited price indexation*. For pension benefits accrued before 6 April 1978 the entire pension has to be revalued by the rate of inflation (as measured by the RPI) up to a maximum of 5 per cent p.a. compounded from the date of leaving the scheme to the date of retirement. For pension benefits accrued on or after 6 April 1978 (when SERPS began), the benefits in excess of the GMP (in the case of contracted-out schemes) are revalued in the same way. The component of the preserved benefit that constitutes the GMP (for both the member and the widow/er) has to be increased from the date of leaving to the date of retirement in one of three ways:

- full revaluation in line with increases in national average earnings;
- increased at 5 per cent p.a. compound together with the payment of a *limited revaluation premium* to the National Insurance Fund to cover increases in national average earnings in excess of 5 per cent p.a.; or
- increased at a *fixed revaluation rate* of 7 per cent p.a. compound from 6 April 1993 (7.5 per cent p.a. compound between 6 April 1988 and 5 April 1993, and 8.5 per cent p.a. compound before 6 April 1988).

These are minimum requirements and do not prevent schemes acting more generously than this.

The 1973 Social Security Act merely preserved the GMP of the departing member (together with the potential GMP for the widow/er); there was no explicit inflation-proofing of the GMP. Under the 1985 act the preserved GMPs for both the member and the widow/er were indexed as above. The 1986 act ensured that the preserved pension in excess of the GMP earned since 1 January 1985 was indexed to retail-price inflation up to 5 per cent. The 1990 act extends this indexing back indefinitely for everyone leaving an occupational scheme (after a date yet to be determined) so long as the scheme has a surplus.

6.4.2.3. *Transfer to a Contracted-In Scheme*

If a member transfers from a contracted-out scheme to a contracted-in scheme after 1 January 1986 he is entitled to a *transfer premium*. The transfer premium represents the part of an occupational pension scheme corresponding to the GMP under SERPS. The transfer premium is used to buy back the employee's rights in SERPS. Before this date the employee was forced to leave the GMP with the old scheme.

6.4.2.4. *Transfer to a Contracted-Out Scheme*

If a member transfers to another contracted-out scheme, he has the right to take his transfer value to his new scheme. This possibility has been available since the 1973 Social Security Act, but for people who changed jobs before 1986 the transfer required the agreement of both schemes. The guaranteed right to a transfer was embodied in the 1985 Social Security Act for those who changed jobs after 1 January 1986 and who entered another approved scheme with more than a year to normal retirement age. The transfer value is generally used to buy a money purchase pension in the new scheme. In the past it was used to buy *added years* in the new scheme. But now well under half the schemes permit added years.

Initially fund trustees were reluctant to accept transfers, partly because they reduced the size of the fund, and partly because they could be sued in later years by the dependants of the original employee if the benefits were thought not to be as large as they could have been. Now trustees are indemnified against this possibility. Also, trustees have recognized that ex-scheme members still have to be administered and provided with information. Since this is expensive, trustees now encourage early leavers to take their transfer values with them rather than leave them as preserved benefits.

The transfer arrangements in the public sector are more highly integrated than in the private sector. Because many public-sector schemes, such as local government, NHS, teachers, police, and fire, as well as many parts of the civil service, are national schemes, they permit completely free internal transfers of pension benefits. In addition, since 1948 a *club transfer system* has been in operation which preserves pension benefits for employees transferring between certain different sections of the public sector, including the nationalized industries and universities. The Government Actuary's Department together with the actuaries of the individual schemes has constructed two sets of transfer-value tables, one for men and the other for women, in order to calculate the value of the pensions transferred between schemes. The system works satisfactorily only if the benefits provision is similar between schemes and if there are approximately an equal number of transfers in each direction. The objective is to achieve a complete transfer of pension rights as opposed to simply the preservation of the pension earned up to the time of the transfer. This means that the transferee receives a year-for-year credit in his new pension scheme which will be evaluated on the basis of his new salary, and this may be higher than his old salary. The government is also prepared to accept membership of the club system by private-sector schemes agreeing to the rules and providing broadly similar benefits as in the public sector.

The club transfer system is divided into three categories:

- *inner club* comprises the main public-sector schemes—civil service, local government, NHS, teachers, police, and fire;
- *outer club* comprises the other public-sector schemes, such as nationalized industries which use the standard transfer-value tables;
- *outside schemes* comprise schemes in the public and private sector which use other tables but accept the reciprocal arrangements of the club.

6.4.2.5. *Section 32 Buy-Out Policy*

As an alternative to a preserved pension in the original scheme, a return of contributions, or a transfer to a new scheme, it is possible as a result of the 1985 Social Security Act for an early leaver to take what has become known as a *section 32 buy-out* (see also Section 7.4.7). A 'buy-out' is a type of insurance policy called a *single-premium annuity bond* taken out by the early leaver, and paid for using the *cash equivalent* of the transfer value he receives. 'Section 32' refers to section 32 of the Finance Act 1981, which first permitted buy-outs. The buy-out becomes attractive in the case where the transfer value is greater than the value of the deferred pension either in the original or in the new scheme. It becomes even more attractive if the transfer value is invested in a successful with-profits or unit-linked policy, so that a larger pension annuity can be purchased at the time of retirement. In the first case annual profits bonuses are added to the value of the policy and, once added, they cannot be taken away. In the second case the value of the policy depends on the value of the units at the time of retirement, so nothing is guaranteed in this case.

The resulting pension depends on both the size of the fund at the time of retirement and the annuity rates available. The fund must be used to buy a pension annuity from an insurance company. There are various possibilities available. It could be an own-life pension only or it could last for the life of the surviving spouse as well; the surviving spouse typically enjoys half-benefits. It could remain constant or increase at a fixed rate of say 5 per cent p.a. It could be unit-linked, index-linked, or with-profits. However, if the pension involves benefits that increase over time, then the initial pension will be lower than with a pension that remains constant over time. In the event of death before retirement, two types of death benefit are generally available: *return of premiums* or *return of fund* which includes all growth to date. If the policy-holder chooses the former option, then he will get a much higher pension if he does reach retirement age, although his beneficiaries will get a much lower sum if he dies in service.

Section 32 schemes must offer a GMP that is increased by either 5 per cent p.a. compound (together with the payment of a *limited revaluation premium* to the National Insurance Fund) or 7 per cent p.a. compound. Most insurance companies receiving transfers into their section 32 schemes invest the GMP component of the transfer value in a non-profit contract. The larger this component, the less that will be available for investing in the potentially more attractive with-profits or unit-linked schemes.

6.4.2.6. *A Personal Pension*

The final choice is to invest the transfer value in a *personal pension scheme*. These are discussed in detail in Chapter 7, but we note that under the 1985 Social Security Act any preserved or deferred pension in a money-purchase personal pension scheme must receive the same treatment in terms of inflation-indexing and investment returns as active pensions remaining in the scheme.

6.4.2.7. *The Determination of the Size of the Transfer Value*

Despite a statutory right to a transfer, there is no legislation relating to the terms of the transfer and this can cause problems. This is because when someone transfers from one pension scheme to another, a *cash equivalent* is transferred from the old to the new scheme. However, the cash equivalent is difficult to determine since there is no simple relationship between the number of *years of pensionable service* earned in the old scheme and the number of *added years* that will be credited to the new scheme. This is because the old scheme will calculate a *deferred pension* based on the earnings at the time of the transfer, whereas the new scheme has to calculate a *projected pension* based on the projected earnings at retirement. Since people generally move jobs because they are offered a higher salary than before, the new pension scheme would prefer a high cash equivalent to be transferred, whereas the old scheme wants to transfer only a low cash equivalent.

There is some choice available to the fund's actuary in determining the size of the transfer value. Typical formulae are based on:

- the value of the leaving member's contributions;
- the capitalized value of the deferred pension at the time of leaving service, possibly with some allowance for future salary increases; or
- if the fund is in deficit, the transfer value might be limited to the member's proportionate share of the fund.

In the second case, the actual transfer value might depend on the relationship between estimated earnings increases and anticipated investment returns. Most actuaries making the calculation assume that earnings rise by 8.5 per cent p.a. compound while investment yields are 9 per cent p.a. compound. But the two schemes might make different assumptions about, say, investment yields, so that the transfer of a given sum of money between schemes could lead to an increase or a reduction in expected benefits.

The greater the difference between investment yields and earnings increases, the lower the transfer value. This follows because the transfer value is intended to purchase a preserved pension at retirement, and the cost of buying a deferred pension annuity falls as investment yields rise. For example, if yields rise from 10 per cent to 13 per cent, this represents a rise of 30 per cent. But the transfer value would fall in value by more than 40 per cent for a man twenty years from retirement with a given preserved pension. So long as interest rates remained at 13 per cent, the lower transfer value would still be sufficient to meet the required preserved pension. But if interest rates subsequently fell back to 10 per cent, the lower transfer value would not then be sufficient.

As a result of these difficulties, the new scheme might be willing to offer only a reduced length of back service or added years compared with the old scheme. This will have the effect of reducing the retirement pension, other things being equal, compared with the old scheme. However, if the employee has changed jobs to achieve a higher salary profile, then it may well be the case that the employee ends up with a higher pension overall, since the higher terminal salary in the new job more than compensates for the shorter length of service.

Whether it is more advantageous for the employee to opt for the transfer value or for the preserved pension depends on the subsequent investment performance in each case. If the transfer value is invested in the new occupational scheme in the form of added years, and the individual receives substantial pay-rises, the added years will generate a correspondingly high pension at retirement. The scheme might also give discretionary pension increases after retirement. If the transfer value is invested in a section 32 buy-out policy or a personal pension, then the pension is based solely on what the fund is worth at retirement, although, in the case of a section 32 policy, there is a guaranteed minimum pension. Leaving the transfer value in the original scheme does not generally result in the largest pension at retirement, although it is possible for the ex-employee to benefit if there is a subsequent distribution of the surplus in the fund.

Because of the uncertainties involved in estimating the size of the projected pension in the new scheme, schemes in recent years have tended not to convert the transfer value into added years. Instead they have chosen to invest the transfer value in a single premium money-purchase scheme, which is less risky from their point of view. If this trend continues, then more and more people, even in supposedly salary-related schemes, will be drawing pensions that are increasingly money-purchase in practice.

6.4.3. THE RIGHTS OF MEMBERS WHO LEAVE SCHEMES INVOLUNTARILY

It is also possible for an individual to leave a scheme on grounds other than by voluntarily changing employment. The main examples here are redundancy and dismissal.

In the case of redundancy, the normal leaving-service benefits discussed above apply. It is also possible for a redundant employee to take a pension from the age of 50 onwards, although the pension is often reduced actuarially to allow for the longer period over which it is likely to be paid. The overall effect of redundancy is generally to induce an actuarial surplus in the fund. This is because most actuaries make provision for salary increases which will not be realized in the event of redundancy. However, if an employee over the age of 50 is granted a pension without actuarial reduction immediately on becoming redundant, then this constitutes an additional liability to the scheme.

In the private sector, 30 per cent of schemes provide for special benefits in the case of redundancy, and in most other private-sector schemes, benefits are provided at the employer's discretion. The most common type of benefit, available to 20 per cent of private-sector members, is for employees made redundant after the age of 50 or 55 to receive an immediate pension based on final salary or accrued service, without loss due to early payment. In the public sector, 50 per cent of schemes have special redundancy benefits, usually based on accrued service without reduction for early retirement but conditional on a minimum period of five years' service.

IDS188 found the following cases in selected schemes as a result of compulsory early retirement:

- *Retirement from the age of 40*:
  this is available in the civil service where the termination of employment may be due to redundancy, 'limited efficiency', or 'inefficiency'; compensation is available as well as a pension and a lump sum.
- *Retirement at 50 for men and women*:
  (a) with normal retirement benefits—local government, teachers, NHS, BBC (BBC subject to ten years' qualifying service);
  (b) with ill-health retirement benefits—coal (staff).

- *Retirement at 50 for women and 55 for men*:
  (a) with normal retirement benefits—steel (staff and manual);
  (b) with ill-health retirement benefits—coal (staff).
- *Retirement at 55 for women and 57 for men*:
  rail (retirement due to redundancy).
- *Retirement at 55 for women and 60 for men*:
  electricity (staff) (subject to twenty-five years' contributory service).

In the case of dismissal, the dismissed employee can seek redress under the 1978 Employment Protection Act. If an employee has been unfairly dismissed, he or she can be awarded compensation by a tribunal. The tribunal will attempt to value the lost pension-rights. This generally depends on the employer's planned contributions to the employee's scheme, although there is some reduction to take account of likely future pensionable employment by the dismissed employee.

6.4.4. STATUTORY RIGHTS ESTABLISHED BY ACT OF PARLIAMENT

There is in fact no comprehensive system of statutory rights for pension-scheme members in Britain. Indeed, there is not even a comprehensive system of supervision for the schemes themselves, although the 1985 Social Security Act established powers for setting up a *registrar of occupational pension schemes* along similar lines to the registrar of companies, and the 1990 Social Security Act established a *pensions ombudsman*. Instead, there is a rather loose system of controls operated by the PSO and the OPB.

The PSO is in practice more interested in ensuring that the surpluses of a scheme are neither generated irregularly nor subsequently used irregularly than with ensuring that members' claims are not weakened by scheme deficits. Its duties, established by the Finance Acts of 1970 and 1971, are to ensure both that the scheme's income and capital gains are derived from legitimate investment and not from trading, and that the capital-gains-tax and income-tax reliefs enjoyed by legitimate schemes are not used by bogus schemes for tax-avoidance purposes.

One important example of the PSO's activities has been its intervention in the attempts of certain companies to 'raid' their pension schemes when they have shown large surpluses. For example, in 1984 the pension scheme of Gomme Holdings (makers of G-Plan furniture) had assets of £8.4m. and future liabilities of only £4.3m. This large net surplus had been the result, on the one hand, of soaring asset values over the previous decade on stock markets both at home and abroad (with the depreciation of sterling adding to the values of overseas assets even further) and, on the other hand, of smaller liabilities caused by a declining industry and work-force, with redundant employees having their pensions frozen at their leaving levels of pay. But the decline in the furniture industry resulted in Gomme having a poor trading record in the early 1980s, and this led it in 1985 to attempt to take out £2.9m. from its employees' pension scheme for its own use. The PSO blocked this move, but other companies were more successful. Also in 1984 the engineering companies B. Elliot and James Neill took £5.25m. and £2m., respectively, from their employees' pension schemes. Dunlop, with a surplus in excess of £44m. in 1983, rather than take cash out, decided to stop putting cash in by introducing a three-year freeze on contributions from April 1985.

The companies' argument was that, since they are expected to make deficiency payments when their pension schemes are in deficit, they should be able to siphon off surpluses when they arise. The Inland Revenue's reply was that by doing this, companies would be able to avoid tax on their profit in good years by putting money into their pension schemes, and then drawing it out in bad years, when the tax liability could be offset by trading losses. The 1986 Finance Act ended systematic surpluses.

The OPB was established by the Social Security Act of 1973 as an independent statutory board with both executive and advisory responsibilities. Its executive responsibilities include the supervision of certain statutory rights of members of schemes, such as those dealing with the preservation of benefits of early leavers or with the equal access of both men and women. More generally, the OPB must be satisfied with a scheme's financial arrangements for contracting out members from the earnings-related component of the state pension scheme. In particular, each scheme must have sufficient resources to provide at least a guaranteed minimum pension equivalent to the earnings-related component. As an additional form of protection, the OPB is able to impose limitations on a scheme's investments, especially on the extent of self-investment in the employing company.

The OPB also gives advice to the secretary of state for social security on matters dealing with the legislation of occupational pension schemes. Three examples of reports prepared by the OPB deal with *Solvency, Disclosure of Information and Member Participation in Occupational Pension Schemes* (Cmnd. 5904, 1975), *Improved Protection for the Occupational Pensions Rights and Expectations of Early Leavers* (Cmnd. 8271, 1981), and *Protecting Pensions—Safeguarding Benefits in a Changing Environment* (CM. 573, 1989).

The first report argued that existing statutory controls covering the contracting-out of occupational schemes were broadly adequate and that additional controls on the funding and investment of the schemes were unnecessary. However, it did recommend that more detailed and systematic information concerning the funding and investment status of the schemes should be made available to members and their trade-union representatives. It also recommended that member participation should be encouraged and that members should be able to sue for breach of trust. The government's reply to the report (*Occupational Pension Schemes: The Role of Members in the Running of Schemes*, Cmnd. 6514, 1976) largely accepted the OPB's views on controls over funding and investment and member participation, and went even further by recommending up to 50 per cent trade-union representation on the boards of trustees of the schemes. However, the National Association of Pension Funds (NAPF), the main representative body of the pensions industry, objected strongly to this on the grounds that this form of interference in the running of schemes could damage their solvency.

The second OPB report on the rights and expectations of early leavers condemned the position of early leavers, whereby even if they only changed jobs once during their working lives, they could end up with pension benefits 40 per cent lower than if they had remained with the same employer. This was because at that time early leavers received frozen benefits based on their salaries at the time of leaving, and these were likely to be much lower than their terminal salaries. The report regarded this as inequitable, especially if members were forced to leave early through redundancy, since it in effect meant that the early leavers were subsidizing the long stayers. It recommended that 'early leavers should receive the same benefits for their years of pensionable service as their fellow members who stay in the same employment to pension age'. This would require the uprating of the frozen benefits to take account of the increase in prices between the time of leaving and the age of retirement. Again, the NAPF objected to the OPB report despite the fact that its own survey in 1980 indicated that 73 per cent of all occupational pension schemes offered no increase on frozen pensions, and the fact that most employees changed jobs about four times during their careers. The main reason for objecting was the increased cost on employers of improving benefits for early leavers. The OPB recognized that there was little hope of employers improving the position of early leavers on a voluntary basis and that legislation would be required. It considered a number of different ways of uprating frozen pension benefits, such as increases in line with average earnings (the minority-report recommendation) or increases in line with average earnings up to a maximum of 5 per cent p.a. compound (the majority-report recommendation).

The third OPB report recommended a move away from discretionary pension benefits and upratings towards guaranteed benefits and upratings. For example, the report argued that trustees should be 'strongly encouraged', although not required by law, to guarantee post-retirement pension-indexing to inflation up to a maximum of 5 per cent p.a. compound. At the time only 20 per cent of schemes guaranteed some form of indexation. As an alternative, companies might consider introducing a *pensioner's option*. This would give the pensioner the option of taking a lower pension at the time of retirement, in return for guaranteed inflationary increases up to 5 per cent p.a. after retirement. If the company was not already providing discretionary increases, the lower pension might begin by being only 67 per cent of the flat-rate pension. If the company was already providing increases on a discretionary basis, conversion to a guaranteed basis might lead to the initial pension being reduced to between 90 per cent and 95 per cent of the discretionary-basis pension. Some companies have such an option, but few pensioners exercise it.

The report also recommended greater protection for pension beneficiaries in the event of a take-over and subsequent winding-up of the pension scheme. Many take-overs occur in the UK because the target company's pension fund is showing a substantial surplus. The report called for a law establishing minimum winding-up benefits, together with inflation-indexing of pensions after retirement up to a maximum of 5 per cent p.a. After meeting these conditions, the report accepted that any surplus in the fund belonged to employers. In addition, the report recommended that job-changers or early leavers (say, as a result of redundancy) should have all their pension rights revalued, instead of just their rights earned after 1 January 1985 (as specified in the 1986 Social Security Act). The report also called for a compulsory registration scheme for pension schemes. The registry should provide both an information and tracing service, and a conciliation and appeals service. But the report fell short of recommending a full pensions-ombudsman scheme, as recommended by, say, the Consumers' Association, on the grounds of cost.

The broad dissatisfaction with the state of the legislation surrounding occupational pension schemes was also reflected in the Wilson Committee's Report to *Review the Functioning of Financial Institutions* (1980). 'The framework within which they operate has grown piecemeal and now needs to be systematised and strengthened. It is unsatisfactory in our view that so much of it should depend on a body of trust law developed for quite other purposes' (p. 324). However, the committee rejected the imposition of a set of detailed statutory controls over pension schemes which, for example, made funding compulsory or put limits on the extent of self-investment, on the grounds that it would be too costly to operate and could have a counter-productive effect on the solvency of the schemes. Instead, it recommended the introduction of a Pension Scheme Act similar to the Companies Act which would indicate the legal duties and obligations of sponsors, scheme trustees, and professional advisers, and which would not only give members (and their representatives) the right to receive information on a regular basis (for example, each time actuarial valuations are made) in order that they might monitor their scheme's management and solvency, but also give them the right of redress in the case of mismanagement, exactly the same as shareholders have in relation to their companies. The committee also recommended, in line with the 1975 OPB report, that up to half the board of trustees of schemes should be appointed by members. Finally, the committee, in recognizing the importance of the collective position of pension schemes in the national economy, recommended that the information made available to members should also be made publicly available, in the same way that companies are obliged to file reports and accounts at Companies House.

Very few of the Wilson Committee's recommendations were implemented. Indeed, some of the things that it was actually opposed to, such as limits on self-investment, have subsequently been implemented. However, the OPB has been more successful. The 1985, 1986, and 1990 Social Security Acts strengthened the rights of early leavers, and the 1986 Occupational Pension Schemes (Disclosure of Information) Regulations and the 1992 Occupational and Personal Pension Schemes (Miscellaneous Amendments) Regulations introduced rights to receive information. The 1990 Social Security Act also introduced partial indexation of pensions after retirement, and it introduced the following measures to protect members of occupational pension schemes: an ombudsman service (even though the OPB thought that this was too expensive), a *register of pension schemes*, a tracing service, and a 5 per-cent ceiling on self-investment (that is, investment in the parent company operating the scheme).

The *pensions ombudsman service* began operating in April 1991. The first pensions ombudsman was Mr Michael Platt, a DSS civil servant. The purpose of the ombudsman service is to consider complaints about private-sector pensions (both occupational and personal) that involve maladministration or disputes over points of law. Complaints must be taken to the ombudsman within three years of them occurring. The ombudsman does not deal with problems arising with the state pension scheme. Nor can he deal with complaints covered by the 1986 Financial Services Act (FSA), such as poor investment performance or excessive commissions, the most common complaints with personal pensions. These complaints would have to be taken to one of the self-regulatory organizations under the FSA: LAUTRO (Life Assurance and Unit Trust Regulatory Organization) in the case of a full-time life-assurance or unit-trust sales agent, and FIMBRA (Financial Intermediaries, Managers and Brokers Regulatory Association) in the case of an independent financial adviser.[2] The ombudsman is the final arbiter. A complainant would first have to approach his scheme's trustees. After that the newly revamped *Occupational Pensions Advisory Service* (OPAS) would have to be approached. The role of OPAS is to conciliate between complainant and scheme, but unlike the ombudsman it cannot enforce a decision. If OPAS fails to find an acceptable solution, the ombudsman is called in.

OPAS is a charity that advises individuals who have problems with their occupational or personal pension scheme. It does not give financial advice or help with negotiating changes to a scheme. In a typical year OPAS receives about 30,000 requests for help. About a third of the requests concern problems with early leavers, 25 per cent involve the amount of benefit or transfer value, 8 per cent deal with winding up or merger, and 6 per cent complain of poor communication between schemes and members and delays in effecting transfers. More than 80 per cent of its enquiries come from people more than 50 years old, and 75 per cent of enquiries come from men. OPAS has had its terms of reference expanded by the 1990 Social Security Act. From April 1991 OPAS has been involved in issues of maladministration, such as companies failing to make contributions into their pension schemes, an action which makes void any insurance-company liability to guarantee scheme benefits. Similarly, OPAS has become involved in cases where companies delay returns to the DSS, which in turn delays rebates to personal pensions. During his first year of operation the pensions ombudsman received more than 2,000 complaints. But he reached decisions in only forty-seven cases, of which eighteen were settled wholly in favour of the complainant. The main causes of complaint were delays in paying transfer values between schemes and problems in winding up schemes when a company fails.

The *pensions tracing service* began in July 1991 and is run by the OPB. The purpose of the service is to help individuals trace their entitlement to company pension benefits earned since 1975. As people move jobs, their pension entitlements might be preserved in the pension schemes of the companies that they left; the entitlement to frozen pensions first came into effect for those leaving schemes after 6 April 1975. By the time that they retire, these companies might have moved, changed names, or disappeared, either through insolvency or take-over. Alternatively, the company might still exist, but the pensioner cannot be traced. In 1990 £2.5bn. was paid out in pensions, and it has been estimated that another £125m. to £250m. (that is, between 5 per cent and 10 per cent of the

---

[2] Both LAUTRO and FIMBRA are shortly to be replaced by the Personal Investment Authority (PIA) which will regulate the provision of financial services to all retail customers.

total) in entitlements was not paid out because either the pensioner could not be traced or the company had vanished.

The new tracing service will catalogue the history of every existing scheme since 6 April 1975 on a computerized data base. It will record every change in the company or organization that manages a scheme. A typical case is where a company becomes insolvent and the company's pension-fund assets are transferred to an insurance company for managing. The insurance company might have to incur substantial costs in tracing eligible pension claimants at pension age. The tracing service should reduce this problem.

The tracing service is funded through an annual levy on all schemes ranging from £5 for small schemes to £600 for those with more than 10,000 members. All schemes with at least two members must inform the service of any change in circumstances on an annual basis.

6.5. Contributions

In this section we examine the contributions that are paid into occupational pension schemes. Unlike SERPS, the contributions into occupational schemes are not fixed. They can differ between schemes, but there are upper limits on contributions imposed by the Inland Revenue (see Section 6.2.2 above).

6.5.1. TYPES OF CONTRIBUTIONS

6.5.1.1. *Principal Contributions*

Most occupational pension schemes are contributory on the part of employees. There are a few non-contributory schemes in both the public sector (principally those of central-government civil servants) and the private sector (mainly for senior executives, known as *top-hat schemes*). There are often wide differences in the rate of contributions: some are flat-rate (that is, a fixed amount independent of income), but most are graduated (that is, a fixed or increasing proportion based on income). The contributions up to Inland Revenue limits attract tax relief at the highest marginal rate paid by the employee: 20 per cent for a lower-rate payer, 25 per cent for a basic-rate payer and 40 per cent for a higher-rate payer. Employer contributions also attract relief from corporation tax.

While employees are limited to paying 15 per cent of their earnings into their company pension schemes, the companies themselves can pay what they like into their schemes and get tax relief. However, if they take money out of the scheme they must pay tax at 40 per cent. The possibility of making unlimited company contributions into a scheme is useful for directors who have built up their companies but have not established a pension scheme. They can make contributions of several times their annual salaries into a scheme, until the fund is sufficiently large to pay the maximum pension commensurate with the number of years' service, up to two-thirds of final salary for twenty years' service.

6.5.1.2. *Additional Voluntary Contributions and Free-Standing Additional Voluntary Contributions*

The 1986 Social Security Act allowed all members of occupational pension schemes to make *additional voluntary contributions* or AVCs to their existing schemes. But by 1991 only 15 per cent of scheme members had chosen to do so. In addition, since October 1987, as a result of the 1987 Finance Act, it has been possible to make *free-standing AVCs* or FSAVCs outside the employer's scheme. The FSAVC schemes are fully portable. So, for example, it is possible to transfer from one FSAVC scheme into another (although it is only possible to have one FSAVC scheme at a time) or into the occupational scheme. Similarly, if an individual transfers from an occupational scheme into a personal pension scheme, it is possible to incorporate the FSAVC into his personal scheme. It is not possible to take out an FSAVC scheme if the employer's scheme is a simplified final-salary scheme (COFSS) (see Section 6.3.1.4 above), or if the member is a controlling director of the company (that is, with 20 per cent or more voting rights). Also, it is only possible to continue contributing to an FSAVC scheme if the contributor remains a full member of the employer's scheme. If the contributor left the employer's scheme and received a return of contributions, he would also have to take a refund of the FSAVC investment. However, it is possible to continue making contributions to an FSAVC while temporarily absent or on secondment, as long as full membership of the employer's scheme is maintained.

Tax relief up to the Inland Revenue limits are permitted on AVCs or FSAVCs even if they are made on an irregular basis. It is even possible to make one-off lump-sum payments. Employees can pay up to 15 per cent of earnings into their combined occupational and AVC or FSAVC schemes, but employers are not permitted to contribute to AVC or FSAVC schemes. Contributions into AVC or FSAVC schemes are made net of basic-rate tax, and the tax element is reclaimed from the Inland Revenue by the institution investing the funds. Any higher rate of tax relief has to be claimed by the policy-holder on his annual tax return. Any excess contributions have to be returned.

If the employer's scheme is offered in addition to SERPS, so that both the employee and employer are paying full national-insurance contributions, then it has been possible since 1 July 1988 for the employee to contract out of SERPS with his own FSAVC scheme and to have part of both his and the employer's NICs redirected into the scheme. However, there is no tax relief on the employee's NICs as there would be for a personal pension.

Most AVCs and all FSAVCs operate on a money-purchase basis, the main exception being public-sector AVC schemes which tend to offer added years towards the final-salary pension. This means that, in general, the pension at retirement will not be related to final salary, nor will it be index-linked. FSAVCs can be provided by insurance companies, unit trusts, banks, and building societies. Insurance companies provide with-profits endowment schemes, unit trusts provide unit-linked schemes, and building societies provide deposit-based schemes. Banks can provide any of these schemes. The deposit-based schemes are the safest, but offer the lowest returns. The best returns over the long run are offered by the unit-linked schemes, whereby the employee's contributions buy units in a fund which is invested in a range of securities: shares, bonds, property, or a mixture of these (that is, managed funds); the value of the units reflects the market value of the securities. In between come the with-profits schemes: investment returns are allocated each year as a bonus which cannot be taken away once it has been allocated; there is also usually a terminal bonus which depends on how well the savings have been invested. In contrast, most companies will offer only one type of AVC, usually a building-society deposit account. Larger companies might offer a with-profits endowment scheme or a unit-linked scheme where the insurance company or unit trust is chosen by the member. In a small number of cases the AVCs are invested in the main pension fund.

The main restriction on AVCs deals with the way in which benefits are paid. Since April 1987 the pension rights from AVCs cannot be commuted into tax-free lump sums as they could before this date (up to a limit of £150,000). They have to be taken as a regular pension. The pension can be taken at any age after 50, although company scheme benefits must be taken at the same time. The Inland Revenue is also concerned that the total benefits from an individual's combined pension schemes do not exceed two-thirds of final salary. The Revenue requires that the individual's principal pension scheme (typically his occupational scheme) police this rule. Any breach of the limit will result in the occupational pension being reduced, so the additional contributions will have been in vain.

However, AVCs and FSAVCs can be used to top up the pension in cases where the individual's occupational scheme will deliver a pension well short of the two-thirds limit. The individual can discover whether this will be the case by asking the employer for a *statement of benefits* which will show any shortfall in pension provision. This may happen if the individual first joined a scheme late in his working life, or changed jobs frequently and received poor transfer values, or is a member of a pension scheme with an accrual rate of less than 1/60th for each year of service, or receives a salary with a large component in overtime or bonus payments which are not taken into account when contributions to the employer's scheme are calculated. Also it is possible for the surplus additional contributions to be used to enhance the pension after retirement. There are two main ways of achieving this. First, the pension could be more fully indexed against inflation than the company is willing to permit ordinarily. Secondly, the company could agree to pay a widow/er's pension up to two-thirds of the member's pension. Most widow/ers' pensions are only half the member's pension. It is also possible for the FSAVC scheme to be used solely for the purpose of providing a spouse's or dependant's pension.

The main disadvantages of FSAVCs compared with AVCs is that they are more expensive to operate. Unlike AVCs, where economies of scale operate, FSAVCs have to be monitored individually. Also, with AVCs the employer generally bears the administration cost, whereas with FSAVCs these costs are borne by the individual. The difference in cost is reflected in Table 6.13. The table shows that the longer the maturity of the scheme, the greater the cost. There could be other hidden costs in FSAVCs that might be incurred if the individual stops saving or retires early.

The 1989 Finance Act changed the rules relating to additional voluntary contributions into occupational schemes. First, the operation and administration of free-standing schemes was made easier, and the trustees of the main scheme could no longer frustrate the free-standing scheme through bureaucratic delays in providing the required information. Secondly, the penalties arising from making excess or surplus contributions were reduced. The returns on the additional contributions can result in the total pension exceeding two-thirds of final salary. Before the act, the company scheme corrected for this by reducing the pension that it paid. Following the act, any surplus pension arising from additional

TABLE 6.13. *Accumulated fund for £1,000 p.a. assuming 10% growth rate less expenses (£)*

	20 yrs.	10 yrs.	5 yrs.	3 yrs.
Company AVC	54,384	15,835	6,145	3,321
FSAVC	52,947	15,415	5,981	3,231

Source: *Daily Telegraph*, 18 Feb. 1989.

contributions is paid to the pensioner after deducting a special tax of 35 per cent for a basic-rate taxpayer and 50 per cent for a higher-rate taxpayer (that is, tax rates that are 10 percentage points higher than the basic and higher tax rates). This means that basic- and higher-rate taxpayers now lose respectively a third and a half of the surplus pension, instead of all of it as before.

6.5.2. STANDARD CONTRIBUTION RATES

GASOPS found that on average about one-quarter of total contributions are derived from employees, while the rest come from employers. But the proportion can vary between schemes, from those in which no employee contribution is made to those in which the total amount of contributions comes from employees.

Table 6.14 shows the proportions of total contributions paid by members in private-sector schemes in 1987. We see that 16 per cent of members pay no explicit contributions, while about 6 per cent of members pay the total amount of contributions toward their pensions. The most common

TABLE 6.14. *Numbers of members paying various proportions of the total contributions: private sector, 1987*

Proportion paid by members (%)	Number of members (thousands)
NA	80
Nil	900
1–9[†]	200
10–19	250
20–29	940
30–39	1,370
40–49	770
50–99	940
100	350
TOTAL	5,800

Notes: * Not applicable because neither employer nor members were contributing in 1987.

[†] Includes schemes in which members contribute for spouse's benefits only or make voluntary contributions only.

Source: GASOPS, Table 6.1.

level of employee contributions is between 30 per cent and 40 per cent of total contributions.

The most common method of determining contributions for contributory contracted-out schemes in both the private and public sectors is a fixed percentage of relevant earnings, which usually excludes national-insurance contributions or volatile components of salary such as overtime payments. In total, 99 per cent of contributory contracted-out schemes apply this mode of calculation. In a few cases, covering about 2 per cent of members in private-sector contracted-out schemes only, the contribution is a given amount which increases with the salary range. With contracted-in schemes, all use the percentage-of-salary method, apart from a few schemes, covering manual workers, which impose a flat contribution independent of salary. A few contracted-out schemes are non-contributory in the sense that contributions are not required for the member's principal pension, although extra benefits such as the widow/er's pension may be contributory: the most notable scheme in this group is that of the civil service. Some contracted-in private-sector schemes are either non-contributory or pay a small fixed contribution of less than £1 per week. For schemes where contributions are calculated according to a percentage of salary, Table 6.15 gives the effective rates of

TABLE 6.15. *Numbers of members paying contributions of various percentages of salary, 1987* (thousands)

%age of salary	Private sector		Public sector	Total
	Contracted-out	Not contracted-out	Contracted-out	
Under 2	40	30	680	750
2 and under 3	190	110	—	300
3 and under 4	310	160	—	470
4 and under 5	500	100	50	650
5 and under 6	1,580	190	150	1,920
6 and under 7	1,100	80	3,250	4,430
7 and over	100	130	350	580
Total paying %ages	3,820	800	4,480	9,100
Non-contributory or other basis	680	500	320	1,500
TOTALS	4,500	1,300	4,800	10,600

Source: GASOPS, Table 6.4.

employee contribution in 1987. The average rate was about 5.5 per cent. In the private sector the most common contribution rate was 5 per cent, while in the public sector it was 6 per cent. The average employee contribution in the private sector in 1987 was £520.

Tables 6.16 and 6.17 give respectively the employee and employer

TABLE 6.16. *Employee contribution-rates in selected schemes*

Scheme	Contribution-rate (%)
Local-government officers	
staff	6.00
manual workers	5.00
Teachers	6.00
NHS	
staff	6.00
manual workers	5.00
Airways	
general staff: male	7.25
female	5.75
pilots, officers, air cabin-crew: male	8.50
female	7.00
BBC	7.50
Coal	
staff: male	6.00
female	5.00
miners	5.00
Electricity	6.00
Gas	
staff	6.00
manual workers: male	3.00
female	2.70
Post Office	6.00
Rail	3.00–5.50
London Transport	
staff	6.00
manual	4.00–4.25
Steel	
staff	8.00
manual	5.75
Water	
staff	6.00
manual	5.00

Source: IDS (1979).

TABLE 6.17. *Employer contribution-rates in selected schemes*

Scheme	Contribution-rate
Local government	13.5% of payroll, comprising 10.75% for new pensions plus 2.75% for increases in existing pensions
Teachers	6.9% plus deficiency payment of 1.5% for 40 years (also an Exchequer supplement of 5%)
NHS	7.5% (also an Exchequer supplement of 5%)
Airways	
general staff: male	15.95%
female	12.65%
	(2.2 times general staff rates)
air cabin-crew: male	25.5%
female	21.0%
	(3 times air cabin-crew rates)
pilots and officers	32.3%
	(3.8 times pilots' and officers' rate)
Coal	
staff	40%, comprising 13% for new pensions and 27% representing deficiency payments
miners	11.95%, comprising 5% for new pensions and 6.95% representing deficiency payments (there is also an Exchequer supplement of 17.5%)
Electricity	
staff	12%
manual	12%
	(2 times employee rate)
Gas	
staff	18% (includes a deficiency payment)
manual	12% (includes a deficiency payment)
Post Office	24%, comprising 11% for new pensions and 13% representing deficiency payments
Rail	7.5%
	(1.5 times average employee rate)
Steel	
staff	16%
manual	10.5%
	(2 times average employee rate)
Water	10.5%
	(1.93 times average employee rate)

Source: IDS (1979).

contribution-rates as percentages of employee salary in a selected range of occupational schemes surveyed in IDS188. While the employee rates remain quite stable over time, the employer rates are much more volatile. Table 6.17 shows that in some schemes employer contribution-rates were quite high in 1977 because schemes were in deficit and deficiency payments had to be made. Such deficits disappeared in the 1980s and the deficiency payments stopped.

The 1992 National Association of Pension Funds survey found that the average employee contribution was 5 per cent of salary, while the average employer contribution was 10 per cent of salary.

6.5.3. THE CIVIL SERVANTS' SCHEME

The largest group of public-sector employees not making any explicit contribution towards their pensions is the civil service, although the widow's pension, introduced into the civil-service scheme in 1949, has a contributory element of 1.5 per cent of salary. Civil servants did make contributions towards their pensions from 1829 until the publication in 1857 of the Report of the Royal Commission to Inquire into the Operation of the Superannuation Act of 1834, which opposed contributions on the grounds that their imposition was a breach of the original contracts of civil servants and also that, in the absence of a fund, contributions were not directly related to a particular future contingency because current civil-servant pensions depended not on their own contributions but on the contributions of future civil servants.

The most recent major review of civil-service contributions was made by the Civil Service Joint Superannuation Review Committee in 1972. It concluded that without a fund (and the cost of establishing a fund for civil servants would be enormous) no useful purpose would be met by the introduction of explicit contributions. However, despite the formal non-contributory nature of their schemes, civil servants' salaries, which had been calculated by the Civil Service Pay Research Unit on the basis of comparability with the private sector, are notionally adjusted to allow for these non-contributory pension benefits.

Nevertheless, there was widespread concern that this notional adjustment, which was set by the government actuary in 1974 at 1.75 per cent of salary, was a completely inadequate representation of the true value of public-sector pensions. In 1976 the House of Commons Expenditure Committee's independent actuary suggested that 5 per cent was a more appropriate figure. The committee also recognized the speculative nature of the problem. Even if the cost of inflation-proofing was fully offset against salary, civil servants were gambling on whether conditions in the future when they retired were likely to be more inflationary than the present, in which case they would gain, or less inflationary, in which case they would lose. In addition, the calculation of the value of the pension was very sensitive to assumptions concerning the course of future interest rates and inflation. The committee concluded that, because of the importance of these calculations, the government actuary should collaborate with other government departments and that the assumptions on which they worked should be published. These recommendations were broadly accepted by the government in March 1978. In particular, it was decided that the value of pension benefits should be notionally set at 7.9 per cent of salary, of which 3.8 per cent was considered to be the value of the inflation-proofing element in those benefits payable at the age of 60, and the remaining 4.1 per cent was the pure superannuation contribution. This notional 7.9 per cent is then deducted from civil-servant salaries in lieu of pension contributions.

6.6. Types of Retirement Benefit

The OPB and PSO stipulate only what minimum and maximum retirement benefits occupational schemes can offer. Different schemes have different methods of calculating and paying retirement benefits. The benefits can be categorized into those given at normal retirement, those for early or late retirement, and finally death benefits.

6.6.1. NORMAL RETIREMENT BENEFITS

6.6.1.1. *Normal Retirement Age*

Pension-scheme members are eligible to receive normal retirement benefits from the *normal retirement age*, and this may vary from scheme to scheme as shown in Table 6.18. For most private-sector schemes the normal retirement age coincides with the state-pension age, that is, 65 for men and 60 for women. In 1987 77 per cent of men and 86 per cent of women could expect to retire at these respective ages. In the public sector, however, the most common retirement age for men is 60, available to 43 per cent of male scheme members, and a further 25 per cent are able to retire between the ages of 60 and 65 years. For women in the public sector, about 52 per cent retire at 60 years. Members of the Armed Forces and others with special fitness requirements generally have a normal retirement age of less than 60 years.

IDS188 found the following normal retirement ages in selected schemes:

- *All at 65*: local government and water, but retirement is optional from the age of 60 for men so long as they have completed twenty-five years' service and for women who have completed at least five years' service.

TABLE 6.18. *Numbers of members of schemes according to normal retirement age* (thousands)

Normal retirement age	Private sector		Public sector		Both sectors	
	1983	1987	1983	1987	1983	1987
Men						
Under 60	—	—	530	500	530	500
60	260	800	1,320	1,200	1,580	2,000
Between 60 and 65	350	230	850	700	1,200	930
65	3,770	3,370	710	400	4,480	3,770
TOTALS	4,380	4,400	3,410	2,800	7,790	7,200
Women						
Under 60	90	10	330	400	420	410
60	1,260	1,210	1,110	1,040	2,370	2,250
Between 60 and 65	30	40	450	550	480	590
65	30	140	10	10	40	150
TOTALS	1,410	1,400	1,900	2,000	3,310	3,400
Combined totals	5,790	5,800	5,310	4,800	11,100	10,600

Source: GASOPS, Table 7.1.

- *Men at 65 and women at 60*: coal (staff and mineworkers), electricity (staff), gas (staff and manual), steel (staff and manual).
- *Men at 63 and women at 60*: airways (excluding pilots and air cabin-crew, who retire at 55).
- *Men at 62 and women at 60*: rail, London Transport (staff).
- *All at 60*: civil service, NHS, teachers, BBC, Post Office.

However, a European Court ruling in May 1990 determined that there could be no discrimination between men and women in terms of retirement age in occupational pension schemes. Such schemes have had to introduce either a common retirement age (for example, 63) or a common retirement decade (such as 60 to 70) for men and women.

6.6.1.2. *Pensionable Salary*

The least common type of normal retirement benefit from an occupational pension scheme is a *money-purchase* pension in which the benefit is a flat-rate benefit depending directly on the amount of contributions paid and the interest earned on these contributions; this, for example, is the kind of benefit that arises out of contributions made to a provident fund and also from a personal pension scheme (see Chapter 7). This method is advantageous where labour mobility is very high because of the precise link between contributions and pension benefit, which is not as necessary for immobile staff.

The most common method of calculating normal retirement benefit is based on a proportion of the *final salary*, that is, it is a graduated benefit which increases with the relevant salary measure. The calculation of the final salary depends on the way in which the employee's *pensionable salary* is calculated for the period prior to retirement. In many cases the definition of pensionable salary excludes fluctuating payments such as bonuses, overtime and shift, and location or accommodation allowances. Where such payments are included, they may be averaged over a number of years in order to derive a more stable measure of their contribution to the pensionable salary. With private-sector contracted-out schemes in 1987, 21 per cent included all payments in their definition of pensionable salary, while the rest excluded some or all of the fluctuating components. In the public sector, only 9 per cent of schemes included all payments.

For a given definition of pensionable salary, the way in which the final salary is related to pensionable salary can vary significantly between schemes, and this can lead to large differences in pensions. For some schemes the final salary can equal the actual annual salary at retirement or it can equal the average salary over a number of years before retirement, although the effect of rapid inflation has led to a reduction in the number of years used in the calculation. In both the private and public sectors an averaging period of one year is the most common method (covering 55 per cent and 96 per cent of employees respectively), although a three-year period is still common for many in the private sector (covering 39 per cent of employees). The remaining workers in the private sector have either a two-year or a five-year averaging period. If the earnings profile of the employee is such that the terminal salary is less than the salary earned in earlier years (for example, a miner who works for the early part of his career underground on the coal-face and later on the surface), then the method of calculation might be based on the *average salary* or some variant such as the best three years in the ten years preceding retirement. In addition, some schemes adjust the resulting average salary to account for inflation up to the date of retirement.

In 1987 more than 90 per cent of private-sector pensions (covering 5.3 million future pensioners) were calculated using the *final-salary* formula and there has been a steady increase in the share of this method since 1971 (see Table 6.19). At the other extreme, only about 500,000 potential pensioners will receive a *money-purchase* pension, although the actual number has quintupled since 1971. Other pension formulae such as

TABLE 6.19. *Numbers of members according to pension formula: private sector* (millions)

Pension formula	1971	1975	1979	1983	1987
Final-salary	4.1	4.6	5.6	5.2	5.3
Average-salary	0.2	0.2	0.1	0.1	—
Salary-range	0.8	0.1	—	—	—
Flat-sum-per-year-of-service	1.1	0.7	0.2	0.1	—
Money-purchase	0.1	0.1	0.2	0.4	0.5
No pension	0.2	0.1	—	—	—
TOTALS	6.5	5.8	6.1	5.8	5.8

Source: GASOPS, Table 7.2.

those based on average salary, salary range, or flat sum per year of service, while once important, are no longer used to any significant extent.

IDS188 found the following variations for calculating pensionable salary in selected schemes:

- *Final year's pay*: rail, London Transport.
- *Final year or average of best three of last ten*: coal (staff), electricity (staff).
- *Best year of last three*: civil service, local government, NHS, gas (manual), Post Office, water.
- *Best 365 days during final 1,095 days*: teachers.
- *Best year within last five*: gas (staff), Post Office.
- *Average of best two years of last five*: airways.
- *Best year within last ten*: gas (staff), Post Office.
- *Average of best three consecutive years in last ten, if better than best of last three years*: Post Office.
- *Best year within last twelve*: steel (staff and manual).
- *Best year within last thirteen*: coal (mineworkers).

Where the relevant pensionable salary relates to an earlier year, this is indexed to the date of retirement using increases in national average earnings.

Senior company executives have found a way of circumventing the limits imposed by final-salary schemes. This is to award themselves substantial salary increases just prior to retirement. For example, in 1988 the chairman of British Gas was awarded a £74,000 salary increase to £185,000 one year before his retirement. His pension at two-thirds of final salary was more than £123,000, that is, £12,000 *more* than his salary a year before retirement.

TABLE 6.20. *Numbers of members with various fractions (including lump-sum equivalents) in final-salary schemes, 1987* (thousands)

Equivalent pension fraction	Private sector		Public sector	Total
	Contracted-out	Not contracted-out		
Better than 60ths (if service less than 40 years)	470	60	650	1,180
60ths	2,990	370	4,000	7,360
Between 60ths and 80ths	350	70	130	550
80ths	690	170	20	880
Less than 80ths	—	110	—	110
TOTALS	4,500	780	4,800	10,080

Source: GASOPS, Table 7.7.

6.6.1.3. *Pension Formula*

Where the pension calculation is based on a proportion of the final or average salary, the actual pension will depend on the number of years of service given. The most common formula is based on the scale of one-sixtieth of the final or average salary for each year of service given, up to a maximum of forty years. This is shown in Table 6.20, which reveals that 66 per cent of private-sector contracted-out schemes and 83 per cent of public-sector schemes are based on the sixtieths scale. There is a tendency for executive staff to have a pensions fraction better than 1/60th, and a tendency for manual staff to have a fraction of 1/80th or less.

Some occupational schemes, when calculating the benefits for their members, take into account the pension that the member will receive from the state system, namely the basic flat-rate pension and, if the scheme is not contracted out, the additional earnings-related pension.

In the private sector, where an adjustment is made, the most common procedure is to reduce the pensionable salary used as the basis for contributions and pensions. Most frequently, the adjustment is related to the basic state pension for a single person. In a third of such cases the deduction from the pensionable salary is equal to the basic state pension, and in another third of cases it is equal to a multiple of one-and-a-half times the basic state pension. In some non-contracted-out schemes the adjustment is also related to the earnings-related component of the state pension. In some schemes there is a deduction from the pension equal to one-eighteenth of the component of final salary which lies between the lower and upper earnings limits permitted by the state scheme for each year of service up to a maximum of twenty years. Other schemes directly reduce their members' pensions by an amount equal to the proportion of the earnings-related pension earned during membership of the scheme. In addition, in some schemes there is a higher pension fraction for the portion of members' final salaries above the upper earnings limit. Some schemes, in both categories, impose a flat-sum deduction to the pensionable salary, usually of about £100 and rarely above £500. GASOPS found that with private-sector contracted-out schemes, 48 per cent made no adjustment, 44 per cent made a deduction in respect of the basic state pension, and 8 per cent made flat-sum deductions. With non-contracted-out schemes, 63 per cent made no adjustment, 15 per cent adjusted pensions to take account of the basic state pension, 14 per cent adjusted pensions to take account of the earnings-related state pension, and 8 per cent made flat-sum deductions.

IDS188 found the following arrangements in selected schemes to account for the state scheme:

- *Basic state pension integrated with occupational pension*: British Rail integrates the state scheme fully with its own scheme to provide a maximum pension of two-thirds of pensionable salary, including the basic state pension, and also a maximum lump sum of one year's pensionable salary.
- *Occupational pension with maximum deduction of £404 p.a.*: London Transport (staff and manual). LT followed the same procedure as BR until 1974, but since then integrates into its own scheme only the value of the basic state pension of £404 p.a. which existed in 1974. The maximum LT pension is two-thirds of pensionable salary plus the basic state pension, less £404 p.a.
- *Occupational pension with maximum deduction of £67.75 p.a.*: civil service, local government, teachers, NHS, water, Post Office (but discontinued service given after 6 April 1978). These schemes are similar to the LT scheme except that £67.75 represents the value of the state pension when compulsory national insurance was introduced in 1948.
- *Occupational schemes with no deductions*: airways, coal (staff and mineworkers), gas (staff and manual), steel (staff and manual).

6.6.1.4. *Commutation Rights*

There are also certain additional pension benefits available on normal retirement which have generally become accepted. The most important is the option of having part of the pension annuity *commuted*, that is, having the rate of annuity reduced in return for a lump sum in cash which is given immediately on retirement. The value of the lump sum is usually up to 3/80ths for each year of service up to a maximum of forty years (and is normally equal to about three years' pension), and the rate of pension is then reduced from the sixtieths scale to the eightieths scale, that is, 1/80th of final or average salary for each year of service up to a maximum of forty years. The lump-sum benefit has been widely available in the public sector for some time, but has only become an important feature of the retirement benefits of the private sector since the 1970s. More than 90 per cent of private-sector members and 95 per cent of public-sector members either have the commutation option or automatically receive a lump sum as well as a pension.

IDS188 found the following schemes offering lump sums:

- *Pension of 1/80th and a lump sum of 3/80ths of pensionable pay for each year of qualifying service*: civil service, local government, NHS, teachers, coal (staff and mineworkers), electricity (staff), Post Office, steel (staff), water.
- *Pension of 1/60th of pensionable pay for each year of qualifying service and the possibility of surrendering part of the pension for a lump sum*: airways (executive pilots and cabin-crew for whom the fraction is 1/56th), BBC, gas (staff and manual); for example, for the BBC the lump sum is ten times the value of the annual pension forgone.

Table 6.21 shows the total amounts spent on pensions in 1987. The table indicates that in addition to the lump-sum retirement benefit, which comprises 20 per cent of total spending on pensions, pensions to former employees comprise 69 per cent of total spending, lump-sum death benefits comprise 3 per cent of spending, and widow/ers' and other dependants' benefits comprise 8 per cent of spending. These benefits are

TABLE 6.21. *Expenditure on pensions in 1987*

	Private sector		Public sector		Total	
	£m.	%	£m.	%	£m.	%
Pensions to former employees	4,550	65	7,200	71	11,750	69
Pensions to dependants of former employees	600	9	850	8	1,450	8
Lump sums on death	350	5	200	2	550	3
Lump sums on retirement	1,950	21	1,950	19	3,400	20
TOTALS	6,950	100	10,200	100	17,150	100

Source: GASOPS, Table 4.1.

roughly similar for both sectors, except that death benefits appear to be a more important feature of private schemes than public schemes.

6.6.2. EARLY- AND LATE-RETIREMENT BENEFITS

6.6.2.1. *Early-Retirement Benefits*

Virtually all occupational schemes allow for the possibility of early retirement as a result of a member's ill health, and will provide a pension under these circumstances. In the private sector about 13 per cent of premature retirement pensions are based on accrued service only (for example, 35/60ths for someone who retired five years early). Some 27 per cent of pensions, usually from smaller schemes, are given on a less favourable basis than this, incorporating a reduction to take account of the fact that the pension is being provided at an earlier age than that of normal retirement: the typical reduction is 6 per cent for each year of early retirement. However, the largest category of premature pensions in the private sector (about 47 per cent) are given on a basis better than accrued service, the best of which are based on full potential service without a reduction for early payment. This category has grown significantly in recent years: in 1971, for example, it comprised only 15 per cent of early-retirement pensions. In nearly 14 per cent of schemes *permanent health insurance* is provided. This normally provides a pension up to normal retirement age only, to be replaced by a pension from the pension fund itself, and, in the most favourable cases, based on service that could have been earned to normal retirement in the absence of ill health. A number of schemes in the private sector require the employee to complete a minimum period of service before becoming eligible for an early-retirement pension. Most schemes have no such waiting period, but of the 16 per cent that do, 10 per cent have a waiting period of five or less years, 5 per cent a period of ten years, and 1 per cent a period of fifteen years.

In the public sector more than 97 per cent of members receive early-retirement pensions based on better-than-accrued service, and the remainder receive them at the level of accrued service without reduction. Most public-sector schemes (86 per cent) have a waiting period of five years, less than 0.2 per cent have a waiting period of ten years, and the rest have no waiting period. The private sector, therefore, appears to be more generous than the public sector in this respect. However, most public-sector schemes usually also grant a special lump-sum payment for early retirement due to ill health in the first five years of employment, and this tends to restore comparability between the two sectors.

Many schemes also provide pensions immediately in the case of voluntary early retirement. There are certain conditions for eligibility, such as that the member must be more than a certain age (for example, 50) or be within a certain period of his normal retirement (for example, five years) and have completed a minimum period of service; also he may require the permission of his employer. In the private sector the largest category of schemes (38 per cent of the total) calculate the early-retirement pension on the basis of service completed by the time of retirement and then apply a reduction to allow for the fact that the member is receiving his pension at an earlier age. At the employer's discretion this reduction can be waived if the early retirement is within two or three years of normal retirement or the member has completed a minimum number of years of service (usually forty years) or has reached the state-pension age. Some pensions (7 per cent) are based on accrued service without a reduction, but often these are not available immediately on early retirement and the member must wait until normal retirement age before receiving his pension. A very small number of pensions (0.5 per cent) are based on full potential service and then reduced, but since the reduction factor is larger, these pensions are approximately equivalent to those based on accrued service with a small reduction. In the public sector the largest category of schemes (44 per cent) do not provide a pension immediately on early retirement; instead, the pension of an early leaver is preserved until the normal retirement date. Others (27 per cent) are based on accrued service without reductions and some (5 per cent) on accrued service with enhancements.

IDS188 found the following variations in selected schemes:

- *Preserved pension payable at normal or minimum retirement age*: civil service, local government, NHS, teachers, coal (mineworkers), Post Office.
- *Preserved pensions (with reduction) payable before normal retirement age*:
  (a) at 55 for women and 60 for men
    1. after ten years' qualifying service: gas (staff and manual);
    2. after twenty-five years' qualifying service: coal (staff), steel (staff and manual);
  (b) at 50 for women and 55 for men: rail, London Transport;
  (c) at 50 for both men and women
    1. after five years' qualifying service: airways;
    2. after ten years' qualifying service: BBC.

6.6.2.2. *Late-Retirement Benefits*

In cases where retirement is deferred beyond normal retirement age, the member's pension is usually also deferred until he actually retires. In the private sector (and also for the nationalized industries) no further contributions are made after the normal retirement age, and this additional period of service is usually not included in the pension calculation (although it is for nearly 10 per cent of schemes). However, the pension, when it is eventually paid, is generally enhanced to allow for both the amount of normal pension forgone and the interest earned on this amount (usually by about 6 per cent for each year's deferment). In 7 per cent of private-sector schemes the member receives a pension at the age of normal retirement despite continuing service. In the public sector the periods of service before and after normal retirement are not distinguished, and so the total amount of service is included in the pension calculation and in addition contributions by both employees and employers are made up to the time of actual retirement. Most public-sector schemes allow for pensions to be paid up to the Inland Revenue's maximum, which is equivalent to forty-five years' eligible service.

People who take early retirement benefit under the 1989 Finance Act. Anyone with twenty years' pensionable service can retire from the age of 50 and still receive a pension of two-thirds of final salary. The tax-free lump sum is calculated as the larger of 225 per cent of the annual pension or 3/80ths of final salary for each year of service up to the age of 50.

6.6.3. DEATH BENEFITS

Another facility that has become more frequently available is the right of assignment, that is, the transferability of the pension rights on the death of the member to his/her widow/er or other dependants in the form of a lump sum and a widow/er's or other dependant's pension. Further, the scheme often returns the member's own contributions, sometimes with interest. In either case inheritance tax is not applicable.

6.6.3.1. *Lump-Sum Death-in-Service Benefits*

In 1987 GASOPS found that most schemes which provided lump-sum death benefits calculated them on the same basis for all members regardless of the member's marital status, sex, or number of dependants. In some schemes the size of the lump sum depended on whether a widow/er's or dependant's pension is also payable. If no such pension is payable, there is generally a refund of contributions. In some cases the size of the lump sum depended directly on the sex or marital status of the member. For example, 94 per cent of schemes provided a lump sum (other than a refund of contributions) when a married male member died in service.

In the private sector most lump-sum benefits paid on death in service are based on a multiple of salary; 81 per cent of married male members are in schemes using this basis. For 8 per cent of male members the lump sum is based on a multiple of salary less the cost of the widow's pension. For 5 per cent the lump sum is based on a fraction of salary times length of service, and for 1 per cent the lump sum is a flat-sum payment. Where the lump sum is based on a multiple of salary, the most common multiple, covering 39 per cent of married male members, is between two and three, though it ranges from between one and two (4 per cent) up to four (26 per cent). The maximum lump sum is four times earnings. A refund of contributions (with or without interest) may be given either in addition to or as a replacement for the lump sum if the former is larger. In 88 per cent of private-sector schemes, lump-sum death benefits do not depend on the marital status of the deceased member. In 10 per cent of schemes the lump sum is lower for unmarried people, while in 2 per cent it is higher.

In the public sector virtually all schemes, regardless of sex or marital status, have a death benefit which depends on a fraction of salary and the length of service, and often the amount of qualifying service is enhanced. This results in a minimum lump sum of one times pensionable salary in the civil-service, local-government, and teachers' schemes and a maximum of three times salary in the airways schemes. In addition to the lump sum, a refund of contributions may also be made, as in the private-sector schemes.

In the public sector, where a lump-sum benefit is given, there is no period of qualifying service. In the private sector 95 per cent of members have no waiting period either: the remainder have a waiting period of between one and ten years.

6.6.3.2. *Widows' and Widowers' Pensions on Death in Service*

The Social Security Pensions Act 1975 required that all contracted-out schemes provide a widow's pension of at least half the guaranteed minimum pension earned by her husband at the time of his death if he died in service. In 1971 only 39 per cent of members were covered for the widow's pension, but by 1987 over 90 per cent were covered. In some schemes, the widow's pension is optional and involves either a higher contribution-rate or a reduced prospective pension for the member. In 82 per cent of private-sector schemes and all public-sector schemes, the widow's pension is based on the member's salary and service. With regard to service, in the private sector the widow's pension is based on actual service given by the time of death in 29 per cent of cases, on partly enhanced service in 13 per cent of cases, and on full potential service in 58 per cent of cases; in the public sector the corresponding figures are 20 per cent, 79 per cent, and 1 per cent. With regard to salary, the most common salary fraction in the private sector (covering 59 per cent of cases) is 1/120th of pensionable salary for each year of service, while in the public sector the most common fraction is 1/160th of pensionable salary for each year of service (covering 95 per cent of public-sector members). In the public sector this usually results, as a minimum, in a widow's pension of half the amount the husband would have received had he retired due to ill health, and then only after a qualifying period of five years: for example, the civil-service, local-government, and teachers' schemes. The most generous widow's pension permitted by the PSO is two-thirds of the maximum pension available to the husband had he retired on grounds of ill health and without a minimum period of qualifying service.

While it is possible for a husband to provide for an increased widow's pension in return for a lower pension for himself, it is generally not possible for the full pension to be restored if the widow's pension is no longer required, say, because the wife died before the husband. Scheme rules usually stipulate that, once an allocation which has been made in favour of a spouse has become effective, say, because the scheme member has retired, it cannot be cancelled, amended, or revoked.

The availability of widowers' pensions increased during the 1980s, and since 6 April 1989 they have been mandatory. By 1987 about 67 per cent of schemes in the private sector and 21 per cent of schemes in the public sector provided for widowers' pensions in all circumstances, and a further 6 per cent and 1.5 per cent of schemes respectively provided pensions only for dependent widowers.

Most schemes in the public sector discontinue the widows' pension if the widow remarries before retirement age, although a few schemes (for example, the BBC scheme) provide widows' pensions for life. In the private sector, on the other hand, in 75 per cent of schemes the status of the widow's pension is unaffected by the widow's remarriage, although in 9 per cent of the schemes it is reduced to the minimum GMP or stopped entirely. If the widow remarries after retirement age, she generally receives more-favourable treatment in respect of the pension. In about 75 per cent of both private- and public-sector schemes, a widow's pension is variously granted in full, granted for service after 1978, or granted unless marriage occurred within six months of death.

The 1992 NAPF survey found that 80 per cent of schemes provided a widow/er's pension of half the member's full prospective pension and this was paid regardless of whether the surviving spouse remarried.

6.6.3.3. *Dependent Children's Benefits on Death in Service*

In the private sector some schemes (37 per cent) either do not make special provision for benefits to children on the death in service of their father, or provide them only if no widow's pension is also payable (13 per cent). The rest provide benefits which are either independent of the amount of the widow's pension (18 per cent) or dependent on this amount (32 per cent). In the public sector 15 per cent of schemes provide children's benefits independent of the widow's pension, and 84 per cent grant benefits which are dependent. The most usual level of benefit in the public sector is one-quarter of the husband's pension for one child and half the pension for two or more children.

6.6.3.4. *Post-Retirement Death Benefits*

Apart from providing benefits on death in service, most schemes also provide benefits in the case where the member dies after retirement. Typically, the widow or widower continues to receive a (usually smaller) pension. In the private sector 91 per cent of schemes will provide a widow's pension in these circumstances, either unconditionally (87 per cent) or in return for a surrender of part of the pension (or lump sum) at retirement (4 per cent). In the public sector all members are eligible for a post-retirement widow's pension.

In both the private and public sectors the value of the pension usually depends on both the length of service and the member's salary (most commonly the scale of 120ths is used in the private sector and 160ths in the public sector). Also, for both sectors the most common pension is one-half of the husband's pension at the time of death, which is payable until his widow's death or until she remarries. In 75 per cent of private-sector and 35 per cent of public-sector schemes, the full pension is guaranteed for five years after retirement, and if the member dies during that period the balance is paid as a lump sum (this is sometimes called a *pension guarantee*). In the schemes surveyed in IDS188, this benefit is available in the coal (staff), electricity (staff), gas (staff), Post Office, and steel (staff and manual) schemes. In the civil-service and local-government schemes (for employees with more than ten years' service), the benefit is equal to the difference between the lump sum and pension paid since retirement.

Finally, widowers' pensions and pensions for other dependants on death after retirement are usually available on the same basis as for death in service.

6.6.4. PENSIONS AND DIVORCE

Divorce can have a drastic effect on the pension that a woman receives in retirement.

Before 1978 working married women were able to pay a reduced rate of national-insurance contributions, but these contributions did not contribute towards a state pension. Instead, such women had to rely on their husband's contributions. Any right to receive a pension ceased when their divorce became absolute. Since 1978 newly married women or married women who begin working again after a break from work have had to pay the full contribution, and so do have the right to receive a state pension.

In terms of occupational pensions, a wife normally has the right to receive a widow's pension equal to half the husband's pension after his death. However, pension schemes do not have to provide for an ex-wife. This means that if the ex-husband remarries, his new wife will benefit from the pension. The ex-wife will lose her maintenance payments when her ex-husband dies, but will receive no pension in compensation.

If the man did not remarry after his divorce, the ex-wife might still have some claim to a widow's pension when he died. This is because the fund's trustees have some discretion over the widow's pension when there is no legal wife around at the time of the man's death. If the ex-wife had been maintained until the ex-husband's death, the trustees might award her a widow's pension. If, however, the man lived with another woman following his divorce, then both women might have a valid claim on the widow's pension.

With self-employed and personal pensions, the husband can choose the beneficiaries. In these cases a woman can ask for widow's benefits to be included in the divorce settlement.

6.7. Indexation of Pensions against Inflation

A particularly important feature of occupational pension schemes is the degree of compensation of the pension in payment against inflation that different schemes award. Some flat-rate benefits, for example, those based on money-purchase schemes, have received no compensation against inflation and so the real value of these benefits is continually decreasing. But most benefits, especially those based on terminal or average salaries, have received at least partial indexation against inflation. Most public-sector pensions have been fully indexed against inflation on an annual basis since 1971.

6.7.1. THE HISTORY OF PENSIONS INDEXATION

The earliest attempt to compensate pensioners for the effects of inflation occurred as a result of the huge inflation that followed the First World War. This was in 1920, when the first Pensions (Increase) Act was passed to relieve the burden suffered by public-sector pensioners with the smallest pensions. The principle was established that, while the pensions of former public servants should not, in general, be changed if circumstances altered after retirement, there would be an exception in periods of rapid inflation when the real values of fixed pensions declined sharply, although only those on the lowest pensions could be so compensated. The Pensions (Increase) Act of 1956 recognized that inflation affected everyone on fixed incomes, and so all public-sector pensions were given increases, although there were still higher percentage increases for the smaller compared with the larger pensions. From 1959 every public-sector pension received the same percentage increase regardless of the size of the pension.

In the 1960s all public-service pensioners were receiving at least partial indexation against inflation. However, the increase in pensions occurred at irregular and unpredictable intervals when the government decided to introduce the necessary Pensions (Increase) Acts, as it did in 1959, 1962, 1965, and 1969. The consequence was that the pensions continually lagged behind inflation. As a result, there was pressure for regular and more frequent reviews of pensions.

In September 1971 the government's white paper *Strategy for Pensions* proposed two-yearly reviews for both state and public-sector pensions. However, in December 1971 the government decided to introduce annual reviews beginning on 1 December 1972, in line with the annual reviews for supplementary benefits. The National Insurance Act of 1971 increased state pensions and national-insurance contributions in line with the cost of living, and was the first act to embody the concept of full compensation, according to some index of inflation. At the same time the administration of public-sector pensions was dealt with in the Pensions (Increase) Act of 1971. This was the act which began the full preservation in real terms of the pensions of all central- and local-government employees. Its specific objectives were to make good the deficiencies resulting from the previous Pensions (Increase) Acts, which had left many public-sector pensions below their initial real values, and to compensate for the rise in the cost of living since the last act in 1969, and to introduce biennial reviews for the purpose of maintaining the purchasing power of public-sector pensions (this was subsequently reduced to annual reviews). The act covered all central- and local-government employees, but excluded the nationalized industries, which had their own arrangements. The act also gave the government the freedom to choose the measure of the cost of living against which pensions were to be increased. In agreement with the trade unions, the government decided to adopt the retail price index as the basis for reviewing the pensions which it provided. This was altered by the Social Security Pensions Act 1975, which specified that the basic component of the state retirement pension would be indexed annually in terms of the preceding year's increase in wages or prices, whichever was greater, while the additional earnings-related component available to non-contracted-out schemes would be increased in line with prices only. The argument which succeeded in bringing about this change was that, in a growing economy, wages tend to grow faster than prices, and that by relating pensions to wages pensioners shared in this growth.

Since public-sector occupational pensions are treated as being equivalent to the additional component of the state scheme, these are also increased in line with prices. In periods of high inflation together with wage restraint, this has resulted in public-sector pensioners receiving more in pension increases than most people in work received in salary increases, including those public-sector workers who replaced them when they retired. By similar reasoning, pensioners in public-sector occupational schemes have also received substantially larger pension increases than their counterparts in private-sector schemes where the pension in excess of the guaranteed minimum pension has not kept in line with increases in the retail price index. While the basic component of the state pension, received by all pensioners in both contracted-in and contracted-out schemes, is indexed, any additional pension derived from membership of an occupational scheme is fully indexed only for public-sector schemes and many schemes of the public corporations, and not for private-sector schemes. In the first ten years after the introduction of index-linking in 1971, public-sector pensions increased by an average of 14 per cent p.a., with a minimum increase of 7.4 per cent, and a maximum increase in 1976 of 26.1 per cent which alone cost the government £180m.

The full indexation of the pensions of public-corporation schemes is not a statutory right granted by parliament but arises from independent decisions made by these corporations in collaboration with their trade unions. Some public corporations use exactly the same formula as for public-sector schemes, while others (including the BBC) retain discretionary powers apart from the granting of a minimum increase, usually 3 per cent. This has led at times to many public-corporation schemes showing a deficit, with the consequent need for deficiency payments from the sponsoring corporation or the secretary of state. For example, the largest public-corporation scheme in Britain (until the splitting up of the corporation in 1981) was the Post Office Staff Superannuation Fund. In the year to 13 March 1980 the scheme received a deficiency payment of £229.7m. from the Post Office and £45m. from the secretary of state for industry.

In 1980 the government established a committee of enquiry into the value of inflation-proofed pensions to the 5 million public-sector employees who received them. The committee, under the chairmanship of Sir Bernard Scott (then deputy chairman of Lloyds Bank and a former chairman of Lucas Industries), reported in early 1981. It concluded that, since 'it is a highly desirable social objective that the standard of living of those in retirement should be protected', and since 'there is no doubt that the occupational pension schemes of the vast majority of public sector employees are superior to the schemes in which nearly all private sector employees found themselves', then it could see nothing wrong with the principle of fully indexed pensions being extended to the private sector (indeed, 'the feeling of injustice so widely held in the private sector must be recognised'), so long as 'the full cost of protecting pensions . . . [is] . . . fully shouldered during working life'. The schemes in the private sector which the Civil Service Pay Research Unit (until it was disbanded in 1983) used as analogues in its pay-and-conditions comparability exercises provided inflation-proofing averaging only 50 per cent to 55 per cent of the rate of inflation. With double-digit inflation this can have devastating consequences for the real values of private-sector pensions.

The Scott Committee realized that it would be more or less impossible for the private-sector schemes to give open-ended commitments in terms of inflation-proofing guarantees, since this could have a serious adverse effect on the long-run solvency of the sponsoring companies. However, the report argued that the government could nevertheless help private-sector pensions in a number of ways. The first was through the guaranteed minimum pension which is fully indexed. The second was to introduce measures which permanently reduced or even eliminated inflation. The third was to improve the real rates of return which could be obtained on the investments held by pension schemes. The committee recognized that the real problem lay with the degree of uncertainty attached to inflation rather than with the level of inflation itself, and it commissioned Professor Richard Brealey and Dr Stuart Hodges of the London Business School to calculate the value to public-sector pensioners of having their pensions fully index-linked in a world in which the rate of inflation was uncertain. The problem for the private sector could be substantially reduced if long-term bonds indexed to inflation were available on the market. The committee therefore recommended that 'the government should look seriously at the case for issuing indexed bonds to cover pension liabilities'.

The first form of government help (through the guaranteed minimum pension) had been introduced in 1978, but was not designed to offer much help to people with above-average incomes. The permanent control of inflation was being tackled by the government's Medium-Term Financial Strategy which had been introduced in the 1980 Budget, and between 1990 and 1992 by UK membership of the Exchange Rate Mechanism of the European Monetary System. The government explicitly took up the third suggestion of the Scott Report by introducing index-linked bonds, beginning in the 1981 Budget with an index-linked 1996 Treasury bond which had a guaranteed real return if held to maturity of 2 per cent.

The Scott Committee could see no good reason why the private sector should not give inflation-proofed pensions so long as they were adequately financed through contributions or investments; after all, 'good pensions, like anything else, have to be earned and paid for during working life'. However, at the present time, 'it is a fact that the private sector employee cannot acquire a pension that has a guarantee of inflation-proofing on any terms'.

This line of reasoning appears to have been largely ignored by private-sector companies. Indeed, public corporations which have been sold off to the private sector have attempted to end the complete index-linking of pensions which their employees had hitherto enjoyed. British Telecom, privatized in November 1984, introduced a new pension scheme for employees joining after 1 April 1986 which removed the automatic right to have their pension benefits inflation-proofed. Its existing 230,000 employees and 82,000 pensioners continued to benefit from inflation-proofing, however. The corporation's justification for doing this was simply that it brought its own pension scheme into line with that operating in the private sector. In 1984 British Airways, while still in the public sector, attempted to buy out the inflation-proofing component of the pensions promised to its 32,000 employees. About half have transferred to a new un-indexed scheme for an average cash compensation of £4,800, representing a cost to BA of around £70m.

6.7.2. CURRENT STATUTORY INDEXATION RULES

The current statutory rules governing the indexation of pensions in payment (including widow/ers' pensions) are contained in the Social Security Acts of 1985, 1986, and 1990 covering minimum increases and in the Finance Acts of 1987 and 1989 covering maximum increases.

The minimum permissible increases under these acts are as follows:

- Since April 1988 the guaranteed minimum pension in payment must be uprated by the occupational scheme by the increase in the retail price index up to a maximum of 3 per cent p.a. compound. If inflation exceeds 3 per cent, the excess is paid by the DSS through the state additional pension, thereby ensuring that the GMP is fully indexed to retail-price inflation. Before April 1988 the GMP paid by an occupational scheme was not revalued after pension age, but was deducted from the notional state additional pension (including increases) and the balance of the notional additional pension paid by the state along with the basic state pension.

- Since April 1992 the excess pension above the GMP must be uprated annually by the scheme by the increase in the retail price index up to a maximum of 5 per cent p.a. compound for service accruing from 6 April 1978. Schemes in surplus have to index their pensions in this way before they can take a contributions holiday.
- In the case where a scheme is wound up, say as a result of a takeover, the existing and preserved pensions must be uprated annually by the increase in the retail price index up to a maximum of 5 per cent p.a. compound. The uprating of the full pension is not obligatory for deferred pensions in ongoing schemes, but only for the GMP; this is designed to reduce corporate take-overs whose sole intention was to extract the surplus in the target's pension scheme.

The maximum permissible increases in pensions in payment are designed to prevent occupational schemes violating their exempt approved status. The general rule is that pensions in payment can be increased to the level of the maximum permitted pension on the retirement date and further increased to account for rises in the retail price index since then. The increases to pensions in payment cannot be made in the form of a tax-free lump sum. Also, a lump sum cannot be adjusted once a pension has been commuted.

Once pensions have reached these maximum limits they cannot be increased further, except to compensate for additional increases in the retail price index. The PSO requires that the *general index of retail prices* is used for this purpose, even though there are other and perhaps more relevant indices, such as the *pensioners' price index.*

6.7.3. CURRENT PRACTICE IN OCCUPATIONAL SCHEMES

The minimum indexation rules listed in the last section are the minimum acceptable under present legislation. Occupational schemes can provide more-generous pension increases than these. In this section we consider current practice in occupational schemes.

With public-sector occupational schemes, the position is clear-cut. Most public-sector schemes index their schemes in accordance with the Pensions (Increase) Acts through Pensions Increase (Review) Orders. This means that the GMP is fully indexed to increases in national average earnings and the excess pension above the GMP is fully indexed to retail prices.

In general, indexation is much less generous in the private sector. Table 6.22 shows the pattern of promised inflation increases in scheme rules as found by GASOPS in 1987. GASOPS found that 55 per cent of schemes *guaranteed* no pension increase at all as a result of inflation.

TABLE 6.22. *Numbers of private-sector pensions according to increases promised by rules, 1987*

Amount of promised increase (%)	Number of pensions (thousands)
5	300
4	110
3	610
2–2.5	40
Proportion of cost of living	60
Full cost of living	170
None	1,610
TOTAL	2,900

Source: GASOPS, Table 9.4.

Only 6 per cent of schemes offered full indexation, and only 10 per cent offered indexation of 5 per cent. This means that in 1987 84 per cent of scheme rules in the private sector were providing for an indexation of their pensions on terms that were not acceptable after April 1988. In addition, of those schemes offering some indexation, 73 per cent applied the indexation only to the pension in excess of the GMP.

However, while scheme rules were not particularly generous in the 1980s, many schemes were providing more-generous increases on a dis-cretionary basis. Table 6.23 shows the pattern of pension increases in 1986, when 80 per cent of schemes awarded some pension increase,

TABLE 6.23. *Numbers of private-sector pensions according to pensions increase in 1986*

Amount of increase (%)	Number of pensions (thousands)
8 or more	110
6 or more but less than 8	160
4 or more but less than 6	980
2 or more but less than 4	810
2 or less	280
No increase	560
TOTAL	2,900

Source: GASOPS, Table 9.2.

whereas from Table 6.22 we see that the scheme rules provide for guaranteed increases in only 45 per cent of schemes. The actual inflation rate was 6.1 per cent in 1985 and 3.4 per cent in 1986. Table 6.23 shows that 28 per cent of schemes awarded increases of 2–4 per cent, 34 per cent of schemes awarded increases of 4–6 per cent, and 9 per cent of schemes awarded increases above 6 per cent. So the majority of schemes were awarding real pension increases in 1986. We can also consider evidence from other sources.

Table 6.24 shows that the largest companies in the UK tend to fully compensate their pensioners for inflation. The average increase over the six years 1980–5 for the top eighty UK companies was 51.5 per cent, about 2 percentage points less than the inflation rate over the period at 53.8 per cent. But many pensioners did much better than inflation. For example, pensioners of the Dowty Group received increases of 90.3 per cent. Public-sector pensioners also did well, with increases of 64.5 per cent on average.

More recent evidence is provided in a report from Income Data Services, *Uprating Pensions in Payment* (November 1989). This report esti-

TABLE 6.24. *Company pension schemes: ten best pension increases 1980–1985*

Company	%age increase
Dowty Group	90.3
Scottish Amicable	85.1
John Lewis	76.0
BAT	71.2
Marks & Spencer	70.4
Glaxo	69.5
W. H. Smith	68.3
Barclays	66.4
Shell	66.0
Lucas (works fund)	64.9
Average (top 80 companies)	51.5
Average (public sector)	64.5
Retail price level	53.8

Note: Covers six-year calendar period from 1 January 1980; increase relates to employee who retires on 1 January 1979.

Source: *Daily Telegraph*, 11 Jan. 1986.

mates that 3.7 million individuals have inflation-proofed pensions. The average increases in pensions between 1986 and 1989 were as follows:

Year	1986	1987	1988	1989
Increase in pensions (%)	4.1	4.1	3.9	5.8
Inflation rate (%)	3.4	4.2	4.9	7.8

Comparing public- and private-sector schemes, IDS found the following pension increases:

	Public-sector pension increases (%)	Private-sector pension increases (%)
1979–81	44.8	24.4
1985–87	9.8	11.3

In the economically difficult years between 1979 and 1981, public-sector pensions were increased at nearly twice the rate of private-sector pensions on average. However, in the economically buoyant years between 1985 and 1987, private-sector pension increases were greater than those in the public sector.

With occupational pension schemes, only the proportion of the pension corresponding to the guaranteed minimum pension has to be indexed up to a maximum of 3 per cent. But IDS found that many companies index the whole of their retired employees' pensions. Only 3 per cent of schemes did not increase pensions at all following retirement, mainly the level-annuity money-purchase schemes of small companies.

With regard to the preserved pensions of early leavers, in the private sector about half of the schemes that gave increases to existing pensioners also compensated preserved pensions, though not necessarily by the same amount; the most common practice is to offer inflation indexing up to a maximum of 5 per cent. In the public sector most preserved pensions are fully indexed to the cost of living until retirement age.

6.8. Comparison with the Rest of the World

The state pension in the UK compares unfavourably with state pensions in the rest of the developed world, especially in the rest of Europe (see Chapter 4). However, when occupational pensions and the effects of differing tax regimes are taken into account, pensioners in the UK are better off than those in the USA and Germany, and only slightly worse off than those in Japan.

Table 6.25 shows net pensions as a percentage of net earnings for individuals on 1.5 times national average earnings, that is, about £22,500 in the UK in 1992. American pensioners can expect to receive 67 per cent of their net pre-retirement earnings, while German pensioners get 74 per

TABLE 6.25. *Net pensions as a percentage of net earnings: for an individual on 1.5 times national average earnings* (%)

USA	67
Germany	74
European Free Trade Association (average)	76
UK	77
Japan	79
European Union (average)	84
France	84
Italy	90
Spain	90
Netherlands	92

Source: Noble Lowndes, *Daily Telegraph*, 9 May 1992.

cent. In the UK the figure is 77 per cent, while the Japanese pensioner can expect to receive 79 per cent. However, in the rest of Europe total pension benefits are much more generous, especially in Italy, Spain, and the Netherlands, where the replacement ratios are 90 per cent or more.

6.9. Summary

- The pension depends on the salary at or near retirement and the number of years of contributions into an occupational scheme. The pension is taxable.
- The pension typically accrues at the rate of 1/60th of final salary for each year of service up to a maximum of forty years' service, thereby giving a maximum pension of two-thirds of final salary.
- Part of the pension can be commuted as a tax-free lump sum at the rate of 3/80ths of final salary for each year of service, up to a maximum of forty years' service, thereby giving a maximum lump sum of 1.5 times final salary. In this case the pension is based on the eightieths scale, with a maximum pension of half final salary.
- The pension can normally start between the ages of 50 and 75 for both men and women.
- There is an earnings limit of £60,000 (in 1989 prices) for the purpose of calculating final salary.
- The pension must be inflation-proofed up to 5 per cent p.a. compound, although the GMP component of the pension must be fully indexed to inflation, the first 3 per cent by the company, with any excess paid by the DSS.

- A spouse's pension has to be provided equal to at least 50 per cent (at most two-thirds) of the member's pension at the time of death. In the event of death in service, the member's dependants receive a pension based on actual service at the time of death.
- Contributions can be paid by both employee and employer, and are tax-deductible.
- The contributions are limited to 17.5 per cent of net relevant earnings up to the age of 50, with a maximum employee contribution of 15 per cent of net relevant earnings; higher limits apply above this age.
- Income and capital gains on the investment in the scheme accumulate free of income and capital-gains taxes, although overseas taxes on overseas investments may have to be paid.

7

Personal Pension Schemes

Personal pension schemes are pension schemes that are organized for individuals or groups of individuals by financial institutions such as banks and insurance companies rather than by the companies for which these individuals work. The pensions offered by such schemes are generally related to the contributions that are paid into them, and as such are known as *defined-contribution* pensions. By 1993 about 5 million people were contributing towards a personal pension scheme, about 25 per cent of those eligible to take out a scheme, but 85 per cent of those likely to benefit most from doing so. Before 1988, the year in which personal pension schemes were introduced, 95 per cent of pension schemes were salary-related. Between 1988 and 1993, 30 per cent of new schemes were personal pension schemes; during 1993 as many as 75 per cent of new schemes were personal pension schemes. In this chapter we discuss some of the main features of personal pension schemes in the United Kingdom.

7.1. The Introduction of Personal Pension Schemes

7.1.1. DEFINED-BENEFIT VERSUS DEFINED-CONTRIBUTION SCHEMES

Pension schemes can be classified according to whether they deliver pensions on the basis of *defined benefits* or on the basis of *defined contributions*.

In recent years in Britain, and as we saw in Chapter 6, most pensions have been of the defined-benefit type. This means that the pensioner receives a pension that is related to some measure of his or her salary at retirement, such as his or her final salary or average salary. The reason for this is clear. Pensions were originally viewed as a relief from poverty. Later they came to be viewed as a form of *income replacement*. This implied that pensioners should be able to sustain in retirement a standard of living similar to that which they enjoyed before retirement. Therefore, in order to guarantee this standard of living pensions were related to salary at retirement. Both occupational pension schemes and SERPS offer defined-benefit schemes.

Another important implication of defined-benefit schemes is that the pension benefit is independent of both the level of contributions made into the scheme and the investment returns on those contributions. If the scheme makes a deficit, the employer (in the case of occupational pension schemes) or the state (in the case of SERPS, the State Earnings-Related Pension Scheme) has to make deficiency payments sufficient to pay the required pensions. If, on the other hand, the scheme makes a surplus, this surplus is legally owned by the employer or the state and does not belong to the pensioners. In the 1980s occupational pension schemes built up substantial surpluses and the 1986 Finance Act placed a limit on the size of these surpluses.

Defined-benefit pensions are nevertheless a fairly recent innovation. Historically, defined-contribution pensions were much more important. Such pensions are based solely on the accumulation of contributions and the rate of return on those contributions. In other words, a fund will be built up while the person is employed. When that person retires the fund will be used to purchase an annuity from a life-assurance company. This annuity will continue until the death of the pensioner. Defined-contribution schemes are also known as *money-purchase* schemes, because once the annuity has been purchased with the accumulated sum of money, it is generally fixed in nominal terms, whatever subsequently happens to the rate of inflation.

A number of factors led to a decline in the popularity of money-purchase schemes during the twentieth century. First, inflation (and especially the huge bout of inflation after the First World War) led to continuous and often substantial declines in the real values of money-purchase pensions. Secondly, if an employee had to take early retirement, say, through ill health, he might not have built up sufficient contributions to buy an adequate pension, so there was some chance that the pensioner could suffer not only ill health but also a very low pension.

Nevertheless, defined-contribution pensions have made a comeback in recent years under new names: *personal pensions* and *portable pensions*. The motivating force behind this renaissance was the right-wing Centre for Policy Studies (CPS), which published a policy document entitled *Personal and Portable Pensions for All* in 1983. The CPS, in wishing to encourage not only individual freedom and choice but also job-mobility at a time of very high unemployment, argued that employees should be allowed to take out personal pensions as an alternative to belonging to their employer's occupational pension scheme. In his Budget speech in March 1987 the chancellor, Mr Nigel Lawson, talked of 'wider pension ownership' and the role of tax reliefs in extending 'popular capitalism' to the area of pensions, as they had done earlier in the decade with 'wider home ownership' and 'wider share ownership'.

7.1.2. THE 1986 SOCIAL SECURITY ACT

The right to take out a defined-contribution pension was enshrined in the 1986 Social Security Act. Personal pension schemes first became available on 1 July 1988, although it was possible to bring forward the starting date of membership to the beginning of the previous tax year. To encourage the take-up of personal pension schemes, the government introduced an incentive bonus for people starting a scheme between 1987–8 and 1992–3 with a reduced incentive bonus between 1993–4 and 1995–6 (see Section 7.5.1 below). Membership of company pension schemes became entirely voluntary from 6 April 1988. Employers could no longer oblige new employees to join their pension schemes as a condition of employment. In addition, existing employees who were members of the employer's scheme could opt out. Employers could set up a new type of occupational pension scheme, based only on contributions.

Existing defined-benefit or final-salary schemes continued to be contracted out of SERPS so long as they provided both a guaranteed minimum pension and a widow/er's pension. But since 1 July 1988 defined-contribution or money-purchase schemes can also be contracted out of SERPS so long as they have collected a minimum level of contributions (such schemes are known as *appropriate personal pension schemes*). Until this date money-purchase schemes were not eligible for contracting out of SERPS. The government's objective was to allow employers to establish their own pension schemes outside SERPS but without having to incur the costs and risks associated with an open-ended final-salary scheme. Personal pensions were therefore open to both the 10.5 million members of SERPS and the 11 million members of occupational schemes.

In order to be accepted as 'appropriate' under the 1986 act and hence issued with an *appropriate scheme certificate* by the Occupational Pensions Board, a personal pension scheme must have as its sole purpose the provision of retirement benefits, death-in-service benefits, spouses' benefits, and so on. There can be no access to benefits in any other circumstances. In particular, there can be no powers to surrender the benefits or assign them to a third party. In addition, the pension must be payable for the life of the member once he has retired, or for a guaranteed period in the event of his death before retirement. The personal pension scheme must be provided by an authorized provider who must offer *standard packages* without any variation from the form agreed with the Inland Revenue. Individual investment packages in which the beneficiary personally directs the investment plan were not permitted by the 1986 act, on the grounds that it would be impossible to ensure that the assets were used solely for the purpose of providing pensions.

However, this was changed by the 1989 Finance Act (see Section 7.4.3 below).

Any person is eligible to take out a personal pension scheme so long as he or she is in employment or self-employed and not already a member of a *sponsored superannuation scheme* in relation to that employment, that is, a general occupational scheme in which an employer makes some contribution to the scheme. However, it is possible to take out a personal pension scheme if the occupational pension scheme to which he or she belongs provides only widow/er's or dependants' pensions or a lump sum on death in service. Further, anyone taking out a personal pension still retains any SERPS benefits that he or she has accumulated.

Employees now have the following personal pension choices which are independent of their employer's scheme (they are discussed in more detail in Section 7.4 below). They can have:

- an appropriate personal pension scheme (also known as a *minimum-contribution* or *rebate-only personal pension scheme*), which is contracted out of SERPS and stands in place of SERPS benefits only; or
- an appropriate personal pension scheme that is also contracted out of SERPS but, as a result of higher contribution-rates, provides more generous benefits than under the above scheme.

Individuals can be members of occupational schemes *and* have personal pensions only in the following circumstances:

- the occupational scheme provides only a widow/er's or dependant's pension and/or a lump sum on death in service;
- the occupational scheme is contracted into SERPS and an appropriate personal pension scheme based only on minimum contributions is used to replace SERPS benefits only (known as a *contracted-in money-purchase* scheme); or
- members of occupational pension schemes can use personal pension schemes for the purpose of receiving transfer payments from previous schemes.

On 1 July 1988, just as personal pension schemes were introduced, so *retirement annuity contracts* or *section 226 schemes* (named after section 226 of the Income and Corporation Taxes Act 1970 in which they were first introduced) for the self-employed and for employees not in occupational pension schemes were withdrawn. Such people can now take out their own personal pension schemes, in the latter case by opting out of SERPS. Section 226 schemes were the predecessors of personal pension schemes, and much of the legislation relating to personal pension schemes was derived from that relating to these retirement annuity contracts.

7.2. **The Legal Structure of Personal Pension Schemes**

7.2.1. THE INLAND REVENUE'S MODEL RULES

Most personal pension schemes have been set up using the Inland Revenue's *model rules*, since any scheme adopting the model rules is automatically granted contracting-out approval from SERPS. Under the model rules, the pension scheme can either be put *in trust* or formed using a *deed poll*. Both methods give beneficiaries enforceable rights in the event of the pension-holder's death, but in the first case the benefits do not form part of the pension-holder's estate, whereas in the second case they do.

7.2.2. TRUSTEES

If a personal pension scheme has been put in trust, one or more *trustees* will have to be appointed. One of the trustees will generally be the scheme member himself. This is because the scheme provides for a pension and decisions about how and when to take this remain under the control of the scheme member. Also, the pension in payment and the tax-free lump sum are personal to the scheme member and cannot be assigned.

The structure of the trust is important in determining what happens to death benefits when the scheme member dies. There are two main types of trust that can be used: a *discretionary trust* and an *interest-in-possession trust*. In both cases it is advisable to have more than one trustee in addition to the scheme member, so that death benefit can be paid to or through the surviving trustee without having to wait for probate. Also in both cases, if there is a widow/er's benefit, it can go only to a legally married wife or dependant. Any lump sum can go to whoever is nominated as a beneficiary by the scheme member in the *expression of wishes* or *nomination statement*, but must be used to buy an annuity. Similarly, if the personal pension scheme has been used to contract out of SERPS, the protected rights, although they cannot be assigned, can still be subject to discretionary disposal conditions in accordance with the trust deeds.

So long as a discretionary trust is drawn up in a way that makes it identical with the type of trust used for pension schemes approved under sections 590–612 of the 1988 Income and Corporation Taxes Act, the trustees have fairly wide powers of discretion in awarding death benefits. Further, there is no interest in possession, so that if trustees change the beneficiary of death benefits away from the individual nominated by the member during his lifetime (which they are entitled to do in a discretionary trust, the expression of wishes or nomination statement providing only a non-binding guide to trustees), there is no inheritance-tax liability, provided the change occurs within two years of death.

With interest-in-possession trusts, the beneficiaries are entitled to the income produced by the trust. This means that the beneficiaries own the capital in the trust, which must be included in their estates for inheritance-tax purposes. Every appointment of a new potential beneficiary reduces the entitlement of the current beneficiaries (in effect, a *potentially exempt transfer* for inheritance-tax purposes occurs), but does not eliminate their inheritance-tax liability, unless they survive for a further seven years.

7.3. The Financial Structure of Personal Pension Schemes

7.3.1. INVESTMENT VEHICLES FOR PERSONAL PENSION SCHEMES

There are three basic types of investment vehicle for personal pension schemes, and the schemes are known as: (i) endowment schemes; (ii) unit-linked schemes; and (iii) deposit administration schemes. They differ according to the method of accumulating and distributing investment returns.

7.3.1.1. *Endowment Schemes*

Endowment schemes are based on *endowment-assurance contracts* with either *with-profits* or *non-profit* options.

The with-profits schemes provide guaranteed benefits at retirement, although the guaranteed benefit is typically only a nominal sum. However, the guaranteed benefits are enhanced by *reversionary bonuses* and *terminal bonuses* which depend on the profitability of the scheme's investments. The reversionary bonuses are usually awarded on an annual basis, and once awarded cannot be withdrawn. The reversionary bonus rates are generally quite stable and do not reflect the exact performance of the scheme's investments in the year that they are awarded. If the bonuses are *simple* bonuses, they are expressed as a percentage of guaranteed benefits; if they are *compound*, they are expressed as a percentage of guaranteed benefits and previously accumulated reversionary bonuses. The terminal bonuses are not added until the scheme matures, and then only if justified by investment performance during the final year of the scheme.

Non-profit schemes aim to give a more guaranteed return than with-profits schemes. They therefore invest in a safer range of assets than with-profits schemes: mainly fixed-interest securities such as government bonds. As a consequence, they have less upside potential.

Endowment schemes can operate a whole range of charges, such as

- an initial charge or capital levy (see Section 7.3.4);
- a management fee;
- an administration fee;
- an annual management charge;
- unit allocation variations which depend on: age at entry, term to selected retirement date, contribution payment frequency, and/or contribution amount.

7.3.1.2. *Unit-Linked Schemes*

There are two main types of *unit-linked scheme*: *unit-trust schemes* and *unitized with-profits schemes* (also called *unit-linked personal pension schemes*).

With unit-trust schemes contributions are used to buy units in one or more unit trusts. These are the most risky type of scheme, since the amount of pension that can be purchased depends entirely on the value of the units on the retirement date: nothing is locked in prior to this date. However, associated with the greater risk is the prospect of greater return, and over the long term unit-trust schemes typically out-perform with-profits endowment schemes by a substantial amount. The value of the unit-trust scheme at retirement depends on both the performance of the investments and the charges made by the management company operating the scheme. The charges made by unit-trust schemes are simply a bid-offer spread (the difference between the price that unit-trusts will buy units from scheme members and the higher price that they will sell units to members) and an annual fund-management fee, ranging from 1.5 per cent for equity funds, through 1.25 per cent for bond funds, to 0.75 per cent for cash funds. The maximum commission is 4 per cent. The main providers of these schemes are Rothschild Asset Management, Professional Life, Gartmore, and Societé Generale Touche Remnant.

Unitized with-profits schemes are a hybrid between unit trusts and with-profits endowment schemes offered by insurance companies. Each contribution is used to buy units in the underlying fund. But at the end of each year the increase in the fund is allocated to scheme members in the form of a bonus and, once allocated, cannot be withdrawn. The bonus will go up and down in line with the growth rate achieved, although some schemes offer a minimum bonus of 4 per cent p.a. Commission rates are likely to be at least 50 per cent of the premium in the first year.

7.3.1.3. *Deposit Administration Schemes*

The safest type of scheme is a *deposit administration scheme*: with this the investments are held in an interest-bearing deposit account paying variable-rate interest gross of tax. Although interest rates vary with market conditions, some schemes offer guarantees. The guarantee can take the form of a minimum interest rate, for example, 4 per cent p.a. throughout the term of the scheme. Alternatively, a higher rate can be guaranteed for a fixed number of years.

Charges with deposit administration schemes typically involve crediting a lower rate of interest throughout the term of the scheme, instead of a fixed charge paid from the initial contributions. While deposit administration schemes are safe, they are likely to offer significantly lower returns over the long term compared with the other schemes above.

7.3.2. PROVIDERS OF PERSONAL PENSION SCHEMES

Personal pension schemes can be provided by life-assurance companies or friendly societies; unit trusts; building societies; and banks. Before the passing of the 1986 Social Security Act, retirement-annuity business could only be offered by insurance companies and friendly societies. Insurance companies have been providing personal pensions to the self-employed since 1956.

Insurance companies typically provide with-profits and non-profit endowment schemes; unit trusts provide unit-linked schemes; and building societies provide deposit administration schemes; banks can provide any of these schemes so long as they have a relationship with a relevant institution, for example, a unit-trust subsidiary.

While banks, building societies, and unit-trust groups have been able to join life-assurance companies in providing personal pensions since 1988, the evidence by 1990 indicated that the predominant position of the life companies had remained largely unchallenged. There were more than 100 life offices offering personal pension schemes in 1990.

The slow growth in direct provision by banks, building societies, and unit-trust groups has been for two main reasons. First, with the market saturated with insurance companies, the market share that has been achieved by new entrants has been quite small. Secondly, the costs of setting up a retail pensions business are high.

However, some of these alternative providers have achieved indirect access into the lucrative personal-pension market, and hence avoided high set-up costs. For example, UBS International Investment (formerly Phillips and Drew Fund Management), the second largest corporate pension-fund manager, manages the pension funds of Acumax, the life-assurance company owned by American Express. Twelve unit-trust groups sell their personal pension schemes through Skandia Life. Fidelity was one of the few unit-trust groups to enter the retail market directly in July 1988; but in August 1993 it sold its personal-pension business to Professional Life (a subsidiary of Skandia Life). Similarly, Gartmore sells its unit-linked pension schemes through Swiss Life. The N. M. Rothschild unit-trust group sells its unit trusts through independent intermediaries. Mercury established its own life company to offer personal pensions; this helped it reduce charges and also allowed it to offer services that only a life office could offer.

On retirement the accumulated savings (which, as with all pension schemes, accumulate free of taxes on income and capital gains) must be used to purchase an annuity from either an insurance company or a friendly society. The scheme must provide the member with an *open-market option* to buy the annuity from an insurance company or a friendly society of his choice and not just the insurance company or friendly society that provided the initial scheme.

Marks and Spencer, the retail chain store, began providing personal pension schemes in 1995 using consultancy and systems support from the Equitable Life Assurance Society.

7.3.3. CATEGORIES OF ASSETS FOR PERSONAL PENSION SCHEMES

When personal pension schemes first started the categories of eligible securities that could be invested in were quite restrictive, mainly quoted UK shares and investment trusts. This was changed by the 1989 Finance Act. It became possible to invest in overseas shares, unquoted UK shares, unit trusts, gilts, and commercial property. The 1990 and 1991 Finance Acts also allowed schemes' transactions in futures and options contracts to be exempt from taxation.

Scheme providers can operate a range of funds specializing in different sectors, and scheme members can usually switch between funds for a small fee. A sophisticated investor could, therefore, switch from one fund to another to benefit from higher expected performance, or to switch into the *cash fund* to protect the investment. Alternatively, the investor might select a *managed fund* in which the investments are moved from one fund to another as opportunities change at the discretion of the fund managers. Sun Life Assurance Company, for example, has eighteen funds to choose from, as listed below:

Pension Managed Fund
The *Pension Managed Fund* has a broad portfolio with freedom to take world-wide holdings in properties, equities, fixed-interest securities, and cash by investing in units of other Sun Life Funds. The emphasis is normally placed on equity investment with the prime objective of capital appreciation as well as a high level of security.

With Profits Fund
The *With Profits Fund* is invested in Sun Life's conventional pension investment portfolio.

Not less than 90% of the declared surplus will be allocated to provide bonuses, at Sun Life's discretion.

The bid price of each unit in the With Profits Fund remains constant after allocation, and when a bonus is declared additional bonus units are added, depending on the number of units held and the length of time they have been held since the last declaration.

Currently, on retirement or death before retirement, a terminal bonus is added to the total bid value of the units. This is calculated as a percentage of your bonus units, and is dependent on the duration of your most recent participation in the Fund.

UK Funds

The *Pension Building Society Fund* provides security and the best rates of interest the managers can obtain. The Fund is invested mainly in building societies, though other deposit-type investments may also be included.

The *Pension Property Fund* is invested in high quality commercial and industrial properties able to attract good tenants and command high rents over the long term.

The *Pension Equity Fund* is invested in ordinary shares of companies, and benefits from capital growth and increases in dividends in times of industrial and commercial growth.

The *Pension Fixed-Interest Fund* holds fixed-income stocks. Prices of such securities fluctuate, and are influenced by changes in other rates of interest as well as investors' expectations regarding future inflation rates.

The *Pension Index-linked Fund* holds index-linked, gilt-edged stocks. It is attractive to investors who want long-term protection from inflation.

The *Pension Cash Fund* offers a temporary home for investment funds when markets are uncertain. It is invested in banks and local authority deposits, treasury bills and the discount and similar markets.

Funds Invested Overseas

The *Pension European Fund* is invested mainly in ordinary shares traded on the stockmarkets of Europe. Fixed-interest securities may also be held.

The *Pension American Equity Fund* is invested in ordinary shares in one of the world's largest investment markets—the US and Canada.

The *Pension US Bonds Fund* holds mainly US government bonds, though US corporate bonds may also be held.

The *Pension Japan Fund* holds mainly ordinary shares but has the flexibility to invest in other assets.

The *Pension Pacific Fund* is mostly invested in ordinary shares quoted in Australia, Singapore, Malaysia and Hong Kong (but not Japan).

The *Pension Far Eastern Fund* invests in the markets available to both the Pacific and Japan Funds. It offers the opportunity to invest in the growing economies of the Far Eastern countries.

The *Pension International Fund* is invested in overseas markets, particularly the US. The aim is to secure long-term capital growth, together with security and stability from a balanced portfolio.

Currency Funds

The *Pension US Dollar Fund*, the *Pension Yen Fund* and the *Pension European Currency Fund* all invest in their respective currencies, providing an opportunity for investors to 'hedge' against sterling whilst maintaining liquidity.[1]

In the with-profits fund, unit prices remain constant over time. With the other funds, unit prices fluctuate. The managed fund is generally regarded as the most suitable for risk-averse investors.

7.3.4. COMMISSION CHARGES

All personal pension schemes involve commission or management charges, and these can be quite high. An initial transfer into a personal scheme might involve costs as high as 25 per cent of the transfer value, with annual commissions of up to 2.5 per cent of the annual premium. This works out, according to the Institute of Actuaries, to commissions varying between 10 per cent and 20 per cent of annual premiums; in contrast, the equivalent costs of running an occupational pension scheme work out at between 5 per cent and 7 per cent of annual premiums. Commissions on a single-premium scheme might only be 4 per cent of the premium, however.

Commissions paid by insurance companies to independent financial intermediaries have increased since the abolition of LAUTRO's maximum commission agreement in December 1989. LAUTRO (the Life Assurance and Unit Trust Regulatory Organization) is the self-regulatory organization for the life-assurance and unit-trust industries established by the 1986 Financial Services Act. LAUTRO has estimated that the commission paid on a twenty-five-year personal pension scheme with monthly premiums of £50 was £366 in 1990, compared with £300 in 1989.

Sometimes the management charges are disguised. This is particularly the case with unit-linked pension schemes. The common practice amongst insurance companies offering unit-linked schemes is to have two classes of units: *accumulation* (or ordinary) *units* and *capital* (or initial) *units*. The capital units carry a much larger share of the costs of managing a pension scheme. This is because there is an annual charge on the capital units (sometimes called a *capital levy*) throughout the life of the scheme (although with some schemes capital units can be converted to accumulation units at the scheme member's *nominated retirement age*, at which time the annual charge ceases). In contrast, there is only an *initial charge* on the accumulation units.

Typically, the first two years' premiums into a scheme (as well as the

---

[1] Sun Life Assurance Society PLC, *Pensions: Light on the Legislation*, Aug. 1987.

first two years of any increase in premiums) are allocated to capital units, although transfer values and single-premium contributions are usually allocated to accumulation units. The annual charge on capital units is generally between 3 per cent and 3.5 per cent of the current value of the units. If only one year's contributions are allocated to capital units, then the annual charge might be as high as 6 per cent. In addition, there is an annual management (or administration) charge of between 0.75 per cent and 1.75 per cent of the value of the fund, and a bid-offer spread on units of around 5 per cent. These charges are extracted by cancelling capital units. The contributions are invested in these units at the *offer price* and, at the *nominated retirement date* (also known as the *vesting date*), the units are cashed in at the *bid price* ruling at that time.

The different effects of accumulation and capital units are shown in the example in Table 7.1. The table shows that the effects of the charges on the capital units can have a striking effect on the overall value of the units after thirty years: £9,890 for capital units and £24,252 for accumulation units. In essence, this is the difference between a 10 per cent investment growth rate and an effective growth rate of 6.5 per cent.

The main alternatives to capital units are reduced allocation units and recurring single premium contracts. With *reduced allocation units*, individuals receive a smaller allocation of units in the early years of a scheme.

TABLE 7.1. *The effect of management charges on unit-linked pension schemes (£)*

Value of units after no. of years	Capital units	Accumulation units
10	3,233	4,327
20	5,654	10,244
30	9,890	24,252

Notes: The figures assume:
- that £1,000 is allocated to both capital and accumulation units at the start of each of the first two years;
- an investment growth rate of 10% p.a.;
- a bid-offer spread of 5%;
- that initial charges are 5% for accumulation units and 0.75% for capital units;
- an annual capital levy of 3.5% for capital units.

Source: Equitable Life Assurance Society, *Daily Telegraph*, 18 Oct. 1986.

A typical scheme might have a 70 per cent allocation in the first two years, so that of every £100 of monthly contributions, only £70 will be invested. Some schemes are even more costly than this with zero allocation in year one and only a 25 per cent allocation in each of years two and three. *Recurring single premium contracts* have the lowest charges of all. This is because they are simply a series of single premium pension schemes and hence carry no extra initial charge other than a 5 per cent bid-offer spread. To illustrate the differences, a £200 per month, 25-year scheme taken out by a 35 year old male when there was a 10 per cent annual return on investments and a 5 per cent bid-offer spread would generate a fund value of £236,000 at age 60 with recurring single premiums, £223,000 with reduced allocation units, and only £212,000 with capital units.

The cost of taking out a section 32 buy-out policy (see section 7.4.7) can also be expensive in terms of commissions. Up to 15 per cent of any transfer value into a section 32 scheme can be taken up by initial charges. Annual commission can be 4 per cent of the annual premium.

7.3.5. SURRENDER VALUES

When someone takes out a personal pension scheme, he or she normally has to nominate a particular retirement date. The difference between the nominated retirement date and the current date fixes the term of the scheme. The scheme provider's investment strategy is designed to deliver a particular fund value on the nominated retirement date and not before. The nominated retirement date becomes the maturity date of the scheme. Scheme members have to make the planned contributions in due time in order for the scheme's providers to achieve their objective. If scheme members cease making contributions before the maturity date and request a return on their investment, they are likely to find that their scheme has a very low *surrender value*.

This is particularly the case for with-profits endowment schemes. Even if the scheme is surrendered only one year before maturity, the surrender value can be substantially below the maturity value. This is because the terminal bonus, which is only awarded if the scheme is maintained until the maturity date, can be very high. Table 7.2 shows the relationship between surrender values and maturity values on with-profits endowment schemes provided by a range of insurance companies. The average terminal bonus is 52.7 per cent of the maturity value, while the average surrender value after twenty-four years of contributing to the scheme is 26.9 per cent less than the maturity value, a value that could be achieved by making contributions for just one more year. There is quite a large

TABLE 7.2. *Surrender values on 25-year with-profits endowment schemes*

Scheme	Maturity value (£)	Terminal bonus as %age of maturity value	Surrender value after 24 years (£)	Surrender value as %age of maturity value
Clerical Medical	41,046	55.6	35,007	85.3
Commercial Union	41,308	29.8	25,862	62.6
Crusader	31,676	48.0	25,812	81.5
Eagle Star	42,067	42.0	35,468	84.3
Equitable Life	33,621	52.4	30,517	90.8
Equity & Law	42,429	63.0	36,029	84.9
Friends' Provident	42,668	57.3	16,447	38.5
General Accident	42,154	52.2	34,867	82.7
GRE	30,928	51.1	26,051	84.2
LAS	35,176	60.9	12,850	36.5
Legal & General	40,421	46.1	32,580	80.6
London Life	37,875	54.0	15,848	41.8
National Mutual	34,207	57.1	13,592	39.7
NPI	31,489	58.2	28,916	91.8
Norwich Union	42,165	45.8	36,867	87.4
Pearl	38,068	63.3	15,556	40.9
Provident Mutual	31,517	53.1	27,471	87.2
Prudential	40,805	56.2	35,768	87.7
Royal Life	32,738	40.6	17,524	53.5
Royal London	42,418	49.6	30,942	72.9
Scottish Amicable	42,158	61.1	34,602	82.1
Scottish Equitable	30,399	50.4	13,345	43.9
Scottish Life	40,109	58.7	34,840	86.9
Scottish Mutual	33,674	50.0	27,318	81.1
Scottish Provident	37,726	51.0	27,874	73.9
Scottish Widows	40,137	52.8	36,222	90.2
Standard Life	43,914	63.0	38,550	87.8
Sun Alliance	35,932	49.6	24,897	69.3
Sun Life	30,830	54.8	24,472	79.4
Average	37,574	52.7	27,452	73.1

Note: Assumptions: male, aged 29, £20 per-month gross premium.

Source: Money Marketing, *Daily Telegraph*, 1 June 1991.

range of variation. The LAS surrender value is only 36.5 per cent of the maturity value, while the NPI surrender value is only 8 per cent below the maturity value.

Surrender values are particularly low if a personal pension scheme is terminated after only a short period of operation. For example, if a scheme is terminated after only one year, the individual might lose 90 per cent of his contributions, because the commissions paid to sales-people are front-end loaded. The individual would lose 40 per cent of his contributions if the scheme was terminated within two years. For example, with the Prudential, premiums of £50 per month would produce a surrender value after two years of £800, compared with total contributions of £1,200. It would not be until the fifth year that the surrender value (£3,300) exceeded contributions (£3,000). However, with rebate-only personal pension schemes the surrender value exceeds contributions from the first year on.

The widespread dissatisfaction with the commissions charged on personal pension schemes led the government to introduce statutory regulations from 1 July 1990, requiring providers of personal pension schemes to publish information on surrender values and the commissions earned by salespeople. All new schemes must indicate the proportion of contributions paid as commission to salespeople and the surrender values in each of the first five years.

However, there was still concern about the high front-end loading of commissions and in July 1993 the Treasury ordered the Securities and Investments Board to prepare a new set of disclosure rules. The Treasury explained: 'The required changes are new rules which will provide a clear and quantified account of the effect of life offices' practices on the value of the policy if cashed in early. New rules will require illustrations of projected returns on life policies using life offices' own recent charges— not industry standard assumptions. Adaptation of the best advice regime [is needed] to allow ... proposals for the automatic disclosure of commission in cash terms at an early stage by all distribution channels.' The new disclosure rule came into force at the beginning of 1995. Commissions have to be disclosed in cash rather than as a percentage of premiums or as a reduction in investment yield; information about the cost of early surrender must also be provided. For example, a life company has to declare that a £50 per month, 25-year endowment scheme might cost £516 initial commission and another £327 over the full term. In addition, if the policy is surrendered within the first six years, there might be no refund of premiums because of penalties and charges.

7.3.6. TRANSFER PENALTIES

Any transfer value into a personal pension scheme or between schemes will be invested in a single lump sum (known as a *single premium*) in one of the three types of schemes: endowment, unit-linked, or deposit administration.

Despite the supposed portability of personal pension schemes, transfers between schemes can be very expensive even for transfers between schemes offered by the same pension-scheme provider. The cost of the transfer can be as much as one-third of the transfer value. For example, Standard Life and Sun Life charge one-third of the transfer value for transfers between their group personal pension schemes and their individual personal pension schemes.

A few schemes, however, have no penalties on transfer to the schemes of other providers. An example is Rothschild Asset Management. Its prospective transfer values for single lump-sum contributions and for monthly contributions are shown in Tables 7.3 and 7.4. These transfer values, which were calculated according to LAUTRO rules, must be paid into another pension scheme and cannot be paid directly to the pension-scheme member. Any transfers will not count for the purpose of Inland Revenue limits on contributions.

7.3.7. INVESTOR PROTECTION

Along with the introduction of personal pension schemes on 1 July 1988 came a whole set of investor-protection rules on product disclosure, best advice for the circumstances of the individual, and cooling-off periods under the auspices of the 1986 Financial Services Act.

TABLE 7.3. *Transfer value of a single lump-sum contribution* (£)

Total contribution including tax credit	Transfer value at end of year				
	1	2	3	4	5
500	520.04	569.36	623.35	682.46	747.18
1,000	1,040.08	1,138.72	1,246.70	1,364.92	1,494.36
1,500	1,560.12	1,708.08	1,870.05	2,047.38	2,241.54
2,000	2,080.16	2,277.44	2,493.40	2,729.84	2,988.72

Note: The figures assume:
- an investment return of 10.75% p.a.;
- an initial management charge of 5% of contributions and a monthly management charge equivalent to 1% p.a. + VAT. Regular contributions are monthly in advance;
- a bid-offer spread of 5%;
- that the basic-rate tax credit is invested at the same time as the contributions; in practice, however, there will be a delay.

Source: Rothschild Asset Management, 1987.

TABLE 7.4. *Transfer value of monthly contributions* (£)

Total contribution including tax credit	Transfer value at end of year				
	1	2	3	4	5
50	598.87	1,254.54	1,972.38	2,758.30	3,618.74
100	1,197.74	2,509.08	3,944.76	5,516.60	7,237.48
150	1,796.61	3,763.62	5,917.14	8,274.90	10,856.22
200	2,395.48	5,018.16	7,889.52	11,033.20	14,474.96

Note: Assumptions as for Table 7.3.

Source: Rothschild Asset Management, 1987.

All investment companies offering investment advice or marketing investment products must:

- be authorized by a *self-regulatory organization* (SRO) or by the Securities and Investments Board (SIB);
- be solvent, honest, and competent;
- always give the best advice to their clients and execute instructions from their clients on the best possible terms;
- keep clients' money in separate accounts; and
- have a proper complaints procedure.

Investors can sue investment companies if they do not abide by these requirements.

Under the Financial Services (Cancellation) Rules 1988, an individual who applies to take out a personal pension has the right to cancel the application up to fourteen days after the application has been accepted. The individual will receive a refund of any contributions made. Nevertheless, individuals should be aware of unscrupulous salespeople, since after the fourteen-day cooling-off period agreements are legally binding, whether or not they are what was originally intended. An example was reported in the national press in September 1991 of an individual who thought that the personal pension scheme that he took out involved a single-premium investment of £5,000, with discretionary additional payments; this would have involved a salesperson's commission of 4 per cent of the investment. In reality, however, the agreement was for annual premium payments of £5,000 for eight years, which involved commissions to the salesperson of 60 per cent of the first year's premium. The individual made three annual payments totalling £15,000 before letting the scheme lapse with a surrender value of only £8,000.

7.4. Types of Personal Pension Scheme

In this section we examine the most important types of personal pension scheme operating in the UK.

7.4.1. APPROPRIATE PERSONAL PENSION SCHEMES

An *appropriate personal pension scheme* is one that has been approved for contracting out of SERPS. When an individual starts an appropriate personal pension scheme, contributions are allocated to two separate funds: a *protected rights fund* and a *personal fund*.

The protected rights fund contains the national-insurance rebates and the 2 per-cent (subsequently reduced to 1 per-cent) government incentive payments (if applicable; see Section 7.5.1 below). This fund is used to provide the *protected rights pension* which is equivalent to the SERPS pension given up. The protected rights pension is therefore similar to the SERPS pension:

- it cannot be taken before state-pension age (65 for men and 60 for women);
- it cannot be commuted for a cash lump sum, unless the total pension provided by the scheme is below £104 p.a.;
- if the scheme member dies before pension payments commence, the protected rights fund must be used to buy a pension for the spouse if the spouse is 45 or over, or has dependent children;
- if the scheme member dies after the protected rights pension has started, the spouse will receive a pension of 50 per cent of the member's pension if the spouse is 45 or over, or has dependent children;
- if there is no spouse aged 45 or over, or no dependent children, then the value of the fund is payable in a lump sum to the beneficiary nominated by the member or to his or her estate if no beneficiary is named;
- the protected rights pension must be increased by the annual rate of increase in the retail price index up to a maximum of 3 per cent per annum. If prices go up by more than 3 per cent per year the DSS will increase the state pension to compensate.

Additional contributions by both employees and employers are placed in the personal fund. The additional contributions can be in the form of a single premium or regular premiums.

7.4.2. REBATE-ONLY PERSONAL PENSION OR CONTRACTED-IN MONEY-PURCHASE SCHEMES

Rebate-only (or *minimum-contribution*) *personal pension schemes* were introduced in the 1988 Finance Act. These schemes operate only a protected rights fund.

Rebate-only schemes can be taken out by anyone who is and wishes to remain a member of a contracted-in occupational pension scheme, but who wishes to leave SERPS. However, additional contributions from the employee or employer are not permitted so long as the individual remains a member of the company scheme. So the pension provided by the protected rights fund may not be sufficient to give an adequate income in retirement. These are sometimes known as *contracted-in money-purchase schemes*.

7.4.3. SELF-INVESTED PERSONAL PENSION SCHEMES

The 1989 Finance Act permitted personal-pension scheme members to manage their own investments. Such schemes are known as *self-invested personal pension schemes* (SIPPSs), or sometimes as *self-managed personal pension schemes*, *own-choice personal pension schemes*, or *self-controlled personal pension schemes*. They are an extension of the small self-administered pension schemes available to company directors and senior executives (see Section 8.3.3). By 1993, about 2,500 SIPPSs had been established with an average value of £200,000.

Existing pension providers still set up the scheme but scheme members will make their own investment selection or use the services of their own stockbroker. In other words, a SIPPS separates the administration function from the investment function. Securities from the following categories can be included in the fund: (i) shares, including overseas shares; (ii) unit and investment trusts; (iii) gilts; (iv) insurance-company managed funds and unit-linked funds; (v) deposit accounts; and (vi) commercial property.

The first SIPPS (called 'Destiny') was introduced in March 1990 by Personal Pension Management (PPM), a subsidiary of merchant bank Guinness Mahon; in 1992, PPM was bought by Provident Life to become Provident Life/PPM. The scheme is available to individuals earning in excess of £20,000 per year who invest a minimum of £3,000 per annum and who either are competent to manage their investments or have their own financial advisers. There is an initial fixed charge of £1,100, an annual fee of £350 (in 1990 prices), and no cancellation charge. The scheme can invest in any suitable investment, such as unit trusts, equities, insurance policies, or commercial property. In addition, the investments can be changed at any time. This contrasts with a conventional scheme, where the only way the individual can change the investments is to surrender the plan, receive a low surrender value, and reinvest in another plan. There are about twenty-five SIPPS providers, the most important being Pointon York and Provident Life. But Provident Life/PPM provides the pensions administration for about half the scheme providers. Prudential Holborn and Britannia Life offer a hybrid SIPPS, whereby a minimum contribution must be invested in these life companies' own funds before other investments can be made. The minimum cost-effective annual contribution for most SIPPSs is £10,000, while the minimum cost-effective lump-sum investment is between £20,000 and £30,000, although the minimum lump sum required to get a good spread of investment risk is £50,000.

The main advantage of a self-managed personal pension scheme is tax-efficiency, as the following examples show. Individuals with a substantial investment portfolio can transfer their assets into a personal pension fund. Although this might generate a capital-gains-tax liability if shares are sold into the fund at a profit, there is full income-tax relief on the value of the funds transferred. Once in the pension fund all income and capital growth from the assets will be free of tax. But the assets have to remain in the fund until retirement.

A partnership planning to buy commercial premises can do so through a SIPPS. The scheme buys the building (using a loan if necessary) and leases it back to the partners at market prices. There are two tax advantages from doing this compared with direct purchase. First, any increase in the value of the property is free of capital-gains tax. Secondly, the rent payable on the property (which must be set on commercial terms) is both a deductible expense for the partnership and income to the pension scheme, and as such grows free of tax. A partnership cannot use a SIPPS to buy its existing commercial premises, however.

Nevertheless, many pension providers appear to be opposed to self-management. For example, Ron Spill, pensions director at Legal and General, said: 'This is an investment opportunity for relatively sophisticated people.' John Woolnough, pensions development manager at Sun Life, said: 'I think it is worst advice for someone with, say, £50 a month to choose their own shares. We have always seen this as something for the more wealthy, professional type of person.' At the Prudential, national operations manager, Alan Smith, said:

Our customer base would not really be interested in managing their own pension portfolio. They much prefer that an expert manager takes the decisions ... People have enough to worry about without having to decide whether they should switch out of Japan into the United Kingdom when they get up in the morning. They may speculate with a bit of extra savings, but for the pension, they like to know that the money is safe. (Quotes from *Daily Telegraph*, 14 October 1989.)

The 1991 Finance Act introduced further restrictions on SIPPSs (and other self-administered pension schemes). Loans from a pension scheme to a business were limited to 25 per cent of the value of the fund in the first two years, and 50 per cent after two years. There was also an effective ban on investment in residential property.

An alternative to a SIPPS is to invest personal pension contributions in a single approved investment trust via a *feeder fund* (that is, a pension scheme whose trust deeds specify what the feeder invests in).

7.4.4. GROUP PERSONAL PENSION SCHEMES

A *group personal pension scheme* is simply a collection of individual personal pension schemes organized by the same employer. The individual schemes are completely portable, so employees can take them with them when they change jobs. They can also decide on an individual basis whether to use their schemes to contract into or out of SERPS.

The main advantage from the employer's position is administrative convenience. He can decide which employees belong to the group scheme, how much to contribute to the schemes of different employees (for example, instead of profit-sharing), automatically deduct employee contributions from payroll, and make a single payment to the company providing the scheme. The only information that the employer needs to provide on individual employees to the scheme provider is: their age, sex, and salary; the proportion of salary contribution from employee and employer; and their expected retirement age. Another advantage is that the employer need make no further contribution to an individual's scheme once that individual has changed employers.

The group plan allows each employee to build up his or her own portable fund independently of how often the employee changes jobs. A typical group fund will be invested in a range of sub-funds, such as a smaller companies fund, an investment trust fund, or a managed fund. However, because they are fully portable, there are few economies of scale in administration costs and so commissions are similar to those for individual schemes.

Group personal pension plans are designed for the employees of small companies with fewer than about 100 employees. There are about half-a-million such companies in the UK, and they employ most of the 6 million of what have been called Britain's 'great unpensioned'.

7.4.5. INDUSTRY-WIDE PORTABLE PENSION SCHEMES

Industry-wide portable pension schemes are designed for employees working in small companies who prefer to have a portable company pension scheme rather than a portable personal pension scheme. Examples are the Engineering Industry Pension Scheme (EIPS) and the British Clothing Industry Association's Pension Scheme (BCIAPS), both launched in 1988.

The EIPS is open to about half-a-million employees in engineering companies not operating occupational pension schemes. It is a money-purchase scheme and is administered by Friends' Provident. The contributions from both employers and employees are invested in with-profits accounts which attract annual bonuses until pension age. Death-in-service benefits are a lump sum equal to two years' earnings and a pension to the surviving spouse. If death occurs after retirement the surviving spouse receives a 50 per cent pension. Employees moving from one participating employer to another will be able to take the full transfer value of their pension with them. Employees leaving the industry will be able to put the full transfer value into their new employer's scheme or into a personal pension scheme.

The BCIAPS is open to around 200,000 employees. It is also a money-purchase scheme and is administered by Save and Prosper. The contributions from both employers and employees will be invested in unit trusts, ranging from a fixed-interest trust to an equity trust. As with standard unit trusts, there is an initial charge of 5 per cent and an annual charge of 1.25 per cent.

Proponents of industry-wide schemes claim that they have advantages over personal pension schemes. The main advantage is that economies of scale can lead to lower operating costs. Also, employers are more likely to make contributions to an industry-wide scheme than to an individual employee's personal pension scheme. Another advantage is that, with the industry-wide scheme, the national-insurance rebate is paid monthly, while with personal pensions the payment of the rebate takes about nine months. Further, industry-wide schemes usually involve free death-in-service benefits, whereas personal pension schemes do not.

7.4.6. TARGETED MONEY-PURCHASE SCHEMES

A recent innovation is the introduction of *targeted money-purchase schemes*. These are money-purchase schemes targeted on the individual needs of scheme members. Typically, they aim to target as closely as possible the pension that a member of a final-salary scheme would get on his or her chosen retirement date. This objective is achieved by a planned strategy of increasing contribution-rates and changing the asset allocation of the fund away from equities towards fixed-income securities throughout the life of the scheme.

In a conventional money-purchase scheme the individual chooses a fixed contribution-rate as a proportion of salary, and these contributions are invested in a single fund depending on the attitude to risk of the individual. The contribution-rate might be around 12 per cent of earnings and the contributions might be invested in a high-risk–high-reward equity fund if the individual is a risk-taker and a low-risk–low-reward bond fund if the individual is risk-averse. In contrast, a targeted money-purchase scheme might have an initial contribution-rate of 7 per cent of salary and be invested entirely in equities. Over time the contribution-rate increases reaching, say, 19 per cent of salary in the year before retirement. In addition, the accumulating assets in the scheme are gradually transferred into fixed-income securities. The aim is to benefit from the higher expected return on shares in the early life of the scheme but to reduce the potential volatility in the value of the fund as retirement approaches by reallocating into less-risky bonds.

This targeting strategy nevertheless remains approximate and might have difficulty in dealing with sudden and unexpected falls in asset values just prior to retirement, or with unanticipated early retirement. However, the Pension Schemes Office (PSO) has recently relaxed the funding arrangements for money-purchase schemes. It now permits trustees to operate a *reserve account*. This account is not allocated to specific members, but can be used to smooth out any volatile market values in pension assets as retirement age approaches. The reserve account, therefore, permits more accurate targeting of the benefits provided by money-purchase schemes.

7.4.7. SECTION 32 BUY-OUT POLICIES

Section 32 buy-outs are single-premium annuity bonds which are issued by insurance companies and used to invest the transfer values of early leavers from occupational pension schemes. They have been available for this purpose since 1981 (see also Section 6.4.2.5).

The 1985 Social Security Act permitted everyone leaving a pension scheme after 1 January 1986 with at least one year to normal retirement to take a buy-out if they wished. The buy-out value had to be equal to the *cash equivalent* of the preserved benefits in the departing scheme. Before 1986 trustees could either refuse a transfer to a buy-out altogether or give a smaller transfer value to buy-out than to another employer's scheme. Now they have to effect the buy-out within six months of a request by the early leaver to do so, otherwise they face penalties.

Section 32 buy-out policies provide an alternative to personal pensions for those who change jobs and do not wish to or are not able to join their new employer's occupational scheme. The pension from a section 32 policy is a guaranteed minimum pension. However, the transfer value available from the employee's former scheme might be so low that the provider of the section 32 pension might not be able to afford the guarantee and so be unwilling to issue the policy. This contrasts with a personal pension scheme, where there is no guaranteed minimum pension: the transfer value is merely given protected rights (see Section 7.5.1 below). But because, with a personal pension, resources do not have to be invested in safe but low-yielding securities in order to deliver the guaranteed pension, it is possible to end up with a higher overall pension. Nevertheless, the tax-free lump sum from a section 32 policy might be higher than with a personal pension. This is because the section 32 lump sum depends on the number of years in the scheme, whereas there is a 25 per cent upper limit on the lump sum from a personal pension scheme.

So the trade-off between a section 32 buy-out pension and a personal pension is between a potentially smaller annuity and a potentially larger lump sum.

7.5. Contributions

Personal pension schemes are subject to both minimum and maximum contributions.

The contributions into a personal pension scheme are related to *net relevant earnings* (as defined in section 646 of the 1988 Income and Corporation Taxes Act). These include salary, overtime payments, bonuses, and the taxable value of certain benefits in kind, such as company cars. For someone who is self-employed, business expenses and trading losses have to be deducted in order to arrive at net relevant earnings.

Net relevant earnings also distinguish between different sources of income. For example, an individual might receive income from both pensionable and non-pensionable employment. The individual might be a member of an occupational pension scheme in respect of his pensionable employment. Nevertheless, he can contribute up to 17.5 per cent of non-pensionable (or 'relevant') earnings into a personal pension scheme. Also, the benefits from the personal pension scheme do not count in determining the maximum benefits payable from the occupational scheme.

The premiums collected by insurance companies from personal-pension scheme members are listed in Table 7.5.

7.5.1. MINIMUM CONTRIBUTIONS

The minimum contributions (as set out in the 1986 Social Security Act) into a personal pension scheme were as follows:

TABLE 7.5. *Premiums from personal-pension scheme members collected by insurance companies, 1987–1992* (£m.)

Year	New annual premiums	New single premiums	DSS rebate
1987	414	812	—
1988	830	815	417
1989	1,084	1,805	1,472
1990	1,067	2,949	948
1991	1,119	3,973	637
1992	1,117	5,166	477

Source: Association of British Insurers, Long-Term Business Statistics, Dec. 1993.

- A rebate on employee national-insurance contributions of 2 per cent of band earnings between the lower and upper earnings limits (for employee national-insurance contributions). Employee national-insurance contributions are not tax-deductible, but the 2 per-cent rebate when made as a contribution to a personal pension scheme attracted tax relief (tax credit) at the basic rate of tax. This implied that the rebate, when grossed up for the basic rate of tax (at 25 per cent) was worth 2.67 per cent. In addition, individuals who took out a personal pension scheme between 1 July 1988 and 5 April 1989 could backdate their contributions to 6 April 1987. Between 6 April 1987 and 5 April 1988 the national-insurance rebate was 2.5 per cent and the basic rate of tax was 27 per cent, so the grossed-up rebate for that financial year was 3.42 per cent. Since April 1993 the national-insurance rebate has been 1.8 per cent or 2.4 per cent grossed up.
- A rebate on employer national-insurance contributions of 3.8 per cent of band earnings. Before 6 April 1988 the rebate was 4.1 per cent. Since April 1993 the rebate has been 3 per cent.
- A *special government incentive bonus* of 2 per cent of band earnings for six years from 1987–8 to 1992–3 on all new company schemes and personal pension schemes started during this period. The special incentive bonus must be used to enhance pension benefits. However, employees who transferred from their employer's occupational pension scheme to personal pension schemes were not eligible for the additional rebate if they had been in their employer's scheme for less than two years; the government wanted to encourage new private-sector schemes, not transfers within the private sector. In April 1993 (as a result of the 1993 Social Security Act) the 2 per-cent incentive was

abolished, but was replaced by an age-related rebate of 1 per cent for those over 30 for the following three years.

The minimum contributions into a personal pension scheme attract tax relief at the basic rate, but do not qualify for higher-rate tax relief. Having received the national-insurance contributions, the DSS will recover the tax relief on the employee's rebate from the Inland Revenue and will pay this amount annually in arrears to the pension-scheme provider, after information on employee earnings has been provided by the employer. The DSS will also pay the employee and employer rebates to the scheme provider within a few months of receiving them. In addition, the government incentive bonus is paid separately by the DSS, in the tax year following that covered by the national-insurance contributions. The minimum contribution-rates for a personal pension scheme are given in Table 7.6 for the period 1987–94.

Table 7.7 shows the value of the state's contribution to a personal pension scheme at different salary levels. For someone earning a salary of £18,200 in 1990–1 (that is, the upper earnings limit for national-insurance contributions in that year), the 2 per-cent employee's rebate and the special bonus were each worth £316.16 and the 3.8 per-cent employer's rebate was worth £600.70. In total, therefore, £1,338.93 could have been invested in a personal pension scheme at no extra cost to the individual. This is the maximum incentive paid by the state to encourage an individual to opt out of SERPS.

The procedure for paying contributions towards a personal pension scheme differs from that operating with contracted-out final-salary

TABLE 7.6. *Minimum contribution-rates into a personal pension scheme as a proportion of band earnings, 1987–1994* (%)

	1987–8	1988–9	1989–90	1990–91	1991–2	1992–3	1993–4
Employee rebate							
(gross)	3.42	2.67	2.67	2.67	2.67	2.67	2.40
(net)	(2.50)	(2.00)	(2.00)	(2.00)	(2.00)	(2.00)	(1.80)
Employer rebate	4.10	3.80	3.80	3.80	3.80	3.80	3.00
Special bonus	2.00	2.00	2.00	2.00	2.00	2.00	1.00*
TOTALS							
(gross)	9.52	8.47	8.47	8.47	8.47	8.47	6.40
(net)	(8.60)	(7.80)	(7.80)	(7.80)	(7.80)	(7.80)	(5.80)

Note: * Available only to someone aged over 30 from 1993–4 to 1995–6.

TABLE 7.7. *Government contributions to a personal pension scheme, 1990–91* (£ p.a.)

Employee earnings	National-insurance rebate*		Tax credit on rebate* (0.67% of salary)	Special bonus*† (2% of salary)	Total state contribution to personal pension scheme* (8.47% of salary)
	Employee (2% of salary)	Employer (3.8% of salary)			
5,000	52.16	99.10	17.47	52.16	220.89
7,500	102.16	194.10	34.22	102.16	432.64
10,000	152.16	289.10	50.97	152.16	644.39
12,500	202.16	384.10	67.72	202.16	856.14
18,200 or above	316.16	600.70	105.91	316.16	1,338.93

Notes: * Paid and calculated on band earnings that exceed the lower earnings limit of £2,392 p.a., but do not exceed the upper earnings limit of £18,200 p.a.; the rate of income tax was 25% in 1990–91.

† The special bonus is equivalent to 2% of the employee's gross earnings between £2,392 and £18,200 p.a.

schemes. In the latter case, employees and employers pay the lower contracted-out rate of national-insurance contributions and then pay contributions directly to their own pension scheme. With personal pensions, employees and employers pay the higher contracted-in rate of national-insurance contributions, even though the personal pension is contracted out of SERPS. The contracted-out rebate, the difference between the contracted-in and contracted-out contribution-rates between the lower and upper earnings limits, is then paid into the personal pension scheme directly by the DSS. So the minimum contribution is exactly the same as the contribution that is made into SERPS.

The DSS does not require any contributions by either employee or employer in addition to the minimum contribution made by the DSS. So employers have no statutory obligation to contribute to an employee's personal pension above the rebate. But they can make additional contributions on a voluntary basis, and they can make such payments conditional on the employee also making additional contributions. The employer can make contributions either regularly or by lump sum (for example, instead of profit-sharing). Further, the regular contributions can be indexed to prices or pay so that they keep up with inflation. The employer can deduct the employee's contributions from pay and make a single payment into the employee's scheme.

Employees have the right to leave an existing pension scheme and to have the transfer value of their existing scheme paid into a personal pension scheme. But employees do not have the right to be readmitted to their employer's scheme at a later date unless the employer agrees. However, they do have the right to re-contract into SERPS on payment of a *personal-pension protected rights premium.* 'Protected rights' is the term given in the 1986 Social Security Act to the rights over the sum that accumulates on the basis of investing the minimum contributions, together with the government's 2 per-cent (or 1 per-cent) incentive payment, if applicable; in other words, it is the portion of the personal-pension benefits that replaces the SERPS benefits.

7.5.2. MAXIMUM CONTRIBUTIONS

The 1986 Social Security Act set upper limits for contributions into personal pension schemes for the purpose of attracting tax relief on contributions (at the highest marginal rate payable by the individual). The maximum contribution-rate was set at 17.5 per cent of net relevant earnings (for both employee and employer combined), if the employee was below 50 years. Higher limits applied for older employees:

Age range	Contribution limits (% of earnings)
50 or less	17.5
51–55	20.0
56–60	22.5
61–74	27.5

The minimum DSS contribution is not included in these limits, but any additional employer's contribution above the national-insurance rebate would be.

The 1989 Finance Act increased contribution limits for those with personal pension schemes aged 36 or over:

Age range	Contribution limits (% of earnings)
35 or less	17.5
36–45	20.0
46–50	25.0
51–55	30.0
56–60	35.0
61–74	40.0

The earnings limit on which contributions qualify for tax relief was set at £60,000 (in 1989 prices), the same as for occupational schemes. Table 7.8 shows the maximum permitted contributions into a personal pension scheme in 1990–91 at different salary levels.

TABLE 7.8. *Maximum contributions to a personal pension scheme for an individual below 36, 1990–91* (£ p.a.)

Employee earnings	State contribution*	Personal contribution[†]	Total contribution
5,000	220.89	875.00	1,095.89
7,500	432.64	1,312.50	1,745.14
10,000	644.39	1,750.00	2,394.39
12,500	856.14	2,187.50	3,043.64
20,000	1,338.93	3,500.00	4,838.93
64,800[‡]	1,338.93	11,340.00	12,678.93

Notes: * 8.47% of band earnings, see Table 7.7.
  [†] 17.5% of net relevant earnings.
  [‡] Maximum salary in 1990–91 on which contributions could be calculated.

Within these limits all contributions qualify for tax relief at the highest marginal rate of income tax payable (under the Income and Corporation Taxes Act 1988). A basic-rate taxpayer pays the contributions net of basic-rate tax, but the scheme invests the gross amount of contributions by reclaiming the tax from the Inland Revenue. The higher-rate taxpayer obtains relief on the basic-rate tax in the same way, but reclaims the higher rate of tax through his tax return. For self-employed individuals or partners in a partnership, contributions are paid gross and all income-tax relief is reclaimed through the tax return. The employer's contributions are allowable against corporation tax or against income tax in the case of sole traders or partnerships.

Table 7.9 shows how tax credits on individual contributions into a

TABLE 7.9. *Tax credits available on individual contributions to a personal pension scheme, 1990–91* (£)

Net contributions	Basic-rate tax credit*	Gross contributions for basic-rate taxpayer	Additional higher-rate tax credit[†]	Gross contributions for higher-rate taxpayer
30.00	10.00	40.00	6.00	46.00
75.00	25.00	100.00	15.00	115.00
100.00	33.33	133.33	20.00	153.33
500.00	166.67	666.67	100.00	766.67

Notes: * Basic rate of income tax at 25% in 1990–91.
  [†] Higher rate of income tax at 40% in 1990–91.

personal pension scheme are calculated. Contributions to a scheme are made out of taxed income. They will be enhanced by an amount corresponding to the highest marginal rate of income tax that has been paid on the income. For a basic-rate taxpayer (at 25 per cent), the tax credit is £33.33 for each £100 of contributions (calculated as $0.25 \times £100/(1 - 0.25)$). For the basic-rate taxpayer the tax credit is automatically reclaimed from the Inland Revenue by the operators of the scheme. For a higher-rate taxpayer (at 40 per cent), the additional tax credit is £20 for each £100 of contributions (calculated as $0.15 \times £100/(1 - 0.25)$), making a total tax credit of £53.33. The additional tax credit is reclaimed from the Inland Revenue through the tax return at the end of each financial year.

7.5.3. REFUNDING EXCESS CONTRIBUTIONS AND CARRY-FORWARD AND CARRY-BACK OF CONTRIBUTIONS

The scheme provider must ensure that the maximum contribution limits are not exceeded, that is, that the scheme is not over-funded. Any excess contributions must be refunded (less tax relief already deducted). Deliberate over-funding is subject to penalties under the 1987 Finance (No. 2) Act. With occupational pension schemes it is possible for a member to receive a refund of contributions if he leaves within two years of service. This refund will not be available to members of personal pension schemes, since these schemes are not associated with any particular contract of employment.

Unused tax relief for the previous six years can be *carried forward* and used to enhance contributions in the current year. If an individual makes contributions to a personal pension scheme in a year when he has no net relevant earnings, then it is possible to *carry back* the tax relief and set contributions against earnings in the previous year.

This facility is particularly useful if there are changes in marginal tax rates during the seven years, as the following example shows. Suppose that a 35-year-old man had net relevant earnings of £45,000 and £50,000 respectively in the tax years 1987–8 and 1988–9. His highest marginal tax rates were 60 per cent and 40 per cent respectively in each of the two years. Suppose further that the man had never contributed to a pension scheme but decided to begin one with a £10,000 contribution in 1988–9. The limit for tax relief is 17.5 per cent of net relevant earnings in each tax year, that is £7,875 in 1987–8 and £8,750 in 1988–9. The man would maximize his tax relief over the two tax years by electing to allocate £7,875 of his £10,000 contributions to 1987–8 and £2,125 to 1988–9. In this way his tax liability over the two years would be reduced by £5,575 (that is, $(£7,875 \times 0.6) + (£2,125 \times 0.4)$). Instead, had he allocated £8,750 to 1988–9 and £1,250 to 1987–8, his tax liability over the two years would have reduced by only £4,250 (that is, (£1,250 × 0.6) + (£8,750 × 0.4)).

7.5.4. SELF-EMPLOYED CONTRIBUTIONS

Self-employed people who are members of personal pension schemes can claim tax relief on their contributions at their highest marginal rate of tax. This is done by presenting the Inland Revenue with a *self-employed premium certificate* (SEPC) from the insurance company or other institution managing their scheme.

The self-employed are taxed on a preceding-year basis (with the tax paid in equal instalments in January and July of the following year). This means that the tax relief on a particular year's contributions can be offset against the income from the preceding year if the individual elects to do this; an election form is sent to the Revenue at the same time as the SEPC. In addition, the self-employed can also *carry forward* unused tax-relief allowances for up to six years or *carry back* additional contributions to the preceding year. In the former case this leads to an increase in the contribution that can be paid in the current year. In the latter case the contributions can be relieved against the previous year's tax liability. In other words, the self-employed can maximize pensions tax relief across seven consecutive tax years.

From April 1996 the self-employed will be taxed on a current-year basis. They will be able to use *self-assessment* and must make a single tax payment to the government in February of the current tax year.

7.5.5. DELAYS IN RECLAIMING NATIONAL-INSURANCE REBATES

One of the main problems that have been identified with personal pension schemes is the time-delays suffered before the rebates from the government become available for investment. With personal pensions, national-insurance contributions must be paid in full and the 1.8 per-cent employee's rebate and 3 per-cent employer's rebate subsequently reclaimed. However, repayments of NICs are not made until the end of the tax year, when employers send in their national-insurance returns to the DSS. However, employers can submit annual returns at any time between April and October. The DSS takes about a month to process returns and send rebates to pension providers. This implies that NICs made in the April of one year might not be available for investment in a personal pension scheme until the November of the following year.

This contrasts with employees in a company pension scheme, who are able to pay their national-insurance contributions net of the 1.8 per-cent rebate. The employer guarantees to pay the employee's rebate, plus the employer's rebate of 3 per cent, plus any additional contributions by the employer within one month. This sum is invested as soon as it is received by the scheme's investment managers.

This rather cumbersome system for calculating and repaying the rebate can lead to both mistakes and delays. This is the conclusion of a Consumers' Association survey published in *Which?* in April 1991. The survey found that one personal-pension scheme member who should have received a rebate of £1,242 instead received only £8.99. Some scheme providers were still receiving rebates from the DSS dating from 1987–8, the first year of contracting out. The scheme provider must provide the member with an annual *protected rights allocation statement.* The Consumers' Association recommends that this statement be checked very thoroughly, since the DSS will not compensate for losses. The Association found that the problems resulted from the DSS not being able to handle the large number of people taking out schemes, and from employers giving incorrect details to the DSS, for example, on the employee's earnings or even the employee's national-insurance number.

7.5.6. PENSION INVESTMENT PROTECTION INSURANCE

There are two types of insurance that can be taken out to protect the pension investment in a personal pension scheme: *life-cover assurance* and *contribution-waiver insurance.*

If a scheme member dies before the pension is drawn, the scheme provider generally allocates to the member's account at the time of death the full bid value of his units plus any bonuses in the case of a with-profits scheme. This sum can then be used to secure benefits for the named beneficiaries of the scheme. However, if the member dies soon after the scheme is started, the sum available for dependants is likely to be very small. Most schemes allow life-cover assurance (that is, term assurance) to be taken out to protect against this possibility. Up to 5 per cent of earnings (under section 637 of the 1988 Income and Corporation Taxes Act and within the limits given in Section 7.5.2. above) can be devoted to life-cover assurance (and the contributions receive tax relief). The life cover would remain in force until either the nominated retirement age or until the pension is drawn. If the member survives until the nominated retirement age, the policy expires worthless and the member receives nothing. The life cover must be purchased from an insurance company, so even if the scheme is taken out with a building society or a unit trust, the contributions pertaining to death benefits must be handed over to an insurance company. The main death-in-service benefits are a lump sum and a minimum pension to the surviving spouse or dependent children. The life-cover benefits might be payable in addition to the bid value of the units in the scheme or inclusive of the bid value of the units to give a fixed total benefit. In either case, it is possible to write the policy in trust for the benefit of the member's dependants, thereby ensuring that the payment of benefits is free from inheritance tax. The bid value of the units is generally payable as a lump sum, with the exception of the portion of the bid value relating to the protected rights which must be used to secure a spouse's pension.

If the spouse is over 45 or there are dependent children, then the money accumulated from the state contributions to the personal pension scheme (that is, NICs, tax credits, or special bonuses) must be used to purchase a widow/er's pension on death in service. The widow's benefit can go only to a legally married wife or a dependant. The lump sum can go to whoever is nominated, but it must be used to buy an annuity. However, these benefits are, like the personal pension itself, money-related and not earnings-related, and so do not automatically increase in line with earnings. But there is no limit to the size of the lump-sum death benefits in the case of a personal pension. In addition, the more that is devoted to death-in-service benefits, the less is available for the scheme member's own pension. In contrast, with a typical occupational scheme the lump-sum death benefit is two-and-a-half times annual earnings, and can be up to four times annual earnings. Similarly, the widow/er's pension is up to half the member's salary at time of death.

Table 7.10 shows some typical monthly premiums for £50,000 of cover. For a 39-year-old male earning £20,000 per year, the maximum contribu-

TABLE 7.10. *Monthly premiums for life-cover assurance (£)*

Scheme	Age 29		Age 39		Age 49	
	Male	Female	Male	Female	Male	Female
Allied Dunbar	10.68	6.34	16.39	8.96	25.54	13.46
Crown Financial	7.50	3.75	15.00	7.12	28.50	11.62
Equitable Life	7.74	5.36	13.37	7.61	23.87	13.86
Friends' Provident	11.37	6.92	17.67	9.75	28.86	15.67
Manulife	12.19	6.94	18.19	8.81	28.69	14.44
Norwich Union	11.05	5.89	16.59	9.04	28.08	16.23

Note: Figures quoted after tax relief, for £50,000 sum assured, for a non-smoker, retiring at 65 if male, or 60 if female.

Source: *Daily Telegraph*, 9 May 1992.

tion for life cover would be £1,000 per year before tax or £750 after tax relief at 25 per cent. This sum would buy £233,800 of life cover from Equitable Life if the man planned to retire at 65. For a 29-year-old woman planning to retire at 60, the life cover would be around £410,000.

Contribution-waiver insurance is designed to give protection in the event that the member is unable to continue making regular contributions following a serious illness or a prolonged disability. The contribution waiver begins six months after a claim and continues until the age of 60, or until the member recovers. The premium for this insurance is about 2.5 per cent of earnings.

As a result of the spread of AIDS, HIV testing has become more common before insurance cover above a certain sum will be granted. In 1991 the typical threshold was £150,000 for single men, £250,000 for married men, and £500,000 for single and married women.

7.6. Normal Retirement Benefits

There are a number of retirement benefits that are available from personal pension schemes. The pension can be taken at any age between 50 and 75, although protected rights benefits (that is, the rights paid for out of the government's free contributions) cannot be taken before state-pension age. In order to take the pension, the scheme member must sign an *authorization and discharge form* from the scheme provider. Non-taxpayers can elect to receive their pensions gross of tax by filling in Inland Revenue form R89.

7.6.1. ANNUITY PENSIONS

7.6.1.1. *Types of Annuity Pensions*

When an individual with a personal pension scheme retires, the cumulated value of the fund in the scheme must be used to buy a *pension annuity* (although 25 per cent of the value of the fund can be commuted as a tax-free lump sum). There are many different terms and types of pension annuity that he or she can choose from; however, because it is mandatory to take an annuity under these circumstances, all the annuities are classified as *compulsory purchase* (or *substitute*) *annuities*.

The first choice concerns the duration or term of the annuity. The greatest income comes from annuities which cease on the death of the annuitant (known as a *single-life annuity* or an *immediate annuity*). But this might turn out to be the worst possible deal if the annuitant dies after only a short period. An alternative is to have payments for a specific period (such as five or ten years) regardless of when the annuitant dies (known as a *single-life annuity with minimum guarantee* or a *temporary annuity*). A variant of this is an annuity *with minimum guarantee and overlap* where both the spouse's income and income during the guarantee period are paid simultaneously. Another alternative is to have the annuity (known as a *joint-life annuity*) continue until the second death, in the case of a married couple. In this respect, it is important to take into account life expectancy, since many people underestimate how long they are likely to live after retirement. The life expectancy of a 60-year-old man is 18.2 years, while that of a 65-year-old man is 14.6 years (the corresponding figures for women are 22 and 18 years respectively). A couple aged 65 and 63 can expect to live another twenty-two years between them.

The second choice concerns the type of annuity. A typical insurance company will offer the following types of annuity:

- *Level annuity*: this pays a fixed amount in nominal terms for the life of the annuitant.
- *Escalating annuity*: an example is a *constant-growth annuity*, where the annuity increases annually at a fixed rate of, say, 5 per cent. The starting pension is much lower than the level-annuity pension.
- *Unit-linked annuity*: the annuity either fluctuates in line with unit prices or is assumed to grow at a constant rate, for example, at 10 per cent p.a.
- *With-profits annuity*: the annuity is based on an assumed annual bonus rate of between 3.5 per cent and 6.5 per cent.
- *Index-linked annuity*: the payments are increased each year in line with the retail price index.

All these annuities can come with the following variations:

- *Contingent benefits*: as with a *joint-life annuity*, where the annuity continues until the death of the surviving spouse; in the event of the member dying first, the annuity sometimes continues at a lower rate, for example, one-half or two-thirds.
- *Minimum guarantee*: the annuity payments are guaranteed for a certain period, such as five years, whether or not the annuitant dies before five years.
- *Capital protection*: the balance of the capital is paid to the annuitant's estate when he dies.

The third choice concerns the frequency and timing of the annuity payment. The main frequency options are: monthly, quarterly, semi-annual and annual. The timing options are: payments in advance (for an *annuity due*) or payments in arrears (for a *deferred annuity*). For a *deferred annuity with proportion*, the annuity on death will pay the proportion owing since the last payment. The less frequent and the later the payment, the higher the annuity.

Table 7.11 shows some typical monthly annuity rates that can be purchased with £50,000. The level annuity provides the largest initial pension, but suffers from having absolutely no protection against inflation. An annual inflation rate of 7 per cent can cut the real value of a pension in half in ten years. Complete protection against inflation is provided by the index-linked annuity, but the cost of this is that the initial pension is much lower than the level pension. With an inflation rate of 7 per cent p.a. it would be 7.1 years before the nominal value of the two pensions was the same. Lying between these two cases is the constant-growth annuity. This is higher than the index-linked annuity and grows at 5 per cent irrespective of the inflation rate. However, it still takes 8.7 years to reach the same pension as the level annuity. The riskiest pensions are those related to the unit-linked and with-profits annuities. This is because the pensions can actually decrease in these cases. But they have the greatest potential for growth. For example, had a unit-linked annuity of £273.08 per month been taken out in 1977 it would have grown to £2,426.61 per month by 1987. But then came the crash in October 1987!

It is possible to have combinations of annuities. For instance, a level annuity could be combined with an index-linked annuity to provide a higher initial pension than a pure index-linked pension, but with at least partial inflation indexing thereafter.

It is also possible to have *phased annuities* (sometimes called *staggered*

TABLE 7.11. *Comparison of annuities: initial monthly pension payable for purchase price of £50,000* (£)

	Man of 65*	Couple of 65 and 63[†]
Level annuity	584.43	451.05
Constant-growth annuity increasing at 5%	382.01	284.61
Index-linked annuity	361.08	260.58
Unit-linked annuity	273.08	180.04
Unit-linked annuity with 10% growth built in	559.88	458.92
With-profits annuity assuming 3.5% bonuses	273.08	180.04
With-profits annuity assuming 6.5% bonuses	559.88	458.92

Notes: * Guaranteed 5 years.
[†] Payable until second death.

Source: Equitable Life, *Daily Telegraph*, 11 Apr. 1987.

vesting) whereby the pension fund is converted into retirement income in phases. In other words, a series of annuities are purchased at regular intervals. This means that it is possible to reduce the risk from retiring when interest rates are low and so having to use the entire fund to buy a low-yielding annuity. In addition, the balance of the fund remains invested under the trust. This gives important inheritance-tax and other advantages. On death, it is possible for the whole of the balance of the fund to be paid as a lump sum to the spouse or to a nominated beneficiary, in each case free from inheritance tax. This contrasts with, say, an annuity with minimum guarantee, whereby the remaining payments are paid out in a lump sum but are not in trust. Only a spouse can receive this particular lump sum free from inheritance tax. Another advantage of phased annuities is that they maximize the size of the lump sum in the case of the early death of the annuitant. With a standard annuity, the annuity ceases when the annuitant dies. It is possible to protect against this, at least in part, by buying an annuity with a minimum guarantee of, say, ten years. But the cost of this guarantee reduces the size of the annuity. A better solution might be phased annuities. While the annuities, unless also guaranteed, cease on the death of the annuitant, the balance of the fund remains in trust. In the case of early death, the bulk of the fund will be intact and available to be paid to a spouse or nominated beneficiary free from inheritance tax.

Annuities from personal pension schemes are taxed under Schedule D of the Income and Corporation Taxes Act 1988. This means that basic-rate income tax is deducted at source in full, even if the pensioner has not used up his or her personal income-tax allowances. Any overpayment of tax has to be reclaimed from the Inland Revenue using forms R40 and R249. This contrasts with occupational pensions which are paid under the pay-as-you-earn (PAYE) system and taxed under Schedule E of the 1988 act. With this system the correct tax liability is calculated each month and deducted from each payment.

7.6.1.2. *Open-Market Option*

Holders of personal pension schemes are entitled to exercise an *open-market option* when they retire (up to one month before retirement). This means that they can take their pension annuity from a different company to the one which accumulated their pension fund. A personal pension has two components: a savings plan which accumulates a fund, and an annuity which delivers the pension on the basis of the size of the accumulated fund. These can be provided by two different institutions (although the pension annuity must be provided by a life-assurance company), and scheme members should select the institution offering the best deal for each component. The open-market option is especially

TABLE 7.12. *Top ten open-market option annuities in 1988: purchase price £10,000, annuity payable monthly, guaranteed five years* (£)

Man of 65	Annuity
General Accident	1,341.48
Norwich Union	1,336.40
Sun Alliance	1,328.52
Equitable Life	1,327.20
Providence Capitol	1,319.64
TSB Insurance	1,318.90
Prudential	1,315.68
Standard Life	1,314.00
Scottish Amicable	1,311.72
Provident Mutual	1,308.72

Source: Planned Savings, *Daily Telegraph*, 28 May 1988.

useful when people have taken out several different schemes and wish to pool their money in order to draw a single pension.

However, the availability of this option does not appear to be widely known about, although it has been available since 1978, and certainly companies offering personal pension schemes do not tend to inform their clients of the option, especially if their pension annuity is not competitive. For example, unit-linked companies tend to provide lower annuities (from their own life companies) than life companies directly. Some companies will actually penalize people if they exercise their open-market option: a charge of 3 per cent is not uncommon. Other companies, however, encourage people to stay with them by offering enhanced annuity rates. Table 7.12 provides an example of some of the best open-market option annuities available (in 1988).

7.6.2. LUMP SUM

Under the 1987 Finance Act the maximum tax-free lump sum that can be drawn from a personal pension scheme is 25 per cent of the value of the fund at the time of retirement, up to a maximum of £150,000, regardless of age. The value of the fund to which this maximum applies covers the total value of benefits, including those to dependants, but it excludes the value of the protected rights of the minimum contributions paid by the DSS. The protected rights of a personal pension scheme are equivalent to the SERPS pension for those who are contracted out.

The 1986 Social Security Act also allowed a maximum tax-free lump sum of 25 per cent, but it was based on a much more generous calculation of the value of the fund at retirement. The change has resulted in a substantial reduction in the lump sum, as the following example shows. Suppose that an individual has built up a fund of £200,000 from his personal contributions, together with another £200,000 from the DSS. Only the £200,000 from personal contributions can be taken into account when calculating the lump sum: that is, £50,000. The remaining balance of £350,000 is used to buy an annual pension. Before the 1987 act the value of the protected rights was included in the calculation of the lump sum, but not the value of the dependants' benefits. If the value of the dependants' benefits in the above example is £50,000, then the calculation of the lump sum before the act was based on a fund value of £350,000 (that is, £200,000 + £200,000 − £50,000), implying a lump sum of £87,500, which in this example is 75 per cent more than became allowable after the act.

The lump sum with a personal pension scheme is also less generous

TABLE 7.13. *Pension possibilities for a man aged 65 retiring with a pension fund of £72,399 (£ p.a.)*

	No lump sum		Lump sum	
	No widow's pension	Widow's pension	No widow's pension	Widow's pension
Tax-free lump sum	—	—	18,099	18,099
Pension for man	9,918	8,615	7,439	6,462
Pension for widow (in event of husband predeceasing her)	—	5,744	—	4,308

Note: The figures assume:
- man aged 65 accumulates fund of £72,399 over 20 years based on £100 per month contributions growing at 10% p.a.;
- all pensions quoted are for a male retiring at age 65, whose wife is aged 63;
- the pensions are payable monthly in advance, and guaranteed to be payable for five years in any event;
- the widow's-pension examples assume that the pension will reduce by one-third on the male death and that payment will be without overlap;
- all pensions are based on annuity rates that were commonly in use during 1987.

Source: Rothschild Asset Management, 1987.

than the scheme operating prior to the introduction of personal pensions, namely the section 226 retirement annuity scheme. With this scheme the lump sum increased with age and was worth about 30 per cent of the accumulated fund. So, for example, a man retiring at 60 with a fund of £100,000 might get £29,373 from a particular insurance company, while a man of 70 would get £34,517 from the same company. An individual with a personal pension scheme fund of £100,000 would only get a lump sum of £25,000, regardless of age. Furthermore, the £150,000 limit to the size of the lump sum applied to each section 226 scheme taken out. It is only possible to have one personal pension scheme at any one time, so it is only possible to have one lump sum. The 1989 Finance Act removed the £150,000 upper limit on the size of the lump sum in personal pension schemes.

Table 7.13 shows the pension possibilities for a man aged 65 retiring with a pension fund of £72,399 offered by Rothschild Asset Management in 1987.

7.7. Early- and Post-Retirement Benefits

7.7.1. EARLY-RETIREMENT BENEFITS

Personal pension schemes do not have specific early-retirement benefits, in contrast with occupational pension schemes. We consider two types of early retirement: voluntary early retirement and early retirement due to ill health.

7.7.1.1. *Voluntary Early Retirement*

With personal pensions it is possible to retire from the age of 50. But the danger is that there may not be a sufficiently large fund built up by the age of 50 to finance an adequate pension over a much longer time span. The pension depends on both the size of the fund at the time of retirement and the actuarial period over which it has to be paid. In turn, the size of the fund depends on the amount of and the return on the contributions that have been paid into the scheme.

The size of the fund may also depend on the relationship between the actual retirement age and the retirement age that the individual nominated when the plan first started. For example, where the scheme has both accumulation units and capital units, the fund available at retirement might be 100 per cent of the value of the accumulation units but only a proportion of the value of the capital units, with that proportion declining the lower the actual age of retirement compared with the nominated retirement age. In the case of one particular insurance company (Target Life), if the nominated retirement age is 65, then the actual age of retirement will affect the value of the capital units included in the fund in the following way:

Age at retirement	Proportion of capital units included (%)
64	93.6
63	87.8
62	82.5
61	77.7
60	73.3

It would be possible with the kind of investment returns available in the 1980s for a 30-year-old man to retire at 50. But in reality retiring at 50 is likely to be expensive. For example, a 30-year-old man could retire at 60 with a £10,000 p.a. pension on contributions of £480 p.a. But he would need to make contributions of £1,500 p.a. (more than three times as much) if he wanted a pension of £10,000 p.a. at 50. In addition, inflation might make the real value of this pension very small in twenty years' time. Also, the man could not get the basic state pension until he was 65 anyway.

7.7.1.2. *Early Retirement due to Ill Health*

Where an individual has to take early retirement through ill health he can still take a pension, but the pension may not be very generous if it is a personal pension. This is true for both with-profits endowment personal pensions and unit-linked personal pensions.

To illustrate, we can consider the case of a man who took out a personal pension scheme when he was 40 but is forced to take early retirement when he is 55 instead of the normal retirement ages of 65. This means that he took out a scheme that was intended to provide benefits after twenty-five years but was obliged to provide them after fifteen years. Many insurance companies providing such schemes on a with-profits basis offer a value after fifteen years similar to that offered by a standard fifteen-year scheme that went to full term. However, some insurance companies offer up to 30 per cent less. Unit-linked schemes also tend to offer less, but not as much less as with-profits schemes.

The explanation offered by the insurance companies is that their expenses are spread over the full term of the scheme, so that, if the scheme does not run to full term, the outstanding expenses still have to be met and this reduces the value of the scheme.

7.7.2. POST-RETIREMENT BENEFITS

It is possible for those people who have not had a pension scheme or have not made the maximum contributions into a self-employed pension scheme to benefit from the tax advantages of beginning a pension scheme *after* the age of retirement. The tax advantages, as always, come from the tax relief on the initial outlay and the tax-free lump sum. In this particular case they are open to people between the ages of 60 and 75. A person aged between 60 and 75 could contribute to the same type of pension scheme as that for a self-employed person. The scheme could take into account not only current earnings but also earnings over the previous six years.

We can illustrate the scheme as follows. An individual aged 60, without any previous pension scheme, makes a contribution of £20,000 to a self-employed pension scheme run by an insurance company. This sum attracts tax relief at the individual's highest marginal rate, say, 40 per cent. The following day he could withdraw a tax-free lump sum of £5,000 (the maximum tax-free lump sum permissible) and the balance as a pension for life. Using typical annuity rates for a 60-year-old man we have the following:

	£
Initial fund	20,000
less tax relief at 40%	(8,000)
Net cost of initial fund after tax relief	12,000
less tax-free lump sum	(5,000)
Net outlay	7,000
Annual pension (gross)	1,985
less tax at 25%	(496)
Annual pension (net)	1,489

For a net outlay of £7,000 the individual will receive an annual pension for life of £1,489, assuming that his tax rate after retirement falls to 25 per cent. This implies an annual return on the investment of 21 per cent.

The initial contribution to the pension scheme has to be made gross. The tax relief has to be claimed by sending a self-employed premium certificate and also an election form (if the contribution is to be treated as having been made in the previous tax year) to the Inland Revenue. Contributions can be carried back and relieved against the previous year's tax liability. Alternatively, unused tax reliefs from the previous six years can be carried forward to increase the level of contributions that can be paid in the current year.

Any individual who is in receipt of earnings and does not have a pension scheme can contribute up to 17.5 per cent of his or her earnings to a pension scheme in each tax year. This proportion increases with age (see Section 7.5.2 above).

Finally, it is possible to take the tax-free lump sum and pension under the scheme without actually retiring, so long as the benefits start before the individual reaches 75.

7.8. Preserved Benefits

Personal pension scheme members are not committed to staying in the same scheme for all their working lives. They are entitled to change schemes, taking their accumulated fund with them. Alternatively, they can leave the accumulated fund with the original scheme. In the latter case, the accumulated fund must generate the same investment yield as the funds accruing to members who remain in the scheme.

7.8.1. DEATH-IN-SERVICE BENEFITS

7.8.1.1. *Return of Premiums or Return of Fund*

Some personal pension schemes operate on a *return-of-premium* basis in the event of death in service, whereas others operate on the basis of a *return of fund*. The latter is distinctly more advantageous.

Return of premiums was fairly common with with-profits pension policies before about 1980. Only slightly more generous were with-profits policies that paid out premiums plus a notional 4 per cent or 5 per cent interest if the scheme-holder died before retirement. Since investment returns of 11 per cent or more are by no means uncommon, this involved a substantial penalty on dying early. Unit-linked pension schemes always provide a return of fund on death in service, although any capital units involved in the scheme are not refunded.

Table 7.14 shows the effects of the two bases for determining return in the event of death in service. The differences between return of premiums and return of fund can be quite substantial. But one advantage of return of premiums is that a marginally higher pension is awarded if the individual does survive to retirement age.

TABLE 7.14. *Projected death-in-service benefits from a with-profits personal pension scheme for a man aged 35 paying £1,000 p.a. to age 60 (£)*

	Return on death*	Annual pension[†]
Return of premiums	25,000	2,366
Return of premiums with 4% interest	43,312	2,326
Return of fund assuming 9% growth	75,362	—
Return of fund assuming 11% growth	100,630	—
Return of fund assuming 13% growth	135,266	2,264

Notes: * Assumes man dies at age 60.
 [†] Assumes man survives and draws pension from age 60.

Source: National Provident, *Daily Telegraph*, 2 May 1987.

Most schemes generally award death benefits on the basis of return of fund after the nominated retirement age. This is true whether or not the individual has retired. So one way of limiting the damage is for an individual to select the earliest possible retirement age in return-of-premium schemes.

If the personal pension scheme member wants to have greater protection than that afforded by either a return of premiums or a return of fund, he can use up to 5 per cent of his earnings to provide for death-in-service benefits. This sum is used to buy life cover (see Section 7.5.6 above).

7.9. Inflation Indexing

7.9.1. INFLATION INDEXING OF PRESERVED BENEFITS

The Social Security Act 1985 requires any preserved or deferred pension in a money-purchase scheme to receive the same treatment in terms of inflation indexing as active pensions remaining in the scheme. In addition, the accrued capital must generate the same investment yield as the capital accruing to active members of the scheme.

7.9.2. INFLATION INDEXING OF PENSIONS IN PAYMENT

The protected rights pension in payment must be increased annually in line with increases in the retail price level up to a maximum of 3 per cent p.a. This also applies to a widow/er's pension.

There are no statutory rules for inflation-proofing of personal pensions in excess of the protected rights pension. As shown in Section 7.6.1, some schemes offer escalating pensions in retirement at the cost of a lower starting pension.

7.10. Taxation Issues

The tax treatment of personal pension schemes is governed by the 1987 Finance (No. 2) Act and the 1989 Finance Act. There is full tax relief on contributions up to 17.5 per cent of salary as the maximum combined employer and employee contributions for employees aged 50 or less. There are higher limits for employees taking out personal pensions at greater ages (see Section 7.5.2). If the scheme is contracted out of SERPS, the minimum contributions paid by the DSS are in addition to the permitted maximum.

The Inland Revenue also allows unused tax relief on an employee's contributions to a personal pension scheme to be carried forward for up to six years, so long as this does not cover a period during which the employee was a member of an occupational pension scheme. This is designed to allow late starters to catch up on their contributions. However, the same carry-forward relief is not available to employers making additional contributions on behalf of employees.

The 1987 act also permitted tax-free lump sums equal to 25 per cent of the total value of the fund, up to a maximum of £150,000, on the retirement of the employee or following the death in service of the employee; in the latter case the lump sum is payable to the spouse. The 1989 act removed the £150,000 maximum to the value of the lump sum.

In the November 1993 Budget, the chancellor announced that the basis for taxing pension annuities would be switched from Schedule D to Schedule E, thereby putting them on the same PAYE basis as retirement pensions from occupational schemes.

7.11. Risks Associated with Personal Pension Schemes

7.11.1. GENERAL RISKS

The main attraction of a money-purchase personal pension scheme is that with high investment returns an individual can end up with a pension that is not limited to two-thirds of final salary. The main risk, of course, is that for a number of reasons the pension is nowhere near as high as with a final-salary scheme. The main reasons for the latter outcome are as follows:

- if the individual left an occupational scheme to join a personal scheme, the transfer value might have been quite low;
- the contributions into the money-purchase scheme are not automatically salary-related as with final-salary schemes; they will be fixed in nominal terms unless they are index-linked in some way;
- the investment returns might turn out to be lower than anticipated, especially after inflation is taken into account;
- the costs of administering the personal scheme could be quite high.

To illustrate some of the risks involved with money-purchase schemes, we can consider the case of a scheme promoted by a particular (unnamed) insurance company. The insurance company's scheme involved a 30-year-old male making contributions of £20 per month. When he retired his pension would be £22,089 p.a. This, it was argued, was well in excess of a pension from a typical final-salary scheme. In addition, the contributions were fixed over time, whereas with a final-salary scheme contributions increase with salary. So, from much lower contributions it was possible to achieve a much higher pension. However, when the scheme is analysed more closely, it is found that it assumes highly optimistic investment returns of 13.5 per cent p.a. for thirty-five years and completely ignores inflation. If an inflation rate of 10.5 per cent is assumed (which still leaves a real rate of return on investments of 3 per cent, quite high by historical standards), the pension is reduced to only £671 p.a. in current prices; this is well below the pension from a typical final-salary scheme.

As another example, we can consider the case of a 40-year-old male earning £45,000 p.a. who asked his pension adviser to conduct a *pension audit* for him. The individual wanted a pension of two-thirds of his final salary and was already contributing £200 per month to a personal pension scheme which had a fund value of £20,000. When he was asked to make forecasts of the future inflation rate and rate of return on his investments, he suggested 7 per cent and 12 per cent p.a. respectively. When this information was keyed into the pension adviser's computer the result was that the individual would receive a pension only equal to 20 per cent of his final salary, or 15 per cent if he took the maximum tax-free lump sum (see Table 7.15). In order to achieve the desired pension of two-thirds of final salary, the individual would have to make contributions of £1,186 gross (£712 net) per month, or 31.63 per cent of his salary, and substantially in excess of the 20 per-cent upper limit on contributions available to a 40-year-old. In the event, the man decided to increase his contributions up to the maximum allowable (that is, £750 gross (£450 net) per month) and also invested a £10,000 lump sum to use up some unused pension relief over the previous six years. His projected pension was then equal to 50 per cent of his retirement salary. Pension audits are provided by companies such as Johnson Fry and Lowndes Lambert Financial Services (formerly Norex Pension Communications).

7.11.2. ADDITIONAL RISKS WITH UNIT-LINKED SCHEMES

The world stock-market crash in October 1987 showed the greater risks from unit-linked pension schemes compared with, say, with-profits endowment pension schemes.

Unit-linked schemes began in the late 1960s with the aim of investing in shares and bonds through the highly diversified vehicle of unit trusts. Between 1974, when the London stock market last suffered a major crash, and 1987, unit-linked schemes have systematically outperformed endowment schemes. However, endowment schemes are less susceptible to security price fluctuations. This is because every year the scheme managers declare a reversionary bonus that is added to the scheme-

TABLE 7.15. *Example of a pension audit*

CURRENT POSITION

Age next birthday	41
Current income p.a.	£45,000
Inflation % p.a.	7.00
Age to retire	60
%age of final income required	66.67
Current fund value	£20,000
Fund growth % p.a.	12.00

POSITION AT RETIREMENT AGE

Income at age 60 p.a.	£162,742
Pension required (66.67%) p.a.	£108,500
(escalating by 7.00% p.a.)	
Pension fund required	£1,085,001

CURRENT PREMIUM

£200.00 p.m. gross, £120.00 p.m. after 40% tax
relief
Premium = 5.33% of gross income

Accumulated pension fund	£326,138
Pension available	£32,614
%age of final income	20.04
or Tax-free lump sum	£81,535
plus reduced pension of	£24,460
%age of final income	15.03

PREMIUM REQUIRED

£1,186.29 p.m. gross, £711.77 p.m. after 40% tax
relief
Premium = 31.63% of gross income

Accumulated pension fund	£1,085,001
Pension available	£108,500
%age of final income	66.67
or Tax-free lump sum	£90,000
plus reduced pension of	£99,500
%age of final income	61.14

ADDITIONAL PREMIUM REQUIRED

£986.29 p.m. gross, £591.77 p.m. net

Source: *Johnson Fry Bulletin*, Oct. 1990.

holder's account, and this cannot be taken away whatever happens to security prices subsequently. On the maturity of the scheme the scheme managers declare a terminal bonus. The set of reversionary bonuses plus the terminal bonus constitute the value of the fund on which the pension is based, but only the terminal bonus will depend on what is happening to security prices on the maturity date of the scheme.

The effects of the 1987 crash can be shown using the following example. A 50-year-old man who had taken out a ten-year pension scheme with a major UK insurance company and retired on Tuesday 13 October 1987 would have been 19 per-cent better off with the company's unit-linked scheme as compared with its endowment scheme. Had the man retired one week later on Tuesday 20 October, the endowment scheme would have beaten the unit-linked scheme by 11 per cent. This is because during the course of the week the value of the unit-linked scheme fell by 25 per cent. In this example both schemes were linked to the company's managed fund, which has a mixture of property and gilts as well as shares. Had the schemes been invested in the company's UK equity fund, the unit-linked scheme would have fallen by even more.

Many people with unit-linked schemes delayed their retirements in the hope that the value of their units would recover. But people aged 75 are prohibited by law from doing this. Had the man in the above example been 75 on Tuesday 20 October 1987, he would have had to cash in his units on that day.

7.12. The Impact of Personal Pension Schemes

7.12.1. SALES OF PERSONAL PENSION SCHEMES

In the first three months following their introduction in July 1988, 550,000 personal pension policies were sold by the 425 insurance company members of the Association of British Insurers (ABI). The total value of premiums collected was £359m., comprising £204m. for regular annual-premium schemes and £155m. for single-premium schemes. The value of the DSS rebates was £229m. In the first full year of operation the total premiums collected were £2,889m., comprising £1,084m. for regular annual-premium schemes and £1,805m. for single-premium schemes. The value of the DSS rebates was £1,472m. By 1990 more than 4.5 million pension schemes had been started. During 1990 ABI members collected total premiums of £4,016m., comprising £1,067m. for regular annual-premium schemes and £2,949m. for single-premium schemes, while the value of DSS rebates was £948m. By 1993, premiums of £6,400m. were being collected from 5 million scheme-holders.

Personal pension scheme providers, especially the insurance companies, have aggressively marketed personal pension schemes to SERPS and occupational pension scheme members. For example, in February 1988 the Prudential Assurance Company began a £7m. marketing cam-

TABLE 7.16. *Sources of new personal pension business 1992*

Method of sale	Annual premiums (%)	Single premiums (%)	Sponsored pension schemes* (%)
1. Independent intermediaries:			
Insurance brokers	25	35	63
Banks insurance services	3	3	1
Building societies insurance services	1	1	†
Accountants	2	3	2
Others	1	2	7
2. Company and appointed representatives:			
Insurance companies:			
Regular employees	24	12	3
Direct sales agents	33	36	21
Banks	3	2	†
Building societies	1	†	†
Others	6	4	1
3. Direct:			
Newspaper advertising	†	†	†
Direct mail	†	1	†
TOTAL	100	100	100

Notes: * Schemes set up by employers for the benefit of employees and which are insured by life companies.
† Less than 0.5 per cent.
Source: Association of British Insurers, June 1993.

paign, a record for any financial product. Table 17.16 reveals the sources of new personal pension business in 1992. It shows the strong dominance of insurance companies with regular employees, direct sales agents, and brokers responsible for 24 per cent, 33 per cent, and 25 per cent respectively of annual-premium business and these groups collectively responsible for 83 per cent of single-premium business. Banks account for only about 6 per cent of sales and building societies for only 2 per cent. Direct selling through newspaper advertising or mail shots is not very important.

The targeting of particular groups has been quite precise. For example, SERPS had about 11 million members in 1988. The government had advised men under 45 and women under 35 to consider personal pension schemes. The potential target group was 7 million people. Of these, 3.5 million earned less than £5,000 per annum and so were not of interest to the insurance companies. This left 3.5 million SERPS targets for the insurance companies, with potential premium income of £2bn. per annum. The insurance companies have also targeted occupational scheme members, despite claims that they do not intend to 'poach' such members. This has incurred the ire of the sponsoring companies.

There is evidence that high pressure sales tactics are being used to persuade members of occupational pension schemes (especially older long-serving members) to switch into unsuitable personal pension schemes: sales agents had sought too little information from potential clients to be able to give them proper advice. In October 1993 the Securities and Investments Board reprimanded the North of England Building Society following a routine inspection of 600 schemes which revealed that one-third of clients had been wrongly advised to switch out of occupational schemes. In November 1993 LAUTRO conducted a survey of personal schemes taken out during the third quarter of 1992 and found that 50,000 schemes had lapsed within one year. In December 1993 the SIB announced it would undertake a more general review of the personal pension schemes of the 500,000 individuals who had transferred £7bn. out of occupational schemes since 1988. Both LAUTRO and the SIB had established working parties to consider possible compensation, which might cost as much as £3bn. As many as 90 per cent of the people who had transferred might have been given inappropriate advice. Miners, teachers, nurses, and police officers were amongst the main targets of sales agents. Many of these people remained working for the same employer; but they switched from a good occupational scheme offering an index-linked pension into a personal scheme towards which the employer did not contribute and which took 25 per cent of the transfer value in commissions and administration charges. An example reported in the press concerned a miner who transferred to a personal pension scheme in 1989 and retired in 1994 aged 60. He has been offered a lump sum of £2,576 and a pension of £734 by his new scheme. Had he stayed in the miner's scheme he would have received a lump sum of £5,125 and a pension of £1,791.

On 1 July 1994, the Securities and Investments Board introduced stricter rules governing transfers between occupational and personal pension schemes. The rules establish the following standards for giving advice:

- pension transfer contracts must include a 14-day cooling-off period during which it is possible to back out of the deal;
- every transfer recommendation must be put down in writing with an explanation of why the pension adviser believes the transfer is a good idea for the individual;
- all pension advisers must use a computerized 'transfer value analysis'

programme to raise the objective nature of the advice and to reduce the degree of subjective judgement;

- the same assumptions must be used to compare occupational and personal pension schemes: for example, it is no longer acceptable to assume high investment returns for personal schemes (thereby 'enhancing' their value) and low inflation rates for index-linked occupational pensions (thereby 'reducing' their value in comparison).

The SIB rules also establish new standards for pension advisers which are designed to root out negligent or corrupt individuals:

- pension transfer business, because of its significance and complexity, has been reclassified as a 'permitted business category', which allows only a restricted group of trained advisers to engage in this activity;
- pension transfer advisers must establish separate and independent units to double-check every transfer recommendation, although small firms of advisers are exempt from this requirement;
- any pension adviser or provider which does more than 1 per cent of its business on an execution-only basis (that is, without advice) must inform the pension regulator as soon as this happens so that the regulator can launch an inquiry;
- the same 1 per cent threshold applies to any pension adviser or provider which claims that clients have insisted on a transfer despite advice not to leave their existing scheme.

7.12.2. OPPOSITION TO PERSONAL PENSION SCHEMES

According to a survey conducted by the Institute of Personnel Management (*Company Pension Intentions*, October 1987), many companies were opposed to the introduction of personal pensions and made great efforts to keep employees in their own schemes. About 63 per cent of those interviewed said that they were either against or neutral-to-against personal pensions. Almost all of them said they would make great efforts to show their employees the benefits of the company occupational scheme and the risks associated with personal pension schemes (such as a stock-market crash). About 97 per cent of those interviewed said they would not top up an employee's personal pension above the legal minimum. According to a survey conducted by Sedgwick Financial Services in 1989, 94 per cent of companies refused to contribute to the personal pension schemes of their employees.

Companies have begun to design their own money-purchase schemes to make them more attractive than personal pension schemes. For example, the Rank Organization puts an 8 per-cent employer's contribution into its own scheme compared with the minimum 3.8 per-cent employer's contribution into a personal pension scheme.

7.12.3. NO SAVINGS TO THE STATE

As we have seen, more than 5 million people had contracted out of SERPS with personal pension schemes by 1993. This means that 85 per cent of the people who were most likely to benefit from contracting out of SERPS had done so. This represents a big increase over the original estimates of those who would contract out made by the DSS. The DSS's estimate was between 0.5 million and 1.75 million.

One of the main objectives of the government in promoting personal pensions was to reduce the cost of SERPS. However, a National Audit Office report published in November 1990 found that the introduction of personal pension schemes, far from saving money, had actually led to a substantial increase in costs to the state. The NAO commissioned the Government Actuary's Department to calculate the likely net cost to the National Insurance Fund of personal pension schemes between April 1987 and April 1993, the period of rebates and special bonuses. The government actuary's calculations showed that the gross cost of the national-insurance rebates and special bonuses was £9.3bn., but the saving in terms of lower SERPS pensions was only £3.4bn., giving a net cost of about £5.9bn. Given that personal-pension scheme providers take between 4 and 13 per cent in commission and charges, this implies that the providers have earned between £375m. and £1.2bn. from rebate-only schemes during this period (all in 1988 prices).

These calculations assumed that everyone who contracts out of SERPS would, as they are entitled to do, re-contract back into SERPS when it was financially advantageous for them to do so, that is, when the special bonus ended in April 1993. The evidence indicated that it would be advantageous for men under 42 and women under 34 earning at least £6,000 p.a. to contract out of SERPS for the period of the special bonus. They could then re-contract into SERPS in April 1993, keeping the benefits of their personal pension scheme. This was because after April 1993 their contributions would buy more pension in SERPS than they would in a personal pension scheme. It was because of the possibility of mass re-contracting back into SERPS that the government decided to extend the special bonus period (albeit on reduced terms) until April 1996.

7.13. Summary

- A personal pension relates to the individual rather than the company and depends on the size of the fund accumulated. There is no limit to the size of the pension that can be received. The pension is taxable.

- The pension can normally start between the ages of 50 and 75 and can be phased in over several years.
- The annuity rates have to be the same for both men and women of the same age, even though women tend to live longer than men.
- The pension must be inflation-proofed up to 3 per cent p.a.
- Up to 25 per cent of the value of the fund can be taken as a tax-free lump sum.
- A widow/er's pension has to be provided equal to 50 per cent of the member's pension at the time of death. In the event of death in service, the member's dependants will receive a benefit based on the value of the protected rights at time of death.
- Contributions can be paid by both employee and employer and are tax-deductible. The minimum employer's contribution is equal to the contracted-out national-insurance rebate.
- The contributions are limited to 17.5 per cent of net relevant earnings for scheme members up to the age of 35; higher limits apply above this age.
- Up to 5 per cent of earnings can be used to purchase life-assurance cover before retirement.
- Income and capital gains on the investments in the scheme accumulate free of income and capital-gains taxes, although overseas taxes on overseas investments may have to be paid.
- Since personal pensions have a uniform rate of minimum contributions regardless of age, this is likely to make them poor alternatives to SERPS for any man over the age of 45 (or any woman over the age of 35) when they take out a pension scheme, assuming an average real rate of return of 0.5 per cent p.a. If the real rate of return rises to 2.5 per cent p.a., then personal pension schemes are not advisable for men over 53 or women over 44.
- When an individual leaves SERPS to take out a personal pension he or she does not lose the SERPS pension accumulated over previous years. He or she will still receive a SERPS pension based on his or her years of membership.

8

Self-Employed, Partners', Executives', and Directors' Pension Schemes

In earlier chapters we discussed the pension schemes available to employees. These cover the vast majority of people in this country. In this chapter we briefly examine the types of pension schemes available to people who are either not employees (the self-employed and partners in partnerships) or who are senior employees (executives) or directors of companies. There are about 40,000 such schemes in the UK.

8.1. Self-Employed and Partners' Pension Schemes

Self-employed individuals and partners in partnerships are not permitted to join SERPS and clearly cannot participate in a company's occupational pension scheme. They can provide for their retirement through the sale of their businesses, or by making provision for retirement in their partnership agreements, or by taking out their own personal pension schemes.

These personal pension schemes are exactly like any other personal pension scheme, with retirement between 50 and 75, and contribution limits of 17.5 per cent of net relevant earnings, which in this case means gross earnings less certain business expenses. They are also much more flexible than the types of *retirement annuity contracts* that were available to the self-employed and partners before the introduction of personal pensions. For example, previously it was not possible to take a transfer value from an occupational scheme to a self-employed scheme and vice versa. Now such transfers are possible. Similarly, if a self-employed person had several jobs he had to keep his pension arrangements separate in the past. Now it is possible for him to have a single personal pension scheme in respect of all his jobs.

8.2. Executive Pension Schemes

Executive pension schemes (EPSs) are used by companies to recruit and retain high-quality senior executives. EPSs therefore offer benefits that are superior to standard pension schemes available to ordinary employees. The following types of additional benefit are available with an EPS:

- A lower normal retirement age: this could be as low as 60 for men and 55 for women (although the age for women will have to be raised progressively to 60 between 2010 and 2020).
- An increased rate of pension accrual: this could be used to provide a two-thirds pension using the Inland Revenue's *accelerated scale* (see Section 6.2.3) for less than forty years' service, indeed for as low as twenty years' service (before 17 March 1987, a full pension could be achieved with only ten years' service).
- An increased tax-free lump sum: as a result of the increased rate of pension accrual, it is possible to receive the maximum tax-free lump sum (of one-and-a-half times final salary) with only twenty years' service (see Section 6.2.3).
- Increased death-in-service benefits: the EPS might offer the maximum permitted lump sum of four times salary plus a return of contributions.
- Increased widow/er's pension: the EPS might offer a pension of two-thirds of the member's pension, instead of the typical half-pension.
- Increased ill-health retirement pension, which could be based on full potential service to normal retirement age.
- Increases in pension fully in line with increases in the retail price index, instead of limited to 5 per cent.

It is clear that EPSs are based on the maximum permissible benefits payable under a scheme approved by the Inland Revenue. Schemes differ between different companies, but few EPSs will offer benefits at the maximum rate in all the above cases. Nevertheless, by their nature EPSs will be more generous than the staff schemes operated by companies.

These benefits can be provided as part of the company's main pension scheme, or through a separate EPS, or through a combination of the main scheme providing standard benefits and an EPS providing the additional or topping-up benefits. There are advantages and disadvantages with each method. For example, confidentiality can be preserved more easily with a separate EPS than with a main scheme. On the other hand, from a funding viewpoint it is often better to have a single scheme, since the costs of the executives' scheme can be hidden away amongst the costs of the general scheme, and the surplus in the general scheme can be used to improve the benefits to executives; with separate schemes the restrictions on surpluses resulting from the 1986 Finance Act apply to each scheme separately.

Most of the extra costs of an EPS will be borne by the company. But it is possible for the executive himself to make a contribution to the EPS through either additional voluntary contributions (AVCs) or a procedure known as *salary sacrifice*. AVCs are subject to the 15 per-cent limit. But this limit can in effect be overcome if the executive voluntarily agrees to give up part of his salary and the company pays an equal amount of money into the pension scheme. The effect of salary sacrifice is to reduce the taxable salary of the executive and for the company to get the same tax relief whether it pays a full salary to the executive or pays a reduced salary and makes an additional pension contribution. However, the effect is also to reduce the executive's pensionable salary for the purpose of calculating pension benefits. In addition, it must not be possible for the executive to use the employer's additional contribution other than for the purpose of providing future pension benefits. Nor must it be possible for the salary sacrifice to be restored at the instigation of the executive.

EPSs have always been a tax-efficient and flexible means of providing a pension and a tax-free lump sum at retirement. However, the 1987 and 1989 Finance Acts placed limits on the benefits that could be drawn from EPSs. The 1987 act limited the tax-free lump sum to £150,000 and increased the number of years' service necessary to qualify for maximum benefits from ten to twenty. Under the 1989 act the maximum tax relief available on an EPS taken out after 1 June 1989 is based on a salary of £60,000 (in 1989 prices), even if the actual salary is larger than this figure. Before 1 June 1989 there was no upper limit to the tax relief available. The £60,000 limit is increased every year in line with inflation. The 1989 act also removed the £150,000 limit to the tax-free lump sum.

EPSs are particularly useful for the purpose of inheritance-tax planning. This is because the lump sums payable under these schemes, as with other approved schemes, are free of inheritance tax. However, the usefulness of EPSs has been reduced by the 1989 Finance Act which placed a £60,000 (in 1989 prices) earnings limit on post-1989 members of EPSs. Nevertheless, the main way in which a senior executive can transfer tax-free wealth to his family, apart from lifetime transfers of gifts and property to a spouse, is through the death benefits from an EPS. This is because the EPS is established under a discretionary trust, so the benefits available after an executive's death will not form part of his estate for inheritance-tax purposes. Although the member can indicate to the trustees in advance of his death his preferences as to who should receive his death benefits, the trustees are not bound by these preferences. However, the whole point of an EPS is that the trustees will abide by the member's preferences and so the member can be fairly assured that his children and grandchildren will be able to receive large sums of money free from inheritance tax if he so wishes.

The 1989 Finance Act also introduced *funded unapproved retirement benefit schemes* (FURBSs) to allow companies to enhance executive pensions. These schemes have no earnings caps, but also have no tax relief (see Section 6.2.5).

8.3. Directors' Pension Schemes

The pension schemes available for directors of companies are generally designed to suit the individual needs of directors, although there are special rules for what are known as 20 per-cent directors. Alternatively, there are group schemes for directors and these are known as small self-administered pension schemes.

Before 1973 controlling directors could not be members of approved pension schemes. They had to take out self-employed retirement annuity contracts, the predecessor of personal pensions. Following the 1973 Finance Act these directors have been permitted to become members of company pension schemes. This helps to explain the current division of directors' schemes into individual schemes and group schemes.

8.3.1. PENSION SCHEMES FOR INDIVIDUAL DIRECTORS

A typical director's pension scheme will have exactly the same structure as an executive pension scheme. In other words, it will be tailor-made to exploit the maximum permitted limits available under an approved pension scheme.

In particular, it can be used in inheritance-tax planning. This is an especially useful feature for directors, since many directors do not actually retire from their companies, but instead continue drawing a salary until their death. In this case all their pension benefits will come in the form of death benefits: hence the importance of inheritance-tax planning.

A director who defers retirement and subsequently dies in service can have his pension benefits paid in one of the following ways:

- a lump sum equal to four times earnings (with earnings limited to £60,000, in 1989 prices), together with a refund of contributions with interest, plus a widow/er's pension; or
- the benefits calculated on the assumption that he had retired on the day before his death, which implies a lump sum equal to five years' pension payments (which is the standard minimum guarantee payment period for pensions), plus a widow/er's pension; any pension payments guaranteed after five years cannot be commuted and must be paid to the deceased's estate as they fall due.

These benefits (with the exception of pension payments guaranteed after five years) will be free of inheritance tax. However, the first option is likely to provide the largest tax-free transfer to the director's descendants.

8.3.2. SPECIAL RULES FOR 20 PER-CENT DIRECTORS

A *20 per-cent director* is a director of a company who on his own or with one or more associates beneficially owns or is able to control directly or indirectly or through other companies 20 per cent or more of the ordinary share capital of the company. An 'associate' covers any relative or partner or the trustees of any settlement to which the director or any relative of the director is a settlor.

If a 20 per-cent director joined an approved pension scheme on or after 1 December 1987 then his pension benefits will be subject to the following restrictions:

- the definition of 'final salary' cannot be based on one year's earnings only, but must be based on earnings averaged over a period of at least three years;
- the earliest age for normal retirement is 60;
- where a director defers drawing his pension beyond his normal retirement date, the pension when paid cannot be higher than the maximum approved pension calculated at his normal retirement age (but the pension cannot be deferred beyond the age of 75).

If, on the other hand, a 20 per-cent director joined an approved scheme before 1 December 1987, then his pension benefits will be subjected only to the first of the above restrictions. Clearly the Inland Revenue is intent on clamping down on the pension benefits available to company directors.

8.3.3. SMALL SELF-ADMINISTERED PENSION SCHEMES

Small self-administered pension schemes (SSAPSs) (also known as *captive pension schemes*) are schemes designed to provide pensions and other benefits for the directors of small companies. Such schemes are limited to twelve members, who are also normally the scheme trustees. They must be operated as *common trust funds*: each member can have a separate account representing a proportion of the total fund, but cannot have specifically earmarked assets. There were about 20,000 SSAPSs in the UK in 1990, managing the pensions of more than 40,000 directors and senior employees. Typical formation costs are between £2,000 and £2,500.

The principal attraction of an SSAPS is the wide investment powers that the directors of a company can exercise, in particular the powers of self-investment. Indeed, self-investment is a considerably more valuable feature of an SSAPS than self-administration. The following forms of self-investment are possible: loans to the company; the purchase of property from the company; and purchase of the company's own shares. SSAPSs hold on average about a quarter of their assets in property and other assets owned by the company. Such self-investment is a vital source of finance for the company.

In the past SSAPSs have often been used as tax-avoidance vehicles, but in 1987 the Inland Revenue began tightening up on their use. Before 1987 the schemes could be used by directors to buy shares, including shares in their own companies, to buy commercial property, and to borrow up to 50 per cent of the pension fund's value on an unsecured basis. From 1987 personal loans to members of the scheme or to anyone with a contingent interest were banned and loan-backs to the company were restricted. It is no longer permissible to invest in company flats, holiday homes, or works of art, for example.

The Inland Revenue also standardized the documentation for SSAPSs. This has reduced the flexibility for designing tax-avoidance features. Finally, the Revenue required all schemes to have an approved trustee, known as a *pensioneer trustee*, who has the responsibility for informing the Revenue of certain types of transactions that take place with the fund's assets. An example of this would be a transaction between the scheme and a director's spouse. This role is filled by companies such as James Hay Pension Trustees, Hornbuckle Mitchell, Mercer Fraser, and Pointon York.

The 1990 Social Security Act introduced further restrictions on self-investment by self-administered pension schemes to no more than 50 per cent of the scheme's assets. However, this restriction does not apply to SSAPSs if the following conditions are met:

- the scheme is for the exclusive benefit of 20 per-cent directors;
- all members of the scheme are trustees of the scheme; and
- investment decisions are required to be unanimously agreed by trustees.

The 1991 Finance Act introduced even more restrictions on these schemes. Loans from a pension scheme to a business are limited to 25 per cent of the value of the fund in the first two years, and 50 per cent after two years. There is also an effective ban on residential property.

However, SSAPSs still remain more flexible than their nearest alternative, self-invested personal pension schemes (SIPPSs) (see Section 7.4.3) for at least two reasons. First, contribution limits are higher with SSAPSs. With SIPPSs, contribution limits range between 17.5 and 40 per cent of earnings, depending on the age of the individual. With SSAPSs, on the other hand, the objective is to provide the maximum pension (two-thirds of final salary and fully index-linked) in the minimum permitted time (20 years). A 40-year-old member of an SSAPS planning to retire at 60 can have annual contributions paid on his behalf that exceed his income, but the same person would have contributions limited to 20 per cent of earnings if he was a member of a SIPPS. Secondly, in February 1994, the Inland Revenue relaxed the rules governing the purchase of pension annuities with SSAPSs. Before this date, scheme members who retired had to purchase their pension annuity within five years. This penalized retirees when annuity rates were low. After this date, the maximum annuity purchase age became 75. This permitted SSAPS members to delay purchasing their annuities until annuity rates were more favourable.

8.3.4. FRIENDLY-SOCIETY PENSION SCHEMES

It is possible to establish a small self-administered pension scheme by setting up a friendly society for the purpose. The Friendly Societies Act of 1974 governs the pension policy while the Trustee Investments Act of 1961 governs the trust investment. The principal condition for setting up a friendly society is that it is formed by at least seven partners in the same partnership, all of whom share the profits of the partnership and contribute to the pension scheme. The partners will also be trustees of the scheme. The registrar of friendly societies does not permit schemes that include both employees and partners, nor schemes involving partners' spouses. Friendly societies can be set up using the services of consulting actuaries for a few thousand pounds.

Friendly-society pension schemes face some of the restrictions of general pension schemes (for example, an upper limit on contributions of 17.5 per cent of earnings), but are otherwise very flexible. For example, the scheme can be operated on a group, pooled basis or the members can pay their contributions into separate accounts which are then invested individually. The pooled fund is unitized, so that the units can be sold by any individual who leaves the partnership.

As another example of the schemes' flexibility there are extremely generous loan-back facilities. It is possible to take out a personal loan equal to 100 per cent of the sum invested (which is secured and charged at a competitive rate), or it is possible to take out a 100 per cent loan to buy residential property. Neither of these possibilities is available in executive pension schemes or standard small self-administered schemes, where any loan-back permitted is limited to 50 per cent. When the scheme is operated on a group basis it is possible to buy company property. The rent paid by the partnership to the friendly society is allowable as an expense for the partnership, but is free of tax for the friendly society, and future capital gains are also free of tax.

There are, however, some constraints on the schemes' investments. For example, there must be a balance between shares, bonds, and property. It is not possible to invest the entire fund in shares, for example.

Finally, the schemes require the authorization of both the registrar of friendly societies and the Inland Revenue.

8.3.5. SELF-ADMINISTERED PENSION SCHEMES FOR CONTROLLING DIRECTORS

SSAPSs have also been set up by insurance companies. Such schemes are generally known as *self-administered pension schemes for controlling directors*. They are hybrid schemes offering some but not all of the features of SSAPSs. For example, there might be greater restrictions on direct investment in property. Also, an insurance company might require that any funds not used for self-investment be invested in insurance policies with the insurance company. Further, the surrender penalties might be high, which effectively locks in the company to a particular insurance company. These schemes are identical to the self-invested personal pension schemes offered by insurance companies (see Section 7.4.3).

9

Pension Choices and Retirement Decisions

In this chapter we compare the different types of pension choices currently open to individuals and companies, and also consider various decisions that have to be made relating to retirement, such as the age of retirement, whether or not to take a lump sum, and what non-pension sources of income might be available during retirement.

9.1. Pension Choices

There is now a very wide range of pension choices open to individuals. They can join their employer's scheme (if he has one), which can be: a contracted-in occupational pension scheme; a contracted-in money-purchase scheme; a contracted-out occupational pension scheme; or a contracted-out money-purchase scheme. They can also top up their occupational pension schemes with additional voluntary contributions or free-standing additional voluntary contributions.

As an alternative, employees now have the following personal-pensions choices, which are independent of their employer's scheme. They can have:

- an appropriate personal pension scheme (known as a minimum-contribution or rebate-only personal pension scheme), which is contracted out of SERPS and stands in place of SERPS benefits;
- an appropriate personal pension scheme that is also contracted out of SERPS but, as a result of higher contribution-rates, provides more generous benefits.

Individuals can be members of occupational schemes *and* have personal pensions only in the following circumstances:

- the occupational scheme provides only a widow/er's pension and/or a lump sum on death in service;
- the occupational scheme is contracted into SERPS and an appropriate personal pension scheme based only on minimum contributions is used to replace SERPS benefits only (sometimes known as a contracted-in money-purchase scheme);
- members of occupational pension schemes can use personal pension schemes for the purpose of receiving transfer payments from previous schemes.

In 1993 there were 21.5 million employees in work in the UK and another 2.5 million people who were self-employed. The pension arrangements of these people were as follows:

- 6.75 million employees entitled to a state pension but not members of a company pension scheme;
- 1.5 million employees in SERPS plus a company pension scheme;
- 9.5 million employees in a company pension scheme that is contracted out of SERPS;
- 3.75 million employees in personal pension schemes;
- 1.25 million self-employed in personal pension schemes;
- 1.25 million self-employed without a personal pension other than the basic state pension.

This means that in 1993 about 70 per cent of pension-scheme members in the UK were members of SERPS or an occupational pension scheme, and 30 per cent were members of personal pension schemes. What factors motivated these choices?

9.1.1. THE CHOICE BETWEEN SERPS AND AN OCCUPATIONAL PENSION SCHEME

The most important choice that a company has to make in respect of the pension scheme that it operates is whether or not to be contracted out of the state earnings-related pension scheme (SERPS). If nothing is done, then all its employees paying national-insurance contributions (NICs) on earnings above the lower earnings limit (LEL) will automatically be members of SERPS. A pension scheme can only contract out of SERPS by applying to the Occupational Pensions Board for a contracting-out certificate.

All employees with sufficient NICs are entitled to the basic state pension, which for a single person is approximately equal to 20 per cent of national average earnings. SERPS provides a maximum pension of only 25 per cent of salary (up to the upper earnings limit, UEL) when the scheme matures in 1998. This in turn implies that the maximum SERPS pension is equivalent to 20 per cent of national average earnings (assuming that the difference between price and wage inflation remains constant). So the total maximum pension available from the combined state schemes is only 40 per cent of national average earnings. (After 1999 the SERPS pension is being reduced to an estimated maximum of 16 per cent of national average earnings.)

Apart from the relatively low pension at retirement, SERPS has a number of other disadvantages. For example, SERPS does not provide:

- income-tax relief on employees' contributions;
- a return of contributions on death before retirement;
- the opportunity to make additional voluntary contributions (although it is possible to take out a personal pension to supplement the SERPS pension);
- any possibility for early retirement before state-pension age;
- a tax-free lump sum at retirement;
- a widow's pension if the widow is under age 45 (unless there is a dependent child).

The main advantage of the state pension is that it is fully indexed to retail-price inflation.

A contracted-out occupational pension scheme, on the other hand, offers a maximum pension of 67 per cent of salary (together with the security of an accumulated fund); but this has to be only partially indexed to inflation up to a maximum of 5 per cent, although companies can, if they have the resources, provide more generous increases, including full indexing (although they may not provide more than full indexing). Furthermore, occupational pension schemes provide all the six benefits listed in the last paragraph.

In return for these pensions, the employee's contribution-rate is 1.8 per cent of earnings for SERPS membership (that is, the implied contribution-rate is equal to the employee's *contracted-out rebate*) and about 5.5 per cent of earnings for membership of an occupational scheme. The employer's contribution-rate is 3 per cent of earnings for SERPS membership (that is, the employer's contracted-out rebate) and about 9.75 per cent of earnings for an occupational scheme. The total cost of SERPS membership is 4.8 per cent of earnings, while the total cost of an occupational pension scheme is 15.25 per cent of earnings on average, more than three times as much.

So, contracted-out schemes provide more generous benefits than contracted-in schemes, but at a higher cost. The state scheme was designed only to provide a minimum level of benefits for those on below-average salaries. Nevertheless, the SERPS pension is provided at very low cost to SERPS members.

When comparing SERPS and an occupational scheme we can draw the following conclusions. SERPS is a suitable pension scheme for employees on modest salaries or for employees who tend to move jobs frequently. It is also suitable for small firms without the system of administration to handle an occupational scheme. However, for more highly paid employees and for larger companies, the benefits of an occupational scheme dominate the simplicity of SERPS.

9.1.2. THE CHOICE BETWEEN SERPS AND A PERSONAL PENSION SCHEME

It is difficult to compare SERPS and personal pension schemes because so many assumptions have to be made about likely investment returns, earnings growth, and inflation. However, it is important to take the following factors into account:

- age: the younger an individual, the greater the time there is for personal pension contributions and for the returns on them to accumulate;
- sex: state pensions for men begin five years later than for women (although as a result of European Court of Justice rulings this will change after 2010);
- special bonus: there was a special incentive in terms of an additional

TABLE 9.1. *Comparison between personal pensions and SERPS* (% of salary)

Age in 1988	Men		Women	
	Personal pension*	SERPS	Personal pension*	SERPS
20	25.4	14.7	18.5	14.6
25	21.9	13.1	15.9	12.8
30	18.7	12.5	13.4	12.0
35	15.9	12.0	11.2	11.5
40	13.3	11.5	9.0	10.7
45	10.7	10.7	6.9	9.6
50	8.1	9.6	4.8	8.9
55	5.6	8.0	2.6	4.0
60	3.1	4.0	—	—

Notes: * Includes national-insurance rebate plus 2% bonus for five years.
  Figures assume:
- salary increases by 6.5% p.a.;
- national-insurance lower earnings limit and upper earnings limit increase by 6.5% p.a.;
- investment return 8.5% p.a.;
- personal pension increases by 3% p.a.;
- personal pension expenses 10% p.a.;
- inflation 5% p.a.;
- allowance is also made for a reducing rebate and tax relief on employee contributions.

Source: Wolanski & Co., *Daily Telegraph*, 18 Oct. 1986.

contracted-out rebate for those taking out personal pensions between 1988 and 1993, followed by a reduced bonus between 1993 and 1996;

• anticipated investment performance: the return that is expected to be generated on personal pension savings, especially in relation to inflation;

• risk: SERPS provides an earnings-related pension at retirement that is guaranteed, whereas a personal pension offers the chance of a higher pension but at the risk that the investment performance of the personal pension scheme might be disastrous.

Table 9.1 presents estimates of the pension (as a proportion of earnings) that could be expected for men and women at different ages from membership of, respectively, a personal pension scheme and SERPS for the same contributions. The assumptions made are listed at the bottom of the table. The table shows that, with these assumptions, men older than 45 years and women older than 35 years are better off staying in SERPS. Employees below these ages can expect to receive larger pensions as a proportion of pay by opting for personal pensions. However, this is not guaranteed. On the other hand, there is no limit to the maximum personal pension that can be achieved. But, unlike the SERPS pension, the personal pension is only partially indexed to inflation up to 3 per cent.

Most members of personal pension schemes will make contributions higher than those implied by Table 9.1. Members of SERPS are not able to do so. On average, contributions into personal pension schemes are about 6 per cent of earnings. The expected personal pension (as a proportion of earnings) is therefore much higher than indicated in the table. This is likely to make personal pension schemes much more attractive than SERPS for higher-paid workers.

9.1.3. THE CHOICE BETWEEN AN OCCUPATIONAL PENSION SCHEME AND A PERSONAL PENSION SCHEME

Perhaps the most important choice that has to be made in terms of pensions is the one between an occupational pension scheme and a personal pension scheme. It is also the most difficult choice to make, because the results of the choice will not be known before the time of retirement, when it is too late to do anything about it.

The main advantages of an occupational pension scheme are:

• the pension is guaranteed to be related to salary at or near retirement; this is especially beneficial for people who enjoy rapid promotion or if there is substantial wage inflation;

• the employer as well as the employee is obliged to contribute to the scheme (unless the scheme is non-contributory, in which case the employee does not even have to contribute); the average employee contribution is 5.5 per cent of salary, but the average employer contribution is 9.75 per cent of salary;

- additional benefits, such as early retirement on grounds of ill health and death-in-service benefits, are automatically provided.

The main disadvantages of an occupational pension scheme are:

- the pension is limited to a fraction of pre-retirement income, at most two-thirds of final salary;
- the pension is linked to a particular contract of employment;
- preserved pension rights or transfer values between schemes tend to be very poor, thereby reducing the overall pension available at retirement (this is probably the most serious disadvantage of occupational schemes);
- the member has no control over the investments in the scheme;
- the accruing pension assets cannot readily be used as security for a loan; in other words, the pension assets are almost completely illiquid until retirement, although this is beginning to change as a result of competition from personal pension schemes;
- an individual can be made redundant, in which case the pension will be linked to the salary at time of redundancy, not at retirement.

The main advantages of a personal pension scheme are:

- there is no limit to the size of the pension at retirement;
- the pension scheme is not linked to any contract of employment;
- the pension scheme is portable, and so can be taken away with a person when he or she changes jobs; so there is no problem with transfer values;
- the member has some control over the investments in the scheme and can choose the plan provider;
- the accruing pension assets can be used as security for a pension loan or pension mortage (see Section 9.1.6 below);
- there was a 2 per-cent special bonus for people taking out personal pensions before 1993 reducing to an age-related 1 per-cent special bonus between 1993 and 1996 (so long as they had not been contracted out of SERPS before);
- the pension scheme is very flexible in terms of changed circumstances; for example, it is possible to reduce or stop making contributions altogether in the event of being made unemployed;
- there is a carry-forward facility, so that it is possible to make higher-than-permitted tax-relieved contributions in the current year based on unused contribution limits over the previous six years;
- there is a carry-back facility, so that it is possible to make contributions in a year when there are no net relevant earnings (say, as a result of

unemployment or maternity leave) and have the contributions set against earnings in the previous tax year.

The main disadvantages of a personal pension scheme are:

- the size of the pension is not guaranteed;
- if the investments perform badly, the pension will be small;
- the employer is not obliged to, and is also not likely to, contribute to a personal pension scheme;
- additional benefits, such as early retirement on the grounds of ill health and death-in-service benefits, require additional contributions (in total up to 5 per cent of earnings can be used to provide for these benefits);
- there is no automatic right to rejoin the employer's scheme;
- the full cost of administering the pension scheme is borne by the member; this cost can be quite high, between 10 per cent and 20 per cent of premiums, in contrast with between 5 per cent and 7 per cent of premiums for occupational schemes;
- if there is dissatisfaction with the investment performance or administration of one personal pension scheme, the costs of transferring to another personal pension scheme could be quite high.

One of the most important factors determining whether it is financially beneficial to join a personal pension scheme is the age at commencement of the scheme. Table 9.2 provides an example of the kind of pension that

TABLE 9.2. *Personal pensions as a percentage of salary at retirement*

Age at commencement (male)	Age 60		Age 65	
	Single life	Joint life	Single life	Joint life
35	45	34	63	45
40	35	26	52	37
45	26	19	40	29
50	17	12	29	21
55	8	6	19	14

Notes: The figures assume:
- 17.5% contributions p.a. of net relevant earnings;
- investment return 9% p.a.;
- salary increases by 8% p.a.;
- post-retirement increases 5% p.a.;
- joint-life pension with wife three years younger;
- annuity rate 10% p.a. and mortality from Table PA(90) of Institute of Actuaries.

Source: Graham Mortgage & Assurance Services, *Daily Telegraph*, 28 June 1986.

can be achieved from a money-purchase personal pension as a proportion of final salary. Assuming that contributions are 17.5 per cent of earnings, earnings increase by 8 per cent p.a., investment returns are 9 per cent p.a., and the pension increases after retirement at 5 per cent p.a., then an unmarried man retiring at 65 could achieve a pension equal to 63 per cent of his retirement salary if he began the scheme at 35, but only 19 per cent of his retirement salary if he began the scheme at 55. If, instead, the man was married with a wife three years younger than himself, then the pension at retirement would be equal to 45 per cent of his final salary if he began the scheme at 35, and only 14 per cent if he began the scheme at 55. Table 9.3 shows the contributions into a personal pension scheme at different commencement ages needed to achieve a pension of two-thirds of final salary at retirement. Only someone joining a personal pension scheme before the age of about 35 is likely to be able to afford the necessary contributions. Anyone starting a personal pension scheme after the age of 40 would not be permitted to make the necessary contributions, since they would exceed the maximum permissible rate. These examples suggest that only very young people will get a pension from a money-purchase scheme that is close to the two-thirds of final pay that they

TABLE 9.3. *Contributions required to achieve a pension of two-thirds of final salary*

Age at commencement (male)	Required contributions (% of salary)	Maximum contributions (% of salary)
25	10.90	17.5
30	13.41	17.5
35	16.81	17.5
40	21.66	20.0
45	28.92	20.0
50	40.81	25.0
55	64.15	30.0
60	129.83	40.0

Note: The figures assume:
- man retiring at age 65;
- no previous contributions into any other pension scheme;
- salary increases by 3% p.a.;
- investment return 6% p.a.

Source: Save and Prosper, *Daily Telegraph*, 13 Nov. 1993.

can get from a final-salary scheme, and even then this pension is not guaranteed.

The choice between an occupational scheme and a personal scheme will be determined mainly by the age of the individual and the individual's attitude to risk. Personal pension schemes will be favoured principally by young people with a low degree of risk aversion. For people who work for a company with a good occupational pension scheme and who intend to remain with the company for the remainder of their careers, the occupational scheme is likely to be the better choice.

9.1.4. THE CHOICE BETWEEN A PERSONAL PENSION SCHEME AND A CONTRACTED-OUT MONEY-PURCHASE SCHEME

An employer's contracted-out money-purchase scheme (COMPS) has a number of potential advantages over a personal pension scheme taken out by an individual employee, even though both are money-purchase schemes and both are contracted out of SERPS. The main advantages are as follows:

- the employer's group scheme is likely, as a result of economies of scale, to be cheaper to administer on a per-capita basis than a personal pension scheme. The government itself has assumed administrative expenses of 7 per cent of premiums for a COMPS and 10 per cent for a personal scheme;
- national-insurance refunds for a COMPS can be paid into the pension fund at the same time that wages or salaries are paid, that is, on a weekly or monthly basis. This is because with this type of scheme NICs are paid net of the refund. However, with personal pensions NICs are paid gross, and the refund does not become available for reinvestment until some time after the end of the tax year. On average there is a delay of about nine months before the refunds are invested in a personal scheme;
- it is more likely that employers will make additional contributions into their own schemes (in addition to the national-insurance rebate) than into a personal pension scheme, especially if those taking out personal schemes are regarded as likely early leavers;
- additional benefits, such as death-in-service benefits, may be provided free in a COMPS; they would cost extra to provide in a personal scheme.

A comparison of the two types of scheme is shown in Table 9.4, using an example which was constructed at the time such schemes first became available. COMPSs became available on 6 April 1988, while personal

TABLE 9.4. *Comparison between personal pensions and COMPSs (%)*

Male age in 1988	Real rate of return over earnings			
	COMPS		Personal pension	
	1%	3%	1%	3%
20	up 65	up 185	up 46	up 155
30	up 51	up 125	up 33	up 102
35	up 36	up 90	up 20	up 70
40	up 21	up 57	up 7	up 41
45	up 5	up 29	down 6	up 16
50	down 11	up 3	down 19	down 6
55	down 22	down 15	down 28	down 22
Crossover age	(47)	(51)	(43)	(49)

Notes: Results for females as for males ten years older.
The figures assume:
- rebate-only schemes;
- tax rate 27%;
- gross investment return 13% p.a.;
- fund at normal retirement date applied on unisex annuity rates at 10% p.a.;
- 3% p.a. increases;
- 50% spouse's pension.

Source: *Daily Telegraph*, 25 Apr. 1987.

schemes taken out before April 1989 could be backdated to 6 April 1987. In the example, both schemes are financed only from rebates of national-insurance contributions. A gross investment return of 13 per cent p.a. is assumed, with a real investment return over earnings of either 1 per cent or 3 per cent, together with annuity rates at normal retirement age of 10 per cent p.a. The pension is assumed to increase at 3 per cent p.a., and there is a 50 per-cent spouse's pension. With these assumptions the table compares the employer's scheme and the personal scheme against a baseline provided by SERPS.

In the case of real investment returns of 1 per cent, men below 47 (women below 37) gain by being in a COMPS compared with being in SERPS. Similarly, men less than 43 (women less than 33) gain from being in a personal scheme compared with being in SERPS. The table also shows how much better off an individual is in a COMPS compared with a personal scheme. For example, a 20-year-old male receives a pension that is 65 per cent higher than a SERPS pension if he is in COMPS, whereas his pension is only 46 per cent higher if he has a personal pension. This implies that a 20-year-old COMPS member can expect to receive a pension that is 13 per cent higher than a comparable personal pension.

9.1.5. THE CHOICE BETWEEN CONTRACTED-OUT MONEY-PURCHASE SCHEMES AND GROUP PERSONAL PENSION SCHEMES

Small employers who would like to operate contracted-out money-purchase schemes for their employees can choose between contracted-out money purchase schemes (COMPSs), based on the guaranteed minimum contribution (GMC) test; and group personal pension schemes (GPPSs).

COMPSs have quite cumbersome administrative arrangements in respect of national-insurance rebates. The GMCs into a COMPS provide *protected rights* for members of the scheme, and so are designed to replicate the rights under SERPS. As a result, a two-tiered administration system is necessary to handle the reduced NICs for employees contracted-out under the COMPS and the full NICs for employees who have chosen to remain in SERPS. If the employer makes only the minimum level of contributions, the payments under the two schemes have to be reconciled on a monthly basis. On the other hand, if the employer pays more than the minimum contributions, rebate reconciliations can be made at the end of the year. Similarly, if an employee joins or leaves a COMPS part of the way through the tax year, the employer is required to identify the minimum contributions for that individual immediately. There are additional problems when an employee wishes to join the company's additional voluntary contribution scheme, because the company has to ensure that excessive benefits are not paid.

GPPSs, on the other hand, are much simpler for the employer to operate, because they are little more than collections of individual personal pensions, so they do not even require audited accounts. Tax relief is also permitted on the employee's portion of the rebate. The disadvantage of a GPPS is that the rebate from the DSS is not usually recovered for several months, unlike the case of a COMPS where the rebate is available immediately for investing. In addition, GPPSs, as with all personal pensions, come under the know-your-client rule of the Financial Services Act, so advisers must conduct a financial profile of every member of the GPPS. Also, employers are not obliged to contribute to a GPPS.

So the choice between a COMPS and a GPPS depends on whether the employer's payroll system is sophisticated enough to handle the national-insurance rebates. If not, a GPPS may be preferred.

9.1.6. THE NON-PENSION BENEFITS OF PENSION SCHEMES

While the most important benefit of a pension scheme is undoubtedly its retirement pension, there are often other benefits from being a member of a pension scheme that are not directly related to the pension. The most significant of these is that the pension assets being accumulated can be used as security for making loans, particularly in the form of pension mortgages and pension loans. These non-pension benefits were originally available only to members of personal pension schemes or their precursors, such as section 226 self-employed schemes. But to prevent defections to personal pension schemes, occupational pension schemes have begun to offer similar benefits.

9.1.6.1. *Pension Mortgages*

Pension mortgages are mortgages of up to thirty-five years raised on the strength of the assets underlying an individual's pension scheme. They began in the early 1980s, when the self-employed and others with individual pension schemes began using their schemes to raise low-cost mortgage finance. In the late 1980s, following the legislation allowing individuals to opt out of their company's occupational scheme, occupational schemes were forced to introduce pension mortgages themselves in an attempt to retain membership within their schemes. Pension mortgages have been available to all home-buyers since April 1988.

An early example of a pension-mortgage scheme was the one devised by consulting actuaries Bacon and Woodrow in 1987 for the employees of occupational schemes advised by them. The mortgage is arranged through the Bank of Scotland, which will lend money against a range of different pension schemes: company final-salary schemes, company money-purchase schemes, executive pension schemes, additional voluntary contribution (AVC) schemes, and personal pension schemes.

Pension mortgages operate by using the tax-free lump sum at retirement to repay the loan capital; the tax-free lump sum was limited to 1.5 times final salary up to a maximum of £150,000 in the 1987 Finance Act, however. The pension mortgage is therefore a standard endowment mortgage with a life-assurance policy. The cost of a pension mortgage comprises the interest on the loan, the premiums on the life policy, and the contributions to the pension scheme. The pension mortgage is, therefore, highly tax-efficient because the pension contributions are fully tax-deductible at the individual's highest marginal tax rate up to an income level of £60,000 (in 1989 prices), although, as with standard endowment mortgages, the insurance premiums are not tax-deductible (life-assurance premium relief (LAPR) of 15 per cent was abolished in the 1984 Budget), and the interest payments on the loan are tax-deductible only up to the first £30,000 of loan (and then only at the basic rate, following the 1991 Budget, and further reduced to the lower rate, following the November 1993 Budget). Nevertheless, a pension mortgage is the least expensive method of paying off a mortgage for all individuals, regardless of their marginal tax rates. This is because of the two advantages that it has over a standard endowment mortgage: tax relief on contributions and an investment fund that is tax-free. These advantages can more than double the return for the same outlay.

The main problem with pension mortgages, however, is that they reduce the pension available at retirement. It is for this reason that Bacon and Woodrow recommend that employees take out an AVC scheme at the same time as taking out a pension mortgage in order to make up for the reduced pension at retirement. The contributions to the AVC scheme also attract tax relief, but the AVC pension benefit must be paid as an annuity and not as a lump sum. AVC schemes also have the advantage that contribution-rates can vary, so that individuals can start off with a low contribution-rate and raise this as their salaries increase.

Table 9.5 shows the monthly contributions to an AVC scheme necessary to finance a pension mortgage. Someone taking out a loan of £100,000 at age 30 can finance this with AVCs of only £22 per month (net) if he is a basic-rate taxpayer and only £17 per month (net) if he is a higher-rate payer, although these contributions grow at 10 per cent p.a.

Nevertheless, pension mortgages are frowned upon by the Inland

TABLE 9.5. *Monthly contributions to an AVC scheme to finance a pension mortgage* (£)

Age when AVCs start	Loan of £30,000				Loan of £100,000			
	25% taxpayer		40% taxpayer		25% taxpayer		40% taxpayer	
	Gross	Net	Gross	Net	Gross	Net	Gross	Net
30	9	7	9	5	29	22	29	17
35	15	11	15	9	49	37	49	29
40	25	19	25	15	80	60	80	48
45	41	31	41	25	138	104	138	83
50	75	56	75	45	250	188	250	150
55	150	113	150	90	498	374	498	299

Note: Assumes that contributions to produce a fund at 65 are sufficient to pay off the loan, assuming AVCs start at ages shown and grow at 10% p.a.

Source: Bacon and Woodrow, *Daily Telegraph*, 28 Mar. 1987.

TABLE 9.6. *The benefits of a pension mortgage: cost of borrowing £30,000 over twenty-five years for a man of 30 in good health and paying income tax at 25% (£)*

Type of mortgage	Total net monthly payment	Surplus cash at end
Level net repayment	227.45*	Nil
Low-cost endowment	222.21†	10,900‡
Pension	243.79§	22,000¶

Notes: Assumes interest rate of 9.75% p.a.

* Includes mortgage protection policy for non-smoker.

† Includes interest and endowment premiums.

‡ Surplus after paying off mortgage. Growth rate of 10.5% p.a. assumed.

§ Includes interest, pension premiums, and insurance for non-smoker over 30 years.

¶ Plus life pension of £18,000 guaranteed for five years, assuming growth rate of 13% p.a.

Source: Abbey National Building Society, *Daily Telegraph*, 2 July 1988.

Revenue. The legislation relating to personal pension schemes stipulates that they must be used 'solely' and not 'mainly' to provide retirement benefits. The Inland Revenue's view is that the aim of the tax concessions is to encourage saving for retirement and not to provide low-cost mortgages. The problem is that any scheme that assigns the lump sum at retirement will not be approved by the Pension Schemes Office. Even the literature that promotes the pension scheme can make no connection between the lump sum and paying off the mortgage. However, provided the lump sum is not assigned it can be used for any purpose, including paying off a mortgage.

The advantage of a pension mortgage is shown in the example illustrated in Table 9.6. A man aged 30 takes out a £30,000 mortgage over twenty-five years at an interest rate of 9.75 per cent. His marginal rate of tax is 25 per cent. There are three ways of repaying the mortgage: a level net repayment mortgage, a low-cost endowment mortgage, and a pension mortgage. The pension mortgage costs slightly more in terms of monthly repayments, but leads to a substantially higher net cash surplus at the end of the loan.

9.1.6.2. *Pension Loans*

Pension loans are an extremely tax-efficient way of raising funds from pension schemes for both individuals and companies. However, different rules apply depending on whether the loan is from a personal pension scheme or from a company pension scheme. The differences are shown in Table 9.7. Personal-pension loans are generally available to individuals with the following types of pension scheme: personal pension schemes, directors' pension schemes, and AVC and FSAVC schemes. The loan does not come from the pension fund itself, but from a bank, building society, or insurance company. The loan must generally be secured. However, the pension-fund assets cannot be used as security for the loan, so security in the form of property, shares, bonds, or a life policy has to be pledged. The first loan schemes came on the market in November 1980.

The loan can be used in a number of ways. The most frequent use is to buy residential property (in other words, the individual is taking out a pension mortgage). Other uses cover the purchase of commercial property, the purchase of shares in a company or partnership, or school fees. The minimum size of the loan is usually £15,001, since any person introducing a client to a lender will need a credit broking licence under the 1974 Consumer Credit Act if the loan is below this amount. There is no pre-set maximum to the size of the loan, although in most cases the loan is limited to a particular multiple (usually 15) of the annual premiums or a particular multiple (usually 2.5) of the policy-holder's salary.

TABLE 9.7. *Types of pension loan*

	Personal loan	Company loan
Eligibility	Personal pension schemes; directors' schemes; AVC and FSAVC schemes.	Small self-administered pension schemes (SSAPSs); executive schemes.
Borrower	Individual.	Company.
Lending source	Bank, building society, insurance company.	SSAPS pension fund; insurance company (with executive schemes).
Purpose	Residential or commercial property; school fees.	Commercial use.
Repayment	Tax-free lump sum or other source.	Company reserves or refinancing.

Source: Allied Dunbar, *Daily Telegraph*, 7 June 1986.

In some cases the loan is related to the size of the fund and can be as high as 100 per cent. The pension loan is repaid when the individual retires from the tax-free lump sum; in other words, the repayment of the capital is free of tax.

Company-pension loans are available from company pension schemes up to 50 per cent of the value of the scheme. Such loans are most frequently associated with small self-administered pension schemes or executive pension schemes which manage the pensions of the owners, controlling directors, or executives of the company. The loan is made by the pension scheme to the company; in other words, it is a *loan-back* arrangement. The loan must be used for commercial purposes, and most loans are used to buy the company property, or to purchase plant and machinery for use in the company. The loan has to be made at market interest rates and must be repaid one year before the directors retire. A loan of this kind provides a very useful source of finance for small companies which might otherwise have serious cash-flow problems. Similar loans are available for partnerships.

Company-pension loans are also available for companies whose directors have personal pension schemes, say, with an insurance company. This time the loan comes from the insurance company rather than the pension fund, but again it is limited to 50 per cent of the value of the fund and must be used for commercial purposes. As with personal-pension loans, tax relief is available on the loan repayments.

The problem with company-pension loans is that they are limited to 50 per cent of the value of the pension fund. With a new company the pension fund is likely to be too small for it to be worthwhile taking out a company-pension loan. For this reason a new type of scheme involving a bridging loan has been devised. One of the early proponents of this type of scheme was the Midland Bank, which began offering loans based on pension policies underwritten by the Sun Life Insurance Company in 1986. The Midland Bank's scheme operates as follows. The bank will offer medium-term loans to credit-worthy companies operating an executive pension scheme. Suppose that the company requires a loan of £100,000 to buy its company property. The loan is an interest-only loan for twelve years. Suppose that after three years the pension fund is sufficiently large to justify a pension loan from the insurance company of £25,000. This sum is used to reduce the bank loan to £75,000. Interest on the bank loan is reduced, but interest on the pension loan has to be paid. As the pension fund grows the bank loan can be replaced with additional pension loans. For example, the bank loan could be paid off in three further tranches of £25,000 every three years. After twelve years the company property is being financed entirely with a company-pension loan. But the pension loan has to be repaid one year before the directors retire. The Midland Bank's minimum bridging loan is £50,000 over ten to fifteen years. Interest on the bank loan and pension loan will be about 3 per cent above base rate.

9.2. Retirement Decisions

The ultimate objective of a pension scheme is, of course, to provide a pension in retirement; in 1993 there were 10 million pensioners in the UK. But there are a number of quite complex decisions about retirement that have to be made. We consider some of them in this section.

9.2.1. DECIDING THE AGE OF RETIREMENT

While people cannot receive their state pension until state retirement age, they can, in principle, take normal retirement at any age between 50 and 75. However, the size of their pension depends on their situation at retirement. If they are members of occupational pension schemes, their pension will depend on their salary at retirement and the number of years of accrued service. If they are members of personal pension schemes, their pension depends on the fund accumulated at retirement. Clearly, the earlier the age of retirement the lower the pension, because contributions have been paid for a shorter period and the pension has to be paid for a longer period. This is true for both occupational and personal pension schemes; although in the case of personal pensions it is conceivable that an extreme fall in stock-market values might reduce the value of the accumulated fund available for paying the pension annuity for someone who delays retirement.

There is another danger for people taking early retirement. If they do not have a pension that is fully index-linked, they will suffer a systematic reduction in the real value of their pension over time whenever inflation is above 3 per cent or 5 per cent, respectively the maximum levels for mandatory pension increases with personal or occupational pensions. An individual with a personal pension scheme also has to decide on the type of annuity (for example, level or escalating) and the insurance company that offers the annuity (that is, the open-market option).

So the decision about when to retire is by no means an easy one to make, since it is not a riskless decision, nor is it easily reversible: most people who retire would not easily find the opportunity of returning to full-time employment.

9.2.2. USING THE LUMP SUM TO BUY AN ANNUITY

When an individual retires he can either take a full pension or commute part of the pension in return for a lump sum. In the latter case, it is possible to use the lump sum to buy an annuity (called a *purchased life annuity*) and to receive a larger overall pension than in the former case. This is because of the way in which annuities are taxed. Part of the annuity is treated as a return of capital, and this element is free of tax. Only the income component of the annuity is subject to tax.

The type of annuity will be the same as for a personal pension annuity (see Section 7.6.1.1), and can, for example, involve joint-life benefit:

1. *Level annuity*. With a level annuity, the return-of-capital element is a fixed amount equal to the following proportion of the capital sum: (1/life expectancy of the annuitant), using the mortality tables PA(90) of the Institute of Actuaries. So, if the annuitant has a life expectancy of ten years, then one-tenth of the capital sum is treated as a tax-free return of capital for each year of the annuity until the annuitant's death.

2. *Escalating* and *index-linked annuities*. With an escalating annuity, the return-of-capital element is a fixed proportion of the annuity. An escalating annuity is one in which the annuity starts at a lower level than the level annuity but increases annually at a fixed rate of, say, 3 per cent or 5 per cent. An index-linked annuity increases in line with inflation. In these cases the annuitant gets partial or complete protection from inflation.

3. *Unit-linked* and *with-profits annuities*. It is also possible to have unit-linked and with-profits annuities, but in these cases the annuity will be variable.

4. *Minimum guarantee annuity*. It is possible to have an annuity where payments are guaranteed for a certain period, such as five years, whether or not the annuitant dies before five years.

5. *Capital-protected annuity*. Alternatively, it is possible to take out a *capital-protected annuity*, where the balance of the capital is paid to the annuitant's estate when he dies. At the time of death the annuity reduces the value of the estate for inheritance-tax purposes. For a higher-rate taxpayer, each £1,000 annuity costs his estate only £600 since the other £400 would have been taken as inheritance tax at death. The capital-protected annuity nevertheless involves a liability for inheritance tax. This can be avoided by having a straight annuity together with a whole life-assurance policy. The premiums on the assurance policy are paid out of part of the income from the annuity. The policy is placed in trust, and upon the death of the annuitant the sum assured goes to the named beneficiaries free of inheritance tax.

We can illustrate the effect of the return-of-capital factor in the case of a level annuity both for a self-employed person and for an employee, using data from Equitable Life. Suppose that a self-employed man of 65 retires with a pension fund of £50,000 with which he could purchase a lifetime annuity of £6,803 p.a. After tax at 25 per cent, the annuity is worth £5,102 p.a. Alternatively, he could take £15,162 as a lump sum, leaving a pension of £4,737 p.a. or £3,553 after tax. The lump sum could be used to buy an annuity of £1,967 p.a. However, £1,054 of this is treated as a tax-free return of capital, leaving only £913 to be taxed. The net income from the annuity is therefore £1,739 p.a. The combined income from the pension and annuity is £5,292 p.a., which is £190 p.a. more than with the pension alone.

Now suppose that a male employee aged 65 retires with the choice between a pension of £10,000 p.a. (£7,500 after tax) or a lump sum of £22,500 and a pension of £7,500 p.a. (£5,625 after tax). The lump sum could be used to purchase an annuity of £2,797, of which £1,460 is treated as a tax-free return of capital, leaving only £1,337 to be taxed. The net income from the annuity is therefore £2,463 p.a. The combined income from the pension and annuity is £8,088 p.a., which is £588 p.a. more than with the pension alone.

These examples seem to illustrate that taking the lump sum is the best choice. But this is not always the case. For example, in the case of an index-linked pension, the pension would increase each year in line with inflation, whereas the annuity from the lump sum is fixed in nominal terms. Sooner or later, the index-linked pension would exceed the fixed pension and annuity.

9.2.3. OTHER SOURCES OF INCOME IN RETIREMENT

9.2.3.1. *Part-Time Employment*

While most people who have retired may not easily find, and may not even want to return to, full-time employment, there are other ways of supplementing the pension in retirement. The most obvious way of doing this is through part-time employment. Income from part-time employment has been called the *fourth pillar* of support in old age, and will become increasingly important as the demographic increase in the ratio of pensioners to workers being experienced in the UK and other advanced countries begins to bite (see Section 10.2.1.1).

9.2.3.2. *Equity Release*

Another important source of income for pensioners is *equity release*. With equity release, home-owners can borrow against the equity in their homes. The resulting loan is used to buy an annuity. A typical equity-release scheme from a building society might lend home-owners aged 60 and over up to 25 per cent of the value of their property. The income from the annuity is fixed to cover the fixed rate of interest on the mortgage, with any surplus available as income to the pensioner. Schemes such as this are usually known as *home-income schemes*. They are relatively safe since they do not involve any accumulation of interest payments. Alternatively, interest on the loan can be deferred or capitalized, so that no interest is payable until the loan exceeds 70 per cent of the value of the equity. This is called a *roll-up loan scheme*. The implied interest rate on the loan is 1 per cent above the standard mortgage rate. This means that with a borrowing rate of 15 per cent, interest payments on the loan would not be required for 7.4 years; if the borrowing rate was 10 per cent, interest payments would not be required for 10.8 years. The danger of a scheme such as this is that the pensioner might have to sell the house or flat in order to repay the loan. The scheme is therefore only suitable for fairly elderly pensioners (over about 70), if they have no other source of finance.

Another alternative is the *reversion scheme*, whereby the pensioner sells the home to an insurance company, for example, and in return is permitted to live in the house and receive an income for life.

One vehicle for achieving equity release that came to be regarded as a poor one for pensioners was the *home-income investment bond* (also known as the *property-reversion bond*). The objective of the bond was to convert the equity in a pensioner's home into income. The home is mortgaged and the proceeds invested in an investment bond issued by an insurance company. The return on the bond would be enough both to pay the interest on the mortgage loan and provide an income for the pensioner. But the bonds performed very badly during the late 1980s as a result of stagnant equity markets, falling house prices, and high interest rates. In many cases the return on the investment bond was insufficient to pay the interest on the loan, let alone provide an income for pensioners. In October 1990 LAUTRO (the Life Assurance and Unit Trust Regulatory Organization) and FIMBRA (the Financial Intermediaries, Managers and Brokers Regulatory Association) effectively banned the product. Some insurance companies even felt obliged to compensate pensioners who bought investment bonds which failed to provide adequate income, and who otherwise would have lost their homes.

9.2.3.3. *Personal Equity Plans*

Personal equity plans (or PEPs) can provide a flexible form of tax-efficient income in retirement, especially if it is believed that income tax rates might go up in the future. In terms of tax treatment, PEPs are the exact inverse of pension schemes. With pension schemes, contributions are subject to tax relief at the highest marginal rate of income tax and they accumulate in a fund that is free from both income and capital gains taxes; but the pension annuity itself is subject to income tax (although any lump sum is tax-free). With PEPs, on the other hand, there is no tax relief on contributions, and the contributions build up in a tax-free fund; but the proceeds from the PEP can be taken as a tax-free lump sum.

For higher rate taxpayers, the front-end relief available from pension schemes is likely to make them more attractive savings vehicles than PEPs, especially if they expect their marginal tax rate to be lower once they retire. However, if tax rates are expected to rise in the future, then for basic rate taxpayers, the future tax benefits from a PEP might be greater than the 25 per cent tax relief gained from current pension contributions.

Another factor is contribution limits, especially when comparing PEPs with AVCs. Contributions into AVCs are restricted to 15 per cent of earnings less any contributions into an occupational scheme; in addition, there is a pensions earnings cap (set at £75,000 in 1993–4). For most people, the PEP limit in 1993–4 of £6,000 per year plus an additional £3,000 in a single company plan will be higher.

However, personal pension schemes may be better than PEPs for older or richer individuals. The contribution limit into personal pension schemes is 17.5 per cent of earnings for people under 50 but rises to 40 per cent for those over 61. In addition, any unused allowances can be carried forward for up to six years, whereas the PEP limit applies to individual tax years. Personal pensions are, however, subject to the earnings cap. For low earners, those working part-time, or those taking career breaks, PEPs may be preferred, since such people are unlikely to make sufficient contributions to render a personal pension scheme worthwhile.

The main advantage of PEPs is their flexibility. The money in personal pension schemes and AVCs is locked in at least until the age of 50, whereas PEPs can be cashed in at any time. In addition, it is possible to switch between funds with PEPs. For example, young people can start a PEP using a capital growth unit trust and then switch to an income fund once they retire.

9.2.3.4. *National Savings Pensioners Guaranteed Income Bonds*

In the November 1993 Budget the government announced that a *National Savings Pensioners Guaranteed Income Bond* would be introduced from the beginning of 1994. The bond is a five-year, fixed-rate investment that pays a monthly income. The interest is paid gross which is beneficial for non-taxpayers on low incomes. It is designed to provide a regular and predictable income stream at a competitive interest rate. It provides an alternative to the fluctuating interest rates available on bank and building society deposits.

9.2.4. PENSION DEFERRAL

Another decision that can be made at normal retirement age is to draw the pension and to continue working. We can examine the advantages and disadvantages of doing this using the state pension scheme.

Individuals reaching state retirement age (65 for men, 60 for women) have the right to defer taking their state retirement pension for up to five years. By doing this their state pension will be enhanced by 1 per cent for every seven weeks deferred, or by approximately 7.4 per cent p.a. If they defer for the full five years, their state pension will be enhanced by 37.3 per cent. An alternative to deferring the pension is to take the pension, save it up, and use the accumulated lump sum to buy an annuity. Which choice is better? The answer depends on interest rates, inflation rates, and life expectancy.

We can consider the following realistic example. Suppose that a man retired aged 65 in 1989 and defers claiming his state retirement pension for five years. Assuming a constant inflation rate of 7.3 per cent p.a., the basic pension would be £62.60 per week in 1994 and this is increased by £23.35 per week or by 37.3 per cent for the man, now aged 70. The £23.35 would itself be increased by the rate of inflation for the remaining life of the pensioner.

His alternative strategy would be to take the pension and invest it in a building society. With an inflation rate of 7.3 per cent and an interest rate of 9.5 per cent after tax, the pension would, with interest reinvested, have accumulated into a lump sum of £16,500 in five years. For a 70-year-old man this would buy a level annuity of £50 per week for life. Since the life expectancy of a 70-year-old man is eleven years, this suggests that in this example taking the pension is better than deferring it, because the level annuity exceeds the additional pension for the whole of the eleven years. Only if the man lives for more than twelve years will the additional deferred pension exceed the annuity.

The opposite result holds for a woman, however. At 65, a woman would be able to buy a level annuity of £40 per week. This would exceed the additional deferred pension for only eight years, and a 65-year-old woman has a life expectancy of seventeen years. On average, therefore, the woman would be better off by deferring the pension.

The general conclusion is that higher inflation rates and greater longevity favour deferring the pension, while lower inflation and shorter longevity favour taking the pension and buying an annuity.

9.2.5. RETIREMENT PLANNING

Retirement planning is gradually becoming a more important issue, according to a survey on retirement attitudes conducted by the Halifax Building Society in February 1991. The survey found that a quarter of the people retiring at the beginning of the 1980s had no personal savings for their retirement. They relied entirely on their state pension. However, of those due to retire in the mid-1990s, only 10 per cent had no personal savings for their retirement.

Table 9.8 shows the sources of income for those already retired. Nine out of every ten pensioners have a state pension. Half the pensioners have company pensions and a quarter can rely on investment income.

Table 9.9 shows the financial provisions made by those planning retirement in the mid-1990s. The Halifax survey found that 42 per cent were making contributions to their company pension scheme and that 8 per cent were making additional voluntary contributions. The survey found that 83 per cent were building up savings in building society or bank deposits. More sophisticated investment strategies included insurance policies (40 per cent), special investment plans (12 per cent), and unit trusts (6 per cent); however, 70 per cent of respondents regarded equity investments as 'too risky'. Property (especially the residential home) was regarded as an important source of investment for retirement by 36 per cent of respondents.

The majority of those either in or close to retirement had a strong aversion to taking out credit. Major consumer-durable items such as cars and electrical appliances had to be purchased prior to retirement and were expected to last. Even those expecting substantial pensions felt that they had to budget carefully after retirement.

Finally, the survey found that most people were not greatly concerned

TABLE 9.8. *Income in retirement*

Source	Pensioners with source (%)
State pension	89
Company pension	52
Part-time job	7
Investments	24
Other	4

Source: Halifax Building Society Retirement Survey, 19 Feb. 1991.

TABLE 9.9. *Financial provisions for retirement*

Source	Individuals with source (%)
Company pension scheme contributions	42
Additional voluntary contributions	8
Savings—building society	50
—bank	33
Property	36
Insurance policy	40
Special investment plan	12
Unit trusts	6
None	16

Source: Halifax Building Society Retirement Survey, 19 Feb. 1991.

about inheritance-tax planning. They would like to leave something to their children, but felt that their children were already better off than they were, and they had, in any case, been told by their children to spend their money on themselves.

9.2.6. THE COST OF CARE IN OLD AGE

Finally in this chapter we will consider an issue that ought to be of concern to all people planning retirement, and this is the cost of care in old age. Three-quarters of those living beyond the age of 85 are severely disabled, requiring either specialist care or residential care. However, in 1991 the average cost for nursing-home care was £13,000 p.a., greatly exceeding the average pension of £8,000 p.a. Clearly, this cost can only be met from non-pension sources. In the past these alternative sources have been savings and home-equity release. More recently insurance companies have begun to design policies that deal with this eventuality. For example, in 1991 Commercial Union launched a policy called 'Third Age Initiative' which is aimed at people over 30. The policy has three options.

The 'Life Plus' option is a life-assurance policy that will pay an annuity if the policy-holder becomes disabled or a lump sum on death. The policy-holder will be considered disabled if he or she is unable to perform four out of six particular daily activities, such as feeding himself or herself or getting out of bed unaided. The payments under this option equal 2 per cent per month of the sum assured for a maximum of fifty months, with the first payment being made three months after a valid claim. For premiums of £50 per month in 1991, a non-smoking 30-year-old male had a guaranteed sum assured of £92,233, equivalent to £1,844 per month for fifty months. However, a 60-year-old woman also paying premiums of £50 per month had a sum assured of only £13,117 or only £262 per month for fifty months, which would not have been sufficient to pay for nursing-home costs.

The 'Well Being' option will pay directly for home care or nursing-home care. This can be paid for as a single premium or in monthly instalments. A 60-year-old man could buy cover of £18,000 per year indefinitely for a monthly premium of £98 or a lump sum of £11,516. The 'Well Being' policy is an insurance policy rather than a life policy, so there is no surrender value.

The 'Health-Wise' option is a medical-insurance policy designed for those over 60. The policy provides cover of up to £60,000 for the treatment of conditions diagnosed after the policy has been taken out. The premiums on this policy are subject to tax relief. The net monthly premium in 1991 for someone aged between 75 and 79 was £53.40 if they lived in London and £29.40 if they lived outside London.

Since 1990, premiums for private health insurance cover benefit from income tax relief at the basic rate for people over 60. However, the government estimated that by 1993, only half a million people out of a total of 12m. people over 60 had taken out private medical insurance.

10

Pensions and Public Policy

In this chapter we examine some of the public-policy issues concerning pensions in the UK. The Conservative government in power since 1979 has made some radical changes to the UK pensions scene. It has been motivated by such factors as the desire to promote individual enterprise in a market economy and the desire to reduce the cost to the state of providing pensions. These factors have led the state to introduce personal pension schemes and, from the turn of the next century, to reduce the benefits payable under the state earnings-related pension scheme. But there are other issues of public concern, ranging from possible inter-generational conflict as the balance of economic power between workers and pensioners changes, through questioning the efficacy of tax subsidies and deciding what to do with pension-fund surpluses and the pensioner victims of inflation, to European Commission directives on the equal treatment of men and women and whether personal pension schemes can be expected to deliver stable pensions in the presence of volatile financial markets. Most recently, in the light of the Maxwell Affair, there has been concern about pension-fund theft by the sponsor.

10.1. Current Government Policy

The Conservative government's objectives have been: to extend choice and flexibility in pensions provision; to encourage more private-sector pensions provision; and to limit the cost to the state, whether through direct public expenditure or tax reliefs. There have been four main factors motivating these objectives.

First, the government has sought to make the pensions system consistent with its overriding policy of promoting the *enterprise economy*. The enterprise economy, amongst other things, requires increased labour mobility and offers people greater choice in planning for their retirement. Both these factors meant that the ties that employees had to their employers' occupational pension schemes needed to be weakened. This weakening of ties has been achieved by a series of measures that have, amongst other things, made occupational-pension scheme membership voluntary, given additional rights to early leavers, required schemes to provide adequate information to members, and introduced personal pension schemes as an alternative to occupational schemes. In addition, greater flexibility and choice in pensions provision have been made possible by the introduction of additional voluntary contribution and top-up schemes.

Secondly, demographic projections indicate that the pensioner population is going to continue to expand relative to the working population. In 1989 there were more than 10 million pensioners and 2.3 workers for every pensioner. By 2035 it is projected that there will be more than 13 million pensioners and only 1.7 workers for every pensioner.

Thirdly, as a consequence of these demographic projections, public expenditure on pensions (both on the basic state pension and the SERPS pension) was in danger of getting out of control. Public expenditure on pensions in 1989 was more than £20bn., about 40 per cent of the total cost of social security. Without the changes to SERPS, it was estimated by the government actuary that by 2054 public expenditure on pensions would have risen to £53bn. in 1989 prices. The total cost of the welfare state rose from 5 per cent of GDP in 1945 to 15 per cent in 1993.

These factors have led the government to attempt to reduce the level of public expenditure devoted to pensions provision, both in the form of direct expenditure and in the form of tax relief. The government has reduced the benefits paid by SERPS after 1999, provided incentives to leave SERPS, and placed limits on the amount of tax relief available on contributions and the benefits that can accrue in pension schemes.

Fourthly, the real living standard of pensioners has been steadily increasing over the last twenty years and is expected to continue increasing. Between 1979 and 1986 pensioners' real net incomes grew by 23 per cent, while between 1970 and 1986 they grew by 45 per cent. This increase was larger than for the population as a whole. It is estimated that about half of this increase came as a result of higher social-security pensions (including increased pensions from SERPS), while half came from higher private incomes in the form of savings and occupational pensions. Between 1979 and 1989 expenditure on social-security benefits paid to pensioners rose by 27 per cent in real terms, reflecting both increased pay-outs under SERPS and an increase of 10 per cent in the number of people receiving a state pension. In 1986 50 per cent of all pensioners and 70 per cent of newly retired pensioners had an occupational pension in addition to the basic state pension; in addition, 70 per cent of all pensioners and 85 per cent of newly retired pensioners were receiving investment income. So while there are still large numbers of pensioners who are very poor, the fact remains that the average pensioner has never been so well off. This fact has provided a further justification, in the government's view, for reducing the level of provision financed by the state.

However, the removal of compulsory membership of occupational pension schemes in 1988 may have the unintended consequence of increasing the cost to the state of pension provision. A National Association of Pension Funds survey in July 1993 indicated that 19 per cent of new employees do not bother to join their employer's scheme immediately, although they may do so eventually. During this period they will accumulate SERPS entitlements that would not have arisen prior to 1988. This represents an additional cost to the state. So the extension of 'choice' may well end up increasing rather than reducing the burden on the state.

The government's attempts to increase pension choice and flexibility, to reduce some of the inequities faced by early leavers and to transfer more of the liability for pension provision to the private sector has brought it into conflict with these private sector providers, even though there remains substantial co-operation and private occupational pension schemes still enjoy substantial tax breaks.

For example, occupational schemes were opposed to the establishment of personal pension schemes. Employers effectively boycotted them by refusing to make employers' contributions towards the personal pension schemes taken out by their employees, even though they would have been willing to put the same contributions on behalf of those same employees into their own schemes. The main reason for this is simple. With occupational schemes, the employer is committed to fund pensions based on final salary. Any surplus in the fund above this liability 'belongs to' the employer. So there is no danger to the employer of making excessive current contributions (that is, of overfunding the pension scheme), because any surplus employer's contributions can be withdrawn at a later stage. However, this is not the case with personal pension schemes. If an employer made contributions to an employee's personal pension scheme which turned out to be 'excessive', there is nothing that the employer can do about it subsequently: this contribution together with the investment return now 'belong to' the employee. So even though employers' contributions are determined to be actuarially fair in the sense that they are set at a level that should not systematically generate a surplus or a deficit, nevertheless employers have refused to put the same contributions into personal pension schemes. As a result, personal schemes are at a severe disadvantage compared with occupational schemes, even though personal schemes offer much greater flexibility to individuals than occupational schemes. There are other possible reasons for refusing to make employers' contributions into personal schemes. For instance, it would limit the huge investing power currently held by occupational schemes, and it would limit the ability of the company to use the pension scheme to attract highly skilled staff or to reward long service.

Occupational schemes were also opposed to extending the rights of early leavers by giving them greater inflation protection for their deferred pensions, on the grounds that this would reduce the ability of the scheme to deliver pensions to loyal long-term employees. Employers have threatened to wind up their schemes if the government imposes any more restrictions on their actions (occupational pension schemes in the UK are voluntary not compulsory). This is not considered to be a serious threat so far, and it is always possible for the government to issue a counter-threat to reduce the occupational schemes' tax breaks even further if they fail to co-operate in achieving greater flexibility in pension provision in the future.

10.2. Other Public-Policy Issues

As we have just seen, the government's policy towards pensions has been dominated by its objectives of reducing state expenditure and encouraging pension choice within the context of private-sector provision. Some of the changes that it has introduced have been motivated by external factors beyond its control (such as demographic changes), while some have been motivated by its attitude to individual enterprise and choice.

There are other public-policy issues that the government has not yet addressed, or at least it has addressed these issues only partially. Some of these relate to external demographic factors, while others can be discussed within the context of the government's attitude to enterprise and choice. All the issues can be examined in terms of potential conflicts or battles between various groups involved in providing or receiving pensions. In addition, most of the issues generally have a financial consequence, and so have an implication for pension funding.

10.2.1. THE BATTLE BETWEEN THE GENERATIONS

10.2.1.1. *What is the Potential for Inter-Generational Conflict?*

The rapid ageing (or *greying*) of the population that will occur in the UK over the next half-century (as well as in other industrialized countries), and is recognized by the government, increases the likelihood of *inter-generational conflict* in a way that the government has not recognized, at least publicly. This factor will affect the cost of both public-sector *and* private-sector pension provision. The government's policy appears to be to transfer as much as possible of this problem to the private sector.

As the ratio of pensioners to workers rises, both state and private pension systems will be obliged to reduce the real value of pensions or increase contribution-rates (equivalent to a forced increase in the savings ratio) or raise the age of normal retirement. If one or more of these things is not done, then the entire pension system will cease to be financially viable.

In the UK and other industrialized countries both the average age of the population and the ratio of pensioners to workers have risen as a result of better health-care increasing life expectancy, the post-war baby boom, and the subsequent decline in fertility rates. In 1950 about 12 per cent of the population was over 65, but by 2025 this proportion will have more than doubled to 25 per cent. It has been estimated that the decline in the ratio of workers to pensioners will require an increase in national-insurance contributions of 50 per cent. While in all industrialized countries there is a net flow of resources from the young to the old, the required increase in resources flowing from young to old is likely to be too large to be politically or socially acceptable.

In the case of Germany, contribution-rates to the state pension scheme would have to rise from 18.5 per cent of workers' income to 42 per cent by 2030. The message here should not be lost on other European Union states as they attempt to harmonize EU pensions to the German standard. In the USA the battle has been joined between the American Association of Retired Persons, which campaigns on behalf of pensioners, and Americans for Generational Equity (AGE), which wants to see the end of social-insurance programmes which benefit the elderly rich at the expense of the young poor.

The evidence indicates that the so-called 'welfare generation', the generation that went through the last war and subsequently extracted a price in the form of the establishment of the 'welfare state', will be the most favoured generation of all time. No generation before it could have hoped, and no generation following it can hope, to achieve the same level of benefits in terms of pensions, health-care, and welfare. The welfare generation contributed very little for these benefits, yet the next generation will not only have to contribute heavily to the welfare generation's pensions, it will experience poorer standards of welfare throughout its own life. Already we can see this in the UK in terms of the systematic decline in the funding of schools and hospitals.

In terms of government policy to alleviate the potential for inter-generational conflict, there would appear to be little room for manœuvre. If the required increase in contribution-rates of the order of 50 per cent is not politically or socially tolerable, then the only two alternatives are increasing the age of normal retirement or reducing the real value of pensions.

Increasing (or even abolishing) the normal retirement age would be a fairly simple and fairly painless solution to the problem. Also, some flexibility in retirement age is desirable, since it is clearly unsatisfactory to oblige all people to retire when they have reached a particular age. Work after the normal retirement age has been called the *fourth pillar* of support in old age (the first three pillars are respectively a state pension, a private pension, and personal savings).

However, the trend in industrialized countries over the last twenty years has been a falling retirement age, rather than an increasing one. For example, since 1970 male employment activity rates in the 55 to 64 age-group have fallen from 87 per cent to 57 per cent in the UK, from 81 per cent to 51 per cent in Germany, and from 74 per cent to 47 per cent in France. This has had the effect of worsening rather than alleviating the problem of funding pensions. The situation is not helped by the reluctance of employers to employ people in their fifties and sixties, preferring instead to take on much younger and cheaper employees. Older employees could do something to help their prospects if they showed some flexibility in terms of, say, remuneration expected and a willingness to adopt new technologies and employment practices.

Reducing the real value of pensions would be a much more difficult policy to implement, although the UK government has managed to reduce the real value of SERPS pensions for those retiring from the beginning of the next century. However, it faced substantial political hostility when it introduced the enabling legislation, and was forced to back down from its original plan of abolishing SERPS altogether.

A future government might find it very difficult politically to make further reductions. Currently in the UK 41 per cent of the electorate is aged 50 or over. By 2025 that proportion will have risen to more than 50 per cent. So the electoral balance of power will soon be held by a group of people much more interested in the size of their pensions than the size of the contributions paid into pension schemes.

10.2.1.2. *How Secure is a Pension Fund Really?*

The long-term benefits of establishing a pension fund would appear to be clear. The individual (together with his or her employer) pays contributions into a fund during the course of his or her working life. These accumulated pension savings, together with the investment returns on the savings, deliver a lump sum at retirement which can be used to purchase a pension annuity from retirement until death. If the value of the fund at retirement is sufficiently large, then the individual can be assured an adequate and stable standard of living during his or her twilight years, without having to rely on either the goodwill of former employers or the state.

In contrast, pay-as-you-go schemes depend not only on the continued goodwill but also on the continued solvency of former employers. The risk facing pensioners in PAYG schemes is that the firm might decline or become insolvent, so that there would be either insufficient or, in the worst case, no current contributors to pay the pensions of retired workers. As we have seen, SERPS has been affected by this problem. While the state scheme cannot go bankrupt as such, its finances can certainly be affected by the *dependency ratio* (the ratio of pensioners to workers).

There is, however, a quite different way of looking at the funding of pension schemes. From this different view, all pension schemes, whether funded or not, are in reality pay-as-you-go schemes. At first sight this may seem a strange notion, but it is related to the way in which the next generation (that is, the current working population) treats the previous generation (that is, the current retired population). Suppose that one generation builds up a fund of assets for its retirement. Its consumption at retirement depends on the 'value' of the fund at retirement. But the fund can only be used to purchase consumer goods that are produced by the next generation. No generation can store for its own retirement the consumer goods that it itself produced. Each generation is wholly dependent on the next generation, not only for the types of goods that it consumes in retirement, but also for the quantity of goods that it is able to consume, since the next generation also chooses the prices of those goods. This leads to another potential for inter-generational conflict, but this time the balance of power rests with the younger generation, since it is always possible for the next generation to reduce the value of the pension funds of the previous generation through inflation.

The point that is being made is that, despite having extracted 'guarantees' about indexed pensions, it is impossible for the generation in retirement to ensure the value of its pension in retirement, because it is impossible for that generation to *pre-commit* the next generation to deliver a particular flow of consumption goods. Since pensioners are interested in the *flow* of real goods and services in retirement, they will be interested in the *flow* of real purchasing power required to finance these goods and services. This is the case whether the pension scheme is 'funded' or 'unfunded'. In this sense, all pensions are pay-as-you-go and a pension fund is in reality only a deferred pay-as-you-go scheme. Instead of using current contributions to pay for pensions, a funded scheme pays for pensions using contributions made forty years before.

While this interpretation of reality cannot be ignored, we must nevertheless ask what the chances are of the current productively active generation decimating the previous generation, and also whether the claims of the retired generation are stronger if it has accumulated a pension fund. The risk faced by current workers in treating pensioners badly is that they could find themselves facing the same treatment when they retire.

Current workers have substantial bargaining power over pensioners. Yet it is also the case that pensioners with a pension fund have some counter-bargaining power. Suppose we have a simple framework in which workers supply all the labour to the production process, and pensioners, via their pension funds, supply all the capital. Both labour and capital are needed to produce goods and services. These goods and services are going to be shared between workers and pensioners according to their relative bargaining power. The claims over these goods and services are undeniably stronger in the case of funded pensioners compared with unfunded pensioners.

10.2.2. THE BATTLE WITH THE STATE OVER TAXATION

10.2.2.1. *Would It Be Better to End Tax Relief on Pension Schemes?*

In tax terms, pension-fund savings are treated more favourably than any other savings vehicle. Contributions into the scheme receive tax relief at the highest marginal rate of income tax. Investment income and realized capital gains within the fund accrue free of income and capital-gains tax respectively. At retirement there is a tax-free lump sum. Only the pension annuity itself is taxed as earned income. Is this favourable tax treatment justified?

The answer to this question depends on whether it would be possible to achieve a reasonable pension at retirement if these tax reliefs were absent. Without them there would be two possibilities: either the pension at retirement would be lower, or the contributions into the scheme would have to be higher. The tax reliefs are therefore a means of transferring purchasing power over time. If a society wishes to be a high-pension society, it can use the tax system to encourage this. The only anomaly in the present system is the tax-free lump sum. If this was taxed at the same rate as the pension annuity, then it would not matter what the size of the lump sum was. If it were not for the tax-free lump sum, the tax treatment of pension schemes would simply be one of *tax deferral*. In other words, all the inflows into the scheme are tax-relieved but the resulting higher outflows from the scheme when it matures would be taxed. The tax liability would merely be deferred and not avoided if the lump sum was also taxed. (The position is slightly more complicated than this because of the possibility of *tax arbitrage*, that is, it is possible for an individual to transfer the tax liability from a period where he or she faces a high marginal tax rate—that is, when he or she is in work—to a period where he or she faces a lower marginal tax rate—that is, when he or she is retired.)

Nevertheless, tax reliefs are a subsidy that can cause distortions elsewhere in the system. In particular, by making savings through a pension scheme more attractive than other forms of saving, tax reliefs discriminate against the direct holding of shares by individuals. While they hold shares indirectly through their pension funds, individuals can exercise no direct influence on the activities of companies by this means. Instead they have to rely on the pension funds themselves to exercise this influence on their behalf. And of course it is not clear that, as investors, individuals would take the same view as their pension funds about the activities of the companies whose shares they own.

Another distortion is that employees become imprisoned within their own occupational schemes. The tax system locks them into a particular scheme and makes it very expensive to move to another one. This reduces labour mobility and so leads to wider inefficiencies in the economy. The introduction of personal pension schemes was designed to overcome this.

As a final example of the distortions caused by tax reliefs, it would, of course, be possible for the current rate of income tax to be lower if the tax subsidies were absent. It has been estimated that in 1990 the tax relief on pension schemes was worth £15bn., equivalent to 10p in the pound off the standard rate of income tax. This would increase current disposable income and might actually increase pension savings (if the positive effect of increasing disposable income outweighed the discouraging effect of a lower net rate of return on pension savings).

On balance, the tax reliefs appear to be justified. Most people, especially the young, appear not to think too much about their pension. By the time they reach retirement, it is too late. Using tax reliefs to encourage people to save for their retirement is on the whole a good thing.

10.2.2.2. *Personal Pensions: Too Successful for their Own Good?*

The success of personal pensions has surprised the government. In 1988 the government estimated that at most 1.75 million people would leave SERPS and take out personal pensions. By the end of 1990 more than 4.5 million people had taken out personal pensions. The government had hoped that the introduction of personal pensions would reduce the cost to the state of providing pensions, but a National Audit Office (NAO) report in November 1990 showed that the opposite was true (see Section 7.12.3).

So, far from saving the state money, personal pensions have turned out to be extremely expensive. The government's main fear is that most personal pension scheme members will re-contract back into SERPS but keep both their personal pensions and the subsidy (special incentive) that was used to get them to leave SERPS initially. So great was the government's fear that in February 1992 it announced that there would be an additional 1 per cent age-related national-insurance rebate for everyone over the age of 30 who remained in a personal-pension scheme and did not re-contract back into SERPS. This additional rebate operates from April 1993, when the 2 per-cent incentive available to all those taking out personal pensions ended, until April 1996. The government estimated that those over 30 would be most likely to re-contract back into SERPS unless they had an additional inducement not to do so.

10.2.3. THE BATTLE BETWEEN THE MEMBERS AND THE SPONSOR

10.2.3.1 *Who Owns the Pension-Fund Assets?*

In final-salary occupational pension schemes, an important issue of concern is the ownership of pension-fund assets. Who owns the assets—the company or the workers? The answer would seem to be obvious: surely it is the workers? After all, the assets represent future pension rights. However, the real answer is more complicated, as the perennial problem of early leavers shows.

When an employee leaves a scheme he or she is entitled to a transfer value which can be transferred to a new scheme or preserved in the original scheme. However, early leavers can often end up with a raw deal, whatever option they choose. In the case of transferring to a new scheme, the transfer value in the new scheme can be worth as little as a quarter of the value that it was worth in the old scheme. This is because the new job usually involves a higher salary, which implies that the associated pension rights are more expensive to acquire. In the case of a preserved pension it is possible to get an even worse deal, as the following case, reported in the press, shows.

A man retired in 1988 aged 65. In 1968 he left a company scheme after ten years' service, leaving behind a frozen pension of £700 p.a. when he was 65. The pension was based on a non-profit policy with an insurance company. In return for combined employee and employer contributions of £2,500, the insurance company had to provide a £700 p.a. pension from 1988. In 1988, when he retired, the man duly received his £700 p.a. pension. But because of inflation it was worth considerably less in real terms than in 1968. The man discovered that in 1988 he could have purchased a £700 p.a. annuity for £5,000. This suggests that the pension fund had just doubled in value over twenty years. Had the £2,500 been invested in a building society it would have grown by 280 per cent, while if it had been invested in shares it would have grown in value by 550 per cent.

This experience demonstrates that early leavers do not have a strong claim on the assets of the fund. The actuaries are free to determine the transfer value. The actuary in the original scheme has an incentive to minimize the transfer value on the grounds that the solvency of the scheme for the 'loyal' employees remaining in the scheme is otherwise put at risk. In the USA the entitlement to a part of the pension is known as *vesting*. The 1974 Employee Retirement Income Security Act (ERISA) imposes minimum standards for vesting. Companies must now offer one of the following: 100 per-cent vesting after ten years of service; 25 per-cent vesting after five years, increasing to 100 per cent after fifteen years; or 50 per-cent vesting when age and service add up to 45, increasing to 100 per cent five years later. There is no equivalent set of standards operating in the UK. What is needed in occupational schemes is a common set of rules to determine transfer values on an equitable basis.

10.2.3.2. *Who Owns the Pension-Fund Surpluses and Deficits?*

In final-salary occupational pension schemes, an important issue concerns the ownership of any actuarial surplus or deficit. Unless the actuary's assumptions are fulfilled exactly, periodic surpluses or deficits are bound to emerge with final-salary schemes.

For example, in the UK the 1970s were characterized by deficits and the 1980s were characterized by very substantial surpluses. The size of the actuarial surplus or deficit is very sensitive to two factors that are difficult to predict: staff turnover and investment returns. The deficits of the 1970s resulted from poor investment returns. The surpluses of the 1980s resulted from very good investment returns and substantial redundancies, especially in manufacturing during 1980 and 1981. The effect of investment returns that are higher than anticipated by the actuary is to increase the value of pension-fund assets. The effect of redundancies is to freeze pension-fund liabilities at the salaries of the workers at the time of redundancy. Although the liabilities are partially indexed to retail-price inflation (up to a maximum of 5 per cent) until retirement age, the indexation is much less than would have occurred if the employees had remained in the scheme until retirement age. This is because the growth in average salaries in the UK exceeds the inflation rate by between 2 and 3 percentage points.

An alternative mechanism to redundancies for capturing the surplus in a pension scheme is to implement a *spin-off termination* of the scheme. This was a procedure attempted in 1986 when Hanson PLC sold its subsidiary Courage to Elders IXL. The Courage pension fund had a surplus of £80m. Hanson attempted to substitute Hanson for Courage as the 'principal company' in the trust deeds of the Courage scheme. It then sought to partially terminate the Courage scheme by setting aside a portion of the fund's assets for the purpose of securing only the accrued benefits of the subsidiary's employees. The remainder of the assets, including most of the surplus, would be left with the existing and deferred pensioners and would be under the control of Hanson. Hanson proposed to keep £70m. of the £80m. surplus for its own benefit or for the benefit of Hanson Group employees.

Hanson's plan went to the High Court and was rejected. Mr Justice Millet held that the Courage pension scheme had been set up for the benefit of Courage employees and the trust deeds could not be changed to substitute Hanson for Courage as the principal employer. Hanson's proposed changes were therefore *ultra vires*. The implication of the *Millet Judgment* is that pension schemes can change their trust deeds to prevent predatory take-overs designed to extract pension-fund surpluses.

Another means of generating a surplus is to *wind up* an existing scheme and replace it with another scheme. By winding up a scheme, liabilities in the form of accrued pension rights become crystallized at the date of the wind-up and, while further contributions also cease, the assets continue to grow. This makes any surplus in the scheme even larger. This was the procedure attempted again by Hanson in 1990. In 1986 Hanson closed the pension scheme of another subsidiary, Imperial Tobacco. New employees had to join a new pension scheme. In 1990 Hanson attempted to persuade members of the old scheme to join the new scheme. The inducement was an improvement in the annual inflation indexing of the pension from a maximum of 5 per cent (in the original scheme) to a maximum of 15 per cent (in the new scheme). The remainder of the surplus would revert to Hanson. Hanson refused to consider proposals by the pensioners for increasing pensions in the original scheme. It argued that the surplus in the original scheme was £130m. and that the cost of the inflation-proofing was £100m. However, an independent report by Pensions Investment Research Consultants prepared for the original scheme's pensioners claimed that the surplus was £230m. and the cost of inflation-proofing would only be £80m.

Hanson's plan again went to the High Court and was again rejected. The vice-chancellor, Sir Nicholas Browne-Wilkinson, held that Hanson had not given 'reasonable and proper' consideration to any of the proposals for improving pensions in the original scheme. The *Browne-Wilkinson Judgment* became a test case about the role of pension funds' management committees. It held that no management committee had the power to state in advance that it would veto all proposed future pension increases.

The solicitor for the pensioners claimed that the decision entitled the pensioners to full indexation of their schemes. Mr Michael Meacher, opposition spokesman for social security, went even further than this. In a letter to Mr Tony Newton, secretary of state for social security, he claimed:

It is becoming clearer by the day that pension fund surpluses must be used exclusively for the benefit of their members and pensioners, that contribution holidays are outlawed unless full inflation-proofing is guaranteed and that scheme members and pensioners have a controlling interest in the management of the fund. (*Daily Telegraph*, 3 November 1990)

A further judicial ruling concerning pension fund surpluses was made in July 1993 when Mr Justice Vinelott blocked a government-inspired move by British Coal to use a pension fund surplus to help finance redundancy payments. The *Vinelott Judgment* stated that British Coal could not allocate its half-share of a £1bn. surplus to pay what it owes its pension scheme for providing early and enhanced payments to redundant managerial and clerical staff. The plan would have broken the scheme's rules because it would have amounted to a 'transfer or payment out' which was prohibited. The judgment effectively meant that British Coal could realise its guaranteed half-share of the surplus only by extending its current ten-year contributions holiday beyond 1997.

However, despite these judicial rulings and the claims of Michael Meacher, the answer to the questions of who legally owns the surplus and who is responsible for the deficit is the company in both cases. In final-salary schemes the best that a scheme member can hope for is a pension based on two-thirds of final salary. Any deficit in the scheme must be made up by the company via a deficiency payment. The 1990 Social Security Act makes the company liable for any fund deficit if a fund is wound up. Any surplus in the scheme is legally owned by the company. It is perfectly entitled to recover that surplus entirely for itself, although it must be careful how it does so, especially in the case of subsidiaries. A company can only recover the surplus immediately by withdrawing it from the scheme if scheme rules permit. However, it can recover the surplus over time and without penalty through an employer-only contributions holiday.

In practice, companies have tended to share some of the surplus with both current members (via employee contributions holidays) and pensioners (via increased pensions). But the lion's share of the surplus is retained by the company. A survey of twenty of the country's largest employers by the opposition Labour party published in March 1991 found that fifteen of them had a surplus in their pension funds. Of these fifteen companies, two have suspended and eleven have reduced employer's contributions. Only two companies cut employees' contributions and only six increased pensions by more than the inflation rate. British Telecom and British Aerospace both suspended their employer contributions, but left employee contributions unchanged and raised pensions by less than inflation. The Post Office, British Rail, ICI, the Electricity Council, and Grand Metropolitan reduced employer contributions but left employee contributions unchanged and raised pensions by less than inflation. Only GEC cut contributions for both itself and its employees and raised the pension by more than inflation. The National Association of Pension Funds annual survey (February 1992) found that in 1991 47 per cent of employers were taking contributions holidays, but 80 per cent of members had no change in their own contribution-rates.

But the point is that scheme members are not legally entitled to share in the successful investments that have been made with their contributions. Given that pension contributions are a form of saving, generally a compulsory form of saving, the fact that the claims of scheme members over their pension assets are quite weak is somewhat surprising.

10.2.3.3. *What Can Be Done for the Victims of Inflation: Pensioners and Early Leavers?*

Inflation can have a devastating effect on the purchasing power of pensions for pensioners not in a fully indexed pension scheme. Until recently most private-sector pensions were increased by less than the inflation rate. For example, between 1984 and 1986 the average increase in pensions was 3.8 per cent and the average inflation rate was 4.8 per cent (*Government Actuary's Survey of Occupational Pension Schemes*, 1991, Table 9.1). However, company pension schemes have been more generous recently: according to the NAPF annual survey, 70 per cent of schemes increased benefits in line with inflation in 1991. Pensioners in money-purchase schemes are particularly badly affected. Also, early leavers can see their preserved pension rights substantially diminished even before they retire.

What can be done about this important problem? The argument of schemes in the private sector is that governments cause inflation and so it is up to governments to do something about the consequences of inflation. The counter-argument is that if there was no inflation, pension schemes would be *obliged* to deliver real pensions; unless, of course, they systematically cut the money value of the pensions that they paid! If they have to deliver real pensions when the inflation rate is zero, why can't they deliver real pensions when the inflation rate is positive?

This argument, it seems, is difficult to buck. Since contributions are proportional to salaries and average salaries grow in real terms by 2–3 per cent, this implies that contributions into schemes also grow in real terms by 2–3 per cent. In addition, fund managers claim to be able to generate long-run real returns on investing the contributions of around 2 per cent. On this basis there would seem to be no acceptable argument for not being able to deliver pensions that are fully indexed to retail-price inflation. This was also the main conclusion of the 1981 Scott Committee of Inquiry into the Value of Pensions. The committee's argument was that so long as people were prepared to make the appropriate contributions, there was no reason not to have full indexation.

10.2.3.4. *How Independent are Pension-Fund Trustees?*

The trustees of pension schemes have a fiduciary duty to act in the best interests of the schemes' beneficiaries. But in occupational pension schemes the trustees are invariably appointed by the companies organizing the schemes: the trustees are often directors of the sponsoring companies. This inevitably leads to a potential conflict of interest. The trustees can be put under pressure to act in a way that benefits the company and does not obviously benefit the pension scheme's members. We can consider several important examples of this.

One deals with the treatment of pension-fund surpluses. The trustees are, in principle, able to devote the entire surplus to enhancing pensions or to reducing employee contributions, thereby directly acting in the interests of the scheme's beneficiaries. Yet invariably, most of the surplus goes towards reducing the employer's contributions, with often only a token gesture towards pensioners and employees. Now, in contractual terms this is perfectly legal. The company is agreeing to deliver a defined-benefit pension at retirement and is obliged to make up any shortfall in achieving this; and the company is the legal owner of the surplus. But it is curious how the trustees invariably accept this position, and how recalcitrant trustees will be replaced with compliant ones if they do not. .

Another important example deals with self-investment, where the pension scheme invests in the parent company. Now, the trustees might well have good reason to invest a portion of the fund in the parent company. They might have good information about the excellent prospects of the company, so purely on grounds of investment criteria the investment might be a good one. Similarly, it might well provide a good incentive to tie the future pensions of employees to the success of the company that they work for. But again the conflict of interest is clear: what might be good for the company (a cheap source of funds) might not be so good for the scheme members (a potentially poor investment return). This potential conflict of interest has sufficiently concerned the government that it has placed an upper limit of 5 per-cent self-investment in the parent company.

Potential conflicts of interest of this kind bring into question the whole system of trust law currently operating in the UK in respect of pension schemes. Genuinely independent trustees would act in the best interests of the pension scheme's members: they could and should be sued if they did not. There is a definite case for reviewing the legal position of trustees. Several proposals have been made in the past. For example, the Occupational Pensions Board might establish model rules for the management of schemes, as was advocated in the Pension Trusts Bill, a private member's bill introduced in the 1986–87 parliamentary session but which fell with the dissolution of parliament in 1987. Another proposal has been compulsory representation on the trust body of different classes of beneficiary. This would help to strengthen the awareness that schemes are trusts in which all members have the same status as beneficiary.

Another obvious solution is to establish a system of pension-scheme administration that is entirely independent of the company. The company would simply deliver employee and employer contributions to the in-dependent scheme administrator and the administrator would do the rest. Now, this does not resolve the problem entirely, since with a final-salary scheme the employer is obliged to make up any shortfall. At least with the present arrangements, where the company's influence over trustees is so strong, it has difficulty in blaming anyone else if things go badly. Clearly, under an independent system of pension-scheme administration, the administrator would be responsible to both the scheme's members and the sponsor for the investment decisions that are made with the contributions.

The issue of trustee independence is discussed further in Section 10.2.3.7 below, dealing with the Maxwell Affair.

10.2.3.5. *The Right to Know?*

The concomitant of the strong influence that companies have over trus-tees is the relatively weak influence that scheme members have over trustees. By and large, pension-scheme members have not tended to organize themselves into effective pressure groups. This is largely because the pensioners and deferred pensioners themselves are usually dispersed geographically, companies are reluctant to give trade unions an active role in representing current employees, and both current employees and pensioners appear to lack the willingness to inform themselves about the activities of their schemes.

Despite the increase in information available to members of pension schemes in recent years, all the evidence tends to suggest that both pensioners and employees are largely ill-informed about their schemes. A typical survey of 1,000 employees in twenty-seven major companies by actuaries Towers, Perrin, Forster and Crosby in 1987 found that 80 per cent of members had never read their pension booklet, 30 per cent did not know what their retirement benefit would be, and 20 per cent did not know how much they paid in contributions. Does this really matter? The answer is probably not, in defined-benefit schemes. Since the employer is agreeing to provide a pension based on final salary, it does not really matter to scheme members how this is achieved. It would probably be better for them to devote their energies to achieving the best possible salary at retirement.

It is far more important for members of defined-contribution personal pension schemes to be informed about the activities of their schemes, since their pensions depend directly on the scheme's performance. Individuals taking out personal pension schemes are likely to be more sophisticated investors than those with occupational schemes, but by the very nature of their contract with the organizer of the scheme they can exercise no collective bargaining power at all. While they can switch out of a poorly performing scheme, the transactions costs of doing so will be quite high.

10.2.3.6. *How Visible Should Pension-Fund Assets and Liabilities Be?*

Another public-policy issue concerns the accounting aspects of pension costs and funds. In the USA accounting standards in respect of pension funds have been well-established for some time: ERISA came into effect in 1974, and the Financial Accounting Standards Board issued Statement of Financial Accounting Standards No. 87, *Employers' Accounting for Pensions* (known as FASB87), in December 1985. FASB87 requires that pension-fund assets and liabilities have to be stated explicitly on companies' balance sheets. Similarly, in Germany pension liabilities are shown on company balance sheets as *book reserves*. In the UK the accounting profession began standardizing accounting practice only in 1988 with the introduction of SSAP24, which stipulated how pension contributions should be treated on a company's profit-and-loss account (see Section 11.4). There is still no requirement for pension-fund assets and liabilities to be stated publicly on the company's balance sheet.

This is clearly a weakness, since it is important for shareholders and pension-scheme members, both actual and potential, to know the true state of the company's pension scheme. While this information is available to scheme members via the three-year valuation reports, the three-year interval is too great for most purposes.

The Accounting Standards Board should consider introducing a new Statement of Standard Accounting Practice (similar to FASB87) dealing with the balance-sheet position of pension-fund assets and liabilities for occupational pension schemes. If companies are going to be taken over in order to cream off their pension-fund surpluses, it seems reasonable that shareholders and pension-scheme members should know about it.

10.2.3.7. *What about Theft by the Sponsor?*

In this section we discuss one of the most remarkable events in recent pension-fund history—an event which has become known as the *Maxwell Affair*.

On 5 November 1991 Mr Robert Maxwell died at sea off the Canary Islands. Within a month his business empire had collapsed. On 4 December 1991 the Serious Fraud Office launched an investigation into how the pension schemes of Maxwell's public companies, Mirror Group Newspapers and Maxwell Communication Corporation, had incurred potential losses of £400m. on loans to his main private companies, Headington Investments and Robert Maxwell Group. In total, during the six months before his death Maxwell had taken £700m. in cash and securities from his public companies and their pension funds. MCC had made loans of £240m. and MGN had made loans of £45m. The MCC pension fund was owed £65m., while the MGN pension fund was owed £350m.

Accountants Coopers and Lybrand Deloitte, auditors to all the Maxwell companies, discovered that the pension funds had been lending shares to the private companies for some time. Initially, the private companies put up collateral to the pension funds of between 125 per cent and 150 per cent of the value of the borrowed shares. But in the six months before he died Maxwell began to sell the collateral. The proceeds should have been used to repay the pension funds, but instead they were used to shore up a collapsing business empire, leaving the pension funds with little likelihood of recovering more than a small proportion of what they were owed. The pension funds had been in surplus prior to the stock lending. By December 1991 they needed £150m. to meet their liabilities to pensioners. The MGN pension fund, for example, had been valued at £520m. and had a surplus of £150m. This had been turned into a deficit of £200m. By December 1991 the MGN pension fund had assets of £170m. and liabilities of £370m.

On 5 December 1991 Headington Investments and Robert Maxwell Group were placed into administrative receivership under the 1986 Insolvency Act at the insistence of the companies' bankers. Accountants Arthur Andersen were appointed as administrator. On 16 December 1991 Maxwell Communication Corporation and Mirror Group Newspapers were also placed into administrative receivership. Accountants Price Waterhouse were appointed as administrator. On 14 February 1992 the MGN and MCC pension schemes were wound up, with members transferred to SERPS with only their guaranteed minimum pensions earned since 1978 protected by the National Insurance Fund; anyone who retired before 1978 did not even get the GMP. On 30 March 1992 the Maxwell Pensions Action Group, which represents 4,500 Maxwell company pensioners, announced that it planned to sue for compensation in the European Court of Justice. The action would be brought under a European Union directive introduced in 1980 which obliges national governments to guarantee the pay and pensions of companies which become insolvent. In total, 32,000 employees and former employees have been affected by the Maxwell collapse, 12,000 from Mirror Group Newspapers and 20,000 from Maxwell's other companies.

Arthur Andersen calculated the asset and liability position of the

Maxwell empire at the time of insolvency as follows. Total debts were estimated at £1.4bn., of which bank loans accounted for £800m. Coopers and Lybrand Deloitte put the figures at £1.6bn. and £900m. respectively. Price Waterhouse subsequently discovered that, between April and July 1991, Maxwell had stripped MCC of all liquid assets, giving its head-office bank account a £105m. overdraft.

The Maxwell assets fell into five main categories:

- Shares in Maxwell Communication Corporation: when MCC's shares were suspended their market value was £226m., so that the 68 per cent of MCC owned by Maxwell was worth £153m. at the time of suspension; another 12 per cent of MCC was held as collateral by the banks, borrowed from the pension funds.
- Shares in Mirror Group Newspapers: when MGN's shares were suspended their market value was £501m., but Arthur Andersen estimated that their real value was only £300m., so the 51 per cent of MGN owned by Maxwell was worth £153m.; another 3.5 per cent of MGN was held as collateral by the banks, borrowed from the pension funds.
- Property: the main properties run by Robert Maxwell Estates were the Mirror Group offices at Holborn Circus, a building in Hangar Lane, and an office in Worship Street, together with vehicles and other tangible assets, such as the corporate yacht (*Lady Ghislaine*), aeroplane, and helicopters, in total valued at £200m.
- Minority holdings in a number of companies, such as 10 per cent of the merchant bank Henry Ansbacher and 6 per cent of Newspaper Publishing which publishes *The Independent* newspaper, in total valued at about £50m.
- Interests in about a dozen media-related operating companies, such as *The European* and *New York Daily News* newspapers and AGB, a market-research company: freed of debt, these would be worth £200m.

So, at the most optimistic, the Maxwell assets are valued at £750m., although the *Financial Times* estimated that £600m. would be more realistic. This left net liabilities of between £650m. and £1bn. The pension funds ranked behind the banks in claims on the companies' assets.

MCC and MGN pensioners were not the only group of pensioners to suffer as a result of the collapse of the Maxwell empire. A number of other pension funds had invested in MCC shares. These included the Post Office, British Airways, Rolls-Royce, Ford, Rover, National Westminster Bank, and Barclays Bank pension funds. In total, these pension funds have lost £200m. on their investments in Maxwell companies.

Initially it was not clear where the missing money had gone, since Maxwell's network of private interests, which involved 430 separate companies, was extremely complicated. Eventually it was discovered that some of the money had been used to finance the cash-hungry activities of Maxwell's private companies, such as *The European* and *New York Daily News*. In addition, the private companies had to make substantial debt repayments. But between £130m. and £339m. of the money was used by the Maxwell private companies in April and July 1991 to buy shares in Maxwell's public company MCC in order to support MCC's share price. This was because £300m. of the £900m. of bank loans to the private companies was secured against Maxwell's own holdings of MCC shares. If the value of these shares fell below 145 per cent of the value of the loans, then the banks required more security to be provided. Any downward pressure on MCC's share price could have put Maxwell's entire empire at risk.

Since operations to support a company's share price are illegal under UK company law, Maxwell used sophisticated ways of concealing his activities. The £130m. to £339m. used to support the MCC share price in April and July 1991 came from three companies in the Maxwell private empire: Bishopsgate Investment Trust, Robert Maxwell Group, and London and Bishopsgate Group. However, the money was paid to overseas companies, such as a company based in Delaware in the USA, after these companies had acquired MCC shares. Money also appears to have been moved through Liechtenstein, Switzerland, and Panama; for example, six secretive Liechtenstein foundations with the names of Corry, Allandra, Bacano, Akim, Kiara, and Jungo were involved, as well as two Swiss companies, Yokasa Finanzierungs and Servex. But the most sophisticated strategy used by Maxwell was the sale of two put options (see Section 12.3.5) on MCC shares to the US investment bank Goldman Sachs. The first put option was issued in August 1990 and expired at the end of November 1990, while the second was issued in January 1991 and expired in February 1991. The effect of the put options was to allow Goldman Sachs to sell MCC shares to Maxwell at a strike price that was higher than the price of MCC shares in the market (for example, the first put option gave Goldman Sachs the right to sell 15.6 million shares to Maxwell at 185p on 30 November, when the market price was around 150p). Goldman Sachs was able to buy MCC shares in the market, exercise its options, and resell the shares to Maxwell at a profit. Goldman Sachs denied that the put options were designed to support the MCC share price. Nevertheless, the options came at an opportune moment for Maxwell. For example, during the life of the first put option the stock market was becoming increasingly concerned about MCC's ability to repay debts due in October 1990, and the share price came under downward pressure. However, substantial purchases of MCC shares in October led to the share price actually rising in October.

While it is not illegal for a public company to buy back its own shares under UK company law, such transactions must be made public and must be made with the agreement of shareholders, even if they are made by indirect means. But Maxwell failed to disclose either to the Stock Exchange or to shareholders that his effective ownership of MCC shares had increased from the publicly disclosed level of 68 per cent to 79 per cent. Under Stock Exchange rules, a publicly quoted company cannot have less than 25 per cent of its shareholdings in public hands. So with 79 per cent of MCC shares owned by Maxwell, the Stock Exchange would have obliged him to take his company private.

It is clear that Robert Maxwell was a very forceful character who ran his companies with an iron fist, keeping his cards very close to his chest. It is said that he operated on a need-to-know basis, but if you needed to know, you never knew. To illustrate this, when Maxwell saved MCC (then called British Printing Corporation) from collapse in 1981, the company gave him the right to make payments without the agreement of other directors. The board passed a resolution stating: 'that the chairman . . . is hereby appointed a committee of the board and that there be . . . delegated to the chairman as such committee all the powers of the board.' All other payments needed authorization by two directors.

Mr Robert Bunn, the finance director of the Maxwell private companies, is quoted as saying, 'through the use of "bullying tactics" and the careful isolation of his senior aides, Mr Maxwell completely controlled the flow of cash to and from his private companies and did so up until his death on November 5'. He went on to say that 'all investment decisions were made by Robert Maxwell—he used to buy and sell shares without talking to other people and we would just get the contract note'. Mr Bunn argued that the treasury departments (of the private companies) which controlled the cash were forbidden to report to anyone other than Mr Maxwell and that he, as finance director, was expressly kept in the dark (quotes from *Financial Times*, 13 December 1991).

The position was no better in the public companies. For example, Maxwell moved between £268m. and £339m. out of MCC in a series of cash transactions that began on 1 April 1991, the day after MCC's financial year-end. Yet MCC directors, including Basil Brookes (finance director), Peter Laister (who became chairman shortly after Maxwell's death), Jean Pierre Anselmini (deputy chairman), and Albert Fuller (head of treasury), apparently failed to question the transfers at a board meeting on 4 July when they signed the previous year's accounts. The Price Waterhouse investigation into MCC discovered 'a series of highly dubious transactions which go back a long time and involve a large number of people'. Mr Laister claimed that Mr Brookes had questioned Maxwell about the size of the loans to the private companies in August 1991, but Maxwell had failed to give satisfactory explanations. Mr Laister also said that he and Lord Rippon, a non-executive director of MCC, had sought advice from city law firm Macfarlanes and managed to force a reduction in the loans to £73m. (quotes from *Daily Telegraph*, 21 December 1991).

This was not the first time that Robert Maxwell had come under the spotlight for mixing up the interests of his private and public companies. Nor was it the first time that he had been involved in creative accounting. In 1971 there had been a Board of Trade inquiry following the calling-off of Maxwell's proposed sale of Pergamon to Leasco. The inquiry concluded that Maxwell was unfit 'to exercise proper stewardship of a publicly-quoted company'.

As a result of Maxwell's reputation, when he sold 49 per cent of his interest in Mirror Group Newspapers through a public offering in May 1991 for £250m., it was necessary for his merchant banker Samuel Montagu to put a 'ring fence' around MGN to prevent cash flowing to the private companies. The MGN ring fence was designed to prevent MGN assets being used for the benefit of the private companies except on an arm's-length basis and on terms that would be demanded of any outside company. In short, the only cash flowing to the private companies would be dividend payments due as a result of their 51 per-cent holding in MGN. MGN was also supposed to have a board of directors that was independent of other Maxwell interests. Yet within weeks of the flotation Maxwell instructed a private Maxwell company to invest surplus MGN cash in gilt-edged stock, and made a £45m. loan to the private companies. There is no evidence that the gilts were ever purchased, and the loan had not been authorized by the MGN board.

Robert Bunn said:

It started to go wrong in terms of the business after the Mirror flotation [in May 1991] when it was clear that the remaining businesses on the private side were primarily loss-making. Consequently, the private side of the group was dependent on dividends and a large disposal programme. Towards the end, Robert Maxwell was driven by cash rather than profitability. (*Financial Times*, 13 December 1991)

In fact, things started to go wrong some time before the Mirror flotation. Maxwell paid far too much ($2.7bn. or £1.9bn.) for the US publishing house Macmillan in November 1988. Most of the financing came from bank loans and the interest payments on the debt soon exceeded the earnings from the company. Maxwell found that he needed to dispose of assets, borrow more external funds, and then 'borrow' from the MCC and MGN pension funds. Maxwell was chasing his own tail in ever-decreasing circles. He was using MCC and MCC pension-fund money to support the MCC share price. At the end of the day there was not enough money in MCC or its pension fund to sustain MCC at its current market value.

When the money ran out, the whole thing folded with astonishing speed.

Robert Maxwell was not the only family member involved in the Maxwell Affair. Also involved were his two sons, Kevin and Ian. Kevin Maxwell was chairman and chief executive of MCC and Ian Maxwell was chairman and chief executive of MGN. On 3 December 1991 they both resigned from these positions. It emerged on 5 December 1991, the same day that the Maxwell private companies were placed into administrative receivership, that the three directors responsible for authorizing the loans from the MGN pension fund to the Maxwell private companies were Robert Maxwell, Kevin Maxwell, and Ian Maxwell. The loans were not illegal, but Robert Maxwell sold the collateral against which the loans were secured, although there has been no suggestion that his sons were aware of these disposals.

The trustee and investment manager to most of the pension funds in both the private and public Maxwell companies was Bishopsgate Investment Management (BIM). (The remaining pension funds were managed by a sister company, London and Bishopsgate International Investment Management.) In total, BIM was responsible for £727m. of pension-fund assets. Directors of BIM included Robert Maxwell and his two sons Kevin and Ian. When BIM went into receivership on 5 December 1991 more than £327m. was unaccounted for. Yet as recently as 18 October 1991 lawyers for the pension-fund trustees wrote to pensioners stating that BIM was an 'authorised investment business which fully complied with guidelines laid down by IMRO'. The liquidator, Robson Rhodes, found that some shares had been transferred from BIM directly to banks as collateral for loans made to Maxwell private companies, while other shares were transferred directly to Maxwell private companies. BIM was replaced as trustees of the Maxwell company pension funds by the Law Debenture Trust Company. In September 1993 Robson Rhodes announced that £29m. was still missing from the MCC pension fund, £117m. was still missing from the MGN pension fund and £293m. was still missing from the remaining Maxwell companies' pension funds.

Robert Bunn argued that 'Kevin is totally embarrassed by the whole situation. It's not a very good legacy to be left' (*Financial Times*, 13 December 1991). However, as *Private Eye* argued at the time:

Kevin Maxwell was a director of most if not all the key private companies as well as of Maxwell Communication Corporation, companies between which the missing millions moved. He handled negotiations with banks for loans. He appears to have signed documents if not cheques involving the movement of money from Mirror Group Newspapers pension fund . . . He is far from a naive dupe, being described as a knowledgeable businessman by those who know him. 'Kevin is a very experienced financier who has put to bed more deals than many in the City', John Holliwell of merchant bankers Henry Ansbacher told *The Observer*. Ansbacher should know, they were long time advisers. So it is hard to believe Kevin Maxwell was ignorant of everything or did not understand the significance of what he did know or of his responsibilities under the Companies Act. Then there are the curiously inaccurate statements he made in the honeymoon period before the missing three quarters of a billion was discovered. Statements like: 'The financial problems are more in the eye of the beholder than they are real'. That slight exaggeration was told to his friends at the *Sunday Times* (10 November). How could someone who worked so close know so little and be so wrong?

On 13 January 1992 the *Financial Times* reported that Kevin Maxwell's signature appeared on an invalid transfer of shares from Bishopsgate Investment Management. The shares in EURIS, a French investment trust, were given to Banque Nationale de Paris as security for a loan to a Maxwell private company. Kevin Maxwell was the sole signatory to the transfer, whereas two signatures were required.

Also on 13 January 1992 the Maxwell brothers appeared before the House of Commons Select Committee on Social Security. They appeared with their counsel, Mr George Carmen QC representing Kevin Maxwell and Mr John Jarvis QC representing Ian Maxwell. The committee's purpose was to discover details of and documentation relating to the hundreds of millions of pounds missing from the Maxwell company pension funds. But the Maxwell brothers refused to answer a single question put by the committee chairman, Frank Field. Asked about documents relating to the pension-fund money, Kevin Maxwell said: 'I wish my counsel to answer.' George Carmen said: 'The answer is plain and clear and respectful, but unambiguous. Mr Kevin Maxwell, on advice, is not going to answer any questions touching on pension funds or documents thereto, and that applies to any questions the committee asks on this matter.' When Ian Maxwell was asked the same question, his counsel replied: 'Having taken legal advice, Mr Ian Maxwell has considered that the risk of answering any questions including questions relating to documents, would prejudice his right to a fair trial.' When Mr Field asked Ian Maxwell which pension funds he belonged to, he replied: 'I decline to answer.' Responding to the same question, Kevin Maxwell's counsel said: 'We shall not answer any question touching upon pension funds and that position is made plain. It will not be answered, however many questions this committee poses this afternoon.' Mr Field concluded the committee meeting by stating that: 'We regard it as immensely serious that our requests for documents or copies of documents have not been produced [*sic*], and we regard it equally seriously that the questions which we put to Ian Maxwell and Kevin Maxwell were not answered.' On 19 February 1992 it was announced that the Maxwell brothers refused to provide written answers to questions from the committee. Constitutional experts regarded the actions of the Maxwell brothers as a contempt of parliament.

The Maxwell brothers' claim of right to silence on the grounds of possible self-incrimination in respect of the pension-fund assets managed by Bishopsgate Investment Management was rejected by the Court of Appeal on 29 January 1992. The Appeal Court ruled that legislation involving the 1985 Companies Act or the 1986 Insolvency Act implicitly removed the privilege against self-incrimination, so that this privilege could not be invoked when facing a reasonable request for information under these acts.

On 18 June 1992 the Maxwell brothers, plus a colleague, Mr Larry Trachtenberg, were charged with conspiracy to defraud and theft involving £135m. of assets belonging to the Mirror Group Pension Trust. On 20 July 1992 Kevin Maxwell was ordered by a judge to refund £406m. to the Maxwell pension funds. Since his declared assets were only £211,000, he was unable to comply with the order. On 3 September 1992 he was declared the UK's biggest-ever bankrupt when a bankruptcy order was made against him for £406m. following a petition filed by the liquidator of Bishopsgate Investment Management. Outside the High Court Kevin Maxwell said:

I stand here bankrupt with a deal of humility. Bankruptcy is a very public humbling. If there is a redeeming feature of the bankruptcy order, it is perhaps that the thousands of people who have suffered loss can take real satisfaction from seeing a former director—and I suppose, above all, a Maxwell—suffer the consequences of their loss personally and in public. Perhaps those concerned believe this alone justifies the cost to creditors of these proceedings, given the very small extent of my estate and my assets.

On 6 October 1992 Robert Bunn was charged with conspiracy to defraud a syndicate of thirty-five banks led by Swiss Bank Corporation and Crédit Lyonnais by pledging the shares in Berlitz International to a third party when they had already been pledged as security for a loan from the banks.

On 8 June 1992 Peter Lilley, the secretary of state for social security, announced an emergency grant of £2.5m. to help Maxwell pension schemes which were unable to maintain payments to pensioners. This was to tide the schemes over until after a court ruling on allocating the £100m. of pension assets recovered by administrators. But Mr Lilley warned that the government would not underwrite fraud. In addition, the scheme would help only Maxwell pensioners, not the 12,000 deferred pensioners of Maxwell pension funds, nor members of funds of companies demerged from the Maxwell group of companies but which had not had their pension-fund assets returned to them. Nevertheless, the £2.5m. grant had been entirely spent by March 1993.

On 13 June 1992 the government established a special Whitehall unit under the chairmanship of Sir John Cuckney, chairman of the 3i Group, to recover the Maxwell pension-fund assets. The unit was responsible for 'persuading' City financial institutions of their 'moral obligation' to contribute to the Maxwell Pensioners Trust aimed at rebuilding Maxwell pension-fund assets. The unit attempted to track down the pension-fund assets that appear to have been transferred to safe havens in Switzerland and Liechtenstein well after Maxwell's death in November 1991. But the institutions were expected to replace any stolen money that could not be traced. The government also called for an international protocol aimed at preventing banking secrecy laws in such countries as Liechtenstein, Luxembourg, Gibraltar, and Switzerland from being used to prevent legitimate criminal investigations. The first contribution into the trust fund was made by the National Association of Pension Funds with £120,000. Several banks refused to contribute to the fund. Credit Suisse, holding £70m. of pension-fund assets as collateral, said it received the assets in good faith and would vigorously contest legal moves by pensioners to have the money returned. Lehman Brothers, holding £30m., said that a donation is 'not on our agenda'. However, within six months the unit had raised more than £5m. The largest single voluntary donation was £1m. from Goldman Sachs. The first payments from the Maxwell Pensioners Trust were made on 2 October 1992 to forty Maxwell pensioners who received *ex-gratia* backdated payments averaging £400 each.

In June 1993 investment management group Invesco MIM was fined a record £750,000 by IMRO and ordered to pay £1.59m. in costs after pleading guilty to 55 breaches of City regulations, including negligence in allowing £77m. of shares from the Maxwell pension schemes to be used as collateral for loans to Maxwell companies. However it refused to comply with a compensation order from the SIB (under Section 61 of the Financial Services Act) to make a donation of more than £2m. to the Maxwell Pensioners Trust.

In July 1993 Goldman Sachs was fined £160,000 by the Securities and Futures Authority and ordered to pay a £56m. without-prejudice contribution to the Maxwell pension funds. Also in July, Guardian Royal Exchange announced that it would refund premiums paid by Maxwell companies for insurance taken out to protect against theft of assets on the grounds that the policies are voidable because 'fraud must have been known to the management of the Maxwell companies at the time of their renewal'.

In September 1993 administrators of the Maxwell company pension funds issued a writ for £100m. against Lehman Brothers International, the investment banking subsidiary of American Express. The writ alleged that Lehmans had entered into stock-lending agreements with BIM in which BIM borrowed US Treasury bills using collateral which belonged to the pension funds and that the Treasury bills were subsequently sold for cash which was deposited in personal accounts belonging to Maxwell. The writ also alleges that Lehmans informed Invesco MIM that these stock-lending arrangements were not normal and that Maxwell was facing financial difficulties. Lehmans rejected the allegations.

In October 1993 the MGN pension fund issued writs for £200m. each against Invesco MIM, Lehman Brothers International and Capel-Cure Myers alleging that each firm was in a position to 'blow the whistle' and inform the fund and the regulators that Maxwell was involved in theft. The three institutions denied the allegations, but in January 1994 paid £32m. to the MGN pension fund in an out-of-court settlement.

Most activities involving money depend largely on trust and the integrity of the participants in those activities. A legal framework of checks and balances can also be in place, but trust and integrity remain the most important factors. When it is discovered that the trust was misplaced and that the integrity of certain participants was non-existent, then this is disappointing. When the matter also involves someone's pension, then the misplaced trust and absence of integrity are distressing. But if there is a failure of integrity and a breach of trust, then what about the checks and balances? Important issues are raised by the Maxwell Affair, the most important of which is the role played by the following in providing those checks and balances: the trustees of the pension funds, the directors of the Maxwell companies, the auditors to the companies and their pension funds, the financial institutions acting on behalf of the companies, and finally, the authorities.

It is quite unsatisfactory that the trustees of the pension schemes of thousands of people are able to act in this cavalier fashion, making unauthorized loans, selling the collateral underlying those loans, secretly buying and selling securities on a whim, and so on. It is also quite unsatisfactory that three of the trustees can come from the same family, when the sponsoring company involves thousands of workers. Others agree. For example, Bryn Davies, an actuary for Union Pension Services, said:

The central problem is the very loose structure of trust law, which was designed to enable medieval knights to protect their family property or to give bread to the poor; it had nothing to do with pensions . . . Now, a lot of people are worried about pensions and there is pressure for the government to be seen to do something. [He went on to say:] There is something structurally wrong when so much power is placed in the hands of the employer. As we have seen, when times get tough, the employer may be subject to a conflict of interest. The best people to look after the scheme members' interest are the scheme members themselves. That is why we believe that at least 50% of trustees should be scheme members. (Quoted from the *Daily Telegraph*, 7 December 1991.)

Sir David Walker, chairman of the Securities and Investments Board, appearing before the House of Commons Trade and Industry Committee in December 1991, argued that, in the light of the Maxwell Affair, there should be a total separation between the company, the trustees of the company's pension fund, and the managers of the pension fund's assets. He argued that it was unsatisfactory that pension-fund trustees were able to manage pension-fund assets. Also in December 1991 Conservative MP Kenneth Hind argued for a far-reaching reform of the rules governing how pension funds are administered. He proposed that: no director or shareholder of the sponsoring company should be a trustee of the associated pension fund; the law should recognize that the pension fund's assets are the property of its contributors; and pension-fund trustees should report annually to each contributor.

The other directors of the Maxwell companies do not appear to come out of this episode with much credit. They have had hundreds of millions of pounds of shareholders' money taken from under their noses in a six-month period and they seem to have done very little to prevent this, even though they were aware that something funny was going on. The non-executive directors whose express purpose is to represent shareholders' interests seem to have been particularly ineffective. It is now essential to ensure that non-executive directors have effective sanctions to restrain the actions of a company chairman or chief executive whose actions appear too wayward, however strong the personality of that chairman or chief executive is. The problem, of course, is that the chairman or chief executive may be desperately trying to save the company from collapse, and no director is going to want to add to the risk of the company failing, even if he feels that the chairman or chief executive is acting illegally.

While auditors do not have a legal obligation to detect fraud, there are a number of issues concerning the role of auditors and audits in the Maxwell Affair. In the case of the Maxwell companies the auditor was Coopers and Lybrand Deloitte. The first issue deals with the accounting practices of the Maxwell companies. For example, it has been argued that the value placed on intangible items such as goodwill, brands, and newspaper titles in the Maxwell companies was far too high. More significantly for the case in point was the fact that many of the movements of cash between the public and private companies and pension funds took place during the financial year ending on 31 March 1991, but the 1990 accounts of the Maxwell companies were never qualified by the auditors.

Yet the whole purpose of preparing accounts is to provide a 'true and fair' picture of a company as a going concern. How is it possible for the 1990 accounts to appear to do just that when the company can collapse barely six months later owing the best part of a billion pounds? The accounting profession via the Accounting Standards Board and the Auditing Practices Committee will have to come up with solutions to this problem.

The second issue concerns potential conflict of interest. While companies are required by law to have their accounts audited, they do not have to use the services of a particular firm of accountants. The auditor always remains the agent of, and depends on the fee income from, the company and the company can always go elsewhere if it is not satisfied with its current auditor. Mr Brandon Gough, chairman and managing partner in Coopers and Lybrand Deloitte, argued that there was no conflict of interest in the Maxwell case. Coopers's fee income from auditing the Maxwell accounts and providing financial advice was £2.4m. in 1991, less than 0.5 per cent of total fee income from all clients. Brandon Gough pointed out that fees would never compromise an audit. Although there had been 'some fairly intensive discussions about accounting methods . . . if we had any major difficulties, we would have qualified the audit'. He argued that the threat of litigation and the unlimited liability of accounting partnerships prevent any compromise of professional standards. Nevertheless, a possible way to deal with potential conflict of interest is to have two separate firms as joint auditors. This, it has been argued, would generate creative tension and eliminate the risk of complacency, although it would raise auditing costs substantially. Brandon Gough's response was that having two separate auditing firms was unnecessary, but it would be a good idea to rotate people on an audit: 'we depend on continuity, but a fresh perspective is valuable.'

The banks believed that they had a stronger claim on the securities that they held as collateral against their loans to Maxwell than the pension funds from which the securities had disappeared. It is now necessary to ensure that the banks and other financial institutions have a duty to exercise 'due diligence' in determining the ownership of securities that are pledged against loans or that they are instructed to sell. This would provide an extra safeguard in the event of failings by trustees, and could be backed up with pension-scheme members having the right to have transactions that can be shown not to be in the best interests of the scheme's beneficiaries declared null and void.

There is a precedent for this. In 1988 most of the assets of the pension fund of Aveling-Barford, an engineering company based in Grantham, were invested in a Royal Life insurance bond, on terms that allowed the broker involved to take out commission of £3m. Royal Life accepted that it should have taken greater care over the actions of its agents and agreed to compensate the pension fund to the tune of £5m.

Giving evidence to the House of Commons Social Security Committee in January 1992, the National Association of Pension Funds argued that pension-fund assets should be held by a custodian trustee independent of the sponsoring company. Mr Brian McMahon, NAPF chairman, said that 'the supervision of an investment manager entrusted with the Mirror Group pension funds was inadequate. We would like to see the Financial Services Act amended to provide protection to pension schemes.' As John Plender said: 'Having failed to deliver a decent state pension scheme, successive governments failed to deliver adequate regulatory arrangements for private occupational pensions' (*Financial Times*, 15 January 1992). An Occupational Pensions Board report in 1989 argued that current controls over pension funds were 'vague, uncertain and discretionary'. Amazingly, IMRO, the regulatory authority for fund managers (which had authorized both BIM and London and Bishopsgate in 1988), visited BIM just six weeks before Robert Maxwell's death and found no problems! For example, it failed to notice that the pension funds had not been unitized (a mandatory accounting procedure that allocates units to each fund on a monthly basis) until six months after BIM began operations in 1988.

The House of Commons Social Security Committee published its report into the Maxwell Affair on 9 March 1992. It was strongly critical of the roles played by the regulatory authorities, financial institutions, professional bodies, and pension-fund trustees, and it called for the members of the Maxwell pension funds to receive compensation, mainly from the banks holding the pension-fund assets as collateral for their loans to Maxwell. In particular, it criticized the actuaries, auditors, and lawyers for having a 'strict compartmentalised view' of their responsibilities and for failing to communicate with each other, despite growing evidence of malpractice: 'Pontius Pilate would have blushed at the spectacle of so many witnesses washing their hands in public before the committee of their responsibilities in this affair.' Mr Frank Field, in introducing the report, argued the Maxwell pension funds would have been safe if only:

- the regulators had acted with a proper degree of suspicion, given the man they were dealing with;
- the directors had carried out their duties fully;
- professional advisers had acted with as much common sense as willingness to pick up their fees;
- insiders had been brave enough to resign and talk;
- newspaper editors had been prepared to stand up to Maxwell's bile and legal 'offences';

- brokers and merchant bankers had cared about their tasks as much as they did about their fees;
- parliament had not been so beguiled by its own rhetoric on the special status of trust law.

The report was also critical of the system of self-regulation operating in the City, stating that the way in which IMRO carried out its duties suggested 'that this aspect of the system of self-regulation is—when the chips are down—little short of a tragic comedy . . . In other words, the system works in those circumstances where there is in fact little need for a regulatory system at all.'

The report's key recommendation was for a royal commission to review pension law and to report on proposals for a new Pension Act. It also made the following recommendations:

- establishment of a new regulatory framework supervised by a strengthened Occupational Pensions Board;
- appointment of independent trustees unrelated to the employing company to hold pension assets;
- annual statements for pension-fund members;
- a right for contributors to veto the transfer of their assets to another scheme;
- all pension-fund accounts to be lodged with the OPB within seven months of the end of the account year;
- the OPB to be given powers to:
  - (a) monitor the appointment and departure of trustees and have the right to veto unsuitable appointments;
  - (b) co-ordinate official bodies concerned with policing funds;
  - (c) co-ordinate the rules of professional advisers;
  - (d) act as a centre for registration of warning signs;
  - (e) operate a system of penalties and fines for those who break the rules; and
  - (f) monitor the winding-up of funds.

On 9 July 1992 the Securities and Investments Board published a report on the role of IMRO in the regulation of two Maxwell companies, Bishopsgate Investment Management and London and Bishopsgate International Investment Management. The SIB's report was in response to an investigation by IMRO into its own role in the affair. In its report IMRO accepted that its standard of supervision was below that required by a financial services regulator. In particular, IMRO acknowledged that:

- its approach to monitoring was too mechanistic;
- its analysis of information was insufficiently critical;
- it failed to recognize the potential risks associated with the companies and to give proper weight to the risks that were identified;

- it was unduly ready to rely on the good faith and professionalism of those with whom it dealt;
- its monitoring activity was insufficiently alert and responsive to information available to it; and
- its response to the crisis after Robert Maxwell's death was inadequate.

The SIB's report was even more critical of IMRO's role. It said: 'IMRO's monitoring failures in this case reveal more than a general lack of market awareness and scepticism in dealing with information about transactions and in monitoring returns.' The SIB considered a suggestion that it withdraw recognition from IMRO, but decided instead to correct its shortcomings. Both the chairman (Mr George Nissen) and the chief executive (Mr John Morgan) of IMRO announced their intention to resign.

The chairman of the SIB, Mr Andrew Large, said that he remained committed to self-regulation. He intended to recruit more industry practitioners to work for the self-regulatory organizations. He also intended to review how the SIB carries out its own regulatory responsibilities and how it monitors the activities of all the SROs in respect of both 'investor protection and efficiency'.

In June 1992 Peter Lilley announced the establishment of the Pension Law Review Committee under the chairmanship of Professor Roy Goode QC of Oxford University. The terms of reference were: to review the framework of law and regulation within which occupational pension schemes operate, taking into account the rights and interests of scheme members, pensioners, and employers; to consider in particular the status and ownership of occupational pension funds and the accountability and roles of trustees, fund managers, auditors, and pension-scheme advisers; and to make recommendations within twelve months.

The committee's objective was not only to study the current framework of pensions legislation based on trust law that was so readily exploited by Robert Maxwell, but to study the ownership of assets in the pension fund, including the ownership of surpluses. Depending on the wording of trust deeds, employers can withdraw money from their own schemes without any obligation to share this with members. It was recognized that reform of the pensions system could not be considered separately from the question of the ownership of assets. The committee was also urged to discuss the safe custody of assets and the question of compensation.

In its submission to the Goode Committee, the National Association of Pension Funds recommended a compulsory compensation scheme for members of occupational pension schemes to protect them in the event that their pension-fund assets are stolen. It recognized that the scheme would cost large employers tens of thousands of pounds per annum. The scheme would pay the promised pension benefits up to a prescribed limit. Trustees would have to ensure that custodians could demonstrate practical independence of the employer. Every fund would be required to pass a solvency test, and under-funded schemes would be required to produce a business plan to ensure that their assets would fund their liabilities within a time-limit. The NAPF proposed that all pension schemes come within the scope of the Investors' Compensation Scheme operated by the Securities and Investments Board, which pays up to £48,000 to each claimant in the event of a company failing.

The Goode Committee submitted its report entitled *Pension Law Reform* (CM2342) in September 1993. In total there were 218 recommendations. The principal recommendations were as follows:

- Trust law should continue to provide the foundation for the interests, rights and duties arising in connection with occupational pension schemes but should be reinforced by a Pensions Act administered by a *pensions regulator*.
- Freedom of trust should be limited so as to ensure the reality of the pension promise, to protect rights accrued in respect of past service and to allow members to make appointments of up to one-third of the trustee board in the case of final-salary schemes and up to two-thirds of the trustee board in the case of money-purchase schemes; scheme members should be allowed to appoint non-members of their scheme as trustees and employers should not be able to remove member trustees who could only be removed by the unanimous decision of the other trustees and the regulator. Trustees should also receive formal training.
- The provision of information for scheme members should be improved both in content and in clarity and presentation.
- The security for members' entitlements should be strengthened by minimum solvency requirements, monitoring by the pensions regulator and scheme auditors and actuaries, restrictions on withdrawals from surplus and, as a last resort, a *compensation scheme* to cover scheme deficits arising from fraud, theft, or other misappropriation. The minimum solvency requirements imply that the fund should have assets at least equal to the sum of the cash equivalent of all active and deferred members' accrued rights (calculated on the same basis as for individual transfer values) plus the cost of buying immediate annuities to meet pension benefits already in payment, together with any pension increases the scheme is required to provide. If the soluency level falls below 90 per cent, a cash injection would be required within three months. The government should also give serious consideration to the introduction of a new type of government-guaranteed security which

could provide more appropriate backing for schemes' index-linked liabilities. The new securities would be called *deferred income government securities* and would have income and capital linked to the retail price index, but with payment of the income deferred for a period. Such securities would permit all deferred pensions to be indexed fully to prices and would greatly facilitate the establishment of solvency standards on a cash equivalents basis.

• On setting up a scheme, the employer should be free to reserve the right to close, freeze or wind up the scheme, to approve or refuse increases in benefit, and to reduce or stop contributions, subject to the minimum solvency requirements.

• The administrative burdens imposed on employers and scheme administrators should wherever possible be reduced, and flexibility increased, through simplification of the law and its administration. In particular, detailed statutory investment rules should be replaced with a general prudent person standard and statutory investment criteria; and there should be a move from excessively detailed and obscurely drafted rules towards more general and clearly expressed statements of principle.

The report argues that:

many of our recommendations do little more than reflect best practice, and, when taken with the simplification measures we have proposed, should add few, if any, financial burdens to a well-run and properly funded scheme. They clarify the rights and responsibilities of all parties associated with the schemes, a clarity which has hitherto been lacking. As a result, both employer and scheme members should feel confident that the pension promise is more secure and that at the same time the employer's future commitments can be limited to what is considered affordable.... The legal regime we have proposed is designed to satisfy four essential criteria: fairness to all parties, security for scheme members, practicality, and the simplification of the law regulating occupational pension schemes and their administration. (pp. 7–8)

In reading the report's recommendations, it seems remarkable that the Goode Committee should have been necessary at all. All the recommendations really do, as the above passage readily acknowledges, is to codify the best practice already operating in the industry and to suggest that the pensions industry introduces a system of regulation and compensation that is now widespread in the rest of the financial services industry; in this sense, the report is not a 'reforming' document at all. It is rather like hearing that, following a series of bad motoring accidents, the government sets up a committee to investigate the problem and fifteen months later produces the Highway Code: motorists should keep left and not drive too close to the car in front; if you wish to get to your destination, you must make sure that you put enough petrol in your tank;

lock valuables away in the boot when you leave the car unattended; the government should establish a proper system of traffic signalling as they have already done on the railways. All very worthy, especially when faced with a fraud on the scale of Maxwell, but one cannot fail to wonder, as we enter the twenty-first century, why this has not been done before for the pensions industry.

In addition, the government has still failed to implement provisions in the 1990 Social Security Act to limit self-investment in the sponsoring company to 5 per cent of pension-fund assets. Once implemented, pension funds are given two years to divest themselves of stocks listed on the Stock Exchange and loans to the sponsoring company, and five years to divest themselves of stocks listed on the unlisted securities market and property.

10.2.4. THE BATTLE OF THE SEXES

In two aspects of their pension arrangements women have historically been treated more favourably than men. These are retirement age and contribution-rates. Historically, women have been allowed to retire earlier than men, yet they live longer than men on average and pay the same contribution-rate towards their pensions. Women may end up with lower pensions on average than men, but this is because they have lower-paid jobs, not because they are treated unfairly in terms of their pension arrangements. Women's pensions have been actuarially more expensive to provide than men's, yet women have not had to pay extra towards them.

In May 1990 the European Court of Justice made a ruling on equal pensions treatment by stating that occupational pension schemes must permit men and women to retire on the same pensions at the same age. Up till this time most company pension schemes, in common with the state scheme itself, had different pension ages for men and women, so that if a man retired before the normal pension age for men he would receive a lower pension (as much as one-third lower) than a woman of the same age in identical circumstances. The ruling was based on the interpretation that contracted-out occupational pensions are equivalent to pay within the definition of Article 119 of the Treaty of Rome and hence subject to the article's equal-treatment provisions. The ruling implies that occupational schemes could no longer avoid having a common pension age simply because the state does not have a common pension age. The first and second EU directives on equality in company pension schemes confirm this implication.

It was agreed at the Maastricht Summit of European heads of government in December 1991 that the ruling applied only to service accruing after 17 May 1990, unless individuals had made a claim for sex discrimination beforehand. This means that most existing male pensioners could not claim compensation from their employers for any discrimination in pensions treatment that they had suffered. The ruling also required the introduction of widowers' pensions that are equivalent to the widows' pensions that are offered by schemes. Similarly, the ruling requires equal treatment in respect of the lump sum at retirement.

As a result of both European Commission directives and European Court rulings, men and women are required to be 'treated equally'. They have to have equal treatment in retirement age and in contribution-rates. In other words, there has to be a common retirement age for men and women, and there cannot be differential contribution-rates to account for the fact that, even with the same retirement age, women will be drawing pensions for a longer period than men on average. It is, of course, arguable that 'equal treatment' could be interpreted as having actuarially fair contribution-rates for men and women, but the European Court has not chosen this interpretation. However, the Equal Treatment Directives did not require amendment of the state-pension age, which for the moment remains 60 for women and 65 for men; that is, women still take the state pension from the age of 60, while men receive it from 65. So there currently exists a distinction between the *retirement age* and the *pension age* in the UK.

It is up to companies to choose their own common retirement age. If they choose 65, the current state-pension age for men, they will save money. If they choose 60, the current state-pension age for women, this will be expensive and lead to substantial reductions in the surpluses built up over the 1980s. The estimated cost of this option is £2bn. p.a. (at 1990 prices) or 15 per cent added to employers' pension costs. Some companies have chosen a common retirement age in between, such as 62 or 63, with the aim of being broadly cost-neutral. For example, the Post Office, British Telecom, and Barclays Bank have decided to introduce a common retirement and pension age with equal pension benefits for both men and women from 60, a position supported by the Equal Opportunities Commission. In contrast, IBM (UK) has fixed a common retirement age of 63.

There are thus three main types of pension arrangements operating in the UK:

- pensions paid from the pension age where the pension age (which can differ for men and women) is less than or equal to the retirement age, with all employees working up to a common retirement age: this means that there might be a common retirement age of 65, with a pension age of 60 for women and 65 for men. Women receive a pension from 60, although they can continue to work until they are 65. This arrangement leads to an increase in taxable income for women, however;

- pensions deferred between the pension age and retirement age with the pension increased actuarially for each additional year worked, but with no additional contributions into the scheme after pension age: this arrangement avoids the potential tax problems of the first one;
- pensions paid from the retirement age with normal contributions and accrual of benefits until this age, whatever the pension age.

The 1992 National Association of Pension Funds survey found that 85 per cent of schemes had equalized the retirement age at 65, and of these 85 per cent permitted retirement at the previous retirement age without a cut in the pension paid.

Whatever the pension age chosen by the company, the state pension cannot be drawn before state-pension age, although it can be deferred for up to five years beyond state-pension age. The main problem with having a common retirement age but different pension ages is that it is generally unfair to men. Suppose that the pension age is 60 for women and 65 for men, and that the common retirement age is 65. This means that women working beyond 60 can have their basic state pension enhanced by 7.4 per cent for each year that retirement is deferred and do not have to pay national-insurance contributions (although their employers continue to pay contributions). In contrast, men have to wait until 65 to get the basic state pension and have to pay national-insurance contributions until they are 65.

The first inequality is that men have to work longer to receive the same basic pension. A woman can qualify for the basic state pension having made (or having been credited with) full NICs for nine-tenths of her maximum working life of forty-four years. A man, on the other hand, has to make (or be credited with) full NICs for nine-tenths of his maximum working life of forty-nine years. A man has to work for 4.5 years longer than a woman to receive the same pension. The second inequality is that women live longer than men. A woman of 60 has a life expectancy of 21.3 years, whereas a man of 65 has a life expectancy of 13.3 years. This means that the average woman will draw her pension for eight years longer than the average man.

A number of other inequalities follow from these two. For example, a woman reaching 60 could decide to continue working rather than retire. She no longer has to pay NICs and, in the mean time, her pension is enhanced at the rate of 7.4 per cent p.a. This means that she will have higher take-home pay and a larger pension at 65 than a man in otherwise identical circumstances. Similarly, while a woman can no longer delay her state pension beyond 65, she could in principle receive both state pension and salary after 65. A man has to wait until he is 70 to receive both state pension and salary. There are similar inequalities in occupational schemes. For example, although the pension can be based on no more than forty years' service, in many schemes contributions are payable until retirement, which means that men can pay contributions for up to five years longer than women.

An alternative to having a single common retirement age in a firm is to have a *retirement decade*, whereby employees, whether men or women, could retire at any age between 60 and 70. The notion of a retirement decade has been proposed by, amongst others, the NAPF in a report called *Equalising State Pension Ages* (March 1991). The NAPF report argues that the central retirement age should be 65, at which age the basic state pension would be payable in full. If people chose to draw their pension before 65, the pension would be reduced to reflect the fact that they would have paid less in contributions and would expect to receive their pension for longer. On the other hand, if people chose to retire after 65, the value of the pension would be enhanced for each year's delay after 65. The payments to pensioners younger than 65 would be made by the occupational schemes, which would be reimbursed by the government in the form of index-linked gilts, once the pensioner had reached the age of 65. The NAPF argued that its proposals would not significantly increase costs. Another proposal, from the Campaign for Equal Pensions, also supports the idea of a retirement decade but wants the full basic state pension payable from 60, at a cost of an additional 2 per cent on NICs.

Another requirement of the Equal Treatment Directives is to have identical annuity rates for men and women of the same age. This has the effect of introducing an 'actuarial inequality' that was not present beforehand. The Association of British Insurers has argued that the traditionally different annuity rates for men and women are based on different life expectancies. The cost of buying an annuity depends on an individual's sex and age and on current rates of interest. Women on average live about four years longer than men. This means that the same lump sum buys a smaller annuity for a woman than for a man of the same age (see, for example, Table 10.1). Equivalently, the same annuity costs a woman more than a man of the same age. In addition, for both men and women the annuity increases with the starting age of the annuitant and with the level of interest rates. In the former case this is because the expected duration of the annuity decreases with the starting age of the annuitant; in the latter case it is because a given sum of money will generate a higher income stream the higher the interest rate. (In contrast with annuities, the greater longevity of women favours them when it comes to life assurance: women pay the same premiums as men four years younger than them.)

TABLE 10.1. *Annuity rates for men and women: gross amount paid half-yearly in arrears on £10,000 (£)*

	Man aged 65	Woman aged 65
Equitable Life	1,558	1,417
Avon Insurance	1,540	1,412
Abbey Life	1,534	1,382
Life Association of Scotland	1,533	1,397

Source: Savings Market, *Daily Telegraph*, 30 Nov. 1985.

The opposite 'actuarial inequality' emerges in respect of the lump sum at retirement. More than 90 per cent of employees elect to convert part of their pension into a tax-free lump sum. Because of their greater life expectancy, women give up a smaller proportion of their pension to receive the same lump sum as men. To illustrate, in a typical pension scheme operating at Inland Revenue approved rates, there are different commutation factors operating, so that a 63-year-old man would have to give up £105.48 of his annual pension in order to receive a lump sum of £1,000, while a 63-year-old woman has to give up only £97.28 for the same sum. (This is because £1,000 buys an annuity of £105.48 for a 63-year-old man, but an annuity of only £97.28 for a 63-year-old woman.)

These inequalities are no longer acceptable under the Equal Treatment Directives. Some schemes in the UK have introduced actuarial equality between men and women, by providing identical pension rights to men and women who have made the same contributions. For example, in 1983 IBM (UK) introduced a common commutation factor for both men and women, whereby a £1,000 lump sum costs both men and women aged 63 the same amount of £103.84 p.a. in reduced pension. Similarly, in 1986 Mecca Leisure introduced common annuity rates for both men and women, based on male mortality statistics.

In June 1991 the government finally accepted the principle that Britain's state-pension ages of 65 for men and 60 for women should be equalized. In December 1991 the Department of Social Security published a consultative document, *Options for Equality in State Pension Ages*. The document examined three possible common state-pension ages for men and women: 60, 63, and 65. The state pension, received by 10 million people and costing £24bn. per year (in 1990 prices), would cost another £3.5bn. per year if men were allowed to retire at 60. Adding in the lost tax and NICs, the additional cost could be as high as £8bn. per year (in 1990 prices). A common pension age of 65 would result in annual savings of about £4bn. to the state, but would lead to women having to work five more years before retiring. A common pension age of 63 would save the Exchequer £500m. per annum. The government also examined the proposal for a retirement decade, with a lower pension if someone retired at 60 and a higher pension if he or she waited until 70; however, it rejected this option on the grounds of greater complexity and the costs that would have to be borne by both employers and the state. The report noted that Germany and Italy will adopt a common pension age of 65 in 2012 and 2016 respectively. In Luxembourg and Spain it is already 65 and in Denmark it is 67. In November 1993 the government announced that it was raising the state-pension age for women from 60 to 65 over a ten-year period beginning in 2010.

10.2.5. THE BATTLE WITH THE MARKETS

The main problem that money-purchase schemes such as personal pension schemes face is that, at the time of retirement, the value of the fund may not be sufficient to buy an adequate pension annuity. The risk is greatest with unit-linked schemes whose value depends entirely on the liquidation value of the assets on the retirement date. If an individual retired on Friday 23 October 1987, he could have ended up with a pension that was 30 per cent less than he would have received had he retired a week earlier on Friday 16 October. The risk is not so large in the case of with-profits endowment schemes, since the reversionary bonuses are guaranteed in all but the final year: what is at risk with these schemes is the terminal bonus. Non-profit schemes are even less risky, and deposit administration schemes have negligible risk.

It is possible to imagine a range of risk-sharing or risk-reducing solutions to the problem posed by unit-linked schemes. An example of a risk-sharing solution is to set the liquidation value of the units at the average value of the units over the preceding twelve months. This would benefit pensioners retiring in a bear market and penalize those retiring in a bull market. An example of a risk-reducing solution would be a dynamic asset allocation strategy that gradually shifted the fund out of high-risk securities such as equities into low-risk securities such as bonds over a period prior to the retirement date. For instance, there could be a 20 per-cent reduction in equity exposure each year for five years prior to retirement. The proceeds could be invested in fixed-interest bonds which mature on (or just prior to) the retirement date, hence locking in the terminal values of the bonds. Bonds will therefore become an increasingly important tool for managing personal pension schemes near maturity, as well as pension funds that have reached maturity.

10.2.6. THE BATTLE OVER CHARGES

The final important battle concerns the costs of operating pension schemes, especially personal pension schemes. The great flexibility offered by personal pension schemes is offset somewhat by the high costs (often disguised) charged by the organizers of the schemes.

With pension schemes organized by insurance companies, the costs fall into three parts: initial commissions, annual management fees, and early surrender values. Annual management fees are generally quite small, although there can be quite large relative differences between different management groups: the typical range is between 0.5 per cent and 1.5 per cent of the fund value. The big differences arise over the methods for extracting initial commissions and for calculating early surrender values. For example, in Chapter 7 we found that pension schemes extracting initial commissions using capital units would end up delivering pensions that were 10 per cent lower than schemes involving recurring single premiums. Also in Chapter 7 we found that surrender values for with-profits endowment schemes were on average 27 per cent below maturity values with just one year to maturity. On top of this, charges can be imposed in a bewildering variety of ways. Apart from initial commissions and annual fund management fees, there can be fixed monthly 'administration' charges and a 'nil allocation' period of up to a year during which none of the member's contributions are allocated to investments. Most of the money collected during the nil allocation period is used to pay sales agents' commissions. Most of these charges are disguised in the small print of the policy documentation.

Pension schemes organized by unit trusts have much simpler charging structures than those organized by insurance companies. Nevertheless, charges can be imposed in a misleading way. This is because unit trusts are required to publish four different prices for their units: the *offer price* (the price that new investors pay for their units), the *bid price* (the price at which existing investors can sell their units), the *cancellation price* (the minimum bid price), and the *initial charge* (the quoted front-end cost of investing in unit trusts).

The initial charge is loaded into the offer price, but if the *bid-offer spread* (the difference between the bid price and the offer price) is greater than the initial charge, then the 'effective' initial charge is greater than the 'quoted' initial charge. The average quoted initial charge on unit trusts is 5 per cent. But if a unit trust's bid price is 85p and its offer price is 93p, then the effective initial charge is 8.60 per cent (of the offer price). In other words, this is the loss that would be incurred if a unit trust was purchased and immediately resold. In July 1993 69.7 per cent of the 1,438 unit trusts operating in the UK had bid-offer spreads exceeding the initial charge (according to a survey by Singer and Friedlander). The worst cases were Barclays Unicorn Property, Morgan Grenfell Genesis, and New Court Smaller Companies with spreads of 8.60, 8.39, and 8.19 per cent respectively. Further, it is possible for the 'effective' bid price (i.e. the cancellation price) to be below the 'quoted' bid price, so that investors do even worse when they sell their units. In July 1993 51.4 per cent of unit trusts had cancellation prices below bid prices.

There is a simple solution to these deceptive practices and that is to adopt a policy of *single pricing*. Both buyers and sellers face the same buying and selling price (equal to the *mid-price* between the bid and offer prices) and in addition there is either a fixed *entry charge* (paid by buyers only) or a fixed *exit charge* (paid by sellers only). Single pricing is already used by some unit trusts such as Singer and Friedlander, and Fidelity to sell offshore unit trusts in the UK. It is also used by *open-ended investment companies* which are common in continental Europe and North America and which will be permitted to operate in the UK in the mid-1990s. Unit trusts are likely to lose market share to these new investment companies unless they adopt single pricing.

Selected References for Part II

Books and Articles

Adam Smith Institute (1984), *Social Security Policy* (Adam Smith Institute, London).

Association of British Insurers (1988*a*), *Company Pension Schemes* (Association of British Insurers, London).

—— (1988*b*), *Personal Pensions: The New Deal* (Association of British Insurers, London).

BENJAMIN, B., HABERMAN, S., HELOWICZ, G., KAYE, G., and WILKIE, D. (1987), *Pensions: The Problems of Today and Tomorrow* (Allen and Unwin, London).

Centre for Policy Studies (1983), *Personal and Portable Pensions for All* (Centre for Policy Studies, London).

COOK, L. (ed.) (1988), 'Your Pension', Supplement, *Daily Telegraph* (11 June).

CRAMB, J. (1988), 'Fingertip Guide to the Revolution', *Financial Weekly* (Apr.).

Department of Employment (1987), 'Pensioners: Incomes and Expenditure 1970–85', *Employment Gazette* (May).

Department of Social Security (1985), *New Pension Choices: The Right Pension for You is Now Yours by Right*, NP40 (HMSO, London).

—— (1988*a*), *New Pensions Choices for Employees*, NP41 (HMSO, London).

—— (1988*b*), *New Pensions Choices for Employers*, NP42 (HMSO, London).

ESCOLME, B., HUDSON, D., and GREENWOOD, P. (1991), *Hosking's Pension Schemes and Retirement Benefits* (Sweet and Maxwell, London).

GOODE, Professor R. (chairman) (1992), *Consultation Document on the Law and Regulation of Occupational Pension Schemes* (Pension Law Review Committee, London, Sept.).

Government Actuary (GASOPS) (1991), *Occupational Pension Schemes 1987: Eighth Survey by the Government Actuary* (HMSO, London).

—— (1993), *Pension Law Reform: Report of the Pension Law Review Committee*, CM. 2342 (HMSO, London, Sept.).

HANCOCK, R., and SUTHERLAND, H. (1992), *Microsimulation Models for Public Policy Analysis* (Suntory-Toyota International Centre for Economics and Related Disciplines, London School of Economics, London).

HARRISON, D. (1992), *Pension Provision in the EC* (Financial Times Business Information, London).

HAY-PLUMB, M., and SHEARER, B. (1987), *Pension Schemes* (Institute of Chartered Accountants in England and Wales, London).

HM Treasury Report (1989), 'Pensions for the Enterprise Economy', *Economic Progress Report*, No. 203 (HM Treasury, London, Aug.).

Income Data Services (IDS) (1976), *Occupational Pensions*, Study 126 (Income Data Services, London, July).

—— (1979), *Public Sector Pensions*, Study 188 (Income Data Services, London, Feb.).

—— (1988), *Occupational Pension Schemes*, Study 421 (Income Data Services, London, Nov.).

—— (1989), *Uprating Pensions in Payment* (IDS Pensions Service, London, Nov.).

LEWIS, D. (1988), *Your Pension* (Penguin, Harmondsworth).

LOWE, J. (1993), *The Which? Guide to Pensions* (Consumers' Association, London).

National Association of Pension Funds, Annual Survey (NAPF, London).

National Audit Office (1990), *The Elderly: Information Requirements for Supporting the Elderly and Implications of Personal Pensions for the National Insurance Fund* (HMSO, London, Nov.).

NAYLOR, B., and FREAN, A. (1988), 'Your Pensions Choices', *Investors Chronicle* (July).

OLDFIELD, M. (ed.) (1988), *The PMI Guide to Pensions* (Heinemann, London).

—— (1993), *Understanding Pensions* (Fourmat, London).

PATERSON, M. (1987), *Pensions: Agenda for Change* (Woodhead-Faulkner, Cambridge).

Pensions Pocket Book (1994) (NTC Publications, Henley-on-Thames).

REARDON, A. M. (1990), *Pensions Guide* (Longman, London).

REARDON, T. (1988), *Planning Your Pension* (Longman, London).

RICHARDSON J. H. (1960), *Economic and Financial Aspects of Social Security* (Allen and Unwin, London).

SCOTT, Sir B. (chairman) (1981), *Report of the Committee of Inquiry into the Value of Pensions*, Cmnd. 8147 (HMSO, London, Feb.).

SERES, J. S. D. (1992), *Pensions: A Practical Guide* (Longman, London).

Tolley's Guide to Personal Pensions and Your New Pensions Choice (1987) (Tolley Publishing, Croydon).

Tolley's Pensions Handbook (1993) (Tolley Publishing, Croydon).

Tolley's Personal Pension and Occupational Pension Schemes: An Employer's Guide (1990) (Tolley Publishing, Croydon).

Tolley's Social Security and State Benefits 1993–94 (1993) (Tolley Publishing, Croydon).

TOULSON, M. (1986), *Managing Pension Schemes* (Gower, Aldershot).

WAINMAN, D. (1992), *Pensions* (Sweet and Maxwell, London).

WALFORD, J. (1988), 'Shedding Light on Personal Pensions', *Money Management* (July).

—— (1989), *Personal Pension Plans* (Financial Times Business Information, London).

WARD, G., and EVANS, A. (1989), *Pensions—Your Way through the Maze* (Institute of Chartered Accountants in England and Wales, London).

WARD, S. (1988), *The Essential Guide to Pensions* (Pluto Press, London).

WILSON, Rt. Hon. Sir H. (chairman) (1980), *Report of the Committee to Review the Functioning of Financial Institutions*, Cmnd. 7937 (HMSO, London, June).

Pamphlets

Annuities and the Open Market Option (Annuity Direct, London).

Annuities and Your Options (Lowndes Lambert Financial Services, London).

Complete Guide to Phased Retirement (Annuity Direct, London).

Staggered Vesting (Lowndes Lambert Financial Services, London).
You and Your Annuity (Annuity Bureau, London).

Journals
Fund Management International (International Business Communications).
Investors Chronicle (Financial Times Business Information).
Money Management Magazine (Financial Times Business Information).
Occupational Pensions (Eclipse Group).
Pensions (United Trade Press).
Pensions and Investment Age (Crain Communications, USA).
Pensions Intelligence (Longman).
Pensions Management (Financial Times Business Information).
Pensions Today (Monitor Press).
Pensions World (Tolley Publishing).

Occupational Pensions Board Reports
Solvency, Disclosure of Information and Member Participation in Occupational Pension Schemes, vol. 1, Cmnd. 5904, Feb. 1975; vol. 2, Cmnd. 5904-I, Apr. 1975; vol. 3, Cmnd. 5904-II, June 1975.
Occupational Pension Schemes—The Role of Members in the Running of Schemes, Cmnd. 6514, June 1976.
Equal Status for Men and Women in Occupational Pension Schemes, Cmnd. 6590, Aug. 1976.
Occupational Pension Scheme Cover for Disabled People, Cmnd. 6849, June 1977.
Improved Protection for the Occupational Pensions Rights and Expectations of Early Leavers, Cmnd. 8271, June 1981.
Greater Security for the Rights and Expectations of Members of Occupational Pension Schemes, Cmnd. 8649, Oct. 1982.
Protecting Pensions: Safeguarding Benefits in a Changing Environment, CM. 573, Feb. 1989.

PART III

PENSION FUNDS IN THE UNITED KINGDOM

Pension funds are part of the long-term investing institutions of the UK. Their purpose is to accumulate assets, the income from and capital values of which are used to pay for the pensions of retired workers. Of about 24 million people with pension rights, about 15 million are in schemes with pension funds. The rest receive their pensions on a pay-as-you-go basis. The income of the pension funds comes mainly from the contributions of both employers and employees and from the rents, dividends, and interest on the assets of the funds. Pension funds are said to be immature *when contributions and investment income exceed pension outflows; they are said to be* mature *when pension outflows are exactly matched by contributions and investment income; they are said to be* overmature *when pension outflows exceed contributions and investment income. In 1980 pension funds were still immature: the value of pension fund assets was about £100bn. but the net acquisition of financial assets was £20bn. that year or 20 per cent of the value of the funds. By 1993 pension funds had almost matured: the net acquisition of financial assets was only £5bn. or 1.25 per cent on total pension fund assets of £400bn.*

In this part of the book we examine UK pension funds, their investments, the performance of those investments, and the consequences of pension funds for capital markets. Chapter 11 looks at the different ways in which pensions can be funded and the different structures that pension funds can have. It also looks at the income-and-expenditure accounts of pension funds, the accounting treatment of pension costs, and the way in which actuarial deficits and surpluses can emerge. Chapter 12 examines the regulatory and investment environment facing pension funds. It discusses the full range of assets that pension funds can invest in, as well as their actual asset holdings over the last thirty years. Chapter 13 begins with a theoretical approach to pension-fund management, performance measurement, and risk management, based on modern portfolio theory. *It concludes with an examination of the main UK pension-fund management groups. Chapter 14 looks at the recent investment performance of both occupational and personal pension funds, and concludes with an examination of some of the problems with investment-performance measurement. Finally, Chapter 15 investigates the consequences of pension funds for capital markets, especially the consequences of the increasing short-termism that has affected pension-fund investment behaviour.*

11

Pension Funding in the United Kingdom

In this chapter we look at the most important features of pension funding in the UK. We begin with an examination of the different ways in which pensions can be financed, the various types of pension fund, and the different funds operating in the private and public sectors. We then examine the accounting framework for pension costs established by the UK Accounting Standards Board in 1988; this framework for the first time standardizes accounting practice in respect of company pension schemes. Occupational pension schemes periodically give rise to actuarial surpluses and deficits. The next part of the chapter presents estimates of the surpluses and deficits that have occurred since the beginning of the 1970s. We consider ways in which companies have attempted to extract the surpluses that their schemes have generated and the role of the 1986 Finance Act in preventing surpluses remaining in pension schemes. Finally, we examine the income-and-expenditure accounts of pension schemes in order to ascertain their financing position.

11.1. What Is Pension Funding?

The best way to answer this question is to compare funding with its alternative, pay-as-you-go.

Pensions may be financed from a reserve or fund which has been built up over a period of years by investing accumulated contributions in earning assets. This is called *accumulation of funds* or *funded financing*. Alternatively, the pension costs of retired employees may be met solely from the current contributions of the employer and of existing employees or from other revenues on a year-to-year basis. This is known as *pay-as-you-go* (PAYG) *financing* or *assessmentism*. Most occupational pension schemes in the UK are now funded (at least partially), and most of those that are not funded are in the public sector. For example, central-government civil servants are in an unfunded scheme which is financed directly by the Exchequer. Most of the remainder of the public sector (local authorities and public corporations) have funded schemes. By definition, personal pension schemes are fully funded. This is because they are money-purchase schemes and the size of the pension depends solely on the size of the fund accumulated at the point of retirement.

The objective of a funded scheme is to build up a fund of investment assets from current income (that is, from the contributions of both employers and employees), so that the earnings from those assets are available to finance the pension obligations of the employer. For a wholly funded scheme, the value of the fund must eventually be sufficient to pay for the total pension liability without additional financing from the employer. When this stage is reached the fund is said to be *mature*. Before this stage is reached the fund is said to be *immature*. The size of the fund, and also the maturity structure of the fund's assets, necessary to match the maturity structure of its liabilities are determined actuarially. They will depend on such factors as: the sex-and-age composition of the membership of the scheme prior to and after retirement; changes in that membership as a result of transfers, withdrawals, normal and premature retirement, and death; the levels of contributions and retirement benefits; the rates of return on the assets; and the rate of inflation.

Under the Inland Revenue rules for exempt approval, the trustees of a pension fund must consult an *actuary* on the valuation of the fund's assets and liabilities, although they do not actually need to appoint an actuary. The actuary has the following responsibilities. He advises on the type of fund suitable both for exempt approval under the 1988 Income and Corporation Taxes Act and for the employer's circumstances: for example, whether or not the scheme should be final-salary or money-purchase, and whether it should be contracted into or contracted out of the State Earnings-Related Pension Scheme (SERPS). The actuary also has to decide on the rate of interest and the rate of wage and price inflation that he will use in his actuarial calculations; the rate of interest will typically be related to the average return expected on investments. Using this interest rate, the actuary then determines the contribution-rate from employees and the employer necessary to finance the projected pension benefits, bearing in mind any minimum or maximum contribution limits that might be operating. The actuary also has to advise on related benefits, such as widow/er's benefit and disability benefit. Finally, and most importantly, the actuary has to conduct regular *actuarial valuations* (usually on a three-yearly basis) to ensure that the scheme is being adequately funded and that it is not producing either an *actuarial deficit* or an *actuarial surplus* (see Section 11.5 below). If the fund is showing a deficit, the actuary will recommend higher contribution-rates for employers and/or employees. If, on the other hand, the fund is showing a surplus of more than 5 per cent of liabilities (the maximum permitted under the 1986 Finance Act), the actuary will recommend ways in which the surplus can be reduced.

In principle, for the scheme to be self-contained and self-financing, it is necessary for the members of the scheme not to begin to receive pensions until the value of assets underlying their accumulated contributions at least equals the expected present value of their future pensions. This means that if an employee joined the scheme half-way through his working life he would have to pay a higher rate of contribution than an employee in the scheme for all his working life if he was to receive the same pension when he retired. In practice, however, most schemes are continuing schemes with both contributions into and pensions received from the funds from the beginning. If new contributions and investment income exceed the current value of pensions being paid, then there will be a net increase in the revenues available for investment, the fund will grow, and a surplus will develop. If, on the other hand, the reverse holds and a deficit develops, the employer will be forced to make *deficiency payments* in order to keep the fund solvent.

Under a PAYG scheme, no substantial fund is built up to meet contingent liabilities. Rather, current contributions are used to finance current pensions directly. Thus, the current work-force finances the pensions of the preceding work-force and relies on the succeeding work-force in turn to pay for its pensions.

The two types of scheme have different costs and benefits. The main advantage of a PAYG scheme is that the initial set-up costs are low since the high cost of setting up the initial fund of investment assets does not have to be met. Further, the running costs of a new PAYG scheme are lower than those for a new funded scheme. In particular, it is less costly to give past-service rights, or to grant pensions based on final salaries, or to increase pensions after retirement when the rate of inflation is high. Also, the administrative cost is lower and the structure of pension finance is simpler with a PAYG scheme.

Eventually, however, as the schemes mature, the advantages of the funded scheme dominate. Tangible assets are created against the real pension liability and these assets provide an investment income which supplements the contributions made by employees and employers, and this ultimately outweighs the lower administrative costs of the PAYG scheme. When a funded scheme is first introduced, all current pensions are financed from current contributions and any surplus of contributions is devoted to purchasing earning assets for the fund. As the fund grows the share of pensions financed from the income of the fund also grows. The fund will continue to grow so long as contributions plus investment income exceed the value of current pensions, since the balance accumulates in the fund.

In addition, even if the employing firm becomes insolvent, the pension fund is legally fully protected, whereas if a firm operating a PAYG scheme goes bankrupt, the scheme merely has a claim on the assets of the firm and comes behind the Inland Revenue, Customs and Excise, and

secured creditors.[1] This is likely to give greater psychological security
to employees in a funded scheme compared with those in a PAYG
scheme who, while nevertheless paying contributions, have no explicit
entitlement to receive pensions and must rely on future generations to
finance their retirement. Funding thereby relieves (or at least reduces)
the burden on future generations.

This is particularly important in the case of a declining industry where
the ratio of pensioners to employees (the dependency ratio) increases
sharply, causing severe problems for a PAYG scheme. In this respect,
funding can be a more stable method of financing pensions than assessmentism. This is because the size of the fund depends on the previous
history of employment in the firm and of contributions made into the
fund. So a firm that is declining may still have a relatively large fund to
finance its large number of pensioners, and it can therefore use this
fund as a buffer to protect the smaller number of current employees
from being asked to make an unacceptable increase in their rate of
contributions. Nevertheless, some pension funds in declining firms or
industries may still face very serious problems.

11.2. Types of Pension Fund

There are various types of pension fund operating in the UK.

11.2.1. PROVIDENT AND POOLED FUNDS

There are *provident funds* and *pooled funds*. With a provident fund, a
separate account is kept for each employee in which all contributions
made by and for him are accumulated and interest added. When the
employee retires he can have the accumulated value of his account converted into an annuity by actuarial calculations based on his life expectancy.
Provident funds are therefore rather like group personal pension schemes.
But most contributory schemes are based on pooled funds in which all
contributions are pooled and invested as a single sum. Some individuals
will, therefore, receive more than is directly proportionate to their contributions while others will correspondingly receive less. However, the

---

[1] The order of priority of pension-scheme members is, first existing pensioners, then early
leavers with deferred benefits, followed by current employees. From the beginning of 1991
an independent trustee has to be appointed to schemes where the company is in liquidation.
But the only requirement of a contracted-out scheme is to provide a guaranteed minimum
pension equivalent to the SERPS benefits forgone, so any new company taking over the
insolvent company would be liable only for this commitment and not for the full extent of
the shortfall in pension-fund assets.

greater diversification of asset holdings that is possible with pooled funds means that for the same contributions it is likely that they will yield higher average pensions than those from provident funds. The distinction between provident funds and pooled funds is clearly more important for defined-contribution schemes, such as personal pension schemes, than for defined-benefit schemes, such as final-salary occupational schemes, where the pension does not depend on the investment performance of the fund.

11.2.2. INTERNAL AND EXTERNAL FUNDS

There are *internally funded schemes* and *externally funded schemes*. An internally funded scheme is one in which the fund invests in its own parent company's assets (that is, *self-investment*). This is accomplished by the firm making an appropriate internal balance-sheet allowance for financing future pensions (a procedure known as *booking* or creating *book reserves*). This procedure is widely used in, for example, Germany, and is permissible in the UK although the 1990 Social Security Act placed a 5 per-cent upper limit on the proportion of internal funding. Some of the disadvantages which apply to PAYG are also valid for internal funding: in particular, if the firm becomes insolvent then the employee's pension is at risk as well as his job. Also, where there is self-investment in the sponsoring company, there may be a conflict of interest between the best interests of the firm and those of the future pensioners in the sense that such internal funds may not be allocated as efficiently as funds acquired from sources external to the firm. On the other hand, some degree of self-investment may well be beneficial. Employees have a tangible stake in the firm and in its future success, and this may help discourage disruptive or inefficient practices by the work-force. In addition, it is possible that self-investment is a fairly economical way of providing funds for investment in industry, and the cost is likely to be much lower than direct access to the capital markets, where there is less reliable information available concerning the particular enterprise than there is internally.

However, most private-sector occupational schemes are externally funded. This means that a *trust fund* is established and *trustees* who are independent of the employer are appointed to supervise the assets of the fund solely in the interests of current and contingent pensioners. The trustees' powers are derived from the Trustee Act of 1925, although they may be modified by the particular *trust deed* establishing the pension-fund trust. In most cases the investment powers of the trustees are mentioned in the deed. Otherwise these powers are specified in the Trustee Investments Act 1961, which limits both the type of investment and the proportion of the fund held in different assets, and, in particular, places strict limits on the amount of self-investment; the limits on self-investment were reinforced by the 1990 Social Security Act. The trustees have a legal obligation to keep accounts and have them audited periodically. In addition, they are required to have three-yearly actuarial reports prepared for the Inland Revenue in order to derive full tax-relief benefits, and also for the Occupational Pensions Board in order to satisfy the contracting-out requirements of the state scheme.

11.2.3. INSURED AND SELF-INSURED FUNDS

There are pension schemes that are *insured* (all of them in the private sector) and others that are non-insured or, more strictly, *self-insured* (sometimes known as *self-administered*).

Most small schemes are arranged through a life-assurance company which undertakes the investments of the fund. The insurance company cannot guarantee the return on the fund but does have long experience in investing life-assurance policies on its own account. Most large schemes are self-administered or self-insured, which means that they undertake their own investing, that is, appoint their own investment managers who consult with stockbrokers, investment banks, or other specialist pension consultants. These schemes are usually either self-trusteed or bank-trusteed. Some small schemes are self-administered, especially those established for partnerships or directors of companies.

In Britain today none of the insured schemes, and only a very small percentage of non-insured schemes, are registered under the Friendly Societies Act. A slightly larger percentage of non-insured schemes are registered by the chief registrar of friendly societies under the Superannuation and Other Trust Funds (Validation) Act 1927. The remainder of the non-insured schemes are set up under trusts established by the Trustee Act 1925.

In very broad terms, private-sector funds comprise two-thirds of the market value of all pension funds. About 20 per cent of the market value of private-sector funds (in 1987 this amounted to £40bn.) is held with insurance companies. The government actuary estimated that life-assurance companies received a net inflow (gross contributions less benefits paid out) of about £3bn. in 1987, either directly as part of their life business or indirectly as part of their separately managed funds. Some of the larger schemes, while self-administering the major proportion of their schemes, do nevertheless have a small part of their investments made by insurance companies: in total about 3 million members are in schemes with some insurance-company participation.

11.3. Funding in the Public and Private Sectors

The biggest difference between private- and public-sector pension schemes is that, whereas most private-sector schemes are funded, the major public-service schemes (those for civil servants, the armed services, police, fire brigades, health service, and teachers) are all unfunded, although paper or *notional funds* are kept for teachers and health-service workers. Other public-sector schemes, in particular those of the local authorities and public corporations, are funded, at least partially.

Income Data Services Study 188 found the following types of scheme operating in the public sector:

- no employee contributions and no funds—the central-government civil service (except spouses' and dependants' benefits) and armed services;
- employee contributions and no funds—police, fire service, central-government civil servants' spouses' and dependants' benefits;
- employee contributions and notional funds—local-authority teachers, National Health Service, and UK Atomic Energy Authority (UKAEA);
- employee contributions and actual funds—local authorities (except teachers, police, and fire service) and public corporations (except UKAEA).

To some extent this diverse outcome has been the result of historical development. For example, with the exception of the civil servants' scheme, all public-sector schemes have developed since 1920; in 1919 a committee, in discussing local-authority schemes, happened to recommend that these should be funded and they have been ever since. While the arguments about whether to fund state schemes or to rely on PAYG have generally tended to favour the former, the outcome has often resulted in the latter, whether discussing state social-security benefits or state employee-retirement benefits. For instance, when the national-insurance scheme was introduced in 1911, the 'sound finance' argument initially won the day but funding was effectively abandoned after several decades. Again, the Beveridge Report of 1942 recommended funding for state retirement pensions, but when they were eventually introduced they were granted to every retired person regardless of his or her previous contribution record and so the fund could not, in practice, operate and grow, and the idea of a fund was formally abandoned in the National Insurance Act of 1959.

The principal justification for not funding in the central-government public services lies both in the permanence of central government and in its virtually unlimited powers of taxation. The services provided by the public sector are likely to continue indefinitely. This means that there is not likely to be the problem encountered in declining industries, where increasingly smaller numbers of current employees have an undue burden in financing the pensions of much larger numbers of former employees. Also, the unlimited capacity of the government to finance itself means that PAYG is in effect merely the current financing of current obligations, that is, a system of finance which is quite consistent with the cash basis of current government accounting practice. This means that current employees need feel no concern that their own pensions will not be paid when they, in turn, come to retire. In the private sector, on the other hand, a fund may be necessary in order to provide such security.

When the Civil Service Joint Superannuation Review Committee examined the case for funding civil servants' pensions in 1972, it recognized the huge problems involved. To begin with, the fund necessary to meet existing pension liabilities would be enormous, requiring a huge additional tranche of public expenditure. Even the funding of future pensions, while leaving existing pensions on PAYG, would be extremely expensive. The committee concluded that in any event there could be no particular advantage to the funding of civil-service pensions since this would do nothing in itself to improve the already high level of security that comes from being a member of a scheme operated by central government.

A particular phenomenon peculiar to the public sector is the notional fund. The teachers' and health-service employees' schemes operate on the basis of notional funding. Both employers and employees make contributions, but any surplus during the year is not kept in separate funds but is lent to the Treasury. The Treasury pays a rate of interest equal to the average yield on long-dated government bonds. Using this rate of interest, the government actuary periodically values the funds and decides whether, given the current level of expenditure on pensions, higher or lower rates of contribution are necessary. Although the Treasury pays the long rate of interest, no real assets are held and so these schemes rely on the government financing pensions as they arise and are therefore, in effect, versions of PAYG schemes.

Another curiosity in the public sector is the scheme operated by local authorities. Each local authority in the UK maintains a fund for its own employees, although increases in pensions are financed from current income via the general rate and its successors the community charge and the council tax. Any alternative to this, such as abandoning the fund in favour of PAYG or notional funding, would involve some form of centrally organized guarantee (as happens, for instance, with the teachers' scheme). This is because such reorganizations as are involved, for example, in boundary changes could otherwise encounter problems in the reallocation of pension liabilities between the newly created authorities. On these grounds, it has been argued that it is desirable for local-authority residents to finance current services at the time that they are consumed and so avoid burdening future generations of residents. In addition, despite possible administrative advantages, local authorities would not welcome the loss of independence that a centrally organized scheme would introduce.

The public corporations have some characteristics in common with private industry and some with the other public services. Many of the public corporations are involved in vital and growing industries in the economy (for example, posts and, until 1984, telecommunications). Others are in declining primary activities such as coal or rail, where problems in the future may be serious. Two examples of declining nationalized industries whose pension funds were in serious difficulties in the 1970s are the coal and rail industries. The policy of British Coal and British Rail has been to fund fully their pension obligations rather than use current financing methods. However, as a result of the rapidly declining membership of these schemes and, in the case of rail, as a result of unsuccessful self-investment in the former unprofitable private railway companies, the funds had insufficient resources to meet their obligations during the 1970s. In both cases the government was forced to step in with deficiency payments. Between 1973 and 1979 the coal fund received £133.6m. and, as a result of the Railways Act 1974, the rail fund received, between 1975 and 1986,' deficiency payments totalling £584m. in 1974 prices. The position of these two funds was, however, improved by the dramatic turn-round in investment fortunes during the 1980s (as can be seen from Table 12.10).

11.4. The Accounting Framework for Pension Costs

In May 1988 the Accounting Standards Board (ASB) published Statement of Standard Accounting Practice No. 24, entitled *Accounting for Pension Costs*. SSAP24 standardizes accounting practice in respect of companies' pension schemes. It came into effect on 1 July 1988.

Before the introduction of SSAP24, a company's profit-and-loss account took into account the contributions payable into the company's pension scheme in the accounting period. But the nature of the contributions could differ for different companies and this could lead to distortions when comparing the accounts of different companies. This is because contributions could represent: normal contributions; normal contributions plus a lump sum to finance a scheme deficit or to enhance benefits; or normal contributions less amounts to amortize a scheme surplus, which if sufficiently large could lead to a contributions holiday. In addition, contributions made during an accounting period might not correspond with the accrual of pension liabilities in the same period, particularly for defined-benefit pensions. This is because pension liabilities are long-term and uncertain. Different pensions are payable depending on whether an employee retires, dies, or leaves service. Similarly, after retirement pension increases can have a large discretionary element.

The purpose of SSAP24, therefore, was to ensure that companies' profit-and-loss accounts reflected the true cost of providing pensions rather than merely the funding (that is, contributions) towards those pensions. This in turn required that the accounts adopt a common set of actuarial assumptions, and so reflect the actuary's best estimate of the cost of providing the anticipated pension benefits.

In operating a pension scheme, a company will have several objectives. First, it will want to ensure that the pension scheme remains solvent at all times by having sufficient assets to meet benefits when they arise. The accepted test for solvency is that, should the scheme be wound up, it would be able to meet all the benefits that employees were entitled to; in other words, there must be no deficiency on a *discontinuance* basis. Secondly, the company will want its contributions to be a stable and relatively constant proportion of its salary bill. These objectives are incorporated into SSAP24, by virtue of the actuarial assumptions made.

The following assumptions have to be made:

- statistical assumptions:
  - rates of mortality;
  - rates of withdrawal from the scheme;
  - rates of retirement (normal, early, ill health);
  - proportions married;
  - rates of new entrants;
  - salary increases due to promotion and merit.
- financial assumptions:
  - rate of price inflation;
  - rate of salary inflation;
  - rates of interest on assets (both income and capital gains);
  - rates of growth of dividends;
  - rates of increase in pensions.

There is usually little disagreement about the statistical assumptions that schemes make. Where there is much more variation, however, is over the financial assumptions. It is common practice to make the financial assumptions in real terms, that is, after taking account of inflation. The normal range of financial assumptions might therefore be as follows:

	Range of rates per annum (%)
Real rate of interest	3–5
Real rate of salary inflation	1–3
Real rate of pension increases	−5–0
Real rate of dividend increases	−2–0

Having produced a particular set of assumptions (known as a *valuation basis*), the actuary will use these to forecast future benefit outgo and investment income. These projected cash flows are then discounted back to the present day, to give the discounted present value of the cash flows (the procedures for doing this are discussed in Blake 1990, chap. 3). In terms of investment assets, it is possible to take the current *market values* of the assets. But a common procedure is to use the *actuarial values* of the assets. The actuarial value is determined by discounting the projected income streams on the assets. The argument that actuaries use for doing this is that both assets and liabilities are valued according to a common consistent set of long-term financial assumptions. In addition, market values can be quite volatile in the short term.

In determining required contribution-rates, two common methods are used: the projected-unit method and the attained-age method.

With the *projected-unit method* (or *accrued-benefits method*), benefits that accrue to members over the following year are estimated, based on projected final salaries at retirement. The normal employer contribution-rate is determined as the ratio of the present value of the following year's accrued benefit (less employee contributions) to the present value of employees' salaries over that year. The benefit accrual is therefore fully funded in the year of accrual. This means that, based on projected final salaries, the assets of the scheme will equal the actuarial value of the benefits accrued. In other words, this method is designed to achieve a funding level of 100 per cent. The normal employer contribution-rate will equal a constant proportion of salaries, so long as the age-and-sex composition of employees stays constant. This in turn requires a regular flow of new entrants into the scheme to prevent the average age of members from rising over time. If it does rise over time, then the contribution-rate will also rise over time.

With the *attained-age method* (or *prospective-benefits method*), both the salaries and benefits earned by employees over their entire future working lives are estimated. The normal employer contribution-rate is determined as the ratio of the present value of expected lifetime benefits (less the present value of employee contributions) to the present value of expected lifetime salaries. This method, therefore, takes account of the future ageing of existing members. Even without new members the contribution-rate using this method will be sufficient to provide the required benefits at the time of retirement.

Because the effect of ageing is taken into account, the attained-age contribution-rate will generally be higher than the projected-unit contribution-rate. As a consequence, assets will tend to be higher than accrued liabilities. This implies that the funding level will be over 100 per cent, reducing to 100 per cent at the date of retirement of the last member. So the main difference between the two methods is that the projected-unit method is designed to achieve exact funding (that is, a funding level of 100 per cent), whereas the attained-age method is designed to achieve a level contribution-rate.

Both methods will be sensitive to the assumptions used to calculate future salaries and benefits. If realized values differ from the assumptions used, there will be an imbalance between assets and liabilities. Any surplus or deficit of assets over liabilities will need to be amortized over the future.

Either method can be used as a basis for determining pension accounting costs under SSAP24. Pension costs can be divided into regular costs and variations from regular costs. *Regular costs* are the costs which, depending on the actuarial method used, fully provide for the expected benefits over the expected working lives of the scheme's members, as determined by the scheme's actuary. Expressed as a proportion of pensionable salaries, regular costs are charged to the profit-and-loss account of each accounting period. *Variations from regular costs* are also determined by the scheme's actuary and result from changes in circumstances, such as

- realized surpluses or deficits;
- changed actuarial assumptions;
- benefit changes or changes in membership conditions;
- increases in pensions in payment or in deferred pensions not provided

  for within existing actuarial assumptions.

SSAP24 requires the variations from regular costs to be spread over the remaining working lives of members. A number of *spreading methods* may be used for this purpose.

The simplest method is the straight-line method which amortizes a variation from regular cost evenly over the average expected remaining working lives for employees in the scheme (denoted by T). Therefore

$$\text{Amount amortized in year } t = \text{Variation cost}/T. \qquad (1)$$

However, the most common method used gives a variation cost that in each year is a constant proportion of employees' salaries:

$$\begin{aligned}
\text{Amount amortized in year } t \\
= (\text{Variation cost} \times \text{Salaries in year } t)/\text{PVS} \qquad (2)
\end{aligned}$$

where PVS is the present value of future salaries expected to be paid over the remaining working lives of employees in the scheme.

The spreading method used clearly affects the allocation of costs to each accounting period. It also affects the balance sheet, since any surplus or deficit after taking account of the variation cost in any accounting period will lead to a balance-sheet provision or accrual. For instance, if an actuarial valuation reveals a deficit of £100,000 at the beginning of the accounting period and the company makes provision in respect of variation cost of £5,000, then the deficit to be accounted for by the company is £95,000.

11.5. Pension-Fund Deficits and Surpluses

11.5.1. ESTIMATING THE DEFICITS AND SURPLUSES

A pension-fund *deficit* occurs whenever the actuarial value of the fund's liabilities in the form of projected future pension payments exceeds the value of its assets. In other words, the liabilities are *under-funded*. A pension-fund *surplus* occurs when the value of the assets exceeds that of the liabilities. In other words, the liabilities are *over-funded*. Given that most occupational schemes are defined-benefit schemes, periodic deficits and surpluses are bound to emerge.

The existence of pension-fund surpluses during the 1980s had been recognized within the actuarial profession for some time, but the first formal estimate of the size of the total surplus was made by Keating and Smyth (1985). Their estimates are given in Table 11.1 for the years 1972–85.

The figures show that there were persistent pension-fund deficits during the 1970s, the largest deficit, of £16.2bn., occurring in 1974 during the depth of the stock-market crash. The deficits declined sharply during the remainder of the 1970s. The first surplus, of £17.7bn., was recorded in 1980. There was a slight fall in the surplus in 1981, but the surplus grew continuously after that to reach nearly £80bn. by 1985. Given that the combined value of UK pension-fund assets in 1985 was about £200bn., this suggests that the surplus in 1985 amounted to about 40 per cent of assets. Using more conservative assumptions, Keating and Smyth estimated the surplus in 1985 to be at least £50bn., or 25 per cent of pension-fund assets, still a staggering amount.

Table 11.1 also estimates the sources of these deficits or surpluses. The main source is what Keating and Smyth call the *asset-market effect*. This is the effect of unanticipated changes in asset prices leading to investment returns either being lower than or greater than allowed for in the actuarial calculations. Keating and Smyth make the assumption that the prices of gilts do not change, and that the prices of UK equities and overseas securities rise in line with inflation. If actual security prices are lower than these expected prices, investment returns will be lower than required fully to fund future pensions and pension funds will move into deficit. If, on

TABLE 11.1. *Pension-fund deficits and surpluses: sources and size* (£bn.)

Year	Redundancy effect	Asset-market effect	Total size
1972	2.1	−2.3	−0.2
1973	2.2	−8.4	−6.2
1974	2.4	−18.6	−16.2
1975	3.8	−14.2	−10.4
1976	5.5	−14.0	−8.5
1977	6.0	−9.0	−3.0
1978	6.5	−9.1	−2.6
1979	8.0	−8.8	−0.8
1980	12.0	5.7	17.7
1981	14.8	−0.5	14.3
1982	17.2	20.4	37.6
1983	20.4	30.2	50.6
1984	22.4	49.5	71.9
1985	24.8	52.5	77.3

Source: Keating and Smyth 1985, Table 1.

the other hand, actual security prices are greater than these expected prices, investment returns will be more than sufficient fully to fund pension liabilities and pension funds will be in surplus. The negative investment returns (both real and nominal) in the 1970s account for the negative asset-market effect for the 1970s in Table 11.1. In the 1980s, however, pension funds generated high positive real returns. This has been partly because of the recovery of UK equity prices. It also resulted from the abolition of exchange controls in 1979 at a time when sterling was very strong. Pension funds began to invest heavily overseas, especially in the US and Japanese markets which saw sharp rises during this period. This, together with the depreciation of sterling since 1981, substantially increased the sterling value of overseas asset holdings. The high positive real returns in the 1980s account for the positive asset-market effect during the first half of the decade.

Redundancies have been the other major source of the funds' surpluses. The *redundancy effect* reduces pension-fund liabilities by more than the reduction of contributions into pension funds. When an employee is made redundant, he is treated as an early leaver in respect of his pension fund. This means that his pension will be related to his salary at the time of redundancy, although it will be increased annually by the smaller of 5 per cent or the rate of inflation. Since salaries generally rise at more than the rate of inflation, this means that the pension liability is much less than if the employee had remained with the company until retirement and collected a pension based on his retirement salary. The reduced pension liability is partially, but not completely, offset by the fact that no further contributions are made into the fund in respect of the employee. The net effect of redundancies, therefore, is to increase the surplus of pension funds. Furthermore, if redundant employees subsequently find pensionable employment elsewhere, then total contributions into pension schemes may not be greatly affected even though total pension liabilities will be reduced. Table 11.1 shows that there was a small positive redundancy effect during the 1970s, but that this rose substantially between 1980 and 1983 as a result of the severe contraction in manufacturing industry in 1980. In 1985 the redundancy effect accounted for one-third of the overall surplus of nearly £80bn., while the asset-market effect accounted for the remaining two-thirds.

Keating and Smyth's estimates were heavily criticized by the actuarial profession: see, for example, Wilkie and Wilson (1986) and the correspondence between Wilkie and Keating in the *Financial Times* (9 and 17 December 1985). The Association of Consulting Actuaries estimated the surplus to be no more than £8bn. (or 4 per cent of the value of pension funds). The main criticisms of Wilkie and Wilson are that nominal increases in asset prices cannot be locked in by pension funds and that the nominal increases in asset prices are in any case accompanied by lower yields on assets. They say that the 'solid returns' on assets were much lower than the 'ephemeral returns' that occurred during the 1980s. With these more cautious valuation assumptions, the surpluses of pension funds were much lower than those reported by Keating and Smyth. The counter-reply of Keating in the *Financial Times* of 17 December 1985 was that during the 1980s there was a sharp increase in both the prices of assets (both gilts and equities) and their real yields, and that this improvement was one of the main reasons for the pension-fund surpluses.

11.5.2. THE 1986 FINANCE ACT

The 1986 Finance Act required that pension-fund surpluses be reduced to no more than 5 per cent of liabilities within five years, beginning in April 1987. This could be achieved in one or more of the following ways:

- reduced contribution payments by current employees (known as an *employees' contributions holiday*);
- reduced contribution payments by the employer (known as an *employer's contributions holiday*);
- enhanced payments to pensioners and deferred pensioners; or

• a return of contributions to employers (but taxed at a special rate of 40 per cent without any offset).

The basis used for establishing whether a surplus existed was the *projected unit credit* basis used by the government actuary for state-pension purposes. When trustees submit actuarial valuations to the Pension Schemes Office, they must also submit an actuarial certificate stating that any surplus in the scheme does not exceed 5 per cent.

The government's intention was that a pension scheme should maintain a fund that was fully sufficient to meet the scheme's accrued pension liabilities together with an adequate margin for contingencies, but that it should not be possible to build up, with the benefit of generous tax reliefs, funds which were greatly in excess of the scheme's accrued liabilities. In requiring the surplus to be reduced, the government did not wish to prohibit a refund to the employer when the trustees deemed this necessary or desirable: for example, where a refund might avert a cash-flow crisis for the employer, or be used to facilitate new investment.

There was some concern, expressed by the Association of Consulting Actuaries (the trade organization representing pension actuaries), the Confederation of British Industry, and the Trades Union Congress that a surplus of only 5 per cent was too low and that the time-limit of five years was too short. Nevertheless, the government refused to modify its position.

Most pension funds have chosen employers' contribution holidays with some small increase in pension payments as the means of reducing their surpluses. We can consider some examples.

In 1986 BTR made profits of £505m. Of this, £17m. came from a cut in employer contributions to group pension schemes inn order to reduce surpluses within the schemes. In 1988 BTR merged the pension schemes of two of its subsidiaries, Thomas Tilling and Dunlop, into the BTR group pension scheme. Thomas Tilling had been taken over in 1983 and Dunlop in 1985. At the time of the Dunlop take-over the surplus in the Dunlop pension scheme was equal to half the value of the company. The surplus in the Thomas Tilling pension scheme in 1988 was £119m. Thomas Tilling pensioners were given a one-off increase in pensions of 10 per cent, costing £4m. This was all they received from the surplus: £57m. was used to reduce employer contributions and £58m. was used to improve benefits in the BTR group pension scheme.

Also in 1986 Metal Box suspended employer contributions to its pension scheme for five years. This benefited profits in 1986 by £7m. and savings over the next five years amounted to £48m. before tax. At the same time, £48m. was used to enhance benefits. Pensions for older pensioners were increased by up to 40 per cent, there were improved early-retirement benefits for men, improved rights for widows, and higher lump sums for death in service. In 1986 Metal Box's pension fund was valued at £550m., and 20 per cent of this (or £110m.) represented the surplus. Again in 1986 Northern Engineering Industries's profits were boosted by £1.5m. to £14.2m. as a result of a freeze on employer contributions to the NEI pension scheme. At the same time pension benefits were improved.

In 1988 British Rail decided to reduce its surplus by enhancing benefits and reducing contributions. The details were as follows:

- contributions were halved from 10 per cent to 5 per cent for employees and from 15 per cent to 7.5 per cent for the employer for an indefinite period;
- there was a 25 per-cent increase in the lump sum payable at retirement;
- there was an extra £2 per-week increase in both current and deferred pensions above that required for inflation-proofing;
- there was an increase in lump-sum death benefits.

The cost of these improvements was estimated at £606m. The BR pension fund was valued at £1.2bn. in 1988 and had the largest surplus of any UK company.

In 1989 Grand Metropolitan announced a pension-fund surplus of £126m. It planned to reduce this surplus by reducing employer contributions by £63m. over the next eleven years. Pre-tax profits were enhanced by more than £10m. in 1989 as a result of this change. In addition, all pensions were raised by at least 7 per cent, with older pensioners getting rises of more than 33 per cent. This accounted for another £63m. of the surplus.

Even small companies found themselves with very large surpluses. For example, Gomme Holdings, makers of G-Plan furniture, had a pension-fund surplus of nearly 100 per cent in 1984. The scheme's assets were £8.4m. and its liabilities were only £4.3m. The surplus came to light when the company, which had experienced a poor trading record during the early 1980s, attempted to withdraw £2.9m. of the surplus for itself. The move was blocked by the Inland Revenue. It was actions such as this which made trustees uncertain over who exactly owned the surplus and led the government to introduce the 1986 Finance Act.

By 1990 the pension-fund surpluses had been reduced substantially from the 40 per cent estimated by Keating and Smyth in 1985 to 22 per cent, as estimated by actuaries Mercer Fraser. This fall has resulted from the combined effects of poor investment returns following the 1987 crash (in 1990, for example, the average fund lost 10 per cent of its value) and increased pension liabilities as a result of legislation emanating from both the UK and Europe. The 1990 Social Security Act requires the inflation-proofing of pensions after retirement, while the European Court's ruling on equal retirement ages for men and women has increased pension costs. In addition, there was a considerable increase in early retirement (without loss of pension) during the 1990–91 recession and this helped to reduce pension fund surpluses even further. By 1993 surpluses had disappeared in many company pension schemes, and in some cases deficits had re-emerged. For example, British Telecom had a deficit of £750m., while the British Rail pension scheme had 'changed from a position five years ago where we had £4m. per working day to invest to one where we have to sell assets of £2m. per week to pay pensioners', according to BR executive David Adams. Between 1994 and 1996, British companies had to increase contributions by an average of 10 per cent of salaries or by £1bn. per year to avoid deficiencies in their schemes.

The manner in which pension-fund surpluses have been treated by companies has led to High Court actions and rulings as the two cases both involving Hanson PLC (then Hanson Trust) showed (see Section 10.2.3.2).

11.6. The Income-and-Expenditure Accounts of UK Pension Schemes

In this section we analyse the financing position of UK pension schemes by examining their income-and-expenditure accounts.

Table 11.2 shows the components of the income-and-expenditure accounts of pension funds in selected years between 1962 and 1992. The table shows the declining share of income coming from contributions (falling from 73 per cent to 57 per cent over the period) and the rising share of income coming from investments (rising from 27 per cent to 43 per cent). The table also shows the declining share of contributions paid by employers and the consequential increase in the share paid by employees. The changing importance of investment income is also discernible. During the 1960s and early 1970s about half the cost of pensions was met from investment income. During the boom period following the 1973–4 stock-market crash, this rose to 83 per cent. However, the increase in the number of pensioners and the improved indexation of their pensions has reduced the share of pensions met from investment income to 66 per cent by 1992. The investment successes of the late 1970s and 1980s are reflected in the last column of Table 11.2, which shows the annual surplus of income over expenditure as a percentage of income. The surplus exceeded 50 per cent during the late 1970s and early 1980s. Pension-fund surpluses had to be reduced following the 1986 Finance Act, and this is reflected in the lower level of surplus in the early 1990s. Finally, we note the quite high costs of administering pension schemes, averaging around 27 per cent of pensions for the whole period.

The next set of tables looks at the pension funds' income-and-expenditure

TABLE 11.2. *Components of the income-and-expenditure accounts of pension funds, 1962–1992 (%)*

Year	Share of income from:		Share of pensions and costs met from investment income	Administrative costs as %age of pensions	Share of contributions between:		Surplus as %age of income
	contributions	investment income			employers	employees	
1962	73	27	48	26	80	20	44
1967	71	29	49	23	80	20	41
1972	72	28	49	24	78	22	43
1977	65	35	77	32	77	23	56
1982	61	39	83	29	74	26	52
1987	61	39	66	28	66	34	41
1992	57	43	66	26	50	50	35

Sources: UK National Accounts Blue Books, 1973 (Table 21); 1984 (Table 4.5); 1993 (Table 4.10).

accounts in some more detail. Table 11.3 presents estimates from the 1987 *Government Actuary's Survey of Occupational Pension Schemes* (GASOPS) of the income–expenditure accounts of both private-sector and public-sector schemes for 1983 and 1987. In both sectors income exceeded expenditure in each year, and so the funds were growing in size. In terms of total income, the private-sector schemes were generating about 30 per cent more income than the public-sector schemes in 1983 and 50 per cent more in 1987. But in terms of income generated from investments rather than current contributions, the private-sector schemes were generating twice as much investment income as public-sector schemes in 1983 and three times as much in 1987, a difference that reflects the greater degree of funding in the private sector than the public sector. The ratio of contributions by employers to those of employees barely changed between 1983 and 1987. But this conceals big differences between the public and private sectors. In the public sector, the employers' relative contribution increased from a multiple of 2.6 to one of 3.0. In the private sector, the ratio fell substantially from 3.5 to 2.8.

In terms of expenditure, pension payments in public-sector schemes are much higher than in private-sector schemes, although the difference declined significantly between 1983 and 1987. In 1983 expenditure on public-sector pensions was more than twice that in the private sector, while in 1987 it was only 60 per cent greater. As a consequence, the net growth of public-sector schemes is much lower than that of private-sector schemes, about 40 per cent of the private-sector growth in 1983 and only 30 per cent in 1987. The net growth in funds was 20 per cent less than total pensions expenditure in the public sector in 1983, and nearly 60 per cent less in 1987, while in the private sector the net growth in funds was four times greater than total pensions expenditure in 1983 and two-and-a-half times higher in 1987. The detailed expenditure items in Table 11.3 indicate that inflation-proofing in the public sector had the greatest effect on pensions to former employees or their dependants and a much smaller effect on the lump sum given on death or retirement. The opposite result tends to hold in the private sector, with the rate of increase in the last two items exceeding that of the first two.

Comparing income and expenditure between 1983 and 1987, we see that, overall, the income of schemes increased by 50 per cent, but expenditure increased by more than 80 per cent. This difference reflects the gradual maturing of pension schemes and also the relative increase in the ratio of pensioners to active members. In addition, the pension-fund surpluses that emerged in the 1980s led employers (particularly those in the private sector) to reduce their contribution-rates significantly, as indicated in the previous section.

Table 11.4 presents estimates of the current accounts of the various

TABLE 11.3. *Estimates of the income and expenditure of pension schemes, 1983 and 1987 (£ million)*

	1983			1987		
	Private sector	Public sector	Total	Private sector	Public sector	Total
Income:						
Employers' contributions	6,200	5,700	11,900	6,650	7,600	14,250
Members' contributions (including additional voluntary contributions)	1,750	2,200	3,950	2,400	2,550	4,950
Transfer payments from other pension schemes	350	200	550	1,550	500	2,050
Rents, dividends, and interest	5,200	2,350	7,550	10,550	3,450	14,000
Miscellaneous income	50	100	150	350	150	500
Total income	13,550	10,550	24,100	21,500	14,250	35,750
Expenditure:						
Pensions to former employees	2,100	4,400	6,500	4,550	7,200	11,750
Pensions to dependants of former employees	250	500	750	600	850	1,450
Lump sums on death	300	150	450	350	200	550
Lump sums on retirement	1,150	1,500	2,650	1,450	1,950	3,400
Transfer payments to other pension schemes or arrangements	350	200	550	1,800	650	2,450
Refunds of contributions to members	100	100	200	150	100	250
State scheme premiums	200	100	300	250	150	400
Expenses and miscellaneous expenditure	300	50	350	1,050	50	1,100
Total expenditure	4,750	7,000	11,750	10,200	11,150	21,350
Excess of income over expenditure	8,800	3,550	12,350	11,300	3,100	14,400
			millions			
Numbers of active members	*5.8*	*5.3*	*11.1*	*5.8*	*4.8*	*10.6*
*Numbers of pensioners**	*2.1*	*2.9*	*5.0*	*2.9*	*3.1*	*6.0*

Note: * Includes widows and other dependants.

Source: GASOPS, Table 4.1.

TABLE 11.4. *Estimates of the income and expenditure of public-sector pension schemes, 1987 (£ million)*

	Public corporations	Central government	Local authorities (f)	Local authorities (u)	Total public sector
Income:					
Employers' contributions	1,390	3,990	850	1,380	7,610
Members' contributions	530	650	590	760	2,530
Transfer payments from other schemes	200	90	160	60	510
Rents, dividends, and interest	2,030	—	1,420	—	3,450
Miscellaneous income	100	—	30	—	130
Total income	4,250	4,730	3,050	2,200	14,230
Expenditure:					
Pensions to former employees	1,370	3,200	1,080	1,530	7,180
Pensions to dependants of former employees	290	350	100	90	830
Lump sums on death	70	60	30	20	180
Lump sums on retirement	470	850	250	390	1,960
Transfer payments to other pension schemes or arrangements	170	190	180	130	670
Refunds of contributions to members	20	40	30	20	110
Miscellaneous expenditure	130	40	20	20	210
Total expenditure	2,520	4,730	1,690	2,200	11,140
Excess of income over expenditure	1,730	—	1,360	—	3,090
					millions
Numbers of active members	*0.9*	*2.00*	*1.10*	*0.8*	*4.8*
Numbers of pensioners*	*0.9*	*1.25*	*0.55*	*0.4*	*3.1*

Notes: * Includes widows and other dependants.

(f) and (u) relate to funded and unfunded local-authority arrangements respectively.

Source: GASOPS, Table 4.2.

different public-sector schemes for 1987. The first point to note is that all central-government schemes and about 40 per cent (in terms of active membership) of local-authority schemes are unfunded and so generate no investment income. In total, about 60 per cent of the active membership of public-sector schemes are in unfunded schemes, and for these it is the employers' net payments which must be adjusted to balance total income with total expenditure.

Table 11.5 shows the income components per member of occupational schemes in 1987. As expected, the unfunded schemes had lower average incomes per member than funded schemes; they also had higher average employer contributions. The lowest average employee contributions were in the central-government scheme (£325 per member p.a.) and this reflects the fact that most central-government employees (in particular civil servants) do not pay direct pension-scheme contributions and instead have a notional amount deducted from their salaries. Investment income per member in the funded schemes varied quite substantially in 1987, ranging from £2,256 per member in the public corporations to £1,291 in local-authority funded schemes.

Table 11.6 shows the average pension and average increase in funds in the different schemes in 1987. The first line shows the average pension for each retired employee, while the third line shows the average amount of pension that is supported by each working employee. The fact that the elements on the third line are smaller than the corresponding elements on the first line indicates that pension schemes are still growing on average. In other words, no sector has more pensioners than currently employed workers, which would be the case if a particular industry, say, were in a steep decline. The average pension is largest for unfunded local-authority pensioners (at £4,542) and lowest for private-sector pensioners (at £1,978). The average pension in 1987 was £3,000 in the public sector and £1,978 in

TABLE 11.5. *Income components per member, 1987* (£)

Outlay per member	Private sector	Public corporations	Central government	Local authorities		Total public sector
				Funded	Unfunded	
Employers' payments	1,147	1,544	1,995	773	1,725	1,585
Members' contributions	414	589	325	536	950	527
Investment income	1,819	2,256	—	1,291	—	719
Total income	3,707	4,722	2,365	2,773	2,750	2,965

Source: Derived from GASOPS, Tables 4.1 and 4.2.

TABLE 11.6. *Pension per member, 1987* (£)

	Private sector	Public corporations	Central government	Local authorities Funded	Local authorities Unfunded	Total public sector
Average pension per retired member	1,978	2,108	3,368	2,332	4,542	3,000
Average dependant's pension	1,000	1,160	1,167	1,152	1,425	1,214
Average pension per active member	888	1,844	1,775	1,073	2,025	1,677
Net growth of fund per active member	1,948	1,922	—	1,236	—	646

Source: Derived from GASOPS, Tables 4.1 and 4.2.

the private sector, which compare with average earnings of £9,300. The average widow/er's or other dependant's pension was £1,214 in the public sector and £1,000 in the private sector. The net growth of fund per active member was highest in the private sector (at £1,948—it almost matched the average pension paid to retired members) and lowest in funded local-authority schemes (at £1,236).

12

Pension-Fund Investments

In this chapter we look at the investment side of pension funds. We begin
with an examination of the regulatory environment that they face. We
show that pension funds face few statutory restrictions on their investment
behaviour and that self-regulation is the guiding principle. Next, we
consider the investment environment faced by pension funds. This is one
of long-term stability with predictable change, but there can also be
substantial volatility in the short run. Following this, we analyse the full
set of assets in which pension funds are permitted to invest. Finally, we
look at the actual asset holdings of UK pension funds and see how these
have changed since the late 1950s. The main long-term capital market
instruments are shares and bonds. Pension funds also hold long-term real
assets, such as property and collectibles (for example, works of art).
There are also a number of relatively new derivative financial instruments
such as futures, options, and swaps whose use is becoming increasingly
important in enhancing pension-fund returns or in reducing risks. Although
pension funds are long-term investors, they do hold some highly liquid
assets and there have been times in the past, when the capital markets
have been depressed, when holdings of liquid assets have been substantial.

12.1. The Regulatory Environment

12.1.1. THE STATUTORY FRAMEWORK

UK pension funds face surprisingly few regulatory restrictions on their
investment behaviour. For example, there is no direct equivalent of the
1974 US Employee Retirement Income Security Act (ERISA), with its
requirement for trustees to adopt a *prudent-man principle*. On the other
hand, there is no state-funded safety net as with the US Pension Benefit
Guaranty Corporation.[1] The main acts of parliament affecting pension-

---

[1] ERISA set up the Pension Benefit Guaranty Corporation (PBGC), a federal insurance
agency which guarantees that employees receive their pensions (up to certain limits) even if
the assets in the pension fund are insufficient and companies are unable to make the
requisite deficiency payments. In 1974 when the PBGC was set up the annual premium was
$1 per employee. This was felt to be sufficient to pay for expected claims. But the
availability of unlimited insurance at negligible cost enabled companies to 'game' the system
by deliberately under-funding their schemes. By 1986 it was estimated that annual premiums

fund investment are the 1961 Trustee Investments Act, which places
limits on the proportion of the fund that may be invested in certain types
of investment, and the 1986 Financial Services Act, which introduced a
framework of self-regulation of the investment practices of all investment
advisers. The 1990 Social Security Act placed a limit on the amount of
self-investment by pension funds in their sponsoring companies of 5 per
cent of fund assets. The 5 per-cent ceiling covers shares, loans, property,
and also money owed by the company to the scheme. The ceiling is
designed to protect pension schemes from the failure of the parent company
and also from hostile take-overs.

Pension funds operate under trust law and so are bound by the trust
deeds of the fund. The trust deeds take precedence over statute law, so,
for example, the trust deeds of most pension funds are drawn to have a
wider scope than the minimum set out in the 1961 Act which, among
other measures, effectively prohibits investments in non-sterling assets.
Pension funds are therefore free to invest in virtually any type of asset,
financial or real, cash or derivative, at home or abroad. In short, they can
invest in anything from old masters to financial futures contracts, and
they can use a whole range of risk-management techniques to hedge their
portfolios (UK pension funds have been using futures and options for
this purpose since 1983). Only explicit speculative trading activities
would invalidate their tax-exemption privileges. If pension funds are 'too
successful' in generating returns, they become subject to the 1986 Finance
Act which limits the value of pension assets to 105 per cent of pension
liabilities. Any surplus above this has to be eliminated through enhanced
pension benefits or contributions holidays.

The main restrictions that pension funds face have nothing to do with
the investment side of their activities. Instead, there are restrictions on
the proportion of salary that can be paid into a pension fund. The
maximum is 17.5 per cent of salary up to a maximum salary of £60,000 (at
1989 prices). There is also an upper limit to the pension benefit and a
restriction on the form in which it can be paid. In the case of final-salary
occupational pension schemes, the maximum pension is two-thirds of final
salary, together with a maximum tax-free lump sum at retirement of 1.5
times salary up to a limit of £90,000 (in 1989 prices). In the case of

of $50 per employee were needed to finance the PBGC. In 1987 the Omnibus Budget
Reconciliation Act imposed stricter standards of minimum funding.

The existence of the PBGC also provided an incentive for firms in financial distress
(healthy firms were prevented from doing this by the 1986 Single Employer Pension Plan
Amendments Act) to invest their pension-fund money in the riskiest assets. This is because
the liability side of their balance sheets is insured. If the risky assets perform well, the
pension fund gains, while if the assets perform badly, the PBGC pays. The crisis in the thrift
industry in the 1980s was caused in exactly the same way, with the Federal Savings and Loan
Corporation facing losses of $500bn.

personal pension schemes there is no limit to the pension, but a limit to the tax-free lump sum of one-quarter of fund assets. Any contributions paid in excess of these limits while permissible do not attract any tax relief. The main concern of the authorities is to prevent pension schemes being used for tax-avoidance purposes.

The authorities are also concerned that pension schemes outside the state system should provide a minimum standard of pension benefits, broadly comparable with the benefits that could be achieved under the state scheme. In the case of occupational schemes these benefits are the *guaranteed minimum pension*, while in the case of personal schemes they are the *protected rights pension*.

Given the restrictions on both contribution inflows and pension outflows, it seems reasonable that the investment practices of pension funds themselves are largely unrestricted. Otherwise it might not be possible to deliver the expected level of pension benefits, given the contribution levels. The only real anomaly in the system is the tax-free nature of the lump sum at retirement. This happened for a curious historical reason, but is otherwise not rational. If the lump sum was taxed at the same rate as the pension, it would not really matter if the entire pension benefit could be taken as a lump sum. There would, of course, be redistributional effects. The present system of a limited lump sum favours longevity and penalizes the early death of pensioners. If the entire pension benefit could be taken as a lump sum equal to the actuarial capitalized value of pension benefits, this would penalize long-lived pensioners, since the size of the lump sum would reflect the average life expectancy of pensioners.

12.1.2. SELF-REGULATION

The main regulatory environment faced by pension funds is therefore one of *self-regulation*. Pension-fund managers do not like to have restrictions placed on their investment decisions other than those placed on them by the trustees, who themselves are subject to the 1961 Trustee Investments Act. But even the trustees are limited in their ability to place restrictions on fund managers. This is because trustees have a fiduciary responsibility under the 1961 act to act in the 'best interests' of the current and future beneficiaries of the fund. What constitutes 'best interests' has been the subject of much debate and even legal dispute, as a famous court case involving the mineworkers' pension fund shows.

12.1.3. THE *MEGARRY JUDGMENT*

The mineworkers' pension fund had a committee of ten trustees drawn equally from the National Coal Board (NCB, now British Coal) and the

National Union of Mineworkers (NUM). In 1982 the NUM, led by its
president Mr Arthur Scargill, declined to endorse that year's investment
proposals submitted by the fund manager. It made alternative proposals
requiring the disinvestment in overseas securities and the prohibition of
investment in energy (especially oil) companies that competed directly
with coal.

The NCB took the NUM to court, arguing that the NUM trustees were
in breach of their fiduciary responsibilities to the Board's pensioners on
the grounds that, in refusing to endorse the 1982 investment proposals,
the NUM trustees were risking the investment performance of the fund
and hence damaging the financial interests of the fund's beneficiaries.
The NUM's counter-argument was that its investment proposals were
directly compatible with the best interests of the fund's beneficiaries.
It argued, for example, that investing in competing energy companies was
harmful to the interests of those working in or retired from the coal
industry. It also argued that investing overseas rather than in Britain was
harmful to the long-term growth of the British economy in general and to
the coal industry in particular.

The case was heard in the High Court by Sir Robert Megarry. The
Megarry Judgment began with a definition of 'best interests':

When the purpose of the trust is to provide financial benefits for the beneficiaries,
as is usually the case, the best interests of the beneficiaries are normally their best
financial interests. In the case of a power of investment, as in the present case, the
power must be exercised so as to yield the best return for the beneficiaries, judged
in relation to the risks of the investments in question. (Megarry 1984, p. 20)

Megarry did concede, however, that there were some cases in which the
best interests of the beneficiaries were not their best financial interests.
This would occur if the beneficiaries had a strong collective aversion
on moral or social grounds to certain types of equity, such as that of
companies engaged in the production of tobacco, alcohol, or armaments
manufacture. In this case, it could be argued that it was better to receive
a lower return from less 'evil and tainted sources'.

Nevertheless, Megarry rejected the NUM's contention that its proposals and the beneficiaries' best interests were compatible. He argued
that the current pensioners had no financial interest in the success of the
coal industry, and neither would future pensioners once they had retired.
Further, he argued that it was the duty of the trustees in the interests of
the beneficiaries to use the full range of investments authorized by the
terms of the trust (under the Trustee Investments Act 1961) to enhance
the fund's return or reduce its risk. Megarry could not see how the
beneficiaries' best interests were served by restricting the range of investments as proposed by the NUM.

12.2. The Investment Environment

UK pension funds' investment environment tends to be characterized by long-term stability and predictable change, but occasional short-term volatility.

12.2.1. LONG-TERM STABILITY

The long-term nature of pension-fund activity and the relatively stable and predictable character of contribution inflows and pension outflows both combine to give pension funds a very wide choice of investment strategy. With regard to inflows, this stability and predictability follow from the contractual nature of the contributions, which means that the inflows are guaranteed over a long period and also that they are less subject to competition from other forms of savings. The long period of time during which contributions are paid allows the investment of these contributions to be made across many business cycles (that is, across many periods of boom and slump) and so leads to a more stable long-run average return than is likely to be achieved over the short term. The question of outflows is also a fairly simple one because pension benefits are reasonably accurately predictable in an actuarial sense. The normal age of retirement of the employee is known from the beginning and the likelihood of premature retirement due to invalidity or the mortality rate both before and after retirement is actuarially predictable. Similarly, with a large enough work-force even the turnover of the work-force can be assessed reasonably accurately. Further, long-term real investment rates and real salary growth rates are also fairly stable, although in the short run investment returns and inflation rates have been extremely volatile in the UK.

These factors of stability and predictability allow the pension fund to select asset portfolios with very long maturity profiles. Indeed, the maturity structure of pension-fund assets is longer than that of any other type of savings institution, including that of insurance companies which, even on their life business, have to deal with short-term endowment policies and also have to make allowance for surrenders, for example. Another implication is that changes in the portfolio can be made purely as a result of changes in investment opportunities and do not need to be forced as a result of sudden and unexpected changes in outflows. If insurance companies, for example, are faced with an increase in the demand for policy loans, they may be forced to switch out of shares. Pension funds, on the other hand, are in a position to change their portfolios gradually and can do so at low cost by appropriately reallocating cash inflows rather than actively switching parts of the existing portfolio; although the latter does take place, of course.

A related factor is the choice of assets open to pension funds, which in principle is considerably wider than that open to insurance companies. For example, on top of their life business, insurance companies are involved in providing policy loans and mortgage loans and these are generally lower-yielding assets; it is possible for pension funds to hold a higher proportion of higher-yielding assets, such as direct property holdings and equity, in their portfolios.

Another very important consideration is the tax status of pension funds. UK pension funds are *gross funds*, which means that they are exempt from capital-gains tax and enjoy (partial) relief from income tax on their investments in the UK and, where double taxation agreements exist, exempt from all capital-gains tax and income tax on their investments held abroad (apart from income tax on dividends, which is generally non-recoverable). This means that total switching costs are much lower for pension funds than for other investors (although dealing and brokerage costs still have to be met) which in turn means that, as circumstances change, pension funds are in a position to achieve their desired portfolios at much lower net cost than other investors, since such portfolio adjustments are not liable to capital-gains tax.

The 1990 Finance Act exempted pension funds (as well as authorized unit trusts) from tax on their trading income from futures, forwards, and options contracts (these instruments are examined in Section 12.3 below). Before the passing of the act, transactions in these instruments made for the purpose of hedging a portfolio (see Chapter 13) were liable for capital-gains tax, while all other transactions were classified as trading and liable for corporation tax. Following the act, all profits from futures, forwards, and options positions are treated as capital gains and pension funds are exempted from capital-gains tax.

The 1993 Finance Act changed the formula for calculating the *tax credits* on dividend payments. Prior to 1993, companies paid *advance corporation tax* (ACT) at the *basic rate* of 25 per cent on their dividend distributions, and at the end of each tax year their *mainstream corporation tax* (MCT) liability was reduced to reflect the ACT already paid. Dividend recipients received a *tax credit* based on the basic rate which non-taxpayers such as pension funds could reclaim in full from the Inland Revenue. However, the 1993 act reduced the ACT rate to 22.5 per cent in 1993–4 and to 20 per cent in 1994–5. Investors' tax credits therefore fell to the *lower rate* of 20 per cent in 1994–5. This had the effect of reducing the income received by non-taxpaying investors including pension funds. Before 1993 every £75 in net dividend payments was equivalent to £100 in gross dividend payments (that is, £75/(1 − 0.25)).

Since April 1994 every £75 in net dividend payments is equivalent to only £93.75 in gross dividend payments (that is, £75/(1 − 0.20)). Pension funds can now reclaim only £18.75 (that is, £93.75 − £75, or 20 per cent of the gross amount of £93.75) instead of the previous amount of £25 (that is, £100 − £75, or 25 per cent of the gross amount of £100). Pension funds' income from equity investment has therefore fallen by 6.25 per cent as a result of this tax change, or by about £600m. in 1993.

12.2.2. PREDICTABLE CHANGE

Pension funds are also subject to change that is reasonably predictable. The most important example of this is the maturing of pension funds. When pension funds are first set up, they are *immature*. They have few pensioners, so that contributions into the funds, together with investment income, exceed pension pay-outs. While they are immature, pension funds will grow very fast. However, over time the ratio of pensioners to contributors (the *dependency ratio*) will increase, causing the growth rate in pension funds to decline. Eventually, pension funds will *mature*, and contributions and investment income will exactly match pension pay-outs. If an industry subsequently declines and the work-force is made redundant, the pension funds in the industry will become *overmature*. While contributions into the funds decline, future pension pay-outs fall by even more, leading to substantial surpluses developing.

12.2.3. SHORT-TERM VOLATILITY

While the investment environment faced by pension funds is generally stable and predictable, this does not imply that it is either static or without any uncertainty. Two examples are the short-term volatility of the real returns on assets, and the volatility of exchange rates.

Table 12.1 shows how volatile the real returns on equities and gilts have been in the UK during the four decades from the 1950s to the 1980s. The average real return on equity for the four decades was 7.9 per cent, while for gilts it was virtually zero. But the range of variation is from −2.1 per cent to 15.6 per cent for equity and from −4.5 per cent to 5.6 per cent for gilts.

The figures in Table 12.1 also indicate how difficult it has been for pension funds to generate systematically positive real returns, although it is essential for their long-term survival that they do so. This is because pension funds have pensions liabilities that are denominated in real terms. Most pensions are initially related to final salaries and are thereafter at least partially index-linked to inflation. The assets of pension funds are

TABLE 12.1. *Real rates of return (before tax) on equities and gilts* (% p.a.)

	Equities	Gilts
Jan. 1950–Dec. 1959	12.6	−1.7
Jan. 1960–Dec. 1969	5.4	0.5
Jan. 1970–Dec. 1979	−2.1	−4.5
Jan. 1980–Dec. 1989	15.6	5.6
Average	7.88	−0.03

Note: The rates of return include both interest and dividend income (treated as reinvested) and capital appreciation or depreciation, and are net of changes in the retail price index.

Sources: Wilson Report (1980, Table 22) and *Financial Statistics* (1991).

financed from the contributions of employers and current employees and also from investment income. Since employee contributions cannot be increased retrospectively, pension funds have always had to be very careful to invest in assets with the best possible returns and so avoid deficits arising. In the 1950s and 1960s it was possible to achieve a positive real return by investing in equities (an average 12.6 per cent p.a. for the 1950s and 5.4 per cent p.a. for the 1960s, which includes dividends and changes in capital values), but the real return on government bonds was much less and in the 1950s was, on average, negative (an average −1.7 per cent p.a.). This explains the massive relative increase in equities in pension-fund portfolios and the corresponding relative decline in government bonds, a trend that was noticed by the Radcliffe Committee as early as 1959. During the 1970s, however, even the real return on equities became negative as a result of low company profitability caused by domestic *stagflation* (low aggregate demand and high inflation at home) and external factors such as the oil crises of 1973 and 1979 which raised costs at home and reduced export demand abroad. The average annual real return on equities during this period was −2.1 per cent. The only other major asset category to outperform UK equities in the 1970s was property, both in its rental and capital-value components, and this is so even when allowance is made for the property crash in 1973–4. The 1980s saw an astonishing turn-round in stock-market fortunes, with annual average real returns on equities of nearly 16 per cent and those on government bonds of nearly 6 per cent. Returns on overseas assets have been even greater in some cases.

So life has been very sweet for pension funds in recent years. But real returns of this size cannot possibly continue: the UK economy is simply not generating sufficient real income to finance them in the long run. There are several reasons why it has not been possible to generate positive real returns on a systematic basis.

The most obvious reason is that, until the introduction of indexed gilts in the Budget of March 1981, no asset had its capital value or its return denominated in real terms. This meant that the only way to attempt to achieve a real return on many assets was to trade in those assets, attempting to take advantage of the cycles (of various terms) in the values of assets in order to generate capital gains. Some assets, for example, developed land and property, gold, and diamonds, generally provide good hedges against inflation as a rule, but their return is not guaranteed and their values can sometimes collapse quite spectacularly (for example, commercial property in 1973–4 and the late 1980s, gold at the end of 1980 following the boom at the beginning of 1980, and diamonds during 1980).

A second reason why in the past it has been difficult to achieve real returns in these circumstances has been that the costs of trading in assets was high. Broking commissions have to be paid on both purchases and sales; and the market-maker's spread (the difference between the bid and offer prices) has to be met. In the 1970s commissions ranged from 0.4 per cent for gilts to 0.8 per cent for equities; and the spread ranged from 0.3 per cent for large company stocks up to 10 per cent for the infrequently traded shares of small companies. This meant that on average it would have cost a pension fund in the 1970s about 1 per cent of the share's value to buy and then immediately resell a typical share. Because of these costs, only about 20 per cent of a pension fund's portfolio was traded in any one year during the 1970s. [Competition following the Big Bang of 1986 has reduced these costs quite substantially. By the 1990s institutional investors could trade commission-free in gilts and in about 25 per cent of deals involving equities, while paying commissions of 0.2 per cent in the remaining 75 per cent of equity deals. Gilt spreads ranged from 0.125 per cent for shorts to 0.25 per cent for longs. Equity spreads ranged from 0.2 to 0.5 per cent. Spreads in illiquid shares had been reduced to about 1 per cent as a result of trading such shares in packages (a procedure known variously as *basket trading*, *portfolio trading*, or *program trading*). The effect of these lower costs has been to increase the average annual turnover of pension fund portfolios to about 50 per cent.]

Thirdly and most importantly, the real rate of return in the economy depends on the growth rate of productivity, that is, real output per worker. This depends on the quantity of capital per worker and the rate of technical progress. But the productivity of capital and the rate of technical progress in turn depend on the resources that are devoted to research and development, and to investment in new production techniques. In the past pension funds have devoted themselves exclusively to portfolio investment, showing very little interest in financing R. & D. or in investment in productive capital. While this type of behaviour may have suited the return objectives of individual funds separately, it may not be sufficient to achieve and sustain a very high rate of return for the economy as a whole, since newer and more productive investment opportunities may miss being financed. Yet pension funds as a whole depend on a high real rate of return for the economy as a whole in order to meet the expectations of their existing members.

One of the criticisms at the time of the 1980 Wilson Committee concerned the investment practices of the long-term financial institutions, especially the pension funds. Since they only held the shares of the top 200 or so companies, it was believed that small companies were denied access to investment finance, or could get it only very expensively via bank loans. The implication was that pension funds were very risk-averse and also very short-sighted, since they were unwilling to help the new firms and industries of the future. They were also considered to be too concerned with short-term income prospects and too sensitive to short-term fluctuations in capital values.

The pension funds' answer to this criticism, which was also largely confirmed by the Wilson Committee itself, was that small companies with a product worth developing and producing did not have any real trouble getting finance. There already existed several channels through which finance for small companies was made available, for example 3i, where the risk is shared between the institutions and the Department of Trade and Industry. This arrangement is largely voluntary and the minority report of the Wilson Committee recommended that the institutions should contribute £1bn. per year to a state investment bank. However, pension funds do not really like dealing in the shares of small companies because they are difficult to research and their shares tend not to be very liquid. Also, it is not clear that small companies relish the thought of institutions holding a large proportion of their share capital. Nevertheless, the larger pension funds began to establish their own venture-capital units at around the time of the Wilson Report (see Section 12.3.3 below).

While pension funds remain immature, they will not be greatly affected by the short-term volatility of investment returns. This is because pension funds are still in the position of having contribution inflows exceeding pension outflows. This in turn means that the funds are not forced to sell

TABLE 12.2. *Selected sterling exchange rates, 1970–1990*

	$US	DM	Yen
1970	2.40	8.74	857.8
1971	2.44	8.53	884.6
1972	2.50	7.98	752.3
1973	2.45	6.54	664.6
1974	2.34	6.05	682.7
1975	2.22	5.45	658.1
1976	1.81	4.55	535.3
1977	1.75	4.05	467.6
1978	1.92	3.85	402.6
1979	2.12	3.89	465.6
1980	2.33	4.23	525.6
1981	2.03	4.56	444.6
1982	1.75	4.24	435.2
1983	1.52	3.87	359.9
1984	1.34	3.79	316.8
1985	1.30	3.78	307.1
1986	1.47	3.18	246.8
1987	1.64	2.94	236.5
1988	1.78	3.12	228.0
1989	1.64	3.08	225.7
1990	1.79	2.88	257.4

Source: *Bank of England Quarterly Bulletin*, various issues.

any of their assets at unfavourable prices in order to meet their liabilities. However, as pension funds mature and the importance of contributions declines, the stability of investment returns becomes a much more important consideration. As the Wilson Committee recognized, the future viability of pension funds 'will depend upon the income from their assets keeping pace with inflation, in other words, upon the real value of their assets in the long run' (Wilson Report 1980, p. 89).

Table 12.2 shows how volatile exchange rates have been in the twenty years since the breakdown of the Bretton Woods fixed exchange-rate system. The table shows the sterling exchange rate against three key currencies, the US dollar, the German mark, and the Japanese yen. Especially volatile has been the sterling–dollar exchange rate. For example, between 1980 and 1985 sterling's value fell by 44 per cent against the dollar (from $2.33 to $1.30), and between 1985 and 1988 it subsequently rose again by 37 per cent (from $1.30 to $1.78). Sterling's value against the Deutschmark and the yen has been dominated by a declining trend, but also with some considerable volatility. Over the period the pound has fallen by 67 per cent against the DM and by 70 per cent against the yen. However, sterling appreciated by 17 per cent against the DM between 1979 and 1981 (from DM3.89 to DM4.56) and by 31 per cent against the yen between 1978 and 1980 (from 402.6 yen to 525.6 yen).

The volatility of exchange rates makes the returns on overseas investments very volatile when measured in sterling terms; and ultimately, of course, UK pensioners will be interested in the sterling value of their pension-fund investments.

The volatility of interest rates, stock-market returns, and exchange rates has led pension funds to engage in risk-management techniques involving futures, options, and swaps. These are discussed in the next section.

12.3. The Components of a Pension-Fund Portfolio

In this section we consider the full range of assets in which a pension fund might consider investing.

12.3.1. MONEY-MARKET SECURITIES

Money-market securities are short-term instruments with maturities of less than one year. There are two main classes: those that are quoted on a *yield basis* and those that are quoted on a *discount basis*.

The most important examples of money-market securities that are quoted on a yield basis are money-market deposits and negotiable certificates of deposit. Such instruments are always issued at par. *Money-market deposits* are fixed-interest fixed-term deposits of up to one year with banks or discount houses. The deposits can be for the following terms: overnight, one week, or one, two, three, four, five, six, nine, or twelve months. They are not negotiable, so cannot be liquidated before maturity. The interest rates on the deposits are fixed for the term and are related to LIBID (the London inter-bank bid rate) of the same term. For example, the one-month deposit rate could be one month LIBID *less* 0.125 per cent. The interest and capital are paid in one lump sum on the maturity day (except for discount-house deposits where interest is paid monthly).

Negotiable certificates of deposit (CDs) are receipts from banks for deposits that have been made with them. The deposits themselves carry a fixed interest rate related to LIBID and have a fixed term to maturity, and so cannot be withdrawn before maturity. But the certificates or receipts on those deposits can be traded in a secondary market, that is, they are negotiable. CDs are therefore very similar to negotiable money-market deposits, although the yields are about 0.25 per cent below the equivalent-term deposit rates because of the added benefit of liquidity. The maturities of CDs are generally between one and three months, although some CDs have maturities in excess of one year (for example, five years). Interest is paid at maturity, except for CDs lasting longer than a year, in which case interest is paid annually. While most CDs are fixed-rate, some have variable interest rates. For example, a six-month CD could have a thirty-day roll-over; this means that the interest rate on the CD is related to six-month LIBID and is fixed for thirty days, and will change every thirty days if LIBID has changed. Pension funds hold CDs in sterling and the major overseas currencies.

Treasury bills, local-authority bills, bills of exchange, bankers' acceptances, and commercial paper are the most important examples of money-market securities that are quoted on a discount basis, that is, they are sold on the basis of a discount to par.

Treasury bills (TBs) are short-term UK government IOUs of three months' duration. On maturity the holder receives the par value of the bill by presenting it to the Bank of England. The proceeds are paid from the National Loans Fund. *Local-authority bills* are similar to TBs but are issued by local authorities. *Bills of exchange* (or *trade bills* or *commercial bills*) are also similar to TBs but are issued by private companies against the sale of goods. They are used to finance trade in the short term.

Bankers' acceptances are written promises issued by borrowers to banks to repay borrowed funds. The lending bank lends funds and in return accepts the bankers' acceptance. The acceptance is negotiable and can be sold in a secondary market. The investor who buys the acceptance can collect the loan on the day that repayment is due. If the borrower should default, the investor has legal recourse to the bank that made the first acceptance. *Commercial paper (CP)* is unsecured promissory notes issued by large corporations. The notes are not backed by any collateral, rather, they rely on the high credit rating of the issuing corporation. Such corporations also tend to maintain credit lines with their banks sufficient to repay all their outstanding commercial paper. CP is therefore a quickly and easily arranged alternative to a bank loan. The sterling commercial-paper market began in 1986.

All these securities are sold at a discount to their par value. On maturity the investor receives the par value. Explicit interest is not paid on discount instruments. However, interest is reflected implicitly in the difference between the discounted issue price and the par value received at maturity.

12.3.2. BONDS AND LOANS

Bonds are capital-market securities and as such have maturities in excess of one year. They are negotiable debt instruments. There are many different types of bonds that can be issued. The most common type is the *straight bond*. This is a bond paying a regular (usually semi-annual), fixed coupon over a fixed period to maturity or redemption, with the return of principal (that is, the par or nominal value of the bond) on the maturity date. All other bonds will be variations on this. The frequency of coupon payments can differ between bonds: for example, some bonds pay coupons quarterly, others pay annual coupons. The coupon-payment terms can differ between bonds: for example, some bonds might not pay coupons at all (such bonds are called *zero-coupon* bonds and they sell at a *deep discount* to their par values, since all the reward from holding the bond comes in the form of capital gain rather than income); some bonds make coupon payments that change over time, for example, because they are linked to current market interest rates (*variable-rate bonds* or *floating-rate notes*) or to an index such as the retail price index (*index-linked bonds*); and some bonds make coupon payments only if the income generated by the firm that issued the bond is sufficient (such bonds are known as *income bonds*; unlike other bond-holders, an income-bond holder cannot put the issuing company into liquidation if a coupon payment is not paid). The redemption terms can differ between bonds: some bonds have a range of possible redemption dates (such bonds are known as *double-dated bonds*) and sometimes the actual date of redemption is chosen by the issuer (*callable bonds*) and sometimes it is chosen by the holder (*puttable bonds*); some bonds have no redemption date at all, so that interest on them will be paid indefinitely (such bonds are known variously as *irredeemables*, *perpetuals*, or *consols*). Some bonds have option features attached to them: callable and puttable bonds are examples of this, as are *convertible bonds* (bonds that can be converted into other types of bonds or into equity) and *bonds with warrants* attached to them (see Section 12.3.5).

Bonds can also be differentiated by their issuer. Most bonds in the UK are issued by the British government in order to finance and manage the national debt; they are commonly known as *gilts*. Then there are bonds that are issued by UK public authorities, especially local authorities. Such bonds are secured on the revenues of the local authorities and are generally not guaranteed by the government. The duration of local-authority bonds is typically between one and five years, although most are for one year and are known as *yearling bonds*.

Private companies also issue bonds, known as *corporate bonds*. There are several classes of corporate bonds. *Debentures* are the most secured form of corporate debt (unlike in the USA, where debentures are unsecured corporate obligations). They are secured by either a *fixed* or a *floating charge* against the assets of the company. *Fixed-charge debentures* specify certain specific assets that are chargeable as security and the company is not permitted to dispose of them; in the event of default the assets are sold and the proceeds used to repay the debenture-holders. *Floating-charge debentures* are secured by a general charge on all the assets of the company. The company is able to dispose freely of assets until a default crystallizes the floating charge, at which time the charge fixes on the assets of the company that are not secured by a fixed charge. Fixed-charge debentures rank above floating-charge debentures in the event of default, but only floating-charge debenture-holders can ask for a company to be declared insolvent under the 1986 Insolvency Act. *Unsecured loan stocks* are corporate bonds that are not secured by either a fixed or floating charge. In the event of liquidation, loan-stock holders rank beneath debenture-holders and preferential creditors (such as the Inland Revenue). *Guaranteed loan stocks* are corporate bonds that are not secured by a fixed or a floating charge, but are guaranteed by a third party, typically the parent company of the issuer.

Bonds can also be distinguished by the currency of denomination. Bonds issued in the UK in sterling by domestic issuers or foreign issuers are known as *domestic* and *foreign* (or *bulldog*) *bonds* respectively. The coupons on domestic bonds are generally paid net of UK basic-rate income tax, whereas the coupons on bulldogs do not generally have tax deducted.

Bonds issued and/or traded in the UK in a currency other than sterling are known as *eurobonds*. The first eurobond was issued in 1963 by the Italian company Autostrada with a coupon of 5.5 per cent and an issue size of $15m. *Eurosterling bonds* were first issued in 1972; they have all the characteristics of eurobonds rather than those of domestic or bulldog bonds, and the main issuers have been UK building societies seeking long-term funds to finance their home loans. The main currencies of issue of eurobonds are US dollars and Japanese yen. They are generally issued by multinational companies, international agencies (such as the World Bank), and sovereign governments, and are generally unsecured. New issues are underwritten and placed with investors by a syndicate of international banks led by a *lead manager bank* (such as Swiss Bank Corporation or Deutsche Bank). The size of a eurobond issue usually lies between $50m. and $100m., with a maturity of about six or seven years. Eurobonds are principally in bearer form, transferable by delivery with no record of holder. The bond certificates have detachable coupon claim tokens and coupon payments are generally paid annually free of UK income tax and withholding tax. Eurobonds are usually listed on the London or Luxembourg stock markets.

The eurobond market has been the most innovative of all bond markets in designing new types of bond, in terms of both coupon payments and redemption proceeds. For example, there are: *dual-currency* bonds, where the coupon payments are in one currency and the redemption proceeds are in another; *currency-change* bonds, where coupons are first paid in one currency and then in another; *deferred-coupon* bonds, where there is a delay in the payment of the first coupon; *multiple-coupon* bonds, where the coupon payments change over the life of the bond (although in a predetermined manner); *fixed-then-floating* bonds, where the coupons change from being fixed-rate to floating-rate; *floating-then-zero* bonds, where the bonds change from being floating-rate coupon bonds to zero-coupon bonds; and *missing-coupon* bonds, where a coupon payment is missed whenever a dividend payment on the issuing corporation's shares is missed.

With *index-linked* or *indexed* bonds, the coupon and principal are linked to a particular index, such as the retail price index (RPI), a commodity price index (for example, oil), or a stock-market index. Index-linked government bonds were first introduced in the UK in March 1981. These bonds were linked to the RPI and were therefore designed to give a constant *real* yield. Initially only pension funds could invest in them, because pension funds had (partially) index-linked pensions to deliver to their pensioners. However, since March 1982 any investor can hold index-linked gilts. Most of the index-linked stocks that have been issued have annual coupon payments of 2 per cent or 2.5 per cent: this is designed to reflect the fact that the long-run real rate of return on the UK capital stock has been about 2.5 per cent.

Pension funds hold all these types of bonds as well as overseas bonds, that is, foreign-currency domestic bonds issued by governments, municipal corporations, and companies. However, some pension funds are prevented by their trust deeds from holding bearer securities.

Loans are non-negotiable debt instruments. Pension funds make long-term loans to local authorities, public and private corporations, and other financial institutions. One such type of loan is a *mortgage* which is used to finance property purchase. Loans are almost always secured with collateral provided by some form of lien. The loan can be on either a fixed or variable interest-rate basis. The term of the loan can be fixed; alternatively, there might be provision for early repayment.

In 1993, the Goode Committee recommended that the government should consider the introduction of a new type of index-linked bond particularly for pension funds. The new bond would be called *deferred income government securities* (DIGS) and would have income and capital linked to the RPI, but the payment of income would be deferred for a period; they could also be issued with a variety of both commencement and redemption dates. Such securities would permit pension funds to invest in assets more closely linked to their liabilities both in real terms and in terms of the timing of cash payments. They would also permit the introduction of deferred pensions that were fully indexed to prices.

12.3.3. SHARES

There are several types of shares that can be held in the firm as specified in the *memorandum* and *articles of association*. The most important type is *ordinary shares* (also called *common stock* or *equity*). Ordinary share-holders are the legal owners of the firm and have voting privileges, the right to receive dividends, and subscription privileges in the event of new shares being issued. When a firm is first established, a certain number of shares will be *authorized*. They will have a *par value*, which in the UK is typically 25p. Some or all of the authorized shares will be issued to shareholders (and are called *issued shares* or *called-up shares*), with an issue price which can exceed the par value but cannot be less than the par value. Any shares that are authorized but not issued are called *unissued shares*. All the issued shares will remain *outstanding* unless they are repurchased by the firm. Large firms will have their ordinary shares listed on the stock market, while the shares of smaller firms may be unlisted.

Most pension funds will hold most of their equity portfolios in UK *listed* shares, but in recent years the largest funds have become more adventurous and have begun investing in the *unlisted* (USM) and *over-the-counter* (OTC) markets. In some cases the risks are great, but so are the potential long-term rewards.

Even more recently the largest pension funds have begun to invest in the *venture-capital* market. Originally the venture-capital market provided start-up equity for new companies, especially in the high-technology sectors. Later it became involved in the later stages of a company's development as well as in most other industrial sectors. One of the most important areas of activity for UK venture capital is *management buy-outs* (MBOs). This contrasts with the USA, where *leveraged buy-outs* (LBOs) financed by *high-yielding bonds* (that is, *junk bonds*) are more important.

There are three main characteristics of a UK venture-capital invest-ment. The first is that the investment is financed by a substantial pro-portion of equity, in order to provide the venture-capital investor with the prospect of significant returns. The second is that the investor takes an active role in the running of the company, through the appointment of a non-executive director. The non-executive director's role is to influence general policy direction and to offer expertise rather than take responsibility for day-to-day operations. The final characteristic is that the investment is a long-term commitment, typically between five and seven years, although the *exit time* can be as long as ten years. It is the long-term commitment of venture capital that makes it an attractive proposition from the viewpoint of pension funds, given the long-term nature of their liabilities.

A pension fund can engage in the venture-capital market either directly by establishing its own venture-capital unit or indirectly through the medium of an independent venture-capital fund. The first method gives the pension fund the greatest degree of influence over the composition of the investment portfolio and over policy issues. But it involves establishing a highly skilled and expensive management team, and it may be difficult to get adequate risk-diversification, especially to begin with. These problems can be alleviated if the pension fund invests in an independent venture-capital fund, although the price of this is reduced influence over the choice of investments.

An example of a venture-capital management group is CIN Venture Managers or CINVEN, which operates the venture-capital operations of the British Coal Pension Fund and the British Rail Pension Fund. CINVEN was set up by the British Coal Pension Fund in 1976 and the pension fund has 3 per cent of its assets (that is, £550m. in 1990) in venture-capital investments. CINVEN is the second-largest venture-capital management group after 3i.

Pension funds have also invested heavily abroad since the ending of exchange controls in 1979. Initially this was in overseas domestic equity markets, but in the second half of the 1980s an international equity market began to develop and this has been used by pension funds. More than 600 shares world-wide have a significant international market. In the UK, domestic equities are traded on *SEAQ* (the Stock Exchange Automated Quotations System) and international equities are traded on *SEAQ International*.

The other important class of shares is *preferred shares*. Preferred shares have many of the characteristics of bonds. In particular, preferred shares offer a fixed dividend, like bonds and unlike ordinary shares. But preferred shares do not guarantee to deliver the dividend payment, and a preferred dividend need not be paid if the firm's earnings are not sufficient to fund it. But if this situation arises, preferred shareholders do not have the right to have the firm declared insolvent, unlike bond-holders. It is this fact that makes preference shareholders legal owners of the firm (along with ordinary shareholders). There are several types of preferred shares. With *cumulative preferred shares*, all unpaid dividend payments cumulate and are paid when earnings are sufficient, unlike standard preferred shares where a dividend is lost if it is not paid in any year. *Participating preferred shareholders* have the right to have their dividends increased above the fixed rate if the firm makes large profits. There are also *redeemable preferred* and *convertible preferred shares*.

12.3.4. FORWARDS AND FUTURES

Forward and futures contracts are examples of *derivative* instruments, that is, they are derivative of a *spot-* or *cash-market* security.

A *forward contract* is an agreement between two counter-parties that fixes the terms of an exchange that will take place between them at some future date. The contract specifies: what is being exchanged (for example, cash for a good, cash for a service, a good for a good, a good for a service, cash for cash, and so on), the price at which the exchange takes place, and the date (or range of dates) in the future at which the exchange takes place. In other words, a forward contract locks in the price today of an exchange that will take place at some future date. A forward contract is therefore a contract for *forward delivery* rather than a contract for immediate or *spot* or *cash delivery*, and generally no money is exchanged between the counter-parties until delivery.

Forward contracts have the advantage of being tailor-made to meet the requirements of the two counter-parties, in terms of both the size of the transaction and the date of forward delivery. However, one disadvantage of a forward contract is that it cannot be cancelled without the agreement of both counter-parties. Similarly, the obligations of one counter-party under the contract cannot generally be transferred to a third party. In short, a forward contract in principle is neither very liquid nor very marketable; however, some forward markets, for example, the forward currency markets in London, are very liquid. Another disadvantage is that there is no guarantee that one counter-party will not default and fail to deliver his obligations under the contract. This is more likely to occur the further away the spot price is at the time of delivery from the price that was agreed at the time the contract was negotiated (that is, from the forward price). It will always be the case that it would have been better for one of the counter-parties not to have taken out the forward contract but to have waited and transacted in the spot or cash market at the time called for delivery. If the spot price is higher than the forward price, the counter-party taking delivery (the buyer) gains and the counter-party making delivery (the seller) loses, and vice versa when the spot price is below the forward price. The greater the difference between the spot and forward prices, the greater the incentive for the losing counter-party to renege (that is, the greater the *credit risk*).

A *futures contract* is also an agreement between two counter-parties that fixes the terms of an exchange that will take place between them at some future date. But it is very different from a forward contract and has been designed to remove many of the disadvantages of forward contracts. But the cost of achieving this has been to remove some of the advantages of forward contracts as well.

Futures contracts are standardized agreements to exchange specific types of good, in specific amounts, and at specific future delivery or maturity dates. For example, there might be only four contracts traded per year, with the following delivery months: March, June, September, and December. This means that the details of the contracts are not negotiable as with forward contracts. However, the big advantage of having a standardized contract is that it can be exchanged between counter-parties very easily. Futures contracts are traded on a central regulated exchange by *open outcry*, whereby traders congregate periodically in a *pit* on the floor of the exchange to buy and sell contracts, with every negotiated price being heard by other traders. When an order is executed, the two traders fill out clearing slips, which are then matched by the exchange. The order is confirmed with customers and a futures contract exists. The number of contracts outstanding at any time is known as the *open interest* at that time.

12.3.5. OPTIONS, WARRANTS, AND CONVERTIBLES

The effect of a futures contract is to fix today the future price of some security. In other words, the price at which a security is traded in the future is locked in today. For many purposes this may be exactly what is required, but for others it is overly restrictive. An investor may be more certain of price rises than price falls, but would nevertheless like to protect against price falls. The solution in this case is to buy an option contract, in this case a put option contract.

An *option* gives to its *holder* the right, but not the obligation, to buy or sell an underlying security at a fixed price (the *exercise price* or *strike price*) at or before a specific date (the *maturity date* or *expiry date*). This right is given by the issuer or *writer* of the option. A *call* option gives the right to *buy* the security while a *put* option gives the right to *sell* the security. In order to give effect to the right to buy or sell, the option has to be *exercised*. A *European* option can only be exercised on the expiry date, whereas an *American* option can be exercised at any time before the expiry date. In return for the insurance offered by the option, a price (that is, the *option premium*) has to be paid.

An *equity warrant* is an option issued by a firm to purchase a given number of shares in that firm at a given exercise price, at any time before the warrant expires. If the warrant is exercised, the firm issues new shares at the exercise price and so raises additional finance. A *bond warrant* is an option to purchase more of the firm's bonds. A warrant generally has a longer maturity than a conventional option (for example, five years), and some warrants are perpetual.

Warrants are usually attached to debt instruments such as bonds (known as *host bonds*). Sometimes they are detachable from these instruments and so can be traded separately; sometimes they are non-detachable. Equity warrants generally do not carry any of the rights of shareholders until they are exercised; for example, they pay no dividends and do not have voting rights. However, warrant-holders are protected from changes to the underlying share price such as those resulting from stock splits or stock dividends through a corresponding adjustment to the exercise price of the warrant (the same is true of ordinary options). Bond warrants can either be exercised into the same class of bonds as the host bond or into a completely different class of bond.

A *convertible* is a bond (or sometimes a preferred share) that is convertible at some future date into ordinary shares (in the case where the convertible is issued by a corporation) or into another bond known as a *conversion bond* (in the case where the issuer is a government). The conversion is at the option of the holder of the convertible, although the conversion can be forced if the convertible is also callable by the firm. A convertible is therefore a means of transforming debt into equity at some future date.

12.3.6. SWAPS

Swaps (or *contracts for differences*) are *synthetic securities* involving combinations of two or more different securities. Most swaps involve combinations of two or more cash-market securities (for example, a fixed interest-rate security combined with a floating interest-rate security, possibly also combined with a currency transaction). However, there are also swaps that involve a futures or forward component, as well as swaps that involve an option component.

Pension funds in the UK have been involved in swap agreements since the late 1960s, when they took out parallel or back-to-back currency loans to finance their overseas investments in a way that was compatible with UK exchange-control regulations then in force. The loan operated as follows. There was a matching agreement between a UK investor and an overseas counter-party, whereby the counter-party purchased overseas assets for the UK investor, who in turn purchased an equivalent amount of sterling assets for the foreign institution. While it involved no direct exchange of principal, this method of overseas investment was clearly very cumbersome and was made even more complicated in the period before June 1979 by additional Bank of England regulations which required every $100 of currency loan to be covered by $115 of dollar assets, with the additional dollar assets being purchased with investment currency at a premium above the official rate.

The back-to-back currency loan was the precursor of the currency swap, the first example of this being between IBM and the World Bank in 1981. The swap market can be said to date from this time. The main types of swap are interest-rate swaps, basis swaps, fixed-rate currency swaps, currency-coupon swaps, and asset swaps. All these swaps work on the principle that different institutions have different comparative advantages, and that as a result there can be gains from the two institutions trading with each other. We will discuss each of them in turn.

Interest-rate swaps are the most important type of swap in terms of volume of transactions. An interest-rate swap is an agreement between two counter-parties to exchange fixed interest-rate payments for floating interest-rate payments in the same currency calculated with reference to an agreed notional amount of principal (hence the alternative name, contract for differences). The principal amount which is equivalent to the value of the underlying assets or liabilities that are 'swapped' is never physically exchanged but is used merely to calculate interest payments. The purpose of the swap is to transform a fixed-rate liability into a floating-rate liability and vice versa. The liability so transformed is therefore a synthetic security comprising the difference between two cash-market liabilities. The floating rate that is used in most interest-rate swaps is calculated with reference to LIBOR (the London inter-bank offer rate). Most interest-rate swaps are in US dollars, but those in yen, sterling, Swiss francs, and Deutschmarks are also important. Interest-rate swaps have a similar structure to interest-rate futures contracts, in the sense that the terms of the future obligations under the swap are determined today.

Basis swaps are the same as floating/floating interest-rate swaps. This means that floating-rate payments calculated on one basis are swapped for floating-rate payments on another basis. The main examples are: the US dollar prime rate–US dollar LIBOR swap; US dollar commercial paper–US dollar LIBOR swap; and the one-month US dollar LIBOR–six-month US dollar LIBOR swap.

Currency swaps are agreements to exchange payments in one currency for those in another. Sometimes the principal is exchanged as well as the interest payments. The structure of a currency swap is similar to a forward contract or futures contract in foreign exchange. There are two types of currency swap: fixed-rate currency swaps and currency-coupon swaps.

Fixed-rate currency swaps have three main components: the principal amounts, the exchange rate, and two fixed interest rates. At the beginning of the swap two principal amounts are 'exchanged' between the two counter-parties at an agreed exchange rate. The exchange rate is usually the spot rate (the average of the bid and offer rates). This exchange of principal can either be 'notional' (no physical exchange takes place) or 'real' (a physical exchange is made). In either case the significance of the principal is that it is used to determine both the interest payments under the swap and the re-exchange of principal when the swap matures. The interest payments that are made depend on both the principal amounts and the interest rates that are fixed at the beginning of the swap. On maturity the principal amounts are re-exchanged between the two counter-parties at the initial exchange rate. Fixed-rate currency swaps, therefore, allow fixed-rate liabilities in one currency to be transformed into fully-hedged fixed-rate synthetic liabilities in another currency.

The other type of currency swap is the *currency-coupon swap* or cross-currency interest-rate swap. It is a combination of an interest-rate swap and a currency swap. The format of the swap is identical to that of a fixed-rate currency swap with both initial and final exchange of principal (at the initially agreed exchange rate), but one or both of the interest payments involved are on a floating-rate basis. So, for example, fixed-rate dollars could be swapped for floating-rate sterling.

Asset swaps combine an asset and a swap to create a synthetic asset. So, for example, a fixed-rate asset can be converted into a floating-rate asset in the same currency or in a different currency.

These are the main types of swap. But there have been other, more complicated swaps that have been executed. *Forward swaps* are swaps that are executed on a future date but the terms are agreed today. A *swaption* is an option on a swap giving the holder the right, but not the obligation, to execute the swap on a future date with the terms agreed today. A *callable swap* gives the fixed-rate payer the right to terminate the swap before the maturity date. An *index swap* is one in which the payments depend on an index, such as the retail price index, a stock index, or an index of bond prices. A *zero-coupon swap* is one in which the fixed-rate payments are compounded over the life of the agreement at some agreed rate of interest and paid on the maturity date.

12.3.7. FORWARD-RATE AGREEMENTS

The market in *forward-rate agreements* (FRAs) began in the early 1980s as an offshoot of the inter-bank market in forward/forward interest-rate agreements. Most FRAs (about 90 per cent) are in sterling or dollars,

although there is a growing market in Deutschmark and yen FRAs.
Virtually all FRAs are quoted in LIBOR. Most are for three-sixes (that
is, three-month LIBOR in three months' time), but there are other
combinations available, for example, nine-fifteens (six-month LIBOR in
nine months' time).

FRAs are equivalent to forward contracts in short-term interest-rate
swaps and so combine many of the features of forward or futures contracts
and of swaps. In other words, FRAs are equivalent to synthetic forward-
swap contracts. An FRA is a contract between two counter-parties to
swap short-term interest-rate payments over an agreed period at some
date in the future. The buyer of an FRA locks in a fixed rate of interest,
while the seller locks in a floating rate. As with a standard swap, no
exchange of principal is involved. Instead, on the settlement date of the
FRA one counter-party makes a single cash payment to compensate the
other counter-party for any difference between the agreed interest rate
and the spot interest rate at that time.

12.3.8. UNIT TRUSTS AND INSURANCE BONDS

A *unit trust* is a financial institution which invests in the securities of other
companies. Its operations are subject to trust law rather than company
law. A unit trust is formed by a trust deed made between the managers
and the trustee. The managers operate and manage the unit trust's
investments and charge a fee for doing so. The trustee, typically a bank
or an insurance company, takes custody of the assets and keeps a register
of unit-trust holders. A unit trust is not permitted to borrow funds to
invest in securities, that is, it cannot engage in gearing.

The unit trust issues units which represent claims on the assets of the
unit trust. The units must be priced to equal the net asset value per unit
in the unit trust. Unit trusts are *open-ended funds*, which means that they
can create or cancel units as demand conditions permit. Unit trusts can
specialize in different sectors of the market (for example, shares or
bonds, UK or Far East) or pursue different investment objectives (for
example, income or capital appreciation). Alternatively, a *balanced* unit
trust will be widely invested across sectors and will aim to achieve high
income with some capital appreciation.

Most unit trusts are authorized by the Department of Trade and
Industry. Until recently authorized unit trusts could only invest in stocks
and shares that were quoted on an approved market. The approved
markets are the listed and unlisted securities markets of Europe, North
America, and the Far East. The investment powers of unit trusts have
been extended by the 1986 Financial Services Act. Authorized unit trusts
can now invest in property, options, futures, and commodities. Previously

only unauthorized offshore unit trusts could make such investments. Unit trusts must still abide by any restrictions contained in their trust deeds. For example, typically no more than 5 per cent of the fund can be invested in any one investment, and the fund can typically hold no more than 10 per cent of the issued share capital of any company.

Pension funds will tend to invest in *exempt unit trusts*, that is, trusts that are exempt from both corporation tax and capital-gains tax. Exempt unit trusts are a suitable investment vehicle for small pension funds, since this enables them to get the maximum benefits from diversification at the lowest cost. A particularly suitable vehicle that enables a small or even medium-sized fund to invest in property is the *exempt property unit trust*. Property is a 'lumpy' investment, and a unit trust is effectively the only way for a small fund to get a weighting in this sector.

An *insurance bond* operates in a very similar way to a unit trust: premiums are paid into the bond and these are used to buy a number of units in a fund which invests in a particular stock market or sector. The price of the bond is related to the total value of assets in the fund and will therefore rise and fall in line with movements in the market or sector. The bonds are issued by insurance companies and come in two main types: *single premium bonds* for lump sum investments and *regular premium bonds*. A variation on the single premium bond is the *distribution bond* which pays an income, usually half yearly. Regular premium bonds typically have two components: *initial* (or *capital*) units and *accumulation* (or *ordinary*) units. The initial units are used as a means of imposing a front-end charge of between 4 and 5 per cent. With accumulation units, all the income from the assets is reinvested; there is also an annual management charge. It is possible to switch between bonds offered by the same insurance company on a bid-price-to-bid-price basis. If a bond is surrendered before the end of the original term, its value will be calculated on the basis of the ruling bid price less a surrender penalty. The income and capital gains on insurance bonds are taxed at the basic rate. Higher rate tax payers can take tax-free withdrawals of up to 5 per cent a year on a cumulative basis, but if the bond is cashed any profit is taxed at a rate equal to the difference between the higher and basic rates of tax. Insurance bonds can be used by pension schemes, but pension contributions will be placed in *exempt units* which will be free of income and capital gains taxes. Lump-sum pension contributions can also be placed in single premium bonds, but not those that make distributions.

12.3.9. INVESTMENT TRUSTS

An *investment trust* is, like a unit trust, a financial institution which invests in the securities of other companies. But, unlike a unit trust, it is not a trust at all; rather, it is a company, subject, as with all other companies, to the provisions of the Companies Acts. In particular, the 1980 Companies Act created a new type of public company, namely the *investment company,* and an investment trust is an example of one of these, since it issues shares to the public.

Investment trusts use their capital and reserves to invest directly in the securities of other companies. A shareholder in an investment trust, therefore, has an indirect interest in the underlying portfolio of securities. As with unit trusts, different investment trusts specialize in different sectors of the market or pursue different investment objectives.

In 1965 the *split-level investment trust* was introduced with two types of equity capital, *income shares* and *capital shares*, and a fixed life (often of twenty years). During the life of the investment trust the income shares receive all the income from the underlying portfolio and the capital shares are entitled to all the assets. When the company is liquidated the income shares are paid out at their par value and the remaining value is paid out to the capital shareholders.

The main differences between investment trusts and unit trusts are as follows. Investment trusts are *closed-end funds*, that is, they have a fixed number of shares which can only be increased through a rights issue; unit trusts are *open-ended* and so can create and cancel units in them as supply-and-demand conditions change. Investment trusts can engage in *gearing*, whereas unit trusts are not allowed to borrow. The prices of shares in investment trusts are determined by market forces, as with the shares of all companies. The prices of unit-trust units, in contrast, are set equal to the net asset value of the underlying portfolio. The prices of investment-trust shares can differ quite substantially from their net asset value. Typically they trade at a substantial discount to net asset value. Unit trusts generally distribute all their income, whereas investment trusts declare dividends which may be low enough to leave some retained earnings in the company.

Investment trusts provide an alternative to unit trusts as a vehicle for pension funds, especially small pension funds, to engage in low-cost diversification. In addition, the discount to net asset value of most investment-trust share prices makes them a cheap way of buying securities.

12.3.10. REAL ASSETS

So far we have examined the main *financial assets* that a pension fund might hold in its portfolio. But it can also invest in *real assets*: principally property, land, and collectibles.

12.3.10.1. *Property*

The main classes of property that pension funds invest in are industrial, commercial, and office property. They do not tend to invest in residential property. Large funds prefer direct property investment, whereas small funds prefer indirect investment through exempt property unit trusts (for example, the Pension Fund Property Unit Trust).

The main objectives of direct property investment are the attainment of a stable rental income and an appreciation of capital value. Large funds tend to select their investments to meet the latter objective, whereas small funds appear to be more concerned with the former. All funds prefer to let their property to substantial tenants, mainly public companies and public authorities, and this preference influences the type of property invested in. In other words the tenant is as important as the property from the investment viewpoint.

Originally pension funds invested in the equity of property companies, but since the 1960s they have begun to invest directly in property, preferably freehold property, but leasehold property with good capital-appreciation prospects is also acceptable. Direct investment offers more influence over both the type of property purchased and the subsequent management of the property than does the investment in property-company shares. Also initially, property holdings were confined to the UK, but with the ending of exchange controls in 1979 pension funds have begun to invest in property overseas, especially in the USA.

In contrast with financial assets, real assets are differentiated by a large number of characteristics. The differences between the shares in two different companies are usually quite small, but the differences between two buildings can be enormous. It is therefore important to specify the set of characteristics underlying property investment. Location, design, and type and conditions of tenure are three of the most important charac- teristics of any property. Of these, location is by far the most significant factor in letting property. If the location of a building is good it can be let even if the design is inadequate. Similarly, a building can become difficult to let because the centre of gravity of activity has shifted in relation to its location. A typical example is the building of a new shopping centre which reduces the popularity of a traditional shopping zone. The design of a building (both internal and external) also has an important influence on rental values. This is because a poorly designed building or, just as important, a building with an out-of-date design, might have to be internally or externally restructured if it is to be let. Rental values also depend on the types and conditions of tenure: freehold or leasehold, length and nature of leasehold, rental review periods, and so on.

Depending on its location, design, and tenure conditions, property is

categorized as either prime or secondary. *Prime property* is in the best
location, is well-designed and in excellent condition, is freehold, and let
to a first-class tenant on a lease with frequent review periods. At any
one time only about 1–2 per cent of property on the market is prime
property; the remainder is *secondary property*, and so is to some extent
less desirable in terms of these three characteristics. This will be reflected
in lower rental values.

Offices, shops, and industrial property have different factors that
should be considered when designing the investment property portfolio.
With offices, the most important factor is ease of access for staff. More
than one-quarter of UK workers work in offices, and half of these are in
the South-East. Proximity to transport routes has a large effect on rental
values. Good design is also important, the most important factors being:
modern and sound construction, good lateral and vertical communication,
efficient heating and ventilation, flexibility in terms of use of space,
and adequate servicing, including computing and telecommunications
facilities. With shops, the most important factors are ease of access
for customers and delivery vehicles, and good storage capabilities. The
location restrictions for shops are less severe than for offices, since profitable shopping sites are not confined to central urban locations. With
shopping types ranging from hypermarkets down to individual units, the
most important type, from the investment viewpoint, is the multiple-shop
complex occupied by national chain-store tenants. Specific features of
such complexes that contribute to the property's value are good customer
access (for example, car-parking facilities), good pedestrian flow (otherwise
customers are not attracted to shopping units on upper levels), good
tenant mix (for example, cafeteria services attract customers to the
complex even though they do not maximize rental income on a unit
basis), good shape, layout, and upper-level access (rectangular units with
wide frontage attract the most walk-in customers, while escalators and
lifts are needed to attract customers to upper levels; atriums give a sense
of openness, even though they are otherwise a 'waste of space'), and
good access by delivery, refuse, and other services.

Industrial property covers light-industrial premises, heavy-industrial
buildings, and warehouses. Only the first and last categories make suitable
investments for pension funds. Heavy-industrial buildings are generally
purpose-built by the companies that intend to use them for production
purposes. The main criterion for industrial property is the ease with
which raw materials can be moved in and finished goods moved out. This
suggests that light-industrial property and warehouses with good rail and
road connections close to conurbations will make the most desirable
investments for pension funds.

Given the heterogeneous nature of property, it is probably not surprising that the property portfolios of pension funds also tend to be very diverse. While many have a general mix of property, some concentrate on office and retail property, with yet others specializing in industrial property.

12.3.10.2. *Land*

In the 1970s pension funds were substantial investors in agricultural land, especially in the rented sector rather than the vacant-possession sector. They acquired farms with sitting tenants and entered into sale and leaseback agreements.

Agricultural land tends to be an attractive investment when inflation is high: the appreciation in land values more than adequately compensates for the low net yields experienced with this type of investment. But if the rate of inflation falls financial assets tend to generate higher real returns than land and without the problems associated with managing farm tenants. This has tended to reduce the attractiveness of investing in agricultural land, and some pension funds have unloaded some of the lower-quality land from their portfolios.

12.3.10.3. *Collectibles*

Collectibles is the name given to small physical assets whose value is expected to increase over time. Collectibles therefore cover works of art, precious metals, porcelain, jewellery, carpets, furniture, rare stamps and coins, antiquities, vintage wines, and so on. Collectibles, mainly in the form of works of art, have been a controversial part of pension-fund portfolios ever since they first started to be collected in the 1970s. The most notable collector has been the British Rail Pension Fund which invested £40m. (or 2 per cent of its funds) in 2,300 items from twenty-two categories, mainly paintings, coins, china, and silver, between 1974 and 1978, and hence earned a reputation for being 'one of Europe's greatest art patrons since the Medici' (Godfrey Barker, *Daily Telegraph*, 28 February 1987).

The British Rail Pension Fund's art collection began in 1974, during the depth of the London equity-market crash, with exchange controls preventing investment abroad, with no index-linked gilts available to insulate the fund from the soaring inflation at home, and with an increase in salaries of 31 per cent. The art collection was an attempt to generate the real returns from physical assets that had apparently disappeared from the holding of financial assets. It was, in the words of the art consultant to the fund, 'a dramatic measure taken in a moment of crisis'.

Despite being copied by many companies throughout Europe and the USA, the British Rail Pension Fund art collection has had a controversial history. First, there was the issue about whether the collection constituted trading or investment. Under Inland Revenue rules, pension funds can only get tax relief on investments, not on trading. The collection was eventually accepted as an investment for the purposes of obtaining tax relief. Secondly, there are the costs of storage and insurance, which are much higher than for financial assets. Thirdly, there is the risk of making poor investment choices which are subsequently difficult to undo. The British Rail fund subsequently admitted that it felt that it had diversified into too many fields. Fourthly, collectibles cannot be disposed of very rapidly, making them a relatively illiquid investment. Fifthly, there are uncertainties about valuation. These investments generate no income, and the return comes entirely from capital appreciation. Given the costs of holding them, the gross return on collectibles has to exceed that on financial assets by a sizeable amount before it dominates the return on financial assets.

The BR Pension Fund decided to sell its collection, beginning in 1987, mainly for the reasons just discussed. In the event it achieved a compound rate of return of 15 per cent p.a. This compared with an average return on all pension-fund investments over the same period of 15.1 per cent p.a. and a return on equities of 18.7 per cent p.a. It turned out that equities had been the better investment, but BR argued that this could not have been known in 1974.

12.4. Different Asset Characteristics and Uses

Pension funds hold some or all of these types of assets in their portfolios. The different assets have different characteristics and different uses. In this section we examine some of these characteristics and uses.

12.4.1. ASSET CHARACTERISTICS

The first characteristic is the *degree of liquidity*. This depends on both the marketability of a security and the transactions costs involved in the liquidation; it also depends on the relative volume of a security coming to the market at any single time. Cash and money-market securities are the most liquid of assets and property the least; between lie, in order of decreasing liquidity, gilts, ordinary shares, options, futures, debentures, loan stock, preference shares, loans, and mortgages.

The second characteristic is the *degree of capital-value certainty* (also called *price risk*). Some assets, such as money-market securities, loans, and mortgages, have a high degree of capital-value certainty in nominal terms. Others, such as fixed-income bonds and index-linked bonds, have capital-value certainty only at maturity, the former in nominal terms, the latter in real terms. Before maturity their capital values move inversely with nominal and real interest rates respectively. Other assets, shares, options, and property, for example, exhibit price risk and so have no capital-value certainty at any stage.

The *degree of income certainty* is the third important characteristic of assets. Money-market securities and fixed-term fixed-income bonds and preference shares have complete or at least a high degree of income certainty, while fixed-rate loans and mortgages only exhibit complete income certainty if there is no early repayment. In contrast, the dividend payments on shares are not guaranteed, and derivative securities such as futures and options make no income payments at all.

The next characteristic is *inflation risk*. Only index-linked bonds offer a complete hedge against inflation. Securities such as ordinary shares, property, and commodities tend to be good inflation hedges over the long term, although this is not guaranteed. Fixed-income bonds, loans, mortgages, cash, and money-market securities are poor inflation hedges, since they all lose value as the price level increases. In between lie variable-rate securities, such as floating-rate notes: if interest rates increase with inflation, the income on variable-rate securities increases to compensate for falling real capital values.

The fifth characteristic is *default risk*. Only government-guaranteed stocks and direct holdings of property are entirely free of default risk. All private-sector securities have some risk of default, unless they are backed by effective collateral. For example, mortgages are fairly safe, since they are backed by property (that is, they are *asset-backed*).

The final characteristic is *currency* (or *exchange-rate*) *risk*. This is the risk that affects all securities held in foreign currencies: fluctuating currency values will lead to fluctuating capital values for all overseas securities when measured in sterling.

12.4.2. ASSET USES

Having discussed the various characteristics that assets possess, we can consider how pension funds use assets in their portfolios. Most assets are used as part of sophisticated portfolio-management strategies, the most important of which are discussed in Chapter 13. The portfolio composition of pension funds differs depending on whether the markets are volatile or stable, and on whether the funds themselves are mature or immature.

Take, for example, money-market securities. Pension funds are, in general, very long-term investors, but they will hold short-term securities for one of two reasons. First, pension funds receive periodic cash-flow payments. These can be dividend payments on their share-holdings, coupon payments on their bond-holdings, rent on their property-holdings, as well as contribution payments from both employees and the sponsoring firm. Such receipts, although fairly predictable, will often be irregular and will generally be in small amounts. It will often be inconvenient to reinvest these payments in the capital markets the moment that they are received. Instead, they will be invested in safe but high-yielding money-market securities until a sufficient amount has been accumulated to invest in longer-term assets.

Secondly, money-market securities are held for the purpose of *market timing*. In periods when the capital markets are depressed, such as during the share-market crashes of 1974–5 and October 1987, pension funds will build up fairly large holdings of liquid assets for strategic reasons. This will be done either by reducing directly their holdings in shares, bonds, and so on, or by refraining from investing cash inflows in such instruments. In either case, liquid-asset holdings are built up in readiness for investing in the capital markets when the bear market bottoms out or a new bull market starts.

In stable markets, immature pension funds will want to go for long-term real growth, that is, they will want to generate a real return on their investments after allowing for inflation. They will also want to maintain a fair degree of liquidity. This will be achieved by having a portfolio dominated by equity. Shares suffer from default risk, but this can be reduced through *diversification*, that is, by holding a widely spread portfolio of shares, both domestically and overseas. Overseas assets will still suffer currency risk, but this risk can be *managed* or *hedged* using *exchange-rate futures, forwards*, or *options*. Shares also suffer from capital-value uncertainty or price risk; this risk can also be hedged using *stock-index futures* and *options*. In addition, over the long term ordinary shares tend to provide good inflation hedges. The price risk associated with bond-holdings is the risk of increases in interest rates, sometimes called *interest-rate risk*; this risk can be hedged with *bond futures* and *options*, or an *asset swap* (see Section 13.2). Pension funds can also write options to generate premium income: for example, during bull markets pension funds can write put options, while during bear markets they can write call options, since in neither case are the options likely to be exercised.

Real assets differ substantially from financial assets in a number of important respects. Direct holdings of real assets tend to be better long-run hedges against inflation than financial assets, even compared with those financial assets such as equity which represent indirect claims against real assets. But against this, the markets for real assets are less liquid than those of financial assets. It is simply not possible to issue new old masters; land can be reclaimed, but this takes time; and buildings can be rebuilt, but this also takes time as well as requiring planning permission.

Similarly, real assets cannot be bought and sold in secondary markets as cheaply or as quickly as can financial assets. Related to this, real assets are not such close substitutes for each other as are financial assets. All this again tends to make real assets suitable only as long-term rather than as short-term, speculative investments. Indeed, in the short term real assets can experience substantial falls in value (both nominal and real), and this risk is difficult both to predict and to hedge against.

As pension funds mature, a different investment strategy is required. Income certainty and capital certainty become more important investment objectives than real capital growth. When pension funds are immature their long-term liabilities can be met with an asset structure dominated by equity. However, as pension funds mature the liabilities become increasingly short-term. Pension pay-outs have to be paid according to a definite schedule, and short-term equity values are too volatile to guarantee meeting this payment schedule. Instead, the asset allocation has to be moved away from equity towards fixed-income and indexed bonds as pension funds mature. This will also have the effect of reducing the likelihood of an actuary's valuation revealing an actuarial deficit, with its consequences for increased contribution-rates.

Related to income certainty is capital-value certainty. Pension funds must ensure that the value of their assets equals the actuarial value of their liabilities. The volatility of equity prices makes this objective much more difficult to achieve with mature funds; even if the equity-price risk can be hedged, this cannot be done without some cost. However, fixed-income bonds can be used to achieve at lower cost the desired objective with respect to capital-value certainty. This is because the volatility of bond prices is much less than that of equity prices, since bond-price movements are tied down by their known value on the maturity date. Before maturity the bond's capital value can be hedged with a *duration-based hedging strategy* using *interest-rate futures* and *options* (see Section 13.12.2.2.1).

Finally, we can consider the use of swaps. One of the most important uses of swaps is as a hedging instrument. For example, a pension fund holding fixed-coupon bonds that expected interest rates to rise could execute an asset swap and earn a return related to LIBOR. Of course, given the capital loss that would be expected on the bonds, it might still be better for the pension fund to sell the bonds rather than undertake the swap. Another use of swaps is as an instrument for asset and liability management. On the liability side swaps can be used to reduce funding costs, while on the asset side they can be used to increase returns. This last factor is of particular value to pension funds.

It is important to examine the risks involved in executing swaps. There are two main types of risk facing the swap counter-parties, *credit risk* and *position* or *market risk*. Credit risk is the risk that the other counter-party defaults on his obligations. Position or market risk is the risk that market interest rates or exchange rates diverge from the rates agreed in the swap, leading to a position loss for one counter-party. While credit as such is not extended when a swap is executed, there is a risk that the promised payments and receipts under the swap are not in fact made. The present value of these future payments and receipts (discounted at the swap interest rate) represents the extent of exposure. Credit risk declines as the swap reaches maturity. Position or market risk, however, varies over the life of the swap according to the extent of movements in interest rates. The two types of risk are not unrelated. For example, a swap might be showing a position gain but the other party then defaults.

The use of derivative instruments such as futures, forwards, and options by pension-fund managers has increased substantially since the passing of the 1990 Finance Act, which exempted them from tax on their trading income from futures, forwards, and options. As a result of this change in the tax regime, turnover on the FTSE100 stock-index futures contract on the London International Financial Futures and Options Exchange (LIFFE) increased by 40 per cent during 1990; and a new FTSE Eurotrack 100 stock-index futures contract was launched in June 1991 (so for the first time stock-index futures contracts are available in the three major markets, the USA, Japan, and Europe).

Stock-index futures are the most frequently used of the derivatives products. Futures involve considerably lower transactions costs than options and, for institutional investors, stock-index futures involve (about 1 per-cent) lower transactions costs than trades involving the underlying stocks. The most important use made of stock-index futures by active pension-fund managers is to make rapid tactical changes to asset allocation through *pre-positioning*. In other words, increased or reduced exposure in any particular market is achieved through the purchase or sale of stock-index futures which locks in, respectively, the purchase or sale price of securities prior to buying or selling them in that market. Stock-index futures can also be used to undertake *overlay strategies*, that is, temporary adjustments in exposure without any subsequent transactions in the underlying cash portfolio. Another important use of stock-index futures is as a temporary repository of surplus cash, thereby ensuring that funds are always invested and so avoiding the risk of missing an upturn.

Forward-currency contracts are the second most frequently used of the derivatives products (the size and efficiency of the forward-currency market in London destroyed the currency futures market in London). Forward-currency contracts are used mainly to hedge short-term exposures in foreign bond markets. They are not used to hedge long-term exposures in equity markets; indeed, currency exposure is often regarded by investors as one of the main benefits of international diversification.

While the use of derivatives is increasing amongst pension-fund managers, it is nevertheless still not as widespread as in the USA. The main reason for this is the reluctance of trustees to use a product that can involve unlimited losses or might involve being 'fleeced by unscrupulous floor traders' (as was proved by the Federal Bureau of Investigation in the case of the Chicago futures markets in the late 1980s). Another reason is the cost of operating computer systems that deal with the administration (clearing, settlement, marking to market, and so on), monitoring, and performance of options and futures positions. Finally there are problems in understanding the complexities of derivatives products (especially options), as well as doubts about the operational effectiveness of derivatives markets when they are needed most: the failure of equity futures markets during the October 1987 crash led to substantial disillusionment in the fund-management profession.

12.5. UK Pension Funds and their Asset Holdings

One of the earliest studies of pension-fund asset holdings was carried out by Professor E. V. Morgan between 1953 and 1955 on behalf of the Association of Superannuation and Pension Funds (now the National Association of Pension Funds), and published in its periodical *Superannuation* in July 1957. A similar study was carried out for the Radcliffe Committee in 1959 (see Table 12.3). The table indicates that for portfolios under their direct control (that is, those not administered by insurance companies) private pension funds had assets valued at £1.658bn. at the end of 1957 and that net inflows to the funds were running at the rate of £198m. p.a. Fixed-interest securities accounted for 55 per cent of assets held, divided between central-government and municipal bonds (43 per cent) and company debentures (12 per cent). Company shares accounted for 25 per cent of the portfolio, property (including mortgages) for 5 per cent, and liquid assets for the remaining 15 per cent.

However, the portfolio composition or *asset allocation* was also changing. The columns representing net investment indicate that a larger proportion of the cash flow was being devoted to company assets (both to shares and debentures) and property, and less was being devoted to government-guaranteed assets. This reflected even at that time the influence of inflation in reducing real pension values, the demand for pensions to be linked to inflation, and the necessary restructuring of the funds' portfolio to meet this demand. In the early part of the century

TABLE 12.3. *Market values of assets held by pension funds, 1957*

Type of asset	Market values of assets, end of 1957		Net investment during 1957	
	£m.	%	£m.	%
British government and government-guaranteed securities	570	34	40	20
Overseas government, provincial, and municipal securities	54	3	2	1
Securities of, and loans to, UK local authorities	98	6	15	8
Company debentures	194	12	34	17
Preference shares	63	4	2	1
Ordinary stocks and shares	351	21	73	37
Mortgages (excluding loans to UK local authorities)	33	2	2	1
Real property (excluding mortgages)	42	3	10	5
Life and annuity policies	1	—	1	1
Cash and other assets	252	15	18	9
TOTAL	1,658	100	198	100

Note: Excludes funds reassured with insurance companies and local-authority funds.

Source: Radcliffe Report (1959, Table 16).

pension-fund investments could safely be restricted by trust deeds to *trustee securities* (mainly fixed-interest bonds with known maturity dates), since pensions were fixed in nominal terms by actuarial calculations. In the post-war period fund managers began to achieve greater freedom over the range of assets that they could hold in their portfolios, and consequently began to select assets whose values, at least theoretically, were supposed to grow in line with inflation, principally company equity. By 1957 pension funds and insurance companies absorbed more equity than the total new capital issues of British companies, thereby demonstrating the importance of these institutions in providing finance for industry.

In contrast, local-authority pension funds at this time were restricted by statute to holding only trustee securities. In 1958 their total assets stood at £435m. and were increasing at the rate of £35m. p.a. Virtually all the assets were held in public-sector securities, two-thirds in local-authority loans and most of the remainder in gilt-edged stock. In 1984 many of these funds had their asset choice increased to include the shares of private-sector companies.

In terms of relative returns on different assets, gilts prices were falling relative to equity prices in 1957, and this also helps to explain the volume of new pension-fund money going into equity. While the funds were unwilling to sell gilts on a falling market (indeed, new gilt purchases were still being made at this time), there can be little doubt that the movements in relative asset proportions in favour of equity were due to these relative return effects. Radcliffe concluded that, even though the funds appeared not to speculate by holding back from investing in long-term assets by temporarily holding liquid assets until prices became more favourable, they nevertheless 'appear to think in terms of interest rates being "high" or "low"'. They appeared to invest all new inflows in long-term assets at the most favourable rates available, but they also appeared to have a 'fairly definite notion of what is a normal rate, and their behaviour is modified in various ways if they feel that current rates are lower than or higher than this normal rate' (Radcliffe Report 1959, p. 91).

Table 12.4 shows the market values of pension funds between 1957 and 1989, disaggregated between private, local-authority, and other public-sector funds (which cover public corporations and nationalized industries). By 1989 the total value of UK pension funds was £254bn., over 120 times their size in 1957. The pension funds quintupled in size during the 1980s alone. A number of noteworthy features can be discerned from the table: the effect on pension-fund values of the UK stock-market crash of 1974 and the subsequent recovery in 1975 is clear; in contrast, the global crash of 1987 had no noticeable effect on pension-fund values; the effect of the government's privatization programme during the 1980s is also clear, with the transfer of nationalized industries to the private sector reducing the relative size of other public-sector funds by one-third during the 1980s; by the end of the decade 70 per cent of pension funds (by value) were in the private sector, while local-authority funds accounted for 14 per cent of the total value, and 16 per cent were in the rest of the public sector.

Table 12.5 presents the asset allocation of pension funds between 1979 and 1990. There have been some striking changes during this period. The most notable difference resulted from the abolition of exchange controls in October 1979. This provided the opportunity for unrestricted investment overseas. In 1979 total investment overseas amounted to 6 per cent of overall funds. In 1990 the proportion was 17 per cent. Most overseas investment is in equity, with only small amounts in international bonds and property. The high point for overseas investment was 1986, when 21 per cent of pension-fund assets were held overseas.

On the domestic front the most notable changes have been the declining

TABLE 12.4. *Market value of pension funds, 1957–1989* (end-year values)

Year	Private-sector funds		Local-authority funds		Other public-sector funds		Total
	£bn.	(%)	£bn.	(%)	£bn.	(%)	£bn.
1957	1.159	(56)	0.397	(19)	0.515	(25)	2.071
1962	2.440	(62)	0.667	(17)	0.852	(21)	3.959
1967	3.879	(61)	1.086	(17)	1.434	(22)	6.399
1972	7.028	(58)	1.934	(16)	3.068	(26)	12.030
1973	7.489	(62)	1.748	(15)	2.813	(23)	12.050
1974	6.307	(62)	1.372	(13)	2.521	(25)	10.200
1975	9.642	(61)	2.134	(13)	4.104	(26)	15.880
1976	11.847	(59)	2.652	(13)	5.516	(28)	20.015
1977	16.983	(59)	3.849	(13)	8.005	(28)	28.837
1978	20.253	(59)	4.303	(13)	9.701	(28)	34.257
1979	23.622	(58)	4.942	(12)	12.261	(30)	40.825
1980	31.543	(58)	6.891	(13)	15.501	(29)	53.935
1981	36.921	(58)	8.167	(13)	18.348	(29)	63.436
1982	48.869	(59)	11.365	(13)	23.964	(28)·	84.198
1983	62.532	(59)	14.274	(13)	29.436	(28)	106.242
1984	80.036	(60)	17.982	(13)	36.384	(27)	134.402
1985	100.076	(64)	20.765	(13)	35.554	(23)	156.395
1986	120.668	(63)	25.401	(13)	43.975	(24)	190.044
1987	132.067	(67)	26.620	(13)	39.612	(20)	198.299
1988	144.562	(67)	29.289	(14)	40.667	(19)	214.518
1989	179.000	(70)	36.600	(14)	38.600	(16)	254.200

Sources: Wilson Report (1980, App. Table 3.50); *Annual Abstract of Statistics* (1985 and 1991, Table 7.17).

importance of fixed-interest bonds and property and the continuing and increasing importance of equity. UK property, the investment jewel of the 1960s and early 1970s, has languished somewhat subsequently. Pension funds have unloaded property from their portfolios, and the weighting has declined from 22 per cent to 10 per cent over the decade (although the weighting in property has stabilized in the last few years). UK fixed-interest stock has declined from a 23 per-cent weighting to a 9 per-cent weighting, reflecting the continued persistence of inflation over the period. The 1980s saw the largest bull phase in UK stock-market history and this explains the weighting in UK equity in excess of 50 per cent.

Table 12.6 shows the cash-flow allocation of pension funds between 1980 and 1990. On average over the decade, 40 per cent of new money

TABLE 12.5. *The asset allocation of pension funds, 1979–1990 (%)*

Year	UK equities	Overseas equities	UK bonds	Overseas bonds	Index-linked bonds	UK property	Overseas property	Cash and deposits	Others
1979	44	6	23	—	—	22	—	4	2
1980	45	9	21	—	—	20	—	3	1
1981	44	12	19	—	0	21	—	3	1
1982	43	14	19	—	3	18	—	2	1
1983	44	17	19	—	3	14	—	3	1
1984	47	16	17	—	3	13	—	3	1
1985	49	17	16	—	3	11	—	3	1
1986	51	20	13	0	3	8	1	3	1
1987	54	14	13	1	3	9	1	4	2
1988	54	17	12	1	3	8	1	3	2
1989	52	14	13	1	3	9	1	5	3
1990	53	15	9	1	3	10	1	6	3

Source: WM Company Annual Review 1990 and Pension Funds and their Advisers (1990, p. 205).

TABLE 12.6. *The cash-flow allocation of pension funds, 1980–1990 (%)*

Year	UK equities	Overseas equities	UK bonds	Overseas bonds	Index-linked bonds	UK property	Overseas property	Cash and others	New money as %age of initial market value
1980	33	23	30	—	—	15	—	-3	19
1981	29	24	26	—	—	16	—	3	15
1982	24	25	22	—	9	15	—	4	13
1983	21	17	31	—	10	9	—	13	12
1984	37	-6	24	—	10	10	—	24	9
1985	37	28	22	—	9	7	—	-4	8
1986	48	25	6	-2	7	2	-1	18	7
1987	91	-16	-9	-1	-9	-5	0	49	5
1988	55	25	-15	7	-2	7	1	21	5
1989	12	83	-42	19	1	5	0	21	5
1990	58	15	-17	37	-3	3	-3	-9	4
Average	40	22	7	5	3	8	0	14	9

Source: WM Company Annual Review 1990.

went into UK equities, 22 per cent into overseas equities, 15 per cent into bonds, and 8 per cent into property, while 14 per cent of new money was held in cash. But the table also reveals substantial volatility in the cash-flow allocation. For example, in 1987 91 per cent of new money went into UK equities, but in 1989 this was reduced to 12 per cent. In contrast, in 1987 the investment in overseas equities was actually being reduced, but in 1989 overseas equity purchases accounted for 83 per cent of new money. The high average investment in cash is largely accounted for by the uncertainties surrounding the 1987 crash, when pension funds attempted to protect themselves by holding nearly half their new money on deposit and disinvesting in all asset categories except UK equities.

There are also some discernible trends in the table. Most notably there is the decline in new money being allocated to UK bonds. Indeed, since 1987 there has been a net disinvestment in UK bonds, although most of this can be explained by the government's budget surplus and its policy of debt repurchase during this period. There was also a fall in the size of the budget surplus in 1990, and this is reflected in the reduced rate of disinvestment in UK bonds in that year. Another trend is the decline in new money being invested in UK property, reflecting the poor returns generated by this sector. A final trend to be noted is the systematic decline in new money as a proportion of the market value of the funds. In 1980 new money equalled 19 per cent of the value of pension funds in that year; by 1990 this had been reduced to 4 per cent. This is explained by the huge increase in asset values during this period, leading to huge surpluses with a consequent reduction in new money as a result of contributions holidays.

Table 12.7 presents figures on the geographical distribution of the overseas assets of pension funds in 1989. North America, historically

TABLE 12.7. *Geographical distribution of the overseas assets of pension funds in 1989* (%)

USA	42
Japan	22
Europe	11
Canada	9
Australia	4
Hong Kong	3
Others	9
TOTAL	100

Source: *Pension Funds and their Advisers* (1989, p. 64).

the first port of call for overseas investment for the UK, still dominates the scene with 51 per cent of the weighting. This is followed by the Far East and Australasia with 29 per cent of the weighting, with Europe having only an 11 per-cent weighting. However, the effects of 1992 and the economic liberalization of Eastern Europe are likely to lead to Europe becoming relatively more important in the near future.

Table 12.8 looks at the size distribution of pension funds in 1989. More than half the pension funds in the UK have a value below £5m., and more than 80 per cent of the funds have a value below £50m. Fewer than 7 per cent of the funds have values in excess of £250m. Yet this small number of very large funds dominate the pension-fund investment scene in the UK. They have command over more than three-quarters of the total value of pension-fund assets in the UK (over £194bn. in 1989). The funds with values below £5m. have a combined value of assets of only 0.3 per cent of the total value of pension-fund assets (about £0.76bn. in 1989).

Table 12.9 examines the asset allocation of UK pension funds in 1990, analysed according to the size of funds. The main distinctions between small and large funds are these: small funds hold a higher proportion of their total assets in cash and other liquid assets than large funds; they hold a higher proportion in UK fixed-interest bonds; they hold a lower proportion in index-linked bonds; they hold a lower proportion in equity (both domestic and overseas); and they hold a lower proportion of their total assets in property (both domestic and overseas) compared with large funds. These differences reflect both the different attitudes to risk and the different requirements for liquidity of small and large funds. Small funds tend to invest in more-liquid, more-divisible, and less-risky assets than large funds. For example, investment in property is 'lumpy' and small

TABLE 12.8. *Number of pension funds and value of assets in 1989, analysed by size of fund*

Size of fund (£m.)	Number of funds (%)	Value of assets (%)
0–5	50.5	0.3
5–10	9.1	0.7
10–25	10.4	1.7
25–50	10.8	3.8
50–100	6.3	5.1
100–250	6.3	11.8
250–1,000	5.1	26.0
1,000+	1.6	50.5

Source: *Pension Funds and their Advisers* (1989, pp. 118–19).

TABLE 12.9. *The asset allocation of pension funds in 1990, analysed by size of fund* (%)

Pension-fund size (£m.)	UK equities	Overseas equities	UK fixed-interest	Overseas fixed-interest	Index-linked gilts	UK property	Overseas property	Cash and deposits	Others
0–5	45.0	12.6	15.3	0.5	0.8	5.2	0.0	7.6	13.0
5–10	50.5	13.5	14.4	0.5	1.4	5.7	0.0	5.9	8.1
10–25	55.3	14.1	11.0	0.7	1.7	3.6	0.3	6.1	7.2
25–50	55.2	16.0	10.6	0.6	2.1	2.9	0.1	6.4	6.1
50–100	55.6	16.9	9.3	0.8	2.6	3.4	0.0	6.5	4.9
100–250	55.1	17.0	10.3	0.7	2.2	5.1	0.1	6.8	2.7
250–1,000	54.5	15.8	8.6	0.9	2.9	7.9	0.4	6.7	2.3
1,000+	50.9	13.7	9.2	0.6	3.4	12.5	1.7	5.0	3.0
Average	52.5	14.8	9.2	0.7	3.1	10.0	1.0	5.7	3.0

Source: Pension Funds and their Advisers (1990, p. 204).

TABLE 12.10. *The top fifty pension funds in 1990*

Position	Value (£m.)	Name of fund
1	12,000.0	British Coal
2	12,000.0	British Telecommunications PLC
3	8,500.0	Electricity Supply
4	7,750.0	Post Office
5	7,000.0	British Railways Board
6	5,800.0	Universities Superannuation Scheme
7	5,750.0	British Gas PLC
8	5,197.9	Barclays Bank PLC
9	4,130.8	Imperial Chemical Industries
10	4,050.1	National Westminster Bank
11	4,046.0	British Steel PLC
12	4,000.0	British Petroleum Company PLC
13	3,819.2	Shell
14	3,346.1	British Airways
15	2,761.2	Lloyds Bank PLC
16	2,533.0	Midland Bank PLC
17	2,217.0	Unilever PLC
18	2,200.0	Water Authorities
19	2,132.9	Strathclyde Regional Council
20	2,059.7	British Broadcasting Corporation
21	2,038.5	Greater Manchester County
22	2,001.6	General Electric Company PLC
23	1,984.0	Merchant Navy
24	1,914.7	British Aerospace
25	1,913.4	Prudential Corporation PLC
26	1,817.4	United Kingdom Atomic Energy Authority
27	1,794.1	Ford Motor Company Ltd.
28	1,745.0	Lucas Industries PLC
29	1,700.0	West Midlands Metropolitan Authorities
30	1,692.0	West Yorkshire Superannuation Fund
31	1,548.5	London Residuary Body
32	1,495.5	Rover Group Ltd.
33	1,468.0	London Regional Transport
34	1,316.3	TSB Group PLC
35	1,222.0	BTR Group
36	1,213.1	Rolls-Royce PLC
37	1,169.6	Imperial Tobacco
38	1,148.2	IBM United Kingdom Ltd.
39	1,145.0	STC PLC
40	1,108.0	Merseyside
41	1,095.0	Sun Alliance Insurance Group
42	1,015.1	Philips
43	997.4	Allied-Lyons

TABLE 12.10. *Continued*

Position	Value (£m.)	Name of fund
44	996.0	Thorn EMI
45	955.7	Grand Metropolitan PLC
46	912.0	Lancashire County Council
47	906.0	Courtaulds PLC
48	881.3	South Yorkshire Pensions Authority
49	870.7	Civil Aviation Authority
50	858.3	Boots Company PLC

Source: *Pension Funds and their Advisers* (1990, p. 187).

TABLE 12.11. *Details of the top three public-sector pension schemes in 1990*

	British Coal		Electricity Supply	Post Office
	Staff scheme	Mine-workers		
Members	26,562	84,291	120,568	198,874
Pensioners	70,217	275,512	93,347	142,300
Deferred pensioners	13,780	268,707	12,313	26,994
Annual contributions (£000)	116,000	308,000	365,200	376,000
Annual investment income (£000)	286,000	278,000	371,300	313,000
Annual expenditure (£000)	268,000	259,000	356,000	394,000
Capital value (£000)	5,821,000	5,252,000	7,774,600	7,323,000
Summary of investments (£000)				
UK equities	2,831,000	2,414,000	3,650,200	3,849,000
British Investment Trust PLC	193,000	171,000	—	—
Overseas equities	635,000	373,000	1,539,600	835,000
UK fixed interest	666,000	714,000	829,000	591,000
Overseas fixed interest	83,000	165,000	12,200	13,000
Index-linked gilts	231,000	220,000	239,300	435,000
UK property	806,000	652,000	835,600	1,280,000
Overseas property	133,000	143,000	144,500	214,000
Cash and deposits	211,000	328,000	382,900	116,000
Agriculture and forestry	—	—	31,100	—
Others (net)	5,000	72,000	109,300	—

Note: The capital values given here may not correspond with those given in Table 12.10 because of differing valuation dates.

Source: *Pension Funds and their Advisers* 1990.

TABLE 12.12. *Details of the top three private-sector pension schemes in 1990*

	British Telecom		British Gas		Barclays Bank
	Staff scheme	New scheme	Staff	BGC scheme	
Members	178,198	48,042	49,152	27,791	90,800
Pensioners	115,387	2	34,200	23,084	18,800
Deferred pensioners	45,891	609	12,788	7,108	19,300
Annual contributions (£000)	575,700	55,871	74,100	34,000	128,529
Annual investment (£000)	468,000	4,868	315,900	88,600	212,487
Annual expenditure (£000)	479,000	583	139,000	42,650	157,368
Capital value (£000)	10,821,700	100,170	4,107,000	1,119,000	5,197,927
Summary of investments (£000)					
UK equities	5,484,200	61,712	2,045,000	586,000	2,572,555
Overseas equities	1,137,900	3,173	653,400	195,800	1,353,277
UK fixed interest	943,700	9,497	495,200	122,300	353,617
Overseas fixed interest	—	—	19,800	11,000	61,349
Index-linked gilts	615,200	4,183	116,800	33,000	—
UK property	1,866,800	—	312,850	69,500	684,781
Overseas property	391,900	—	68,750	—	87,184
Cash and deposits	434,700	31,138	369,300	81,500	185,449
Others (net)	(52,700)	(9,533)	25,900	19,900	868

Note: The capital values given here may not correspond with those given in Table 12.10 because of differing valuation dates.

Source: Pension Funds and their Advisers 1990.

TABLE 12.13. *Value of private-sector funds per member, 1987*

Size of fund (£m.)	Average value per member (£000)
Over 1,000	60
500–1,000	34
250–500	44
100–250	30
50–100	28
10–50	26
Under 10	NA

Source: Derived from GASOPS, Table 4.3.

funds find it difficult to achieve adequate risk-diversification by investing directly in property. As we argued above, their preferred method of achieving sufficient diversification is to invest in property unit trusts.

12.5.1. THE LEADING PENSION FUNDS IN THE UK

Table 12.10 lists the top fifty pension funds in the UK in 1990. There were forty-two funds with assets of more than £1bn. The largest funds are those of current and former nationalized industries. The largest pension funds are those of British Coal[2] (formerly the National Coal Board) and British Telecom (privatized in 1984), with assets of £12bn. After this come the schemes of four nationalized industries: electricity generation (privatized in 1990), the Post Office, British Railways, and the universities. Following these come the schemes of the largest private-sector companies in the UK, a list that is dominated by the schemes of the banking and insurance sectors, the oil sector, the chemical and electrical sectors, and the automobile sector. Interspersed among these are the schemes of the largest metropolitan authorities. The top fifty schemes had assets in excess of £142bn in 1990.

Tables 12.11 and 12.12 present details of the investments of the top

[2] The coal industry in the UK is in terminal decline, but the industry's pension fund has a huge actuarial surplus. In April 1993 the government and British Coal introduced a plan to use £1bn. of the surplus to finance redundancy payments for thousands of miners. Prior to this the redundancy payments had been financed from general taxation. British Coal said that it was right for it to consider if part of the surplus could be used to relieve the burden on taxpayers; but the opposition Labour Party said that the plan 'makes miners pay for their own redundancy packages'. The plan was subsequently rejected by the High Court.

Pension-Fund Investments

three public-sector and private-sector schemes in the UK. In the public sector these are the British Coal, Electricity Supply, and Post Office schemes; in the private sector, the British Telecom, British Gas, and Barclays Bank schemes.

Table 12.13 shows the average value of private-sector funds per member in 1987. The average value generally increases with the size of the funds. In the smallest schemes the average value per member was £26,000, while in the largest schemes with assets in excess of £1bn. the average value per member was £60,000.

13

Pension-Fund Management

This chapter discusses the functions of pension-fund managers and the ways in which they assess and execute the pension trustees' portfolio preferences. It then discusses the two main types of fund-management strategies, passive and active, particularly as they apply to share and bond portfolios. We also examine how to measure and assess pension-fund performance. We then examine how pension funds undertake hedging or risk-management strategies to protect the value of their pension-fund assets. Finally, we examine the leading pension-fund management groups in the UK. (The chapter assumes that the reader has some understanding of *modern portfolio theory* (MPT); this is explained in some detail in Blake 1990.)

13.1. The Functions of Pension-Fund Management

A *pension-fund manager* is an individual who, or company which, runs a pension fund on behalf of the trustees of a pension scheme. The fund manager can be directly employed by the pension scheme or can be an independent organization under contract to the scheme.

The functions of the fund manager are:

- portfolio structuring and analysis—using the trustees' objectives and constraints (in particular the constraints imposed by the pension fund's liabilities) to structure an optimal portfolio, and then analysing the portfolio's expected return and risk;
- portfolio adjustment—selecting the set of asset purchases and sales as circumstances change;
- portfolio-performance measurement and attribution—measuring the actual performance of the portfolio, identifying the sources of the performance, and comparing the performance against that of a predetermined bench-mark portfolio. This function is usually undertaken by an organization independent of the manager running the pension fund;
- risk management—using hedging instruments (in particular, futures, options, and swap contracts) to hedge the interest-rate, stock-market (beta), and currency risks involved in both domestic and international investment.

In the UK the activities of pension-fund managers are regulated by IMRO (the Investment Managers Regulatory Organization) under the 1986 Financial Services Act.

13.2. Fund-Management Styles

There are a number of different management styles that a fund manager can follow. Which one is appropriate depends on the size of the fund and the preferences of the trustees, and also the size and preferences of the fund-management group itself.

Small pension funds may decide to have their portfolios managed by insurance companies (these are called *insurance-managed portfolios*). Sometimes the funds are *pooled*. This increases the degree of *diversification*, but there is no individual attention given to any particular portfolio: every member of the pool has the same set of investments and gets the same return. Pooled funds typically operate through two types of legal entity, namely *exempt unit trusts* which are established under a trust deed and *managed pension funds* which are a particular type of insurance contract. Each entity is designed to share the same exemptions from income and capital-gains tax as fully approved pension funds. The same advantages that apply to pooling in general also apply to this particular type of investment pooling, namely that trading can take place more economically at lower unit cost because of the larger volumes traded and, in principle, the portfolio can be more effectively diversified since a wider spectrum of assets can be held in the pool than could be held by a small pension fund operating alone. Alternatively the funds are *segregated* and different funds will have different investments. Large pension funds will either have their investments managed directly through an appointed fund manager or indirectly through a single or group of external financial intermediaries, such as an investment bank (this is known as uninsured or strictly *self-insured fund management*).

The most common management style is known as *balanced management*. With this style, the fund manager is responsible for deciding on both the general asset categories that are invested in (such as shares, bonds, or money-market instruments) and the individual securities within each asset category that are invested in (for example, ICI shares or medium-term gilts). The first decision is known as the *asset-allocation* decision and the second is known as the *security-selection* decision. The balanced-management approach can apply whether the pension fund is small and part of an insurance-managed pool or whether it is large and employs its own fund-management group.

The problem with balanced managers is that they cannot be experts in all markets, especially on a global basis. One solution is to have *specialist managers* in each sector who take the security-selection decision. Sitting above the specialists will be an *asset-allocation manager* and possibly an *overlay manager* whose role is to make temporary changes to asset allocation using futures and options contracts (see Section 13.12 below). Another solution is to have *split-funding*. This means that a number of balanced managers are appointed. While this does not solve the problem of insufficient expertise in all markets, it forces managers to compete against each other. However, the danger of this is that they may be induced to over-trade the portfolio (this is known as *churning*), so that transactions costs might be excessive. In addition, a *risk manager* has to sit above the individual managers to ensure overall risk control.

There are two main types of portfolio-management strategies: passive and active.

Passive portfolio management involves a *buy-and-hold strategy*, that is, buying a portfolio of securities and holding them for a long period of time, with only minor and infrequent adjustment to the portfolio over time. Passive portfolio management is consistent with two conditions being satisfied in the securities market: *efficiency* and *homogeneity of expectations*. If securities markets are efficient, then securities will be fairly priced at all times. There will be no misvalued securities and hence no incentive to trade actively in securities. Similarly, if securities markets are characterized by investors who have homogeneous (that is, identical) expectations of the risks and returns on securities, then again there is no incentive to trade actively in securities.

Active portfolio management involves frequent and sometimes substantial adjustments to the portfolio. Active managers do not believe that securities markets are continuously efficient. Instead, they believe that securities can be misvalued, so that trading in them can lead to excess returns (even after adjusting for risk and transactions costs). Alternatively, active managers believe that there are *heterogeneous* (that is, divergent) *expectations* of risks and returns on securities and that they have better estimates than the rest of the market of the true risks and returns on securities. Again, they attempt to use their better estimates to generate excess returns. In short, the objective of active managers is to 'beat the market'.

It is often questioned whether pension funds should invest abroad when their liabilities are denominated in sterling. Yet there are a number of reasons that can be put forward to support the case for international investment.

The first and most important reason deals with the benefits of diversification. Pension-fund managers, in spite of the nature of their liabilities, will generally be interested in achieving a high level of return for a given level of risk. Risks can be reduced by diversification of the portfolio across a range of assets. Diversification within one country can eliminate the *unsystematic risk* that results from the differential performance of individual firms and sectors. But diversification within one country cannot reduce the *systematic risk* that results from the common effect that the performance of the economy as a whole has on all firms. However, to the extent that the performances of different national economies are not perfectly correlated, each country's systematic risk becomes a diversifiable risk in a global context. Such risk can be reduced by holding a global-market portfolio.

Not only can international investment reduce risk, it can also enhance returns in a number of ways. For example, some countries (such as Germany and Japan) might be more successful economically than the home economy of the fund and hence offer higher investment returns. Similarly, if the share of profits in national income changes differentially across countries, then international investment provides a hedge against any fall in the domestic profit share and therefore in equity values. Furthermore, there are certain high-value economic activities (for example, gold and oil extraction) which might not be undertaken in the home economy.

These examples apply mainly to equity investments, rather than to investments in the other main asset categories, bonds and property. Bond markets tend to be much more globally integrated than equity markets, so the benefits from international diversification are reduced, although not entirely eliminated. Property investment, on the other hand, might actually be more risky abroad than it is domestically. This is because it is less liquid and more dependent on local knowledge than either equity or bonds.

While there are undoubted benefits with international investment, there are also additional risks. The most important of these is *currency* (or *exchange-rate*) *risk*, the risk that the domestic currency might appreciate relative to the currency in which the overseas investment is held and so reduce the return on that investment when measured in the domestic currency. (This risk can be hedged with forward, futures, or options contracts.) There are other types of risk. *Settlement risk* is the risk that either payment or securities may not be delivered following a transaction; this risk could be high in less-developed financial markets. *Liquidity risk* is the risk that an investor might find himself locked into a particular foreign investment because of the narrowness of the market for that investment, which makes it difficult to liquidate the investment. *Transfer risk* (sometimes called *political risk*) is the risk of being locked into a particular overseas market as a result of an unanticipated imposition of exchange controls. The last three risks can be avoided altogether by disregarding certain markets (such as those in the Third World or even middle-income countries such as Turkey or Korea), while currency risk is unlikely to overcome the benefits from international diversification.

Davis (1991a) reports the responses to a questionnaire on attitudes to international investment by a group of London fund managers. Most of them emphasized the benefits of risk reduction from international investment rather than the prospects of higher returns. Most fund managers felt that the global markets had become much more efficient during the 1980s, partly as a result of their own activities helping to equalize returns across national economies. Nevertheless, the fund managers recognized that anomalies existed and often persisted, especially in the *emerging markets* of the Far East and Latin America, but also in an advanced economy such as Japan.

Although most fund managers believed that the global markets were efficient, they did not take this to its logical conclusion and invest their assets in a *global portfolio*. A number of candidates have been put forward as global portfolios. One candidate uses portfolio weightings based on relative market capitalizations; this would lead to an allocation in UK assets well below 10 per cent. Another uses portfolio weightings based on the share of imports in the consumption basket purchased by pensioners; given that UK pensioners consume a relatively high proportion of UK goods, this implies a much larger weighting in UK assets.

So, if UK fund managers do not invest in a global portfolio, what determines their international asset allocation? In the case of pension funds, the nature of the liabilities remains the most important factor. Pension-fund managers are aware of the risks of asset–liability mismatch, since the size of the 'final salary' depends on UK growth and inflation. This led many pension-fund managers to invest heavily in UK equity. However, not all pension-fund managers felt this way. Some held the view that the efficiency of markets and the convergence of different national economies was now so great that so long as a pension fund held 'real assets' some currency mismatching was acceptable.

Other influences on the international asset allocation were the behaviour of other fund managers and the pressure from trustees not to underperform the median fund. This tended to encourage a *herding* approach to portfolio structuring, as opposed to a *contrarian* approach. However, some fund managers pointed out that through an 'education process' trustees could be led by successive steps to accept the level of international exposure desired all along by the fund managers.

Once the domestic–international portfolio split had been made (and with the fund managers interviewed the international component ranged from 12 per cent to 35 per cent), the next decision concerned which overseas markets and assets to invest in. The fund managers tended to adopt a hierarchical decision-making process: first determining core holdings in the three major markets of North America, Europe, and the Far East; then the asset-allocation split between equities, bonds, and property; and finally the stock-selection decision of which particular equities, bonds, and properties to invest in. Sometimes the asset-allocation decision was made before the country decision. To many of the pension-fund managers bonds were not regarded as particularly important. Similarly, the emerging markets of the Far East, India, Latin America, Eastern Europe, and even Greece or Spain were considered to be of marginal importance to some pension-fund managers. The main reasons put forward were illiquidity (difficulties in withdrawing or even investing much money), settlement problems, and political instability.

13.3. Asset–Liability Modelling and Management

Asset–liability modelling is a quantitative technique used by some pension funds to structure their asset portfolio by paying due regard to the structure of their liabilities. It is a relatively new modelling technique, beginning in earnest in 1988. But by 1990 a survey by Greenwich Associates found that 30 per cent of pension funds were using asset–liability modelling in one form or another.

Asset–liability modelling begins by making forecasts about how a pension fund's liabilities are going to accrue over a particular time horizon, that might be five, ten, or fifteen years ahead. To do this, assumptions concerning salary-growth rates, staff turnover, and the age distribution and sex composition of the work-force have to be made. Then forecasts concerning the funding position of the pension scheme have to be made. This involves making projections of future contribution-rates and also assessing the value of assets in relation to accrued liabilities. These forecasts and projections are made under different scenarios concerning likely outcomes. Typically, three scenarios are adopted: most likely, best-case, and worst-case. This provides a realistic range of possible outcomes, and in the last case spells out the extent of the risks that the pension-fund trustees face.

There are two main uses of asset–liability modelling. The first is to indicate the consequences of adopting any particular investment strategy. The second is to discover alternative strategies that increase the probability of meeting the fund's objectives (this is known as *asset–liability management*). Proponents of asset–liability modelling argue that the strategy allows pension funds to generate higher returns without any consequential increase in risk.

The modelling exercises might indicate, for example, that if current investment returns are sustained, there would be no need to change the employer contribution-rate over the next five years. However, the worst-case scenario might indicate that the employer contribution-rate might have to rise by 10 per cent over the next five years. The exercise therefore allows the employer to plan for this possibility. As another illustration, the modelling exercise might indicate that, because a pension fund is maturing, it should switch out of equities into fixed-income bonds, which are more likely to meet pension liabilities with lower risk of employer deficiency payments.

While all this seems eminently sensible, the technique is not without its critics. As with many long-term forecasting exercises, the predictions are only as good as the assumptions used to generate them. Some claim that the assumptions made about future investment returns are likely to be so unreliable that the modelling exercise provides very little of value. Less sceptical proponents of asset–liability modelling argue that the 'models are to be used and not believed', with the usefulness of the technique being 'to provide a disciplined quantitative framework for qualitative discussions on investment policies' (Roger Urwin, *Financial Times*, 18 April 1991).

Another problem encountered with the technique comes from fund managers who are concerned that it gives an unwarranted role to actuaries in designing investment strategies, in particular asset-allocation strategies. Actuaries have always played a role in determining a pension scheme's liabilities. But with the advent of asset–liability modelling, actuaries have begun to play a role in establishing the long-term asset allocation over, say, a ten-year horizon. Fund managers claim they are being reduced to the subsidiary role of determining short-term asset allocation and stock selection relative to this new long-term bench-mark. However, not all fund managers are critical of this redefinition of respective roles. Many have positively welcomed the formal separation of long-term policy decisions from short-term tactical decisions that asset–liability modelling allows.

Another potential problem concerns the interpretation of performance measurement in the light of the technique. Asset–liability modelling justifies different pension funds pursuing very different investment policies. For example, small, fast-growing funds might pursue very aggressive investment policies, while large mature funds might adopt passive investment policies. This makes it very difficult to interpret a single performance league table drawn up on the assumption that all funds are pursuing the same objective of maximizing returns. Performance-measurement services have begun to take this into account by constructing peer-group performance league tables, drawn up for subgroups of funds following similar objectives.

Urwin, in the article cited above, believes that despite these problems, the future of asset–liability management is assured and is likely to become a majority practice as natural as performance measurement (see Section 13.9 below and Chapter 14) has become.

13.4. Different Fund-Management Strategies for Defined-Benefit and Defined-Contribution Schemes

We can expect to see fund managers of personal pension schemes pursuing rather different investment strategies from those of fund managers of occupational schemes.

Managers of occupational schemes are *net investors*. They have contingent liabilities, in the sense that they have pension liabilities related to final salary. They must, therefore, construct and manage an asset portfolio that has the greatest chance of meeting these liabilities. They are partially insulated from this commitment as a consequence of the employer's obligation to make deficiency payments in the event that the assets are insufficient to meet liabilities. However, the protection is only partial, since the employer is likely to change the fund manager if he or she under-performs to this extent.

Managers of personal pension schemes, in contrast, face no such constraints. They are in effect *gross investors*. They do not have specific contingent liabilities to take into account. Their objective is to do the best they can with the contributions they receive. The pension depends entirely on the sum of money accumulated at the time of retirement. The fund never shows a deficit and never shows a surplus. If the fund manager has made poor investment decisions, the size of the fund will be low and the resulting pension will be small. But by the time that this is known, it is too late.

This does not, of course, mean that fund managers will necessarily prefer to manage personal pension schemes. If their performance figures are published and are consistently poor, they will lose business and ultimately go out of business. But the point remains that personal-pension-scheme managers face fewer constraints and are likely to be monitored less intensively and possibly less critically (because their clients are geographically dispersed and collectively unorganized) than managers of occupational schemes.

13.5. Determining the Trustees' Objectives and Constraints

One of the first tasks of the pension-fund manager (once he or she has been awarded the *mandate* from the pension-fund trustees) is to determine the trustees' objectives and constraints. It is important to do this for at least three reasons. First, it is a prerequisite for the initial structuring of the portfolio. Secondly, it will influence the kinds of portfolio adjustments that can be made. Thirdly, because it affects the initial portfolio structure, it will also influence the portfolio's subsequent performance.

The trustees' objectives and constraints can usually be expressed as follows. While these objectives and constraints apply mainly to occupational schemes, they are also relevant for personal schemes, although personal-pension scheme members do not typically express their objectives and constraints in this form. An example of a questionnaire designed to identify the objectives and constraints of trustees is given in the appendix to this chapter.

1. *Risk–Reward Profile*. The risk–reward profile of the fund (or the required rate of return on the fund's assets consistent with an acceptable degree of variability in asset values) can only be determined once the liabilities of the fund have been specified. The fund's actuaries determine long-term pension obligations and the acceptable level of risk, usually expressed in terms of a minimum acceptable value to the fund. While the complete specification of the risk–reward profile is rarely communicated to the fund manager (indeed, it is rarely understood by the trustees themselves), the fund manager must nevertheless determine a level of portfolio risk consistent with the degree of risk aversion specified by the trustees. The principal aim of a pension fund has been stated to be 'to achieve the maximum investment return which is consistent with the security of the fund' (Wolanski 1980, p. 18). A similar aim holds for defined-contribution schemes, although with such schemes the liabilities do not provide such an important constraint.

2. *Time Horizon*. While the time horizon for pension funds themselves is extremely long (in excess of thirty years for immature funds), the time horizon relevant for trustees, and therefore for pension-fund management groups, is much shorter: usually between three and five years. This is because this is the typical duration of a mandate.

3. *Mandate Restrictions*. The mandate also specifies other aspects of the trustees' preferences. For example, it can state the countries or companies whose securities cannot be invested in, for example, South Africa, and the shares of defence, tobacco, alcoholic-beverage, or, indeed, rival companies. It can also state the type or quality of securities that cannot be invested in, for example, options, warrants, preference stock, or unsecured debt.

4. *Pension-Scheme Resources*. The fund manager also has to take into account the resources made available by the trustees, both in terms of the initial value of the fund and in terms of the flow of contribution payments

that are going to be received. The size of the fund limits the type of investments that may be suitable. For example, a small fund is unlikely to invest directly in commercial property, while the trustees of a large fund are less likely to want large holdings in unit trusts.

All the above factors will affect the initial portfolio, adjustments to the portfolio, and subsequent performance. It is important for both the trustees and the fund manager to be aware of this from the outset. It is important to isolate the performance of the fund manager from, say, the restrictions placed on him or her by the trustees.

The most important characteristic that the fund manager has to identify is the trustees' attitude to risk, which in *modern portfolio theory* (MPT) is expressed in terms of either a *degree of risk tolerance* or a *degree of risk aversion*. The higher the degree of risk tolerance (the lower the degree of risk aversion) the greater the degree of risk (and expected return) that can be sustained in the pension fund.

A standard procedure for inferring the trustees' degree of risk tolerance is to ask them to select their preferred combination of general asset categories, say, the preferred mixture of shares and bonds. To help the trustees, they could be given the *portfolio opportunity set* derived from holding different combinations of shares and bonds. This is shown in Fig. 13.1 as the curved line *BPS*. At *B*, the portfolio is invested 100 per cent in bonds (the least risky portfolio), while at *S* the portfolio is invested 100 per cent in shares (the most risky portfolio). Suppose the trustees pick a particular mix, say 60 per-cent shares to 40 per-cent bonds. This portfolio is represented by point *P* in Fig. 13.1. The portfolio manager now has some idea of the *normal* (or *strategic* or *target*) *mix* of shares and bonds. He or she also has some idea of the trustees' degree of risk tolerance. This is because *P* must be a tangency point between the portfolio opportunity set and the trustees' *indifference curve* in *mean–variance space* (that is, the trade-off between return and risk that leaves the trustees with the same level of *expected utility* or welfare). The indifference curve can be represented by the equation:

$$\bar{r}_p = \bar{u} + \frac{1}{R_T}\sigma_p^2 \tag{1}$$

where

$\bar{r}_p$ = expected (or mean) return on portfolio;

σ_p^2 = variance of return on portfolio (the most common measure of risk in MPT);

$\bar{u}$ = intercept (measures *expected utility* level from portfolio *P* in units of expected return);

R_T = degree of risk tolerance (= 1/degree of risk aversion).

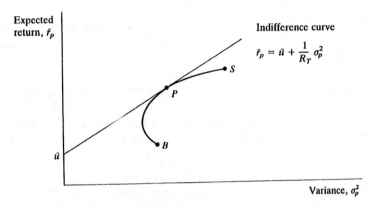

Fig. 13.1. Inferring the trustees' risk tolerance

If the degree of risk tolerance is assumed to be constant, then the indifference curve is linear as shown in (1). If we know P, we can calculate the slope of the line tangent at P and, given this, derive the trustees' degree of risk tolerance:

$$R_T = \frac{1}{\text{Slope of line tangent at } P}. \tag{2}$$

The higher the degree of risk tolerance, the flatter the indifference curve and the closer portfolio P will be to S. In other words, the higher the degree of risk tolerance, the greater the amount of risk that can be sustained in the portfolio.

Rewriting (1) gives:

$$\bar{u} = \bar{r}_p - \frac{1}{R_T} \sigma_p^2 \tag{3}$$

or

$$\text{Expected utility} = \text{Expected return} - \text{Risk penalty}. \tag{4}$$

This shows that the *expected utility* of the portfolio is equivalent to the *risk-adjusted expected return* on the portfolio. It is derived by subtracting a *risk penalty* from the expected return, where the risk penalty depends on the portfolio risk and the trustees' risk tolerance. For example, if $\bar{r}_p = 0.17$ (17 per cent), $\sigma_p = 0.30$ (30 per cent), and $R_T = 3$, then:

$$\bar{u} = 0.17 - \tfrac{1}{3}(0.30)^2 = 0.14 \ (14\%).$$

Note that $R_T = 3$ implies that $1/R_T = 1/3$; in other words, the trustees have to be compensated with one-third of a point increase in expected return to compensate them for taking on a one-point increase in variance in order for them to remain indifferent and have the same expected utility (see (1) and Fig. 13.1).

If the pension fund is *immature* (so that employee and employer contributions and investment income are more than sufficient to meet pension pay-outs), the trustees are likely to have a fairly high degree of risk tolerance. In this case the fund manager's objective is to select the portfolio that maximizes expected utility given by (3). It can be shown that if:

$\bar{r}_s, \bar{r}_b$ = expected returns on shares and bonds;
σ_s^2, σ_b^2 = variance of returns on shares and bonds;
$\quad \sigma_{sb}$ = covariance between returns on shares and bonds;
θ_s, θ_b = proportion of the portfolio in shares and bonds (with $\theta_b = 1 - \theta_s$)

then the optimal proportion of the portfolio invested in shares is given by:

$$\theta_s^* = \frac{\sigma_b^2 - \sigma_{sb}}{(\sigma_s^2 - 2\sigma_{sb} + \sigma_b^2)} + \frac{\bar{r}_s - \bar{r}_b}{2(\sigma_s^2 - 2\sigma_{sb} + \sigma_b^2)} R_T. \tag{5}$$

The proportion of the portfolio invested in shares increases linearly with the degree of risk tolerance, R_T, and with the spread between the expected returns on shares and bonds.

On the other hand, if the pension fund is *mature* (so that contributions and investment income are only just sufficient to meet pension pay-outs) then the trustees will be concerned about minimizing the mismatching between assets and liabilities. In other words, the trustees are concerned that the value of the assets (or equivalently the return on the assets) in the portfolio should never be less than the value of the liabilities (or equivalently the pay-out on the pension liabilities). This type of behaviour is known as *safety-first* portfolio behaviour.[1]

Of course, in a world of risk it is not possible to guarantee that the return on the assets will never be less than the pay-out on the liabilities. Instead, the fund manager will attempt to minimize the *probability* that the return on the assets will be less than the pay-out on the liabilities, that is:

$$\text{min. probability } (r_p < r_\ell) \tag{6}$$

---

[1] The trustees of some mature pension funds (in particular those with very high degrees of risk tolerance) might still be more interested in expected utility maximization than in safety-first investment behaviour. This is because surplus investment returns can be used to reduce the employer's contributions into the scheme and in the limit lead to a complete contributions holiday for the employer. In other words, the pension fund can be used as an investment vehicle for the employer as well as for the provision of pensions for the employees.

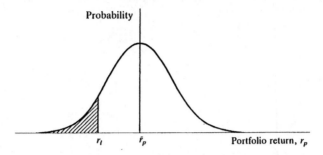

Fig. 13.2. The safety-first investment criterion

where

r_p = rate of return on portfolio of assets;
r_ℓ = rate of pay-out on pension liabilities.

If the portfolio return is generated by the *normal* (or Gaussian) *distribution*, then the optimum portfolio would be the one for which the expected return on the portfolio, $\bar{r}_p$, is the maximum number of standard deviations away from r_ℓ. This is demonstrated in Fig. 13.2. The shaded area is the probability of the return on the portfolio being less than r_ℓ. This area is minimized when the number of *standard deviations* between $\bar{r}_p$ and r_ℓ is maximized. Since the number of standard deviations between $\bar{r}_p$ and r_ℓ is given by $(\bar{r}_p - r_\ell)/\sigma_p$, then (6) is equivalent to:

$$\max k = \frac{\bar{r}_p - r_\ell}{\sigma_p}. \tag{7}$$

To illustrate, suppose that $r_\ell = 0.1$ (10 per cent) and we have the following two portfolios:

	Portfolio *A*	Portfolio *B*
$\bar{r}_p$	0.17	0.20
σ_p	0.30	0.35

For portfolio *A*, we have:

$$\frac{\bar{r}_p - r_\ell}{\sigma_p} = 0.23$$

while for portfolio *B*, we have:

$$\frac{\bar{r}_p - r_\ell}{\sigma_p} = 0.29;$$

therefore portfolio *B* is preferred.

All portfolios having the same value k in (7) will be equally preferred under the safety-first criterion, and this fact allows us to construct indif-

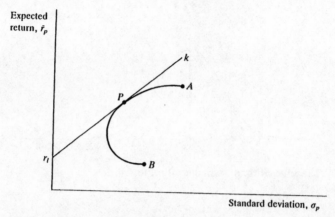

Fig. 13.3. The optimal safety–first portfolio

ference curves in mean–standard-deviation space, under the safety-first criterion. Rearranging the expression in (7), we get:

$$\bar{r}_p = r_\ell + k\sigma_p. \tag{8}$$

Fig. 13.3 shows how the optimal portfolio is selected. The optimal portfolio P is the tangency portfolio between the indifference curve and the portfolio opportunity set APB.

Having determined the trustees' objectives and constraints, the fund manager is now in a position to manage the pension fund. However, it is likely that the share portfolio and the bond portfolio will be managed separately. In addition, the fund manager has to decide whether to manage the fund passively or actively. We will consider all these factors in turn.

13.6. Passive Fund Management

In this section we will examine the passive management of share and bond portfolios. We will assume initially that the pension fund is immature (so that the trustees are interested in maximizing a risk–return utility function), and subsequently that the pension fund is mature (so that the trustees are interested in safety first).

13.6.1. PASSIVE FUND MANAGEMENT FOR EXPECTED UTILITY MAXIMIZING TRUSTEES

We will assume that the trustees are concerned only with risk and return and that their degree of risk tolerance has been assessed. We will also assume that there is a consensus view of the expected returns and risks associated with different securities. Finally, we will assume that it is possible for investors to borrow and lend at the same riskless interest rate. In short, we have the stylized world of MPT in which stock markets are efficient. Such a world justifies passive fund management as the appropriate management technique, since investors cannot expect to earn positive (risk-adjusted) excess returns from actively trading securities after adjusting for transactions costs. There are two main types of passive strategy: *buy-and-hold* and *index matching* (or *indexing*).

Buy-and-hold involves the purchase of securities and holding on to them indefinitely or, in the case of fixed-maturity securities (such as money-market instruments and bonds), until maturity, and then replacing them with similar securities. The return from a buy-and-hold strategy will be dominated by income flows (that is, dividend and coupon payments), and in the case of shares, by *long-term* capital growth. Expectations of *short-term* capital gains or losses are ignored: in the case of bonds, capital gains and losses are ignored altogether, because at maturity only the par value of the bond will be received.

Since there is a consensus view that all securities are fairly priced at all times, it does not really matter which securities are bought and held. However, by only buying and holding a few securities, a substantial amount of diversifiable risk might remain in the resulting portfolio. A version of buy-and-hold that eliminates diversifiable risk is index matching.

Index matching involves the construction of an *index fund* which is designed to replicate the performance of the market index. The optimal portfolio is determined (depending on the degree of risk tolerance) as a combination of a riskless asset and the index fund. This is shown in Fig. 13.4, which depicts the *capital market line* (which shows the equilibrium relationship between expected return on the portfolio and portfolio risk as measured by the standard deviation of return on the portfolio; see also equation (30) below), and where M is the consensus view of the *market portfolio* and C is the riskless asset. Given the trustees' indifference curve (and degree of risk tolerance), the optimal portfolio P is invested in the following proportions: θ_m in the market portfolio and $(1 - \theta_m)$ in the riskless asset. It can be shown (see Blake 1990, p. 290) that:

$$\theta_m = \frac{1}{2}\left(\frac{\bar{r}_m - r_f}{\sigma_m^2}\right) R_T \tag{9}$$

where

$\bar{r}_m$ = consensus expected return on the market;
σ_m^2 = consensus variance of the return on the market;
r_f = return on the riskless asset (for example, Treasury bills).

For example, if $\bar{r}_m = 0.18$ (18 per cent), $\sigma_m = 0.35$ (35 per cent), $r_f = 0.1$ (10 per cent), and $R_T = 3$, then $\theta_m = 0.98$, that is, 98 per cent of the fund

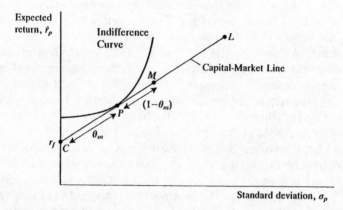

Fig. 13.4. Passive portfolio management

is invested in the market and 2 per cent is invested in the riskless asset. (Note that, if the indifference curve is linear in expected-return–variance space, as in Fig. 13.1, then it will be convex when it is redrawn in expected-return–standard-deviation space, as in Fig. 13.4.)

There are several types of indexing that are possible.

Complete indexing involves the construction of an index fund which exactly matches the underlying market portfolio. In the case of shares this could be the FT-A All Share Index; in the case of bonds it could be the Salomon Brothers Bond Index; in the case of an international portfolio it could be the Morgan Stanley Capital International Index. Complete indexing is very expensive. For example, the FT-A All Share Index contains more than 800 securities weighted according to their relative market proportions. To construct a portfolio of 800 securities with the same proportions as the index would involve extremely high brokerage commissions (which are ignored by the underlying index). Also, the constituents of the index change quite frequently and so the re-balancing of the index fund (that is, selling the deleted securities and purchasing the added securities) involves dealing spreads as well as brokerage commissions (and these are also ignored by the underlying index). A bond-index fund is even more expensive to construct. Over time, the average maturity of a bond index will decline unless new long-maturing bonds are added to replace those that mature and automatically drop out of the index. All this shows that complete indexing is not feasible. Three alternatives have been suggested: stratified sampling, factor matching, and commingling.

Stratified sampling involves the construction of an index fund based on a sample of securities from the total population comprising the index. The idea is to divide the total set of securities into sectors or strata (which are, for example, industry-based for shares or maturity-based for bonds). An overall sample proportion is selected, for example, 5 per cent. Then the top 5 per cent of securities that have the highest correlation with the market index are included in the index fund. This procedure limits initial transactions costs and subsequent re-balancing costs, but increases the risks of *tracking error*, the error in not exactly replicating the market index.

Factor matching (or *risk matching*) is more sophisticated than stratified sampling. Stratified sampling involves selecting securities on the basis of a single factor, for example, industry grouping or maturity range. Factor matching involves the construction of an index fund using securities selected on the basis of a number of factors (or risk indices). The first factor is generally the level of systematic or market risk, so the selected portfolio must be chosen to have the same variance of return as the market (see below). The other factors (in the case of shares) could be sector breakdown, dividend pattern, firm size, and financial structure (that is, debt/equity ratio). The selected index fund would be a portfolio of, say, fifty securities which matches the market in terms of the above five factors and has the highest correlation with the market.

Commingling involves the use of *commingled funds* such as *unit trusts* or *investment trusts* rather than the explicit formation of an index fund. Commingling may be especially suitable for small pension funds and may provide an acceptable compromise between the transactions costs of complete indexing and the tracking error of stratified sampling.

Apart from the transactions costs involved in setting up and re-balancing, there are other problems with running an index fund. The most important one concerns income payments on the securities. The total return on an index includes not only capital gains but also income in the form of dividend or coupon payments. In order to match the performance of the index in terms of income, the index fund would have to have the same pattern of income payments as the index. It would also have to make the same reinvestment assumptions as the index. Since the index fund was constructed to replicate the capital structure of the index, it is unlikely to replicate the income pattern (unless exact matching was used). Similarly, the index assumes that gross income payments are reinvested costlessly back into the index on the day that each security becomes ex-dividend. In practice, however, these assumptions are violated in four ways. First, the dividend or coupon payment is not made until an average of six weeks after the ex-dividend date. Secondly, the payment is received net of tax (non-taxpaying investors such as pension funds have to wait even longer before receiving a tax rebate). Thirdly, there are dealing costs of reinvesting income payments. Fourthly, the income payments on different securities are going to be trickling in all the time, and no fund manager is going to invest small sums of money on the day they are received. Instead, the small sums are going to be accumulated until a suitable large sum is available for reinvestment. The effect of all these factors is that the index fund will begin to drift away from the index and will eventually have to be re-balanced. Another problem concerns the effect of changing the constituents of the index. When the announcement of the change is made, the price of the security being deleted falls, while the price of the security being added rises. These effects can cause major tracking errors between the index fund and the index.

All these factors lead to the index fund invariably under-performing the index. So it appears that passive fund managers cannot even match the index, let alone beat it. But this appearance is deceptive. The appropriate test is how well an index-fund manager performs on a risk-adjusted and transactions-cost-adjusted basis compared with a fund manager pursuing an active strategy.

Despite these problems, passive fund management is becoming increasingly important as a management strategy. And it is also a sensible strategy if there is a consensus about the market portfolio's expected return and risk. The only occasions on which a passive fund manager goes into active mode is when either (i) the client's preferences change or (ii) the consensus concerning the market portfolio's expected return and risk changes. The first case leads to a new combination of the riskless asset and the index fund. The second case leads to a re-balancing of the existing index fund.

13.6.2. PASSIVE FUND MANAGEMENT FOR SAFETY-FIRST TRUSTEES

The trustees of a mature pension fund will want to ensure that the present value of the fund's assets is at least as great as the present value of the pension liabilities. The stream of future pension liabilities is reasonably predictable: actuaries are able to make good forecasts of the future number of pensioners and, since most pensions are only partially indexed against inflation, it is relatively easy to predict the growth in the value of pensions. This suggests that it is desirable to ensure that the future cash flows from assets required to meet the pension payments are also reasonably predictable. This, in turn, suggests that bonds should play a significant role in the portfolios of mature pension funds. Indeed, in the past, when pensions were not indexed at all, fixed-coupon bonds were the ideal vehicle for meeting pension funds' needs. Today, when there is some indexing of pensions, pension funds will need to have indexed bonds and shares in their portfolios as well. In this section we will consider some of the passive strategies suitable for the bond portfolios of safety-first trustees. The two main types of strategies are immunization and cash-flow matching.

Classical immunization (or *duration matching*) involves the construction of a bond portfolio which has an assured return over a given investment horizon (equal to that of the pay-out on the fund's liabilities) regardless of changes in the level of interest rates. Equivalently, it involves the construction of a bond portfolio with a present value equal to (or, even better, never less than) the present value of the liabilities regardless of changes in the level of interest rates. In short, the bond portfolio is *immunized* against interest-rate changes.

Fig. 13.5 shows the effect of immunization in terms of the present values of assets and liabilities. A is the logarithmic *present-value profile* for the portfolio of fixed-income bonds and L is the logarithmic present-value profile for the liabilities. When the current interest rate is r_0, the values of the bonds and the liabilities are both P_0. When interest rates rise, the present values of both the bonds and liabilities fall. The present value of the bonds falls in order to match the increase in yields when coupon payments are fixed. The present value of the liabilities falls because lower contributions need to be collected as the interest earned on them increases. Similarly, when interest rates fall, the present values of both the bonds and liabilities rise. But the important point to note is that, whatever happens to interest rates, the present value of the bonds is never less than the present value of the liabilities: indeed, except when the interest rate is r_0, the present value of the bonds always exceeds that of the liabilities. This result arises for two reasons: the bond portfolio is constructed to have the same *duration* and (at least) the same *convexity* as

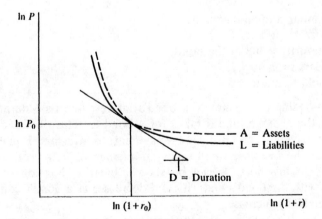

Fig. 13.5. Classical immunization in terms of present values

the liabilities. Duration measures the slope of the present-value profile at any given interest rate, while convexity measures the curvature.

Duration and convexity are first- and second-order measures of *interest-rate risk*. This is because they measure the interest-rate sensitivity of the present-value profile: the lower the duration and the greater the convexity, the less sensitive the bonds and liabilities are to interest-rate changes, that is, the lower the degree of interest-rate risk that they contain. As interest rates rise, the present value of the portfolio falls, but the return from reinvesting the portfolio's cash flows (coupon payments and maturing bonds) increases. A perfectly immunized portfolio exactly balances these offsetting effects, that is, exactly offsets interest-rate risk with *reinvestment risk*. By constructing the bond portfolio to have a duration equal to the specified investment horizon, both the return on the portfolio and the value of the portfolio will be immunized against interest-rate changes. We can demonstrate these results using a portfolio containing a single bond.

We will consider a bond with five years to maturity, a current value of £114.28, an annual coupon payment of £13.77, and a yield to maturity of 10 per cent. The duration of the bond (see Blake 1990, chap. 5) is given by:

$$
\begin{aligned}
\text{Duration} &= \frac{d}{P}\left(\frac{(1+rm)^{T+1} - (1+rm) - rm.T}{(rm)^2(1+rm)^T}\right) + \frac{B}{P}\frac{T}{(1+rm)^T} \\
&= \frac{13.77}{114.28}\left(\frac{(1.1)^6 - (1.1) - 0.1(5)}{(0.1)^2(1.1)^5}\right) + \frac{100}{114.28}\frac{5}{(1.1)^5} \\
&= 4 \text{ years}
\end{aligned}
\tag{10}
$$

where
  d = annual coupon payment;
  P = current price of the bond;
  B = maturity value of the bond;
  T = years to maturity;
  rm = yield to maturity.

As well as being a measure of a bond's interest-rate risk, duration also measures the average time it takes for a bond to return cash flows (that is, coupon payments and principal repayment) to investors. Equation (10) shows that the five-year bond takes an average of four years to return cash-flows to investors. It can be shown that the duration of a bond increases with the bond's maturity and decreases as a bond's coupon and yield to maturity increase.

If this bond is held for exactly the same time as its duration (that is, four years) and then sold, its value in four years' time will be the same

TABLE 13.1. *The value of the bond in year 4 as reinvestment rates change*

Year	Cash flow	Reinvestment rates		
		9%	10%	11%
1	13.77	$13.77 (1.09)^3$	$13.77 (1.1)^3$	$13.77 (1.11)^3$
2	13.77	$13.77 (1.09)^2$	$13.77 (1.1)^2$	$13.77 (1.11)^2$
3	13.77	$13.77 (1.09)$	$13.77 (1.1)$	$13.77 (1.11)$
4	13.77	13.77	13.77	13.77
5	113.77	$113.77 (1.09)^{-1}$	$113.77 (1.1)^{-1}$	$113.77 (1.11)^{-1}$
Year 4 value		167.30	167.30	167.30

whatever happens to interest rates (that is, reinvestment rates). This can be seen from Table 13.1.

So whatever happens to reinvestment rates, the value of the bond in year 4 is always equal to £167.30. This follows because as interest rates change, the change in the income component of the value of the bond is always offset by the change in the capital component of the bond's value, where the bond is valued at its duration date (that is, year 4). The income component is given by the sum of the first four elements of the above table:

$$\text{Income component} = £13.77((1 + rm)^3 + (1 + rm)^2 + (1 + rm) + 1).$$

The capital component is given by the last element of the table:

$$\text{Capital component} = £113.77(1 + rm)^{-1}.$$

If the interest rate falls from 10 per cent to 9 per cent, the income component falls by £0.95 and the capital component rises by £0.95. Similarly, if the interest rate rises from 10 per cent to 11 per cent, the income component increases by £0.93 and the capital component falls by £0.93.

If the bond had been held for any other period than its duration, the value of the bond would not be independent of the interest rate. For example, had the bond been held to maturity, the year 5 value of the bond would be £182.40 (at 9 per cent), £184.10 (at 10 per cent), and £185.80 (at 11 per cent).

It follows from the fact that the year 4 value of the bond is constant, regardless of interest rates, that the return from holding the bond must also be constant, regardless of interest rates, if the holding period is equal to the bond's duration. The initial cost of the bond is £114.28 and the terminal value is £167.30, therefore the rate of return over four years is:

$$\text{Rate of return} = (167.30/114.28)^{1/4} - 1$$
$$= 0.10 \text{ (i.e. 10\%)}$$

equal to the original yield to maturity on the bond. By holding a bond for its duration, it is possible to lock in the initial yield to maturity.

Now, if a pension fund has liabilities of £100,000 which arise in four years' time, the fund manager could recommend that the trustees invest in a portfolio of 598 (that is, £100,000/£167.30) of these bonds.

The same principles apply to portfolios of bonds. The duration of a portfolio of bonds is simply the weighted sum of the durations on the individual bonds:

$$D_p = \sum_{i=1}^{N} \theta_i D_i \tag{11}$$

where

D_p = duration of the portfolio with N bonds;
D_i = duration of ith bond;
θ_i = proportion (by value) of ith bond in the portfolio.

It is possible to construct a portfolio with a specified duration from a whole range of bonds with different durations. For example, the portfolio could be constructed from bonds with durations close to that of the liability (this is called a *focused* or *bullet portfolio*), or it could be constructed from bonds with durations distant from that of the liability (this is known as a *barbell portfolio*). Consider, for example, a liability with a duration of ten years and a set of bonds with durations of four, nine, eleven, and fifteen years, respectively. A focused portfolio would contain the nine- and eleven-year duration bonds with weights of 50 per cent each, giving a duration of:

$$0.50(9) + 0.50(11) = 10 \text{ years.}$$

A barbell portfolio would consist of the four- and fifteen-year duration bonds with weights of 45.5 per cent and 54.5 per cent respectively, giving a duration of:

$$0.455(4) + 0.545(15) = 10 \text{ years.}$$

The advantage of a barbell strategy is that a much wider range of portfolios with different durations can be constructed compared with a focused strategy. However, the disadvantage of the barbell strategy is that it has greater *immunization risk* than the focused strategy.

Immunization risk arises whenever there are non-parallel shifts in the yield curve. As the last example showed, the immunization effect works because there were parallel shifts in the yield curve, that is, the reinvestment rate fell from 10 per cent to 9 per cent at each maturity. If this does not happen, then matching the duration to the investment horizon no longer guarantees immunization. Non-parallel shifts in the yield curve will lead to the income component of the value of the portfolio changing either too much or too little compared with the change in the capital component, that is, there will be immunization risk. This risk is reduced if the durations of the individual bonds in the immunizing portfolio are close to that of the liabilities (that is, if a focused portfolio is used). In this case, non-parallel yield-curve shifts will affect the individual bonds and the liabilities in a similar way. The effects of non-parallel yield-curve shifts are divergent if the durations of the individual bonds in the immunizing portfolio are distant from that of the liabilities (as in a barbell portfolio), even though the duration of the portfolio itself is the same as that of the liabilities.

While immunization is usually regarded as a passive strategy, the portfolio will have to be periodically re-balanced and therefore an immunization strategy has certain active elements. There are two main reasons for rebalancing: (i) changes in interest rates and (ii) the passage of time. Immunization is only effective for small changes in interest rates. As the change in interest rates increases, the effectiveness of immunization decreases. However, the discrepancy always favours the portfolio holder, as shown in Fig. 13.6. For example, if the interest rate falls from 10 per cent to 5 per cent, the year 4 value of the portfolio in the last example rises to £167.70, while if the interest rate rises to 20 per cent, the value of the portfolio rises to £168.73. The passage of time will automatically reduce the duration of the portfolio. But the reduction in duration may not occur at the same rate as time decays. For example, after one year the duration of the portfolio might decline by only 0.8 years. So periodi-

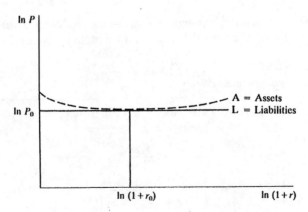

Fig. 13.6. Classical immunization in terms of investment horizon values

cally the portfolio has to be re-balanced with respect to both the new reinvestment rate and the remaining investment horizon.

So far we have considered the construction of an immunized portfolio to meet a single liability at a single future date. But a pension fund has to meet a schedule of liabilities over time. This involves the construction of a *dedicated portfolio* which is capable of meeting the schedule of liabilities from both the income and capital components and which declines to zero on the payment of the last liability. There are two ways of dedicating a portfolio: multi-period immunization and cash-flow matching.

When there are multiple liabilities, it is no longer sufficient simply to match the duration of the portfolio to the average duration of the liabilities as in classical immunization. Instead, it is necessary for each liability payment to be individually immunized (that is, duration-matched) by a portfolio payment stream. The procedure for doing this is known as *multi-period immunization*.

A very simple alternative to multi-period immunization is *cash-flow matching*. This involves finding the lowest-cost portfolio that generates a pattern of cash flows that exactly matches the pattern of liability payments. The procedure for doing this is as follows. A bond (the lowest-cost if more than one is available) is purchased with the same maturity and value as the last liability payment. The coupon payments on the bond help to finance the earlier liabilities. Taking these coupon payments into account, another bond (again the lowest-cost) is purchased with the same maturity as the penultimate liability payment. Working backwards in this way, all the liabilities can be matched by payments on the bonds in the portfolio. To illustrate, annual liability payments of £1,000 for three years could be met by the purchase of nine 11.11 per-cent three-year bonds, eight 12.50 per-cent two-year bonds, and seven 14.29 per-cent one-year bonds (see Table 13.2).

There are two main advantages of cash-flow matching over immunization. First, there is no need for duration matching. Secondly, there is

TABLE 13.2. *Cash-flow matching*

Number of bonds	Coupon (%)	Maturity (years)	Cash flows (£)		
			Year 1	Year 2	Year 3
9	11.11	3	100	100	1,000
8	12.50	2	100	900	—
7	14.29	1	800	—	—
TOTAL			1,000	1,000	1,000

no need to re-balance the portfolio as interest rates change or with the passage of time, as there is with immunization. Cash-flow matching is therefore a pure passive buy-and-hold strategy. However, in the real world it is unlikely that bonds exist with the appropriate maturity dates and coupon payments. To guarantee that the liabilities are paid when due in the absence of perfect matching, the cash-flow matching strategy would have to be over-funded. In this case an immunization strategy might well end up meeting the required objectives at lower cost.

Horizon matching is a combination of cash-flow matching and immunization. For example, a fund manager might construct a portfolio which cash-flow matches the liabilities for the next four quarters, but which is immunized for the remaining investment horizon. At the end of the four quarters the portfolio is re-balanced to cash-flow match over the subsequent four quarters, and again immunized for the remaining period.

13.7. Active Fund Management

Active fund management is suitable for immature pension funds whose trustees have a high degree of risk tolerance and are therefore interested in maximizing expected utility. However, mature pension funds might be actively managed in the expectation of reducing employers' contributions. Further, there are different active strategies for the share and bond portfolios.

13.7.1. ACTIVE SHARE-FUND MANAGEMENT

A portfolio will be actively managed whenever it is believed that there are misvalued securities around, or when there are heterogeneous expectations of the risks and returns on securities, so that there is no consensus view of the market portfolio. Expectations of price movements are vitally important with active management. This contrasts with passive management, where expectations are less important but where risk aversion dominates behaviour. Active fund management operates around four activities: *country selection, asset allocation, security selection* (sometimes called *stock-picking*), and *market timing*.

To simplify the problem of constructing the portfolio, the fund manager breaks it down into a number of stages. At the first stage, called the *country-selection* stage, the fund manager decides what proportion of the total portfolio to devote to each country: for example, 80 per cent to the UK, 8 per cent to the USA, 6 per cent to Japan, 4 per cent to Germany, and 2 per cent to Australia. At the second stage, called the *asset-allocation* stage, he or she decides the proportions of each country portfolio devoted to broad asset categories: such as shares, bonds, and money-market securities. The optimal asset-allocation decision has been demonstrated before (see equation (5)). It depends on the trustees' degree of risk tolerance and on the fund manager's estimates of the risks and returns on shares and bonds. The asset-allocation decision is extremely important since it dominates the performance of most portfolios. This is because returns on securities within each asset category are usually highly correlated, that is, they generally rise together or fall together. This implies that selecting the best-performing asset category is more important for performance than selecting the best-performing securities within each asset category. However, restrictions placed on them by trustees may mean that fund managers do not have a completely free hand in making their asset-allocation decisions.

Having decided the asset allocation, the fund manager can then proceed to the third stage, called the *security-selection* stage. At this stage the fund manager in charge of a particular asset category selects securities from that category. This is done independently of the securities being selected within another category, so that any cross-category correlations between bonds and shares are completely ignored when forming the share and bond portfolios. This common feature of hierarchical or stage-by-stage decision-making is known as *separability*: the bond portfolio is separable from the share portfolio.

There is sometimes an intermediate stage between asset allocation and security selection, known as *sector selection* (or group selection). At this stage funds are allocated to different sectors of each category before individual securities are selected from within those sectors. So, for example, with bonds the sectors could be short-term, medium-term, and long-term bonds. With shares, the sectors could be the components of the Standard Industrial Classification (for example, banks, breweries, electrical, textiles, and so on). It is also possible that some fund-management groups use a different hierarchical ordering: for example, the asset-allocation decision might be made before the country-selection decision.

We will assume that the asset-allocation decision (and where appropriate the country- and sector-selection decision) has been made (according to equation (5) above). We can therefore concentrate attention on the security-selection decision. Security selection is important whenever fund managers are prepared to accept the overall consensus for the market as a whole but believe that certain individual securities are misvalued. In other words, most shares are fairly priced but a few are either underpriced or overpriced. A good stock-picker believes he or she knows which securities are misvalued. An overpriced security has an expected return that is less than, or a risk estimate that is more than, the market consensus estimate, while an underpriced security has an expected return that is more than, or a risk estimate that is less than, the market consensus estimate.

In MPT the fair price of a security is determined using the *capital-asset pricing model* (CAPM) and the *security-market line* (SML). A security is said to be fairly priced when its *equilibrium expected return* ($\bar{r}_i^*$) is given by:

$$\bar{r}_i^* = r_f + (\bar{r}_m - r_f)\beta_i \tag{12}$$

where
  β_i = beta of the ith security, defined as the ratio of the *covariance* between the return on the security and the return on the market (σ_{im}) to the *variance* of the return on the market (σ_m^2), that is, $\beta_i = \sigma_{im}/\sigma_m^2$.

This is the formula for the capital-asset pricing model. It states that the equilibrium return on a risky security is equal to the risk-free return (r_f) plus a *risk premium* which equals the product of the *market-risk premium* ($\bar{r}_m - r_f$) and the *beta* of the security (β_i).

The *beta* of a security measures the security's embodiment of *systematic risk* (or *market risk*). The higher the systematic risk, the higher the beta and the greater the expected return on the security has to be in order for the security to be held in equilibrium. The total risk of a security can be decomposed into the security's systematic risk plus its *specific* risk:

Total risk = Systematic risk + Specific risk

or

$$\sigma_i^2 = \beta_i^2 \sigma_m^2 + \eta_i^2 \tag{13}$$

where
  σ_i^2 = variance of the return on the ith security;
  η_i^2 = specific risk of the ith security.

Because the specific risk of a security can be eliminated by low-cost diversification (that is, it is diversifiable), this component of total risk will not be 'priced' in equilibrium. Only the component of total risk (namely, the systematic risk) that is correlated with the market and hence undiversifiable, because market risk is undiversifiable, will be priced in equilibrium.

The graphical representation of the CAPM is called the security-market line (see Fig. 13.7). Both the CAPM and the SML show that the expected (or required) return on a risky security increases linearly with the security's beta (since the market-risk premium is common to all securities). When a security is fairly priced, it will lie along the SML.

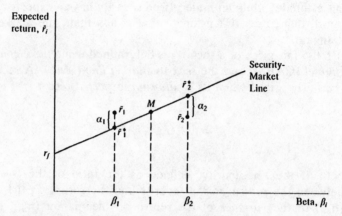

Fig. 13.7. Security selection: alpha values for shares

The beta for a portfolio of securities (β_p) is the weighted average of the betas of the individual securities:

$$\beta_p = \sum_{i=1}^{N} \theta_i \beta_i \tag{14}$$

where

θ_i = proportion (by value) of the ith security in the portfolio.

The difference between the return expected by the fund manager ($\bar{r}_i$) and the equilibrium expected return as given by equation (12) is known as the *alpha* of the security:

$$\alpha_i = \bar{r}_i - \bar{r}_i^* \tag{15}$$

where

α_i = alpha of the ith security.

For example, suppose that $\bar{r}_m = 0.18$ (18 per cent), $r_f = 0.10$ (10 per cent), and $\beta_1 = 0.75$, then $\bar{r}_1^* = 0.16$ (16 per cent). If $\bar{r}_1 = 0.17$ (17 per cent), then $\alpha_1 = 0.01$ (that is, 1 per cent). This means that the security offers a 1 per cent higher return than it should have and is therefore underpriced.

When a security's alpha is positive, the security is underpriced. When a security's alpha is negative, the security is overpriced. When a security is fairly priced, its alpha is zero (see Fig. 13.7). The alpha for the portfolio (α_p) is the weighted average of the alphas of the individual securities in the portfolio:

$$\alpha_p = \sum_{i=1}^{N} \theta_i \alpha_i \tag{16}$$

where
  θ_i = proportion (by value) of the ith security in the portfolio.

The objective of a stock-picker is to select portfolios of securities with positive alphas, a procedure which has been called 'the quest for alpha'. In other words, the stock-picker will construct portfolios of securities which, in comparison with the market portfolio, have less-than-proportionate weightings in the overpriced (negative-alpha) securities (since they are expected to fall in price) and more-than-proportionate weightings in the underpriced (positive-alpha) securities (since they are expected to rise in price).

A fund manager engages in security selection when he or she accepts the overall consensus for the market portfolio but believes that individual securities are misvalued. A fund manager engages in *market timing* when he or she does not accept the consensus about the market portfolio. In other words, he or she is more bullish or more bearish than the market. Market timing is equivalent to adjusting the beta of the portfolio over time (see Fig. 13.8). If the fund manager is expecting a bull market, he or she wants to increase the beta of the portfolio (that is, to make it more *aggressive*). If he or she is expecting a bear market, he or she wants to reduce the beta of the portfolio (that is, to make it more *defensive*). One way of doing this would be to buy high-beta shares in a bull market and sell them in a bear market. However, the transactions costs involved would make this an expensive strategy. An alternative is to keep the portfolio of risky assets constant and to raise or lower beta by lowering or raising the proportion of the portfolio held in cash. This can be a cheaper alternative, since moving into or out of cash is generally cheaper than

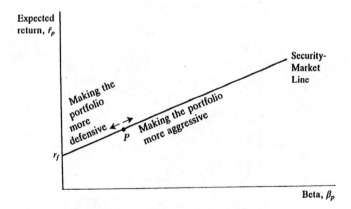

Fig. 13.8. Market timing

moving between different shares. An even cheaper alternative is to use futures or options (this is discussed in Sections 13.8 and 13.12 below).

13.7.2. ACTIVE BOND-FUND MANAGEMENT

As with shares, a bond fund will be actively managed whenever there are misvalued bonds around, or when there are heterogeneous expectations about the risks and returns on bonds, so that there is no consensus view of the market portfolio for bonds. Similarly, with the asset-allocation decision having been made, active bond-fund management operates around the activities of security selection and market timing. However, there is a difference between share- and bond-portfolio managers. Most share managers engage in security selection, whereas most bond managers engage in market timing.

A bond-picker will construct portfolios of bonds which, in comparison with the market portfolio, have less-than-proportionate weightings in the overpriced bonds (since they are expected to fall in price) and more-than-proportionate weightings in the underpriced bonds (since they are expected to rise in price). In other words, the portfolio has relatively low weightings in negative-alpha bonds and relatively high weightings in positive-alpha bonds (see equation (15)), where alpha is defined with respect to the *bond-market line* (see Fig. 13.9). For example, suppose that $\bar{r}_m \doteq 0.12$ (12 per cent) and $r_f = 0.10$ (10 per cent), then the equation for the bondmarket line is:

$$\begin{aligned} \bar{r}_i^* &= r_f + (\bar{r}_m - r_f)D_i/D_m \\ &= 0.10 + (0.02)D_i/D_m \end{aligned} \qquad (17)$$

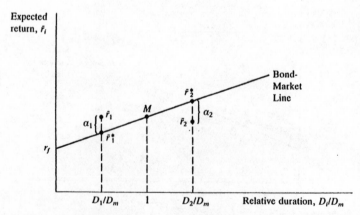

Fig. 13.9. Security selection: alpha values for bonds

where
$\bar{r}_i^*$ = equilibrium expected return on the ith bond;
D_i/D_m = relative duration of ith bond (where D_m is the duration of the market portfolio of bonds).

If for Bond 1, $D_1/D_m = 0.5$, then $\bar{r}_1^* = 0.11$ (11 per cent). If $\bar{r}_1 = 0.12$ (12 per cent), then $\alpha_1 = 0.01$ (that is, 1 per cent). The bond offers a 1 per-cent higher return than it should have and is therefore underpriced.

A market timer engages in active management when he or she does not accept the consensus for the market portfolio, and is either more bullish or more bearish than the market. Expectations of interest-rate changes are, therefore, a crucial input into successful market timing. A bond-market timer is interested in adjusting the relative duration of his or her portfolio over time (market timing with bonds is sometimes called *duration switching* or *rate-anticipation switching*). If the fund manager is expecting a bull market because he or she is expecting a fall in the general level of interest rates, he or she wants to increase the duration of the portfolio by replacing low-duration bonds with high-duration bonds. If the fund manager is expecting a bear market because he or she is ex-pecting a rise in the general level of interest rates, he or she wants to reduce the duration of the portfolio by replacing high-duration bonds with low-duration bonds.

Active bond-portfolio management is generally not as profitable as active share-portfolio management. There are several reasons for this. First, there are more shares than bonds traded in the UK. The most liquid bonds are UK government bonds and then only at certain maturi-ties. Because of active trading in these bonds, they are less likely to be mispriced. In addition, the volatility of bond prices is generally much less than that of share prices, so the opportunity for substantial mispricing of bonds is in any case much less than for shares. Further, with only a few bonds suitable for active trading, the portfolio consisting of those bonds will be relatively un-diversified and will therefore be relatively risky, thereby reducing the risk-adjusted excess returns from active trading. The costs of active bond-portfolio management can also be reduced by using futures and options (see Section 13.12 below).

Bond-portfolio adjustment involves the purchase and sale of bonds, that is, the *switching* or *swapping* of bonds. There are two main classes of bond switches: *anomaly switches* and *policy switches*. An anomaly switch is a switch between two bonds with very *similar* characteristics but whose prices (or yields) are out of line with each other. A policy switch is a switch between two *dissimilar* bonds because of an anticipated change in the structure of the market (for example, quality ratings are expected to change) which is expected to lead to a change in the relative prices (or yields) of the two bonds. Policy switches involve greater expected returns, but also greater potential risks, than anomaly switches.

The simplest example of an anomaly switch is a *substitution switch*. This involves the exchange of two bonds which are similar in terms of maturity, coupon and quality rating, and every other characteristic, but which differ in terms of price (or yield). Since two similar bonds should trade at the same price and yield, then whenever a price (or yield) difference occurs, an arbitrage opportunity emerges. The 'dear' bond is sold short and the 'cheap' bond is purchased. Later, if and when the anomaly has been eliminated, the reverse set of transactions are made in order to close-out the position. The time taken for the elimination of the anomaly is known as the *work-out period*. The work-out period is important for calculating the rate of return on the switch. The shorter the work-out period, the greater the annualized rate of return. If the position has to be held until maturity before the anomaly is corrected, the annualized return from the switch may be negligible.

Table 13.3 illustrates a typical substitution switch. If, historically, the difference between the prices of two bonds A and B has never been more than £0.50 and the difference between the yields to maturity has never been more than 0.10 per cent (that is, ten basis points), then clearly at date 1 an anomaly exists and so a substitution switch is made. The cheaper Bond B is purchased and the dearer Bond A is sold short. By date 2 the anomaly has been eliminated. Bond A was correctly priced and its price has not changed between the two dates. Bond B was underpriced and its price rises by £1, while its yield falls by twenty basis points. If dates 1 and 2 are a year apart, the rate of return on capital employed of £100 is only 1 per cent. However, if the two dates are one month apart, the annualized rate of return is 12.68 per cent. It is important to note that this switch involves the short sale of one bond *and* the purchase of another bond: there is a *relative* mispricing between the bonds, but it is impossible to know in advance which bond is *absolutely* mispriced.

TABLE 13.3. *A substitution switch*

	Date 1			Date 2			Profit	
	Action	Price (£)	Yield (%)	Action	Price (£)	Yield (%)	Price (£)	Yield (%)
Bond A	Sell	100	10.00	Buy	100	10.00	0	0.00
Bond B	Buy	99	10.20	Sell	100	10.00	1	0.20
TOTAL							1	0.20

If the coupon and maturity of the two bonds are similar, then a substitution swap involves a one-for-one exchange of bonds. However, if there are substantial differences in coupon or maturity, then the duration of the two bonds will differ. This will lead to different responses if the general level of interest rates changes during the life of the switch. It will therefore be necessary to weight the switch in such a way that it is hedged from changes in the level of interest rates but still exposed to changes in the anomalous yield-differential between the bonds.

To illustrate, suppose that Bond A in the last example has a duration of ten years, while Bond B has a duration of two years. This means that Bond A is five times more responsive to interest-rate fluctuations than Bond B. To protect against unanticipated shifts in interest rates, the relative investment in the two bonds is determined as follows:

Investment in Bond A/Investment in Bond B

= Duration of Bond B/Duration of Bond A. (18)

Expressing this in terms of nominal amounts:

Nominal of Bond B bought

= Nominal of Bond A sold

$$\times \frac{\text{Duration of Bond A} \times \text{Price of Bond A}}{\text{Duration of Bond B} \times \text{Price of Bond B}}$$

$\simeq 5 \times$ Nominal of Bond A sold. (19)

So for every Bond A sold, five of Bond B have to be bought. Consider what would happen if there was a one-for-one exchange and interest rates fell by 1 per cent. The price of Bond A would rise by 10 per cent (that is, 1 per cent times its duration of ten), from £100 to £1·10. The price of Bond B would rise by 2 per cent (that is, 1 per cent times its duration of two), from £99 to £101. Suppose also that the price of Bond B rose by another £1 to £102 to correct the anomaly. So, although the relative mispricing has been corrected, the substitution switch has made a loss of £8. Similarly, differences in coupon rates between the two bonds will affect the profitability of the switch and this has to be taken into account.

Another type of anomaly switch is a *pure yield–pick-up switch*. This simply involves the sale of a bond with a given yield to maturity and the purchase of a similar bond with a higher yield to maturity. With this switch there is no expectation of any yield or price correction, so no reverse transactions take place at a later date.

Policy switches are designed to take advantage of an anticipated change. The change could be (i) a shift in interest rates; (ii) a change in the structure of the yield curve; (iii) a change in a bond's quality rating; or (iv) a change in sector relationships. A shift in interest rates is exactly

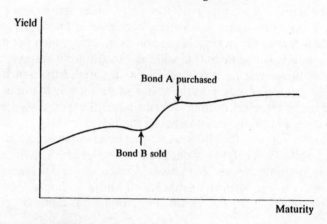

Fig. 13.10. Bond switching

what a market timer is looking out for. So switching from low-duration to high-duration bonds if interest rates are expected to fall is an example of a policy switch (as we have seen, it is also known as a *duration switch* or *rate-anticipation switch*). The other changes listed above lead to what are known as *inter-market* (or *inter-sector*) *spread switches*. We can give some examples.

Normally the yield curve is a smooth relationship between yield and maturity. But occasionally there may be humps or dips in the yield curve, as in Fig. 13.10. If the humps and dips are expected to disappear, then the prices of bonds (for example, Bond A) on the hump can be expected to rise (their yields will fall) and the prices of bonds (for example, Bond B) in the dip can be expected to fall (their yields will rise). So one example of a switch is the purchase of Bond A and the short sale of Bond B.

A bond whose quality rating is expected to fall will fall in price. To prevent a capital loss, it can be switched for a bond whose quality rating is expected to rise or to remain unchanged.

An example of a change in sector relationships is a change in taxes affecting two sectors. For instance, one sector (for example, the domestic-bond sector) might have withholding taxes on coupon payments, whereas another sector (for example, the eurobond sector) might not. If it is anticipated either that withholding tax will be applied to all sectors or that it will be withdrawn from all sectors, then another switch is possible.

13.8. Mixed Active–Passive Fund Management

So far we have considered pure passive and pure active strategies, but it is possible for fund managers to use mixtures of the two. For example, the asset-allocation decision can be passive, but the fund manager actively engages in security selection. This is known as a *security-selection style* of management. Alternatively, the fund manager might construct passive portfolios of individual securities, but make active asset-allocation decisions. This is known as an *asset-allocation style* of management.

Another mixed strategy is *core–satellite* portfolio management. This is a management strategy pursued by very large funds. The fund manager has a large *core portfolio* that is never traded, because doing so would result in adverse market movements. But surrounding the core portfolio are a number of smaller *satellite portfolios*. The satellite portfolios are actively managed and even have the ability to take short positions, because they can borrow securities from the core portfolio, that is, they can go short against the core (see Fig. 13.11).

With bond portfolios, an example of a mixed strategy is *contingent immunization*. The fund manager begins with an active strategy, and continues in this mode until the end of the investment horizon or until the return on the active strategy falls below a threshold level, at which point the bond portfolio is immunized for the remainder of the investment horizon.

Another type of mixed active–passive strategy involves options and futures. With one version of this strategy, fund managers have passive portfolios of cash-market securities. The portfolio is not traded because of the high transactions costs of trading in the cash market. Instead, the fund managers trade a view on individual securities by buying or selling individual stock options. Similarly, they can engage in market timing and shift the beta of their share portfolio (or the duration of their bond portfolio) by buying or selling stock-index or gilt options and futures (this is illustrated in Section 13.12 below). This is because transactions costs are low (at least for institutional investors) and liquidity is generally high in the markets for derivatives.

With another version of this strategy, what are called *equitized cash portfolios* are constructed. The entire value of the portfolio is held pas-

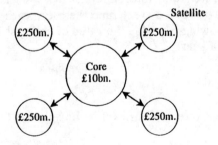

Fig. 13.11. Core–satellite portfolios

sively in money-market instruments. The active part of the strategy is performed entirely with futures. Yet another version is known as a *90–10 portfolio*. In this case 90 per cent of the portfolio is held in cash and 10 per cent in options. With money-market interest rates at around 10 per cent, the strategy locks in the initial value of the portfolio (since £90(1 + 0.1) ≈ £100), but gains from the intrinsic value of the options if they expire in-the-money.

13.9. Performance Measurement

At the end of each year (sometimes at the end of each quarter) the pension-fund manager's performance is going to be measured. Sometimes this function is performed by the fund manager himself or herself; more generally it is performed by an independent performance-measurement service. The questions that are important for assessing how well a fund manager performs are:

- How do we measure the *ex-post* returns on his or her portfolio?
- How do we measure the risk-adjusted returns on his or her portfolio?
- How do we assess these risk-adjusted returns?

To answer these questions, we need to examine returns, risks, and benchmarks of comparison.

13.9.1. *EX-POST* RETURNS

There are two ways in which *ex-post* returns on the fund can be measured: *time-weighted rates of return* (or geometric means), and *money-weighted* (or *value-weighted*) *rates of return* (or internal rates of return). The simplest method is the money-weighted rate of return, but the preferred method is the time-weighted rate of return, since this controls for cash inflows and outflows which are beyond the control of the fund manager. However, the time-weighted rate of return has the disadvantage of requiring the fund to be valued every time there is a cash flow.

Consider the following, showing the value of and cash flow from a fund over the course of a year:

Time	0	6 months	1 year
Value of fund	V_0	V_1	V_2
Cash flow	—	CF	—

The money-weighted rate of return (r) is the solution to (assuming compound interest):

$$V_2 = V_0(1 + r) + CF(1 + r)^{1/2} \qquad (20)$$

or to (assuming simple interest):

$$V_2 = V_0(1 + r) + CF(1 + \tfrac{1}{2}r); \tag{21}$$

in the latter case, this implies that:

$$\text{Money-weighted rate of return} = \frac{V_2 - (V_0 + CF)}{V_0 + \tfrac{1}{2}CF}. \tag{22}$$

The time-weighted rate of return is defined as:

$$\text{Time-weighted rate of return} = \frac{V_1}{V_0} \frac{V_2}{V_1 + CF} - 1. \tag{23}$$

If the semi-annual rate of return on the portfolio equals r_1 for the first six months and r_2 for the second six months then we have:

$$V_1 = V_0(1 + r_1) \tag{24}$$

and

$$\begin{aligned} V_2 &= (V_1 + CF)(1 + r_2) \\ &= (V_0(1 + r_1) + CF)(1 + r_2). \end{aligned} \tag{25}$$

Substituting (24) and (25) into (23) gives:

Time-weighted rate of return

$$\begin{aligned} &= \frac{V_0(1 + r_1)}{V_0} \left(\frac{(V_0(1 + r_1) + CF)(1 + r_2)}{V_0(1 + r_1) + CF} \right) - 1 \\ &= (1 + r_1)(1 + r_2) - 1 \end{aligned} \tag{26}$$

which is a chain-linking of returns between cash flows.

TABLE 13.4. *Example of time-weighted rate of return*

Time	0	6 months	1 year
Share-price index	(1.0)	(0.8)	(1.2)
Cash flow into Fund A	20	—	—
Value of Fund A including cash flow	120	96	144
Cash flow into Fund B	10	10	—
Value of Fund B including cash flow	110	98	147

It is clear that the time-weighted rate of return reflects accurately the rate of return realized on the portfolio. The cash flow could be an inflow ($CF > 0$) such as a dividend payment or a contribution payment from the employer, or an outflow ($CF < 0$) such as a pension pay-out. Both inflows and outflows are beyond the control of the fund manager and their effects should be excluded from influencing the performance of the fund.

We can illustrate this using the example in Table 13.4 where the initial value of two funds is £100. Both funds receive £20 during the year but the timing of the cash flows is different: Fund B receives cash at a time when shares are relatively cheap.

The money-weighted rate of return can be calculated as follows:

Money-weighted rate of return on Fund A
$$= \frac{V_2 - (V_0 + CF_1)}{(V_0 + CF_1)}$$
$$= \frac{144}{120} - 1$$
$$= 0.20 \ (20\%)$$

Money-weighted rate of return on Fund B
$$= \frac{V_2 - (V_0 + CF_1 + CF_2)}{V_0 + CF_1 + \frac{1}{2}CF_2}$$
$$= \frac{147 - 120}{115}$$
$$= 0.2348 \ (23.48\%).$$

So the Fund B manager is performing better than the Fund A manager according to the money-weighted rate of return measure.

The time-weighted rate of return is calculated as follows:

Time-weighted rate of return on Fund A
$$= \frac{V_1}{(V_0 + CF_1)} \frac{V_2}{V_1} - 1$$
$$= \frac{96}{120} \frac{144}{96} - 1$$
$$= 0.20 \ (20\%)$$

Time-weighted rate of return on Fund B
$$= \frac{V_1}{(V_0 + CF_1)} \frac{V_2}{(V_1 + CF_2)} - 1$$
$$= \frac{88}{110} \frac{147}{98} - 1$$
$$= 0.20 \ (20\%).$$

The time-weighted rate of return of 20 per cent is the same in both cases. This reflects the true performance of both funds over the period, since they were both invested in the same shares. (Note that the money-weighted and time-weighted rates of return are the same when there is no intermediate cash flow, as in the case of Fund A.)

13.9.2. ADJUSTING FOR RISK

The *ex-post* rate of return has to be adjusted for the fund's exposure to risk. The appropriate measure of risk depends on whether the beneficiaries of the fund's investments have other well-diversified investments or whether this is their only set of investments. In the first case, the *systematic risk* (beta) of the fund is the best measure of risk. In the second case, the *total risk* (standard deviation) of the fund is best. If the portfolio is a bond portfolio, then the appropriate measure of market risk is *relative duration*.

13.9.3. BENCH-MARKS OF COMPARISON

In order to assess how well a pension-fund manager is performing, we need one or more bench-marks of comparison. Once we have determined appropriate bench-marks we can then compare whether the fund manager outperformed, matched, or under performed the bench-marks on a risk-adjusted basis.

An appropriate bench-mark is one that is consistent with the preferences of the fund's trustees and the fund's tax status. For example, a different bench-mark is appropriate if the fund is a *gross fund* (and does not pay income or capital-gains tax, as with a pension fund) than if it is a *net fund* (and so does pay income and capital-gains tax, such as the fund of a general insurance company). Similarly, the general market index will not be appropriate as a bench-mark if the trustees have a preference for high-income securities and an aversion to shares in rival companies or, for moral reasons, the shares in (for example) tobacco companies. Yet again, the FT-A All Share Index would not be an appropriate bench-mark if half the securities were held overseas. There will, therefore, be different bench-marks for different funds and for different fund managers. For example, consistent with the asset-allocation decision, there will be a share bench-mark for the share-fund manager and a bond bench-mark for the bond-fund manager.

So the bench-mark will be an index of one kind or another. It is important to understand the structure of the relevant index. We can distinguish between *absolute* and *relative* indices, between *price-weighted*

TABLE 13.5. *Example of index construction*

Day	Share number	Price (£)	Number of shares (millions)	Capitalization (£m.)
1	1	0.65	50	32.50
	2	0.82	50	41.00
	3	1.15	75	86.25
	4	0.25	100	25.00
	Sum =	2.87		Sum = 184.75
2	1	0.70	50	35.00
	2	0.78	50	39.00
	3	1.23	75	92.25
	4	0.21	100	21.00
	Sum =	2.92		Sum = 187.25

and *value-weighted* indices, and between *arithmetic* and *geometric* indices. These can be explained using Table 13.5, which contains the input for an index containing four shares. If day 1 is the base date, then the base price-weighted absolute index is given by:

$$\text{Index} = \frac{2.87}{0.0287} = 100$$

and the base value-weighted absolute index is given by:

$$\text{Index} = \frac{184.75}{1.8475} = 100.$$

On day 2 the *price-weighted absolute index* is:

$$\text{Index} = \frac{2.92}{0.0287} = 101.74$$

while the *value-weighted absolute index* is:

$$\text{Index} = \frac{187.25}{1.8475} = 101.35.$$

The day 2-to-day 1 price-relatives for the four shares are given by:

Share number	Price-relative
1	1.0769 (0.70/0.65)
2	0.9512 (0.78/0.82)
3	1.0696 (1.23/1.15)
4	0.8400 (0.21/0.25).

The *equal-weight arithmetic relative index* for day 2 is:

$$\text{Index} = \frac{1.0769 + 0.9512 + 1.0696 + 0.8400}{4} \times 100 = 98.44.$$

The *equal-weight geometric relative index* for day 2 is:

$$\text{Index} = [(1.0769)(0.9512)(1.0696)(0.8400)]^{1/4} \times 100 = 97.95.$$

So the four indices give quite different results even across just one day's price movements, with two rising and two actually falling. So it is important that the returns on the portfolio are constructed in the same way as the bench-mark index. For example, the FT-A All Share and the FTSE100 Indices are value-weighted arithmetic absolute, whereas the FT30 Index and the FT Government Securities Index are equal-weight geometric relative.

Not only is a pension-fund manager's performance compared with the return on a market index, it is also compared relative to the performance of other pension-fund managers. This provides a second bench-mark of comparison. Pension-fund managers are generally ranked in order of decreasing returns, and the objective of every fund manager is to be in the first *quartile* of performance, and certainly to be above the *median* fund. Of course, only half the funds can beat the median fund!

There is often a third bench-mark against which the performance of a pension-fund manager is compared. This is the rate of inflation in the retail price index. So another test is whether the fund manager can generate a portfolio return sufficient to beat inflation and therefore provide a positive real return to the fund. An even more stringent bench-mark is the rate of wage inflation as measured by increases in the index of national average earnings; this is because wage inflation is typically 2 percentage points higher than price inflation, reflecting the fact that real wages in the UK grow at about 2 per cent p.a. This performance measure is consistent with a pension fund's liabilities, which in the case of final-salary schemes increase on average at the rate of wage inflation.

13.10. Measures of Portfolio Performance

13.10.1. PERFORMANCE MEASURES BASED ON RISK-ADJUSTED EXCESS RETURNS

There are three performance measures based on risk-adjusted excess returns (that is, returns in excess of the riskless rate of interest), each one distinguished by the risk measure used.

The first is the *excess return to volatility measure,* also known as the *Sharpe measure* (Sharpe 1966). This uses the total risk measure:

$$\text{Excess return to volatility (Sharpe)} = \frac{r_p - r_f}{\sigma_p} \qquad (27)$$

where

r_p = average return on the portfolio (usually geometric mean) over an interval (typically the last twenty quarters);

σ_p = total risk as measured by the standard deviation of the return on the portfolio (calculated over the last twenty quarters). Note: the geometric mean is used to construct the average return, but the arithmetic mean must be used to construct the standard deviation;

r_f = average risk-free return (usually geometric mean) over the same interval.

The Sharpe measure is illustrated in Fig. 13.12. *BM* is the bench-mark portfolio (it could be the market portfolio). *A*, *B*, *C*, and *D* are four portfolios. Portfolios *A* and *B* beat the bench-mark on a risk-adjusted basis, while portfolios *C* and *D* under-perform the market. Portfolio *A* is the best (that is, is ranked highest according to the Sharpe measure) and Portfolio *D* is the worst. The ranking of the portfolios on a risk-adjusted basis is *A*, *B*, *C*, *D*; but the ranking of the portfolios without adjusting for risk is *B*, *C*, *A*, *D*. This shows the importance of adjusting for risk. Portfolio *C*, for example, was exposed to substantial risk during the year, but did not generate sufficient returns to justify that exposure.

The second performance measure is the *excess return to beta measure*, also known as the *Treynor measure* (Treynor 1965). This uses the systematic risk measure:

$$\text{Excess return to beta (Treynor)} = \frac{r_p - r_f}{\beta_p} \qquad (28)$$

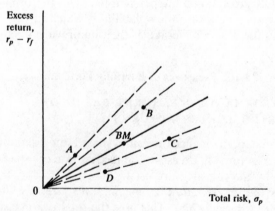

Fig. 13.12. Excess return to volatility

where

β_p = beta of the portfolio (calculated over the last twenty quarters).

This is illustrated in Fig. 13.13.

The third is the *excess return to relative duration measure*, a measure suitable for bond portfolios:

$$\text{Excess return to relative duration} = \frac{r_p - r_f}{D_p/D_m} \qquad (29)$$

where

D_p/D_m = duration of bond portfolio relative to duration of the market.

This is illustrated in Fig. 13.14.

How should these measures be interpreted? Let us compare the Sharpe and Treynor measures. Suppose that the Sharpe and Treynor measures for an individual fund and for the market are as follows:

	Individual fund	Market
Sharpe	1.3	1.6
Treynor	5.0	4.0

Comparing Treynor measures, the individual fund manager is good at market timing, but comparing Sharpe measures, is less good at security selection: he has taken on a lot of specific risk (which could have been diversified away) and has not been adequately rewarded for doing so.

13.10.2. PERFORMANCE MEASURES BASED ON ALPHA

As an alternative to ranking portfolios according to their risk-adjusted returns in excess of the riskless rate, it is possible to rank portfolios

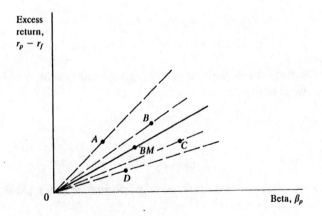

Fig. 13.13. Excess return to beta

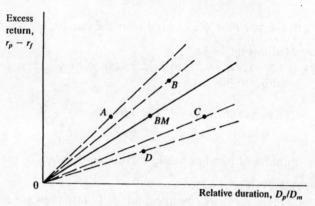

Fig. 13.14. Excess return to relative duration

according to their alpha values. Again, three different performance measures are available depending on the risk measure used.

If the risk measure is total risk, the appropriate alpha value is defined with respect to the capital market line:

$$\bar{r}_p = r_f + \left(\frac{\bar{r}_m - r_f}{\sigma_m}\right)\sigma_p \tag{30}$$

where
$\bar{r}_p$ = expected return on the portfolio;
$\bar{r}_m$ = expected return on the market;
σ_m = standard deviation of the market.

The corresponding alpha is:

$$\alpha_\sigma = r_p - \bar{r}_p. \tag{31}$$

This is shown in Fig. 13.15. The best-performing fund is the one with the largest alpha.

If the risk measure is systematic risk, the relevant alpha is defined with respect to the security market line:

$$\bar{r}_p = r_f + (\bar{r}_m - r_f)\beta_p \tag{32}$$

so that:

$$\alpha_\beta = r_p - \bar{r}_p. \tag{33}$$

This is known as the *Jensen differential performance index* (Jensen 1969). It is illustrated in Fig. 13.16.

If the risk measure is relative duration, the relevant alpha value is defined with respect to the bond market line:

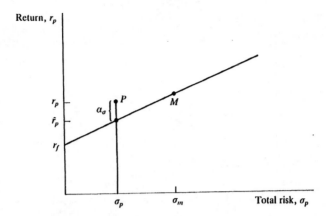

Fig. 13.15. Alpha defined on volatility

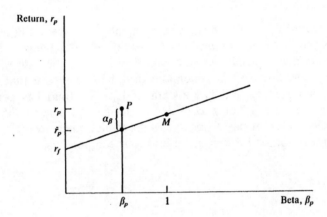

Fig. 13.16. Alpha defined on systematic risk

$$\bar{r}_p = r_f + (\bar{r}_m - r_f)\frac{D_p}{D_m} \tag{34}$$

so that:

$$\alpha_D = r_p - \bar{r}_p. \tag{35}$$

This is illustrated in Fig. 13.17.

13.11. The Decomposition of Total Return

Having discussed various measures of the performance of a fund, the next task is to identify the sources of that performance. This involves breaking

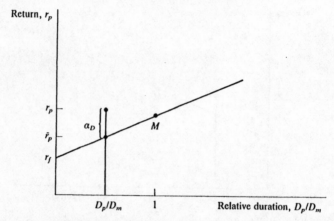

Fig. 13.17. Alpha defined on relative duration

down the total return into various components. One way of doing this is known as the *Fama decomposition of total return* (after Fama 1972).

The Fama decomposition is shown in Fig. 13.18 in the case where the relevant measure of risk is systematic risk, beta. Suppose that Fund P generates a return r_p and has a beta of β_p. The fund has performed well over the period being considered. Using the Jensen differential performance index, it has a positive alpha value, equal to $(r_p - r_2)$. The total return r_p can be broken down into four components:

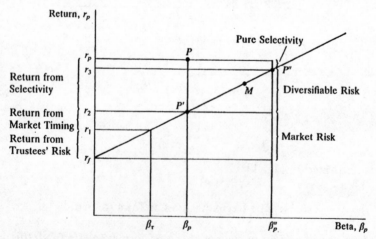

Fig. 13.18. Fama decomposition of total return

Return on the portfolio
= Riskless rate
+ Return from trustees' risk
+ Return from market timing
+ Return from security selection.   (36)

The first component of the return on the portfolio is the riskless rate, r_f: all fund managers expect to earn at least the riskless rate.

The second component of portfolio return is the return from the trustees' risk. The fund manager will have assessed the trustees' degree of risk tolerance to correspond with a beta measure of β_τ, say. The trustees are therefore expecting a return on the portfolio of at least r_1. The return from the trustees' risk is therefore $(r_1 - r_f)$.

The third component is the return from market timing. This is also known as the return from the fund manager's risk. This is because the pension-fund manager has chosen (or at least ended up with) a portfolio with a beta of β_p which differs from that expected by the trustees. The fund manager has implicitly taken a more bullish view of the market than the trustees. He or she has consequently decided to raise the beta of the portfolio above that expected by the trustees. He or she has done this· by selecting a portfolio with a larger proportion invested in the market portfolio and a smaller proportion invested in the riskless asset than the trustees would have selected. In other words, the fund manager has engaged in market timing. With a portfolio beta of β_p, the expected return is r_2, so that the return from market timing is $(r_2 - r_1)$.

The fourth component is the return from selectivity (that is, the return from security selection). It is equal to $(r_p - r_2)$ and is known as the return from selectivity for the following reason. Consider portfolios P and P' in Fig. 13.18. They both have the same amount of market risk, because they both have the same beta, β_p. However, they have different total risks. Portfolio P' contains no diversifiable risk since it lies on the security market line. Portfolio P, however, lies above the SML. It is therefore not a linear combination of the market portfolio and the riskless asset (only portfolios along the SML are). In other words, P differs from P' because P's manager has engaged in active security selection. This has resulted in portfolio P earning an additional return, but the fund manager has had to take on diversifiable risk to do so.

Is the extra return worth the risk? To answer this question we need to compare portfolio P with another portfolio which lies on the SML and which has the same total risk. Suppose that this other portfolio is P''. P'' is found as follows. Suppose that the total risk of P and P'' is $\sigma_p^2 = 30$. Since P'' lies on the SML, we know that all the risk of P'' is undiversifiable and that this is equal to $(\beta_p'')^2\sigma_m^2$ (see equation (13)). If $\sigma_m^2 = 25$, it follows that:

$$\beta_p'' = \sigma_p/\sigma_m = \left(\frac{30}{25}\right)^{1/2} = 1.1.$$

The return on P'' is r_3 (given that the beta of P'' is β_p''), while the return on P is r_p. Since r_p is greater than r_3, it means that the risk from selecting P was worthwhile. The additional return from taking on additional diversifiable risk is $(r_3 - r_2)$. But the portfolio P fund manager has done even better than this, and earned an additional return $(r_p - r_3)$, known as the return from pure selectivity.

Fig. 13.18 can also be used to show a different decomposition from that given by equation (36). The return $(r_2 - r_f)$ is the return from taking on market risk: it is equal to the sum of the returns from the trustees' risk and the manager's risk. Similarly, the return from security selection can be broken down into the return from diversifiable risk and the return from pure selectivity. Therefore an alternative decomposition to equation (36) is:

> Return on the portfolio
> = Riskless rate
> + Return from market risk
> + Return from diversifiable risk
> + Return from pure selectivity.   (37)

The Fama decomposition was done in terms of beta and is therefore important for share portfolios. It is possible to perform a similar decomposition in terms of bond portfolios using relative duration (see, for example, Fong, Pearson, and Vasicek 1983).

We can illustrate the Fama decomposition using the following data on a pension fund based on the previous twenty quarters:

$$\begin{array}{ll} r_p = 20\% & r_m = 16\% \\ \sigma_p = 15\% & \sigma_m = 12\% \\ \beta_p = 0.9 & r_f = 10\%. \end{array}$$

The trustees' desired beta is given as $\beta_\tau = 0.8$. Using this, we can calculate the expected return on the trustees' desired portfolio. A beta of 0.8 implies a portfolio that is 80 per-cent invested in the market and 20 percent invested in the riskless asset. Therefore:

$$r_1 = 0.2(10) + 0.8(16)$$
$$= 14.8\%.$$

This means a return from trustees' risk of:

$$r_1 - r_f = 14.8 - 10.0$$
$$= 4.8\%.$$

However, the actual beta of the portfolio is 0.9, implying that it is 90 per-cent invested in the market and 10 per-cent invested in the riskless asset. This in turn implies an expected return on the actual portfolio of:

$$r_2 = 0.1(10) + 0.9(16)$$
$$= 15.4\%.$$

This gives a return from market timing of:

$$r_2 - r_1 = 15.4 - 14.8$$
$$= 0.6\%.$$

The next step is to find the portfolio P'' with the same total risk as the pension-fund portfolio P. This portfolio has a beta of:

$$\beta_p'' = \sigma_p/\sigma_m$$
$$= 15/12$$
$$= 1.25.$$

Portfolio P'' is invested 125 per cent in the market and -25 per cent in the riskless asset (that is, with borrowings at the riskless interest rate equal to 25 per cent of the fund's value). The expected return on this portfolio is:

$$r_3 = -0.25(10) + 1.25(16)$$
$$= 17.5\%.$$

Therefore the return from diversifiable risk is:

$$r_3 - r_2 = 17.5 - 15.4$$
$$= 2.1\%.$$

This leaves the return from pure selectivity as:

$$r_p - r_3 = 20.0 - 17.5$$
$$= 2.5\%.$$

The decomposition of total return can be used to identify the different skills involved in active fund management. For example, one pension-fund manager might be good at market timing but poor at stock selection. The evidence for this would be that his $(r_2 - r_1)$ was positive but his $(r_p - r_2)$ was negative. He should therefore be recommended to invest in an index fund but be able to select his own combination of the index fund and the riskless asset. Another pension-fund manager might be good at stock selection but poor at market timing. He should be allowed to choose his own securities but someone else should choose the combination of the resulting portfolio of risky securities and the riskless asset.

13.12. Hedging

13.12.1. THE OBJECTIVE OF HEDGING

The objective of *hedging* (or *risk management*) is to transfer risk from one individual or corporation to another individual or corporation. The person offloading the risk is the *hedger*; the person taking on the risk is the *speculator* or *trader*.

The hedger is concerned with adverse movements in security prices or with increases in volatility which increase the overall riskiness of his or her position. For example, if a pension fund has a long position (net asset position) in cash-market securities, the fund manager will be concerned about the prices of those securities falling and will want to protect against this possibility. Alternatively, if the pension fund has a short position (net liability position) in cash-market securities, the fund manager will be concerned about rising prices and will want to protect against this possibility.

In order to hedge successfully and so transfer all (or at least most) risk, the hedger will have to select a suitable hedging instrument. A good hedging instrument will be one whose price movements mirror closely those of the underlying cash-market securities. Two of the most suitable hedging instruments will therefore be instruments that are derivative upon cash-market securities, namely financial futures and options.

Financial futures and options were first introduced in the early 1970s in response to the huge increase in interest- and exchange-rate volatility that resulted from the ending of fixed exchange rates and the increase in world inflation rates. The first hedging instruments were therefore designed to hedge against adverse movements in interest rates and exchange rates. Later, the introduction of (exchange-traded) options on individual shares, and options and futures on stock-market indices allowed share-price movements to be hedged as well.

Pension funds have been involved in hedging since the early 1980s. However, the Inland Revenue initially treated pension-fund activities using futures and options as trading and hence not exempt from taxation. This severely limited these activities. But the 1990 Social Security Act exempted pension-fund profits from futures and options from taxation, and this has significantly increased their use.

13.12.2. HEDGING WITH FUTURES

Futures contracts can be used to hedge interest-rate risk (both short-term and long-term), stock-market risk, and exchange-rate risk. There are some simple rules for hedging with futures:

- if *short cash* (that is, expecting a cash inflow and worried that prices will rise or interest rates will fall), then *buy futures* (that is, put on a *long hedge*);
- if *long cash* (that is, holding cash or securities and worried that prices will fall or interest rates will rise), then *sell futures* (that is, put on a *short hedge*).

The number of futures contracts required to hedge a cash position is determined as follows. We construct a *hedge portfolio* from a long position in the cash security and a short position in h units of the corresponding futures contract (where h is the *hedge ratio*). If the initial cash position is a short one, then the hedge portfolio involves a long position in h units of the futures contract. In the first case, the value of the hedge portfolio (P^h) is given by

$$P^h = P^s - hP^f \tag{38}$$

where P^s is the value of the cash security and P^f is the value of the futures contract. The optimal hedge ratio is determined to ensure that the hedge portfolio is riskless, or, in other words, has a constant value independent of whether the value of the cash security rises or falls. This requires:

$$\Delta P^h = \Delta P^s - h\Delta P^f$$
$$= 0 \tag{39}$$

(where Δ denotes a change in the value of), so that the hedge ratio is determined as:

$$h = \frac{\Delta P^s}{\Delta P^f}. \tag{40}$$

Equation (40) says that the hedge ratio is set equal to the ratio of the volatility of the price of the underlying cash-market security being hedged to the volatility of the futures contract being used to hedge it. If the price of the cash-market security tends to be more volatile than that of the futures contract, then the hedge ratio will exceed unity, so that more futures contracts will be needed to hedge the underlying cash position than the face value of that position. The opposite holds if futures are more volatile than cash.

The number of futures contracts necessary to hedge a cash security is given by:

$$\text{Number of contracts} = \frac{\text{Face value of cash exposure}}{\text{Face value of futures contract}} \times h \quad (41)$$

that is, the number of contracts equals the hedge ratio scaled up by the ratio of the face value of the cash exposure to the face value of the futures contracts. With the number of contracts determined in this way, the hedge will be *perfect* (that is, completely riskless for small changes in security prices). This is depicted in Fig. 13.19 which shows the value of a hedged portfolio comprising a long position in cash securities (P^s) and a short position in h futures contracts (P^f). If the hedge is put on when the value of the cash portfolio is P_0^s, then the hedged position locks in a portfolio value P_0^h equal to the futures price P_0^f at the time the hedge is implemented. This value is locked in so long as the hedge is maintained until the expiry date of the futures contracts, whatever subsequently happens to the value of the underlying securities.

13.12.2.1. *Hedging with Stock-Index Futures*

13.12.2.1.1. *Full Hedging* Stock-index futures contracts (such as the FTSE100 contract on LIFFE—the London International Financial Futures and Options Exchange) can be used to hedge the systematic risk from holding equity portfolios. We can illustrate the use of such contracts with the following example.

Suppose that on 1 April a pension-fund manager is uncertain about where the market is going over the next three months and wishes to hedge £1m. of his equity portfolio which has a beta of 1.15. On 1 April the FTSE100 index is standing at 2,204.0 and the value of the June contract on LIFFE is 2,300.0. Because the fund manager is long in the cash market, he will need to be short in the futures market to hedge the portfolio. The fund manager has to calculate the number of futures contracts that have to be sold in order to hedge the portfolio. He has to

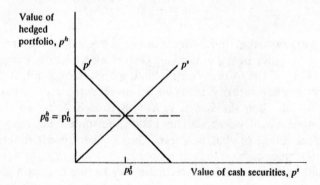

Fig. 13.19. Hedging with futures

calculate the cost of putting on the hedge and he also has to calculate the value of the portfolio that he is locking in.

Since the value of each one-point movement (known as a *tick*) in the LIFFE FTSE100 contract is worth £25, the fund manager will need to sell futures contracts according to the following formula:

$$\text{Number of contracts} = \frac{\text{Face value of cash exposure}}{\text{Face value of futures contract}} \times \beta_p$$

$$= \frac{\text{Face value of cash exposure}}{\text{Tick value} \times \text{Futures price}} \times \beta_p \quad (42)$$

where β_p, the beta of the portfolio, is the hedge ratio. Using the data in the example, this means that the fund manager needs to sell:

$$\text{Number of contracts} = \frac{£1,000,000}{£25 \times 2,300.0} \times 1.15$$

$$= 20 \text{ June contracts}$$

to hedge the portfolio exactly. Because the portfolio beta exceeds unity, more contracts will be needed for a perfect hedge than if the portfolio exactly matched the market index and had a beta of unity.

The portfolio value that the fund manager is locking in is based on the index value of the June contract, namely 2,300.0 (so long as the futures contract is held to expiry). The fund manager knows that, whatever happens to the cash-market index between 1 April and 30 June, his hedged portfolio will have a value on 30 June determined by:

Terminal value of hedged fund

= Initial value of hedged fund

$$\times \left[1 + \left(\frac{P^f(1 \text{ April}) - P^s(1 \text{ April})}{P^s(1 \text{ April})} \right) \times \beta_p \right] \quad (43)$$

where
P^f = futures index or price;
P^s = cash index or price.

That is:

Terminal value of hedged fund

$$= £1,000,000 \times \left[1 + \left(\frac{2,300.0 - 2,204.0}{2,204.0} \right) \times 1.15 \right]$$

$$= £1,050,091.$$

The fund manager cannot use futures contracts to lock in the current value (as of 1 April) of the cash index; he can only lock in the current value (as of 1 April) of the futures index for 30 June. The reason why the portfolio value is fixed for 30 June is that the cash and futures positions are exactly offsetting. If the cash index rises between 1 April and 30 June, the value of the cash portfolio rises by an amount which exactly offsets the fall in the value of the futures contracts. The opposite holds for a fall in the index over the period.

We have considered the case of a pension-fund manager who has a long cash portfolio, and is worried that equity prices will fall; he therefore sells futures. Another pension-fund manager might be expecting a cash inflow into his fund in the near future and is worried that equity prices will rise before the cash inflow arrives. He is therefore said to be short cash and will want to hedge this position by buying futures contracts.

13.12.2.1.2. *Partial Hedging* In the last subsection, we considered the case of a pension-fund manager who hedged the full value of his portfolio in order to eliminate the systematic risk contained in it. He could instead have hedged only part of his portfolio. Depending on how it is done, partial hedging is equivalent to active fund management and it is a way of engaging in active fund management much more cheaply than can be done in the cash market. We can consider a number of active portfolio strategies as partial hedges: changing asset allocation, market timing, and security selection. These strategies are collectively known as *overlay strategies*.

A cheap and simple way of changing the asset allocation of the portfolio between shares, bonds, and money-market securities is by buying or selling futures contracts. Suppose, for example, that a pension-fund manager wanted to increase the proportion of shares in the portfolio. He could do this by first buying stock-index futures contracts. This locks in the prices of shares prior to buying them in the market. This strategy is also known as *pre-positioning*.

Market timing with an equity portfolio is equivalent to beta trading, that is, trading in and out of high-beta stocks depending on whether the fund manager's views are bullish or bearish. This strategy is expensive in terms of transactions costs, however, and identical results can be achieved much more cheaply using stock-index futures contracts. This can be seen from the perfect-hedge example given above. The £1m. portfolio, which was fully hedged by selling twenty futures contracts, was entirely unresponsive to market movements and so had a beta of zero, exactly the same as the riskless asset. But any portfolio beta can be achieved with appropriate use of futures contracts. The portfolio beta with futures (β_{pf}) is given by:

$$\beta_{pf} = \beta_p + \theta_f \beta_f \qquad (44)$$

where $\theta_f \beta_f / \beta_p$ is the proportion of the portfolio covered by futures ($\theta_f > 0$ if futures are purchased, $\theta_f < 0$ if futures are sold), and β_f is the beta for the futures contract. (Normally we would set $\beta_f = 1$, but in practice stock-index futures contracts are slightly more volatile than the underlying index, implying that $\beta_f = 1.1$ approximately.) In the above example, a portfolio beta of 0.8 could be achieved by selling six futures contracts (that is, $20 \times (-0.35)/1.15 \simeq -6$, since $\theta_f = -0.35$), while a portfolio beta of 2.0 could be achieved by buying fifteen contracts (that is, $20 \times 0.85/1.15 \simeq 15$, since $\theta_f = 0.85$).

A third active strategy is security selection. Stock-index futures allow the fund manager who is skilled at security selection to separate this activity from market timing. By holding a long position in shares and an appropriate short position in stock-index futures, the fund manager can remove any market risk from holding the shares but retain the specific risk. He or she will do this if he or she believes the particular share is underpriced relative to the market. In other words, he or she is putting on a *relative-performance bet* and has constructed a *relative-performance portfolio*. If he or she is correct he or she will earn an appropriate return to security selection. With stock-index futures contracts it is possible to hedge the systematic risk of a portfolio but not the specific risk in the individual shares in the portfolio. In order to hedge this non-systematic risk it is necessary to use individual stock options. (This strategy will be discussed in Section 13.12.3.1.)

13.12.2.2. *Hedging with Bond Futures*

13.12.2.2.1. *Full Hedging* Bond futures contracts (such as the long gilt contract on LIFFE) can be used to hedge the systematic risk or the interest-rate risk from holding bond portfolios. Suppose that a fund manager believes that interest rates will rise and that as a consequence the value of his bond portfolio will fall. One alternative would be to dispose of the bonds and repurchase them after interest rates have risen. But this would involve transactions costs, and also there is no guarantee of being able to repurchase the same portfolio of bonds. A much cheaper alternative is for the fund manager to use the long gilt futures contract to temporarily 'step outside' his portfolio.

Bond futures contracts are priced off the *cheapest-to-deliver* (CTD) bond from the range of deliverable bonds. If the price of the CTD bond changes, so does the futures price and in the same direction. The relationship between changes in the futures price and the price of the CTD bond (see, for example, Blake 1990, chap. 8) is given by:

$$\Delta P^f = \frac{1}{PF_{\text{CTD}}} \Delta P_{\text{CTD}} \tag{45}$$

where

ΔP^f = change in the price of the long gilt future;

ΔP_{CTD} = change in the price of the CTD bond;

PF_{CTD} = price factor for the CTD bond (which converts the CTD bond into a bond with a yield to maturity of 9 per cent as required by the LIFFE long gilt futures contract).

It follows from equation (45) that the futures price moves by less than the cash bond if the price factor (PF_{CTD}) exceeds unity and by more otherwise. This relationship can be used to hedge CTD bonds. However, it should be remembered that the relationship is approximate because it excludes any allowance for accrued interest and so on.

Suppose that on 1 April a pension-fund manager is expecting a cash inflow of about £1.20m. in two months' time which he intends investing in the CTD bond (which we suppose to be Treasury 12.5 per-cent 2013–15 with a price factor of 1.3032131 and currently trading at £118 per £100 nominal). He is concerned that yields will fall and gilt prices will rise against him. Because he is short cash, he decides to hedge his exposure by purchasing long gilt futures contracts on LIFFE. To do this he buys June contracts according to the following formula:

$$\text{Number of contracts} = \frac{\text{Face value of cash exposure}}{\text{Face value of futures contract}} \times PF_{CTD} \quad (46)$$

where $h = PF_{CTD}$ is the hedge ratio and where

$$\text{Face value of cash exposure} = \frac{\text{Market value of cash exposure}}{P_{CTD}}$$

where P_{CTD} is the market price of the CTD bond. That is,

$$\text{Number of contracts} = \frac{£1,000,000}{£50,000} \times 1.3032131 = 26$$

since the long gilt futures contract on LIFFE has a face value of £50,000. Note that the number of contracts depends on the face value of the futures contract *and* the face value of the cash exposure. Since P_{CTD} is £118 per £100 nominal, a market exposure of around £1.2m. is equivalent to a nominal exposure of around £1m. (that is, £1m. $\simeq$ £1.2m./1.18).

When a bond other than the CTD bond is being hedged the duration of both bonds must be taken into account (this procedure is known as *duration-based hedging*). Duration is defined by equation (10) above and measures the interest-rate sensitivity of the price of a bond. It is easy to show that the following relationship between a bond's price, its yield to maturity, and its duration holds (see, for example, Blake 1990, chap. 5):

$$\Delta P = (-D) \times P \times \Delta rm/(1 + rm) \qquad (47)$$

where
   D = duration of a bond;
   P = price of a bond;
   rm = yield to maturity on a bond.

Equation (47) shows that for a given change in yield, the change in the price of a bond is greater the greater its duration. Therefore, the more price-sensitive the bond to be hedged is compared with the CTD bond, the larger the number of futures contracts that will be needed to hedge that bond. Suppose that the bond to be hedged is the Treasury 13.5 per-cent 2013 (denoted by the subscript H below), then the *duration hedge ratio* is given by:

$$DHR = \frac{\Delta P_H}{\Delta P_{CTD}} = \frac{D_H \times P_H \times \Delta rm_H \times (1 + rm_{CTD})}{D_{CTD} \times P_{CTD} \times \Delta rm_{CTD} \times (1 + rm_H)}. \qquad (48)$$

This ratio can be simplified if we assume parallel yield-curve movements (that is, $\Delta rm_{CTD} = \Delta rm_H$):

$$DHR = \frac{\Delta P_H}{\Delta P_{CTD}} = \frac{D_H \times P_H \times (1 + rm_{CTD})}{D_{CTD} \times P_{CTD} \times (1 + rm_H)}. \qquad (49)$$

It can be simplified even further if we assume parallel percentage-yield-curve movements (i.e. $\Delta rm_{CTD}/(1 + rm_{CTD}) = \Delta rm_H/(1 + rm_H)$):

$$DHR = \frac{\Delta P_H}{\Delta P_{CTD}} = \frac{D_H \times P_H}{D_{CTD} \times P_{CTD}}. \qquad (50)$$

Using (50) and assuming that P_H = £126.25, D_{CTD} = 11.6 years and D_H = 13 years, then:

$$DHR = \frac{13 \times 126.25}{11.6 \times 118.00} = 1.199.$$

In terms of duration, the Treasury 13.5 per-cent 2013 bond is equivalent to 1.2 CTD bonds in the sense that it is about 20 per-cent more volatile than the CTD bond. This suggests that the appropriate number of con-tracts required to hedge this bond is given by:

$$\text{Number of contracts} = \frac{\text{Face value of cash exposure}}{\text{Face value of futures contract}} \times PF_{CTD} \times DHR \qquad (51)$$

that is (assuming again a nominal exposure of £1,000,000):

$$\text{Number of contracts} = \frac{£1,000,000}{£50,000} \times 1.3032131 \times 1.199$$

$$= 31 \text{ contracts.}$$

In terms of hedging bond portfolios, again it is possible to use duration-based hedging. Suppose that the duration of the portfolio (see equation (11) above) is 14.2 years and the weighted average price (per £100 nominal) of the bonds in the portfolio is £110.125. Then the appropriate duration hedge ratio for the portfolio is

$$DHR_p = \frac{D_p \times P_p}{D_{CTD} \times P_{CTD}} \tag{52}$$

where

D_p = duration of the portfolio;
P_p = weighted average price of the bonds in the portfolio;

that is,

$$DHR_p = \frac{14.2 \times 110.125}{11.6 \times 118.00} = 1.142.$$

The number of futures contracts necessary to hedge a £10m. bond portfolio is given by:

$$\text{Number of contracts}$$
$$= \frac{\text{Face value of cash exposure}}{\text{Face value of futures contract}} \times PF_{CTD} \times DHR_p$$
$$= \frac{£10,000,000}{£50,000} \times 1.3032131 \times 1.142$$
$$= 298.$$

13.12.2.2.2. *Partial Hedging* Using the gilt futures contract for partial hedging provides the fund manager with a relatively inexpensive vehicle for engaging in active bond-fund management or overlay.

Take, for example, market timing. With a bond portfolio, market timing is equivalent to *duration trading*. At the onset of a bear market the bond manager might trade out of high-duration bonds into low-duration bonds. This is expensive in terms of transactions costs. A much cheaper alternative is to use futures contracts to hedge the portfolio. In this way, any desired bond-fund duration target can be achieved. For example, a perfect hedge consisting of long cash bonds and (the appropriate number of) short contracts in gilt futures will have a zero net change in capital value whatever happens to underlying interest rates. The duration of the hedge will be zero. Any desired duration can be achieved using

$$D_{pf} = D_p + \theta_f D_f \tag{53}$$

where D_{pf} is the duration of the portfolio hedged with futures, D_f is the duration of the futures contract (equal to the duration of the CTD bond) and $\theta_f D_f / D_p$ is the proportion of the portfolio hedged with futures.

So it is clear how hedging is equivalent to market timing. Futures can be used to move the bond portfolio's duration about while keeping the underlying cash-bond portfolio fixed. If the pension-fund manager thinks that interest rates are going to fall he or she buys futures; if he or she thinks that they are going to rise, he or she sells futures.

Another activist strategy using futures contracts is *pre-positioning*, that is, locking in prices prior to buying or selling a bond. Suppose that a pension-fund manager wishes to purchase a substantial amount of a particular gilt (say £200m.). If he attempted to do this in a single tranche, market makers would exploit this by hiking up the price against him. On the other hand, if he attempted to purchase the required amount in £20m. tranches over two or three days, general market prices might have moved against him. The solution is for the fund manager to pre-position using futures contracts and then to purchase the bond in tranches when they become available on the market. In order to pre-position £200m. of the bond, the fund manager would purchase 4,000 futures contracts. He would then purchase the bond in tranches and simultaneously sell an equivalent number of futures contracts. This strategy fully protects the fund manager against falls in interest rates. Similarly, if the fund manager wished to sell a substantial amount of a particular gilt, he could pre-position by first selling an equivalent number of futures contracts and then buy them back as the cash bonds were sold. Pre-positioning is a particularly effective strategy when the futures market is more liquid than the cash market. This is true of the Treasury bond market in the USA. However, the long gilt futures market on LIFFE is not (yet) as liquid as the underlying cash gilt market, so that prepositioning on LIFFE may not be as easy as it is in the USA.

Futures can also be used to aid another activist strategy, bond selection. Suppose that an analysis of the yield curve suggests that the Treasury 8 per-cent 2019 is relatively underpriced. The pension-fund manager would like to remove any market risk and trade only what he believes to be the relative mispricing of this bond; in other words, he would like to place a *relative-performance bet* against the market. With equities this is easy because the stock-index futures contract involves a market index. With bonds, on the other hand, the relative-performance bet is against the CTD bond, not a bond-market index. This is because the bond futures contract is priced off the CTD bond rather than an index. So a bond relative-performance bet cannot entirely remove market risk. Nevertheless, the procedure for placing the bet is simple. Because the Treasury 8 per-cent 2019 bond is underpriced, the fund manager buys the gilt and sells an equivalent number of futures contracts. Had the gilt been relatively overpriced rather than underpriced, the procedure for placing the bet is theoretically more complicated. In the USA the bet is feasible because of the existence of a *repurchase market* in government bonds. In the UK, which currently lacks a repurchase market, the placing of relative-performance bets on overpriced bonds is virtually impossible unless the fund manager runs a satellite portfolio within a core–satellite configuration. This is because of the difficulty of shorting the overpriced bond. With a repurchase market it is possible to short the bond by *reversing* it into the repurchase market and buying futures contracts against the reverse position. Once the relative mispricing had corrected itself (say after three days), the bond would be *repoed* out of the repurchase market.

13.12.2.3. *Hedging with Currency Futures*

Hedging exchange-rate risk with currency futures contracts is an alternative to hedging with forward contracts. To illustrate the use of currency futures, we can consider the case of a pension-fund manager who is expecting dividend payments on his US investments of $3m. It is now 1 April and the dividend payments are due on 1 June. They will be repatriated immediately, and the fund manager is concerned that sterling will rise against the dollar between 1 April and 1 June. To hedge against this risk the fund manager decides to buy sterling currency futures contracts on the International Monetary Market (IMM) of the Chicago Mercantile Exchange (CME) which have a contract size of £62,500 traded against the dollar (that is, the fund manager is short cash sterling and therefore needs to be long sterling contracts to hedge the exposure).

Suppose that on 1 April the spot exchange rate is $1.75 per £, and the June IMM futures price is $1.77. At the spot exchange rate the dividend payments are valued at £1,714,285.71 (that is, $3,000,000/$1.75) in sterling. The number of sterling contracts necessary to hedge this exposure is determined as follows:

$$\text{Number of contracts} = \frac{\text{Face value of cash exposure (sterling)}}{\text{Face value of futures contract (sterling)}} \quad (54)$$

that is,

$$\text{Number of contracts} = \frac{£1,714,285.71}{£62,500} = 27.$$

So a short exposure of £1,714,285.71 can be hedged by buying twenty-seven sterling futures contracts. The contracts have a sterling value of

£1,687,500 (that is, 27 × £62,500) and a dollar value of $2,986,875 (that is, £1,687,500 × $1.77).

13.12.3. HEDGING WITH OPTIONS

Hedging using options can be a more flexible alternative to hedging using futures. Futures are used when the amount and timing of the exposure are known with certainty: a futures contract locks in the price of a specific amount of an asset at a specific future date. Options can be used when either the amount or the timing of the exposure is not known with certainty. Options can also be used when the hedger wants to protect against adverse price movements but would like to benefit from favourable price movements: with futures, the hedger gains when prices move in one direction but loses when prices move in the opposite direction. In addition to being able to hedge interest-rate risk, stock-market risk, and exchange-rate risk, it is also possible to use options contracts to hedge the specific risks of individual securities (a hedging possibility not generally available using futures). (Note that *call options* give the right but not the obligation to buy the underlying security, while *put options* give the right but not the obligation to sell the underlying security.)

13.12.3.1. *Hedging with Individual Stock Options*

The simplest way for a pension-fund manager to hedge a long position in ABC shares is to purchase an at-the-money put option with an *exercise price* equal to the current price of the share. Figure 13.20 shows the profit-and-loss profile for this combination when the share price is trading at 115p (shown by the dashed line). The fund manager is protected (at the cost of the premium on the put) if the share price falls below 115p and

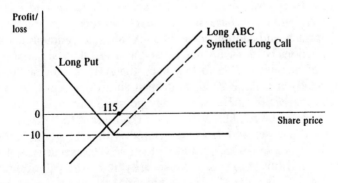

Fig. 13.20. A fixed hedge using a long at-the-money put

keeps the gains he would make if the share price rises above 115p. But this profit-and-loss profile is exactly the same as that of a long-call option. In other words, the combination of a *long share* and a *long put* is equivalent to a *synthetic long call*.

The pension-fund manager has a number of alternatives to hedge a portfolio of ABC shares. He could hold on to ABC and buy an at-the-money put. Alternatively, he could sell ABC and buy an at-the-money call. Obviously, he will do whatever is cheaper, taking into account transactions costs. Suppose that on 1 April, with ABC trading at 115p, the June 115p call is trading at 12p and the June 115p put at 10p. The riskless rate of interest is 10 per cent and ABC has annual dividends of 6 per cent (assume quarterly dividends are paid at the end of each quarter). We can consider the two hedging alternatives.

The first alternative involves holding on to ABC, earning the dividends, and buying the put option. The net cash flow per share from this position as of 30 June is as follows:

Purchase of 115p put option on 1 April × interest factor:	$-10 \times (1 + 0.1(91/365))$
Dividends on ABC on 30 June:	$115 \times 0.06(91/365)$
	$-8.53p$

The second alternative involves selling ABC and investing the proceeds at 10 per cent and buying the call option. The net cash flow per share from this position as of 30 June is as follows:

Interest on ABC sale:	$115 \times 0.1(91/365)$
Purchase of 115p call option on 1 April × interest factor:	$-12 \times (1 + 0.1(91/365))$
	$-9.43p$

So the first alternative is less expensive than the second: it is better to hold on to ABC and buy the put. This solution is likely to be reinforced when transactions costs are taken into account. The second alternative involves a sale and a purchase and so incurs two sets of transactions costs involving spreads and commissions. The first alternative involves only one set of transactions costs. A further disadvantage of the second alternative is the risk of not being able to buy back the ABC shares at the end of June, especially if a large block had been sold on 1 April. At the end of June the market for ABC stock may be quite thin and a large block of shares may not be readily available on the market to be repurchased.

To avoid the costs and risks associated with selling the underlying security, there is a hedging alternative to selling the security and buying call options, and this is to retain the security and write call options. This is illustrated in Fig. 13.21. The combination is a *synthetic short put* and the hedger is protected from a limited decline in the price of ABC

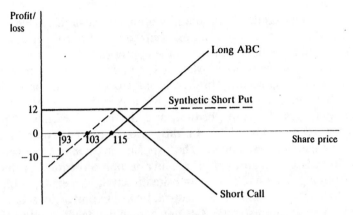

Fig. 13.21. A fixed hedge using a short at-the-money call

shares because of the premium earned from writing the call option. The premium on the June call option is 12p and this protects the hedger from a 12p fall in the share price.

Comparing Figs. 13.20 and 13.21, it is clear that the share price would have to fall to less than 93p (or by more than 19 per cent) before hedging with a short call leads to larger losses than hedging with a long put. Nevertheless, the long put (Fig. 13.20) gives complete downside protection, whatever the fall in the share price, and has better upside potential in the event of the share price rising rather than falling. We can see that the profit on the short call (Fig. 13.21) is limited to 12p whatever the rise in the share price, whereas with the long put (Fig. 13.20), the upside potential is unlimited.

So we have the following simple rules for hedging with options:

- if the cash position is adversely affected by *falling* prices, then *buy puts* or *sell calls*;
- if the cash position is adversely affected by *rising* prices, then *sell puts* or *buy calls*.

But when should we use options in preference to futures? The answer depends (i) on whether the exposure in terms of amount or timing is certain or uncertain, and (ii) on whether the exposure is symmetrical or asymmetrical.

The exposure is *certain* (both in amount and timing), for example, for a pension-fund manager planning to repatriate dividends denominated in dollars on a given future date and wishing to guarantee the sterling value of the dividends. In this case a currency futures or forward contract is the appropriate hedging instrument. On the other hand, a pension-fund manager wanting to reduce the volatility of his or her fund's value through a partial hedge faces an *uncertain* exposure over an *uncertain* time interval. In this case an options contract is the appropriate hedging instrument.

The exposure is *symmetrical* when it is equally responsive to a rise or fall in the underlying security price. This means that a price move in one direction benefits the cash position, while a price move in the opposite direction damages the cash position, and the hedger wishes to protect against the second possibility. In this case, a futures contract is the appropriate hedging instrument. The exposure is *asymmetrical* when the cash position is damaged by a price move in one direction but does not benefit from a price move in the opposite direction. An example of this is a bank that has provided an interest-rate cap guarantee to a borrower: the bank loses if interest rates fall but does not benefit if interest rates rise. In this case, an options contract is the appropriate hedging instrument.

Once an options hedge has been chosen, the next step is to decide whether to use a fixed hedge or a ratio hedge.

A *fixed hedge* is a one-off options hedge designed to limit the maximum loss on the hedged position, but to benefit from any upside potential. In other words, a fixed options hedge is rather like an insurance policy: in return for a premium, the minimum value of a cash position is guaranteed. A fixed hedge hedges the full amount of the actual or expected exposure and the hedge is maintained until the exposure is eliminated, at which point the options are either sold or exercised. The hedges illustrated in Figs. 13.20 and 13.21 above were examples of fixed hedges.

A *ratio* (or *delta-neutral*) *hedge* is designed to establish and preserve a combined cash-and-options position that is delta-neutral over time. The *delta* of an option measures the responsiveness of the option price (P^o) to changes in the price of the underlying security (P^s):

$$\text{Delta} = \frac{\Delta P^o}{\Delta P^s}. \tag{55}$$

We know from equation (40) above that the hedge ratio is determined by (using equation (55)):

$$h = \frac{\Delta P^s}{\Delta P^o} = \frac{1}{\text{Delta}}. \tag{56}$$

Since delta is the inverse of the hedge ratio, a delta-neutral hedge is one in which the ratio between the number of options and the number of securities being hedged is always kept equal to the inverse of the option delta. This implies that a ratio hedge has to be re-balanced whenever the option delta changes.

To illustrate, we will consider a ratio hedge involving a combination of a long position in ABC shares and a long position in put options. The number of put-option contracts necessary to hedge the ABC shares is determined as follows:

$$\text{Number of contracts} = \frac{\text{Number of shares}}{\text{Option delta} \times 1,000}. \qquad (57)$$

Since the standard options-contract size is for 1,000 shares (in the UK), we must divide the number of shares by 1,000. In addition, because the delta of an option is always less than unity, more options contracts will be required to construct a ratio hedge than a fixed hedge. For example, if the delta of the put option used to hedge 30,000 ABC shares is 0.75, then the number of put options required to construct the ratio hedge is given by:

$$\text{Number of contracts} = \frac{30,000}{0.75 \times 1,000} = 40 \text{ contracts}$$

equivalent to 1.33 (that is, 1/0.75) contracts per 1,000 shares (compared with a fixed hedge which uses 1 contract per 1,000 shares).

Fig. 13.22 illustrates a ratio hedge using 1.33 long at-the-money puts per 1,000 ABC shares. It shows both the short-term profit-and-loss profile and the profit-and-loss profile at expiration. In the short term the hedge is both delta-neutral and *gamma-positive*, so that it shows a short-term profit whether the price of ABC shares rises or falls (*gamma* measures the change in an option's delta as the price of the underlying security changes). As the share price changes, the ratio hedge will have to be re-balanced. The process of *ratio-hedge management* is illustrated in Fig. 13.23. The initial position is at *A*. Suppose that after several weeks the

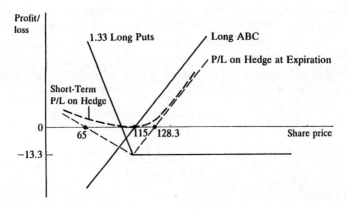

Fig. 13.22. A ratio hedge using at-the-money puts

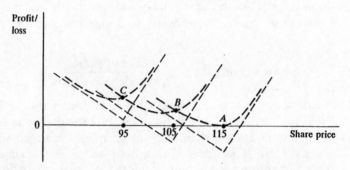

Fig. 13.23. Ratio-hedge management

share price had fallen to 105p, so that the hedger is sitting on a profit. However this profit is not guaranteed, so the hedger will want to lock in the profit by re-balancing the hedge at B with respect to the new option delta. The hedge is again re-balanced at C when the share price falls to 95p, and a further profit is locked in.

Because frequent re-balancing will be an expensive process, it is advisable to use a ratio hedge only when a cheaper alternative is not available, that is, when it is desired to hedge a cash position continuously over time rather than for a specific date. When a specific sum is going to be hedged for a specific date, then a fixed options hedge or even a futures hedge should be used.

13.12.3.2. *Hedging with Stock-Index Options*

The aim of hedging with individual stock options is to hedge the specific (or non-systematic) risks of individual shares. The aim of hedging with stock-index options, on the other hand, is to hedge the systematic (or market) risk of a portfolio of shares. We must therefore take into account the beta of the portfolio being hedged. The specific risks attached to the individual shares in the portfolio remain unhedged by this strategy.

The number of contracts needed to hedge a portfolio of shares is determined as follows. For a fixed hedge:

$$\text{Number of contracts} = \frac{\text{Face value of cash exposure}}{\text{Face value of index}} \times \beta_P$$

$$= \frac{\text{Face value of cash exposure}}{\text{Tick value} \times \text{Index level}} \times \beta_P. \quad (58)$$

For a ratio hedge:

$$\text{Number of contracts} = \frac{\text{Face value of cash exposure}}{\text{Face value of index}} \times \frac{\beta_P}{\text{Option delta}}. \quad (59)$$

To illustrate, we will suppose that on 15 July a pension-fund manager has a £5m. portfolio with a beta of 1.15 which he intends to hedge by buying LIFFE November 1850 put options on the FTSE100 index (which have a tick value of £10). The closing index on 15 July is 1825.00 and the fund manager intends employing a fixed hedge. The number of contracts to hedge the portfolio is found using (58):

$$\text{Number of contracts} = \frac{£5,000,000}{£10 \times 1825.00} \times 1.15 = 315.$$

Hedging with individual stock options eliminates all risks, while hedging with stock-index options eliminates only systematic risk. A pension-fund manager who hedges the systematic risk in his portfolio is therefore taking on a *relative-performance bet* against the market. He is eliminating the market risk in his portfolio but leaving it exposed to specific risk which, if he is good at security selection, he will be very pleased to do. In short, he is hoping to beat the market, having eliminated market risk.

13.12.3.3. *Hedging with Bond Options*

It is possible to hedge long-term interest-rate risk using options on bond futures. The following rules apply:

- calculate the best futures hedge;
- for a fixed hedge, replace the futures hedge with the same number of options contracts;
- for a ratio hedge:

$$\text{Number of contracts} = \frac{\text{Number of contracts in futures hedge}}{\text{Option delta}} \quad (60)$$

where the number of contracts in the futures contract is given by equation (51) above.

In the bond-portfolio example above, 298 futures contracts were needed to hedge the portfolio. As an alternative, the portfolio could be hedged using 298 put options on the futures contracts. If the delta of the put options is 0.82, then 363 put-options contracts would be needed for a ratio hedge.

13.12.3.4. *Hedging with Currency Options*

As with other types of options hedges, hedging with currency options is useful when the hedger wants to insure against downside exchange-rate risk, but wants to preserve some of the benefits of favourable exchange-rate movements. For example, the Philadelphia Stock Exchange sterling currency option has a contract size of £31,250 traded against the dollar.

To illustrate, we will consider a UK pension-fund manager with a US portfolio valued at $1m. on 1 April when the current exchange rate is

$1.59 and the three-month forward rate is $1.65 per £. Suppose that he decides to hedge half the portfolio against a rise in sterling over the next three months (the fund manager is short sterling cash and therefore needs to be long call options and/or short put options; if he is both long calls and short puts, he has created *synthetic long futures*). A fixed hedge would involve the purchase of the following number of Philadelphia SE June 1.60 sterling call options contracts (that is, with an exercise price of $1.60 per £1):

$$\text{Number of contracts} = \frac{\text{Face value of cash exposure (sterling)}}{\text{Face value of option contract (sterling)}} \quad (61)$$

that is,

$$\begin{aligned}
\text{Number of contracts} &= \frac{\$500,000/\$1.59}{£31,250} \\
&= \frac{£314,465.41}{£31,250} \\
&= 10.
\end{aligned}$$

If the *option premium* is 3.5 cents per £, then the total cost of the contracts is $10,937.50 (that is, 10 contracts × $0.035 premium × £31,250). If, instead, a ratio hedge is used and the option delta is 0.435 then 23 contracts (that is, 10/0.435) will have to be purchased and this will raise the cost of the hedge to $25,156.25.

The cost of the options, therefore, lies between 2.2 per cent (that is, $10,937.50/$500,000) and 5.0 per cent (that is, $25,156.25/$500,000) of the fund being hedged. Since this is usually much greater than the cost of forward cover (about 0.5 per cent of the value of the exposure), options are generally less favoured than forward cover. Because of the option premium, the effective exchange rate locked in by the option is $1.635 (that is, exercise price of $1.60 + premium of $0.035).

13.12.4. HEDGING WITH SWAPS

Swaps provide an alternative to futures and options as hedging instruments. For example, a pension-fund manager with fixed coupon bonds in his portfolio who expected a temporary rise in interest rates could execute an *asset swap* and hence earn a return related to market rates.

This can be illustrated as follows. Suppose that the pension-fund manager holds £50m. nominal of bonds trading at par with a coupon of £10 per £100 nominal. He executes an asset swap with a bank whereby he retains ownership of the bonds, but makes fixed-rate payments to the bank of 9.75 per cent on £50m. and in return receives floating-rate payments from the bank equal to LIBOR (the London Inter-Bank Offer Rate). The cash flows involved in this transaction from the pension fund's point of view are as follows. The pension fund:

- earns from the fixed coupon bond   10%
- pays to the bank   (9.75%)
- receives from the bank   LIBOR

LIBOR + 0.25%

and so receives floating-rate payments on £50m. of LIBOR plus 0.25 per cent. In other words, the pension fund has transformed its fixed-coupon bonds into *synthetic floating-rate notes* (FRNs) yielding LIBOR plus 0.25 per cent.

If at the time of the swap LIBOR was 9.50 per cent, then the synthetic FRNs would yield 9.75 per cent, which is less than the yield on the fixed-coupon bonds. If, however, immediately after the swap had taken place LIBOR rose to 10.50 per cent, then the synthetic FRNs would yield 10.75 per cent. This is a yield of 0.75 per cent higher than that on the fixed-coupon bonds, equivalent to £375,000 p.a. on £50m. The increase in yields would reduce the value of the underlying bonds, of course, but the pension-fund manager believes that the increase in interest rates is only temporary, say, because the government has imposed a temporary credit squeeze. If this squeeze is expected to last about eighteen months, at which time interest rates are expected to return to their original levels, the fund manager could unwind the swap. Bond prices would return to their original levels and the fund manager would have saved the costs involved in selling the bonds before rates rise and repurchasing them before rates subsequently fall again; this was the only procedure available to fund managers to protect themselves against rising interest rates before the introduction of swaps, futures, and options.

13.13. Pension-Fund Managers

13.13.1. THE LEADING PENSION-FUND MANAGEMENT GROUPS

Table 13.6 lists the top twenty-five pension-fund management groups in the UK in 1989 in terms of value of funds under management. Most (fourteen out of twenty-five) are subsidiaries of UK investment banks. The investment-banking subsidiaries of the four high-street retail banks (Barclays, National Westminster, Lloyds, and Midland) are represented in this subset. Seven are specialist fund managers (Henderson, Gartmore,

TABLE 13.6. *Leading pension-fund managers*

	Value of segregated funds at 31 December			Total funds (£bn., 1989)*	Number of pension-fund clients		
	1989 (£m.)	1988 (£m.)	%age change		1989	1988	%age change
Mercury Asset Management	23,616	17,754	33.0	33.82	580	553	4.9
Phillips & Drew Fund Mngt.†‡	14,242	10,620	34.1	16.26	196	185	5.9
Barclays de Zoete Wedd Investment Mngt.	13,600	9,600	41.7	19.90	128	118	8.5
Schroder Investment Mngt.‡	11,800	8,700	35.6	22.20	133	130	2.3
County Natwest Investment Mngt.§	9,464	7,840	20.7	12.29	106	122	−13.1
Robert Fleming Asset Mngt.	9,295	9,240	0.6	21.10	143	147	−2.7
Prudential Portfolio Managers ¶	9,100	6,100	49.2	34.60	56	39	43.6
Morgan Grenfell Investment Mngt.	6,453	5,243	23.1	17.16	96	98	−2.0
Henderson Pension-Fund Mngt.‖	5,464	4,917	11.1	8.83	168	195	−13.8
Baring Investment Mngt.	5,229	4,264	22.6	6.78	116	109	6.4
Gartmore Investment Mngt.	4,447	2,700	64.7	6.72	114	105	8.6
Lloyds Investment Mngt†	4,333	3,768	15.0	6.40	54	51	5.9
MIM	3,365	2,616	28.6	9.89	132	125	5.6
Midland Montagu Asset Mngt.‡	3,121	2,396	30.3	4.48	9	12	−25.0
N. M. Rothschild Asset Mngt.	2,700	2,700	0.0	9.07	75	81	−7.4
Murray Johnstone Pension Mngt.	2,666	2,100	26.9	4.70	55	57	−3.5
Kleinwort Benson Investment Mngt†	2,641	2,324	13.6	9.24	68	74	−8.1

Cazenove Fund Management	2,630	1,770	48.6	5.50	60	59	1.7
Hambros Bank†‡	2,500	2,000	25.0	4.50	48	48	0.0
Queen Anne's Gate Asset Mngt.**	2,300	1,800	27.7	2.30	9	1	n/a
Lazard Investors‡	2,000	1,800	11.1	4.10	36	34	5.9
Capital House Investment Mngt.	1,880	1,500	25.3	2.70	50	46	8.7
Eagle Star	1,754	1,465	19.7	11.80	23	22	4.5
Hill Samuel Investment Mngt.†‡	1,617	1,505	7.4	16.48	36	33	9.1
Baillie Gifford & Co. Investment Mngt.	1,576	1,042	51.3	3.49	38	35	8.6
TOTAL	147,793	115,764	27.7	294.31	2,529	2,479	2.0

Notes: * Total funds managed by group, including non-pension funds.

† 1988 data changed by the fund manager. Fund manager now called UBS International Investment.

‡ 1988 number of clients changed by the fund manager.

§ Of the net 16 clients lost, a total of 5 did not meet minimum fund-size requirements. Fund manager now called Natwest Investment Mngt.

¶ Includes Prudential Staff Pension Fund.

‖ These figures exclude the Henderson Pensions Managed Fund which is valued at £77m. and has 44 clients.

** In September 1989 reconstructed as an investment-management company to manage pension funds of the former Water Authorities; prior to September 1989, Queen Anne's Gate managed £1.8bn. of the Water Authorities' superannuation fund; percentage increase in number of clients is therefore not applicable.

Source: Financial Times Survey on Pension Fund Investments, 3 May 1990.

MIM, Murray Johnstone, Queen Anne's Gate, Capital House, and Baillie Gifford). Only two insurance companies (Prudential and Eagle Star) are represented in the top twenty-five. Three of the pension-fund management groups are foreign-owned: the broking house Phillips and Drew is owned by the Union Bank of Switzerland; the investment bank Morgan Grenfell is owned by Deutsche Bank; and the specialist fund manager Gartmore is owned by Banque Indosuez.

The largest pension-fund management group in 1989 was Mercury Asset Management, owned by investment bank S. G. Warburg. It had 580 pension-fund clients with a total £23.62bn. under management, which represented 70 per cent of the total of £33.82bn. under management; the average funds per client was £40.7m., which is quite small. The management group with the largest funds per client was Midland Montagu Asset Management, with only nine clients but £3.12bn. under management, giving average funds per client of £347m.

In total, the top twenty-five groups managed pension-fund assets of £148bn. in 1989, an increase of nearly 28 per cent over the previous year. Fifty per cent of the funds managed by the top twenty-five are owned by pension funds. Given that the total value of UK pension funds in 1989 was around £250bn., this suggests that the top twenty-five fund managers manage 60 per cent of UK pension funds. In terms of clients, there were 2,529 clients in 1989, with average funds of £58.4m. The total number of clients increased by only 2 per cent compared with the previous year. Given the often quite substantial changes in clients experienced by individual fund managers (for example, the Prudential increased its client list by 43.6 per cent while Henderson lost 13.8 per cent of its clients between 1988 and 1989), this suggests that there are often frequent changes of fund manager within the group, but no net movement to fund managers outside the group.

The Hyman Robertson pension fund management survey for 1993 found that concentration among pension fund managers was increasing. The top five fund managers had increased their share of the market by 6 per cent during the previous five years.

13.13.2. SELECTING THE FUND MANAGER

The marketing of fund-management services has become extremely important in the 1980s. Taylor (1986) describes some aspects of the marketing process. Marketing has four main functions: (i) to keep the fund-management team aware of new business opportunities resulting from legislative and capital-market developments, or the activities of competitors; (ii) the origination of new business; (iii) the design and implementation of new products and advertising campaigns; and (iv) to ensure that existing clients receive adequate attention.

The origination of new business begins with identifying a potential client, in this case a company whose pension fund requires managing. The first task is to identify key personnel in the company, using such sources as industry directories or independent consultants. The next step is to obtain a foothold and make contact with the *gatekeeper*, the person in the company whose role is to filter out potential fund managers and recommend a short list to his superior, usually the finance director. This initial contact can be made by direct communication (*cold calling*), through an established relationship, or again using consultants. The gatekeeper typically reports to a pensions subcommittee which in turn reports successively to the finance committee, the main board, and the pension-fund trustees. The next step is to exploit the foothold with the aim of taking part in the series of presentations known as the *beauty contest*, which ultimately lead through preliminary and final heats to the award of the mandate. As the fund manager crosses each hurdle the complexity of the presentations increases, since the client's emphasis inevitably switches from the elimination of unsuitable managers to the identification of each competitor's favourable characteristics. The ultimate choice usually depends to some extent on personal prejudice or the 'rapport' generated between the client and the fund-management team.

Once the mandate has been won, *client maintenance* becomes another very important task of marketing. This requires constant effort, helped both by efficient administration of the account by a designated *account executive* and, of course, by successful investment performance.

During the 1980s the most important determinant used by trustees for selecting the management group for their pension fund was good investment performance over the preceding two or three years. Without this, it has proved almost impossible for a management group to win a new mandate. Similarly, managers with recent poor investment performance are likely to lose clients.

Investment performance depends to a large extent on the investment style of the management group. As we have seen, the main investment styles are balanced management, asset-allocation management, stock-selection management, and index matching. The first three are active management styles, where the intention is to beat the market. The last is a passive management style, where the objective is to match the market. Mercury Asset Management, for example, practises a traditional balanced management style. Robert Fleming, in contrast, practises a stock-selection management style based on UK equities; in 1989 this strategy led to poor performance. The retail banks tend to use index matching.

Yet all the evidence shows that past investment performance has no implication for future investment performance and is therefore unlikely to provide a good guide to selecting a fund manager (see Section 14.1.2.3). A recent piece of evidence for this comes from a report by consultants Mercer Fraser, *Past Performance in Perspective* (1989). The report indicates that most fund managers' investment performance tends to exhibit a cyclical pattern, with a run of good years followed by a run of poor years. No fund-management group can expect to deliver systematically good performance over an extended period. The implication is that to replace a manager after a few years of poor performance may turn out to be a short-sighted strategy. On the other hand, there is no guarantee that good performance will ultimately be delivered. There appears to be a definite asymmetry in performance, since a poor management team is capable of delivering systematically poor performance indefinitely. So it is always difficult to distinguish poor cyclical from poor trend performance at least in the short term, say two to three years.

Another problem is that associated with being a victim of one's own success. Successful management teams will attract new clients, and this will eventually require the management team to be expanded. Since it is difficult to achieve this with new appointments of the same calibre, subsequent performance may suffer. Two examples of this in the 1980s were Robert Fleming and Henderson. Both had had a long tradition of good performance and in the early 1980s took on new pension-fund clients. Performance in the mid-1980s was disappointing for both existing and new clients, and by the end of the 1980s many clients had transferred to other managers. Both groups were forced to restructure and reduce the scale of their operations in order to recover performance.

Another feature of the 1980s has been the change in the selection process for fund managers. Originally pension-fund mandates were won through personal contacts between trustees (largely the employing company directors) and managers. This tended to favour traditional merchant banks. During the 1980s mandates began to be awarded through open competition. As elsewhere in the UK financial services industry during the 1980s, relationship deals have begun to be replaced by transactional deals. This tended to favour newcomers and weaken the position of the traditional fund-management groups.

It appears that lessons from the 1980s will be learned for the 1990s. Fund managers will not be judged solely on the basis of past performance, since this will inevitably lead to disappointment. Fund management is an activity that depends critically on both individual skill and judgment, and team co-operation. So the factors that will be taken into account in assessing fund-management groups will be the quality of personnel, the quality of the organization's management, the investment style of the group, and the resources devoted to investment administration and communication with trustees.

13.13.3. CHARGES FOR FUND MANAGEMENT

Table 13.7 shows the typical level of fees that are charged by fund-management groups on funds of different sizes. For funds valued at £10m., the average direct fee is 0.36 per cent of the fund value or £36,000; for funds valued at £100m., the average direct fee is 0.17 per cent or £174,000. However, when other costs, such as administration and stockbrokers' commissions, are added on, charges increase to 0.56 per cent (or £56,000) for a typical £10m. fund, and to 0.33 per cent (or £330,000) for a typical £100m. fund. It is possible for a fund to avoid

TABLE 13.7. *Total costs of investment management to the client*

	£10m. fund		£100m. fund	
	(£)	% of fund	(£)	% of fund
All managers on Bacon & Woodrow Database				
Direct fees	36,000	0.36	174,000	0.17
UK commissions	6,000		55,000	
Overseas charges	1,000		22,000	
Overseas commissions	3,000		52,000	
Unit-trust fees	8,000		18,000	
Administration	2,000		9,000	
TOTAL	56,000	0.56	330,000	0.33
Total excluding commissions	47,000	0.47	224,000	0.22
The ten largest managers				
Direct fees	40,000	0.40	159,000	0.16
UK commissions	2,000		22,000	
Overseas charges	2,000		41,000	
Overseas commissions	2,000		40,000	
Unit-trust fees	12,000		52,000	
Administration	nil		nil	
TOTAL	58,000	0.58	314,000	0.31
Total excluding commissions	54,000	0.54	252,000	0.25

Source: Bacon & Woodrow, *Financial Times*, 3 May 1990.

paying brokers' commissions in the UK by dealing directly with market-makers on a net basis. However, this would mean that the fund manager would not then get the benefit of any of the research services provided by the broker and which are provided free to clients and hence reduce the effective cost of dealing through the broker.

Fund managers typically charge an extra 0.5 per cent for dealing in overseas securities. This additional charge provides an incentive for managers to engage in churning, that is, excessive trading in overseas securities. According to *Financial Statistics*, the overseas equity portfolios of UK pension funds are turned over more than twice as frequently as their UK equity portfolios. Some fund managers also follow the practice of placing overseas investments in unit trusts, which involve a management charge of around 1 per cent. So, many overseas investments involve double charging.

In contrast, very low charges operate with index funds. For UK index funds charges as low as 0.03 per cent can be negotiated. For overseas index funds charges typically lie between 0.10 per cent and 0.15 per cent.

Specialized active managers charge quite high fees, often in excess of 0.5 per cent. Performance is essential with active fund management, and increasingly the fee is performance-related. Typically there is a flat fee plus a variable fee that is related to the excess over an index or to league-table performance (for example, being in the top quartile).

13.13.4. FUND-MANAGEMENT INFORMATION-AND-ANALYSIS SERVICES

Whatever type of investment strategy is pursued by pension funds, whether it be insured or self-insured, segregated or pooled, pension-fund trustees and managers will be well aware that the performance of their funds will depend very much on the quality of the financial advice that they receive. And it is clear that with the onset of information technology more and more resources will be devoted to the collection, analysis, and dissemination of financial data. There are two main types of service available to pension funds.

13.13.4.1. *Statistical Services*

The first of these is *statistical services*, which include daily or weekly analyses of important markets, especially the bond and shares markets. The first major providers of these services were stockbrokers who compete for business on a non-price basis. Generally this information is provided free of charge, with the stockbroker relying for his income on the commission from any deals which may result from his advice being taken (this is known as *soft-commission* business).

Besides those provided free of charge by stockbrokers, there are a number of statistical services for which the client pays directly. These can be either paper-based services or computer-based real-time services. A leader in the field of printed paper statistical services is Extel, which provides and updates a set of cards with comprehensive information on both quoted and unquoted companies. Extel and Inter-Bond also collate information on the bond market in the form of bond manuals. Chart Analysis and Investment Research of Cambridge provides a charts service and McCarthy Information provides a news-cutting service. Further information is available from the Financial Times Information Service. Statistics relating to the property market are less widespread. For example, estate agents Jones Laing Wootton, a major supplier in this field, are able only to collect information relating to properties which they themselves manage. Their data on capital values and rental yields have to be corrected for differing review periods and reversion dates, and so are reasonably reflective of the whole economy only so long as their properties form a representative sample.

The availability of modern information technology and the sheer volume of financial information from the world's financial markets have led to the rapid spread and predominance of the computer-based provision of and analyses of statistical information. One of the first uses of computers was in the immediate dissemination of stock-market prices to stockbrokers. Later more detailed information on price, yield, and price–earnings ratios was provided. Later still a complete range of information on the state of the major stock markets, foreign-exchange markets, and money markets was provided. The Reuters' Stockmaster, Videomaster, and Monitor services were examples of these three developments in the USA. Similar services are provided by Telerate, Morgan Stanley Capital International, Bloombergs, Wright Investor Services, Ford Investment Services, and Bechtel Information Services. These services' main purpose was simply the rapid provision of information for dealers. Another type of service was necessary to analyse the information. In the UK Datastream and Fintel (owned by the *Financial Times* and Extel) are major suppliers of such analytical information on the main stock markets of the world. For example, fund managers can use the service to search for shares which match certain yield, P/E (price–earnings ratio), and growth-rate requirements. The Stock Exchange itself has developed Topic which supplies information on the top shares on both the London and main overseas stock exchanges.

13.13.4.2. *Research-and-Analysis Services*

The second set of services available to pension-fund investment managers are *research-and-analysis services*. These are mainly provided by stockbrokers who undertake research at the level of the economy, at the level of the industry, and at the level of the firm. There are also international specialist providers of these services such as Frank Russell.

At the economy level stockbrokers analyse the current performance and future prospects of the British and other major world economies and how these are reflected in the state of their stock markets in respect of both shares and bonds. Sophisticated econometric modelling and forecasting techniques are frequently used. From the different stock-market views, fund managers are then able to get some idea of which economies are likely to offer the best investment opportunities over the course of the next year or so. At the industry level stockbrokers analyse the key industrial sectors of the economy in terms of current and likely future profitability, especially in relation to the remainder of the economy. And finally, at the company level stockbrokers look at the prospects of different firms in the industry with a view to determining whether different company shares being traded on the stock exchange are relatively cheap or relatively expensive. Again, fund managers can then synthesize these various sources of information in order to ascertain which industries and subsequently which companies within those industries offer the brightest prospects in the near future.

Stockbrokers will tend to concentrate their research efforts on shares which are readily marketable. This means dealing in the shares of companies with large stock-market capitalizations rather than the less-liquid shares of smaller companies, where trading can adversely affect the share price and it is possible to become locked in to such companies. Another problem is that trustees usually place limits on the proportions of any company held by the fund, and it is easy to reach these limits for small companies. For all these reasons the shares of smaller companies are under-researched and under-traded, with most stock-market activity taking place in the country's largest 200–300 companies.

Appendix: Investment-Objectives Questionnaire

1. How would you describe your outlook for the economy over the next 5 years?
   a. Very positive
   b. Somewhat positive
   c. Neither positive nor negative
   d. Somewhat negative
   e. Very negative
   f. I am undecided

2. How do you feel about investing in common stocks in general?
   a. I think stocks are very attractive and should occupy a dominant position in our portfolio.
   b. Common stocks should have a place in our investment portfolio.
   c. I think stocks are relatively risky and their use should be limited.
   d. I think stocks should be used very sparingly, if at all.

3. How would you generally categorize your investment objectives?
   a. Growth—Maximum growth of capital with little or no income considerations.
   b. Growth with income—Primary emphasis on capital growth of the fund with some focus on income.
   c. Income.

4. Does the portfolio have current income objectives (interest plus dividends)?
   No income objective
   3%
   4%
   5%
   6%
   7%
   Other. If other please describe.

5. Some plans have a need for growing investment 'income' (i.e., dividends and interest) over time. Do the plan's assets have a need for growth in 'income'? (Yes/No.)

6. If your investment manager is very positive on the outlook for common stocks, what is the maximum percentage of your portfolio you would allow to be invested in common stocks?
   0%
   20%
   40%
   60%
   80%
   100%

   In Bonds?
   0%
   20%
   40%
   60%
   80%
   100%

7. If your investment manager is very negative on the outlook for common stocks, what is the minimum percentage of your portfolio you would allow to be invested in common stocks?
   0%
   20%
   40%
   60%
   80%
   100%

In Bonds?
0%
20%
40%
60%
80%
100%

8. a. What average annual 'absolute' rate of return (as opposed to return 'relative' to a market index) do you consider to be the investment objective for a fund, on a long-term basis?
   12–14% p.a.
   10–11.9% p.a.
   8–9.9% p.a.
   6–7.9% p.a.
   Other.
   b. An increase in investment return is usually associated with an increase in the acceptable level of fluctuation of the portfolio value cycle to market cycle. Would you be willing to accept a wider possible range of fluctuation in an attempt to achieve a higher return? (Yes/No.)

9. If a target rate of return over and above the inflation rate has been established, please specify.
   Not determined
   Keep pace with inflation
   1% above inflation
   2% above inflation
   3% above inflation
   4–5% above inflation
   Other. If other, please describe.

10. Plan 'risk' can be defined in different ways. Please indicate below the single item that best describes how you tend to view risk.
    a. The possibility of not meeting the actuarial assumption (if a pension plan).
    b. The possibility of not achieving an established larger rate of return.
    c. Not at least equalling the rate of inflation.
    d. High degree of fluctuation in the value of the portfolio within a market cycle.
    e. The chance of a great loss in the value of an individual security regardless of how well the overall portfolio might perform.
    f. Other. If other, please specify.

11. The primary emphasis in examining the investment performance for the account should be on:
    a. Comparing actual returns to an 'absolute' percent return target.
    b. 'Relative' comparison. That is, comparing the actual account returns to various market indexes.

c. Using both 'absolute' and 'relative' measures.

d. I have no real preferences.

12. Bond interest varies with quality and length of maturity of the bond. What bond quality do you feel is appropriate for the portfolio?
All AAA rated
None lower than AA
None lower than A
None lower than BAA

13. The time period used in evaluating investment return has a significant impact on the probability of realizing the stated return objective. The longer used, the better chance that up and down market cycles will average out to your desired return. What investment time horizon seems most appropriate for the account?
a. Ten years or more
b. Five years
c. Three years
d. A complete market cycle
e. I do not know

14. What regularity of direct contact with your adviser is preferable?
Meetings
Annually
Semiannually
Quarterly
When deemed necessary by either the investment manager or client.

Written or oral communication
Quarterly
More frequently than quarterly
When deemed necessary by investment manager or client.

15. Is geographic location of your manager important to you? (Yes/No.)
Comment.

16. Would you consider investing a portion of the assets in tangible vehicles? (Yes/No.)
If yes, which of the following? real estate; oil and gas; precious metals; other.

17. Would you be inclined to consider the use of put and call option strategies to increase portfolio income and/or reduce volatility? (Yes/No.)

(*Source*: Shearson Lehman Brothers, 1990.)

14

Pension-Fund Investment Performance

The measurement of the investment performance of occupational pension funds was not seriously undertaken in the UK until the beginning of the 1970s. It was not until then that the trustees of pension funds became sufficiently aware of the relative performance of different pension funds to begin to have their own performance measured in some systematic way. More recently personal pensions have come on to the scene, and their investment performance also has to be measured.

The two main pension-fund performance measurement services in the UK are the WM Company and Combined Actuarial Performance Services (CAPS). The WM Company, which began providing performance-measurement services in 1975, was originally part of Edinburgh stock-brokers Wood McKenzie, but now WM stands for World Markets and the company is owned by Bankers Trust. CAPS is operated by consultant actuaries R. Watson, Mercer Fraser, Bacon and Woodrow, and Noble Lowndes. CAPS began monitoring performance in 1970. There are also a number of much smaller services operated by companies such as Wyatt, and Godwins. In addition, an analysis of the data contained in the Pension Fund Survey published in *Financial Statistics* is provided by UBS International Investment (formerly Phillips and Drew Fund Management) in its annual publication *Pension Fund Indicators: A Long Term Perspective on Pension Fund Investment*.

In this chapter we investigate the recent performance of UK occupational pension funds and personal pension schemes.

14.1. The Investment Performance of Occupational Pension Funds

In this section we examine the recent investment performance of occupational pension funds using data from *Pension Fund Indicators*, the WM Company, and CAPS.

14.1.1. THE DISTRIBUTION OF RETURNS ON PENSION FUNDS

Table 14.1 examines the annual rates of return on pension funds between 1963 and 1990. In particular, it looks at the returns generated by the average private-sector and average local-authority funds over this period.

TABLE 14.1. *Annual rates of return on UK pension funds, 1963–1990* (%)

Year	Average private-sector pension fund	Average local-authority pension fund	Inflation	
			Wages and salaries	Retail prices
1963	11.5	—	5.0	2.2
1964	−3.2	—	4.8	4.3
1965	7.0	—	6.4	4.9
1966	−0.2	—	5.7	3.3
1967	18.8	18.5	7.0	2.6
1968	25.3	23.7	6.6	6.3
1969	−8.4	−8.5	8.8	4.7
1970	0.5	0.0	13.7	7.9
1971	38.4	36.5	8.8	8.9
1972	9.3	8.5	15.9	7.7
1973	−17.1	−21.3	12.9	10.7
1974	−31.0	−31.9	29.1	18.9
1975	63.8	70.9	19.1	25.0
1976	6.8	5.7	11.4	15.1
1977	38.9	43.3	9.3	12.2
1978	6.6	4.8	13.4	8.4
1979	8.6	8.5	19.6	17.2
1980	26.4	27.5	19.3	15.2
1981	11.1	10.7	10.2	12.0
1982	30.0	32.5	7.9	5.4
1983	22.3	23.7	8.0	5.3
1984	21.9	23.0	6.5	4.6
1985	15.2	16.0	8.9	5.6
1986	22.7	24.1	9.3	3.8
1987	6.7	5.9	8.1	3.7
1988	15.4	15.3	11.0	6.8
1989	28.0	28.5	7.3	7.7
1990	−11.6	−12.3	10.1	9.3
1963–79	8.2	8.9	11.4	9.2
1980–90	16.5	17.0	9.7	7.2
1963–90	11.4	12.7*	10.7	8.4

Note: * Excluding 1963–66.

Source: *Pension Fund Indicators* (1991).

What is especially notable is the large swings in performance in the 1960s and 1970s. The boom years of 1967 and 1968 were followed by poor performance in 1969 and 1970. In 1971 there was a substantial recovery in performance, resulting from the property-led Barber boom, with an average return on assets of around 37 per cent. This was followed two years later by the property crash of 1973–4, which resulted in the value of the average pension fund's assets being cut by 50 per cent. There was a remarkable recovery in 1975 (with returns of 60–70 per cent), and this was followed in 1977 by the Healey boom, when returns of around 40 per cent are recorded.

The average annual return on pension-fund assets in the 1960s and 1970s was 8.2 per cent for private-sector funds and 8.9 per cent for local-authority funds. But this is in nominal terms. When price inflation (which averaged 9.2 per cent p.a. in the 1960s and 1970s) is taken into account, the typical pension fund made a loss in real terms of an average 1 per cent p.a. When the return on pension-fund assets is compared with wage-and-salary inflation, the picture is even grimmer. The nominal growth rate in wages and salaries, which averaged 11.4 per cent p.a. in the 1960s and 1970s, exceeded the returns being generated by pension funds by about 3 per cent p.a. Given that most pension schemes offer pensions related to final salary, this was clearly a very worrying state of affairs. It led to most pension schemes being in actuarial deficit, requiring substantial deficiency payments from employing companies in order to remain solvent.

In the 1980s, however, the story was very different. This was a decade of high stable returns both in nominal and real terms. The only important exception to this was 1987, which witnessed the global stock-market crash in October. But even this crash was nowhere near as severe as the one in 1973 and 1974, when pension funds actually lost value. In 1987 the crash came towards the end of a year which had enjoyed substantial returns, and the crash itself was not sufficient to lead to an overall loss being made on the year taken as a whole. (Performance in 1990 was actually worse than in 1987, with returns of around −12 per cent recorded.)

The average annual nominal return generated during the 1980s was 16.5 per cent for private-sector funds and 17.0 per cent for local-authority funds. Correcting for inflation, given an average price-inflation rate of 7.2 per cent, this implies average annual real returns of 9.3 per cent and 9.8 per cent respectively. Pension-fund returns even exceed wage-and-salary inflation by about 7 per cent on average.

This provides a remarkable contrast with the 1960s and 1970s. It also partly accounts for the substantial pension-fund surpluses that built up during the early 1980s. The rest of the explanation lies in the huge redundancies that were occurring during the same period. These had the effect of dramatically reducing pension-fund liabilities, since the pensions of redundant workers are related to the salary of the worker at the time of redundancy, but the pensions are not payable until the individual reaches normal retirement age. The resulting actuarial surpluses became so large that in 1986 the chancellor forced the funds to take measures to reduce the size of the surpluses to no more than 5 per cent of liabilities within five years. There were four means available: reduced employers' contributions; reduced employees' contributions; enhanced pensions; or a repatriation of surplus funds to the employer. Most schemes chose to have contributions holidays (especially employers' contributions holidays) rather than to enhance pensions. This has had the effect of substantially reducing cash inflows into the UK financial markets.

Taking the 1960s, 1970s, and 1980s together, the overall picture is less spectacular. Average annual pension-fund returns range between 11.4 per cent and 12.7 per cent. After price inflation is taken into account, private-sector pension funds averaged returns of 3 per cent p.a. in real terms, while local-authority funds averaged 4.3 per cent. The premium over wage inflation was even smaller, 0.7 per cent and 2 per cent p.a. respectively. Over the long run, therefore, pension funds are not likely to sustain the performance of the 1980s.

When compared with the best possible investment performance, that resulting from perfect knowledge of future asset returns, the actual performance of pension funds is likely to seem rather poor. Lever (1981) reminds us of the possibilities during a particularly dramatic period for the UK Stock Exchange. If £1m. had been invested in equities on 1 January 1973 it would have been worth less than £350,000 on 31 December 1974, including reinvested dividends, but if it had been invested in a deposit earning the minimum lending rate of the Bank of England it would have been worth £1.25m. By 31 May 1975 the equity portfolio would have been valued at £750,000 and the deposit would have risen to £1.3m. But if, at the end of 1974, the deposit had been switched into equities, then the fund would have been worth £2.75m. on 31 May 1975, giving an overall rate of return of about 52 per cent p.a. compared with −11 per cent p.a. for the all-equity portfolio and 11 per cent p.a. for the all-cash portfolio.

The distribution of pension-fund returns between 1970 and 1990 is given in Table 14.2. The table shows the maximum and minimum returns achieved in each year. The distribution of returns between these limits is shown by the median and upper and lower quartile rates of return. The median return is presented rather than the average return, since the latter can be distorted by freak results in the tails of the distribution. If the distribution of returns is right-skewed, the average will exceed the median, while the opposite will hold if it is left-skewed. The median return over the twenty-one-year period was 15 per cent. This means that every £1m. invested in the median fund in 1970 was worth nearly £19m. by 1990. An investment of £1m. in 1970 which subsequently achieved the same annual return as the best-performing fund for each year would be worth £340m. by 1990. In contrast, an investment of £1m. in 1970 which subsequently

TABLE 14.2. *Distribution of returns on pension funds, 1970–1990* (%)

Year	Minimum	Lower quartile	Median	Upper quartile	Maximum	Range
1970	−6	−4	1	1	5	11
1971	25	36	38	42	51	26
1972	6	11	13	16	22	16
1973	−29	−25	−22	−20	−10	19
1974	−47	−35	−31	−21	1	48
1975	12	52	66	79	104	92
1976	−9	2	4	6	14	23
1977	16	35	39	43	52	36
1978	−2	5	6	8	22	24
1979	−3	7	8	10	21	24
1980	11	26	28	30	43	32
1981	1	9	11	13	25	24
1982	9	28	31	34	44	35
1983	2	21	24	26	40	38
1984	8	18	20	22	33	25
1985	−12	14	16	18	49	61
1986	−4	22	24	26	51	55
1987	−25	0	2	5	39	64
1988	−14	10	12	14	29	43
1989	−10	29	32	34	42	52
1990	−16	−12	−10	−9	−7	9
Average	−4	12	15	18	32	36

Sources: Hager (1980) and CAPS *General Reports* (various).

achieved the same annual return as the worst-performing fund for each year would be worth only £424,000 in 1990. These results show that the average range of returns (that is, the difference between the maximum and minimum returns) was a massive 36 percentage points; even the average inter-quartile range was 6 percentage points, or 40 per cent of the median return. While, as we shall see later, the chance of the same fund being either the top-performing fund or the worst-performing fund for twenty-one years in a row is negligible, these results are illustrative of the widely differing performances of occupational pension funds in the UK.

14.1.2. EXPLAINING THE DISTRIBUTION OF RETURNS

14.1.2.1. *Some Hypotheses*

A number of hypotheses have been put forward to explain these differences in performance:

- there might be a relationship between performance and cash inflows;
- there might be a relationship between performance and the size of the fund;

TABLE 14.3. *Pension funds monitored by the WM Company, 1990*

Size-range (£m.)	No. of funds	Value (£m.)
0–5	230	644
5–15	498	4,714
15–100	551	22,245
100–1,000	243	62,292
1,000+	37	119,246
TOTAL	1,559	209,141

Source: WM Company Annual Review 1990.

- there might be a relationship between performance and the type of fund manager;
- there might be a relationship between performance and the asset-allocation strategy pursued by the fund manager;
- there might be a relationship between performance and activity (the degree of trading in the portfolio);
- there might be a relationship between performance and the security-selection decisions of the fund manager;
- there might be a relationship between performance and the market-timing strategies of the fund manager;
- some fund managers might consistently perform better than others.

We will investigate these hypotheses using evidence provided mainly by the pension funds monitored by the WM Company, but also with supporting evidence from CAPS.[1]

14.1.2.2. *Related Data on Performance*

In 1990 the WM Company monitored the portfolios of 1,559 pension funds with a total market value of £209bn., which represents three-quarters of the total value of directly invested pension schemes in the UK. Table 14.3 shows the distribution of these funds (which WM calls the *WM universe*) according to size. The range is from 230 funds with assets below £5m. (with an average size of £2.8m.) to thirty-seven funds with assets in excess of £1bn. (with an average size of £3.2 bn.). The overall average fund size is £134m.

Table 14.4 shows the average returns generated by the WM universe in

---

[1] The distribution of returns on the funds monitored by WM is very similar to those monitored by CAPS. Table 14.2 presents CAPS returns because CAPS has been monitoring returns for a longer period than WM.

TABLE 14.4. *Average returns on pension-fund asset categories, 1985 and 1990 (%)*

Asset category	Returns			Standard deviation 10 yrs.
	1985	1990	10 yrs.	
UK equities	19.8	−9.8	18.5	13.9
Overseas equities	10.8	−27.3	14.7	23.4
UK bonds	12.6	7.9	14.0	14.0
Overseas bonds	—	−1.4	—	—
Index-linked	0.2	3.9	—	—
Cash/Other	19.9	12.6	11.1	4.8
TOTAL (excluding property)	16.1	−10.8	16.0	13.7
UK property	3.6	−7.5	11.4	10.7
Overseas property	—	−12.7	—	—
TOTAL (including property)	14.5	−10.6	15.1	12.3
Retail price index	5.7	9.3	6.4	2.6
Average earnings index	8.9	10.1	8.6	1.2

Source: *WM Company Annual Review* 1990.

1985, in 1990, and for the ten-year period 1981–90. The year 1985 was a good one for the funds. They returned 20 per cent on both their UK equity holdings and cash deposits. Only UK property and index-linked bonds turned in pedestrian performances. In total, the funds generated a return of 16.1 per cent if property is excluded and 14.5 per cent if property is included, thus comfortably beating inflation, whether measured by prices or wages. In contrast, in 1990 investment performance was little short of disastrous, with all asset categories losing money with the exception of UK bonds, index-linked bonds and cash deposits; performance overseas was particularly poor. Overall, the funds lost nearly 11 per cent of their value in nominal terms and about 20 per cent in real terms.

The average performance of the pension funds during the 1980s as a whole, however, was impressive, with strong contributions from each asset category, particularly UK equities. The average annual return was 15.1 per cent. Given that the average inflation rate was 6.4 per cent, this suggests that the funds monitored by WM generated annual real returns of nearly 9 per cent during the 1980s. Returns of this size could not last indefinitely, as the results for 1990 showed.

Table 14.4 also shows the annualized *standard deviation* of the returns over the ten-year period 1981–90. Standard deviations measure the *volatility* of asset returns: the higher the standard deviation, the greater the volatility. Standard deviations have the following interpretation (which assumes that the returns on assets follow the *normal distribution*). We can expect the actual return on an asset to lie within one standard deviation of the average return on the asset in two out of every three years. Similarly, we can expect the actual return on an asset to lie within two standard deviations of the average return on the asset in nineteen out of every twenty years. For example, in any three-year period we can expect the return on UK equities to lie in the range 4.6~32.4 per cent (that is, 18.5 ± 13.9) for two years, and outside the range for one year. Similarly, in any twenty-year period, we can expect the return on UK equities to lie in the range −9.3~46.3 per cent (that is, 18.5 ± 27.8) for nineteen years and outside the range for just one year. Clearly, the smaller the standard deviation the narrower the range of variation. The standard deviation increases with the riskiness of the asset. Table 14.4 shows that overseas equities were the most risky assets held in pension-fund portfolios during the 1980s and cash deposits were the least. This is not surprising. What is perhaps more surprising is that UK equities and UK bonds had the same degree of risk during the 1980s, at 14 per cent p.a. Given that the return on UK equities exceeded that on UK bonds by 4.5 percentage points, this suggests that UK bonds did not generate a return consistent with their degree of risk.

Table 14.5 shows the distribution of returns made by the WM universe of pension funds on their asset holdings during 1990. As would be expected, the *median fund* (the 50th-percentile firm) made returns very similar to the weighted average returns given in Table 14.4. The total return (including property) made by the median fund was −10.4 per cent. The worst-performing funds made returns of less than −15.8 per cent, and the best-performing funds made returns of more than −6.5 per cent.

The distribution of the total return is very close to the distribution of the return on UK equities. This is because pension-fund portfolios were heavily weighted with UK equities during 1990, as Table 14.6 shows. The weighting in UK equities increased from 53 per cent to 54 per cent during the year. This was in spite of the fall in the values of UK equity holdings by £13.9bn. from £127bn. to £113.1bn. The explanation for this is that, although their capital values fell, £4.7bn. of new money was devoted to purchases of UK equities during the year.

Table 14.6 also shows that the asset allocation was broadly stable during 1990, with the exception of overseas equities, which ended the year with a portfolio weighting of 18 per cent, 3 percentage points less than at the beginning of the year. The explanation for this lies principally in a rate of return approaching −30 per cent. Nevertheless, 15 per cent of

TABLE 14.5. *Distribution of returns on pension-fund asset categories, 1990*

Asset category	Percentiles				
	95th	75th	50th	25th	5th
UK equities	−15.7	−11.3	−9.3	−7.3	−5.0
Overseas equities	−32.2	−29.6	−27.2	−24.5	−20.0
UK bonds	−1.2	6.1	8.2	10.3	20.9
Overseas bonds	−11.9	−6.7	−0.7	5.3	8.7
Index-linked	−3.9	1.9	3.5	5.5	9.9
Cash/Other	7.7	12.7	13.9	14.8	16.4
TOTAL (excluding property)	−16.1	−12.5	−10.5	−9.1	−6.5
UK property	−14.8	−13.7	−8.5	−2.6	6.4
Overseas property	−20.4	−16.4	−16.4	−13.4	−1.0
TOTAL (including property)	−15.8	−12.4	−10.4	−9.1	−6.5

Source: *WM Company Annual Review* 1990.

cash flow was devoted to increases in overseas equity holdings. The cash-flow allocation also indicates a substantial switching away from UK bonds into overseas bonds. Overseas bond holdings almost doubled in 1990 from £3.5bn. to £6.2bn. The table also identifies the sources of asset returns. Particularly noticeable are the substantial falls in capital values experienced by equities, and the very low level of dividend income earned by overseas equities.

Table 14.7 shows the asset-allocation decisions of the WM universe during the 1980s. What is noticeable is the systematic increase in the weighting of UK equities and the systematic falls in the weightings of UK bonds and property. The fall in UK bond holdings has been mainly at the expense of overseas bond holdings: by 1990 overseas bond holdings (which only began in a significant way in 1987) were up to half those of UK bond holdings. The pension funds' holdings of index-linked bonds have been very stable at 3 per cent. In contrast, the holdings of overseas equities have been quite volatile: particularly noticeable is the dramatic fall in weighting in 1987 as a result of the October global stock-market crash. Also noticeable is the increased weighting in cash and other liquid assets in bad years, such as 1987 and 1990.

The cash-flow allocation was much more volatile than the asset allocation during the 1980s, as Table 14.8 shows. The pension funds' objective appeared to be to use cash flow to establish and then maintain a par-

TABLE 14.6. *Asset allocation, source of return, and cash-flow allocation, 1990*

Asset category	Asset allocation				Source of return			Cash-flow allocation	
	Initial		Final		Capital	Income	Total		
	£bn.	%	£bn.	%	£bn.	£bn.	%	£bn.	%
UK equities	127.0	53	113.1	54	−18.6	6.1	−9.8	4.7	58
Overseas equities	50.8	21	37.4	18	−14.6	0.8	−27.3	1.2	15
UK bonds	14.6	6	12.8	6	−0.1	1.5	7.9	−1.4	−17
Overseas bonds	3.5	2	6.2	3	−0.3	0.3	−1.4	2.9	37
Index-linked	5.7	2	5.5	3	0.0	0.2	3.9	−0.3	−3
UK property	19.6	8	17.4	8	−2.5	1.0	−7.5	0.2	3
Overseas property	2.2	1	1.6	1	−0.3	0.1	−12.7	−0.2	−3
Cash/Other	13.7	6	14.4	7	0.0	1.9	12.6	0.7	9
Currency instruments	−0.0	0	−0.0	0	0.1	−0.0	N/A	−0.0	−0
TOTAL	237.9	100	209.1	100	−36.8	11.9	−10.6	8.1	100

N/A = not applicable.
Source: WM Company Annual Review 1990.

TABLE 14.7. *Asset allocation, 1980–1990 (%)*

Asset category	1980	1981	1982	1983	1984	1985	1986	1987	1988	1989	1990
UK equities	45	44	43	44	47	49	51	54	53	53	54
Overseas equities	9	12	14	17	16	17	20	14	16	21	18
UK bonds	21	19	19	19	17	16	13	13	10	6	6
Overseas bonds	—	—	—	—	—	—	0	1	1	2	3
Index-linked	—	—	3	3	3	3	3	3	3	2	3
UK property	20	21	18	14	13	11	8	9	10	9	8
Overseas property	—	—	—	—	—	—	1	1	1	1	1
Cash/Other	4	4	3	4	4	4	4	6	6	6	7

Source: WM Company Annual Review 1990.

TABLE 14.8. *Cash-flow allocation, 1981–1990 (%)*

Asset category	1981	1982	1983	1984	1985	1986	1987	1988	1989	1990
UK equities	29	24	21	37	37	48	91	55	12	58
Overseas equities	24	25	17	–6	28	25	–16	25	83	15
UK bonds	26	22	31	24	22	6	–9	–15	–42	–17
Overseas bonds	—	—	—	—	—	–2	–1	7	19	37
Index-linked	—	9	10	10	9	7	–9	–2	1	–3
UK property	16	15	9	10	·7	2	–5	7	5	3
Overseas property	—	—	—	—	—	–1	0	1	0	–3
Cash/Other	3	4	13	24	–4	18	49	21	21	9
Currency instruments	—	—	—	—	—	–2	–1	–0	0	–0
Cash-flow ratio*	15	13	12	9	8	7	5	5	5	3

* New money as percentage of initial market value.
Source: WM Company Annual Review 1990.

ticular desired asset allocation. So, for example, the funds wanted to achieve and then maintain a weighting in UK equities of around 54 per cent, from a beginning-of-decade baseline of around 44 per cent. But because UK share prices were rising more rapidly than the values of other asset categories during the decade, this objective could be achieved with a less-than-proportionate allocation of new cash. Between 1981 and 1986 pension funds devoted only one-third of new cash to UK equity purchases. Similarly, the very stable relative holdings of index-linked bonds have been achieved by combinations of quite substantial cash investments and disinvestments on a year-to-year basis. Finally, Table 14.8 reveals the continual maturing of the funds with a systematic decline in new money invested as a proportion of the funds' market value. In 1981 cash inflows equalled 15 per cent of market value. By 1990 this figure had fallen to 3 per cent, as a result of contribution holidays mainly by employers.

14.1.2.3. *Testing the Hypotheses*

In this section we will investigate the hypotheses listed above concerning the distribution of returns generated by pension funds.

The first hypothesis suggested that there might be a relationship between performance and cash inflows: the higher the cash inflows relative to fund size, the greater the opportunity to make tactical investments and consequently the higher the return. The evidence for this is mixed. For individual funds, CAPS found that there was 'no evidence that the rate of growth of a fund [that is, the size of the cash-flow ratio] had influenced its performance' (*Pension Fund Investment Performance General Report*, 1985, p. 24). However, for pension funds as a whole, the evidence of recent years suggests some weak support for the hypothesis. Table 14.8 shows that there has been a steady decline in the cash-flow ratio between 1981 and 1990. The reduced pressure of new cash coming to the markets has had the effect of tempering price rises and reducing returns. From Table 14.2, we see that the returns on the median fund were lower at the end of the decade than at the beginning. The correlation coefficient between the size of the cash-flow ratio and the returns on the median fund is quite high at 43 per cent, providing some evidence for the hypothesis.

Table 14.9 investigates whether investment performance depends on the size of the fund. It is possible that large funds will generate greater returns because they can afford more-sophisticated and more-skilled fund managers. On the other hand, small funds might be managed more carefully and intensively just because they are small. The evidence in Table 14.9 indicates that large funds lost marginally less in 1990 than small funds (−10.3 per cent against −11.4 per cent), but that for the decade as a whole small funds made marginally more than large funds (15.5 per cent against 15.0 per cent). But these differences are probably

TABLE 14.9. *Returns by size-range of funds (%)*

Size-range (£m.):	0–5		5–15		15–100		100–1,000		1,000+		Total	
	1990	10 yrs.	1990	10 yrs.	1990	10 yrs.	1990	10 yrs.	1990	10 yrs.	1990	10 yrs.
UK equities	-10.4	18.2	-9.4	18.1	-9.5	18.1	-10.0	18.1	-9.8	18.7	-9.8	18.5
Overseas equities	-26.8	13.5	-26.8	13.9	-26.7	13.9	-27.0	13.9	-27.7	15.4	-27.3	14.7
UK bonds	7.2	13.4	7.9	13.6	7.1	13.5	6.1	13.8	8.6	14.2	7.9	14.0
Overseas bonds	-0.7	—	0.9	—	0.6	—	-1.1	—	-3.3	—	-1.4	—
Index-linked	4.5	—	3.8	—	3.4	—	3.8	—	3.9	—	3.9	—
TOTAL (excluding property)	-11.4	15.8	-10.7	15.9	-10.7	15.8	-11.3	15.9	-10.6	16.2	-10.8	16.0
UK property	-11.0	9.7	-9.5	10.0	-8.9	9.9	-4.7	11.4	-8.1	11.4	-7.5	11.4
TOTAL (including property)	-11.4	15.5	-10.7	15.5	-10.7	15.5	-10.9	15.4	-10.3	15.0	-10.6	15.1

Source: WM Company Annual Review 1990.

TABLE 14.10. *Asset allocation by size-range of funds* (%)

Size-range (£m.):	0–5		5–15		15–100		100–1,000		1,000+		Total	
	1980	1990	1980	1990	1980	1990	1980	1990	1980	1990	1980	1990
UK equities	53	59	51	57	54	57	48	56	42	52	45	54
Overseas equities	12	20	13	20	12	20	11	20	8	17	9	18
UK bonds	23	6	22	5	24	5	23	5	20	7	21	6
Overseas bonds	—	3	—	5	—	5	—	5	—	2	—	3
Index-linked	—	1	—	1	—	2	—	2	—	3	—	3
Cash/Other	5	9	6	10	4	9	4	6	5	6	5	7
TOTAL (excluding property)	93	98	92	98	94	98	86	94	75	87	80	91
UK property	7	2	8	2	6	2	13	6	25	11	20	8
TOTAL (including property)	100	100	100	100	100	100	100	100	100	100	100	100

Source: WM Company Annual Review 1990.

not statistically significant: the striking feature is the broad similarity between the returns of funds of different sizes.

Table 14.10 shows how funds of different sizes make their asset-allocation decisions and how these have changed between 1980 and 1990. The following points emerge from the table. The most important point is that small funds hold a greater weighting in equities (both UK and overseas) and in cash than large funds, and a much smaller weighting in property. This suggests that small funds are more liquid than large funds. The composition of the property portfolio also differs between small and large funds. For example, large funds hold 67 per cent of their property portfolio in UK direct property (such as offices, shops, and industrial property), 27 per cent in UK property unit trusts, and 6 per cent in overseas property. The small funds hold all their property investments in UK property unit trusts. However, during the 1980s all funds whatever their size increased UK and overseas equity holdings and reduced UK bond and property holdings.

However, despite the differences in asset allocation between small and large funds, this has not resulted in substantial differences in return. So we can conclude that there is no relationship between performance and size of fund.

Tables 14.11–15 examine pension-fund investment behaviour and performance according to type of investment manager. According to Table 14.11, 56 per cent of funds were internally managed in 1990, either wholly or partly. Another 32 per cent of funds were managed by financial conglomerates such as investment banks or insurance companies (offering either managed/pooled funds or segregated funds, where the insurance

TABLE 14.11. *Type of investment management, 1986 and 1990 (%)*

	Proportion of total	
	1986	1990
Internal	30	27
Part internal/external	29	29
Two or more managers	4	6
Financial conglomerates	23	22
Life-company managed	4	4
Life-company segregated	5	6
Independent managers	4	5

Source: *WM Company Annual Review* 1990.

company acts purely as an investment manager with no insurance factor in the services provided). Only 5 per cent of funds had totally independent boutique managers, and another 6 per cent of funds were managed by two or more competing fund managers. This distribution of fund managers had not changed very much since 1986, the only real discernible change being relatively fewer 'internally managed funds and relatively more independently managed and jointly managed funds.

Table 14.12 shows the total returns generated by the different types of fund manager between 1986 and 1990. The table shows that there is some similarity of return, both on a year-to-year basis and over a five-year average. The average return, in terms of total assets, ranges from 10.5 per cent for joint and independent fund managers to 11.3–11.4 per cent for internally managed and life-company managed funds. However, the following differences are discernible. Internally managed funds and life-company managed funds clearly pursue more conservative investment strategies than other fund managers. Their returns are lower on average in good years (such as 1986 and 1989) and higher on average in bad years (such as 1987 and 1990). The riskiest investment strategies are pursued by independent managers: they tend to achieve the best returns in good years and the worst returns in bad years. The final points to note are that financial conglomerates produce very average returns, and that the strategy of having two or more competing fund managers is not particularly successful, the average returns from this strategy being amongst the lowest. The best performance over a five-year period came from internally managed and life-company managed funds (but only by a short head). How much, if at all, do these differences in performance result from different asset-allocation strategies? And how much, if at all, do they result from different trading strategies? Tables 14.13–15 seek to answer these questions.

Table 14.13 indicates some quite substantial differences in asset-allocation patterns between different types of fund manager. For example, between 1985 and 1990 internally managed funds held on average 12.5 per cent of their assets in UK property, whereas independent managers held only 2 per cent. Internally managed funds and life-company managed funds held above-average weightings in UK bonds and UK property and below-average weightings in UK equities, reflecting the investment conservatism that was revealed in Table 14.12. In contrast, independent managers, seen in Table 14.12 to have the most volatile returns, held well-above-average weightings in the riskiest securities, equities, and below-average weightings in the safest securities, UK bonds. Funds managed by financial conglomerates and joint-managed funds also had above-average weightings in equities and below-average weightings in the other assets. Again, this is the strategy that gives above-average

TABLE 14.12. *Returns according to type of investment management, 1986–1990 (%)*

	Total (excluding property)						Total assets					
	1986	1987	1988	1989	1990	5 yrs.	1986	1987	1988	1989	1990	5 yrs.
Internal	24.6	3.4	12.2	31.4	−10.7	11.1	22.1	4.6	14.8	29.8	−10.2	11.3
Part internal/external	23.4	2.6	12.3	31.5	−10.2	10.9	21.1	3.8	14.2	29.7	−10.0	10.9
Two or more managers	24.2	1.5	10.8	31.4	−10.0	10.6	23.3	2.0	11.3	30.7	−9.9	10.5
Financial conglomerates	25.0	1.6	12.3	32.3	−11.3	10.8	23.6	2.1	13.0	31.6	−11.0	10.8
Life-company managed	25.3	4.0	11.1	29.9	−9.4	11.2	24.0	5.3	14.2	27.6	−10.0	11.4
Life-company segregated	25.9	2.6	11.5	31.1	−13.0	10.4	24.7	3.7	13.2	29.9	−12.4	10.7
Independent managers	25.3	0.4	11.0	33.2	−11.2	10.6	24.7	0.4	11.3	32.9	−11.2	10.5
Average	24.5	2.4	12.1	31.6	−10.8	10.9	22.5	3.4	13.8	30.3	−10.6	10.9

Source: WM Company Annual Review 1990.

TABLE 14.13. *Asset allocation according to type of investment management, 1985–1990 (%)*

	UK equities						Overseas equities						UK bonds						Index-linked						UK property					
	1985	1986	1987	1988	1989	1990	1985	1986	1987	1988	1989	1990	1985	1986	1987	1988	1989	1990	1985	1986	1987	1988	1989	1990	1985	1986	1987	1988	1989	1990
Internal	47	48	50	51	51	53	14	17	13	15	19	16	15	13	12	11	8	10	3	3	3	3	2	1	14	12	13	13	12	11
Part internal/external	47	49	52	51	52	53	15	17	13	15	19	16	15	13	12	10	6	6	5	4	4	4	3	4	12	10	11	12	11	11
Two or more managers	53	54	59	57	56	56	20	24	16	19	25	20	15	12	12	9	4	4	2	2	2	2	3	2	5	3	3	4	3	3
Financial conglomerates	52	54	58	56	56	56	20	23	16	19	24	20	15	12	13	9	5	5	2	3	1	1	1	1	6	4	4	4	5	6
Life-company managed	47	50	52	46	45	45	20	22	17	15	21	16	21	17	18	21	14	13	3	0	0	0	0	1	6	7	10	14	13	13
Life-company segregated	53	54	57	56	58	59	16	21	14	17	21	18	19	14	14	11	6	4	1	1	2	2	1	3	9	7	8	10	9	8
Independent managers	53	54	60	58	56	57	23	26	17	21	28	23	16	12	12	9	3	4	1	1	1	3	4	2	3	2	1	2	2	1
Average	49	51	54	53	53	54	17	20	14	16	21	18	16	13	13	10	6	6	3	3	3	3	2	3	10	8	9	10	9	8

Source: WM Company Annual Review 1990.

returns in good years and below-average returns in bad years. Over the second half of the 1980s, however, the asset-allocation strategy pursued by internally managed and life-company managed funds generated the highest average returns; although the difference between the best and worst performers was less than 1 percentage point on average.

The diversity of asset-allocation strategies by different fund-management groups during the second half of the 1980s contrasts with the convergence of strategies during the preceding decade. This convergence of strategies began after the 1973–4 UK stock-market collapse and recovery. The outcome of this experience was that the previous quite-varied investment strategies pursued by different pension funds led to such dramatically differing performances that fund managers were more or less 'embarrassed' into following broadly similar strategies to avoid being caught out on a limb. This was also justified on the grounds that since pension funds have similar index-linked long-term liabilities, there will consequently be a natural set of assets (that is, 'a preferred habitat') in which to hold their funds. This set of assets will be such as to match most readily the nature and maturity structure of the liabilities and will clearly be dominated by such assets as equity, which in the long run should achieve the real returns necessary to meet the pension liabilities. It has therefore been argued (Lever 1981) that fund managers should only leave this preferred habitat to avoid losses or when outstanding capital-gains potentials arise elsewhere, and should return to the fold when such gains have been fully exploited. It would appear that the boom years of the 1980s, when pension funds were generating more-than-adequate real returns, have again encouraged more individualistic investment strategies. It would be interesting to see whether a return to leaner times restores the common investment strategy. Nevertheless, in terms of the hypothesis concerning the distribution of pension-fund returns, we can conclude that the different asset-allocation strategies pursued by different types of fund manager do explain some of the differences in pension-fund returns.

Table 14.14 shows the activity rates of the pension funds during the 1980s. Activity measures the pension funds' turnover of securities in excess of the net investment of new money. It is measured in terms of average capital employed (that is, the value of the average fund):

Activity = (Purchases + Sales − Net investment)/Value of average fund
= Turnover − (Net investment/Value of average fund).

The table reveals that pension funds were far from passive investors during the 1980s. Even during the quietest year, 1982, activity exceeded 50 per cent for the average fund. During the busiest year, 1987, activity reached 123 per cent. This means that the average fund turned over its

TABLE 14.14. *Activity rates, 1981–1990 (%)*

	1981	1982	1983	1984	1985	1986	1987	1988	1989	1990	10 yrs.
UK equities	23	29	29	51	54	56	80	58	77	42	50
Overseas equities	52	53	80	82	100	118	132	113	126	78	93
UK bonds	150	164	128	114	189	189	244	195	201	196	177
Overseas bonds	—	—	—	—	—	492	355	404	237	239	345*
Index-linked	—	107	93	92	124	95	156	124	91	97	109**
TOTAL	55	52	54	65	93	96	123	95	103	68	80

*   5 yrs.
** 9 yrs.
Source: WM Company Annual Review 1990.

portfolio of assets one-and-a-quarter times in 1987, after allowing for investments from new cash.

Activity rates within individual asset categories were even more striking. Trading in UK equities was quite 'quiet' during the decade, the average activity rate being 50 per cent. In contrast, the pension funds' bond portfolios were very actively traded: the average activity rate in UK bonds was 177 per cent during the 1980s, while that in overseas bonds was 345 per cent between 1986 and 1990. Unlike share prices, bond prices do not trend over time. This suggests that bonds have to be more actively traded than equities in order to realize capital gains or to avoid capital losses. Do the greater activity rates generate higher returns? Comparing the ten-year average columns in Tables 14.4 and 14.14, we see that the opposite holds: UK equities with the lowest average activity rate (50 per cent) had the highest average return (18.5 per cent), while UK bonds had the highest average activity rate (177 per cent) and the lowest average returns (14 per cent).

Table 14.15 reveals substantial differences in activity rates between different fund managers. For example, between 1986 and 1990 the average activity rate for internally managed funds in UK equities was 40 per cent, whereas the corresponding activity rate for independent managers was 104 per cent, two-and-a-half times greater. On average, internally managed and life-company managed funds had below-average activity rates, whereas the other types of fund manager had above-average rates. In particular, where managers were competing against each other, as in the case of joint managers or part internal/part external managers, activity rates were very high. The evidence indicates that above-average activity rates are not associated with above-average returns. Table 14.12 shows that the highest average returns were earned by internally managed and life-company managed funds which had the lowest average activity rates.

TABLE 14.15. *Activity rates according to type of investment management, 1986–1990 (%)*

	UK equities					Overseas equities					UK bonds					Index-linked					Total				
	1986	1987	1988	1989	1990	1986	1987	1988	1989	1990	1986	1987	1988	1989	1990	1986	1987	1988	1989	1990	1986	1987	1988	1989	1990
Internal	37	43	33	48	40	86	93	77	88	60	141	166	119	105	201	46	58	73	47	112	67	76	61	69	47
Part internal/external	58	104	64	84	47	146	165	143	168	111	245	304	266	326	239	105	124	106	85	70	113	152	112	135	76
Two or more managers	85	93	98	106	74	122	122	136	137	105	158	176	183	260	194	109	317	190	114	130	108	124	126	135	102
Financial conglomerates	82	78	65	84	44	154	139	103	110	67	205	289	220	174	218	134	337	257	98	130	124	133	102	107	62
Life-company managed	74	94	60	57	61	96	95	185	107	61	156	126	112	94	99	129	373	99	235	187	106	103	103	85	84
Life-company segregated	57	70	67	69	67	82	99	114	131	112	278	272	265	297	262	92	257	190	268	94	112	118	114	142	100
Independent managers	117	134	87	111	69	148	139	136	106	75	131	157	131	104	178	176	214	66	26	53	130	147	105	120	89
Average	56	80	58	77	42	118	132	113	126	78	189	244	195	201	196	95	156	124	91	97	96	123	95	103	68

Source: WM Company Annual Review 1990.

TABLE 14.16. *Decomposition of relative performance (%)*

Contribution to relative performance from	Top quartile		Bottom quartile	
	1981–5	1986–90	1981–5	1986–90
Initial asset allocation	67	−4	9	0
Security selection	27	83	−109	−100
Changing asset allocation and market timing	6	21	0	0

Source: **WM Company Annual Review** 1990.

This confirms the evidence of Table 14.14 above. In conclusion, therefore, we find that high activity rates, either within asset categories or by type of fund manager, are associated with below-average returns.

Table 14.16 decomposes the relative performance of the top-quartile and bottom-quartile funds into three effects: the effect of the initial asset allocation; of security selection; and of changing asset allocation and market timing. The initial asset allocation is the beginning-of-period mix of broad asset categories (that is, equities, bonds, domestic, overseas, and so on). Security selection is the particular securities, sectors, or countries chosen. Within a given asset allocation the potential choice of individual securities is very large indeed. There are thousands of UK shares, hundreds of UK bonds, and dozens of overseas markets from which to make individual selections. The third potential source of return comes from changes to the asset allocation during the year and from the timing of purchase-and-sale decisions (that is, attempting to buy low and sell high). The procedure for calculating this decomposition (known as the *Fama decomposition*) is given in Chapter 13.

The decomposition of relative performance for the top quartile and bottom quartile funds is done for two periods, 1981–5 and 1986–90. The results indicate that, for the worst-performing funds, the principal cause of their poor performance in both sub-periods was bad security selection. The initial asset allocation and changing asset allocation and market timing during the year contributed little or nothing to the performance. For the top-quartile funds, the principal source of their above-average performance was good initial asset allocation (accounting for 67 per cent of the above-average return) in the first sub-period and good security selection (accounting for 83 per cent of the above-average return) in the second. Changing asset allocation during the year and the effects of market timing accounted for at most 21 per cent of the above-average return.

TABLE 14.17. *Returns relative to the market index, 1981–1990 (%)*

	1981	1982	1983	1984	1985	1986	1987	1988	1989	1990	10 yrs. annualized
WM UK equities	14.3	30.7	28.4	29.8	19.8	25.9	7.1	10.4	36.0	−9.8	18.5
FT-A All Share Index	13.7	29.1	29.1	31.9	20.4	27.4	8.0	11.5	36.1	−9.7	19.0
WM UK equities relative to index	0.6	1.6	−0.7	−2.1	−0.6	−1.5	−0.9	−1.1	−0.1	−0.1	−0.5
WM overseas equities	16.3	27.3	40.5	21.1	10.8	37.2	−18.5	23.4	40.3	−27.3	14.7
FT-A World Index (excluding UK)	20.9	32.0	37.9	32.3	12.9	40.8	−9.3	31.0	31.5	−32.8	17.1
WM overseas equities relative to index	−4.6	−4.7	2.6	−11.2	−2.1	−3.6	−9.2	−7.6	8.8	5.5	−2.4
WM UK bonds	2.4	52.6	16.2	10.4	12.6	12.5	16.4	8.2	7.4	7.9	14.0
British Government Stocks Index	1.6	54.4	16.4	7.2	11.3	11.5	15.2	6.7	8.2	9.6	13.5
WM UK bonds relative to index	0.8	−1.8	−0.2	3.2	1.3	1.0	1.2	1.5	−0.8	−1.7	0.5
WM UK property	14.4	8.9	8.7	12.3	3.6	7.3	19.4	32.8	18.2	−7.5	11.4
WM Property Performance Service Index	17.1	12.7	3.9	8.2	7.5	7.0	12.2	25.6	30.8	9.2	13.1
WM UK property relative to index	−2.7	−3.8	4.8	4.1	−3.9	0.3	7.2	7.2	−12.6	−16.7	−1.7

Source: WM Company Annual Review 1990.

Another test of the significance of market timing is provided in Table 14.17, which shows the relative performance of the WM universe in UK and overseas equities, UK bonds, and UK property. In each case performance is measured against a market bench-mark such as the FT-A All Share Index. In the asset categories given in Table 14.17, the WM pension funds under-performed the index in three out of four cases. Over a ten-year period they failed to beat the market in UK equities (by −0.5 per cent), overseas equities (by −2.4 per cent), and UK property (by −1.7 per cent). They managed to beat the market only in UK bonds (by 0.5 per cent). However, the returns generated by the market indices in Table 14.17 cannot be directly compared with those generated by the funds, because the former avoid transactions costs whereas the latter cannot. The funds have to pay brokerage commissions when they invest new money and pay commissions and bid-offer spreads when they trade in assets. In contrast, the index is constructed using middle prices without taking commissions into account. This, of course, makes it more difficult to beat the market. Nevertheless, for all their sophisticated techniques and expertise, the evidence shows that pension-fund managers cannot systematically match the market, let alone time the market and beat it. Even in the case of UK bonds, where the average excess return is 0.5 per cent, the fund managers under-performed the market in four out of ten years, despite the activity rates reported in Table 14.16. So we can conclude that pension-fund performance is not related to market timing.

One of the ways in which trustees review the performance of their fund managers is through the consistency of performance over a number of years. Table 14.18 shows, for the two five-year periods 1980–4 and 1985–9, the distribution of funds monitored by CAPS according to the

TABLE 14.18. *Consistency of performance* (%)

Number of years of above-average performance	Total fund		UK equities	
	1980–4	1985–9	1980–4	1985–9
5	3	3	2	5
4	25	18	14	18
3	26	28	35	26
2	25	34	31	27
1	15	14	15	18
0	6	3	3	6
	100	100	100	100

Source: *CAPS General Reports*, 1985 and 1989.

number of years in which the performance of a fund was above average (that is, exceeded the return on the median fund for that year). It shows that only 3 per cent of funds had above-average returns in all five years of each sub-period. Similarly, only 6 per cent and 3 per cent respectively of funds had below-average returns in all five years of each sub-period. Again, in both sub-periods about half the funds had above-average returns in three or more years and about half had above-average returns in two or fewer years. This distribution of total fund returns is similar to the distribution that would arise if above-average returns occurred entirely by chance, that is, if there was no systematic component to fund performance over time. A similar pattern emerges with the funds' UK equity performance: only 2 per cent and 5 per cent respectively of funds had above-average performance in all years of each sub-period. So there is very little evidence for consistency of performance by pension-fund managers, and consistency of performance therefore cannot be an explanation for the distribution of pension-fund returns.

Summarizing our results, we find that:

- there is no relationship between performance and cash inflows at the level of the individual pension fund, but, in aggregate, a reduction in cash inflow can reduce price pressures on the whole market and reduce returns;
- there is no relationship between performance and fund size, despite significant differences in asset-allocation patterns between small and large funds;
- there appears to be a relationship between performance and type of fund manager, but this was largely because of the different investment-management strategies pursued;
- there appears to be a relationship between performance and the asset-allocation strategies of pension funds: high-risk asset allocations have performed better in boom years and worse in slump years than conservative asset allocations; overall, during the period under investigation, the conservative strategy has led to the highest overall return;
- there is a relationship between performance and activity: during the period of investigation, high levels of activity, whether by asset type or fund-management type, were associated with below-average returns;
- there is a relationship between performance and security selection: while above-average returns were not always associated with good security-selection decisions, we found that below-average returns were always associated with bad security-selection decisions;
- there was no systematic relationship between performance and the market-timing strategies of fund managers;
- there was no evidence that fund managers could systematically deliver superior performance over extended periods.

14.2. The Investment Performance of Personal Pension Schemes

The performance of personal-pension-scheme investments is important for two reasons. First and most importantly, the size of the pension at retirement depends solely on the value of the investment fund at retirement. This, of course, contrasts with the pension from a final-salary occupational scheme which, by definition, is independent of the performance of the pension fund. Secondly, past performance is often used as a guide to future projections and hence as a means of advertising different pension-scheme providers' products. Related to this, past performance can be used to compare different categories of investment vehicle, such as unit-linked managed funds and with-profits insurance funds.

The principal difference between unit-linked funds and with-profits funds is that the former fluctuate in value in line with the underlying investments, whereas with the latter the value increases systematically as a result of annual reversionary bonuses and terminal bonuses. The objective of with-profits funds is to deliver stable performance, so that in good years some profits are retained in order to finance bonuses in bad years. In a bull market, unit-linked funds ought to deliver superior performance to that of with-profits funds holding similar investments. The opposite should be true in a bear market.

Another difference is that with-profits funds tend to have a more diversified range of investments than unit-linked funds, with the possible exception of unit-linked managed funds. This is because unit-linked funds tend to specialize in particular sectors or geographical areas, such as technology or Japan. Such specialist unit-linked funds, therefore, tend to be highly risky, either delivering a performance that is above average if the right sector or geographical area is picked, or delivering a performance that is disastrous if the wrong sector or geographical area is selected.

The exception is unit-linked managed funds. With such funds the investment is spread across a diversified range of securities, such as equities, gilts, and property, and as such will have a very similar investment spread and, consequently, investment performance, to equivalent with-profits funds. Indeed, when unit-linked managed funds first appeared, they were specifically structured to match with-profits funds. Therefore, because they are less risky, most people choosing unit-linked funds choose the managed fund.

The advantage of both managed and with-profits funds is that the funds' managers have the discretion to change the asset mix as circumstances change. During the 1980s, for example, managed funds became more equity-oriented, with, in some cases, equities exceeding 75 per cent

TABLE 14.19. *The performance of unit-linked managed funds and with-profits insurance funds, 1986: value of fund to man retiring aged 65 for annual premium of £500 (£)*

Best performance over 5 years

Unit-linked managed funds		With-profits funds	
Target	5,195	Friends' Provident	4,958
Standard Life	4,243	London Life	4,629
Confederation Life	4,198	Equitable Life	4,346
City of Westminster	4,137	Scottish Amicable	4,311
London & Manchester	4,122	Medical Sickness	4,289
Pearl	4,099	Standard Life	4,273
Sun Life	4,083	National Mutual	4,216
GRE	4,001	General Accident	4,204
Save & Prosper	3,979	Scottish Life	4,152
Provincial Life	3,965	Scottish Widows	4,150

Best performance over 10 years

Unit-linked managed funds		With-profits funds	
Confederation Life	14,294	Scottish Widows	14,807
Albany Life	13,869	Norwich Union	14,288
Lloyds Life	13,132	Equity & Law	14,044
Allied Dunbar	12,745	Scottish Amicable	13,950
Imperial Life	12,606	Standard Life	13,934
Save & Prosper	12,539	Equitable Life	13,612
Sun Life of Canada	12,375	National Mutual	13,103
Schroder Life	12,320	Scottish Equitable	12,840
Merchant Investors	11,857	NPI	12,787
Abbey	10,834	Scottish Mutual	12,461

Source: Policy Market and Planned Savings, *Daily Telegraph*, 1 Feb. 1986.

of the asset mix. In contrast, the typical with-profits fund was more than 50 per cent invested in gilts and property. This meant that for the first seven years of the 1980s unit-linked managed funds are likely to have out-performed with-profits funds. However, with-profits funds were more resilient during the stock-market crash of October 1987 as a result.

We can examine the recent performance of with-profits, unit-linked managed, and specialist unit-linked funds using Tables 14.19–22.

Table 14.19 shows the performance of unit-linked managed and with-profits funds over five and ten years up to 1986, for a 65-year-old male who retired in 1986 having paid premiums of £500 p.a. With the exception of the Target unit-linked managed fund over five years (which appears to be something of an outlier, since it does not even appear in the top ten list over ten years), the main pattern that emerges is that with-profits funds have on average out-performed managed funds over both the five-year horizon and the ten-year horizon. For example, the Standard Life with-profits fund out-performs the Standard Life managed fund by £30 over five years. Yet this covers the period of the longest bull market in the history of the British stock market, where the reverse result might have been expected. The second feature that emerges is that there seems to be very little consistency of performance by fund managers. No fund-management group can deliver top performance in both managed funds and with-profits funds over both five-year and ten-year horizons. In terms of managed-fund performance alone, only Confederation Life was in the top ten over both the five- and ten-year horizons. In terms of with-profits funds, the consistency of performance is a little better, but only Equitable Life, National Mutual, Scottish Amicable, Scottish Widows, and Standard Life managed to achieve top-ten rankings over both horizons.

Table 14.20 updates the information contained in Table 14.19, by

TABLE 14.20. *Performance of unit-linked managed funds and with-profits insurance funds, 1989: value of fund to man retiring aged 65 for annual premium of £500 (£)*

Best performance over 5 years

Unit-linked managed funds		With-profits funds	
Provident Mutual	4,166	Friends' Provident	4,494
Albany Life	4,131	Scottish Amicable	4,452
Sun Life	4,085	National Mutual	4,439
Confederation Life	3,929	Norwich Union	4,439
Friends' Provident	3,625	Medical Sickness	4,285

Source: Policy Market, *Daily Telegraph*, 14 Jan. 1989.

TABLE 14.21. *Performance of specialist unit-linked funds, 1989: value of fund to man retiring aged 65 for annual premium of £500 (£)*

Best and worst unit-linked performance over 5 years

Best company	Fund		Worst company	Fund	
Albany	Japanese	5,156	M&G	Pacific	2,385
Target	Property	5,028	Scottish Equitable	Index-linked	2,304
Provident Mutual	UK equity	4,937	Prolific	N. American	2,138
Royal Life	Equity	4,829	Prolific	Technology	2,124
Sun Life	Equity	4,612	Liberty Life	American	2,001

Source: Policy Market, *Daily Telegraph*, 14 Jan. 1989.

looking at five-year performance for unit-linked managed and with-profits funds up to 1989. This therefore covers the period of the 1987 crash. The table shows the greater resilience to the crash of the with-profits funds compared with the managed funds: all the with-profits funds out-performed the best managed fund. The table also shows the general lack of consistency of performance over time of the fund-management groups. The notable exceptions are Confederation Life (among managed funds) and National Mutual and Scottish Amicable (among with-profits funds) which make three appearances in Tables 14.19 and 14.20.

Table 14.21 shows the extremes of performance by specialist unit-linked funds over the five years up to 1989. The best specialist funds out-performed both the best unit-linked managed funds and the best with-profits funds by a substantial margin. The worst specialist funds performed disastrously, not even returning the initial contributions of £2,500. But it is difficult to judge in advance which are the best sectors or geographical areas to be in. The table appears to indicate that being in the right sector or geographical area is more important for performance than being with the right fund-management group. So, for example, between 1984 and 1989 it was right to be in UK equity or Japan and wrong to be in technology stocks or the USA, regardless of the group managing the fund.

Table 14.22 shows the best and worst performance of personal pension schemes over a four-year period from 1 July 1988, when personal pension schemes were first introduced. Of the forty funds surveyed, more than half generated returns lower than the sums invested after taking into account transactions costs. The best-performing funds were those invested in deposits and fixed-interest securities. The worst-performing funds were in equities. The table shows the performance of the best and worst managed funds and equity funds in the case of a male paying £50 per

TABLE 14.22. *Best and worst personal pension scheme performance, 1988–1992 (£)*

	Managed fund*		Managed fund†		Equity fund*		Equity fund†	
Best five								
1	Rothschild	2,868	Providence Capital	1,553	Rothschild	2,896	Providence Capital	2,125
2	Liberty Life	2,568	Rothschild	1,464	Liberty Life	2,772	Liberty Life	1,592
3	LAS	2,554	National Mutual	1,425	Scottish Equitable	2,658	National Mutual	1,494
4	Norwich Union	2,530	Liberty Life	1,393	Norwich Union	2,654	Rothschild	1,490
5	Prosperity Life	2,489	Tunbridge	1,369	Friends' Provident	2,632	L and M	1,398
Worst five								
1	Prolific	2,187	LAS	1,088	Prolific	2,071	Prolific	1,097
2	Sun Alliance	2,182	MGM	1,076	MGM	2,052	General Accident	1,038
3	Target Life	2,166	Target Life	1,066	Cannon Lincoln	2,048	Prudential	993
4	Cannon Lincoln	1,957	General Accident	1,052	Providence Capital	2,005	MGM	922
5	Providence Capital	1,957	Prudential	986	Irish Life	1,937	Target Life	830

Notes: The figures assume:
- retirement funds are based on a policy taken out on 1 July 1988, with a retirement age of 65 on 1 July 1992;
- male paying * £50 per month, † £1,000 single premium.

Source: Money Marketing Unit-Linked Survey 1992, Sept.

month or a lump sum of £1,000 on 1 July 1988 and retiring on 1 July 1992. In the case of the funds receiving monthly contributions, only the top five funds generate returns exceeding the total contributions of £2,400. In the case of the funds receiving single premiums, the best managed fund generates an annual return of 12 per cent and the best equity fund generates an annual return of 21 per cent. The worst funds generate losses of 0.35 per cent and 4.6 per cent p.a. respectively. There is also an interesting consistency of performance by Rothschild and Liberty Life at the top and by Prolific, MGM and Target Life at the bottom. It should also be noted that this performance covers the period of the worst recession in the UK since the 1930s, with the shares in most companies performing particularly badly. Over a long period of time, such as twenty-five to forty years, equities on average out-perform Treasury bills by about 6 per cent p.a. (that is, the *equity risk premium* is 6 per cent), and this tends to make equities a suitable long-term investment for pension schemes.

The implication of all this for personal-pension-scheme investors is this. Risk-averse investors should go for with-profits funds or unit-linked managed funds or for a mixture of the two. Only risk-loving investors should contemplate the more speculative specialist unit-linked funds. As retirement approaches, all pension investors should switch all funds to a with-profits fund to avoid any catastrophic fall in fund values.

14.3. Some Problems with Performance Measurement

In this section we outline some of the problems associated with investment performance measurement as practised in the UK.

14.3.1. HOW TO MEASURE INVESTMENT PERFORMANCE

The first problem, of course, is how to measure investment performance. Pension funds will be concerned with the total combined returns on their portfolios, that is, with both income and capital gains or losses. Since most pension funds are gross funds they do not have to pay income tax or capital-gains tax, so income and capital gains can be treated equally in the portfolio which implies that market value, rather than book or face value, is the relevant measure of capital value. There are two possible ways of measuring total rates of return: the money-weighted rate of return and the time-weighted rate of return. As we saw in Section 13.9, the second measure is the more appropriate.

Typically, the returns are calculated both with and without the property portfolios of the funds. The returns are then ranked in order of decreasing returns. The objective of every fund manager is to be above the *median* fund, and ideally to be in the *first quartile* of funds. On the face of it this would seem to be a straightforward exercise. But all is not what it seems. The most important problem is that fund returns are not adjusted for the *risk exposure* that they have taken to generate those returns. This is both surprising and not so surprising at the same time. Risk has the very peculiar property of being all-pervasive before the event and entirely unimportant after the event. What is completely unknowable before an investment decision is made becomes entirely obvious afterwards as time unfolds. With the wisdom of hindsight we could all have predicted whether a particular investment was going to be successful or unsuccessful. So why not just report *ex-post* performance? After all, it is only realized investment performance that investors can benefit from. It is only the actual cash in the kitty that can be used to buy goods. What is the point of saying that a pension-fund manager generated a return of 30 per cent last year, but that after adjusting for risk he or she lost 10 per cent?

Well, the point of adjusting for risk is that a pension-fund manager, along with every other investor, has to make investment decisions before the world becomes obvious. The fund manager has to use his or her skill and judgement to select the best-performing assets before it is known which were the best-performing assets. Good investment performance could be the result of good skill and judgement, or it could be the result of just good luck. By adjusting portfolio performance for the risk exposure taken to generate the return, it is possible to differentiate, however imperfectly, between skill and luck. Why should a skilled and conservative fund manager not receive due credit compared with an unskilled and reckless fund manager, just because the latter had the good fortune to generate a superior (unadjusted) return? There is, of course, no good reason. In addition, there is no good reason *not* to report risk-adjusted returns.

The procedures for calculating *risk-adjusted returns* (also based on modern portfolio theory) are now well established (see Chapter 13), and risk-adjusted returns have been reported on US funds for some time. So pension-fund trustees should now insist that not only the risk-adjusted returns on the portfolio are reported but also the *performance attribution*, that is, the identification of the sources of portfolio performance, is reported.

14.3.2. METHODS OF COMPARISON

A second practical problem confronting performance monitors is that of the method of comparison. Once the rate of return has been calculated for a particular fund, how should this be compared with that of other funds or with some other yardstick such as a notional fund or an index fund? There is little point in measuring performance unless there is also some means of comparing that performance. The most obvious way is to make comparisons with other funds with similar characteristics, the most important of which are the type of liabilities, the restrictions placed on the investment manager by the trustees, the overall fund size, and the rate of cash inflow. British pension funds are in the enviable position of facing few real constraints in practice. They are not liquidity-constrained because, although pension funds have final-salary type liabilities, contributions currently exceed these liabilities and will continue to do so in the foreseeable future, and so the funds are free to pursue very long-term investment strategies. In addition, trustee restrictions are really only investment guidelines and can generally be changed should investment opportunities dictate. Further, it appears that the total fund size and rate of cash inflow have little discernible effect on performance. Thus, for all these reasons pension funds are sufficiently similar in characteristics to be directly comparable in terms of their performance.

Once performance comparisons have been made between actual pension funds and their respective investment managers, the next step is to compare the performance of actual funds with that of a notional fund. A notional fund is an artificial fund constructed from assets with a particular mix, the mix designed to represent some long-run optimal allocation between assets. For example, a fund comprising 60 per-cent equities and 40 per-cent fixed interest would constitute a 60:40 notional fund. The aim would be to compare the performance of an actual fund with that of the notionäl fund. There are problems, however, concerning the treatment of the notional fund that have to be dealt with. For example, should the notional fund be re-balanced periodically to preserve the 60:40 ratio? And if so, are the consequential brokerage expenses taken into account? The most sensible solution seems to be to leave the actual notional fund mix alone but to invest new cash inflows in the 60:40 ratio.

The third method of comparison is with a market index itself, such as the FT-Actuaries All Share Index. This leads to the idea of the index fund, a fund constructed from all the shares in a particular sector, usually related to the market value of those shares, in which additions to and deductions from the fund are made according to some pre-set formula. The aim would then be for the actual pension fund to out-perform, or at least to perform as well as, the index fund. The evidence suggests that it is very difficult to do this on a systematic basis. The most likely reason for this lies in the *efficient-markets hypothesis* which predicts that it is impossible to systematically 'beat the market'. This follows because the information about companies acquired by investment analysts for institutional clients such as pension funds soon becomes discounted in company share prices and hence cannot be systematically exploited. This is reinforced by the dichotomized nature of the stock market, in which institutional investors trade in the shares of only a small number (about 200 or 300) of the largest companies, leaving the rest of the market largely unresearched and consequently untraded. This concentration of analysis in such a small number of shares by investors with such large funds at their disposal, together with high dealing costs, makes it very likely that significant share trading (that is, high activity) may actually reduce rather than enhance overall fund performance. (We found evidence for this above.) Further, since many fund managers' fees are related to dealing volume, this may lead to a bias to over-trade (that is, churn) the portfolio. For all these reasons, some funds have adopted a policy of passive fund management in which the objective is to achieve a performance as close to the market average as possible. To this end they construct their portfolio as an index fund in which purchases are made according to a particular formula, not related to normal investment criteria, although the actual shareholdings and the timing of purchases and sales are left to the discretion of the investment manager, with the overall aim of achieving the return on the FT-Actuaries All Share Index. It is much easier to do this in the USA than in the UK, because brokers' commissions are much lower there and also because the spread between bid and offer prices is much smaller. These factors make it feasible for small and medium-sized funds to engage in the strategy to the extent that is required to approximate the market index, namely, the purchase of as many constituents of the market index as possible. As a result, in the UK the index fund is likely to perform slightly worse than the selected index compared with the same fund in the USA.

14.3.3. DIFFICULTIES OF COMPARISON

The two main services, CAPS and WM, measure performance in slightly different ways, and this makes direct comparison between them misleading. For example, they measure the rate of return on the FT-Actuaries All Share Index, the principal bench-mark for UK equity performance, in different ways. In 1989, for instance, CAPS measured the rate of return on the index at 35.5 per cent, while WM measured it at 36.1 per cent. The discrepancy resulted from the different treatment of dividends received on the shares in the index. While the difference is only 0.6 percentage points, this is nevertheless highly significant for fund managers operating index-matching funds.

14.3.4. SELECTION BIAS

Another problem with performance measurement that has come to prominence in recent years is *selection bias*. The argument here is that funds should only be included in a particular *universe* of funds whose performance is being measured if all the funds are pursuing the same objectives and face the same investment restrictions. This argument has led to fund managers selectively withdrawing poorly performing funds retrospectively from the universe on the grounds that, after all, their performance was atypical. This, in turn, leads to what is known as *median drift*, whereby the average measured performance for a particular year is revised upwards over time. So, for example, it is possible to see a fund-management group with a dozen funds remove the two worst funds from the calculation on the grounds that these funds were 'atypical' and thereby increase the average or median performance of the remaining funds in their stable. The performance-measurement services are largely powerless to prevent this happening, since a fund-management group is a client of the service and free to choose how it interprets its performance.

Nevertheless, as a result of growing dissatisfaction with the misuse of performance statistics, the National Association of Pension Funds set up the Stonefrost Committee to establish consistent standards for the presentation of performance measures. The committee proposed, for example, that fund performance should distinguish between property and non-property investments, but did not accept that different weightings should be given to realized and unrealized capital gains. Unfortunately, the committee also rejected the presentation of returns on a risk-adjusted basis: '"Volatility" and "risk" are often used too loosely. What may be "volatility" to one contributor to the investment management function may or may not be "risk" to another. We have failed to identify methods of expressing "risk" as simply as methods of measuring "returns".' (National Association of Pension Funds Report, 1990*b*, p. 7.)

The underlying reason for this temptation to misuse performance statistics is the pressure on fund managers to deliver good performance in the short term, the so-called *short-termism* problem. There has been a tendency both to appoint and to dismiss fund managers on the basis of very short-term performance. The argument is that, given the dominance in the stock market of pension funds and other institutional investors, the pressure to achieve good short-term performance can lead to substantial distortions in the capital markets. Companies are pressing their pension-fund managers to deliver superior short-term performance, and the fund managers, who are investing in the shares of these very same companies, are in turn pressing the companies to act in a way that leads to their share

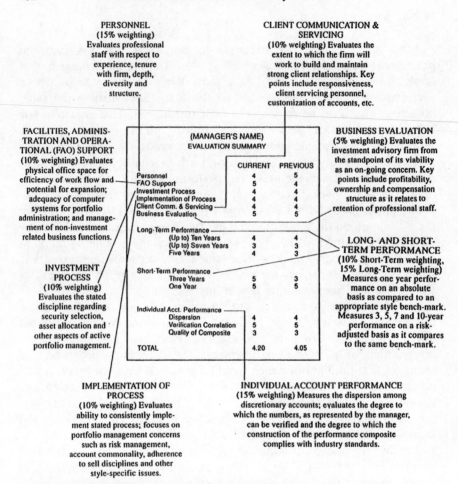

FIG. 14.1. Fund-manager performance evaluation summary
(*Source*: Shearson Lehman Brothers Consulting Group Institutional Services, 1991.)

prices increasing in the short term. So anything that tends to reduce the share price in the short term, such as the financing of a long-term investment programme, is criticized. (This problem is discussed in more detail in the next chapter.)

14.3.5. ANONYMITY

Another striking feature of performance measurement is anonymity. While performance-measurement services report the performance of their client pension funds, they do so in such a way that the performance of any particular fund cannot be identified publicly. This means that it is not possible to identify exactly who the best- and worst-performing fund managers are. It is not possible, therefore, to identify whether a particular fund manager has been able to deliver systematically good or bad performance over a number of years. Nor is it possible to determine whether one particular management style (balanced, specialist, passive, and so on) proved superior to any other. This is clearly unsatisfactory. Every scheme member should know how well his or her fund manager is performing. This is particularly true for members of personal pension schemes whose pensions depend directly on how good their fund managers are. Fund managers' performance is evaluated publicly in the USA; an example of an evaluation summary is given in Fig. 14.1.

15

The Consequences of Pension Funds for Capital Markets

Given the size of pension funds, we cannot ignore their consequences for capital markets. Some of these consequences are good, while some are bad. Pension funds have a very important role to play in ensuring that capital markets operate efficiently. They also, in principle, provide a stable source of finance for long-term investment in British industry. However, in recent years the investment behaviour of pension funds, along with that of other institutional investors, has been dominated by *short-termism*, that is, the obsession with generating short-term investment returns whatever the longer-term costs. In this chapter we analyse some of these costs. In particular, we examine the costs of ignoring long-term investment opportunities, the consequences of hostile take-over bids, the issue of pre-emption rights, and the incentive that short-termism offers to engage in fraud and malpractice. We also consider the increased volatility in capital markets caused by the reduction in pension-fund *surpluses* and by the increasing *maturity* of pension funds. We end the chapter with an examination of some of the solutions to short-termism that have been proposed.

15.1. The Good Consequences of Pension Funds

15.1.1. HELPING TO MAKE CAPITAL MARKETS EFFICIENT

Pension funds and insurance companies are two of the most important *institutional investors* in the UK. Institutional investors have an essential role to play in ensuring the *efficient* operation of capital markets. An efficiently operating capital market has the following characteristics. It is *liquid*, which means that it is trading securities in sufficient volume and with sufficient frequency that most investors believe that they can liquidate their investments in securities very rapidly; in other words, when investors buy securities they are not locked in to holding those securities for long periods. An efficient capital market is also one that *values securities fairly*. When an investor buys or sells a security he or she will want to pay or receive a fair price. An efficient capital market is also one that is *well-regulated*, in the sense that it operates to the highest professional standards and is free from widespread fraud and malpractice. Finally, an efficient capital market is *innovative* and responsive to the changing needs of investors, rapidly responding to their needs for new risk-management tools or index-matching strategies, for example.

Institutional investors have an incentive to ensure that all these characteristics hold. This is because they have such huge sums of money invested. Smaller investors, by comparison, would also like to operate in an efficient capital market, but are unable to bring the same pressure to bear. The existence of large institutional investors with large sums of money will encourage the development of a system of competing *financial intermediaries* providing services in broking, market-making, research, and so on that the institutional investors demand. And it is the competing financial intermediaries whose actions ensure that the capital markets are efficient.

15.1.2. PROVIDING A LARGE, LOYAL SHAREHOLDER BASE FOR FINANCING REAL INVESTMENT

Institutional investors' ownership of UK companies' equity has increased from less than 30 per cent in the early 1960s to more than 60 per cent in the early 1990s. It has been estimated that about fifty top fund managers have effective control (51 per cent) of UK industry. Pension funds themselves own 30 per cent of UK industry. This means that, through their pension funds, companies own about one-third of each other.

If the pension-fund holdings are held passively, the effect on both companies and the economy can be beneficial. Companies will have a large, loyal shareholder base and this will allow companies to plan and undertake long-term investment projects that increase the long-term profitability of the company and have long-term benefits for shareholders. In this way, a virtuous circle is created. Pension funds, therefore, have an important role in channelling *savings* towards *investment*. Pension savings can be used to finance investment projects which increase the country's capital stock, and hence increase its productive base. Pension funds do not tend to be directly involved in the investment projects themselves (that is, in *direct investment*). Instead, they usually purchase and hold in their portfolios the securities (shares, bonds, and so on) that are issued by the companies undertaking the investment projects (that is, *portfolio investment*). Nevertheless, pension funds provide an efficient conduit for collecting together the pension savings of employees and directing them into real investment.

The passive-shareholder strategy is not without its problems, however. If the bulk of the shares in a firm are not traded, analysts and brokers have no incentive to undertake research into the firm's activities. Without continuous research and monitoring the share price ceases to reflect the true value of the company. In other words, the markets are in danger of becoming *inefficient*. This is believed to be what happened to Bond Corporation of Australia, for example. Most of the shares in Bond Corp. were held by a small number of institutional investors and were not heavily traded. Analysts and brokers effectively stopped researching the company. The problems with the company only began to emerge when it bought a large stake in Lonrho of London and Lonrho retaliated by commissioning an investigation into Bond Corp.'s finances. The rest, as they say, is history.

15.2. **The Bad Consequences of Pension Funds**

The bad influences of pension funds are at least as great as the good influences. They can be summarized in one word: *short-termism*, the concentration on short-term performance at the expense of long-term investment, and a resulting destabilizing effect on capital markets.

15.2.1. IGNORING LONG-TERM INVESTMENT OPPORTUNITIES

The Wilson Committee to Review the Functioning of Financial Institutions made these comments about pension funds:

In law, their first concern must be to safeguard the long-term interests of their members and beneficiaries. It is, however, possible for fiduciary obligations to be interpreted too narrowly. Though the institutions may individually have no obligation to invest any particular quantity of new savings in the creation of future real resources, the prospect that growth in the UK economy over the next two decades might be inadequate to satisfy present expectations should be a cause of considerable concern to them. The exercise of responsibility which is the obverse of the considerable financial power which they now collectively possess may require them to take a more active role than in the past . . . in more actively seeking profitable outlets for funds and in otherwise contributing to the solutions of the problems that we have been discussing. (1980, pp. 259–60)

The investment strategy of pension funds, especially in respect of their substantial investments overseas since 1979 and their apparent unwillingness to invest in British industry, has been widely criticized by others, most notably by those on the left politically. The main criticism has been that pension funds have been too concerned with short-term investment returns and not sufficiently concerned with the long-term future of the British economy. In other words, pension funds have been accused of short-termism. There is now pressure on pension funds and other institutional investors to examine the social dimension of their investment policies.

The Wilson Committee and others (for example, Minns 1980) argued that pension funds did not invest sufficiently in small companies, and that as a result small companies found it difficult to raise adequate funding for expansion (this is the so-called *Macmillan gap*). The pension funds' defence against this criticism rested on the argument that the costs of investing in small companies were much higher than those of investing in large companies. The reason for this is as follows. Small companies are difficult, and therefore expensive, to research because small companies are generally relatively new and so do not have a long track record. Also, their shares may not be very liquid. Further, pension-fund trustees place limits on the proportion of a company's equity in which a fund can invest. For example, a pension fund might not be permitted by its trustees to hold more than 5 per cent of any company's equity. For a company with equity valued at £1m., the investment limit is £50,000. A large pension fund might have £500m. of contributions and investment income to invest per year. This could be invested in 10,000 million-pound companies or it could be invested in fifty large companies. It is not hard to see why the pension fund is going to prefer the latter to the former strategy, even if it could find 10,000 companies to invest in.

Minns found that, because pension funds prefer to invest in large firms, they also prefer to invest in sectors dominated by large firms. Since the financial sector has a larger proportion of large firms than other sectors, such as the capital-goods sector, pension funds have tended to invest in the financial sector in preference to, say, the capital-goods sector, which is the sector that provides the engine for growth in the economy.

Related to the criticism that pension funds are unwilling to invest in small companies is the criticism that pension funds have been unwilling to supply risk-taking *venture capital* to small unquoted companies engaged in new, high-risk ventures. Venture capital usually involves the direct involvement of the investor in the venture. Not only does the investor supply seed-corn finance, he or she also supplies business skills necessary to support the inventive talent of the company founder. This can help to reduce the risks involved in the venture. The reward for the provision of finance and business skills is long-term capital growth. The problem with pension funds is that, while they have substantial resources to invest, they do not generally have the necessary business expertise to provide the required support. As a result, pension funds remain largely portfolio investors rather than direct investors. In other words, they prefer to invest in equity from which they can make a quick exit if necessary, rather than make a long-term commitment to a particular firm.

Not only do pension funds tend to avoid the risks of direct investment, they tend also to be risk-averse when it comes to portfolio investment. They seek the maximum return with the minimum of risk, and the investment managers of pension funds tend to be extremely conservative investors, devoid of entrepreneurial spirit. As Helowicz has said, pension funds

do not have any expertise in the business of, or a commitment to, the companies in which they invest. Shares will be bought and sold on the basis of the potential financial return. It therefore follows that the potential social and economic implications of an investment decision have little influence on that decision. (Benjamin *et al.* 1987, p. 98)

The Megarry Judgment (see Section 12.1.3) has had the important effect of associating the best interests of pension beneficiaries with their best financial interests. This in turn means that pension funds must pursue investment policies that maximize return, given risk. It also follows that it becomes difficult, if not impossible, to adopt what has become known as a *socially-responsible-investment* (SRI) strategy. This is a strategy that avoids certain types of investment on ethical, political, or religious grounds, and instead invests in socially valuable projects that emphasize, say, job creation.

Such investments can be made on the basis of recommendations from organizations such as the Ethical Investment Research and Information Service (EIRIS). EIRIS, for example, has a list of around 200 SRI companies, all of which are included in the FT-Actuaries All Share Index. The list contains mainly small companies and excludes companies with interests in tobacco and brewing. It also excludes the finance sector, such as banks and insurance companies. Funds based on the EIRIS list have in the past out-performed the FT-Actuaries All Share Index, so SRI does not necessarily imply low returns. Nevertheless, the Megarry Judgment does make it difficult to propose SRI policies that are based on explicit exclusions of particular shares or sectors.

Pension funds have in recent years also responded to some of the other criticisms that have been mentioned above. For example, some of the larger funds have established venture-capital divisions.

15.2.2. HOSTILE TAKE-OVER BIDS

The UK stock market is the least regulated in the world when it comes to take-over bids. References to the Monopolies and Mergers Commission have been based in the 1980s only on competition considerations, rather than on public-interest considerations, the traditional reason for a reference.

The large shareholdings of pension funds have provided the source of equity to win corporate control in the event of hostile take-overs. Pension funds have been blamed for selling out to the bidder and hence being responsible for control being handed over to a predator, often from a country that would not permit similar behaviour (for example, the Nestlé take-over of Rowntree in 1988 would not have been permitted in Switzerland). The incentive to support the predator lies in the huge rise in the share price at the time of the bid and the almost certain fall subsequently, if the bid fails. Thus, by supporting the bid the pension funds have been accused of short-termism of the worst kind. Institutional investors have been accused of relying on take-overs to resolve the problem of poor management of a company rather than by directly intervening in the boardroom themselves.

A vicious circle is created. Companies are forced to divert their energies to counter potential take-over threats. Investment projects cannot be undertaken if they damage the share price in the short term. Share prices can be quite volatile. It is this unattractive scenario that has persuaded many medium-sized unquoted companies not to seek a quotation on the London Stock Exchange.

One recent example of the exercise of pension-fund market power was the hostile take-over of Globe Investment Trust in July 1990 by the British Coal Pension Fund, which had held 28.5 per cent of the equity in Globe since the mid-1970s. Globe was the largest investment trust in the UK, with a market capitalization of £1.1bn., and the only investment trust in the FTSE 100 index of leading shares. The battle for Globe was won largely because other institutional investors agreed to sell their shareholdings to the British Coal Pension Fund. For example, POSTEL, the Post Office pension fund, sold its 2 per-cent shareholding, Prudential its 5 per-cent holding, Standard Life its 5 per-cent holding, and Legal and General its 1.5 per-cent holding. Globe spent £7.5m. on its bid defence.

The explanation for why the British Coal Pension Fund was interested in an investment trust such as Globe is simple. Investment-trust shares in the UK have historically traded in the market at a discount to their net asset value. Sometimes this discount has been as high as 30 per cent. In the early 1990s it fell to about half this amount. Nevertheless, a 15 per-cent discount on the net asset value of securities that are easy to value since they are quoted on the stock market remains a very attractive target for an institutional investor.

This aspect of short-termism is a direct consequence of the companies themselves demanding that their own pension funds beat the average, when no more than half of them can do this. They cannot then really complain when fund managers capitalize on the large price rises resulting from take-over bids by selling their stakes in an attempt to beat the average, knowing that if the bid fails the share price will sink back again.

The mutual influence that companies and their pension funds have over each other is now so great that the consequences can have a destabilizing effect on UK equity markets and can damage confidence in British boardrooms. This compares strikingly with the position in Japan, where Japanese companies also built up cross-holdings in each other during the 1960s and 1970s. The extent of the cross-holdings is about 38 per cent, slightly more than in Britain. Yet the Japanese cross-investment is never used in a destabilizing manner and certainly is never involved in a hostile take-over.

The implication of all this is that market pressures can be very effective in ensuring that companies operate in the interests of shareholders. However, the large shareholdings of pension funds set overambitious performance targets which can be used to destabilize the very companies which set those targets.

It should be noted, however, that not all commentators are critical of hostile take-overs. For example, Evan Davis and Graham Bannock of the David Hume Institute were commissioned by the Joseph Rowntree Foundation to assess the consequences of the take-over of Rowntree by Nestlé. In their report (Davis and Bannock 1991), they state their view that it was 'sad that a UK concern built up over 120 years can lose its independence in a few months'. But they concluded that the take-over did 'some benefit and no significant harm' to the UK economy, with the main losers being Swiss shareholders of Nestlé who ended up paying an inflated price for Rowntree. Nestlé kept up the good relations with workers that Rowntree had long established, and introduced some improvements, such as a free health-screening service. The research centre doubled in size and capital spending rose sharply. Although employment fell, it fell by less than in the same period prior to the bid. In short, the report argues that there are good and bad take-overs, and that no bid should be prevented just because the target company is large or protests loudly. Other commentators go further. For example, US economist and Nobel Laureate Paul Samuelson argues that: 'Takeovers, like bankruptcy, represent one of nature's methods of eliminating dead wood in the struggle for survival.'

15.2.3. THE ISSUE OF PRE-EMPTION RIGHTS

Pension funds, through their shareholdings, can exercise a powerful influence on the behaviour of the companies in which they hold shares. A recent example of this has been the issue of pre-emption rights which have been enshrined in numerous Companies Acts.

Pre-emption rights are the rights attached to existing shareholdings when a company seeks to raise additional finance by issuing new shares. Historically, pre-emption rights have meant that existing shareholders have had to be offered the right to buy any new shares in direct proportion to their shareholdings before the shares are offered to new shareholders (pre-emption means 'buy before'). In this way, shareholders are protected from any dilution of their rights or controls over the company. Any deviation from this practice, or *disapplication* as it is called, must have specific shareholder approval.

However, many leading company directors and corporate treasurers have been arguing for greater flexibility in company financing, with greater freedom to raise equity finance through new funding techniques such as *bought deals* and *overseas placings*. Company directors have been supported in this argument by the main securities houses in the City, which would earn fees from these new financing techniques.

The main argument put forward by the companies and securities houses in favour of relaxing pre-emption rights is that the rights restrict the growth of companies, since expansion is limited to the extent that existing shareholders are willing to buy the new shares. Also, rights issues are lengthy and cumbersome procedures. Another argument is that most shareholders are British investors, and that pre-emption rights effectively limit companies to raising funds in the UK equity market, which is less than 10 per cent of the world equity market.

UK companies were, therefore, being forced to ignore a vast overseas pool of investment funds. Having a presence in overseas equity markets helped to enhance the reputation of UK companies overseas and lowered the cost of other financing operations, such as commercial paper. In addition, because of this restricted access to the markets, larger price discounts had to be offered on rights issues to existing shareholders to induce them to take up the issue than would be necessary in the case of a wider distribution. Institutional investors were, therefore, really acting in their own self-interest by demanding the preservation of pre-emption rights. This was doubly so when it is recognized that institutional investors also largely underwrite the rights issues and hence receive underwriting fees which would not be necessary if the company could access a wider market.

Stock Exchange rules permit shareholders to forgo some of their pre-emption rights, and in the past companies have been able to issue up to 2.5 per cent of their existing share capital without a reference to existing shareholders. In other words, 2.5 per cent of share capital could be disapplied. But in October 1986, at the time of Big Bang, the Stock Exchange relaxed its rules. The Association of British Insurers (ABI) accepted a ceiling of 5 per cent. The National Association of Pension Funds also accepted the 5 per cent ceiling, but with the proviso that no more than 12.5 per cent of equity could be disapplied over five years. Together, pension funds and insurance companies own 55 per cent of UK equity. But within months the ABI had reduced its ceiling to 2.5 per cent again in the face of substantial new equity issues by companies in the form of placings, equity warrants, and euroconvertible bonds. In April 1987 Fisons was forced to withdraw an international issue targeted at European and Japanese investors in the face of pressure from institutional investors. Also in April 1987 C. H. Beazer was forced to reduce its issue of American depository receipts.

The Stock Exchange was forced to mediate between the protagonists. In October 1987 it issued new guidelines which were approved by the Association of Corporate Treasurers, the NAPF, and the ABI. The guidelines permit a listed company to issue up to 5 per cent of its equity capital in any one year and up to 7.5 per cent over three years, without having to offer pre-emption rights. However, the discount at which the new shares are sold must not exceed 5 per cent of the share price (including underwriting fees, typically 2 per cent) at the time of the announcement. The guidelines cover such financing techniques as warrants and euroconvertible bonds, which had in the past been used to overcome pre-emption ceilings. In addition, the guideline limits can be exceeded in exceptional circumstances and after consultation with shareholders.

The guidelines seemed to work quite well. An example of this was the financing arrangement for Next by Salomon Brothers with the placing of euroconvertible bonds by way of a rights issue in September 1987. The bonds were placed with institutional investors at home and abroad, but the bonds placed with domestic institutions were subject to *claw-back*. This meant that existing shareholders could buy back the bonds from the institutions at a claw-back offer price. Any shareholders who did not wish to participate in the offer could sell their nil-paid rights in the market.

15.2.4. THE DANGERS OF FRAUD AND MALPRACTICE

The introduction of personal pension schemes has led to a substantial increase in the number of companies offering such schemes. This increase in competition has the beneficial effect of ensuring that the commissions charged by these companies are more competitively determined. However, it also increases the risk of fraud. The UK financial-services industry is by and large a reasonably safe place to invest. The 1986 Financial Services Act has established a system of self-regulation, and there are heavy penalties for conducting investment business without being authorized. Nevertheless, every now and again there are substantial frauds perpetrated on unwitting investors. The case of gilts specialists Barlow Clowes comes immediately to mind. (Peter Clowes was sentenced to ten years' imprisonment in February 1992.) While the Barlow Clowes case did not involve personal pension schemes, it did involve the savings of many retired investors, and it also revealed the quite astonishing naïvety of even fairly sophisticated private investors.

The *caveat-emptor* warning is as valid today as ever. Whenever such cases emerge there are always calls for tighter regulation, yet there is always the danger of too much regulation. And ever since the Financial Services Act came into force, there have been claims that the UK financial-services industry is over-regulated and warnings that parts of the industry might move to less-regulated centres in Europe.

The balance between too much and too little regulation is a difficult one to set. And the pressures for the industry to move in one direction or another will change with the extent of fraud that materializes. Nevertheless, that balance does have to be set and to be set within a Europe-wide context. It is clearly good for the whole market that investors should have faith in the integrity of the market. But it is also good for investors that the market should not be so over-regulated that the benefits of competition have disappeared.

Even if fraud is not widespread, there is still the possibility of mal-practice of one kind or another. Malpractice is a definite consequence of short-termism. One example is *churning*, the procedure of excessive trading in the asset portfolio in an attempt to generate superior short-term performance. The problem is that churning attracts substantial transactions costs, which tend to reduce the net return on the fund to below that which would have occurred had the portfolio not been traded (as we saw in the last chapter). Churning can also lead to excessive share-price volatility, which is of little use to anyone except speculators.

15.2.5. THE CONSEQUENCES OF REDUCING PENSION-FUND SURPLUSES AND THE INCREASING MATURITY OF PENSION FUNDS

Another potentially destabilizing influence on the markets has resulted from the reduction in pension-fund surpluses. This has taken place largely through the mechanism of employer contributions holidays. This has had the effect of dramatically reducing the flow of new money into the stock markets, which has had two consequences.

First, the pressure on the prices of domestic securities has been con-tained. A substantial proportion of the price rises in the UK markets during the 1980s up until 1987 was due to the weight of new money (in the form of pension contributions and insurance premiums) from institutional investors. When that flow (at least from pension funds) was curtailed from the start of 1987, the pressure for further price rises was also curtailed. As a result, and notwithstanding the crash of October 1987, the UK markets were fairly flat for the remainder of the decade.

Secondly, the reduced flow of contributions has reduced the ability of fund managers to re-balance their asset portfolios using only new money. Traditionally fund managers have been able to re-balance their portfolios away from, say, domestic bonds to overseas equities simply by using the new money to buy overseas equities. With lower cash inflows, fund managers would have to sell domestic bonds in order to increase their portfolio weightings in overseas equities. This strategy raises costs, however, since commissions on turnover are increased.

The increasing maturity of pension funds could also have a destabilizing effect on capital markets. As pension funds mature, asset-liability management becomes more important and, as a consequence, the optimal structure of pension-fund portfolios changes. Maturing pension funds will need to reduce their weighting in equities and increase their weighting in fixed-income bonds in order to reduce the risk of not being able to meet their liabilities when they fall due. In other words, immunization strategies become more important for maturing pension funds (see Section 13.6.2).

If pension funds reduce their demand for equities and increase their demand for bonds, this will cause equity prices to fall and bond prices to rise. So the immediate effect of pension-fund maturity is increased volatility in asset prices.

The longer-term effect might be for companies to reduce the supply of new equity coming to the market and to increase the supply of debt. In other words, companies might respond to these changes in demand by changing their capital structures in favour of greater *leverage* or *gearing*. However, greater corporate leverage has the effect of increasing the riskiness of corporate bonds by reducing the *equity shield*. So the increasing maturity of pension funds might have the perverse result of reducing the effectiveness of the very immunization strategies that are required by the increasing maturity of pension funds.

15.2.6. POOR RELATIONSHIPS BETWEEN TRUSTEES AND INVESTMENT MANAGERS

Under the 1961 Trustee Investments Act, trustees have a legal responsibility to ensure the pension fund is soundly invested. In practice, trustees delegate this responsibility to a professional investment-management company. The trustees provide general investment guidelines, and the investment manager undertakes the day-to-day management of the fund.

The relationship between trustees and investment managers is frequently an unhappy one. This is likely to be the case when one of the parties has no real understanding of the other's role. Typically, the trustees have little understanding of investment management, yet they have to provide general investment guidelines and also assess the subsequent performance of the fund manager. If the trustees are unskilled in executing these functions, the fund manager can be (or can at least feel) unfairly treated.

The main investment guidelines set by trustees are asset-allocation guidelines (principally the proportions of the fund devoted to bonds and equity) and country-allocation guidelines (the proportions of the fund devoted to the various domestic and overseas markets). These are extremely important areas, since subsequent investment performance depends critically on the initial asset and country allocations made. Indeed, the evidence indicates that the asset-allocation and country-allocation decisions dominate investment performance and have a much more important effect than the stock-selection decision (as we saw in the last chapter).

Now, the optimal asset- and country-allocation decisions depend on the investor's attitude to risk. The greater the investor's aversion to risk, the greater the fund's investment in low-risk securities such as government bonds and the less the fund's investment in high-risk securities such as equities; similarly, the greater the fund's investment in stable economies, the less in high-risk economies. However, the lower the fund's risk profile, the lower its expected return; in other words, the lower its expected performance.

The first task of the fund manager after winning the mandate from the trustees is to determine the trustees' attitude to risk. This in itself is an extremely complicated exercise, but the fund manager will invariably be left with the impression that the trustees are 'fairly risk-averse'. This suggests that an investment portfolio should be constructed which has fairly low risk and consequently modest returns on average. Nevertheless, the fund manager can also be confident that when the portfolio's subsequent performance is assessed, the trustees will be critical of the fund manager if their fund's return is below average.

From the fund manager's viewpoint the poor return was the result of the trustees' expressed aversion to risk, but the trustees will have conveniently forgotten this point. Hence, the fund manager may feel that he or she has been unfairly treated by a set of people largely ignorant of the effect that their constraints place on his or her performance.

From the trustees' viewpoint, the fund manager will have promised, during the negotiations leading to the award of the mandate, to bring substantial expertise and experience to the task of managing the pension fund. The fund manager will also have negotiated an attractive management fee, typically based on the end-year value of the fund. In return, the trustees will have reminded the fund manager of their legal responsibilities in respect of the fund, but will then expect the fund manager to deliver on his or her promises.

If the subsequent performance of the fund is poor, the problem of identifying the source of the poor performance is not easy. It could be the result of the constraints imposed by the trustees, poor investment-management decisions, or just bad luck.

Since the mid-1980s the relationship between trustees and fund managers has begun to change quite dramatically. Gone are the days when the chairman of a company whose pension fund needed managing and the chairman of a merchant bank arranged a deal over a cosy drink at their club. As a result of the widespread use of performance-measurement services and the importation of aggressive Wall Street marketing practices, the fund-management process has become very competitive. Now a fund manager must deliver performance or risk being fired.

15.3. Solving the Problem?

The National Association of Pension Funds was sufficiently concerned about the deterioration in the relationship between pension-fund managers and company chairmen (a relationship that has been described as the *Barbarians at the Gate* versus the *Sybarites in the Boardroom*) to publish the opinions of leading 'protagonists' on both sides in a report entitled *Creative Tension?* (National Association of Pension Funds 1990*a*).

Some company directors wished to outlaw short-termist behaviour by fund managers. For example, Sir Hector Laing of United Biscuits suggested that shareholders should be denied voting rights until they have held shares for twelve months. Jonathan Charkham of the Bank of England argued that many pension-fund managers tended to act as punters rather than as stewards of their clients' investments. If shareholders expect company directors to be accountable to them, they must behave responsibly in return. Lord Tombs of Rolls-Royce complained of institutional investors who never bothered to turn up to companies' annual general meetings.

One counter-argument is that company directors frequently forget that it is the shareholders and not the company directors themselves who actually own the company. Sir James Ball of Legal and General argued that, until recent years, shareholders had been 'considerably neglected by companies'. Sir Martin Jacomb of Barclays de Zoete Wedd criticized boards which admitted to bad news only when the market forced it out of them. In extreme cases they then get their own back on shareholders by asking for share dealings to be suspended.

Another counter-argument is that shareholders have every right to keep their company directors in check and that it is only the threat of take-overs that forces company directors to act in the best interests of their shareholders. At other times shareholders appear unable or unwilling to exercise their rights. A recent example of this was the failed take-over bid for BAT Industries by Hoylake, led by Sir James Goldsmith, during 1989–90. Hoylake argued that BAT was being inefficiently run by its management, and that it could release the 'hidden value' in BAT by replacing the management. This hidden value would be shared between existing BAT shareholders and Hoylake. In the event, BAT's management succeeded in defeating the bid and keeping their jobs by implementing the very strategies that Hoylake intended to adopt. The obvious question is: why was the Hoylake bid necessary before they did this?

The real problem is the separation between ownership and control. Shareholders own the company but they are not involved in the day-to-day running of it. Also, shareholders (and this includes institutional shareholders) do not tend to have any expertise in company management *per se*. This is inevitable in large companies. But what is not inevitable is that shareholders should feel completely divorced from their company's management. David Hopkinson of the M&G unit-trust group argues for continuous contact between management and shareholders, especially institutional investors. Another solution, proposed by Sir James Ball and Sir Adrian Cadbury of Cadbury-Schweppes, is to have independent non-executive directors on company boards with their role written into company law. This would certainly cement some degree of long-termism, but company boards have always tended to resist this type of outside interference. Also, institutional investors have the power to insist on independent directors even without a change in the law, but have in the past chosen not to exercise this power. Instead, they have relied on market forces in the form of take-over bids to see that inadequate managements were replaced.

However, very recently institutional investors (through the auspices of the Institutional Shareholders Committee) have begun to take direct action in the managements of companies if they have become dissatisfied with company performance. In the past dissatisfied institutional investors would simply have sold their shares; they have now begun to fire the chairman. For example, in May 1991 institutional investors removed John Fletcher as chairman and chief executive of the Budgens supermarket group, and in June 1991 they removed John Hardman as chairman and chief executive of the Asda supermarket group. In the case of Asda, the institutional investors, which included the Prudential, Schroders, and Scottish Widows, demanded a separation of the roles of chairman and chief executive and the appointment of more non-executive directors to represent the interests of the main shareholders.

Nevertheless, the problem of short-termism in the UK has not been resolved and, moreover, does not look like going away. Pension-scheme members are entitled to expect that their pension funds do not act in a way that destabilizes the very companies for which they work. Nor should it be forgotten just how pension funds have achieved their strong position. It is as a result of the huge tax advantages which pension funds enjoy, and which have been used over the last thirty years to decimate private shareholders, the very group of investors who historically have provided such a loyal and stabilizing influence on the companies that they invested in.

If pension funds and other institutional investors continue to behave irresponsibly, there is no reason why they should continue to do so with the benefit of huge subsidies from the taxpayer.

Selected References for Part III

ALTMAN, R. M., and ATKINSON, A. B. (1982), 'State Pensions, Taxation and Retirement Income, 1981–2031', in M. Fogarty (ed.), *Retirement Policy: The Next Fifty Years* (Heinemann, London).

ATKINSON, A. B. (1991), *The Development of State Pensions in the United Kingdom*, Welfare State Programme Discussion Paper No. WSP/58 (Suntory-Toyota International Centre for Economics and Related Disciplines, London School of Economics, London).

Bank of England Quarterly Bulletin (1986), 'Asset Groupings of Life Assurance and Pension Funds' (Dec.).

BENJAMIN, B., HABERMAN, S., HELOWICZ, G., KAYE, G., and WILKIE, D. (1987), *Pensions: The Problems of Today and Tomorrow* (Allen and Unwin, London).

BLAKE, D. (1990), *Financial Market Analysis* (McGraw-Hill, London).

—— (1992), *Modelling Pension Fund Investment Behaviour* (Routledge, London).

BODIE, Z. (1991), 'The Effect of Pension Funds on US Capital Markets' mimeo. (Boston University, Boston, Mass.).

CARNE, P. G. C., and OGWUAZOR, P. P. E. (1989), 'A Guide to Accounting Standards: Accounting for Pension Costs' *Accountants Digest* (Institute of Chartered Accountants in England and Wales, London, Winter).

CREEDY, J. (1982), *State Pensions in Britain* (Cambridge University Press, Cambridge).

DAVIS, E., and BANNOCK, G. (1991), *Corporate Takeovers and the Public Interest* (David Hume Institute, Edinburgh).

DAVIS, E. P. (1988), *Financial Market Activity of Life Insurance Companies and Pension Funds* (Bank of International Settlements Economic Papers No. 21, Basle).

—— (1991a), 'International Diversification of Institutional Investors', *Journal of International Securities Markets* (Summer), 143–67.

—— (1991b), 'The Development of Pension Funds: An International Comparison', *Bank of England Quarterly Bulletin* (Aug.), 380–90.

—— (1992a), 'The Development of Pension Funds in the Major Industrial Countries', in *Planning for Retirement in Europe* (Centre for European Policy Studies, Brussels).

—— (1992b), 'The Structure, Regulation and Performance of Pension Funds in Nine Industrial Countries' (Bank of England Discussion Paper, London).

ESCOLME, B., HUDSON, D., and GREENWOOD, P. (1991), *Hosking's Pension Schemes and Retirement Benefits* (Sweet and Maxwell, London).

FABOZZI, F. J. (ed.) (1990), *Pension Fund Investment Management* (McGraw-Hill, London).

FAMA, E. (1972), 'Components of Investment Performance', *Journal of Finance* 17, 551–67.

Financial Times Survey (1990), *Pension Fund Investment* (May).

—— (1991), *Pension Fund Investment* (Apr.).

FONG, H. G., PEARSON, C., and VASICEK, O. (1983), 'Bond Performance: Analysing Sources of Returns', *Journal of Portfolio Management* (Spring), 46–50.

GIARINI, O. (ed.) (1990), *Studies on the Four Pillars* (Geneva Papers on Risk and Insurance No. 55, Apr.).

GOODE, PROFESSOR R. (chairman) (1993), *Pension Law Reform: Report of the Pension Law Review Committee*, CM. 2342 (HMSO, London, Sept.).

Government Actuary (1990), *National Insurance Fund Long Term Estimate* (HMSO, London).

—— (GASOPS) (1991), *Occupational Pension Schemes 1987: Eighth Survey by the Government Actuary* (HMSO, London).

HAGER, D. P. (1980), *Measurement of Pension Fund Investment Performance* (Bacon and Woodrow, Consulting Actuaries, Jan.).

—— and LEVER, C. D. (1989), *Pension Fund Investment* (Butterworths, London).

Income Data Services (IDS) (1979), *Public Sector Pensions*, Study 188 (Income Data Services, London, Feb.).

JENSEN, M. (1969), 'Risk, the Pricing of Capital Assets and the Evaluation of Investment Portfolios', *Journal of Business* 42, 167–247.

JOHNSON, P., CONRAD, C., and THOMSON, D. (eds.) (1989), *Workers versus Pensioners: Intergenerational Justice in an Ageing World* (Manchester University Press, Manchester).

JOLLANS, A. (1991), *European Community Action in the Field of Pension Funds* (Commission of the European Communities, Brussels).

KEATING, G., and SMYTH, M. (1985), 'The Pension Fund Surpluses', *Financial Outlook* 3 (Gower Publishing, Aldershot, Nov.), 4–10.

LEVER, C. D. (1981), *Musings of a Scoreboard Operator—Some Reflections on Our Measurement of Investment Performance Service* (Bacon and Woodrow, Consulting Actuaries, London, Mar.).

MEGARRY, Sir R. (1984), *Judgment in the Matter of the Trusts of the Mineworkers' Pension Scheme*, CH 1983, M No. 5498.

MINNS, R. (1980), *Pension Funds and British Capitalism* (Heinemann, London).

National Association of Pension Funds Yearbook (1989) (National Association of Pension Funds, London).

National Association of Pension Funds Report (1990a), *Creative Tension?* (National Association of Pension Funds, London, Feb.).

—— (1990b), *Investment Performance Measurement* (Report of the Stonefrost Committee of Enquiry) (National Association of Pension Funds, London, Dec.).

—— (1991), *Equalising State Pension Ages* (National Association of Pension Funds, London, Mar.).

National Audit Office (1990), *The Elderly: Information Requirements for Supporting the Elderly and Implications of Personal Pensions for the National Insurance Fund* (HMSO, London, Nov.).

Pension Funds and their Advisers (1990) (AP Information Services, London).

Pension Fund Indicators—A Long-Term Perspective on Pension Fund Investment (1991) (Phillips and Drew Fund Management, London, Apr.).

PRODANO, S. (1987), *Pension Funds: Investment and Performance* (Gower, Aldershot).

RADCLIFFE, Rt. Hon. the Lord (chairman) (1959), *Report of the Committee on the Working of the Monetary System*, Cmnd. 827 (HMSO, London, Aug.).

SCOTT, Sir B. (chairman) (1981), *Report of the Committee of Inquiry into the Value of Pensions*, Cmnd. 8147 (HMSO, London, Feb.).

SHARPE, W. F. (1966), 'Mutual Fund Performance', *Journal of Business* 39, 119–38.

SHEPHERD, A. G. (ed.) (1987), *Pension Fund Investment* (Woodhead-Faulkner, Cambridge).

SOUTHALL, S., and PUNTER, J. (1985), *A Pension Scheme Wind-Up: Legitimate Act or Smash and Grab?* (Mercer Fraser, London).

TAYLOR, C. (1986), *The Marketing of Fund Management Services* (Portfolio Management Division, Fuji International Finance, London).

Tolley's Accounting for Pension Costs (1993) (Tolley Publishing, Croydon).

Tolley's Income Tax 1993–94 (1993) (Tolley Publishing, Croydon).

TREYNOR, J. (1965), 'How to Rate Management of Investment Funds', *Harvard Business Review* 43, 63–75.

WM Company Annual Review: UK Pension Fund Service (1991) (The World Markets Company, Edinburgh).

WILKIE, D., and WILSON, A. (1986), 'The Pension Fund Surpluses: A Comment', *Financial Outlook* 3 (Gower Publishing, Aldershot, July), 4–8.

WILSON, Rt. Hon. Sir H. (chairman) (1980), *Report of the Committee to Review the Functioning of Financial Institutions*, Cmnd. 7937 (HMSO, London, June).

WOLANSKI, H. (1980), *Pension Funds and their Advisers* (AP Financial Registers, London).

PART IV

THE FUTURE

In the final part of the book we look into the future. Chapter 16 analyses the changes that might take place as a result of a Labour government being elected in the UK; it also looks at developments in Europe and the USA and how these might affect UK pension funds. Finally, in the light of the problems with the existing framework of UK pension schemes that have emerged in the earlier parts of the book, we propose in Chapter 17 a new fifteen-point ideal pension scheme.

16

Future Developments

In this chapter we look briefly into a crystal ball in order to see what the future might hold for UK pension schemes and funds. As we have seen, the political party in power has a commanding influence over the UK pensions framework, so the first task is to examine the pensions proposals that a future Labour government would implement. We have also seen that the European Union has an increasing influence on the domestic legislation of Member States, so the next task is to examine developments at the EU level. Finally, we look at developments in the USA, the leading innovator in the field of pension schemes and pension funding.

16.1. The Proposals of a Future Labour Government

The Conservative government in power since 1979 has introduced some very radical changes to the pensions system in the UK. A Labour government would reverse many, although not all, of these changes, according to the Labour Party's *Policy Review for the 1990s*.

The most important change would be to revamp SERPS, the State Earnings-Related Pension Scheme. In particular, a Labour government would reintroduce a SERPS pension based on the best twenty years of earnings, rather than on career-revalued earnings. It would also be possible to pay additional contributions into SERPS in order to enhance benefits or to fill in gaps in the contributions record. In addition, the self-employed would be permitted to join SERPS for the first time. State pensions would be increased annually in line with earnings instead of prices. In addition, the single-person and married-couple pensions would rise by respectively £5 and £8 per week immediately a Labour government came into office. These changes would be financed through the introduction of a 50 per-cent rate of income tax on gross earnings above £40,000 p.a. and the removal of the ceiling on employee national-insurance contributions; at the same time, the 2 per-cent rate of employee national-insurance contributions on earnings below the lower earnings limit would be abolished.

A Labour government would require occupational pension schemes to revalue their pensions automatically in line with inflation. Not fully index-linking benefits is regarded by the Labour Party as 'a form of legalised expropriation', since pensions are a form of deferred pay. However, in the event of a 'real economic crisis', the requirement fully to index benefits could be temporarily waived. The 1990 Social Security Act requires occupational pensions to be up-rated in line with inflation, but only up to a limit of 5 per cent p.a. Over the last twenty-five years inflation in the UK has averaged 8.7 per cent p.a. A Labour government would also introduce legislation to prevent companies recovering any surpluses in their schemes.

A Labour government would enable employees to have half the voting rights on boards of trustees. In June 1991 Michael Meacher, Labour's social-security spokesman, announced that 'a pension fund is the property of present and former employees. Our proposal for 50 per cent representation by employees on boards of trustees will ensure that employers cannot treat funds as theirs to do with as they wish.' As shown in Section 16.2.2.2 below, 50 per-cent representation is quite common in Europe. In addition, a Labour government would curb the activities of pension funds and other institutional investors to prevent hostile take-overs of UK companies.

The Labour Party would remove the 'artificial bribes' in the form of additional national-insurance rebates which are being used to encourage people to contract out of SERPS and take out personal pension schemes. This would reduce the optimal age of re-contracting back into SERPS from 45 to 40 for men and from 40 to 35 for women. It would also change the status of personal pension schemes (and contracted-out money-purchase schemes) from one based on the payment of guaranteed minimum contributions, to one based on the provision of a guaranteed minimum pension. In addition, it would restrict tax relief on pension contributions to the basic rate of income tax.

In the past pension rights have not usually been taken into account in the case of divorce, and so by default have been split according to who has made the contributions. This generally means that the man benefits most. But the Matrimonial Causes Act 1973 requires pension rights to be taken into account in a divorce settlement. The Labour Party wants to go further and have pension assets divided equally between each partner in the event of divorce. In the case where more than a single marriage is involved, pension rights to wives and ex-wives would be based on the relative duration of their marriages.

16.2. Developments in the European Union

16.2.1. CURRENT PENSION ARRANGEMENTS IN EUROPE

Table 16.1 shows the type of occupational pension schemes available in other Member States of the European Union. Where they exist, most occupational schemes are defined-benefit schemes. The main exception is Denmark, where most pension schemes are based on defined contributions; there are also defined-contribution schemes in Belgium. In Italy, however, almost everyone gets very high social-security pensions, and occupational pension schemes are available only for senior executives.

TABLE 16.1. *Occupational pension schemes in the European Union*

Country	Types of scheme	Methods of financing
Belgium	Employer-funded arrangements. Both defined contribution and defined benefit.	Small employers—generally insured arrangements. Medium employers— deposit administration contracts. Large employers—private directly invested schemes called ABSLs.
Denmark	Employer-funded arrangements. Mainly defined contribution.	Most employers small, so most plans insured.
France	Based on a points system, approximates to career-average revalued benefit.	Industry-wide schemes financed on a pay-as-you-go basis.
Germany	Defined-benefit arrangements.	Book reserve on employer's balance sheet with compulsory insolvency insurance. Some direct insurance arrangements with insurance companies.
Greece	Senior employees, defined benefit. For other employees, high social-security benefits adequate, little occupational-scheme coverage. In some industries there are industry-wide union plans.	Deposit administration contracts.

TABLE 16.1. *Continued*

Country	Types of scheme	Methods of financing
Ireland	Employer-funded arrangements. Mainly defined benefit.	Similar to United Kingdom. Directly invested schemes and insured arrangements.
Italy	Very high social-security benefits—few occupational schemes, only for senior executives.	Where schemes exist— group insurance.
Luxembourg	Very high social-security benefits—few occupational schemes.	Where schemes exist— group insurance or book reserves.
Netherlands	Law requires any pension promise to be funded. Individual employer and industry-wide schemes common.	Directly invested schemes and insured arrangements.
Portugal	Defined-benefit schemes.	Schemes existing prior to 1986—pay-as-you-go common. New schemes post-1986 required to be funded. Group insurance policies common.
Spain	Defined-benefit schemes supplement social-security system.	To be tax qualified, a scheme must be funded. Pay-as-you-go with or without book reserves is still common. Directly invested schemes. Deposit administration contracts. Since 1987 book reserves and deposit administration schemes classed as non-qualified schemes.

Source: Escolme *et al.* (1991, pp. 203–4).

It is estimated that the value of pension funds in the EU exceeds 700bn. ECUs (Jollans 1991). Of this, over half is accounted for by UK pension funds and another 25 per cent by Dutch pension funds. Pension funds are also relatively important in Ireland, Denmark, and to a lesser extent in Belgium. However, they are not widespread in the rest of the EU. In France, for example, pensions are mostly provided on a pay-as-you-go basis. In Germany, on the other hand, pension schemes are financed through *book reserves* on company balance sheets (together with compulsory insolvency insurance). Elsewhere in the EU, where funding exists, most schemes are based on deposit administration, that is, contracts with low-risk deposit-taking institutions (see also Davis 1991; 1992*a*,*b*).

16.2.2. PROPOSALS FOR 1992 AND AFTER

In terms of future developments within the European Union, there are two main themes. Both relate to the Single European Market after 1992. The first theme deals with state-pension and social-security benefits, and the second deals with pension funds.

16.2.2.1. *The Community Charter*

In terms of state-pension and social-security benefits, current EU thinking is expressed in the 1989 *Community Charter of the Fundamental Social Rights of Workers.*[1] The Charter states that (quoted from Atkinson 1991, p. 1):

1. Every worker of the European Union must, at the time of retirement, be able to enjoy resources affording him or her a decent standard of living (para. 24).
2. Any person who has reached retirement age but who is not entitled to a pension or who does not have other means of subsistence, must be entitled to sufficient resources and to medical and social assistance specifically suited to his or her needs (para. 25).

As Atkinson argues, the first principle requires that each Member State's pension system guarantees to provide an earnings-related pension with a reasonable *income-replacement ratio*, that is, a pension that is a reasonable proportion of final salary. The second principle requires that, even in the absence of a specific pension entitlement, individuals are entitled to a minimum level of resources. The Charter does not put precise figures to

---

[1] There are twelve fundamental social rights: freedom of movement for EU nationals; freedom to choose and engage in an occupation and to be fairly remunerated; improvement of living and working conditions; social protection; freedom of association and collective bargaining; vocational training; equal treatment; information, consultation, and participation; protection of health and safety at the workplace; protection of children and young persons; protection of the elderly; and protection for the disabled.

these objectives, nor does it require all Member States to provide exactly the same pension and social-security benefits, although it is clear that the ultimate objective is convergence towards the best pension and social-security benefits on offer in the EU.

In the UK context these objectives are addressed through a combination of a mixed flat-rate/earnings-related *state social-security pension scheme*, and *income support*, a means-tested system of social assistance. The full basic flat-rate pension is about 16 per cent of the average earnings of male full-time employees. An individual with lifetime average earnings equal to male national-average earnings at the date of retirement will receive a total state pension equal to 33 per cent of final gross salary, that is, a gross replacement ratio of 33 per cent (corresponding to a net replacement ratio of 42.5 per cent). An individual on half national-average male earnings has a gross replacement ratio of 45 per cent, while someone on one-and-a-half times national-average male earnings has a gross replacement ratio of 28.5 per cent.

The UK state pension scheme is much less generous than that typically operating in the rest of Europe. For example, in Germany the median gross replacement ratio is 55.8 per cent (corresponding to a net replacement ratio of 65 per cent), while in France the gross replacement ratio lies between 59 per cent and 71 per cent in the private sector and averages 61 per cent in the public sector. The Italian state pension is 2 per cent of earnings for each year of contributions, payable from the age of 55 for women and 60 for men. After forty years' service the pension is therefore 80 per cent of earnings. This contrasts with the full UK basic flat-rate state pension of £52 per week (in 1991–2), earned after 40 to 45 years of work from the age of 60 for women and 65 for men and which equals only 16 per cent of average earnings. In addition, the contribution-rate is less than 1 per cent of earnings in Italy compared with 9 per cent in the UK.

Furthermore, the UK basic flat-rate pension will systematically fall over time as a proportion of average earnings. This follows from the Thatcher government's switch in the early 1980s from a policy of indexing pension increases to the higher of wage or price inflation, to one of indexing pension increases to price inflation only. The government actuary (1990) has calculated that if real earnings grow at 1.5 per cent p.a., then the basic pension falls from 16 per cent of average earnings in 1990 to 8 per cent in 2040. If real earnings grow at 2.5 per cent p.a., the basic pension falls to 8 per cent of average earnings in 2018. With pensions linked to prices, the government actuary calculates that the combined employee and employer Class 1 national-insurance contribution falls from 19.1 per cent of relevant earnings in 1990–1 to 14.1 per cent of relevant earnings in 2050–1. However, with pensions linked to earnings rather than prices, the combined contribution increases from 19.1 per cent to 24.5 per cent.

Not only has the UK government reduced the relative value of the basic state pension, it has also, as a result of the 1986 Social Security Act, reduced the value of the state earnings-related pension from the year 1999. The effect of the act was to reduce the formula for calculating the SERPS pension from 25 per cent of the best twenty years' earnings to 20 per cent of career earnings (although both are revalued using an earnings index). Creedy (1982) has calculated that pensions based on the best twenty years' earnings are about 20 per cent higher than pensions based on career earnings. Atkinson (1991) has calculated that someone whose best twenty years' earnings are 1.2 times average male earnings will have his pension cut from 42 per cent of final gross earnings (52 per cent of net earnings) to 33 per cent of final gross earnings (42.5 per cent of net earnings) following the 1986 act. The SERPS pension is low compared with the pension available from occupational pension schemes, where the best pension available is equal to 67 per cent of final salary.

Atkinson also questions whether personal pensions are compatible with the Community Charter's first objective of ensuring that every retired worker has sufficient resources to afford a decent standard of living. He argues that:

With personal pensions ... there is no guaranteed pension at retirement ... There must be concern about those who are unlucky in their choice of investments: there is no redistribution between those whose investments have performed well and those whose turn out to be less well chosen. A guarantee is replaced by a lottery. The uncertainty surrounds both the capital sum which will be available at retirement and the rate of annuity which it will purchase. (1991, p. 20)

In terms of the Charter's second principle, the provision of a minimum level of resources in retirement, the government has sought to meet this through income support, the latest in a long line of means-tested minimum-level benefits stretching back to the Poor Laws. However, Atkinson points out that a substantial proportion of those entitled to these benefits do not claim them. In 1985 the DSS estimated that the take-up rate for supplementary pensions was only 79 per cent, implying that £100m. went unclaimed in that year. It was expected that the effect of SERPS would be to reduce the need for supplementary benefit in retirement as SERPS entitlements built up. Altman and Atkinson (1982) estimated that the original SERPS would reduce the predicted number of people with incomes below the supplementary-benefit level in 2016 from 2.7 million to below 1 million. Atkinson argues that 'in its current scaled-

down version, [SERPS] will be less effective, and low incomes among a
minority of the elderly are likely to be a continuing problem in the next
century' (1991, p. 24).

Atkinson concludes by saying that the UK state-pension system fails to
meet the objectives of the Community Charter. The SERPS pension
offers a replacement ratio that is low both by European standards and in
comparison with occupational schemes. Also, the means-tested income
support fails to provide a fully effective safety net. Further, personal
pensions, by definition, cannot provide a guaranteed minimum pension.
In addition, the UK government refused to sign the Social Chapter of the
Maastricht Treaty in December 1991.

16.2.2.2. *Europe-Wide Pension Funds*

The second area of future developments concerning the EU covers pension funds. EU thinking in this, as well as many other fields, is dominated
by the principle of *subsidiarity*. Subsidiarity means that matters which *can*
be dealt with satisfactorily at national level *should* be dealt with at
national level, and the EU should not intervene unnecessarily. Subsidiarity
has replaced the earlier principle of *harmonization*, which required the
convergence of policies among Member States.

Jollans (1991) offered some reasons why there were limits to subsidiarity in terms of pension provision. He argued that companies could
employ staff in different Member States without having to establish separate companies in each state. The employees could be paid across national
borders. But pensions, which the European Court of Justice has established as being deferred pay, could not easily be provided across national
borders. One company with operations in each Member State had to
establish twelve separate pension schemes and funds. This meant that
an employee who moved between Member States could not remain in
the same pension scheme, even where he or she was working for the same
employer.

Jollans also pointed out the problems faced by pension funds operating
at the European level, particularly in respect of their investment activities. They were in practice limited to investment managers selected
from the home state. They were also limited in their choice of cross-
border investments by regulations that discriminate in favour of local
investments. For example, investments in other Member States were
often subject to withholding taxes which could not be reclaimed by
pension funds, even though they were tax-exempt investors.

In October 1991 the First Pension Funds Directive was approved by the
European Commission. It embodied the following objectives for both
private-sector and public-sector pension funds in a European context
from the beginning of 1993:

1. the freedom for cross-border investment management of pension funds: Member States are no longer able to require that a pension fund be managed locally, and multinational companies are able to manage their European pension funds on a group basis with a single fund and a single fund manager; and
2. the freedom for cross-border investment of pension-fund assets: Member States can no longer require a minimum investment in a specific category of asset or in a specific location, nor can they require that more than 60 per cent of a fund's liabilities be matched in terms of assets in the same currency (the maximum was 80 per cent in the case of money-purchase schemes, and ECU-denominated assets could match any EU currency).

These objectives related specifically to pension funds as separately constituted entities that accumulate investment funds, and therefore excluded book-reserve systems and pay-as-you-go systems of funding. In France this definition included the 'caisses de retraite', while in Italy it included the 'casse di previdenza' and the 'fondi speciali di previdenza'. But it principally referred to the pension funds of the UK, the Netherlands, and Ireland.

The first objective, freedom of services for cross-border investment management, is already sanctioned by the Treaty of Rome. Indeed, providers of investment-management services have the right to offer their services throughout Europe on the basis of a single licence, through the Second Banking Directive, the Third Life Assurance Directive, and the Investment Services Directive which implemented the Treaty principle. However, in some Member States it was not possible for pension funds to accept investment-management services from a provider not established in the same Member State.

The second objective, freedom of cross-border investment of assets, is also sanctioned in general terms by the Treaty of Rome and has been implemented in the Capital Markets Directive. This directive removed direct restrictions on transferring funds across borders and indirect barriers limiting these transactions. The directive did permit two exceptions:

- restrictions on exceptionally large short-term capital movements, which could disturb foreign-exchange markets or domestic liquidity; and
- restrictions based on prudential reasons for the protection of the consumers of financial services.

The second exception has been used by Member States to impose restrictions that, according to Jollans, 'go well beyond what can be justified on prudential grounds' (1991, p. 5). Jollans, reflecting the Commission's view, argues that for a pension fund with liabilities denominated in real terms, the most prudential investment policy is one which is widely diversified. The Commission therefore took the view that the exceptions to the Capital Markets Directive that could be justified on prudential grounds should be strictly limited.

The Commission's original proposals had suggested full cross-border pensions provision: 'The possibility to belong to a pension fund established in another Member State without legal or financial discrimination is an important freedom and a necessary measure for the completion of the internal market.' They also embodied two further objectives that did not subsequently appear in the First Pension Funds Directive:

3. the freedom for cross-border membership of pension funds; and
4. the freedom for cross-border protection of benefits on changes of employment.

It soon became clear that these last two objectives were too ambitious to implement in the short term.

For example, the third objective, freedom of cross-border membership, requires *mutual recognition* of the different legal and supervisory systems between Member States on the basis of:

- certain common investment principles in respect of:
  (a) matching assets and liabilities,
  (b) spreading of risk through diversification,
  (c) maintaining sufficient liquidity, and
  (d) limitations on self-investment in the sponsoring company;
- agreement on a minimum funding standard that ensures the protection of members' rights; and
- periodic disclosure of accounts and actuarial reports.

Member States have to be satisfied that the legal and supervisory systems in other Member States give adequate protection to their citizens who take out contracts with financial institutions that do not come under their direct control.

A related issue is mutual fiscal recognition. Given the tax reliefs that are available in some Member States on pension contributions and investments, a principal concern of the tax authorities in any country is to prevent over-funding and the abuse of tax privileges. Further, there are wide differences in the tax treatment of pension contributions and vesting requirements between different Member States: in Germany and Luxembourg there is no employee tax relief on contributions; in Belgium the investment income from pension funds is taxed; and in Germany pension schemes have stringent vesting requirements, with a qualifying period of ten years' employment and no pension entitlement for employees leaving before the age of 35. In addition, a Pension Funds Directive involving tax proposals requires unanimous rather than qualified-majority approval. In the light of previous experience, unanimous agreement might take twenty years of negotiation to achieve.

Another related issue is employee participation. Currently Member States either have no legal requirements for member participation or have a requirement to have a specific level (usually 50 per cent) of representation on the decision-making body of the pension fund. In the case of Spain more than 50 per-cent participation is required. In the former case there is usually some level of participation. The Commission's original proposals set a target of 50 per-cent participation, but also recognized the sensitivities of Member States in this matter and the scope for obstruction by certain Member States in achieving this target.

The third objective has been delayed until the implementation of a Second Pension Funds Directive. The fourth objective, the freedom of cross-border protection of benefits from pension funds on changing employment, has also been delayed. But the Commission has no proposals dealing with the level of benefits from pension funds. The Commission accepts that the level of pension-fund benefits, as with the level of wages, is a matter of subsidiarity rather than harmonization within the Community.

The First Pension Funds Directive is generally regarded as only a first step towards full liberalization. Apart from the objectives that were not implemented, there was no attempt to move towards 'passports' for pension-scheme providers of the kind given to banks under the Banking Directive; the passport grants to any institution recognized as competent to operate in one Member State the right to operate throughout the EU. Also there is no plan to establish a central verification body: national governments are left to monitor compliance, leading to the possibility of divergent standards developing. Nevertheless, Hoffman (1992) argues that the Pension Funds Directive, along with the other capital-liberalization directives, could lead to a tripling of cross-border investment, from 350bn. ECUs to 1 trillion ECUs. He argues that there would be some profound consequences:

A pool of savings in the developed world would be liberated for investment opportunities throughout the world; the institutional shareholder would become a force throughout European industry, with the result that many companies [would] become subject to shareholder control for effectively the first time; and there would be a growing demand for ECU-denominated equities. (p. 1)

Davis (1993) also forecasts a financial revolution in continental Europe in the near future. His starting point is Europe's ageing population which will make the state funding of pensions increasingly onerous if dramatic changes are not made soon. But he sees a tremendous opportunity for continental capital markets if a system of private-sector pension funding takes over from the current state-operated pay-as-you-go schemes. As contributions flow into private-sector pension funds, this will be translated into a demand for the equity of European companies. The French, for example, have realised that the privatisation programme that they announced in the early 1990s will not be successful unless institutional investors such as pension funds are there on the other side to bid for the equity up for sale. In addition private-sector companies will choose to issue equity in response to this new source of demand. This will lead to substantial changes in the financial structure of continental European companies with sharp falls in debt/equity ratios predicted as equity financing replaces debt financing.

The activities of pension funds may also increase the allocative efficiency of Europe's financial markets. Increased equity trading may reduce stock market volatility and increase liquidity. Historically stock market volatility has been higher in France and Germany than it has been in the UK or the US (the standard deviations of annual real total returns between 1967 and 1990 were 26.9 per cent for France, 20.3 per cent for Germany, 18.9 per cent for the UK, and 14.4 per cent for the US). This is because foreigners have dominated trading on continental exchanges. The introduction of European pension funds would ensure a stable but active investor base as well as increasing the size and depth of the equity market. This in turn would help to increase liquidity, i.e. the ability to trade in large size without adverse movements in price and at low transactions costs. The present lack of liquidity in continental exchanges is reflected in the success of SEAQ International in London which in 1993 executed 50 per cent of French and Italian and 30 per cent of German share transactions.

A final dramatic impact of European pension funds will be to reduce the domination by banks of continental companies, especially German companies, both in terms of main-board membership and the ratio of bank loans in financial structure. The arguments that have been put forward in favour of bank domination are that companies can obtain secure, long-term debt finance for investment and research and development, and that banks are more willing than markets to rescue companies in trouble. As a consequence of this, there is very little public disclosure of information by companies, there is a preference for insider control and the close holding of company shares, and an informal rather than a rule-based system for conducting financial relations. Pension funds will not be willing to accept subordination to banks and are therefore likely to seek to overturn the whole continental system. Davis (op. cit.) believes that this could lead to a convergence of the continental financial system to the 'Anglo-Saxon' model operated by the US and the UK which gives primacy to equity-holders as ultimate owners of the firm. Equity-holders demand higher and more stable dividend payments, more public disclosure of information by companies, the removal of underperforming managers, equal voting rights for all shares, pre-emption rights, and equal treatment in takeovers. To back up these demands, pension funds would require the establishment of a regulatory framework in continental Europe that covered takeovers, insider information, dual classes of shares, and the equal treatment of creditors in bankruptcy to protect the funds' corporate bond holdings. However, these changes might also introduce some of the problems associated with the Anglo-Saxon model, in particular short-termism, the willingness to sell shares to predators in hostile takeovers and the preference for short-term dividends over long-term investment and research and development: the savings ratio is much lower in Anglo-Saxon than in continental financial systems.

16.3. Lessons from the United States

US pension funds are huge: in 1988 two-thirds of the world's pension assets were held in US pension funds. They are five times larger by value of assets than UK pension funds. Developments in US pension funds provide lessons for the UK and the rest of the world (Bodie 1991; Davis 1991).

16.3.1. INNOVATIONS IN FINANCIAL PRODUCTS, INTERMEDIARIES, AND STRATEGIES

One of the main developments in the USA over the last twenty years has been an explosion of new financial products (that is, *financial innovations*), especially *hedging* or *risk-management* products (see Section 13.12). There have been two major factors underlying this explosion. The first was the increasing volatility of interest rates and exchange rates beginning in the early 1970s. The second was the passing of the Employee Retirement Income Security Act (ERISA) in 1974. ERISA codified the legal status of companies' obligations in defined-benefit pension schemes. It also imposed minimum funding requirements on the basis of a *prudent-man principle*. Pension funds now had a legal obligation to match assets and liabilities, and failure to do so meant that companies could be sued. The first factor provided pension funds with the opportunity to engage in risk-management activities. The second provided them with the need to do so.

This demand for hedging instruments by pension funds was met by the creation of new types of hedging instruments, particularly those suitable for the *immunization* of portfolios and the *duration matching* of assets to liabilities (see Section 13.6.2). Thus a multitude of new hedging instruments, mainly fixed-income bond products and stock-index derivative products, came on to the market. Two of the most important examples of fixed-income bond products are *guaranteed income contracts* (GICs) and *collateralized mortgage obligations* (CMOs).

GICs are zero-coupon bonds of up to six years' maturity issued by insurance companies to pension funds. GICs guarantee a nominal rate of return to the investor, but also offer the investor the option of withdrawing money early with no penalty. They are particularly useful in defined-contribution schemes. The insurance companies themselves hedge the interest-rate risk by investing in fixed-income securities.

CMOs are packaged securitized mortgages issued in tranches to reduce the *prepayment risk* associated with standard mortgage-backed securities. The fast-pay tranche gets interest plus *all* the capital repayments on the mortgages until the principal on this tranche is fully redeemed; it is the shortest-maturity tranche. In the interim, the other tranches receive interest only. Once the fast-pay tranche has been repaid, the second tranche receives *all* capital repayments, until it too is fully redeemed. This process continues until the last tranche, known as the slow-pay or Z-tranche, receives capital repayments once all the earlier tranches have been redeemed; it is the longest-maturity tranche. The advantage of CMOs to pension funds is that they allow them to invest in fixed-income securities with known maturities that are fully asset-backed. (These and other types of new financial products are explained in more detail in Rivett and Speak 1991.)

In contrast to these successful innovations, there have also been innovations that have failed, again as a result of pension funds. The most notable of these have been long-term inflation-protected securities such as *CPI-linked bonds*. There have been many potential issuers of such bonds, but the market has failed because of insufficient demand from pension funds and other institutional investors. Bodie (1990) regards this as evidence that US pension funds do not view their liabilities as indexed for inflation. Alternatively, he says, it is evidence that people already have enough inflation insurance for their retirement. US social-security retirement benefits are indexed to retail prices, and much personal saving is invested in residential property which is a good long-term inflation hedge. In terms of inflation indexation the UK is ahead of the USA. The UK government has issued index-linked bonds since 1981 and has required limited but mandatory indexation of occupational pensions since 1988.

Not only have US pension funds prompted the introduction of many new financial products, they have also led to the introduction of new financial intermediaries and investment strategies. The most important new type of financial intermediary is the specialist *asset–liability-management company* devoted to the management of pension-fund assets (see Section 13.3). One of the most important new investment strategies is *index matching*. This is the strategy of managing a portfolio so as to match the performance of a stock- or bond-market index. This is a strategy that is suitable for very large pension funds which cannot engage in active portfolio trading in any significant way, since the size of their transactions is likely to lead to the market moving adversely against them (for more details see Section 13.6.1).

16.3.2. DISRUPTIONS TO SECURITY MARKETS AND COMPANIES

Security-market volatility, especially that at the time of the October 1987 stock-market crash, was blamed on a combination of a *stock-index arbitrage* strategy known as *program trading* and a *dynamic hedging* strategy called *portfolio insurance* (see, for example, Blake 1990, chap. 16). If the value of the futures stock-index gets out of line with the cash stock-index, a stock index-arbitrage opportunity emerges. To exploit such opportunities, sophisticated computer programs were developed to signal buy or sell instructions. With large numbers of investors sending buy or sell instructions to the market at the same time, this could lead to huge shifts in security prices and hence to increased stock-market volatility. At the same time, pension funds used dynamic hedging strategies to protect themselves against *shortfall risk*, the risk of the value of their assets falling below that of their liabilities. This involves the funds automatically liquidating their share portfolios as markets start to fall. This will tend to accentuate any market downturn and, indeed, has been put forward as the principal cause of the 1987 crash.

US pension funds have also been blamed for *short-termism*. In particular, they have been criticized for excessive *churning* and *speculation*. Indeed, in 1989 Congress passed the Excessive Churning and Speculation Act which penalizes these activities by taxing the short-term capital gains of pension funds. Senator Kassebaum, one of the sponsors of the act, argues that: 'The legislation is designed to encourage pension fund managers to adopt a better long-term investment strategy...Absent such a change, we face the stark prospect of losing our status as a major industrial player.'

Another aspect of short-termism for which pension funds have been heavily criticized is that, although they are substantial owners of the stock of many corporations, they do not become involved enough in the management of those corporations. If they are dissatisfied with a company's action or performance, they have in the past simply sold the company's shares rather than challenged the company's management. In other words, they abdicate their shareholder voting rights or their rights to *corporate governance*.

This criticism of pension funds in the USA, reported by Bodie as recently as May 1991, is also common in the UK. However, it does not correspond with the perception of US pension funds in the UK. Consider the following comment made in a British national newspaper in July 1991:

The Americans are coming. The top 60 American pension funds with $300 billion under management expect to increase their holdings of UK and European stocks from 5% to 20% of their portfolios in a couple of years. Americans just *lurve* corporate governance. They are not averse to highly public rows with entrenched managements if necessary and they take [shareholders'] democracy very seriously. (City Comment, *Daily Telegraph*, 13 July 1991)

The evidence that the City commentator provided for this assertion was this: 'One British company with 20% of its shares held by Americans found that foreigners outvoted domestic shareholders at the annual meeting. Only 10% of the British shareholders bothered to vote, while more than half the Americans did.'

Whoever's view is closer to the truth, the commentator goes on to point out that continental European companies are in for an even bigger shock. These companies have traditionally been able to call upon networks of friendly shareholders to support management against either hostile take-overs or any acts of shareholder democracy that the bulk of shareholders might try to exercise. In addition, voting restrictions are widespread across Europe. The European Commission has tried to tackle this problem by working on a new Company Law Directive that is designed to abolish two-tier share structures and limited voting rights. In the UK, the Cadbury Committee proposed a code of best practice for companies that included the appointment of independent non-executive directors to represent the interests of shareholders by guarding against undue concentrations of power in the boardroom, and by ensuring the proper disclosure of relevant information (Cadbury 1992).

16.3.3. WHAT ARE THE LESSONS?

Many of the developments from the USA are similar to those that have occurred in the UK. For example, the development of specialist pension asset–liability-management companies, and the complaints about short-termism, churning, and speculation are strikingly common to both US and UK pension funds.

In contrast, the UK seems to be ahead of the USA in terms of the inflation indexation of both pensions and accrued pension rights. Equally in contrast, US capital markets are considerably more sophisticated and inventive than those in the UK and Europe. (Anyone who disputes this should read Michael Lewis's *Liar's Poker*.) Many innovations in the US security markets are peculiar to the USA; for example, collateralized mortgage obligations were developed essentially because US residential mortgages are issued at fixed interest rates, in contrast with the UK where most residential mortgages are floating-rate. However, most of the US financial innovations, especially in the fields of risk management and asset-liability management, are very useful to UK pension funds. In addition, US attitudes to corporate governance are likely to have a significant, if not altogether welcome or desirable, impact on the management of UK companies. If, as our City commentator believes, the Americans are coming, then UK corporate managements are in for a big surprise. Whether this will be for the long-term good of the UK economy, however, is a different matter.

17

The Ideal Pension Scheme

As we saw in Chapter 10 on public policy, the Conservative government has gone some way to weakening the control that companies have over occupational pension schemes and has also done much to increase the choice that individuals have over their pensions. But more needs to be done. In the light of our subsequent analysis, is it possible to design an ideal pension scheme?

An ideal pension scheme is one that is not attached to a particular contract of employment. In other words, it is *not* an occupational pension scheme. It seems as strange to attach a pension scheme to a particular contract of employment as it would be to attach, say, a savings scheme to a particular contract of employment. What would we think if, when we started working for a company, the employer insisted that we deposit all our savings with the company? What would we think if the employer also insisted that we could only get our savings back when we left the company, but if we left before we actually retired we would get some unspecified sum of money returned to us? Again, what would we think if the employer also stated that the rate of return that we received on our savings would be both unspecified and unrelated to the rate of return that he or she received from investing our savings, or that, in the unfortunate event that the company went bankrupt or the employer ran off with the assets, we might actually lose all our savings? In truth, we would not dream of leaving our life savings with an employer, so why should we leave our pension savings with an employer?

Another question that we should constantly ask is: why should a pension be different from any other personal finance decision that we make? Why should it so differ from mortgage, insurance, car-purchase, or savings-and-investment decisions that it requires the constant interference of the employer? After all, a pension scheme is nothing more than a long-term savings scheme designed to build up a fund that can be used to buy an annuity when we retire.

An ideal pension scheme has the following fifteen characteristics:[1]

1. It is fully portable and therefore completely independent of the company.

2. Adequate contributions related to the employee's salary and age are

[1] For a comparison of this ideal scheme with the actual Australian pension system, see the appendix to this chapter.

made into the scheme by both the employee and the current employer. These contributions are tax-deductible up to separate limits for the employee and employer. There might be a conventional or standard contribution-rate for the employee which is less than the maximum, but the employee would be free to make additional voluntary contributions (or indeed to reduce contributions if circumstances required). There would also be a conventional or standard contribution-rate for the employer, but again more-generous employers might be induced to make additional contributions. Contributions in excess of the employee and employer limits would be permitted but would not attract tax relief. The employer's contributions would cease when the employee left the company. The employer would then be contributing to the employee's future pension only in proportion to the time that the employee worked for the company and in proportion to the value of the employee's work (assuming, of course, that the employee's salary measures this).

3. The scheme would be administered by an independent pension-scheme administrator, independent of both the employing company and the investment manager of the fund. This would be necessary to ensure adherence to tax-relief limits and safe custody of the scheme assets. The scheme administrator would have to be advised by actuaries to ensure that contributions were adequate. A system of competing scheme administrators could be established. However, the scheme administrators would operate according to a standardized set of deeds, similar to company articles of association. They would also be subject to annual audits.

4. The pension fund containing the pension assets would be managed by one or more fund-management groups. The fund-management group(s) would be selected on the basis of their investment track record. The idea is to benefit from *diversification*. Just as individuals tend to place their savings with a variety of competing institutions, so they could place their accumulating pension assets with competing institutions. This could be done either on a discretionary or a non-discretionary basis. Depending on their attitude to risk, individuals could select a high-risk investment strategy or a low-risk investment strategy, or some combination of the two. If they become dissatisfied with a fund manager, they could transfer to a new one. They would not be tied to a particular institution.

5. Pension-fund management groups would operate on a similar basis to unit trusts in the UK (or mutual funds in the USA). They would collect, pool, and invest contributions on behalf of individuals. In return, the individual would be allocated accumulation units whose transfer values (calculated on the basis of *single pricing*) were published on a daily basis. The individual could transfer his or her pension assets between fund managers simply by selling existing units in the current scheme and purchasing units in the preferred scheme. This resolves the problem of

transfer values: they are executed at market values. In practice, the scheme administrator would have to execute these instructions to ensure that the proceeds were duly reinvested and not spent before retirement age.

6. The investment income and realized capital gains in the fund would accrue free of income and capital-gains tax.

7. The pension age would be flexible and not necessarily linked to actual retirement. In other words, an individual could draw the pension without actually having retired. However, the individual should be warned about the dangers of retiring too early: the pension might not be sufficient to provide an adequate standard of living.

8. At pension age the scheme administrator would sell the pension units and use the proceeds to buy an index-linked pension annuity from an insurance company. The size of the pension annuity would depend on: (i) the size of the accumulated fund at retirement; (ii) the age of retirement and hence the life expectancy of the individual; and (iii) the anticipated inflation rate.

9. The pension scheme would therefore, in practice, be a money-purchase scheme. However, there is no reason, in principle, why a pension scheme related to salary could not be designed (in effect a *targeted money-purchase scheme*). It could not be a strict final-salary scheme, since it would always be possible for an individual to negotiate a 'final' salary with his or her employer that was well in excess of previous salary experience and hence the contribution record. Nevertheless, it would be perfectly possible to design a scheme that was based on *career-revalued earnings*. The revaluation factor could be related to national average earnings (as with SERPS, the state earnings-related pension scheme), retail prices, or indeed, investment returns; the latter case results in a pension that is very close to the standard money-purchase pension. Salary-based schemes are clearly feasible because in the long term, real investment rates and the real growth rate in earnings (and therefore in contributions) are positive: in fact, in the UK they both average between 2 per cent and 3 per cent. Given these rates, an appropriate contribution-rate, and a sufficiently long contribution record, the required fund size at retirement can be expected with a high degree of probability. After all, this is nothing more than what occupational pension schemes already promise. What is being proposed here is that the scheme should be provided by the market, rather than by the company. After all, no company can promise what the market will not ultimately provide. There is also no reason to restrict the pension to the type of rigid 'two-thirds of final salary' formula of conventional occupational schemes, so the individual would be able to choose a particular contribution-rate to target

a particular income-replacement ratio (although, as we have already mentioned, contributions above a particular level would not attract tax relief).

10. The pension annuity would be fully linked to retail-price inflation. There is no real reason why real pensions cannot be guaranteed. (If the inflation rate was zero, pension schemes would automatically be delivering real pensions, unless they actually *cut* the money value of those pensions. If pension schemes can deliver real pensions when there is no inflation, why can they not do so when the inflation rate is positive?) Since the state is largely responsible for inflation, it might be necessary for the state to insure pension increases above a certain rate of inflation. This might be necessary if, during some periods, investment returns did not keep up with inflation. Nevertheless, compensation for inflation is a valuable right and the state might charge an insurance premium in return for providing this right.

11. Part of the pension entitlement could be taken as a lump sum. There is no real reason why this should be free of income tax. If the lump sum were subject to income tax, there would be no real reason why there should be any limit to the size of the lump sum; although it should be made quite clear to individuals that if they spend all the lump sum immediately, they will spend the rest of their days in penury!

12. As part of the pension scheme, it would be possible to buy related pension benefits such as death-in-service benefits and a spouse's pension.

13. Pension-scheme members would be provided with full and regular information about their schemes in precisely the same way that shareholders receive information about their companies. The information would cover:

- the state of employee and employer contributions into the scheme;
- the type of assets in the pension fund;
- the rates of return generated on the assets;
- the fees or commissions charged by the scheme administrator and pension-fund manager.

14. The remuneration to the organizations involved in providing operating services to the schemes (that is, scheme administrators, fund managers, and annuity providers) would be determined competitively, but should not be *front-end loaded*. In other words, there should not be a high initial fixed cost that in effect ties an individual to a particular (and possibly inefficient or uncompetitive) organization providing, say, fund-management services.

15. The pension industry would be supervised by a *pensions regulator* who would also operate a *compensation scheme* to compensate scheme

members in the event of fraud or malpractice.[2] The new regulator would combine the role of the Occupational Pensions Board and the registrar of pension schemes who is responsible for holding details of all pension schemes and deferred pensioners in the country. The compensation scheme would be financed by a levy on all pension schemes.

What are the advantages of the ideal pension scheme? The most important advantage is that it individualizes or personalizes pension arrangements in precisely the same way that most of the other financial matters that we face are personalized. In doing this, it eliminates all the potential conflicts of interest between the employee and the company, or between the early leaver and the long stayer. Further, it explicitly identifies where responsibilities lie:

- the responsibility of the employee and the employer for making adequate and timely contributions;
- the responsibility of the independent scheme administrator for operating the scheme;
- the responsibility of the fund manager for running the pension fund for the benefit of the pensioner;
- the responsibility of the insurance company for providing the pension annuity;
- the responsibility of the state for compensating the pensioner for causing 'excessive' inflation and for regulating the industry.

One potential disadvantage with this scheme concerns the size of fees and commissions charged by those institutions involved in servicing it. The evidence with personal pension schemes indicates that these fees and commissions can be excessive, that is, they may not be determined competitively (see Section 10.2.6). Great care would be needed to ensure that individual scheme members were not subject to excessive charges. Publication of fees and commissions would help to achieve this. However, the main disadvantage of the scheme is that it cannot *guarantee* a pension at retirement that is linked to 'final salary' as with occupational pension schemes. While there is much to be said for having a standard of living in retirement that is related to the standard of living just prior to retirement, the ideal pension-fund scheme outlined above would certainly be good enough in practice to warrant replacing the entire system of occupational pension schemes.

Finally, we should ask how the present pension system in the UK should be changed. Given existing expectations about final-salary pensions and also the huge size of pension funds, it might not be realistic

---

[2] The Goode Report (1993) has also recommended the introduction of a pensions regulator and a compensation scheme.

to introduce radical change instantaneously. It may be that existing occupational schemes should be closed to new members and allowed to die a natural death, although a natural death would take the best part of a century to occur. A much more radical proposal would be to introduce the change-over immediately. Companies would either recover surpluses or fund deficits, and the remaining pension-fund assets would be divided up according to accrued rights and allocated to personal pension funds (in other words *unitized*). To reduce break-up costs and financial-market uncertainty, it might be sensible for occupational pension schemes to establish themselves as independent scheme administrators administering the individual funds of the former occupational schemes. They could immediately compete for new business, but individuals would be free to transfer their units elsewhere. Natural inertia would minimize financial-market disruption.

The ideal pension scheme has much to recommend it, both to countries with existing occupational pension funds, such as the UK, the USA, and Holland, and to countries contemplating the introduction of formal pension funds, such as Italy. There have been other suggestions for individualizing pension schemes: for example, American-style individual retirement accounts and personal investment pools (suggested by Lord Vinson and Philip Chappell of the Centre for Policy Studies). Vinson argues that all existing funds should be required to give an annual statement to members, showing transfer value based on service to date. He suggests that all members should have the chance at least annually to take the full transfer value into a separate fund, whether or not they remain in their employer's service. This, he argues, would solve the twin problems of portability and ownership: 'we would take billions of pounds that are nobody's money and turn it into somebody's money.' Even some senior members of the Labour Party are beginning to recognize both the desirability and long-term inevitability of personal pensions (Field and Owen, 1993).

Protagonists of occupational pension schemes claim that few personal-pension scheme members would end up with pensions worth two-thirds of final salary. The counter-question is: when the rights of early leavers are so poor and when the average individual changes jobs four times during his or her career, how many members of occupational schemes actually end up with such a pension under current arrangements?

To implement the ideal pensions scheme will take a *Pension Schemes Act*. This was first suggested to the Wilson Committee in 1980 but the pension funds persuaded the Committee against it. There can be no further delay!

Appendix: The Australian Pension System

Having designed this ideal pension scheme, I discovered (from Professor David M. Knox, Director of the Centre for Actuarial Studies at the University of Melbourne) that the Australian pension system already embodies most of these characteristics.

While there is no universal state-pension or earnings-related scheme in Australia, there is a means-tested pension payable from 65 (for men) and 60 (for women) and a compulsory private-sector occupational-pensions industry. The compulsory system, supplemented by optional additional superannuation, is fully funded and administered and invested in the private sector, subject to various controls. The pensions industry is regulated by the Insurance and Superannuation Commission (ISC) under the Superannuation Industry (Supervision) Act (SIS) which came into effect on 1 July 1993. A fund is only eligible to receive tax concessions if it elects to become a 'regulated superannuation fund', which is a fund subject to regulation by the ISC. Such an election once made is irrevocable.

In terms of the fifteen desirable characteristics for a pension scheme, the Australian system bears the following comparisons:

1. The compulsory employer contributions are vested with the employee as a legal entitlement. Upon resignation employees may transfer them to a new fund or to specially approved roll-over (or holding) funds which earn market rates. The accumulated contributions cannot be accessed until age 55, rising to age 60 in the future.

2. Employers *must* contribute at least 5 per cent (or 3 per cent for small employers) of earnings into a complying superannuation fund. This figure will rise to 9 per cent at the end of the century. They may contribute more than this, if they so desire. The cost is tax-deductible but subject to a 15 per-cent contributions tax, payable by the fund. Many employees contribute but it is not compulsory. There are very limited tax incentives. Employee contributions are made from after-tax pay.

3. The SIS Act requires a set of covenants to be incorporated into trust deeds which specify the duties and powers of trustees. Trustees (50 per cent of whom must be employee representatives) are required to:

(a) act honestly in all matters concerning the entity;

(b) exercise, in relation to all matters affecting the entity, the same degree of care, skill, and diligence as an ordinary prudent person experienced in business would exercise in dealing with the property of another person for whom the person felt morally bound to provide;

(c) ensure that the trustees' duties and powers are performed and exercised in the best interests of the beneficiaries;

(d) keep the money and other assets of the entity separate from any money and assets, respectively, that are not held on trust;

(e) not enter into any contract, or do any other act or thing, that would prevent the trustee from, or hinder the trustee in, properly performing or exercising the trustee's functions and powers; and

(f) allow a beneficiary access to any prescribed information or any prescribed documents.

4. The SIS Act also gives trustees responsibility for the management of the fund assets. In particular, trustees are required to formulate and give effect to an investment strategy that has regard to the whole of the circumstances of the entity including, but not limited to, the following:

(a) the risk involved in making, and the likely return from, investments;

(b) the composition of the entity's investments as a whole, including the extent to which the investments are diverse or involve the entity in being exposed to risks from inadequate diversification;

(c) the liquidity of the entity's investments, having regard to expected cash-flow requirements;

(d) the likely return from the entity's investments, having regard to its objectives and its expected cash-flow requirements; and

(e) the ability of the entity to discharge its existing and prospective liabilities.

5. Australian pension schemes are effectively unitized: every member is credited with interest (which must be linked to the fund earning rate) on a half-yearly basis.

6. The investment income in Australian pension schemes does not accrue free of tax. It is taxed at 15 per cent, less certain credits which lead to a net tax rate of 5–10 per cent.

7. The pension age (access age) currently lies between 55 and 65, although this is expected to increase to between 60 and 70 in the future.

8. Most Australians take their pension benefits in the form of a lump sum at retirement (which is taxed at either 0 per cent or 15 per cent depending on circumstances), rather than a pension annuity (which is taxed at the highest marginal rate, less a 15 per-cent rebate to offset the contributions tax).

9. The vast majority of Australian schemes are defined-contribution plans. Some of the major plans are defined-benefit, but the introduction of a minimum contribution-rate, expressed as a percentage of salary, leads many employers to a defined-contribution arrangement.

10. The index-linking of annuities is not widespread in Australia.

11. There is no lump-sum limit in Australia, except in respect of maximum benefits which affect only a small minority of employees.

12. Death-in-service and spouse's pensions are normal in Australia.

13. Australian funds must now provide considerable information to members on an annual basis, including information on:

(a) vested benefits;

(b) amount of net earnings in the period;

(c) current death benefit;

(d) amount of fees deducted;

(e) a statement relating to the accounts of the fund;

(f) any asset that exceeds 5 per cent of the fund's assets;

(g) a statement of the investment objectives of the trustees for the fund; and

(h) the names of the trustees and any appointed managers.

14. Most funds now operate with annual administration and investment charges.

15. The SIS Act contains provisions which enable financial assistance to be given to funds which have suffered a loss as a result of fraud or theft. A fund may apply to the Treasurer of the Australian government for

assistance only if it has suffered a loss as a result of fraudulent conduct or theft, which loss has caused substantial diminution of the fund leading to difficulties in the payment of benefits. If the Treasurer determines to grant assistance to such a fund, then the cost will be met by a levy on the superannuation industry.

Selected References for Part IV

ALTMAN, R. M., and ATKINSON, A. B. (1982), 'State Pensions, Taxation and Retirement Income, 1981–2031', in M. Fogarty (ed.), *Retirement Policy: The Next Fifty Years* (Heinemann, London).

ATKINSON, A. B. (1991), *The Development of State Pensions in the United Kingdom*, Welfare State Programme Discussion Paper No. WSP/58 (Suntory-Toyota International Centre for Economics and Related Disciplines, London School of Economics, London).

BLAKE, D. (1990), *Financial Market Analysis* (McGraw-Hill, London).

BODIE, Z. (1990), 'Inflation, Index-Linked Bonds and Asset Allocation', *Journal of Portfolio Management* 16, 48–53.

—— (1991), 'The Effect of Pension Funds on US Capital Markets', mimeo. (Boston University, Boston, Mass.).

CADBURY, Sir A. (chairman) (1992), *Report of the Committee to Review the Financial Aspects of Corporate Governance* (Gee, London).

CREEDY, J. (1982), *State Pensions in Britain* (Cambridge University Press, Cambridge).

DAVIS, E. P. (1991), 'The Development of Pension Funds: An International Comparison', *Bank of England Quarterly Bulletin* (Aug.), 380–90.

—— (1992a), 'The Development of Pension Funds in the Major Industrial Countries', in *Planning for Retirement in Europe* (Centre for European Policy Studies, Brussels).

—— (1992b), 'The Structure, Regulation and Performance of Pension Funds in Nine Industrial Countries' (Bank of England Discussion Paper, London).

—— (1993), 'The Development of Pension Funds: An Approaching Financial Revolution for Continental Europe', in R. O'Brien (ed.) *Finance and the International Economy* (Oxford University Press, Oxford).

ESCOLME, B., HUDSON, D., and GREENWOOD, P. (1991), *Hosking's Pension Schemes and Retirement Benefits* (Sweet and Maxwell, London).

FIELD, F., and OWEN, M. (1993), 'Private Pensions for All: Squaring the Circle' (Fabian Society Discussion Paper No. 16, London).

GOODE, PROFESSOR R. (chairman) (1993), *Pension Law Reform: Report of the Pension Law Review Committee*, CM. 2342 (HMSO, London, Sept.).

Government Actuary (1990), *National Insurance Fund Long Term Estimate* (HMSO, London).

HARRISON, D. (1992), *Pension Provision in the EC* (Financial Times Business Information, London).

HOFFMAN, J. (1992), *Towards a Single European Capital Market* (CSFB Economics, Credit Suisse First Boston, London).

HM Treasury Report (1989), 'Pensions for the Enterprise Economy', *Economic Progress Report*, No. 203 (HM Treasury, London, Aug.).

JOLLANS, A. (1991), *European Community Action in the Field of Pension Funds* (Commission of the European Communities, Brussels).

Lewis, M. (1989), *Liar's Poker* (Hodder and Stoughton, London).

Mortensen, J. (ed.) (1992), *The Future of Pensions in the European Community* (Centre for Economic Policy Studies, Brussels).

Rivett, P., and Speak, P. (eds.) (1991), *The Financial Jungle—A Guide to Financial Instruments* (Coopers and Lybrand Deloitte, London).

Wilson, Rt. Hon. Sir H. (Chairman) (1980), *Report of the Committee to Review the Functioning of Financial Institutions*, Cmnd. 7937 (HMSO, London, June).

APPENDIX: PENSIONS-RELATED ORGANIZATIONS

ANNUITY BUREAU
Enterprise House, 59–65 Upper Ground, London SE1 9PQ
Telephone: 0171-620 4090

ANNUITY DIRECT
32–38 Scrutton Street, London EC2A 4RQ
Telephone: 0171-375 1175

ASSOCIATION OF BRITISH INSURERS
51 Gresham Street, London EC2V 7HQ
Telephone: 0171-600 3333

ASSOCIATION OF CONSULTING ACTUARIES
1 Wardrobe Place, London EC4V 5AH
Telephone: 0171-248 3163

ASSOCIATION OF INVESTMENT TRUST COMPANIES
Park House, 16 Finsbury Circus, London EC2M 7DJ
Telephone: 0171-588 5347

ASSOCIATION OF PENSION LAWYERS
c/o Paul Stannard, 10 Snow Hill, London EC1A 2AL
Telephone: 0171-248 9133

ASSOCIATION OF PENSIONEER TRUSTEES
c/o Suntrust Ltd., St James Barton, Bristol BS99 7SL
Telephone: 01179-426911

ASSOCIATION OF UNIT TRUSTS AND INVESTMENT FUNDS
65 Kingsway, London WC2B 6TD
Telephone: 0171-831 0898

BANKING OMBUDSMAN
70 Grays Inn Road, London WC1X 8NB
Telephone: 0171-404 9944

BENEFITS AGENCY
c/o Department of Social Security, Quarry House, Quarry Hill, Leeds LS2 7UE
Telephone: 01132 324000

BRITISH BANKERS ASSOCIATION
10 Lombard Street, London EC3 9EL
Telephone: 0171-623 4001

BUILDING SOCIETIES ASSOCIATION
3 Saville Row, London W1X 1AF
Telephone: 0171-437 0655

BUILDING SOCIETIES OMBUDSMAN
Grosvenor Gardens House, 35–37 Grosvenor Gardens, London SW1X 7AW
Telephone: 0171-931 0044

CENTRAL PENSIONS BRANCH
c/o Department of Social Security, Benton Park Road, Newcastle upon Tyne
NE98 1YX
Telephone: 0191-213 5000

CONTRACTED OUT EMPLOYMENT GROUP (COEG)
c/o Department of Social Security, Benton Park Road, Newcastle upon Tyne
NE98 1YX
Telephone: 0191-213 5000

CONTRIBUTIONS AGENCY
c/o Department of Social Security, Benton Park Road, Newcastle upon Tyne
NE98 1YX
Telephone: 0191-213 5000

DEPARTMENT OF SOCIAL SECURITY
Richmond House, 79 Whitehall, London SW1A 2NS
Telephone: 0171-210 3000

FACULTY OF ACTUARIES IN SCOTLAND
23A St Andrew Square, Edinburgh EH2 1AQ
Telephone: 0131-557 1575

**FINANCIAL INTERMEDIARIES, MANAGERS AND
BROKERS REGULATORY ASSOCIATION**
Hertsmere House, Hertsmere Road, London E14 4AB
Telephone: 0171-538 8860

GOVERNMENT ACTUARY'S DEPARTMENT
22 Kingsway, London WC2B 6LE
Telephone: 0171-242 6828

INSTITUTE OF ACTUARIES
Staple Inn Hall, High Holborn, London WC1V 7QJ
Telephone: 0171-242 0106

INSURANCE OMBUDSMAN
City Gate 1, 135 Park Street, London SE1 9EA
Telephone: 0171-928 4488

**INVESTMENT MANAGERS REGULATORY
ORGANIZATION**
Broadwalk House, Appold Street, London EC2A 2AA
Telephone: 0171-628 6022

INVESTMENT OMBUDSMAN
6 Frederick's Place, London EC2R 8BT
Telephone: 0171-796 3065

**LIFE ASSURANCE AND UNIT TRUST REGULATORY
ORGANIZATION**
Centre Point, 103 New Oxford Street, London WC1A 1QH
Telephone: 0171-379 0444

LOWNDES LAMBERT FINANCIAL SERVICES
Norex Court, 195 Marsh Wall, London E14 9SG
Telephone: 0171-512 1000

NATIONAL ASSOCIATION OF PENSION FUNDS LTD.
12–18 Grosvenor Gardens, London SW1W 0DH
Telephone: 0171-730 0585

OCCUPATIONAL PENSION POLICY GROUP
c/o Department of Social Security, Adelphi, 1–11 John Adam Street,
London WC2N 6HT
Telephone: 0171-962 8000

OCCUPATIONAL PENSIONS ADVISORY SERVICE
11 Belgrave Road, London SW1V 1BR
Telephone: 0171-233 8080

OCCUPATIONAL PENSIONS BOARD
Scottish Life House, PO Box 2EE, Newcastle upon Tyne NE99 2EE
Telephone: 0191-225 6414

OVERSEAS BRANCH
c/o Department of Social Security, Benton Park Road, Newcastle upon Tyne
NE98 1YX
Telephone: 0191-213 5000

PENSION SCHEMES OFFICE (INLAND REVENUE)
Lynwood Road, Thames Ditton, Surrey KT7 0DP
Telephone: 0181-398 4242

PENSIONS AND INVESTMENTS RESEARCH CONSULTANTS LTD.
Challenor House, 19–21 Clerkenwell Close, London EC1R 0AA
Telephone: 0171-972 9060

PENSIONS MANAGEMENT INSTITUTE
PMI House, 4–10 Artillery Lane, London E1 7LS
Telephone: 0171-247 1452

PENSIONS OMBUDSMAN
11 Belgrave Road, London SW1V 1RB
Telephone: 0171-834 9144

PENSIONS RESEARCH ACCOUNTANTS GROUP (PRAG)
c/o MNPA, Ashcombe House, The Crescent, Leatherhead, Surrey KT22 8LQ
Telephone: 01372-438600

PERSONAL PENSION GROUP
c/o Department of Social Security, Alfred Wilson House, Waterloo Street,
Newcastle upon Tyne NE1 1XB
Telephone: 0191-213 5000

PUBLIC SECTOR TRANSFER CLUB
c/o HM Treasury, Civil Service Pension Division, Room 11, Alencon Link,
Basingstoke R21 1JB
Telephone: 01628-521249

REGISTRAR OF PENSION SCHEMES
PO Box 1NN, Newcastle upon Tyne NE99 1NN
Telephone: 0191-225 6393

SECURITIES AND FUTURES AUTHORITY
Cottons Centre, Cottons Lane, London SE1 2QG
Telephone: 0171-378 9000

SECURITIES AND INVESTMENTS BOARD
2 Bunhill Row, London EC1Y 8RA
Telephone: 0171-638 1240

SOCIETY OF PENSION CONSULTANTS
Ludgate House, Ludgate Circus, London EC4A 2AB
Telephone: 0171-353 1688

GLOSSARY

This 'Pensions Terminology' is reproduced with the kind permission of the Pensions Management Institute as copyright-holder.

The following abbreviations are used throughout the Glossary:

DSS	Department of Social Security
FA	Finance Act
OPB	Occupational Pensions Board
S	Section (of an Act)
PSO	Pension Schemes Office
SSA 73	Social Security Act 1973
SSPA 75	Social Security Pensions Act 1975
FSA 86	Financial Services Act 1986
SSA 86	Social Security Act 1986
ICTA 88	Income and Corporation Taxes Act 1988
SORP 1	Statement of Recommended Practice 1
SSAP 24	Statement of Standard Accounting Practice 24
SSA 90	Social Security Act 1990
JOM	Joint Office Memorandum

2% INCENTIVE

Payments which SSA 86 requires the DSS to make in certain cases to an appropriate personal pension scheme or a newly contracted out occupational pension scheme. Subsequently reduced to a 1% incentive for those over 30 from April 1993.

20% DIRECTOR

A term sometimes used to refer to a **controlling director**.

87–89 MEMBER

An alternative term for a **Class B Member**.

ACCELERATED ACCRUAL

Provision by a scheme of an accrual rate greater than one sixtieth of pensionable earnings for each year of pensionable service. Also used as an alternative term for **uplifted 60ths**.

ACCOUNTING BASES

The methods developed for applying fundamental accounting concepts to financial transactions for determining the accounting period in which income and expenditure should be recognised and the amounts of assets and liabilities in the balance sheet or net assets statement.

ACCOUNTING POLICIES
The specific accounting bases adopted to present fairly the financial results and position of an entity.

*For a typical larger pension scheme, these might include decisions on accounting for conversion of foreign currency, the valuation of investments and recognition of dividend income, and the extent to which the **cash basis** is used.*

ACCOUNTING STANDARDS BOARD (ASB)
The successor organisation to the **Accounting Standards Committee** which is now responsible for producing accounting standards. Previously published as 'Statements of Standard Accounting Practice' (SSAPs), accounting standards are now issued by the ASB as 'Financial Reporting Standards' (FRSs), though the ASB has adopted standards extant at the time it came into existence. Standards are preceded by 'Discussion Papers' and 'Exposure Drafts' (EDs).

ACCOUNTING STANDARDS COMMITTEE (ASC)
The organisation responsible until July 1990 for the issue of Statements of Standard Accounting Practice (SSAPs) which are mandatory and Statements of Recommended Practice (SORPs) which are non-mandatory.

In August 1990, the Accounting Standards Committee was replaced by the Accounting Standards Board.

ACCRUAL RATE
The rate at which pension benefit builds up as pensionable service is completed in a **defined benefit scheme**.

ACCRUALS CONCEPT
The accounting principle whereby revenues and costs are recognised as they are earned or incurred, rather than when money is received or paid.

*See also **matching**.*

ACCRUED BENEFITS
The benefits for service up to a given point in time, whether **vested rights** or not. They may be calculated in relation to current earnings or projected earnings.

Allowance may also be made for revaluation and/or pension increases required by the scheme rules or legislation.

ACCRUED BENEFITS VALUATION METHOD
A **valuation method** in which the **actuarial liability** at the valuation date relates to:

(a) the benefits for current and deferred pensioners and their dependants, allowing where appropriate for future increases, and
(b) the **accrued benefits** for members in service on the valuation date.

A recommended contribution rate may allow for earnings and service projected to the end of a specified period (the control period). In that case allowance may be made for replacing members assumed to leave during that period.

ACCRUED RIGHTS

A term sometimes used to describe **accrued benefits**.

The term is given specific definitions for the purposes of preservation (SSA 73), contracting out and the Disclosure Regulations (SSPA 75).

ACCRUED RIGHTS PREMIUM (ARP)

A type of **state scheme premium** which may be paid for a member below **state pensionable age** when a scheme which is contracted out by reference to the provision of a **GMP** ceases to be contracted out. In return for the ARP, the state scheme will take over the obligation to provide a **GMP**.

ACCUMULATED CONTRIBUTIONS

The total of contributions paid by a member of a pension scheme during a given period, enhanced where appropriate by interest. In a money purchase scheme the term may also include the employer's contributions.

ACTIVE INVESTMENT MANAGEMENT

A style of managing a portfolio which is designed to achieve, over a period of time, performance which is superior to index-based performance benchmarks.

ACTIVE MEMBER

A member of a pension scheme who is at present accruing benefits under that scheme in respect of current service.

ACTUARIAL ASSUMPTIONS

The set of assumptions as to rates of return, inflation, increase in earnings, mortality etc, used by the actuary in an actuarial valuation or other actuarial calculations.

ACTUARIAL BASIS

A term commonly used to mean valuation method and/or actuarial assumptions.

ACTUARIAL CERTIFICATE

A certificate given by an actuary, and arising out of actuarial work.

Particular examples are:

(a) *the certificate in respect of the OPB solvency test which is required for some contracted out schemes;*
(b) *the certificate given to the PSO in connection with the rules for dealing with pension scheme surpluses under ICTA 88.*

ACTUARIAL DEFICIENCY

The excess of the **actuarial liability** over the **actuarial value of assets**, on the basis of the **valuation method** used.

If an actuarial report refers to a surplus or deficiency, it must be studied to ascertain precisely what assets and liabilities have been taken into account. In a stricter sense, the terms surplus and deficiency might be used in relation to the results of a discontinuance valuation.

ACTUARIAL INCREASE
An enhancement of benefits to compensate for the deferment of pension beyond the **normal pension date**.

ACTUARIAL LIABILITY
The value placed on the liability of a pension fund for outgoings due after the **valuation date**.

See prospective benefits valuation method and accrued benefits valuation method.

ACTUARIAL REDUCTION
A reduction made to a member's accrued pension benefits in order to offset any additional cost arising from their payment in advance of the **normal pension date**.

ACTUARIAL REPORT
A report on an actuarial valuation, or actuarial advice on the financial effects of changes in a pension scheme.

A report on an actuarial valuation must conform to actuarial guidance issued by the Institute and the Faculty of Actuaries.

ACTUARIAL STATEMENT
The statement required by the Disclosure Regulations to be included in the **annual report**. It must show in the prescribed form the security of the accrued and prospective rights of members and be signed by an actuary.

ACTUARIAL SURPLUS
The excess of the **actuarial value of assets** over the **actuarial liability** on the basis of the valuation method used.

See notes under actuarial deficiency.

ACTUARIAL UNDERTAKING
A name commonly used for an undertaking given in a prescribed form by an employer to inform the actuary whether any of the specified events, which are likely to invalidate any certificate required by the OPB for contracting out purposes, have occurred.

ACTUARIAL VALUATION
An investigation by an actuary into the ability of a pension scheme to meet its liabilities. This is usually to assess the **funding level** and a **recommended contribution rate** based on comparing the **actuarial value of assets** and the **actuarial liability**.

ACTUARIAL VALUE OF ASSETS
The value placed on the assets by the actuary. This may be market value, **present value** of estimated income and proceeds of sales or redemption, or some other value.

ACTUARIAL VALUE OF FUTURE CONTRIBUTIONS
The **present value** of assumed future contributions and income therefrom.

ACTUARIAL VALUE OF LIABILITIES
See **actuarial liability**.

ACTUARY
An adviser on financial questions involving probabilities relating to mortality and other contingencies.

For statutory purposes in the UK, the term automatically includes Fellows of the Institute of Actuaries and of the Faculty of Actuaries. Persons with other actuarial qualifications may be approved by the Secretary of State for a specific purpose of the legislation.

ADDED YEARS
The provision of extra pension benefit by reference to an additional period of pensionable service in a **defined benefit scheme**, arising from the receipt of a transfer payment, the paying of additional voluntary contributions or by way of **augmentation**.

ADDITIONAL COMPONENT
An alternative term for **additional pension**.

ADDITIONAL PENSION
The earnings-related element of the state pension, over and above the **basic pension**.

ADDITIONAL VOLUNTARY CONTRIBUTIONS (AVCs)
Contributions over and above a member's normal contributions if any, which the member elects to pay to the scheme in order to secure additional benefits, either **added years** or **money purchase**.

See also free standing additional voluntary contributions.

ADMINISTRATOR
The person or persons regarded by the PSO and, where relevant, the OPB, as responsible for the management of a pension scheme.

The term may also refer to the person who manages the day to day administration of the scheme.

AGGREGATE METHOD
A valuation method in which the recommended contribution rate is obtained

directly as that which, if paid on behalf of existing members over their future periods of active membership, would provide for the excess of the present value of all their benefits over the actuarial value of assets.

ALLOCATION

1. The facility for a member to give up (or allocate) part of his/her pension in exchange for a pension payable to the member's spouse or dependant.

    or

2. The process for the application of payments to the benefits of individuals under an insured scheme using controlled funding.

ALTERNATIVES TO SHORT SERVICE BENEFIT

Benefits or options permitted as a partial or complete substitute for **short service benefit** under the preservation requirements of SSA 73.

AMORTISATION

An accountancy term for the reduction in value of an asset, such as leasehold property, caused by the passage of time. If the cause is not solely related to time the corresponding term is depreciation.

*Sometimes used to mean the spreading of an **actuarial surplus** or **deficiency** over an appropriate period or the discharge of a liability by instalments.*

ANNUAL PREMIUM METHOD

See **level annual premium method**.

ANNUAL REPORT

The means by which the trustees of a pension scheme communicate financial and other information about the scheme to members, employers and other interested parties.

The term is used in particular to describe the specific information which is required to be made available by trustees in relation to each scheme year under the Disclosure Regulations. This must include a copy of the audited accounts and of the latest actuarial statement and other information specified including a financial review by the trustees and an investment report. It may contain additional information not required by the Regulations.

Trustees often publish a simplified annual report for members containing the above material suitably summarised and, perhaps, illustrated.

ANNUITY

A series of payments, which may be subject to increases, made at stated intervals until a particular event occurs. This event is most commonly the end of a specified period or the death of the person receiving the annuity.

ANNUITY OPTION

The right to apply the proceeds of an insurance policy to buy an annuity in various pre-specified ways.

See guaranteed annuity option, open market option and tied annuity option.

ANTI-FRANKING REQUIREMENTS

The requirements which ban the practice of franking at one time followed by some schemes, whereby the statutory increases in **GMP** were offset against other scheme benefits, rather than being added to a member's total benefits.

The requirements are covered in Ss 41A–41E of SSPA 75 and details of the requirements and permitted exceptions are given in JOM 78 para 165 and JOM 77 paras 170–196 and paras 212–213.

APPOINTED DAY (A-day)

The date from which **final salary schemes** are required to provide **limited price indexation** of pensions in payment in accordance with SSA 90.

The term also has the more general meaning of the date on which any legislation comes into force.

APPROPRIATE ADDITIONS

Amounts to be added when calculating the minimum benefit for the purpose of **anti-franking requirements** in respect of any further benefit accruing after contracted out employment ceases or any enhancement of the benefits in excess of the **GMP** due to postponed payment.

APPROPRIATE PERSONAL PENSION SCHEME (APPS)

A personal pension scheme or free standing AVC scheme granted an appropriate scheme certificate by the OPB, enabling its members to use it for the purpose of contracting out.

APPROPRIATE SCHEME CERTIFICATE

The certificate issued by the OPB to a personal pension scheme or to a free standing AVC scheme confirming that the scheme satisfies the conditions required for contracting out.

APPROVED SCHEME

A retirement benefits scheme which is approved by the Inland Revenue under Chapter I of Part XIV of ICTA 88, including a free standing AVC scheme. The term may also be used to describe a personal pension scheme approved under Chapter IV of that Part.

*See also **exempt approved scheme**.*

ARTICLE 119

Article 119 of the Treaty of Rome, providing that men and women are entitled to equal pay for equal work.

*See also **Barber judgment**.*

ASSET ALLOCATION STRATEGY
The long term apportionment of pension scheme assets between the various investment classes such as equities, fixed interest and cash.

ASSETS
The items such as investments, debtors, and cash to which the trustees of a pension scheme have title.

ATTAINED AGE METHOD
A prospective benefit valuation method in which the **actuarial liability** makes allowance for projected earnings. The **standard contribution rate** is that necessary to cover the cost of all benefits which will accrue to existing members after the **valuation date** by reference to total earnings throughout their future working lifetime projected to the dates on which benefits become payable.

AUDITING GUIDELINES
Guidelines issued by the Auditing Practices Committee (APC) to give guidance to auditors on particular commercial or legal circumstances.

The APC was replaced in April 1991 by the Auditing Practices Board (APB), which adopted the existing guidelines.

AUGMENTATION
The provision of additional benefits in respect of particular members, normally where the cost is borne by the pension scheme and/or the employer.

AVERAGE EARNINGS SCHEME
See **career average scheme**.

AVERAGE REMAINING SERVICE LIFE
As defined by **SSAP 24**, a weighted average of the expected future service of the current members of the scheme up to their normal pension dates or expected dates of earlier withdrawal or death in service.

BALANCE SHEET
A financial statement of the assets and liabilities of an entity at a particular date designed to give a **true and fair view** of the state of affairs.

In a pension scheme, a net assets statement is preferred on the grounds that a balance sheet without the actuarial liability does not give a true and fair view.

BAND (OR BANDED) EARNINGS
An alternative term for **upper band earnings**.

BARBER JUDGMENT
The judgment of the European Court of Justice in the case of Barber v.

Guardian Royal Exchange on 17 May 1990, which held that pensions count as pay for the purposes of **Article 119**.

BASIC COMPONENT
An alternative term for **basic pension**.

BASIC PENSION
The single person's flat rate state pension paid to all who have met the minimum national-insurance contribution requirements. A widow, widower or in some cases a married woman may also claim a basic state pension on the contribution record of his or her spouse.

BENEFICIARY
A person entitled to benefit under a pension scheme or who will become entitled on the happening of a specified event.

BENEFIT STATEMENT
A statement or estimate of benefits payable in respect of an individual on the occurrence of specified events.

BENEFITS AGENCY
A self contained unit within the DSS set up to handle claims, to administer the payment of benefits, and to conduct reviews and appeals.

BENEFITS IN KIND
Any benefits other than cash provided as remuneration for an employment.

BLOCK TRANSFER
See **bulk transfer**.

BONUS CREDIT
For the purposes of the preservation requirements of SSA 73, a retrospective award of or improvement in retirement benefit.

BOOK COST
In portfolio valuations, the historic cost—or the average of the historic cost—at which stocks and shares were purchased.

BOOK RESERVE SCHEME
A term used to describe an unfunded occupational pension scheme which is accounted for by a **provision** in the employer's accounts.

BOOK VALUE
An ambiguous term which may be used to mean **book cost, historical cost, carrying value** or **net book value**.

BRIDGING PENSION
An additional pension paid from a scheme between retirement and **state pen-**

sionable age, which is usually replaced by the state pension payable from that age.

BULK TRANSFER

The transfer of a group of members, not necessarily with their consent, from one pension scheme to another, usually with an enhanced transfer payment in comparison with an individual's **cash equivalent**.

The PSO must be consulted about any such transfer payments.

BUY BACK

A term used to describe the payment of a type of **state scheme premium** by means of which a member's rights to SERPS are fully reinstated.

BUY OUT

The purchase by pension scheme trustees of an insurance policy or bond in the name of a member or other beneficiary, in lieu of entitlement to benefit from the scheme, following termination of the member's pensionable service.

Sometimes also used to refer to the purchase of an insurance policy in the name of the trustees.

CANCELLATION NOTICE

A document issued to the investor by the **pension provider** outlining the contract particulars, and the investor's legal right to cancel the contract without penalty within a specified period of receiving the notice.

Introduced for some pension contracts under FSA 86 and SSA 86.

CAPITALISED VALUE

An alternative term for **present value**.

CAREER AVERAGE SCHEME

A scheme where the benefit for each year of membership is related to the pensionable earnings for that year.

CARRY BACK

The election by a member of a personal pension scheme or a retirement annuity policy holder to have a contribution or part of it treated as having been paid in the tax year immediately prior to that in which it was paid, or, in the absence of **net relevant earnings** in that year, in the tax year before that.

CARRY FORWARD

The election by a member of a personal pension scheme or a retirement annuity policy holder to carry forward unused relief where contributions (other than those of the employer) exceed the maximum allowable amount relievable against **net relevant earnings**.

CARRYING VALUE
The amount at which an asset is stated in the accounting records and financial statements of an entity. It may comprise cost less depreciation or may be a revalued amount.

CASH ACCUMULATION POLICY
An alternative term for **deposit administration**.

CASH BASIS
A method of accounting under which the transactions are accounted for only at the time money is received or paid. This is in contrast to the **accruals concept**.

CASH EQUIVALENT
The amount which a member of a pension scheme may under Schedule 1A of SSPA 75 require to be applied as a transfer payment to another permitted pension scheme or to a buy out policy.

CASH OPTION
An alternative term for **commutation**.

CENTRALISED SCHEME
A pension scheme operated on behalf of several employers.

CERTIFICATE OF EXISTENCE
A document confirming that a person entitled to a pension is still alive.

At the same time, confirmation may be sought about other conditions affecting entitlement.

CERTIFIED AMOUNT (CA)
That part of a **contributions equivalent premium** which may be recovered out of any refund of scheme contributions to the member.

CLASS A (OR B OR C) MEMBERS
Terms derived from specimen rules issued by the PSO, applying to members of occupational schemes who joined during specified periods.

Differing Inland Revenue limits apply to each Class.

Class A Members of schemes established on or after 14 March 1989 and all new members of earlier schemes joining on or after 1 June 1989.

Class B Members of schemes established before 14 March 1989 who joined between 17 March 1987 and 31 May 1989.

Class C Members who joined schemes before 17 March 1987.

A member may be exempt from treatment as a Class A or B member under transitional arrangements. Class B members or (where scheme rules permit) Class C members may elect to be treated as Class A members, but will then be subject to the **earnings cap**.

CLOSED SCHEME

A pension scheme which does not admit new members.

Contributions may or may not continue and benefits may or may not be provided for future service.

COMMINGLED FUND

A term sometimes used to describe a **common investment fund** or an **exempt unit trust**.

COMMON INVESTMENT FUND

An arrangement whereby the assets of two or more pension schemes, operated by a single employer or a group of employers, are pooled for investment.

COMMUTATION

The giving up of a part or all of the pension payable from retirement for an immediate cash sum.

COMMUTATION FACTORS

Factors used to determine the amount of pension which needs to be forgone in order to provide a given lump sum benefit.

COMPLIANCE AUDIT

1. An audit carried out to ensure compliance with the rules and regulations imposed by the Financial Services Act.

2. An audit at the instigation of the Inland Revenue's PSO to ensure compliance with Revenue rules and practices as described in JOM 102.

COMPULSORY PURCHASE ANNUITY (CPA)

An annuity which must be purchased at retirement for a member retiring from service.

CONCENTRATION OF INVESTMENT

Placing a significant proportion of the assets of a pension scheme in any single investment.

The amounts requiring compulsory disclosure and reporting are laid down by the OPB and the Disclosure Regulations.

CONSULTING ACTUARY

An **actuary** whose sole or main business is consultancy.

CONTINUATION OPTION

A facility offered by an insurance company which insures a scheme's death benefits, whereby a member leaving the scheme can effect a life assurance policy without evidence of health.

Formerly very common, but now becoming less usual.

CONTINUED RIGHTS
The term used in the **Practice Notes** to refer to the rights of scheme members who continue to be subject to pre existing Inland Revenue limits, including both **pre 17 March 1987 continued rights** and **pre 1 June 1989 continued rights**.

CONTRACT OUT
To use a statutory arrangement under which members of a pension scheme which meets certain conditions obtain rights under it in place of part of their earnings related state scheme benefits. Contributions to the state scheme are reduced in respect of such employees or, in the case of a personal pension scheme or free standing AVC scheme, partly repaid to the scheme.

CONTRACTED OUT EMPLOYMENTS GROUP (COEG)
The division of the DSS which deals principally with termination of contracted out employment and related matters.

CONTRACTED OUT MONEY PURCHASE SCHEME (COMPS)
A **money purchase scheme** which is contracted out, usually by reference to the provision of **protected rights**.

A money purchase scheme can also be contracted out by reference to the provision of a GMP, but would then be viewed by the OPB as a COSRS, not as a COMPS.

CONTRACTED OUT PROTECTED RIGHTS PREMIUM (COPRP)
A type of **state scheme premium** which may be paid by a money purchase scheme which is contracted out by reference to the provision of **protected rights**, in order to purchase benefits under the state scheme for a member, if the scheme ceases to be contracted out.

CONTRACTED OUT REBATE
1. The amount by which the employers' and employees' national-insurance contributions are reduced in respect of employees who are contracted out by virtue of their membership of an occupational pension scheme.

2. The equivalent payment made by the DSS as **minimum contributions** to a personal pension scheme.

CONTRACTED OUT SALARY RELATED SCHEME (COSRS)
An occupational pension scheme which is contracted out by reference to the provision of a **GMP**.

CONTRACTING OUT CERTIFICATE
The certificate issued by the OPB, in respect of an occupational pension scheme which satisfies the conditions for contracting out, confirming the employees in the employments named in the certificate are to be treated as being in contracted out employment.

CONTRIBUTIONS AGENCY
A self-contained unit within the DSS set up to advise employers on their national-insurance contributions, to ensure that employers and self employed people pay their proper contributions, and to maintain accurate contributions records.

CONTRIBUTIONS EQUIVALENT PREMIUM (CEP)
A type of **state scheme premium** which may be paid when a member leaves with less than two years **qualifying service** (or five years for a leaver before 6 April 1988), in return for which the state scheme will take over the obligation to provide his/her **GMP**.

CONTRIBUTION HOLIDAY
A period during which employers' and/or members' contributions are temporarily suspended, normally when the fund is in surplus. The term is sometimes used loosely when contributions continue to be paid but at a reduced rate.

CONTRIBUTORY SCHEME
A scheme which requires contributions from active members unless such contributions are temporarily suspended during a **contribution holiday**.

CONTROLLED FUNDING
A **funding plan** which has regard to the pension scheme's liabilities as a whole rather than those for individual members.

This term is most commonly used in connection with insured final salary schemes.

CONTROLLING DIRECTOR (20% DIRECTOR)
A director who, together with his associates, owns or controls 20% or more of the ordinary shares of the employing company. Special restrictions apply to controlling directors who are members of approved schemes. The full definition is set out in the **Practice Notes** (IR12 (1991)).

The term 20% director is used in IR12 (1979), which also contains references to former controlling directors as defined in earlier legislation.

COOLING OFF NOTICE
An alternative term for **cancellation notice**.

CORPORATE TRUSTEE
A company which acts as a trustee.

CREDITORS
Amounts owed by an entity in accordance with the accruals concept, i.e. amounts due but not paid.

Acceptable alternative terms for use by a pension scheme are 'current liabilities', 'accounts payable' or 'amounts payable'.

CROSS-REGIME TRANSFER
An alternative term for **inter-regime transfer**.

CURRENT FUNDING LEVEL
The **funding level**, at the present time, where the **actuarial liability** in respect of active members is taken as the present value of accrued benefits calculated in relation to current earnings, revalued as for preserved pensions on the statutory basis (or such higher basis as has been promised).

CURRENT UNIT METHOD
An accrued benefits valuation method in which the **actuarial liability** is based on earnings at the **valuation date**. The standard contribution rate is that necessary to cover the cost of benefits which will accrue in the year following the valuation date by reference to earnings projected to the end of that year.

CUSTODIAN TRUSTEE
A trustee responsible for holding the assets of a trust, other trustees being responsible for the management of the trust including the investment decisions.

*See also **trust corporation**.*

DEBTORS
Amounts owing to an entity e.g. amounts due but not received. The term may also include sums paid in advance of expenditure being incurred in accordance with the **accruals concept**.

Acceptable alternative terms for use by a pension scheme are 'current assets' or 'amounts receivable'.

DECLARATION OF TRUST
A formal document or part of a document establishing the trusts of a pension scheme.

DEED
See **trust deed**.

DEED OF ADHERENCE
A legal document admitting a new employer to a scheme and containing an undertaking by the new employer to comply with the provisions of the scheme.

DEED OF APPOINTMENT
A legal document by which a new trustee is appointed.

DEED OF COVENANT
A term sometimes used for **deed of adherence**.

DEEMED GMP
The **GMP** which must be provided for contracted out service from 6 April 1991

for married women and widows paying reduced rate national-insurance contributions.

DEFERRED ANNUITY
An annuity which commences from a future date.

DEFERRED PENSIONER
A person entitled to **preserved benefits**. Sometimes referred to as a deferred member.

DEFERRED RETIREMENT
An alternative term for **postponed retirement** or **late retirement**.

DEFICIENCY
See **actuarial deficiency**.

DEFINED BENEFIT SCHEME
A pension scheme in which the rules specify the benefits to be paid, and the scheme is financed accordingly.

DEFINED CONTRIBUTION SCHEME
An alternative term for a **money purchase scheme**.

DEFINITIVE TRUST DEED
The detailed trust deed which follows an **interim trust deed**.

DEPENDANT
A person who is financially dependent on a member or pensioner or was so at the time of death or retirement of the member or pensioner.

For PSO purposes, a spouse qualifies automatically as a dependant and a child of the member or pensioner may always be regarded as a dependant until attaining the age of 18 or ceasing to receive full time educational or vocational training, if later.

DEPENDANT'S (PENSION) OPTION
An alternative term for **allocation**.

DEPOSIT ADMINISTRATION
An insurance policy under which contributions, net of expense charges, are accumulated in a pool to which interest and usually bonuses are added. The proceeds are applied to provide pensions and other benefits as they become due.

DERIVATIVES
A generic term for financial instruments used in the management of portfolios such as **futures contracts** and **options**.

DETERMINATION

1. Exercise of a statutory power, usually by the OPB or the Secretary of State, either to take action in specified circumstances or to decide whether in certain situations the requirements of the law are met.

2. The term is sometimes used as an alternative term for **winding up**.

DIRECT INVESTMENT

A term used to describe the method of investment for a **self administered scheme** by which the securities are held directly in the name of the trustees and do not involve any form of insurance contract.

DISABILITY BENEFIT

A benefit paid to an employee who is unable to work for medical reasons, e.g. from a pension scheme, an **ill health early retirement benefit**; from an employer, a benefit consequent on an injury at work; or from an employer or an insurance policy, a **prolonged disability** payment.

DISCLOSURE REGULATIONS

Regulations issued under SSPA 75 requiring disclosure of information about pension schemes and benefits to interested parties.

The term is also used to describe the regulations requiring disclosure of information in relation to insurance policies.

DISCONTINUANCE

The cessation of contributions to a pension scheme leading either to **winding up** or to the scheme becoming a **frozen scheme**.

DISCONTINUANCE FUNDING VALUATION METHOD

An out of date term for **current unit method**.

DISCONTINUANCE VALUATION

An **actuarial valuation** carried out to assess the position if the scheme were to be discontinued and the trustees were to wind up in accordance with the requirements of the **trust instrument**. The valuation may take into account the possible exercise of any discretion to augment benefits.

DISCRETIONARY INCREASE

An increase in a pension in payment or in a preserved benefit arising other than from a system of **escalation** or **indexation**. Such an increase may be of a regular or an ad hoc nature.

DISCRETIONARY SCHEME

A scheme in which the employees to be offered membership are selected by the employer. Often the benefits, or the contributions from which they are to be provided, are also decided individually for each member.

DISREGARD
See **state pension disregard**.

DOCUMENTATION CERTIFICATE
A form of certificate used, in lieu of submitting detailed scheme documentation, either in seeking Inland Revenue approval in certain cases (an IR documentation certificate) or to satisfy contracting out requirements (an OPB documentation certificate).

DYNAMISATION/DYNAMISM
1. A term sometimes used to describe escalation or indexation.

2. Also used to describe index linking of earnings, either for calculating scheme benefits, or for determining **final remuneration** for the purpose of PSO limitations.

EARLIER SERVICE COMPONENT
For the purposes of **limited price indexation** under SSA 90, that part of the pension benefit under a **final salary scheme** which is attributable to service before the **Appointed Day**.

EARLY LEAVER
A person who ceases to be an active member of a pension scheme, other than on death, without being granted an immediate retirement benefit.

EARLY RETIREMENT
The retirement of a member with immediate retirement benefit, before normal pension date.

*The benefit may be reduced because of early payment. See also **ill health early retirement**.*

EARMARKED POLICY
A term used in the **Practice Notes** to denote a policy held by a pension scheme, where each annuity or sum assured is earmarked to provide benefits for or in respect of an individual member.

EARNINGS CAP
Limitation introduced by FA 1989 on the amount of remuneration on which the benefits and contributions of a **Class A Member** may be based. This was set at £60,000 for tax year 1989/90, and is increased annually in line with prices. The same limitation applies to **net relevant earnings** for all members of personal pension schemes.

EARNINGS FACTOR (EF)
A notional amount of earnings used for the purpose of calculating state scheme benefits or **GMPs**.

EARNINGS LIMITS
See **lower earnings limit** and **upper earnings limit**.

ELIGIBILITY
The conditions which must be met for a person to be a member of a scheme or to receive a particular benefit. These may, for example, relate to age, service, status and type of employment.

EMPLOYER
The person or body with whom the member of a pension scheme has a contract of employment relevant to that scheme.

This term is to be preferred to 'company' as having more general application in the context of pension schemes.

ENDOWMENT ASSURANCE POLICY
A policy which provides a lump sum at a fixed future date or on earlier death.

ENHANCED COMMUTATION FACTOR
A term used in the **Practice Notes** to denote a commutation factor that includes allowance for prospective pension increases for which provision is made in the rules of the scheme.

ENTRY AGE METHOD
A prospective benefits valuation method in which the new entrant contribution rate is taken as the **standard contribution rate**.

ENTRY DATE
The date on which an employee is permitted to join a pension scheme.

EQUAL ACCESS
Identical entry conditions for each sex. This is required by SSPA 75.

EQUAL TREATMENT
The principle requiring one sex to be treated no less favourably than the other, as embodied in EC Council Directive 86/378.

EQUIVALENT PENSION BENEFIT (EPB)
The benefit which must be provided for an employee who was contracted out of the former **graduated pension scheme**.

See also payment in lieu.

ESCALATION
A system whereby pensions in payment and/or preserved benefits are automatically increased at regular intervals and at a fixed percentage rate. The percentage may be restricted to the increase in a specified index.

EX GRATIA BENEFIT
A benefit provided by the employer which he is not legally required to provide.

EXCHANGE OF LETTERS
A term used where a letter from an employer to an employee constitutes part or all of the documentation for an **individual arrangement,** and a copy is signed by the employee to signify acknowledgement of its terms.

Where the letter does not itself incorporate a declaration of trust, it will usually be coupled with a formal declaration of trust to ensure that the arrangement is legally enforceable.

EXECUTIVE SCHEME
A scheme for selected directors or employees.
*See also **discretionary scheme**.*

EXEMPT APPROVED SCHEME
An approved scheme other than a personal pension scheme which is established under irrevocable trusts (or exceptionally, subject to a formal direction under S592(1)(b) of ICTA 88) thus giving rise to the tax reliefs specified in ICTA 88.

EXEMPT UNIT TRUST
A unitised form of investment normally managed by an investment organisation specifically designed for pension funds and charities which enjoys the same tax advantages as a directly invested pension fund's assets.

EXPERIENCE DEFICIENCY/SURPLUS
An actuarial deficiency or surplus which arises because events have not co-incided with the actuarial assumptions made for the last valuation.

EXPRESSION OF WISH
A means by which a member can indicate a preference as to who should receive any lump sum death benefit. The choice is not binding on the trustees, and as a result Inheritance Tax is normally avoided.

EXTERNAL INVESTMENT MANAGER
An **investment manager,** normally a third party, not employed solely by the trustees or by the employer.

FAS 87
The US Financial Accounting Standards Board's statement which deals with accounting for pension costs in employers' accounts. FAS 88 applies to employers' accounts when a scheme is wound up or if benefits are settled on termination of employment.

FINAL AVERAGE EARNINGS
See **final pensionable earnings**.

FINAL EARNINGS SCHEME
An alternative name for a **final salary scheme**.

FINAL PENSIONABLE EARNINGS/PAY/SALARY
The pensionable earnings, at or near retirement or leaving service, on which the pension is calculated in a **final salary scheme**. The earnings may be based on the average over a number of consecutive years prior to retirement.

FINAL REMUNERATION
The term used by the PSO for the maximum amount of earnings which it will permit to be used for the purpose of calculating maximum approvable benefits.

*The permissible alternatives are set out fully in the **Practice Notes**.*

*See also **earnings cap**.*

FINAL SALARY SCHEME
A pension scheme where the benefit is calculated by reference to the member's pensionable earnings for a period ending at or before normal pension date or leaving service, usually also based on pensionable service.

FIXED REVALUATION RATE
The rate by which a contracted out scheme may revalue **GMP** between termination of contracted out employment and state pensionable age as one of the alternatives to applying **Section 21 Orders**.

The rate changes periodically. It was 8.5% for members leaving up to 5 April 1988 and 7.5% for members leaving between 6 April 1988 and 5 April 1993. It has been 7% since 6 April 1993.

FLAT RATE SCHEME
A pension scheme which provides benefits for each year of pensionable service not related to earnings.

FORGOING
An alternative term for **salary sacrifice**.

FRANKING
See **anti franking requirements**.

FREE COVER
The maximum amount of death or disability benefit which an insurance company covering a group of lives is prepared to insure for each individual without production of evidence of health.

FREE STANDING AVC SCHEME
A scheme established by a **pension provider** to accept free standing additional voluntary contributions.

FREE STANDING ADDITIONAL VOLUNTARY CONTRIBUTIONS (FSAVCs)

Contributions to a pension contract separate from a company pension scheme effected by an active member of that scheme. Benefits are secured with a **pension provider** by contributions from the member only.

FROZEN BENEFIT

A **preserved benefit**, strictly one not subject to **revaluation**.

FROZEN SCHEME

A **closed scheme** where no further contributions are payable and members are entitled to **preserved benefits**.

FULLY INSURED SCHEME

A scheme where the trustees have effected an insurance contract in respect of each member which guarantees benefits corresponding at all times to those promised under the rules.

Sometimes incorrectly used to mean insured scheme.

FUNDING

The provision in advance for future liabilities by the accumulation of assets, normally external to the employer's business.

FUNDING LEVEL

The relationship at a specified date between the **actuarial value of assets** and the **actuarial liability**.

The funding level may be calculated separately in respect of different categories of liability, e.g. pensions in payment and AVCs.

FUNDING OBJECTIVE

See **funding plan**.

FUNDING PLAN

The arrangement of the incidence over time of payments with the aim of meeting the future cost of a given set of benefits.

Possible objectives of a funding plan might be that, if the actuarial assumptions are borne out by events:
(a) A specified funding level should be reached by a given date.
(b) The level of contributions should remain constant, or should after a planned period be the standard contribution rate required by the valuation method used in the actuarial valuation.

FUNDING RATE

A term sometimes used to describe the **recommended contribution rate**.

FUTURES CONTRACT
A contract which binds two parties in a sale or purchase at a specified future date at a price which is fixed at the time the contract is effected.

GLOBAL CUSTODIAN
An independent third party who undertakes the role of holding and accounting for securities in a portfolio on behalf of an investment manager or trustees.

GRADED SCHEDULE SCHEME
An alternative term for **salary grade scheme**.

GRADUATED PENSION SCHEME
The state earnings related scheme which commenced on 3 April 1961 and terminated on 5 April 1975.

GROUP PERSONAL PENSION SCHEME
An arrangement made for the employees of a particular employer to participate in a personal pension scheme on a grouped basis. This is not a separate scheme; merely a collecting arrangement.

GROUP POLICY
An insurance policy in respect of more than one individual.

GUARANTEED ANNUITY OPTION
The right to apply the proceeds of an insurance policy to buy an annuity at a rate guaranteed in the policy.

GUARANTEED MINIMUM PENSION (GMP)
The minimum pension which an occupational pension scheme must provide as one of the conditions of contracting out (unless it is contracted out through the provision of **protected rights**).

For an employee contracted out under any occupational or personal pension scheme an amount equal to the GMP is deducted from his/her benefits under the state scheme.

GUARANTEED PENSION
A term which may be used to describe the minimum benefit available from an insurance policy.

*Also sometimes used to denote **minimum pension** or **pension guarantee**.*

GUIDANCE NOTES (GN)
1. Notes published by the PSO describing the requirements for tax approval in respect of specified types of schemes, in particular those relating to personal pension schemes (IR76).
*See also **Practice Notes**.*

2. Notes published by professional bodies such as the Institute of Actuaries, advising their members on the appropriate course of action in specified circumstances.

HANCOCK ANNUITY

A term describing a certain kind of annuity purchased by the employer at the time of an employee's retirement, the capital cost of which is normally allowed for tax relief in the year of purchase.

HEADROOM CHECK

A funding check to ensure **IR** limits are not exceeded within a **free standing AVC scheme**. This check is carried out prior to payment of contributions in certain circumstances, notably where the proposed gross contribution is £2,400 p.a. or more. Full requirements are set out in the free standing AVC scheme supplement to the **Practice Notes**.

HISTORICAL COST

A term meaning that the amount at which an asset or liability is stated in the accounts is the cost of acquiring or producing it, sometimes less depreciation.

According to SORP 1 and the Disclosure Regulations, the assets of a pension scheme should be stated at market value.

HYBRID SCHEME

A pension scheme in which the benefit is calculated usually as the better of two alternatives, for example on a final earnings and a money purchase basis.

ILL HEALTH EARLY RETIREMENT

Retirement on medical grounds before **normal pension date**. The benefit may exceed that payable on early retirement in other circumstances.

IMMEDIATE ANNUITY

An annuity which commences immediately or shortly after its purchase.

INCENTIVE PAYMENT

See **2% incentive**.

INDEPENDENT TRUSTEE

An individual or corporate body with no direct or indirect involvement with the pension scheme, sponsoring employer, or members, other than performing the duties of the trustee.

Under provisions introduced by SSA 90, an independent trustee is required to be appointed where an employer has become insolvent.

INDEX LINKING

A term describing adjustment in line with an index (usually of prices or earnings). In relation to pensions, an alternative term for **indexation**.

INDEXATION

1. A system whereby pensions in payment and/or preserved benefits are automatically increased at regular intervals by reference to a specified index of prices or earnings.

   *The term is also occasionally used in relation to index linking of final pensionable earnings or final remuneration: see explanation under **dynamisation**.*

2. It is also in common use as a method of investment management where the objective is to produce a return equal or close to that of a chosen stock market index.

INDIRECT DISCRIMINATION

The unequal treatment of one sex in relation to the other by applying conditions which, while not directly discriminatory, are more likely to be met by one sex than the other.

INDIVIDUAL ARRANGEMENT

An occupational pension scheme with only one member where the documentation, often an **exchange of letters**, relates only to that member.

An employer may have several individual arrangements for different employees.

INDUSTRY WIDE SCHEME

A **centralised scheme** for non-associated employers in a particular industry.

INFLATION PROOFING

A term commonly used to describe **indexation**.

INLAND REVENUE LIMITS RULE

A rule, which must be included in the rules of an approved occupational pension scheme, specifying the **maximum approvable benefits** for members.

INSURED SCHEME

A pension scheme where the sole long term investment medium is an insurance policy (other than a **managed fund** policy).

INTEGRATION

The design of pension scheme benefits to take into account all or part of the state scheme benefits which the member is deemed to receive.

*One form of integration involves a **state pension disregard**.*

INTERIM TRUST DEED

A form of trust deed commonly used to establish a pension scheme on broadly stated terms leaving the detailed provisions and the rules to be provided later by a **definitive trust deed**.

A scheme may be established by other methods, for example by a board resolution, declaration of trust or exchange of letters.

INTER-REGIME TRANSFERS
Transfers between different types of approved pension arrangements.

The Inland Revenue requirements relating to such transfers are set out in the Practice Notes.

INVESTMENT
The process by which contributions and net income are used to increase the value of pension fund assets by means of cash deposits, the purchase and sale of equities, fixed interest stocks, bonds, property and other authorised investments.

INVESTMENT INCOME
The income derived from dividends, interest or rents from the investment of assets.

INVESTMENT MANAGEMENT AGREEMENT
The document in which an investment manager sets out the basis upon which it will manage a portfolio. The document is normally countersigned on behalf of the pension fund trustees and forms the legal and regulatory framework for the relationship between the trustees and the investment manager.

INVESTMENT MANAGER
An individual or body to which the investment of the whole or part of the assets is delegated by the trustees in accordance with the provisions of the scheme documentation.

INVESTMENT PERFORMANCE MEASUREMENT
The comparison of the rate of return of a given pension fund over a period with one or more of:

(a) the notional return of a model fund;
(b) the actual rates of return of other funds; or
(c) the movement in stock market indices;

over the same period.

INVESTMENT POLICY/STRATEGY
The periodic decisions regarding the types and proportions of assets in which a pension fund is invested.

INVESTMENT REPORT
A document communicating details of the assets of a fund, their deployment and changes, together with reasons.

INVESTMENT TRUST
A company quoted on a Stock Exchange, whose business is the process of investing in a wide range of securities, normally equities. The value of its shares reflects the underlying value of its portfolio of investments.

JOINT OFFICE
The Joint Office of the OPB and SFO which existed prior to 1 August 1991, when they shared the same premises.

JOINT OFFICE MEMORANDA (JOM)
Explanatory memoranda issued by the Joint Office prior to its cessation on 31 July 1991.

LATE RETIREMENT
The retirement of a member, with immediate retirement benefit, after **normal pension date**.

The benefit may be increased because of late payment.

LATER EARNINGS ADDITION
An amount to be added when calculating the minimum benefit for the purpose of **anti-franking requirements** where a member continues in pensionable service after contracted out employment ceases and the level of earnings is higher when he/she retires or leaves than on ceasing to be contracted out.

LATER SERVICE COMPONENT
For the purposes of **limited price indexation** under SSA 90, that part of the pension benefit under a **final salary scheme** which is attributable to service after the **Appointed Day**.

LETTER OF EXCHANGE
See **exchange of letters**.

LEVEL ANNUAL CONTRIBUTION BASIS
An alternative term for **level annual premium method**.

LEVEL ANNUAL PREMIUM METHOD
A method of determining the premiums payable under an insurance contract with the object of keeping the premium for each individual at a constant rate until there is a change in circumstances.

LEVEL OF FUNDING
An alternative term for **funding level**.

LEVY
A levy introduced by SSA 90, based on the active membership of occupational and personal pension schemes, to help meet the costs of the **Pensions Ombudsman** and the **Register**.

LIABILITIES
Amounts which a pension scheme has an obligation to pay now or in the future. The amounts may not be immediately ascertainable and some liabilities may be dependent on the occurrence of future events.

LIFE ASSURANCE SCHEME
A scheme which provides a benefit only on the death of a member (normally on death in service).

LIMITED PRICE INDEXATION (LPI)
The requirement under SSA 90 to increase pensions (other than **money purchase** benefits) in excess of **GMP** under a **final salary scheme**, once in payment, by 5% per annum or RPI if less. The requirement applies automatically to pensions accrued after the **Appointed Day**. It also applies to pensions accrued before the **Appointed Day** to the extent that surplus within the scheme is identified and required to be used for such purpose.

LIMITED REVALUATION PREMIUM (LRP)
A type of **state scheme premium** which may be paid when a member of a scheme contracted out by means of the **GMP** test ceases to be in contracted out employment. In return for this premium any subsequent revaluation of **GMP** up to state pensionable age above a specified level (currently 5 per cent p.a.) would be provided by the state scheme instead of under the occupational scheme. This is one of the alternatives to applying **Section 21 Orders**.

LINKED QUALIFYING SERVICE
Actual service in a previous scheme which gives rise to a **transfer credit**, which ranks as **qualifying service**.

LONG SERVICE BENEFIT
The term used in the preservation requirements of SSA 73 to describe the benefit payable at **normal pension age**, with which **short service benefit** must be compared.

LOWER EARNINGS LIMIT (LEL)
The minimum amount, approximately equivalent to the **basic pension**, which must be earned in any pay period before national-insurance contributions are payable.

LUMP SUM CERTIFICATE
A certificate which must be provided by a transferring scheme in certain circumstances, described in the **Practice Notes**, stating the maximum lump sum available from a transfer payment.

MANAGED FUND
An investment contract by means of which an insurance company offers participation in one or more pooled funds. Also used to denote an arrangement where the scheme assets are invested on similar lines to unit trusts by an external investment manager.

MARKET LEVEL INDICATOR (MLI)
An index giving a weighted comparison of values of equities and fixed interest

securities. Market level indicators are used to adjust the amount of some state scheme premiums.

MARKET VALUE
The price at which an asset might reasonably be expected to be sold in an open market.

Although 'current market value' should be defined by reference to actual current conditions of the market, for practical purposes other considerations may be postulated, e.g. adopting a 'willing buyer, willing seller' basis.

MASTER POLICY
An alternative term for **group policy**.

MATCHING
1. The policy of selecting investments of a nature, incidence or currency similar to that of the expected outgoings.

2. An accounting term, meaning that revenue and costs are matched with one another or 'hedged' so far as their relationship can be established or justifiably assumed.

MAXIMUM APPROVABLE BENEFIT
The maximum benefit for an individual which is allowable under an approved scheme (other than a personal pension scheme or a simplified defined contribution scheme).

MEMBER
A person who has been admitted to membership of a pension scheme and is entitled to benefit under the scheme. Sometimes narrowly used to refer only to an **active member**.

For some statutory purposes the term 'members' may include employees who are prospective members.

MEMBER PARTICIPATION
The active participation of members in the affairs of a pension scheme. This may be directly through representation on the trustee body, or indirectly through joint consultative committees with an employer.

MEMBER'S NORMAL CONTRIBUTIONS
The regular contributions required from an active member by the scheme rules.

MINIMUM BENEFIT
An amount of benefit which a scheme promises if the normal benefit for a particular member would be smaller.

MINIMUM CONTRIBUTIONS
1. Contributions payable to a personal pension scheme or to a free standing

AVC scheme by the DSS in respect of a member who has elected to contract out. The contributions consist of a partial rebate of national-insurance contributions, together with the **2% incentive** where applicable.

2. The term could also be used in respect of any minimum amount which a member is required to contribute in order to be a member of an occupational or personal pension scheme, or in order to make additional voluntary contributions.

MINIMUM CONTRIBUTIONS SCHEME

A rebate only personal pension scheme or a contracted out money purchase scheme to which only payments to the same level as the rebate are made.

See rebate only personal pension scheme.

MINIMUM PAYMENTS

The minimum amount which an employer must pay into a money purchase scheme which is contracted out through the provision of **protected rights**. This amount corresponds to the reduction in national-insurance contributions which applies in respect of employees who are contracted out.

MINIMUM PENSION

See **minimum benefit**.

MODEL RULES

Specimen rules produced by the OPB and/or the PSO for certain categories of pension schemes to facilitate approval and/or the issue of a contracting out or appropriate scheme certificate.

MODIFIED PREMIUM VALUE

A **premium value** which excludes the loadings made by the insurer in premium rating for initial expenses, such as issue expenses, commission and stamp duty.

MONEY PURCHASE

The determination of an individual member's benefits by reference to contributions paid into the scheme in respect of that member, usually increased by an amount based on the investment return on those contributions.

MONEY PURCHASE CONTRACTED OUT SCHEME

The term used in SSPA 75 (as amended by SSA 86) to describe a **money purchase scheme** which is contracted out through the provision of **protected rights**.

MONEY PURCHASE SCHEME

A scheme where the benefits are determined on a **money purchase** basis.

MONEY PURCHASE UNDERPIN
A minimum benefit provided in a defined benefit scheme, calculated on a **money purchase** basis.

*See also **hybrid scheme**.*

MOVEMENT OF FUNDS STATEMENT
A statement within the annual accounts of a pension scheme which reconciles the changes in the net assets with income and expenditure and changes in market value.

N/NS × P CERTIFICATE
A certificate obtained by administrators of a personal pension scheme from trustees of an occupational pension scheme in respect of a transfer payment for a **controlling director**, higher earner or a member over age 45, to certify that the transfer value covers the individual's total accrued rights and that these are within IR limits.

NET ASSETS STATEMENT
A summary of the net assets (assets less liabilities) of a pension scheme usually presented as part of the audited accounts in the **annual report**.

This does not take account of the liabilities to pay benefits in future as this is properly reflected in the actuarial valuation.

According to SORP 1 and the Disclosure Regulations, the assets of a pension scheme should be stated at market value.

NET BOOK VALUE (NBV)
The historical cost of a fixed asset less depreciation.

NET RELEVANT EARNINGS
Earnings from self employment or non pensionable employment after deducting losses and certain business charges on income, used in determining the maximum contributions to a **retirement annuity** or **personal pension scheme** which qualify for tax relief.

With effect from tax year 1989–90 net relevant earnings have been restricted by the **earnings cap**. The maximum contribution below the cap is currently 17.5 per cent of net relevant earnings with higher percentage limits for persons aged over 35, if contributing to a personal pension scheme, or 50, if contributing to a retirement annuity.

NEW CODE
An obsolete term originally distinguishing pension arrangements made under FA 70 from those made under earlier legislation (**old code**).

NEW ENTRANT CONTRIBUTION RATE
A rate of contribution estimated as being sufficient to provide benefits for future entrants, including any contribution required from the members.

NEW MONEY

The flow into a fund of contributions and transfer payments less outgoings. Normally not considered to include income from existing assets.

NIL CERTIFICATE

A certificate indicating that a transfer value is not to be used to provide retirement benefits in lump sum form, such as on a transfer from a **free standing AVC scheme**.

NOMINATION

The naming by a member of the person to whom he/she wishes any death benefit to be paid. The scheme documentation will indicate whether this is binding on the trustees or merely for their consideration. In the latter case (which is the more common) the term **expression of wish** is to be preferred.

NON APPROVED SCHEME

An alternative term for an **unapproved scheme**.

NON CONTRIBUTORY SCHEME

A pension scheme which does not require contributions from its active members.

Not to be confused with a contributory scheme where contributions are suspended during a **contribution holiday**.

NORMAL PENSION AGE (NPA)

The age by reference to which the **normal pension date** is determined.

SSA 73 defines the term for the purposes of the preservation requirements as the earliest age at which a member is entitled as of right to receive unreduced benefits on retirement.

NORMAL PENSION DATE (NPD)

The date at which a member of a pension scheme normally becomes entitled to receive his/her retirement benefits.

NORMAL RETIREMENT AGE (NRA)

For employment purposes, the age at which employees holding a particular position normally retire from service. This is usually (but not always) the same as **normal pension age**.

NORMAL RETIREMENT DATE (NRD)

Commonly used with the same meaning as **normal pension date**.

OCCUPATIONAL PENSION SCHEME

An arrangement subject to SSA 73, organised by an employer or on behalf of a group of employers to provide pensions and/or other benefits for or in respect of one or more employees on leaving service or on death or retirement.

A more detailed definition is to be found in S51(3)(a) SSA 73.

OCCUPATIONAL PENSIONS ADVISORY SERVICE (OPAS)

A grant aided body providing free help and advice to members of the public who have problems concerning their rights under either occupational or personal pension schemes. Its independent service is provided by a network of local volunteer advisers.

OCCUPATIONAL PENSIONS BOARD (OPB)

A statutory body set up under SSA 73, with functions derived from that Act and SSPA 75. The Board is responsible for issuing **contracting out** or **appropriate scheme certificates** for pension schemes which meet the statutory requirements, for supervising those schemes to ensure that **GMPs** and protected rights are secure and for ensuring that **equal access** and **preservation** requirements are satisfied. The Board is required to report to the Secretary of State when he/she seeks their advice and to comment on draft regulations affecting occupational pension schemes.

The Board can make grants to persons or organisations who give advice or assistance in connection with occupational or personal pensions activities, and it has been appointed as the Registrar of Occupational and Personal Pension Schemes. The Board can, on application, authorise or direct occupational or personal pension schemes to be modified or wound up, e.g. in cases where the power to do so does not exist in the trust deed.

OLD CODE

The legislation before FA 70 relating to approval of occupational pension schemes, and the corresponding Inland Revenue practice.

See also new code.

OPEN MARKET OPTION

The option to apply the proceeds of an insurance contract to buy an annuity at a current market rate from the same or another insurance company.

OPTING OUT

A decision by an employee to leave or not to join an occupational pension scheme of the employer.

This was made a statutory right from 6 April 1988 under SSA 86.

OPTION

A derivative financial instrument under which the payment of a sum of money gives a right, but not an obligation, to buy or sell something at an agreed price on or before a specified date.

ORDINARY ANNUAL CONTRIBUTIONS

A term used in the **Practice Notes** to denote the contributions payable to an occupational pension scheme by the employer on a regular basis in accordance with the scheme documentation.

OVERLAP
The term describing an arrangement whereby a pension for a dependant becomes payable in addition to the **pension guarantee** until the end of the guarantee period.

OVERRIDING LEGISLATION
The application of statutory requirements to pension schemes by means of provisions which directly override scheme rules.

Examples include revaluation, anti-franking requirements, rights to a cash equivalent under SSPA 75 and the provisions of ICTA 88 and FA 1989 relating to schemes approved before 23 July 1987 and 27 July 1989 respectively.

PACE OF FUNDING
The rate of progress towards the objective of the **funding plan**.

PAID UP BENEFIT
A **preserved benefit** which is irrevocably secured for an individual member under a contract of insurance under which premiums have ceased to be payable in respect of that member.

PARTIALLY APPROVED SCHEME
A pension scheme only partially approved by the PSO because it provides some benefits which are not approvable, for example for overseas employees.

Not to be confused with partial loss of tax exemptions which occurs under Schedule 22 of ICTA 88 if a pension scheme which is excessively overfunded fails to take action to reduce the surplus.

PASSIVE INVESTMENT MANAGEMENT
A style of managing a portfolio which involves little activity and is normally linked to a particular index so that the portfolio value moves with that index.

PAST SERVICE
Service before a given date. Sometimes used to denote service before entry into the pension scheme.

PAST SERVICE BENEFIT
A benefit granted for **past service** and/or **pre scheme service**.

PAST SERVICE RESERVE
A term generally used to describe the **present value** of all benefits accrued at the **valuation date** by reference to earnings projected to the dates on which benefits become payable.

PAY AS YOU GO (PAYG)
An arrangement under which benefits are paid out of revenue and no funding is made for future liabilities.

The state scheme is pay as you go.

PAYMENT IN LIEU (PIL)

A payment made to the National Insurance Fund for a member who ceased to be contracted out of the former **graduated pension scheme**, where the **equivalent pension benefit** was not preserved within the pension scheme.

PENSION COST

Under **SSAP 24** the cost of providing pensions, which is charged to the profit and loss account of the employer over the expected service lives or **average remaining service life** of employees in the scheme. The amount may be more or less than the actual payments made to the pension scheme.

PENSION FRACTION

The fraction of pensionable earnings for each year of pensionable service which forms the basis of the pension in a final salary scheme or an average earnings scheme.

PENSION FUND

Strictly speaking the assets of a pension scheme but very often used to denote the pension scheme itself.

PENSION GUARANTEE

An arrangement whereby on the early death of a pensioner, the pension scheme pays a further sum or sums to meet a guaranteed total. This total may be established by relation to, for instance, the late member's accumulated contributions or a multiple of the annual rate of pension.

PENSION INCREASE

An increase in a pension in payment.

Such an increase may arise as a result of escalation or indexation, or may be a discretionary increase. In practice the term may also embrace revaluation of preserved benefits.

PENSION MORTGAGE

A mortgage where the lender anticipates the borrower drawing sufficient cash by way of **commutation** from a pension scheme or retirement annuity to cover repayment of the loan. There can be no formal link between the loan and the anticipated cash sum.

PENSION PROVIDER

A body by which a personal pension scheme or free standing AVC scheme must be established in order to be approved by the Inland Revenue.

PENSION SCHEME

An occupational pension scheme, a personal pension scheme or a free standing AVC scheme.

PENSION SCHEMES OFFICE (PSO)

The office of the Inland Revenue which deals with the approval of pension schemes under the relevant tax legislation.

*Prior to 1 April 1992 known as the **Superannuation Funds Office (SFO)**.*

PENSION TAX RELIEF AT SOURCE (PTRAS)

The procedure whereby contributions to an occupational pension scheme are deducted from the member's pay before tax is calculated under PAYE, giving immediate tax relief at the highest applicable rate. Such relief is also available for contributions to personal pension schemes but at basic rate only, relief at higher rates having to be separately claimed.

PENSIONABLE AGE

The term used in legislation to denote **state pensionable age**.

PENSIONABLE EARNINGS

The earnings on which benefits and/or contributions are calculated.

*One or more elements of earnings (e.g. overtime) may be excluded, and/or there may be a **state pension disregard**.*

PENSIONABLE EMPLOYMENT

An alternative term for **pensionable service**.

PENSIONABLE SERVICE

The period of service which is taken into account in calculating pension benefit.

SSA 73 gives the term a statutory definition for the purposes of preservation, which also applies for the purposes of the revaluation and transfer payment requirements of SSPA 75.

PENSIONEER TRUSTEE

An individual or company with pensions experience appointed in accordance with the requirements relating to the approval of **small self administered schemes** under ICTA 88 to act as a trustee of such a scheme.

PENSIONER

A person who is currently receiving a pension from a pension scheme.

PENSIONER'S RIGHTS PREMIUM (PRP)

A type of **state scheme premium** which may be paid for a member or pensioner over state pensionable age when a **defined benefit scheme** ceases to be contracted out, in return for which the state scheme will take over the obligation to provide his/her **GMP**.

PENSIONS OMBUDSMAN

A post created under SSA 90 to deal with complaints against, and disputes with, occupational and personal pension schemes. The person appointed is completely independent and acts as an impartial adjudicator.

PERMANENT HEALTH INSURANCE (PHI)
An alternative term for **prolonged disability insurance**.

PERMITTED INVESTMENTS
In general the type and classes of investment allowed to trustees under a trust deed and rules. More specifically the investments stipulated by the Inland Revenue in connection with individual pension arrangements such as personal pension and small self administered schemes.

PERMITTED MAXIMUM
The term used in legislation to describe the **earnings cap**.

PERSONAL PENSION
An alternative term for a **personal pension arrangement**.

The term is also frequently used to describe a retirement annuity effected under the tax legislation in force before July 1988.

PERSONAL PENSION ARRANGEMENT
An individual contract made under a **personal pension scheme**.

PERSONAL PENSION CONTRIBUTIONS CERTIFICATE
A certificate issued by a personal pension scheme provider to the member to enable that member to provide his/her Inspector of Taxes with evidence of membership and contributions.

PERSONAL PENSION PROTECTED RIGHTS PREMIUM (PPPRP)
A type of **state scheme premium** which may be paid by a personal pension scheme for a member if the scheme ceases to be contracted out.

PERSONAL PENSION SCHEME (PPS)
Usually used to mean a scheme approved under Chapter IV of Part XIV of ICTA 88, under which individuals who are self employed or in non pensionable employment, not in an occupational pension scheme, make pension provision usually by means of unit trust or deposit account contracts.

See also self invested personal pension.

SSA 86 uses a slightly different definition which excludes a scheme open only to the self employed but also includes a free standing AVC scheme.

POST 89 MEMBER
An alternative term for a **Class A Member**.

POST 89 REGIME

The package of maximum approvable benefits introduced by FA 1989, details of which appear in the **Practice Notes**.

See also Class A Member.

POSTPONED RETIREMENT

The situation where a member has remained in employment beyond normal pension date and payment of the pension has not yet commenced.

PRACTICE NOTES (PN)

Notes on the approval of occupational pension schemes by the PSO, currently issued as IR12 (1991). Schemes approved before November 1991 continue to be subject to the earlier **Practice Notes** (IR12 (1979)), but may choose to adopt certain parts of the later **Practice Notes**.

PRE 1 JUNE 1989 CONTINUED RIGHTS

The rights of a member of an occupational pension scheme who continues to be subject to the Inland Revenue maximum benefit limits which were generally applicable between 17 March 1987 and 31 May 1989.

*The full definition is set out in the **Practice Notes**.*

*The rights include exemption from the **earnings cap**, as for pre 17 March 1987 Continued Rights, but there are restrictions on commutation, and maximum pension is only available after 20 years' service.*

See also Class B Member.

PRE 17 MARCH 1987 CONTINUED RIGHTS

The rights of a member of an occupational pension scheme who continues to be subject to the Inland Revenue maximum benefit limits which were generally applicable before 17 March 1987.

*The full definition is set out in the **Practice Notes**.*

*The rights include exemption from the **earnings cap** and an Inland Revenue maximum pension based on 10 or more years' service.*

See also Class C Member.

PRE 87 MEMBER

An alternative term for a **Class C Member**.

PRE AWARD DYNAMISM

A term sometimes used to describe **revaluation** of preserved benefits between leaving a scheme and retirement.

PRE SCHEME SERVICE

Service before the start of the relevant pension scheme or before entry into membership.

PREMIUM VALUE
A basis of valuation (of a long term insurance policy) for pension scheme accounting purposes, based on an equivalent single premium.

See Appendix 2 of SORP 1.

PREPAYMENT (PENSION)
An asset on the balance sheet of the employer's accounts usually representing the excess of funding payments over the amount calculated by the actuary as being his best estimate under **SSAP 24** of the costs of providing pensions. It sometimes reflects or includes negative pension cost and/or a surplus included in the balance sheet under the transitional provisions of **SSAP 24**.

PRESENT VALUE
The total of the amounts of a series of future payments or receipts discounted at interest to a current date, usually the **valuation date**, and allowing for the probabilities of payment or receipt.

PRESERVATION
The granting by a scheme of **preserved benefits**, in particular in accordance with minimum requirements specified by SSA 73.

PRESERVED BENEFITS
Benefits arising on an individual ceasing to be an **active member** of a pension scheme, payable at a later date.

PRINCIPAL EMPLOYER
The term commonly used in scheme documentation for the particular participating employer in which is vested special powers or duties in relation to such matters as the appointment of the trustees, amendments and winding up. Usually this will be the employer which established the scheme or its successor in business.

PRIORITY LIABILITIES
Benefits and other liabilities which are given precedence in accordance with the **priority rule** when a scheme is wound up.

Under S40(3) SSPA 75 a contracted out salary related scheme must contain a rule which gives priority, in the event of the scheme winding up, to GMPs and certain other liabilities.

PRIORITY RULE
The provisions contained in the scheme documentation setting out the order of precedence to be followed if the scheme is wound up with insufficient assets to meet all liabilities.

PRIVATELY INVESTED SCHEME
A term sometimes used to describe a **self administered scheme**.

PROCEEDS OF POLICY SCHEME

A money purchase scheme where the benefits promised to the members are those which can be provided from the proceeds of an insurance contract effected in respect of each member.

PROJECTED ACCRUED BENEFIT METHOD

A valuation method which compares the accrued **actuarial liability** with the value placed on the scheme assets for valuation purposes. The **actuarial liability** is based on service up to the **valuation date** and makes allowance for projected earnings. Used only in the context of the Pension Scheme Surpluses (Valuation) Regulations 1987 (SI 1987 No. 442).

PROJECTED UNIT METHOD

An accrued benefits valuation method in which the **actuarial liability** makes allowance for projected earnings. The **standard contribution rate** is that necessary to cover the cost of all benefits which will accrue in the year following the **valuation date** by reference to earnings projected to the dates on which benefits become payable.

This is known in the US as projected unit credit method.

PROLONGED DISABILITY INSURANCE (PDI)

Insurance effected outside a pension scheme against long term sickness or disability, providing a regular income during such periods of absence before retirement.

Normally, the income becomes payable only after a minimum period. Not to be confused with ill health early retirement.

PROSPECTIVE BENEFITS VALUATION METHOD

A **valuation method** in which the **actuarial liability** is the **present value** of:

(a) the benefits for current and deferred pensioners and their dependants, allowing where appropriate for future pension increases, and

(b) the benefits which active members will receive in respect of both past and future service, allowing for projected earnings up to their assumed exit dates and, where appropriate, for pension increases thereafter,

less the **present value** of future contributions payable in respect of current members at the **standard contribution rate**.

PROTECTED RIGHTS

The benefits under an appropriate personal pension scheme or a money purchase contracted out scheme, deriving respectively from at least the **minimum contributions** or **minimum payments**, which are provided in a specified form as a necessary condition for contracting out.

The term may also be used in a general sense to describe rights given to certain members on change of rules or change of pension scheme which are superior to those of a new entrant.

PROTECTED RIGHTS ANNUITY

The pension provided from **protected rights** under an appropriate personal pension scheme or a money purchase contracted out scheme by purchase from an insurance company or friendly society.

PROTECTED SPOUSE

A widow or widower of a member of a money purchase contracted out scheme or an appropriate personal pension scheme who is either aged 45 or more, or aged under 45 with dependent child(ren).

PROVISION

1. An amount written off to provide for depreciation or diminution in value of assets.

2. An amount retained as reasonably necessary to provide for any liability or loss which is likely to be incurred but the amount or date of which is uncertain. (See Companies Act 1985, Schedule 4 para 88.)

See also reserve. Pension costs in employers' accounts should be actuarially assessed. If, as a result, there is a provision, the balance sheet formats of the Companies Act require it to be described under the heading 'Provisions for liabilities' as 'Pensions and similar obligations'.

PROVISIONAL APPROVAL

1. The allowing of tax relief on a provisional basis in respect of employee contributions where an occupational pension scheme is set up under interim documentation. The **Practice Notes** do not use the term. Strictly, Inland Revenue approval is not granted until definitive scheme documentation has been examined.

2. The granting of provisional approval in respect of a personal pension scheme pursuant to S655(5) ICTA 88 and the Personal Pension Schemes (Provisional Approval) Regulations 1987.

PUBLIC SECTOR PENSION SCHEME

An occupational pension scheme for employees of central or local government, a nationalised industry or other statutory body.

PUBLIC SECTOR TRANSFER ARRANGEMENTS

The arrangements of the **transfer club** to which certain schemes mainly in the public sector belong.

PUBLIC SERVICE PENSION SCHEME

A **public sector pension scheme** the particulars of which are statutorily defined, for example the schemes for the civil service, local authorities, the police and fire services.

PURCHASED LIFE ANNUITY (PLA)

An annuity purchased privately by an individual. In accordance with S656 ICTA 88, instalments of the annuity are subject to tax only in part.

QUALIFYING PERIOD
An alternative term for **waiting period**.

QUALIFYING SERVICE
The term defined in SSA 73 denoting the service to be taken into account to entitle a member to **short service benefit**. The current condition is for at least two years' qualifying service. If a transfer has been received from a personal pension scheme, the member is treated immediately as being entitled to short service benefits.

See also linked qualifying service.

RATE OF RETURN
The change in value of an investment over a period, taking into account both the income from it and the change in its market value. Normally expressed as an equivalent annual rate.

REAL RATE OF RETURN
The difference between the **rate of return** of an investment and a selected measure of inflation over the same period.

The measure of inflation used should be specified, but will often be the index of retail prices or of national average earnings.

REBATE ONLY PERSONAL PENSION SCHEME (ROPP)
An **appropriate personal pension scheme** which is funded solely by rebates of national-insurance contributions payable by the DSS to the pension provider in due course as a result of an election to contract out.

RECOGNISED OCCUPATION
An occupation for which the PSO may be able to agree a pension age earlier than 50 under an occupational or personal pension scheme.

RECOGNISED PROFESSIONAL BODY (RPB)
A professional body recognised by the Securities and Investments Board as regulating and supervising for the purposes of FSA 86 those of its members who undertake investment business activities.

RECOMMENDED CONTRIBUTION RATE
The contribution rate recommended by the actuary. It is usually obtained by adjusting the standard contribution rate for differences between the **actuarial liability** and the **actuarial value of assets** taking into account the objectives of the funding plan.

The pension scheme's auditor is required to state in the audit report whether the employers have been paying the contributions recommended by the actuary.

RECURRENT SINGLE PREMIUM METHOD
An alternative term for **single premium method**.

REGISTER

The register of occupational and personal pension schemes maintained by the Occupational Pensions Board pursuant to SSA 90 and the Register of Occupational and Personal Pension Schemes Regulations 1990.

Schemes required to register include free standing AVC schemes, unfunded schemes and overseas schemes. Paid up or frozen schemes are required to register, but are not required to pay the levy.

REGULAR PENSION COST

An accounting term defined in **SSAP 24** as meaning the consistent ongoing cost recognised under the actuarial method used.

REINSURANCE

The practice whereby one insurer insures with another risks it has accepted so as to offset the impact of part or all of the expected claims.

The term may be used loosely to describe the insurance, e.g. stop loss, taken out by trustees of a self administered scheme to offset the effects of excessive death benefit claims.

RELEVANT BENEFITS

The term used in ICTA 88 and the **Practice Notes** to describe the types of benefits which are within the tax regime governing occupational pension schemes.

The full definition is set out in S612(1) ICTA 88, and covers any type of financial benefit given in connection with retirement, death or termination of service. The definition does not include benefits provided only in the event of accidental death or disablement during service.

RELEVANT EARNINGS

See **net relevant earnings**.

REQUISITE BENEFITS

The scale of benefits which an occupational pension scheme was originally required to provide as one of the conditions of contracting out. The requirement to provide requisite benefits was removed in November 1986.

RESERVE

An amount appropriated from the profits of a business and set aside on the balance sheet as part of the capital employed.

*Any amount which ought properly to be regarded as a **provision** should not be included in a reserve.*

RETAINED BENEFITS

Retirement or death benefits in respect of an employee deriving from an earlier period of employment or self employment. In some circumstances retained benefits must be taken into account in the **maximum approvable benefits**.

RETIREMENT ANNUITY

An annuity contract, between an insurance company or friendly society and a self employed individual or a person in non pensionable employment, which was established before 1 July 1988 and is approved under Chapter III of Part XIV ICTA 88.

RETIREMENT BENEFITS SCHEME

An arrangement for the provision of benefits consisting of or including **relevant benefits**.

The full definition is set out in S611 ICTA 88.

REVALUATION

1. The application, particularly to preserved benefits, of **indexation, escalation** or the awarding of **discretionary increases**. SSPA 75 imposes revaluation in the calculation of **GMP** and of preserved benefits other than **GMP**.

2. An accounting term for the revision of the **carrying value** of an asset, usually having regard to its **market value**.

REVALUED EARNINGS

A term used to describe **index linking** of earnings for calculating benefits.

REVALUED EARNINGS SCHEME

A pension scheme where the benefits are based on earnings for a given period revalued in direct proportion to a specific index of prices or earnings.

A notable example is the earnings related component of the state pension scheme.

REVENUE UNDERTAKING

A written undertaking given by the administrators of an approved scheme agreeing to notify the Inland Revenue of certain information or to refer to them before taking certain specified actions.

REVERSIONARY ANNUITY

An annuity which commences to be paid on the death of a specified person, normally to a spouse or a dependant.

RULES

The detailed provisions of a pension scheme, brought into operation by a definitive trust deed or in some other formal way, for example by a trustees' resolution.

SALARY GRADE SCHEME

A type of **average earnings scheme** in which the benefit for each year of service depends on the range into which the member's earnings fell during that year.

SALARY RELATED SCHEME

A **defined benefit scheme** in which benefits are related to earnings, i.e. a final salary scheme or an average earnings scheme.

SALARY SACRIFICE

An agreement (which the Inland Revenue requires to be in writing) between the employer and employee whereby the employee forgoes part of his/her earnings in return for a corresponding contribution by the employer to a pension scheme.

*This is not the same as an **additional voluntary contribution**.*

SECTION 21 ORDERS

The Orders issued each year in accordance with S21 SSPA 75 specifying the rates of increase to be applied to the earnings factors on which the additional pension and **GMPs** are based. This revaluation is based on the increase in national average earnings.

*In respect of early leavers, see also **fixed revaluation rate** and **limited revaluation premium**.*

SECTION 32 POLICY

The term used widely to describe an insurance policy used for **buy out** purposes where the member chooses the insurance company.

The term came into use as a result of S32 FA 81, which gave prominence to the possibility of effecting such policies (now contained in S591 ICTA 88).

SECTION 49 SCHEME

An occupational pension scheme which was formerly contracted out and which is still subject to supervision by the OPB under S49 SSPA 75.

SECTION 226 ANNUITY

An alternative term for **retirement annuity**.

SECURITIES AND INVESTMENTS BOARD (SIB)

The chief regulator of financial services set up under the Financial Services Act 1986. The board is responsible for laying down the broad framework for investor regulation and is the supervisory body for self regulatory organisations such as IMRO.

SEGMENTATION

A practice under which one or more arrangements are effected simultaneously to allow phased drawing of benefits by an individual who joins a personal pension scheme, or who prior to 1 July 1988 effected a retirement annuity contract.

SEGREGATED FUND

An arrangement whereby the investments of a particular pension scheme are managed by an external investment manager independently of other funds under its control. Often used to indicate an individual portfolio of stocks and shares in contrast to a pooled fund.

SELF ADMINISTERED SCHEME

A pension scheme where the assets are invested, other than wholly by payment of insurance premiums, by the trustees, an in house manager or an external investment manager.

Although on the face of it the term self administered should refer to the method of administering contributions and benefits, in practice the term has become solely related to the way in which the investments are managed.

SELF ADMINISTERED PERSONAL PENSION

A term sometimes used to mean **self invested personal pension**.

SELF EMPLOYED ANNUITY

An alternative term for **retirement annuity**.

SELF INVESTED PERSONAL PENSION (SIPP)

A personal pension under which the member has freedom to control investments.

The requirements governing self invested personal pensions are set out in JOM 101.

SELF INVESTMENT

A term used to describe the investment of a scheme's assets in employer related investments.

A 5% limit is imposed on employer related investments by SSA 90 (with certain exemptions). The PSO imposes separate restrictions on self investment by small self administered schemes. Requirements as to disclosure and reporting of self investment are laid down by the OPB and the Disclosure Regulations.

SELF REGULATORY ORGANISATION (SRO)

A body authorised by the Securities and Investments Board to regulate and supervise investment business or financial service activities.

SERVICE

A period of employment with one or more connected employers.

SHORT SERVICE BENEFIT (SSB)

The benefit which must be provided for an **early leaver** under the preservation requirements of SSA 73.

SIMPLIFIED DEFINED CONTRIBUTION SCHEME (SDCS)
A money purchase scheme subject to the simplified approval procedure described in Part 22 of the **Practice Notes**.

SIMPLIFIED FINAL SALARY SCHEME (SFSS)
A final earnings scheme subject to the simplified approval procedure described in JOM 94 subsequently withdrawn because of lack of demand.

SINGLE PREMIUM METHOD
A method of determining the premiums payable under an insurance contract with the object of meeting each year the cost of the benefit relating to that year.

SMALL SELF ADMINISTERED SCHEME (SSAS)
A self administered occupational pension scheme with few members (generally less than 12) which is subject on this account to certain special conditions for approval under ICTA 88.

SOLVENCY TEST
An actuarial calculation to determine whether the assets of the scheme are sufficient to meet the statutory obligations to the members under the rules of the scheme.

SPECIAL CONTRIBUTIONS
Contributions payable by the employer or by the members for a limited period or as a single payment, often to provide new benefits or to meet deficiencies.

STANDARD CONTRIBUTION RATE
The contribution rate required by a particular valuation method before taking into account any differences between the **actuarial liability** and the **actuarial value of assets**.

STATE EARNINGS RELATED PENSION SCHEME (SERPS)
A term widely used to describe the additional pension provisions of the state pension scheme.

STATE PENSION AGE (SPA)
See **state pensionable age**.

STATE PENSION DISREGARD
A reduction in pension or pensionable earnings to achieve **integration**.

STATE PENSIONABLE AGE
The date from which pensions are normally payable by the state scheme, currently the 65th birthday for men and the 60th birthday for women.

STATE SCHEME PREMIUM
A payment made to the state scheme in certain circumstances. The categories

of state scheme premium are: accrued rights premium, contracted out protected rights premium, contributions equivalent premium, limited revaluation premium, pensioner's rights premium, personal pension protected rights premium, transfer premium.

STATEMENT OF RECOMMENDED PRACTICE 1 (SORP 1)

Usually referred to as SORP 1, Statement of Recommended Practice 1 'Pension scheme accounts' was issued in 1986 by the Accounting Standards Committee and gives guidance to current best accounting practice for pension schemes. Its recommendations were effectively made mandatory by the **Disclosure Regulations**.

STATEMENT OF STANDARD ACCOUNTING PRACTICE 24 (SSAP 24)

The accounting standard which deals with the accounting for and the disclosure of pension costs and commitments in the financial statements of employers in respect of arrangements for the provision of retirement benefits for their employees.

STATUTORY DISCHARGE

The discharge provided in respect of a member who exercises the statutory right to a **cash equivalent** under SSPA 75.

STATUTORY SCHEME

A scheme (usually in the public sector) established by Act of Parliament.

STATUTORY TRANSFER

Making a **transfer payment** in a case where the member has a right to require such a payment under SSPA 75.

STOCK LENDING

The process by which stock is released to a third party in return for valid security and a fee for so doing. This is normally undertaken on a short term basis.

STOCK SELECTION

The process of selecting which stocks are included in a portfolio.

SUPERANNUATION FUNDS OFFICE (SFO)

See **Pension Schemes Office (PSO)**.

SURPLUS

See actuarial surplus.

Rather confusingly, the term may also be used to describe an excess of income over expenditure in a scheme's annual accounts.

SURRENDER
1. A term used in relation to the cancellation of an insurance policy by the payment of a 'surrender value'.

2. A term sometimes used to describe **allocation** or **commutation**.

TAX RELIEF AT SOURCE
See **pension tax relief at source**.

TERM ASSURANCE POLICY
A policy which provides a lump sum on death only before a specified date.

Sometimes referred to as term insurance policy.

TERMINAL FUNDING
An arrangement whereby a payment to meet the present value of a benefit is made only at or about the time when the benefit is due to commence.

Not common in the UK except in respect of discretionary pension increases.

TIED ANNUITY OPTION
The option to apply the proceeds of an insurance contract to buy an annuity from the original insurer at its current market rate as an alternative to exercising a **guaranteed annuity option**.

TOP HAT SCHEME
An alternative term for **executive scheme**.

TOP UP PENSION SCHEME
A pension scheme providing benefits which supplement those provided under another scheme.

*The term is used in Inland Revenue guidance notes to refer to an **unapproved** scheme.*

TOTAL EARNINGS SCHEME
A type of average earnings scheme where the pension is a specified fraction of the member's aggregate earnings throughout the period of membership.

TRACKING FUND
A fund which, using computer software, seeks to match investment performance to a particular stock market index.

TRANSFER CLUB
A group of employers and occupational pension schemes which has agreed to a common basis of transfer payments.

TRANSFER CREDIT
Under SSA 73 and SSPA 75 the benefit purchased by a transfer payment. The

effect on **qualifying service** is to link that part of the previous pensionable service which gave rise to the transfer payment to the service in the receiving scheme.

TRANSFER PAYMENT

A payment made from a pension scheme to another pension scheme, or to an insurance company to purchase a **buy out** policy, in lieu of benefits which have accrued to the member or members concerned, to enable the receiving arrangement to provide alternative benefits.

The transfer payment may be made in accordance with the scheme rules or in exercise of a member's statutory rights under SSPA 75.

TRANSFER PREMIUM

A type of **state scheme premium** which can be paid when accrued benefits in excess of **GMPs** have been transferred to an occupational pension scheme which is not contracted out.

TRANSFER VALUE

The amount of the **transfer payment**, usually based on actuarial advice, which the trustees are prepared to make to another pension scheme or an insurance company.

TRIVIAL PENSION

A pension which is so small that it can be commuted in full without prejudicing the approval of the scheme by the PSO.

The maximum amount of pension which may be commuted on account of triviality is also governed by preservation and contracting out requirements.

TRUE AND FAIR VIEW

Certain legislation requires accounts to show a true and fair view. This is generally understood as requiring accounts to contain information in sufficient quantity and quality as to satisfy the reasonable expectations of the readers. Compliance with accounting principles and standards is integral to this concept.

According to the Disclosure Regulations and SORP 1, the accounts of a UK pension scheme should present a true and fair view.

TRUST

A legal concept whereby property is held by one or more persons (the trustees) for the benefit of others (the beneficiaries) for the purposes specified by the trust instrument. The trustees may also be beneficiaries.

TRUST CORPORATION

A company empowered under the Public Trustee Act 1906 to act as **custodian trustee** and which is expected to provide professional expertise in managing trusts.

TRUST DEED
A legal document, executed in the form of a deed, which establishes, regulates or amends a trust.

See also interim trust deed and definitive trust deed.

TRUST INSTRUMENT
A trust deed or other document or series of documents, by which a trust is created and the provisions governing the trust are prescribed.

TRUSTEE
An individual or company appointed to carry out the purposes of a trust in accordance with the provisions of the trust instrument and general principles of trust law.

TRUSTEE REPORT
A report by the trustees describing various aspects of a pension scheme. It may form part of the **annual report**.

UNAPPROVED SCHEME
An occupational pension scheme which is not designed for approval by the Inland Revenue. Following FA 89 an employer may provide benefits for an employee under an unapproved scheme without those benefits being taken into account in calculating **maximum approvable benefits** under an **approved scheme**. Such a scheme may be used to provide benefits on earnings in excess of the **earnings cap**. The Inland Revenue has published guidance notes on the tax treatment of unapproved schemes.

The term is sometimes also used to refer to a scheme which is awaiting approval.

UNFUNDED SCHEME
A pension scheme for which the employer does not set aside and accumulate assets in advance of the benefits commencing to be paid. The basis may be **pay as you go** or **terminal funding**.

UNIFORM ACCRUAL
The treatment of retirement benefits as being earned equally over the period of potential pensionable service to normal pension date, especially for the purposes of the preservation requirements of SSA 73.

UNISEX ANNUITY RATES
Annuity rates which do not distinguish between gender.

UNISTATUS ANNUITY RATES
Annuity rates which do not distinguish between gender, marital status or the existence of dependants.

UNIT LINKED PENSION SCHEME
A scheme, often an individual arrangement, where the amount of the retirement benefits is related to the performance of a specified unitised fund, usually through the medium of an insurance policy.

UNIT TRUST
A trust set up under the supervision of the Department of Trade and Industry. Its portfolio of investments is unitised to enable investors to buy in to the trust or to redeem an earlier investment. The price of units is determined by the managers based on the net asset value of the fund.

UNTIED ANNUITY OPTION
An alternative term for **open market option**.

UPLIFTED 60ths
Benefits in excess of one sixtieth of final remuneration for each year of service to the extent permitted by the PSO in an approved occupational pension scheme (only allowable in respect of members with **pre 17 March 1987 continued rights**).

UPPER BAND EARNINGS
Earnings between the **lower earnings limit** and the **upper earnings limit** on which the **additional pension** is calculated.

Also used in the calculation of a GMP.

UPPER EARNINGS LIMIT (UEL)
The maximum amount of earnings (equal to approximately seven times the **lower earnings limit**) on which national-insurance contributions are payable by employees.

UPPER TIER EARNINGS
An alternative term for **upper band earnings**.

VALUATION BALANCE SHEET
A comparison of the **actuarial value of assets** with the **actuarial liability** showing the elements of these amounts in the form of a balance sheet, with an amount for surplus or deficiency as a balancing item.

The results of an actuarial valuation may be presented in other ways.

VALUATION BASIS
A term commonly used by actuaries to mean **valuation method** and/or **actuarial assumptions**.

VALUATION DATE
The date by reference to which the **actuarial valuation** is carried out.

VALUATION METHOD
An approach used by the actuary in an **actuarial valuation**. The main categories of approach are described under **accrued benefits valuation method** and **prospective benefits valuation method**. A variety of methods can be used but the method or methods used in a particular case should be adequately described in the actuarial report.

VALUATION REPORT
See **actuarial report**.

VALUE FOR MONEY
A minimum benefit which is related to the member's contributions. SSA 73 preservation requirements originally included such a minimum, but this was removed by amending regulations from 1 January 1986.

VESTED RIGHTS
(a) For active members, benefits to which they would unconditionally be entitled on leaving the scheme;
(b) for deferred pensioners, their preserved benefits;
(c) for pensioners, pensions to which they are entitled;

including where appropriate the related benefits for spouses or other dependants.

WAITING PERIOD
A period of service specified in the rules which an employee must serve before being entitled to join the pension scheme or to receive a particular benefit.

In some pension schemes the waiting period before being entitled to join may automatically count as pensionable service. Not to be confused with **qualifying service**.

WAIVER OF PREMIUM OPTION
A benefit available under some personal pension schemes and retirement annuity contracts, whereby the pension provider undertakes to credit regular premiums to the individual's contract if he or she becomes unable to contribute because of lack of relevant earnings arising from incapacity.

WIDOW'S/WIDOWER'S GUARANTEED MINIMUM PENSION (WGMP)
The minimum pension which an occupational pension scheme (other than a **money purchase contracted out scheme**) must provide for the surviving spouse of a member as one of the conditions of contracting out.

WIDOW'S/WIDOWER'S (PENSION) OPTION
An alternative term for **allocation** in favour of a spouse.

WINDING UP
The process of terminating a pension scheme, usually by applying the assets to

the purchase of immediate and deferred annuities for the beneficiaries, or by transferring the assets and liabilities to another pension scheme, in accordance with the scheme documentation.

See also priority rule.

WITH PROFITS POLICY
An insurance policy under which a share of the surpluses disclosed by actuarial valuations of the insurance company's life and pensions business is payable as an addition to the guaranteed benefits or in reduction of future premiums.

WITH PROPORTION
The term describing an arrangement whereby on the death of a person receiving an annuity paid in arrears, a proportionate payment becomes due from the date of the last full payment up to the date of death.

INDEX